Y0-DKP-264

Special Edition
USING
Visual C++™ 4

Mark Evans
Property of Biological and Agricultural
Engineering Dept.

November

Tue Wed T
        1   2
7   8   9
14 15 16 17 18

☐ Jan
■ Feb
☐ Mar
☐ Apr
■ May
☐ Jun

Food   Gas   Motel

que®

ODBC Oracle Driver Setup

Special Edition

USING
Visual C++™ 4

Written by

Chane Cullens
Mark Davidson
Paul Robichaux
Chris Corry
Steve Potts
Kate Gregory

QUE®

Special Edition Using Visual C++ 4

Copyright© 1996 by Que® Corporation

Library of Congress Catalog Number: 95-72548

ISBN: 1-7897-0401-3

99 98 97 96   6 5 4 3 2 1

Interpretation of the printing code: The rightmost double-digit number is the year of the book's printing; the rightmost single-digit number, the number of the book's printing. For example, a printing code of 96-1 shows that the first printing of the book occurred in 1996.

Screen Reproductions in this book were created by using Collage Plus from Inner Media, Inc., Hollis, New Hampshire.

Composed in *Stone Serif* and *MCPdigital* by Que Corporation

Credits

President and Publisher
Roland Elgey

Associate Publisher
Joseph B. Wikert

Editorial Services Director
Liz Keaffaber

Managing Editor
Sandy Doell

Director of Marketing
Lynn E. Zingraf

Senior Series Director
Chris Nelson

Title Manager
Bryan Gambrel

Acquisitions Editor
Fred Slone

Product Director
Nancy D. Price

Production Editors
Noelle Gasco
Andy Saff

Copy Editor
Patrick Kanouse

Assistant Product Marketing Manager
Kim Margolis

Technical Editor
Jeff Bankston

Technical Specialist
Nadeem Muhammed

Acquisitions Coodinator
Angela Kozlowski

Operations Coordinator
Patty J. Brooks

Cover Designer
Dan Armstrong

Book Designer
Kim Scott

Copywriter
Jennifer Reese

Production Team
Steve Adams
Michael Brumitt
Michael Dietsch
Chad Dressler
Jason Hand
Michael Henry
Clint Lahnen
Paula Lowell
Brian-Kent Proffitt
Julie Quinn
Laura Robbins
Bobbi Satterfield
S.A. Springer

Editorial Assistant
Michelle Newcomb

Indexer
Gina Brown

About the Authors

Chane Cullens is Bristol Technology's Wind/U product manager. Chane has more than 12 years of experience in C++ programming, including designing and implementing graphical applications in Windows and Motif, as well as other portable APIs. He coauthored *Cross Platform Development with Visual C++*, and has been published on C++ programming in *Dr. Dobb's Journal*. Chane can be reached on the Internet at Chane@Bristol.com.

Mark Davidson has been developing with Borland products since Turbo Pascal for CP/M and has been using Borland C++ since it was Turbo C 1.0. He has been writing Windows applications since the days of Windows 2.0. Currently, he works for Sony Electronic Publishing, where he develops Windows as well as Macintosh applications.

Chris Corry is a Principal working in the Center for Advanced Technologies at American Management Systems of Fairfax, Virginia. Although his professional interests span a wide range of topics, he spends the majority of his time investigating object-oriented programming techniques, software component standards like OLE and OpenDoc, and distributed object technologies. He was a contributing author to *Killer Borland C++ 4* and *Special Edition Using Visual C++ 2*, published by Que, and *OS/2 Unleashed*, published by Sams Publishing.

Paul Robichaux, who has been an Internet user since 1986 and a software developer since 1983, is currently a software consultant for Intergraph Corporation, where he writes Windows NT and Windows 95 applications. In his spare time, he writes books and Macintosh applications. He can be reached via e-mail at perobich@ingr.com.

Steve Potts received a degree in Computer Science from Georgia Tech. He has been designing and writing software systems for 12 years. He is a consultant in Windows-based technologies, and owns NoBoredom Classes, a computer education firm in Atlanta, Georgia.

Kate Gregory works in Visual C++ (specializing in Internet applications), teaches Internet and C++ programming courses, and writes. With her husband Brian, Kate has a computer consulting and software development business in rural Ontario, Canada. They develop Internet applications in Visual C++—their current project is a newsreader. She teaches Internet and C++ programming courses, and this is her second book for Que. Kate can be reached at kate@gregcons.com.

We'd Like to Hear from You!

As part of our continuing effort to produce books of the highest possible quality, Que would like to hear your comments. To stay competitive, we *really* want you, as a computer book reader and user, to let us know what you like or dislike most about this book or other Que products.

You can mail comments, ideas, or suggestions for improving future editions to the address below, or send us a fax at (317) 581-4663. For the online-inclined, Macmillan Computer Publishing has a forum on CompuServe (type **GO QUEBOOKS** at any prompt) through which our staff and authors are available for questions and comments. The address of our Internet site is **http://www.mcp.com** (World Wide Web).

In addition to exploring our forum, please feel free to contact me personally to discuss your opinions of this book: on CompuServe, I'm at 75767,2543, and on the Internet, I'm **nprice@que.mcp.com**.

Thanks in advance—your comments will help us to continue publishing the best books available on computer topics in today's market.

Nancy D. Price
Product Director
Que Corporation
201 W. 103rd Street
Indianapolis, Indiana 46290
USA

Contents at a Glance

Visual C++ Tools

Using MFC

OLE

Custom Controls

Advanced Programming

Contents

4 Debugging Visual C++ Applications   103

II Using the Microsoft Foundation Class Library   125

5 Introducing MFC   127

6 Using MFC   187

III Object Linking and Embedding   219

7 Introduction to OLE   221

8 OLE and the Microsoft Foundation Classes   247

17 Writing ODBC and DAO Applications in Visual C++   567

18 Run-Time Type Identification (RTTI)   593

Introduction

The success of Windows 95 has raised the required level of graphical user interface (GUI) sophistication that every application expects of users. As a programmer, the price that you must pay for this refined GUI interface is a dramatic increase in the programming effort required.

Windows 95 and Windows NT programs are more complicated and larger than similar Windows 3.1 programs. Because of this added complexity, programmers must overcome a formidable learning curve to program Windows 95 applications. To help Windows programmers, Microsoft has made its Visual C++ development environment more sophisticated. With Visual C++, version 4, Microsoft has redesigned the programming environment and created the Developer Studio, made the AppWizard extensible, increased the integration of the ClassWizard, and added the Component Gallery to make it easier to integrate prebuilt solutions. These utilities make it easy to create advanced Windows programs. Microsoft has also worked with several other companies to extend the Developer Studio to make the task of creating and debugging sophisticated GUI applications easier than ever. For example, if you are having problems debugging, you drop in Nu-Mega's BoundsChecker; if you are looking for additional prebuilt components, you drop in VisualComponent's spreadsheet or charting components. The formula is simple:

Visual C++ + Reuse + Leverage = World Class Application

Is This Book for You?

This book is aimed at readers who already are familiar with C++, Windows, and the basics of Windows programming. Prior knowledge of the Microsoft Foundation Classes (MFC) is a plus but not a requirement. This book covers many programming topics that use C++ and MFC. If you use only the C compiler portion of the Visual C++ product, this book *is not for you!* Because of the huge amount of available information, covering every aspect of Visual C++ and the MFC library in any one book is impossible.

Hardware and Software Requirements

As its title suggests, this book is for programmers who are using Visual C++ 4. To use Visual C++ 4, you must be running Microsoft Windows 95, Microsoft Windows NT 3.51, or a newer operating system. Therefore, you must have a powerful computer, the minimum requirements being a computer based on the 486 microprocessor with 16M RAM, a 400M hard drive, a super-VGA graphics adapter, and a mouse input device.

What's in This Book?

This book contains 18 chapters. This section briefly describes what you will find in each of these elements.

Part I, "Visual C++ Tools," consists of Chapters 1 through 4. This first part offers the basic information that you need to work with the Visual C++ Developer Studio, AppWizard, ClassWizard, and debugging tools, and the integrated AppStudio utilities. In addition, this part of the book introduces you to the classes in the MFC library.

Chapter 1, "Getting Started with Visual C++," gets you quickly up to speed with working in Visual C++. You learn how to install the compiler, and how to use the editor, toolbars, Help system, and integrated online Help system. You also get started writing your own program with AppWizard.

Chapter 2, "Using the Visual C++ Developer Studio," discusses the new Developer Studio and its various options. These options enable you to manage files, edit text, view information, manage program project files, browse through program declarations and class definitions, conduct debugging sessions, invoke programming tools, fine-tune the various components (including the compiler, linker, and resource compiler), and manage the Developer Studio environment.

Chapter 3, "Using AppStudio," focuses on using the integrated resource editors to create and edit program resources, including menus, dialog boxes, icons, bitmaps, and string tables. This chapter shows you how to use the resource editors to modify an existing menu resource, add a new dialog box resource, and create a new form view.

Chapter 4, "Debugging Visual C++ Applications," presents the Visual C++ Developer Studio debugger and discusses setting breakpoints, as well as the use of conditional and unconditional breakpoints. In addition, the chapter looks at using the function call stack, mixing assembly code with C++ statements, and managing the new display windows.

Part II, "Using the Microsoft Foundation Class Library," consists of Chapters 5 and 6. This part presents the classes in the MFC library that support the visual programming controls, such as command buttons, edit boxes, and list boxes.

Chapter 5, "Introducing MFC," shows you the code that AppWizard creates and exactly how it works. You learn what classes make up the Microsoft Foundation Class library, and you find out how to add custom functionality to your programs.

Chapter 6, "Using MFC," takes the skeleton MFC application generated in Chapter 5 and makes a real Windows application: a simple text file viewer. The code shows you how to make MFC applications read text files, display text, handle scrolling, and handle printing with print preview support.

Part III, "Object Linking and Embedding," consists of Chapters 7 through 9. This part presents information about writing programs that make use of OLE 2 technology. You learn about the components of OLE and how to write OLE-enabled programs.

Chapter 7, "Introduction to OLE," discusses the features found in OLE 2. You learn about the many technologies that make up OLE and how OLE fits into Microsoft's plan for component software.

Chapter 8, "OLE and the Microsoft Foundation Classes," presents the code for OLE container and server applications. You learn how to use the AppWizard to make adding OLE to your application easy, and also find out how to modify the code that the AppWizard creates.

Chapter 9, "OLE Automation," focuses on one part of Object Linking and Embedding, OLE Automation, which gives you a way to manipulate an application's objects from outside the application. You learn how to use OLE Automation to control other applications and how to expose your programs' functions to other servers.

Part IV, "Custom Controls," consists of Chapters 10 and 11. This part of the book shows you how to create OLE custom controls using Visual C++.

Chapter 10, "Using the ControlWizard," guides you through the process of using the newest Visual C++ wizard to generate skeletons for OLE custom controls.

Chapter 11, "Building OLE Controls," takes you step-by-step through the process of writing OLE custom controls as you add functionality to the control skeleton that you generate in Chapter 10.

Part V, "Advanced Windows Programming," includes Chapters 12 through 18. This part of the book shows you how to access Visual C++'s advanced features, including exceptions, templates, memory management, database applications, and advanced debugging techniques.

Chapter 12, "Cross-Platform Development," explains the transition from Win16 to Win32 and how to write portable applications for Win32 on Macintosh and UNIX operating systems.

Chapter 13, "Exception Handling," focuses on the new C++ exception-handling capabilities that Microsoft has added to Visual C++.

Chapter 14, "Mastering Templates," focuses on the new C++ template capabilities that Microsoft has added to Visual C++.

Chapter 15, "Memory-Management Techniques," teaches you how to program to the new Win32 flat memory model. After reading this chapter, you will be able to choose between C memory allocation and C++ memory allocation, and understand how OLE 2 uses memory.

Chapter 16, "Advanced Debugging Techniques," describes some of the advanced features available in the Visual C++ integrated debugger. The chapter also offers some tips on designing applications correctly and thus avoiding the need for advanced debugging techniques.

Chapter 17, "Writing ODBC and DAO Applications in Visual C++," teaches you how to gain access to the Open Database Connectivity standard that is built in to Visual C++ and the MFC libraries.

Chapter 18, "Run-Time Type Identification (RTTI)," shows you how RTTI can provide a variety of important services that can help make your code more robust and portable.

The companion CD includes a bonus chapter, Chapter 19, "Using Common Controls with MFC." This chapter explains how to use the new sophisticated controls that Visual C++ supports.

Conventions Used in This Book

To enhance the usability of this book, the following typographical conventions have been used:

- Words or phrases defined for the first time appear in *italic*. Words or phrases that you are asked to type appear in **bold.** Code listings, syntax, screen displays and on-screen messages appear in a special monospace typeface.

- Names of classes, functions, variables, messages, macros, and so on also appear in a special monospace typeface.

- In syntax examples, variables or placeholders appear in a special *monospace italic* typeface, and optional items appear in brackets ([ ]).

- A code continuation character (➡) is used when a code line is too long to fit within the margins of this book. This symbol simply indicates that due to page constraints, a code line has been broken that normally would appear on a single line.

We hope this book helps you in working with Visual C++ to build MFC-based Windows applications. Good luck in your programming endeavors.

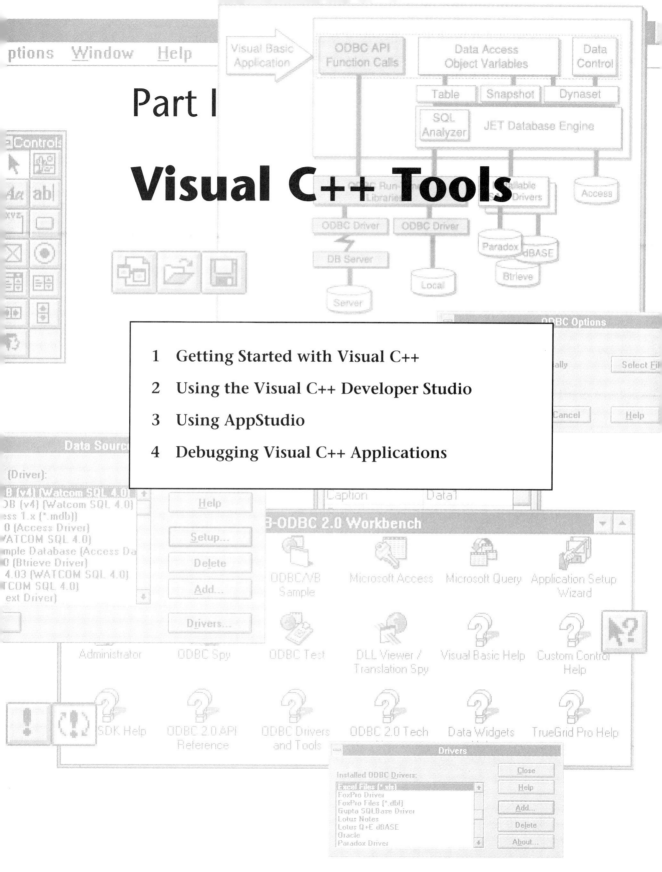

Part I

Visual C++ Tools

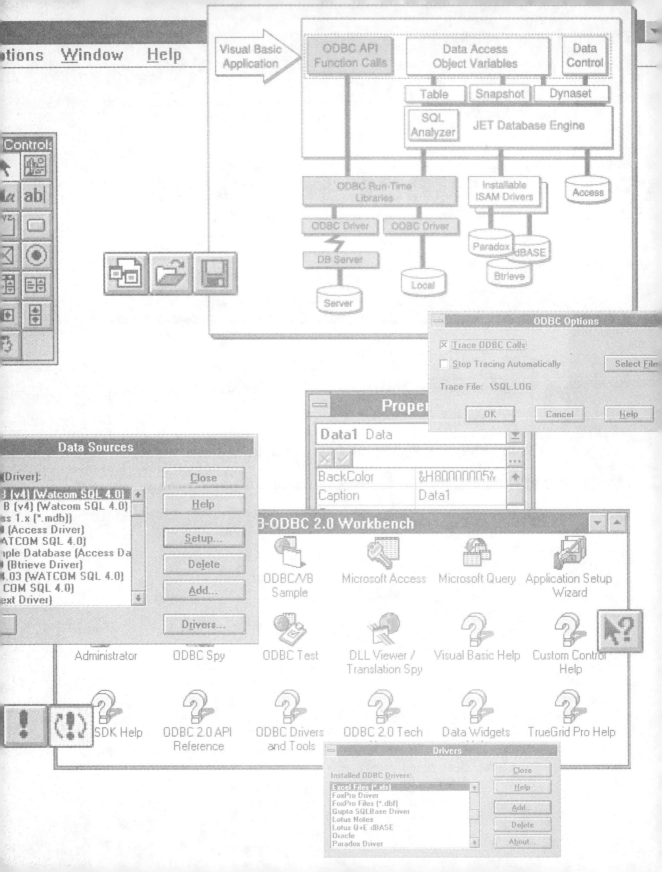

Getting Started with Visual C++

Visual C++ has always been a large application, and it can be a little intimidating at first. Before plunging into the details of how to use the Developer Studio, Visual C++, and the Microsoft Foundation Classes (MFC), this chapter introduces you to Visual C++ 4 by covering the following topics:

- The compiler's new features
- How to work inside the Developer Studio
- How to get started programming using AppWizard

When you've finished this chapter, you'll have a general understanding of what you'll learn in the following chapters.

About Visual C++

Visual C++ 4 is the second major release of Microsoft's 32-bit, native-mode, C++ programming tool with a Windows-hosted integrated development environment (named Developer Studio). With its integrated design environment, Visual C++ gets you programming faster because of its built-in visual programming tools.

The Visual C++ package includes much more than a built-in compiler and editor. Windows is a special graphical environment that uses resources such as icons, cursors, and bitmaps. Visual C++ enables you to create and modify these resources, all in one complete environment.

The tools in the Visual C++ package (see fig. 1.1) include the following:

- The compiler and tools for modifying Windows resources and generating code.
- Spy++, which enables you to trace Windows messages, Windows classes, and internal Windows information.
- MFC Tracer, which enables you to control information related to debugging programs that are based on the Microsoft Foundation Classes (MFC).

- PView (Process Viewer), which enables you to view the details about threads of execution (or processes) that are running.

- WinDiff, which shows the difference between two files. This resource is especially useful for showing how two different source files are related.

- Integrated InfoViewer, which provides online access to the manuals' entire text.

- Technical Support, another Windows help file that contains information from Microsoft's technical support staff on how to use Visual C++ product support.

- Release Notes, which presents last-minute information related to Visual C++.

- Help Workshop, which helps you compile, test, and report help files and edit project and contents files.

- MFC Migration Kit, with which you can move C-based applications into the MFC world.

- Microsoft Roadmap, for finding information on Microsoft products, programs, and services.

Fig. 1.1

Explorer Visual C++ group icons.

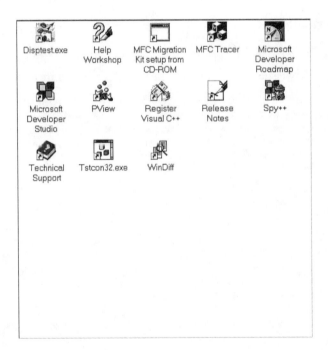

The Visual C++ setup under Windows 95 also creates a Visual C++ 4.0 Taskbar menu item, which expands to include several of the aforementioned tools (see fig. 1.2).

Fig. 1.2

The Visual C++ Taskbar menu.

Now that you've seen the programs, tools, and utilities that come with Visual C++, the next section describes what's new and exciting with this version of Visual C++.

Features That Are Especially Hot

Visual C++ has many features to offer. Some, however, are especially noteworthy:

- Integrated AppStudio. Resource editors are now part of the Developer Studio (see Chapter 3, "Using AppStudio," for more information).

- Customizable AppWizard. This feature enables you to generate projects to meet company- or industry-specific requirements (see Chapter 5, "Introducing MFC," for more information).

- Customizable, dockable toolbars. This feature makes interacting with the environment as easy as clicking a mouse. You can also create new toolbars. This chapter discusses these aspects of toolbars.

- Code generation for creating 32-bit applications for Windows, using the Win32 API.

- Better-integrated debugging capabilities. You now can debug container and server OLE applications. Also, Just in Time (JIT) debugging enables Visual C++ to debug any program, whether or not the program has debug information.

- The Microsoft Foundation Class libraries, version 4.0.

- Integrated online help and Books Online, with 15,000 pages of documentation.

- An incremental compiler that compiles only the functions that have changed.

- Incremental linking, which makes the project build cycle quicker on projects that have already been linked.

- C++ language additions: standard template library (STL), run-time type information (RTTI), and namespaces.

System Requirements

Visual C++ requires the following minimum configuration:

- A PC with an 80386 or higher processor (Microsoft recommends an 80486).
- Windows 95 or Microsoft Windows NT version 3.51 or later.
- A VGA monitor (Microsoft recommends a Super VGA monitor).
- 16M of available memory (Microsoft recommends 20M).
- A CD-ROM drive.
- A hard disk with about 100M disk space, or with enough space to install the options that you need. The Setup program lets you select installation options and tells you the disk space requirements for the options that you select.

If you are developing and testing applications for Win32s, you also need either a dual-boot computer or a separate computer with the following:

- Microsoft Windows or Microsoft Windows for Workgroups running in enhanced mode.
- MS-DOS version 5.0 or later.

You must install the Win32s dynamic-link libraries (DLLs) on the computer that you plan to use for testing and debugging Win32s programs. For example, if you plan to use a second computer for testing and debugging Win32s programs, you must install the Win32s DLLs and debugger on the second computer.

Once you have an understanding of the basic system necessary to run Visual C++, you are ready to install the package.

Installing Visual C++

Microsoft's excellent installation utility makes installing Visual C++ an easy task. All you do is tell the Setup program which subdirectory of the hard drive is to receive the program. Then specify which options you want to install. After you specify a couple of options, the utility handles the rest of the work of copying files and installing system registration information for you.

Running the Setup Program

To begin the installation process, put the Visual C++ installation CD-ROM in your CD-ROM drive, choose Run from the Windows 95 taskbar, or switch to Program Manager and choose File, Run. You then see the Run dialog box. In the Open text box, type the following:

```
n:\MSDEV\Setup.exe
```

where *n* is the letter of the drive that contains the Visual C++ disc. Choose the OK button or press Enter when you finish typing the Setup program's command line.

When the installation program starts, it displays a Welcome dialog box (see fig. 1.3) that explains what the Setup program is about to do and how long it will take. Click the <u>N</u>ext button to display the Software License Agreement dialog box (see fig. 1.4).

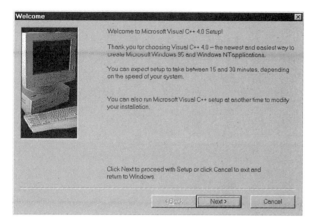

Fig. 1.3

The Welcome dialog box.

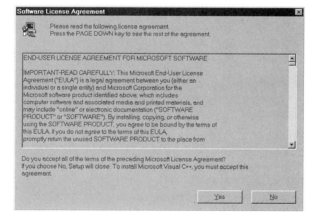

Fig. 1.4

The Software License Agreement dialog box.

After reading the license agreement, click <u>Y</u>es to display the Registration dialog box (see fig. 1.5). Then click the <u>N</u>ext button to display the Installation Options dialog box (see fig. 1.6).

Fig. 1.5

The Registration dialog box.

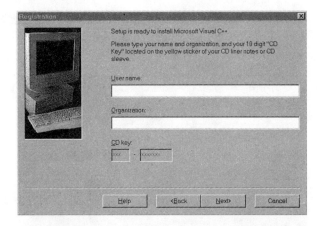

Fig. 1.6

The Installation Options dialog box.

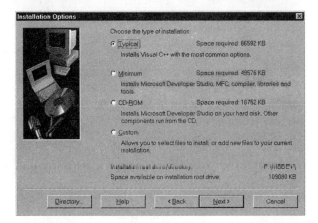

The Installation Options dialog box presents four main choices:

■ Typical installation installs the most commonly used options. This installation requires 100M of disk space.

■ Minimum installation installs on your hard drive the minimum files necessary to run Visual C++. This installation requires 60M of disk space.

■ CD-ROM installation installs the Developer Studio on your system. All other features are accessed from your CD-ROM drive. With this option, you must have the Visual C++ disk available every time that you use the compiler. This installation requires only 5M of disk space.

■ Custom installation enables you to choose which files to install.

Notice that, near the bottom-right corner of the screen, the Installation Options dialog box displays the amount of disk space available on your current disk drive. To change the current disk drive, click the Directory button. Then, in the Change

Directory dialog box (see fig. 1.7), specify the new drive and directory in which you want to install Visual C++.

Fig. 1.7

The Change Directory dialog box.

In most cases, you probably will choose <u>T</u>ypical, <u>M</u>inimum, or CD-<u>R</u>OM installation.

Next, the Setup program displays a final dialog box (see fig. 1.8) informing you that the program is about to start coping files.

Fig. 1.8

The dialog box that the Setup program displays when ready to copy files.

At this point, you can simply sit back as the Setup program copies the files to your hard disk. If you choose <u>C</u>ustom installation, you have several other options, which the next section discusses.

Using Custom Installation

If you choose <u>C</u>ustom installation from the Installation Options dialog box, the Setup program displays the Custom installation dialog box (see fig. 1.9).

To install the Microsoft Visual C++ development environment in the \MSDEV\BIN directory, you can click the Microsoft Developer Studio check box.

Click the Microsoft Visual C++ Build Tools check box to install the compiler, other build tools, and include files. If you choose the OLE Controls check box, the Setup program installs support for OLE controls in dialog boxes created with MFC.

Fig. 1.9

*The Custom installation
dialog box.*

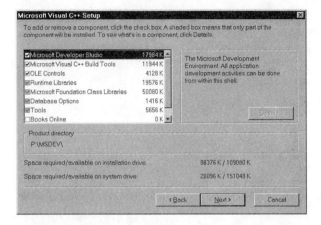

Click the Runtime Libraries check box to specify which run-time libraries to install
and whether to install the run-time libraries' source code. To access these options,
click the Details button in the Custom installation dialog box. You then see the
Runtime Libraries dialog box (see fig. 1.10).

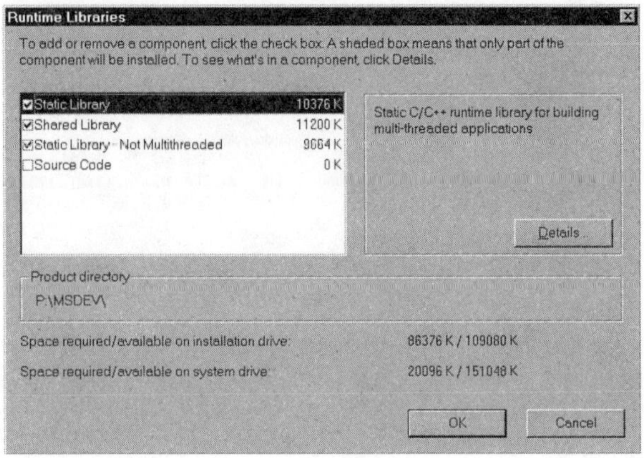

Fig. 1.10

*The Runtime Libraries
dialog box.*

To install the Microsoft Foundation Class library files, click the Microsoft Foundation
Class Libraries check box in the Custom installation dialog box. The Setup program
installs these libraries in the \MSDEV\MFC directory and the Windows SYSTEM directory. After selecting this check box, you can click the Details button to open the
Microsoft Foundation Class Libraries dialog box and select which files to install
(see fig. 1.11).

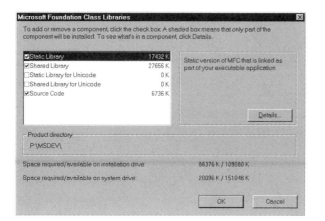

Fig. 1.11

The Microsoft Foundation Class Libraries dialog box.

Choose the Custom installation dialog box's Database Options check box to specify the database support to install. Click Details to see the Database Options dialog box (see fig. 1.12).

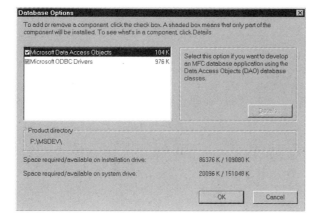

Fig. 1.12

The Database Options dialog box.

Visual C++ 4 supports both Open Database Connectivity (ODBC) and Microsoft Data Access Objects (DAO). *DAO* is the data access engine used by other Microsoft applications, such as Access and Visual Basic. To choose which ODBC drivers to install, select the Microsoft ODBC Drivers check box and click the Details button. You then see the Microsoft ODBC Drivers dialog box (see fig. 1.13).

The Custom installation dialog box's Tools check box enables you to install Windows and OLE development tools. After selecting this check box, you can click the Details button to open the Tools dialog box (see fig. 1.14) and select the tools to install. The Setup program installs the tools in the \MSDEV\BIN directory. The Tools dialog box has check boxes for five categories of tools that you can install: Spy++, Tracer, Win32 SDK Tools, Profiler, and OLE Development Tools.

Fig. 1.13

*The Microsoft ODBC
Drivers dialog box.*

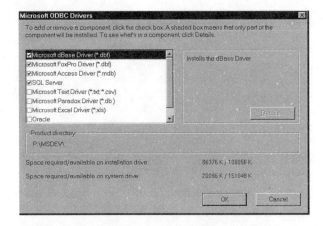

Fig. 1.14

The Tools dialog box.

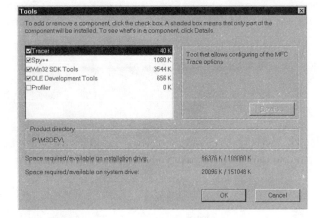

The Custom Installation dialog box's Books Online check box enables you to install help files associated with Visual C++—a total of 15,000 pages.

This covers all the options that you can set with a Custom installation. At this point, you can click the Next button and complete the installation as discussed earlier. If you choose all the options available in the Custom installation dialog box, you will need more than 290M of free disk space.

Introducing Visual C++

With Visual C++, you do your programming work in one convenient environment. The Visual C++ environment integrates all the tools you need so that you can be a productive and efficient programmer. This section introduces you to the Visual C++ Developer Studio and helps you to start using its features immediately.

Starting Developer Studio

Starting Visual C++ is easy. After completing installation, you start Visual C++ by running the Microsoft Developer Studio. When you invoke the Developer Studio, a graphical image with a copyright message displays. After a few seconds, this splash screen disappears and the program loads. The screen should display the empty Visual C++ desktop. Welcome to Developer Studio!

Before you start writing programs, take a moment to examine the menus, toolbars, and editor windowing system. The menu at the top of the window serves as a gateway to the features in Visual C++.

The Developer Studio offers a multiple-document interface (MDI) to display several windows at the same time. You can open more than one editor window to view different files at the same time. You might load two programs into multiple windows and use one program's information to write statements in another.

Using the Editor

The Developer Studio starts without any editor windows open. An *editor window* enables you to type and modify your program code. The editor window's title bar contains the name of the file that you are editing. When you create a new file without giving it a name, the Developer Studio creates an editor window with the name Text1.

An *active editor window* with no current activity is ready to accept input. Before typing the text, place the cursor in the editor window's top-left corner. As you start to type, the text appears at the current cursor location in the editor window.

The editor begins in *Insert mode*, which means that as you type, text is inserted at the cursor. In *Overwrite mode*, you type over existing text. To toggle between Insert mode and Overwrite mode, press Ins on your keyboard.

The Developer Studio editor is intuitive and easy to use. What you type appears on the screen at the cursor. Press Enter to insert a new line and move the cursor to the start of the next line. Pressing Backspace deletes the character to the left of the cursor. Pressing Delete removes the character directly at the cursor. Press Page Up or Page Down to scroll the window up or down one screen at a time, respectively. The Developer Studio programmer's editor enables you to cut, copy, and paste text by using menu commands and shortcuts, as well as the drag-and-drop editing technique. The latter feature is similar to the editing features provided by such word processors as Word for Windows. With drag-and-drop editing, you can highlight and left-click a section of text, move the cursor to a new position while continuing to hold down the mouse button, and then release the mouse button at the point to which you want to move the text. If you want to copy the text (instead of moving it), hold down the Ctrl key while you are performing the drag-and-drop operation. This handy form of editing is new to programmer's tools.

If you don't want to use drag-and-drop editing, you can use the more traditional editor commands (many programmers prefer to use their typing fingers when programming instead of "mousing around").

> **Note**
>
> An undo buffer is provided to enable you to undo and redo selected editing actions.

Using the Search Options

To find a specific sequence of characters, choose Edit, Find. The Find dialog box appears (see fig. 1.15). Type the string for which you want to search, and specify any of the various Search options (you learn about the Search options in detail in Chapter 2, "Using the Visual C++ Developer Studio").

Fig. 1.15

The Find dialog box.

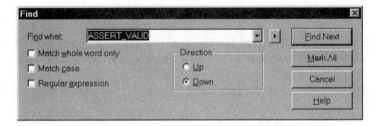

After entering your text, choose the Find Next button to begin your search. The Find feature then highlights any instance of the text that it finds. If the Find feature does not find an instance of the text, a dialog box tells you that no text was found.

> **Note**
>
> To find a text string in several files at once, choose File, Find in Files.

To do a search-and-replace operation, choose Edit, Replace. The options in the resulting Replace dialog box (see fig. 1.16) are similar to those in the Find dialog box. Along with the text for which you are searching, enter the replacement text. Then click the Find Next button.

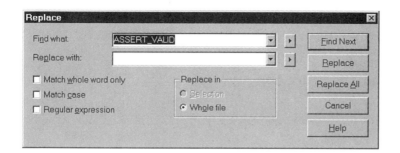

Fig. 1.16

The Replace dialog box.

The editor prompts you before executing a search-and-replace operation. You can always choose Cancel to abort the operation. The search-and-replace functions are among the operations most commonly used by programmers.

Using Toolbars

Toolbars provide a quick way to choose commonly used menu commands with the mouse. The toolbars initially appear under the main menu bar as a horizontal group of buttons. To use them, move the cursor to the appropriate button and click.

There are eight standard toolbars, and you can create additional ones. Figure 1.17 shows the standard toolbars, which include the following:

- The Standard toolbar contains general tools for working in the Developer Studio.
- The Project toolbar contains tools for rebuilding projects.
- The Resource toolbar contains tools for editing project resources.
- The Edit toolbar contains tools for editing documents.
- The Debug toolbar contains tools for debugging your program.
- The Browse toolbar contains tools for using the C++ Browse tool.
- The InfoViewer toolbar contains tools for using the online books.
- The InfoViewer Contents toolbar contains tools for navigating in the online books contents window.

The toolbars are context-sensitive. Which buttons a toolbar displays and whether those buttons are enabled or disabled depend on the state of the Developer Studio. For example, if the debugger is active, the tools on the Debug toolbar become active; otherwise, they are disabled.

If a toolbar is *dockable,* you can choose where to place it on the screen. You can choose to let the toolbar *float* (so that it's always on top of all other windows) or to *dock* it to the side of the Developer Studio (see fig. 1.18). When docked, a toolbar no longer contains a title that describes its function.

Fig. 1.17

The eight standard toolbars.

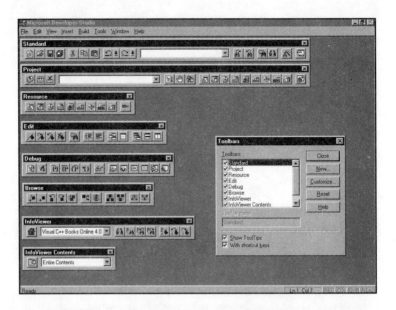

Fig. 1.18

Toolbars docked to the Developer Studio.

You control which toolbars are active by choosing Toolbars from the Tools menu. The Toolbars dialog box appears. You can choose which toolbars are currently displayed. As a shortcut, you can right-click a toolbar, which then displays a menu that enables you to choose which toolbars are available for your use.

Getting Online Help

The Developer Studio does not use the Windows Help system. To implement online help, the Developer Studio instead uses advanced hypertext technology to include online references for the predefined C and C++ language definitions, MFC, Windows API function calls, and more (see fig. 1.19). The hypertext technology is embedded in the Developer Studio.

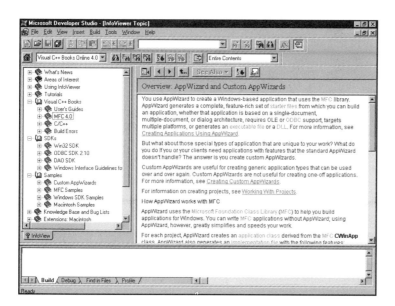

Fig. 1.19

The InfoViewer online help system.

I

Visual C++ Tools

To access context-sensitive help, just place the the cursor over a word, phrase, keyword, or function name, and then press F1. The information pops up in a window. To search for information, choose the Search option from the Help menu.

When using the Developer Studio, if you want specific information on a keyword, use the hypertext help system. This system gives you immediate access to related information. Words within the help system's text can be linked to other, related information. All hypertext links display in a different color (usually green). When you move the cursor over these special links, it changes to a hand. You can then click the link to display the related information.

InfoViewer, the new online documentation system, is now an integral part of the Developer Studio, not the separate application that it was in Visual C++ 2. The workspace window's InfoView pane displays the table of contents for Books Online. Help topics appear in an MDI child window, the InfoViewer topic window. With this new integration, you can now accomplish the following:

- View both your source window and a topic window without having to switch between applications
- Easily copy text from a topic window into a source window, using either the Clipboard or a drag-and-drop operation

Working with Project Files

Visual C++ organizes programs into projects. A *project* consists of the source files required for an application, along with the specifications for building that program. Each project can specify multiple targets to build from its source files. A target specifies such things as the type of application to build, the platform on which it is to run, and the tool settings to use when building. The inclusion of multiple targets enables you to extend a project's scope but still maintain a consistent source-code base from which to work.

The Developer Studio includes a project window, which displays a project's contents in several views. By default, the project workspace window contains the panes listed in table 1.1.

Table 1.1   The Panes of the Project Workspace Window

Pane Title	Description
FileView	Displays the project configurations that you have created. Expanding the top-level folders shows files within the project.
ResourceView	Displays the resource files included in the project. Expanding the top-level folders shows the resource types in the files (see fig. 1.20).
ClassView	Displays the C++ classes defined in your projects. Expanding the top-level folders shows classes; expanding a class shows its members.
InfoView	Displays the table of contents for online help. Expanding the top-level folders shows books and topics.

Fig. 1.20

The project workspace window in ResourceView.

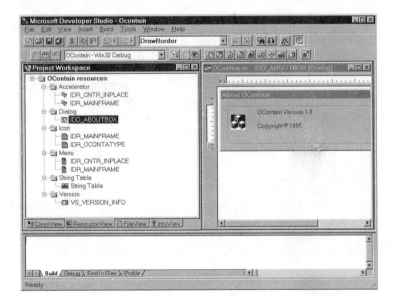

Project workspaces are stored in a file with the extension .MDP. Although these are text files, you usually don't modify the files yourself. You let the Developer Studio load and display the information in the file for you. Through dialog boxes, you can specify which files to add to a project.

After specifying the project's files, the targets that your project is to build, and the tool settings for those targets, you can build the project with the commands in the Build menu.

Creating Applications with AppWizard

AppWizard, a built-in Visual C++ utility, helps you quickly start projects by creating a skeleton application for you. The skeleton is built around the Microsoft Foundation Classes and incorporates support for features that you specify, like Windows Sockets or OLE 2.0.

When you use AppWizard, it creates a feature-rich project for you that contains all the files necessary for a basic application. To create a new project and to access AppWizard, choose File, New.

The New dialog box appears. Choose Project Workspace from the list of available options. The New Project Workspace dialog box appears (see fig. 1.21). In the Name text box, type **My First App**. Then click the Create button.

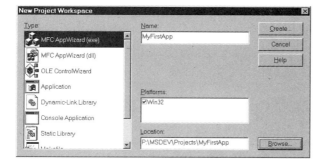

Fig. 1.21

The New Project Workspace dialog box.

At this point, you go through a series of six steps, each of which asks you about the application that you want to create (see fig. 1.22 for step 1). To accept the default value, click the Next button through all six steps. Then click the Finish button to create the source code for the application as well as the new project file.

After creating your project, you can compile the new program by choosing Build, Build, or by pressing Shift+F8). As the project is being compiled, the output window at the bottom of the screen displays status information (see fig. 1.23). When the program finishes compiling, choose Build, Execute (or press Ctrl+F5). Your finished program should look something like that shown in figure 1.24.

Fig. 1.22

*Step 1 of the MFC
AppWizard.*

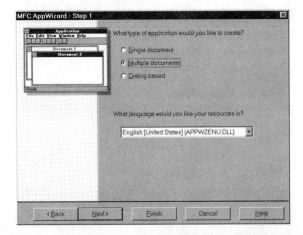

Fig. 1.23

*The output window located
at the bottom of the screen
displays status information
as your project compiles.*

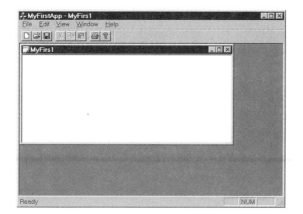

Fig. 1.24

Your first program, created by AppWizard.

Configuration Options

Before finishing this chapter, take a look at the ways that you can customize the Developer Studio. The Tools menu has several commands that you can use to customize the Developer Studio, including the Customize and Options commands.

The Customize command displays the Customize dialog box (see fig. 1.25). This tabbed dialog box provides options to customize the toolbars, the options on the Tools menu, and keyboard commands. By clicking the tabs at the top of the dialog box, you select the items that you want to customize.

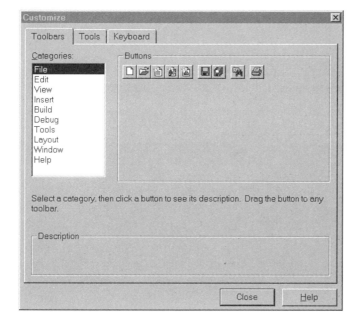

Fig. 1.25

The Customize dialog box.

The Options command displays the Options dialog box (see fig. 1.26), another tabbed dialog box that lets you set options related to the Developer Studio environment. The tabs are Editor, Tabs, Debug, Compatibility, Directories, Workspace, Format, and InfoViewer.

Fig. 1.26

The Options dialog box.

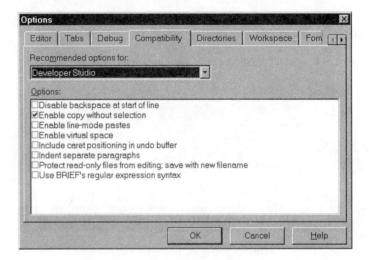

By setting the selections in the Customize and Options dialog boxes, you can configure the Developer Studio to work the way that you want.

From Here...

This chapter got you up and running with Visual C++. You learned how to install the compiler, how to use the editors, how to access the Help system, and how to create, compile, and run your first program using the AppWizard and Developer Studio.

Depending on what your main interests are, you should move on to various places in the rest of the book:

- If you are new to Visual C++, see Chapter 2, "Using the Visual C++ Developer Studio."

- To learn how to build your application with the AppWizard, see Chapter 3, "Using AppStudio."

- To learn more about debugging with Visual C++, see Chapter 4, "Debugging Visual C++ Applications."

- For more information about programming with the Microsoft Foundation Classes, see Chapter 5, "Introducing MFC."

- For a discussion of Object Linking and Embedding, see Chapter 7, "Introduction to OLE."

- To learn about advanced programming techniques, see Chapter 10, "Using the ControlWizard."

CHAPTER 2

Using the Visual C++ Developer Studio

You begin working with Visual C++ by loading the Developer Studio. With the Developer Studio, you do your programming work in one convenient environment. Visual C++ and Microsoft's FORTRAN compilers "plug in" to Developer Studio; the Developer Studio integrates all the tools you need so that you can be a productive and efficient programmer. It seems fitting, therefore, to introduce you to this program-development environment.

Keep in mind that the Developer Studio offers commands of different levels of sophistication. Some commands perform general tasks, such as file management. Other commands perform more advanced programming tasks, such as debugging or resource editing.

In this chapter, you learn how to load the Developer Studio and work with Developer Studio commands. You also learn about the following Developer Studio menus:

- The File menu commands let you manage the various kinds of source files that are involved in creating a program.
- The Edit menu provides commands for editing text, including search and replace operations.
- The View menu lets you toggle between the available source, class, and InfoViewer views of your project.
- The Insert menu provides commands for adding new files and resources to your project.
- The Build menu (which changes to Debug when you are using the debugger) lets you build or rebuild your project and set the options for the compiler, linker, and project.
- The Tools menu is where you access tools like Spy++ (or any tool you choose to add). You can also customize the Studio's toolbars and options.
- The Window menu enables you to quickly pick a window and bring it to the front, or to arrange all the windows to make best use of your monitor.
- The Help menu is your gateway to the Developer Studio's extensive online Help.

The discussion of the advanced Developer Studio commands includes simple examples that should familiarize you with these commands and how they work. When necessary, some of the more advanced commands are discussed in more detail later in this book.

Loading the Developer Studio

Loading the Developer Studio is easy. You can simply double-click the Visual C++ icon. You can usually find this icon within the Microsoft Visual C++ entry on the Start button by choosing Start, Programs, Microsoft Visual C++ 4.0, Microsoft Developer Studio. Alternatively, you can choose Start, Run and enter the following command:

C:\MSDEV\BIN\MSDEV.EXE

This command assumes that you have installed Visual C++ in the default drive C and in the default directory \MSDEV. (No command-line switches are available for loading the Developer Studio.)

Figure 2.1 shows the Developer Studio.

Fig. 2.1

The Developer Studio's main screen.

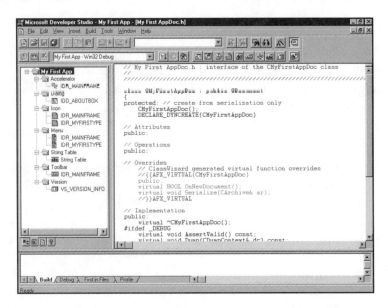

The Menu System

The menu system has the features that you need to manage your programming tasks efficiently. In the menu system, you find utilities and features for handling files and for editing, running, and compiling your programs.

Some menu commands are context-sensitive. Therefore, depending on the state of your work, certain menu options are available and others are not. The options that are not available are shown in gray.

Often a command in the main level of the menus leads to another option. Each menu command followed by ellipses (...) displays a dialog box. In the dialog box, you can set additional options to control the command. The dialog boxes enable you to make several choices at once to affect the command's behavior. Table 2.1 summarizes the menus and their commands.

Table 2.1 Developer Studio's Main Menus	
Menu	**Purpose**
File	Use these commands to open, save, create, and print program files. Choose File, Exit to exit the Developer Studio.
Edit	Use these commands to cut, copy, paste, and clear text in the edit windows. You can use this menu to undo or redo the previous editor operations and to search and replace text.
View	Use these commands to view information about the project, to start the Class Wizard, and to control which windows and toolbars are visible.
Insert	Use these commands to add resources, files, and prebuilt functionality into your project.
Build	Use these commands to compile and organize your projects.
Debug	Use these commands to troubleshoot your programs with the Visual C++ debugger. The menu's commands enable you to single-step and trace through your code, view variable values, set watch points, and look at the call stack.
Tools	Use these commands to customize the Developer Studio toolbars and environment and to record macro keystrokes. You can also add other tools and utilities that are not part of the Developer Studio to this menu for easy access.
Window	Use these commands to manage the various windows that appear in the Developer Studio. You can select which editor window to make active, arrange edit windows on the desktop, or close all open windows.
Help	Use these commands to access the powerful online help system. You can find help for every aspect of the MFC class libraries, the Windows API, the C and C++ languages, and C and C++ run-time library routines.

Now that you have reviewed each main menu item, the following sections examine the options available for each top-level menu command, explain what they do, and give you an idea of how they operate.

The File Menu

The File menu commands enable you manage the various kinds of source files that are involved in creating a program. The File menu includes the following commands: New, Open, Close, Open Workspace, Close Workspace, Save, Save As, Save All, Find in

Files, Page Setup, Print, and Exit. The menu also contains the most-recently used files and workspaces so you can easily revisit files or workspaces that you have previously edited.

> **Note**
>
> As you start using the Developer Studio, you will notice new items (which are numbered starting from 1) added on this menu between the Print and Exit options. These are program files with which you have recently worked. Selecting the number associated with the file (or moving the menu bar over the item and pressing Enter) instantly loads the file. The benefit is that you don't have to retype the file name.

The New Command (Ctrl+N)

The New command displays a dialog box (see fig. 2.2) that enables you to open a new source window.

Fig. 2.2

The New dialog box.

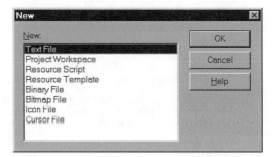

From the New dialog box, you can choose one of the following types of files:

- Text File creates a C (.c) or C++ (.cpp) source-code file or any type of ASCII text file (.txt).

- Project Workspace creates a new Developer Studio project workspace (.mdp) file. When you are working on an application, you must have a project created that gives the compiler information about the application that you are creating.

- Resource Script stores information about the resources (dialog boxes, bitmaps, icons, cursors, and strings) associated with an application. You add resources to this file with the Insert, Resource command.

- Resource Template creates a new file for resource templates. You add resources to this file with the Insert, Resource command, modify them, and then save the file in the Templates directory under your Developer Studio installation directory. Subsequently, the resources that you have created appear in the list of resources in the Insert Resource dialog box.

- Binary File enables you to create and edit binary files. The resulting editor window lets you enter only numerical values in hexadecimal notation.

- Bitmap File creates a new Windows bitmap (.bmp) file and opens the bitmap resource editor.

- Icon File creates a new Windows icon (.ico) file and opens the icon resource editor.

- Cursor File creates a new Windows cursor (.cur) file and opens the cursor resource editor.

After you select a file type and click the OK button, the Developer Studio creates a new editor window. When you are creating a new project file, the New Project dialog box appears, which enables you to specify information about the application that you are creating.

Each window in the Developer Studio contains a title that consists of the name of the associated file. When you create a new code or text window, Developer Studio initially uses the temporary name text1.cpp. The second new code or text window is named text2.cpp, and so on. Source windows are numbered beginning with 1.

Compiled Files

When you create a new project file (.mdp) by choosing File, New, Visual C++ enables you to choose which type of application you want to generate. Visual C++ 4 enables you to generate the following kinds of programs and libraries:

- Microsoft Foundation Classes (MFC) applications built with the AppWizard (.exe)

- MFC dynamic link libraries built with the AppWizard (.dll)

- OLE custom controls (.exe)

- "Plain" Windows applications (.exe)

- Windows dynamic link libraries (.dll)

- Console-mode applications (.exe)

- Static libraries (.lib)

- Makefiles (.mak)

- Custom AppWizard applications (.awx)

Console-mode applications emulate MS-DOS (text-based) applications in Windows. The emulation is not complete; it excludes cursor-control and keyboard-scanning techniques. However, you can write short DOS-like C and C++ programs on the fly and compile them into console-mode applications. With such applications, you can use the C++ stream input/output (I/O) and the standard C I/O library.

The Open Command (Ctrl+O)

With Visual C++ 4, you open all file types by choosing File, Open. The list of file types in the Open File dialog box includes the following:

- Common files (.c, .cpp, .cxx, .h, .rc)
- Source files (.c, .cpp, .cxx)
- Include files (.h, .hpp, .hxx, .inl)
- Definition files (.def)
- Project workspaces (.mdp)
- Resource files (.rc, .rct, .res)
- Image files (.bmp, .dib, .ico, .cur)
- Executable files (.exe, .dll, .ocx)
- Browse info files (.bsc)
- Object description files (.odl)
- All files (*.*)

Developer Studio knows what type of editor to open for each file type.

The Open command invokes the Open File dialog box, which enables you to open files for viewing or editing. In the File Name text box, you type the name of a file located on any existing drive and directory. You can use wild-card characters as necessary. Beneath the File Name text box is a list box that displays all files (in the currently selected path) that match the wild card that you entered.

The Close Command (Ctrl+F4)

Choose File, Close to close the currently selected (or *active*) window. If you have updated the window but have not saved it, Visual C++ prompts you to save the window's contents. You can close all open windows without exiting the Developer Studio by choosing Window, Close All.

The Open Workspace Command

The Open Workspace command enables you to open the following:

- Project workspaces (.mdp)
- Makefiles (.mak)
- Executable files (.exe)
- All files (*.*)

When you open an existing project workspace, Visual C++ restores all the environment settings to the state that they were in when you last saved the project workspace.

The Close Workspace Command

Use the Close Workspace command to close the currently active workspace. If necessary, Developer Studio prompts for actions concerning the windows that are open and the files that you have modified—whether or not you included them in a project.

The Save Command (Ctrl+S)

The Save command writes the currently active window's contents to disk. If the active window is new and has not yet had a disk file name associated with it, this item invokes the Save As dialog box to request the name of the associated file.

The Save As Command

Choosing File, Save As invokes the Save As dialog box (see fig. 2.3), which prompts you to specify a new file name for the active window. The Save As dialog box, which is similar to the Open dialog box, enables you to select the output file's drive, directory, and name.

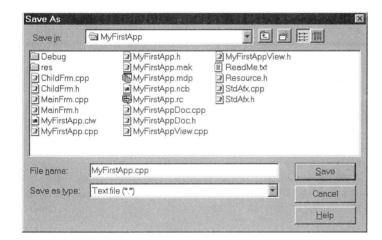

Fig. 2.3

The Save As dialog box.

The Save All Command

The Save All command provides a convenient way to save all the source windows currently active in the Developer Studio. This command ensures that you save all open windows to disk with a minimum of effort. If you frequently have to save the files on which you are working because of possible power interruptions, you will appreciate this command.

> **Note**
>
> The Developer Studio can automatically save files before compiling files. To enable this feature, choose Tools, Options and then select the Save before Running Tools check box. If you want Developer Studio to confirm which files you want saved, select the Prompt before Saving Files check box.

The Find In Files Command

Choose File, Find In Files to open the Find In Files dialog box (see fig. 2.4), in which you can search for a sequence of characters in one or more files. You specify the files to search by indicating the type of file and the folders in which to search. You can use regular expressions to match character patterns in the selected files. The output window displays the search results. When the search finishes, you can open a file that contains a match by double-clicking the entry in the output window.

Fig. 2.4

The Find In Files dialog box.

The Page Setup Command

Choose File, Page Setup to open the Page Setup dialog box, in which you can specify how the printed output of your source code will appear. The dialog box enables you to specify a header (which is printed at the top of each source-code page), a footer (printed at the bottom of each page), and the size of the margins on the left, top, right, and bottom sides of the page.

Both the Header and Footer text boxes can contain special codes that you can use to customize the look of the printed page. Table 2.2 shows the codes that you can use to format the header and footer. For example, if you enter the string **&l&f** for the header and the string **&c&p** for the footer, the output page displays a left-justified file name in the header and a centered page number in the footer.

Table 2.2	Header and Footer Formatting Codes
Format Code	**Description**
&f	File name
&p	Page number of the current page
&t	Current system time

Format Code	Description
&d	Current system date
&l	Left-justified
&c	Centered
&r	Right-justified

> **Note**
>
> The format codes are not case-sensitive.

The Page Setup dialog box does contain default values, so you need not enter any text to use the printing features available within the Developer Studio.

The Print Command (Ctrl+P)

Choose File, Print to open the Print dialog box (see fig. 2.5), which enables you to produce a printout of the contents of the currently active window. In the dialog box, you can choose the entire contents of the active window (the All radio button) or only text that is currently selected (the Selection radio button).

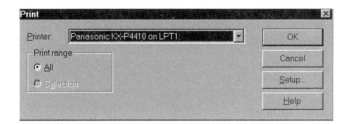

Fig. 2.5

The Print dialog box.

In addition, the Print dialog box contains a drop-down list box that displays the list of currently available printers. You can manipulate the setup of the currently selected printer by clicking the Setup command button.

The Setup command button invokes the Printer Setup dialog box (see fig. 2.6). This dialog box (which might look different than the one shown in fig. 2.6, depending on the type of printer that you are using) enables you to select printing parameters, such as the paper size, paper source, graphics resolution, number of copies, memory, output orientation, font cartridges, and fonts.

The Exit Command (Alt+F4)

The last command in the File menu is Exit, which closes all the source windows and then closes the Developer Studio. If you haven't yet saved any source windows in the Developer Studio, it prompts you to save them before exiting.

Fig. 2.6

The Printer Setup dialog box.

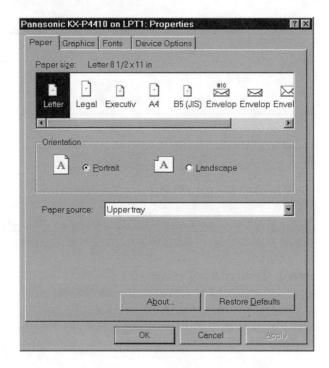

The Edit Menu

The Edit menu commands support text editing and searching. The menu contains the following commands: Undo, Redo, Cut, Copy, Paste, Delete, Select All, Find, Replace, Go To, InfoViewer Bookmarks, Breakpoints, and Properties.

The Undo Command (Ctrl+Z)

You use the Undo command to reverse the effect of your most recent editing operation. The actual number of editing actions that you can undo depends on the size of your undo buffer. This buffer has a default size of 64K. You set this value by modifying information in the system Registry.

For Windows NT, the Registry Editor is REGEDT32.EXE, and for Windows 95, the Registry Editor is REGEDIT.EXE (see fig. 2.7). The undo buffer size is stored in the following path:

```
My Computer\HKEY_CURRENT_USER\Software\Microsoft\Developer
        \Text Editor\UndoRedoSize
```

The Redo Command (Ctrl+Y)

The Redo command enables you to counteract the effects of the Undo command. You use Redo to restore the results of the editing actions that you just reversed with Undo. (This command should be particularly useful to programmers who get bleary-eyed from long hours in front of the computer.)

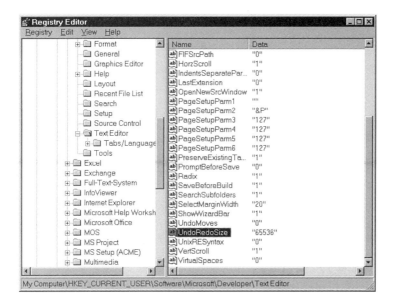

Fig. 2.7

Changing the undo buffer size with REGEDIT.

The Cut Command (Ctrl+X)

By choosing Edit, Cut, you can delete a block of selected text and write it to the Windows Clipboard (overwriting the Clipboard's previous contents). You then use the Paste command to insert the deleted text in one or more locations in a source window. The Cut and Paste commands are useful to move text from one location to another both within a single source window and between source windows.

The Copy Command (Ctrl+C)

You use the Copy command to copy a block of selected text into the Windows Clipboard (overwriting the Clipboard's previous contents). You then use the Paste command to insert the copied text in one or more locations in the same source window or in other windows. The shortcut key combination for Copy command is Ctrl+C, and you can also use the related icon on the toolbar.

The Paste Command (Ctrl+V)

The Paste command lets you insert the Clipboard's contents at the current cursor location. If you have any currently highlighted text, the command deletes the text and inserts the Clipboard's contents. You use the Paste command with the Cut and Copy commands to move and copy text, respectively.

The Delete Command (Del)

The Delete menu command deletes text without copying it to the Clipboard. If no text is selected, Delete removes the character to the right of the keyboard cursor.

> **Note**
>
> Use the Undo command to reverse the action of the Delete command. Undo is available in this situation because Delete copies the deleted characters to the undo buffer.

The Select All Command

Choose the Select All menu item to select the contents of an entire editor window. When you choose this command, the entire source buffer is highlighted and the cursor moves to the end of the window. You can then use the Cut, Copy, Delete, and Paste commands to manipulate the highlighted text.

You will find the Select All command most helpful when you are creating new applications that rely on code previously written from previous projects. There is no shortcut key combination for this menu item.

The Find Command (Ctrl+F3)

You can use the Find command to perform versatile text searches ranging from simple text to sophisticated text patterns known as *regular expressions*. You also can use the Find command to locate text and then set a bookmark on the line that contains the matching text. (You'll learn more about bookmarks later in this chapter.)

When you choose Edit, Find, the Find dialog box displays (see fig. 2.8). In the Find What combo box, you enter the text or text pattern for which you want to search. You can recall previously entered text items by choosing them from the associated drop-down list.

Fig. 2.8

The Find dialog box.

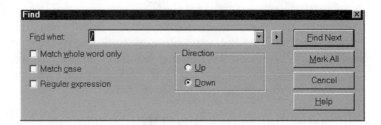

To fine-tune the operation of the Find dialog box, you can select the following options:

- The Match Whole Word Only check box determines whether the matching text should match an entire word.
- The Match Case check box specifies whether the search is case-sensitive.
- The Regular Expression check box determines whether to treat the search text as a regular expression. You can click the small right-arrow bitmap next to the Find

What combo box to display a drop-down list of common regular expressions that you might need when searching through your code. Select an expression from the list to use it.

- The Direction group (consisting of the Up and Down options) determines the search direction.

The dialog box has two buttons that trigger different kinds of searches. The Find Next button finds the next matching text. The Mark All button searches for the matching text and sets a bookmark for each matching line.

After starting a search, you can press the F3 key to continue searching for other occurrences of the same text string without having to redisplay the dialog box.

You can use toolbar buttons to display the Find dialog box, search for new text, or search for the next occurrence of specified text. The toolbar contains a combo box that enables you to recall a previous search string or to enter a new one. To conduct another text search, click the toolbar's Binocular button. The Developer Studio then performs the text search based on the most recent settings in the Find dialog box.

Regular Expressions

Regular expressions are special strings that contain text patterns. You use these patterns to search for a range of strings. Regular expressions use special characters to specify the text pattern. The Developer Studio supports the following characters:

.   Represents any individual character. For example, the pattern `m..t` matches *meat, meet, ment,* and any other four-character word that starts with *m* and ends with *t*.

*   Matches zero or more of the characters or the expression preceding the asterisk. For example, the pattern `Robin*son` matches *Robinson* and *Robison.*

+   Matches one or more of the characters or the expression preceding the plus character. For example, the pattern `Sham+as` matches *Shammas* and *Shamas.*

^   Matches a pattern at the beginning of a line. For example, the pattern `^if` matches only a code line that starts with the characters *if.*

\$ Matches a pattern at the end of a line. For example, the pattern `-1)$` matches any line that ends with the string *–1).*

[]   Matches any of the characters appearing in the brackets or any range of ASCII characters delimited by a hyphen. For example, the pattern `199[0-9]` matches 1990 through 1999. The pattern `me[aen]t` matches *meat, meet,* and *ment,* but not *melt.*

\{\}   Matches any sequence of characters between the escaped braces. For example, the text pattern `\{ba\}*by` matches *by, baby, bababy,* and *babababy* in the word *babababy.*

\   Specifies that the preceding character be treated as a normal character and not as part of the pattern characters. For example, the pattern `\[i\]` matches the string *[i].*

The Replace Command

You can use the Replace command to replace both simple text and text patterns. This command invokes the Replace dialog box (see fig. 2.9).

Fig. 2.9

The Replace dialog box.

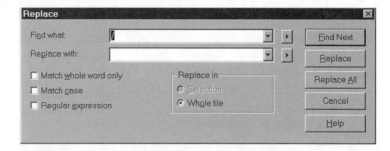

The Replace dialog box has two combo boxes, Find What and Replace With. In these controls, you can enter the search-and-replacement text. The Replace dialog box has the same check box options as the Find dialog box.

The Replace dialog box has several command buttons. The Replace button changes the currently selected text to the replacement text. By clicking the Replace All button, you can search and replace text all in one fell swoop.

Caution

Use the Find Next command button when you are replacing text that matches a text pattern. By using this approach, you can view the matching text before you replace it. To be doubly safe, work on a copy of the source code and not the original. By using this precaution, you have the luxury of resorting to the original document, if necessary, with little effort. The Undo command also works with Replace.

The Go To Command (Ctrl+G)

The Go To menu item enables you to move to a specific item within an editor window. When you select the Go To option, the Go To dialog box displays (see fig. 2.10).

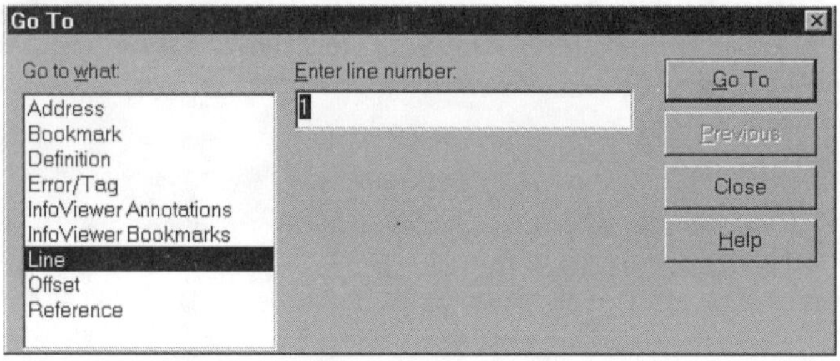

Fig. 2.10

The Go To dialog box.

The Go To dialog box's Go To <u>W</u>hat list box enables you to select what you want to move to. Table 2.3 describes the available selections.

Table 2.3	Moving around in Source Files by Using the Go To Dialog Box	
Go To What Selection	**What You Must Provide**	**Comments**
&f	Any filename	
Address	An address expression	Use any valid debugger expression.
Bookmark	A bookmark name	Use the bookmark name.
Definition	Identifer whose definition you want to see	Browse information must be enabled for this to work.
Error/Tag	An error or tag from the list provided	Jumps to the selected error or tag.
InfoView Annotations	Name of an InfoViewer annotated topic	Visits the annotated topic.
InfoViewer Bookmarks	Name of an InfoViewer bookmark	Jumps to the specified bookmark.
Line	Line number	Use 99999 to go to the last source line. The line number must be a decimal number.
Offset	Decimal or hex number	Use any decimal or hexidecimal number; the number is the number of lines that you want to move.
Reference	Identifer whose reference you want to see	Browse information must be enabled for this to work.

By watching the Developer Studio status line at the bottom of the screen, you can view the line number on which the cursor is currently placed.

The InfoViewer Bookmarks Command

Use the <u>I</u>nfoViewer Bookmarks command to visit and create a set of bookmarks in the online documentation. With an InfoViewer bookmark, the Name field is the help topic's title and the Book field is the book's name.

The Bookmarks Command

The Developer Studio's bookmarks are similar to the bookmarks that you use when reading your favorite Stephen King novel. Their purpose is to mark important locations in your work that you want to return to later.

Just as you can dog-ear several pages in a novel, Developer Studio enables you to set bookmarks in multiple locations of your source code. You just might find that the electronic bookmarks that you use in Developer Studio are even more helpful than the ones that you use for your leisure-time reading.

To work with bookmarks in the Developer Studio, you use the buttons in the Bookmarks dialog box. The Edit, Bookmarks command displays the Bookmarks dialog box.

Using Named and Unnamed Bookmarks. Developer Studio includes support for two types of bookmarks. Named bookmarks have individual names; you access them through the Edit, Go To command and the Bookmarks dialog box's Go To button. Named bookmarks are saved as part of your source file, so they stay around until you manually delete them. Unnamed bookmarks are temporary; they are erased when you close or reload the file. You access unnamed bookmarks with shortcut keys as discussed below.

Adding New Bookmarks. The Add button in the Bookmarks dialog box enables you to create a new named bookmark. You use this command to mark specific lines of code manually, perhaps to show the lines to a colleague.

To create the bookmark, put the cursor on the line to which you want the bookmark to point, and then select Edit, Bookmarks. When the Bookmarks dialog box appears, type the name of your new bookmark into the Name field, then click Add. The bookmark will appear in the Bookmarks dialog box's list.

To set an unnamed bookmark, put the cursor on the line that you want marked and use the BookmarkToggle command. By default, Developer Studio binds this command to Ctrl+F2. When you set an unnamed bookmark, the Developer Studio displays a small icon in the left margin of the editor window.

> **Note**
>
> You can change the shortcut key for almost any Developer Studio command with the Tools, Customize command. See the section "The Customize Command" for more details.

You can also set unnamed bookmarks with the Find dialog box by using its Mark All button. The Find command will set a bookmark for each occurrence of the search string.

> **Note**
>
> When you choose the Mark All button in the Find dialog box, Visual C++ adds all the new bookmarks and does not automatically remove the existing ones.

Removing Bookmarks. When you finish with a bookmark, you can delete it. Developer Studio enables you to delete one or more bookmarks by selecting them in the Bookmarks dialog box's bookmark list and clicking the Close button.

To remove an unnamed bookmark, put the cursor on the line that you want marked and use the BookmarkToggle command. (Remember, the default binding for this command is Ctrl+F2.)

Navigating to Bookmarks. To go to a named bookmark, you can do one of two things:

- Use the Edit, Go To command as discussed in the "The Go To Command" section.
- Open the Bookmarks dialog box by choosing Edit, Bookmarks, then select the bookmark to which you want to jump, and click Go To.

To move between unnamed bookmarks, you can use the Next and Previous Bookmark commands. Next Bookmark moves the cursor to the next line that contains a bookmark. This command's shortcut key is F2. Similarly, the Previous Bookmark command moves the cursor to the previous line that contains a bookmark. The shortcut key combination for this command is Shift+F2.

Jumping to Bookmarks. After you've added bookmarks in your files, you can quickly jump to any of them.

The Breakpoints Command (Ctrl+B)

The Breakpoints command invokes the Breakpoints dialog box, shown in figure 2.11. This dialog box helps you manage the breakpoints in your source code. The dialog box contains command buttons to add, remove, disable, and clear breakpoints. The Developer Studio supports several types of breakpoints, including the following:

- At a specific location if an expression is true
- At a specific location if an expression has changed
- At the current statement if an expression is true
- At the current statement if an expression has changed
- At WndProc if a specific message is received

The Breakpoint dialog box enables you to specify the type of breakpoint, its location (file or line number), and the tested expression.

The Properties Command (Alt+Enter)

Use the Properties command for displaying information about the currently active window. When you choose this option, the Properties dialog box opens, displaying information about the active editor window.

Fig. 2.11

The Breakpoints dialog box.

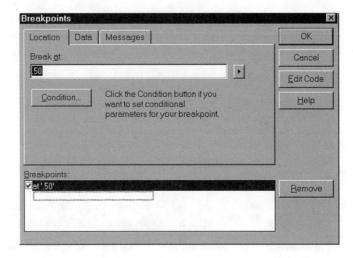

The information displayed is context-sensitive; it varies according to the type of window currently open. For example, if you are editing a C or C++ source-code file, the Properties menu item displays a dialog box that shows the full path and file name associated with the editor window (the title bar displays only the file name), the read-only status of the file, and the type of highlighting to use for the file. However, if you are editing a dialog box (using the built-in AppStudio utility), the Properties dialog box displays information about the dialog box that you are editing.

You use the Properties dialog box in a variety of different situations. As you work through this book, you will learn other uses for this dialog box's items.

The View Menu

The View menu commands support viewing the information in your project workspace in a variety of ways and controlling which windows and toolbars to display. The menu contains the following commands: ClassWizard, Resource Symbols, Resource Includes, Full Screen, Toolbars, InfoViewer Query Results, InfoViewer History List, Project Workspace, InfoViewer Topic, Output, Watch, Variables, Registers, Memory, Call Stack, and Disassembly.

The ClassWizard Command (Ctrl+W)

The ClassWizard (see fig. 2.12) is a powerful feature of Visual C++ that helps you quickly generate MFC-based classes and functions that you can use in your C++ programs. The ClassWizard helps you manage the creation and editing of code by handling messages related to your application. It also helps you create dialog boxes by mapping associated data values to member variables in your class.

You learn about using ClassWizard (as well as a related tool, AppWizard) in Chapters 5 and 6 of this book.

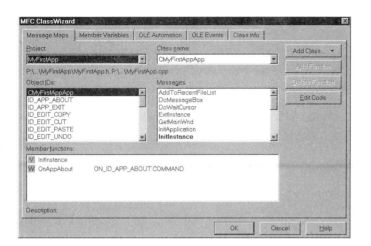

Fig. 2.12

The MFC ClassWizard.

The Resource Symbols Command

The Resource Symbols command displays the Symbol Browser dialog box (see fig. 2.13), which helps you manage the symbols defined and used by your program.

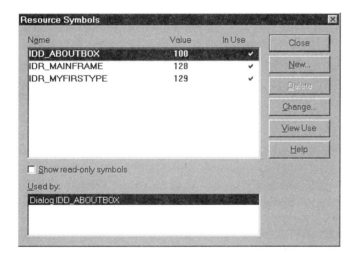

Fig. 2.13

The Resource Symbols dialog box.

The dialog box lists the symbolic constant, along with the numeric values associated with the symbol, for each resource. Helpfully, the list tells you whether the symbol is being used. This feature is handy when you are debugging or optimizing a project to ensure that you are using the symbols you expected.

By clicking the New button, you can add a new symbol to those associated with your project. You then type the symbol name and the value to associate with the symbol. To change the value associated with a symbol, click the Change button. By clicking the View Use button, you can also view the instances in your code that use a symbol.

The Resource Includes Command

The Resource Includes command enables you to change the name of the symbol's header file. By choosing this menu item, you open the Set Includes dialog box, which enables you to type the new name for the header file that is to contain symbol name declarations. Although this feature can be handy when fine-tuning your programs, you probably will not often use this option.

The Full Screen Command

The Full Screen menu item enables you to use the text editor and other resource editors in full-screen mode. When you initially select full-screen mode, a toolbar button with a small graphic of a computer screen displays. You can toggle full-screen mode on and off by clicking this button. You can also press the Esc key to end full-screen mode.

The Toolbars Command

The Toolbars menu item enables you to choose which toolbars are available for use. After invoking this command, you can choose from a dialog box that lists the following standard toolbars:

- Standard
- Project
- Resource
- Edit
- Debug
- Browse
- InfoViewer
- InfoViewer Contents

Each of these options controls the display of its associated toolbar. You can turn each toolbar on or off by clicking the check box next to its name in the dialog box. For each toolbar, you can choose whether to display ToolTips by checking the Show Tool Tips check box. A ToolTip is the message that describes what a toolbar button does; the message appears when you hold the cursor over a toolbar for more than a second without moving it. If you want the ToolTips to include the shortcut keys for buttons, check the With Shortcut Keys box too.

By clicking the New button in the Toolbars dialog box, you can create your own named toolbar. When you click New, you are prompted to name your new toolbar. Developer Studio then displays the new toolbar and the Customize dialog box appears. See the section "The Customize Command" to find out what to do next.

Developer Studio also enables you to customize the standard toolbars. If you want to customize an existing toolbar, select it in the Toolbars dialog box and click Customize.

The InfoViewer Query Results Command

The InfoViewer Query Results menu item displays the online help Query Results window. Double-click the name of a topic to go there directly. You can keep the Query Results list open as you read the topic by *pinning* it—click the push-pin button near the upper-left corner of the list window. By default, the results list is sorted based on the number of matches (or *hits*) found in each topic, in descending order; the number in the first column indicates the topic's rank. To sort the results list by book title, click the Book button at the top of the second column. To sort the results list by the topic title, click the Topic button at the top of the third column. To revert to sorting by the number of hits, click the Order button above the first column. To see the history list, click the History List tab at the bottom of the window.

The InfoViewer History List Command

The InfoViewer History List menu item displays the online help History List window. InfoViewer keeps track of the topics that you've previously viewed, so you can easily return to those topics. Double-click the topic's name to go directly to that topic. You can keep the History list open while you view another topic by pinning it; click the push-pin button near the upper-left corner of the History list's window. By default, the History list displays the topics in the order that you visited them, starting with the most recently visited. To sort the results list by book title, click the Book button at the top of the second column. To sort the results list by the topic title, click the Topic button at the top of the third column. To see the query results, click the Query Results tab at the bottom of the window.

The Project Workspace Command (Alt+0)

The Project Workspace menu item displays the Project Workspace window. In this powerful and flexible window, you can view and manipulate all parts of your projects. Separate panes—ClassView, ResourceView, FileView, and InfoView—display your classes, resources, files, and online help. From these views, you can navigate to member functions, open resources, or even set the default project. The docking Project Workspace window is the site of operations for your development tasks.

The InfoViewer Topic Command (Alt+1)

The InfoViewer Topic menu item displays the InfoViewer main output window. Any InfoViewer Topic window provides several ways to get related information. Table 2.4 describes the toolbar buttons that enable you to find the information.

Table 2.4 The Toolbar Buttons Available from InfoViewer Topic Windows

Icon(s)	Function
◀ ▶	These toolbar buttons move you to the topic that precedes or follows the current one, as listed in the table of contents. The keyboard shortcuts are Ctrl+Shift+P and Ctrl+Shift+N, respectively.
📋◀	This toolbar button expands and scrolls the table of contents to show you where the current topic is, relative to the rest of the table of contents. The keyboard shortcut is Ctrl+S. You can also have this synchronization done automatically by setting the Track Topic in InfoView check box in the Workspace tab of the Tools, Options dialog box; see the section "The Options Command" for more details.
t..	This toolbar button returns you to the last topic that you viewed; you can backtrack up to 50 steps. The keyboard shortcut is Ctrl+B. You can also see a list of previously viewed topics; see "The InfoViewer History List Command" for more details.
See Also ▼	This toolbar button displays a drop-down list that contains related topics. The keyboard shortcut is Ctrl+Shift+S.

Note

Before using these toolbar buttons, make sure that the table of contents has been synchronized. Otherwise, the topic selected in the table of contents might not be related to the topic that you are currently viewing.

Words or phrases highlighted in color are *hot links*. Clicking a hot link can either move you to another topic or display a pop-up window. The keyboard shortcut is to press Tab to move to the next hot link in the topic text, and press Enter to activate the hot link and jump to the corresponding topic. By default, hot links to other topics are green, and pop-ups are gray. To change the coloring, see the section "Customizing Developer Studio."

If you want to learn more about a word that is not a hot link, click the word and then press the F1 key. The effect of this action is the same as pressing F1 after selecting a word in a source window: It searches the help index for the word and displays the topic indexed under that word.

The Output Command (Alt+2)

The Output command displays the output window. This window displays the progress of compiling and linking source files or building a project, and all the warnings and error messages associated with these processes. The output window is a read-only window.

The Watch Command (Alt+3)

The Watch command opens the Watch window, which you can use to view the values of variables during a debugging session. The fastest way to start watching a variable is by using the QuickWatch dialog box (see the section "The QuickWatch Command" for full details). You can also type the names of the variables that you want to watch into any empty slot in the Name column of the Watch window. You must type each watched variable on a separate line, and you can delete only an entire line or entire structured variable or class instance. The Watch window does not allow partial deletion of watched items. The shortcut key for the Watch command is Alt+3.

The Variables Command (Alt+4)

The View, Variables command offers a convenient display of the values of variables that are local to the currently executing function or member function. The command automatically includes the local variables of the currently executing function and displays their values; all you have to do is display the Variables window.

If you want to look at the value of local variables in functions "higher" in the call chain than the current function, you can select the variable context from the Variables window's Context pull-down list. Moreover, when the current function returns to its caller function, or calls another function, the Variables window updates its contents to show the local variables of the new current function.

The Registers Command (Alt+5)

By choosing View, Registers, you can display the current values of the microprocessor registers. This dump is useful when checking parameters for calls to functions written in x86 assembly or other languages.

The Memory Command (Alt+6)

The Memory menu item displays a raw hexadecimal dump of memory. After you specify the address to display, Visual C++ opens a window that shows the contents of memory starting from the specified address.

The Call Stack Command (Alt+7)

By choosing View, Call Stack, you display the Call Stack window (see fig. 2.14). This window shows the chain listing all the functions that have been called to reach the current statement in your program. The most recently called function is located at the top of the list.

The Disassembly Command (Alt+8)

The Disassembly menu item opens an editor window that contains the actual assembly language code that Visual C++ creates when compiling your C and C++ source code. Although the assembly language source code frightens many programmers, examining it can be useful, if only to appreciate the work that the compiler is saving you from doing (after all, aren't you happy that you can write in a high-level language such as C++ instead of having to write directly in assembly language?). More importantly, disassembling code is also useful for optimizing code manually.

Fig. 2.14

The Call Stack dialog box.

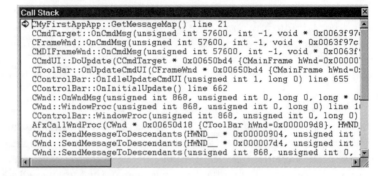

The Insert Menu

The Insert menu commands enable you to insert information into your project workspace in a variety of ways. The menu contains the following commands: File, Resource, Resource Copy, Files into Project, Project, and Component.

The File Command

Choose Insert, File to insert a file into the currently active window. This command provides an efficient way to import old source code into your current project. Developer Studio then displays the Insert File dialog box, in which you can choose individual files to add to your project.

The Resource Command (Ctrl+R)

The Resource command displays the Insert Resource dialog box (see fig. 2.15), with which you can add a new resource to your application.

Fig. 2.15

The Insert Resource dialog box.

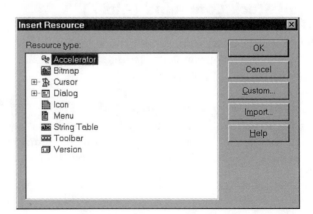

To create a new resource, choose the type of resource that you want:

- Accelerator lets you create keyboard-accelerator resources for binding keys to commands.
- Bitmap creates Windows bitmap picture images.
- Cursor creates cursor images.
- Dialog creates dialog boxes.
- Icon creates a standard Windows icon to represent your program visually in the Program Manager, Start menu, and so forth.
- Menu enables you to create menu bars and pull-down menus.
- String Table lets you group text strings and store them as a single resource.
- Toolbar gives you access to a bitmap editor tailored for toolbar editing.
- Version creates program version information.
- Custom creates user-defined resource types. You use the Developer Studio binary editor to modify a user-defined resource.

When you select a resource type and click OK, Developer Studio creates a new resource of whatever type you selected, switches to the Resource View tab if it's not already active, and opens the appropriate resource editor for your new resource.

After you choose the type of resource that you want to create, click the OK button. Developer Studio then creates the new resource, switches to the Resource View tab if it's not already active, and opens the associated editor window.

The Resource Copy Command

Choose the Resource Copy menu item to duplicate a resource defined in an existing resource file. If you copy a resource with a different language (such as English or French) or conditional definition, the resource's language or condition is shown after the symbol name in the project window. A symbol identifies the condition under which this copy of the resource is used.

The Files into Project Command

The Files into Project menu item invokes the Insert Files into Project dialog box (see fig. 2.16). This dialog box enables you to add or delete files in the project. The Insert Files into Project dialog box works just like the Insert File dialog box that you learned about earlier in this chapter, except that here you can add many files at once.

Fig. 2.16

The Insert Files into Project dialog box.

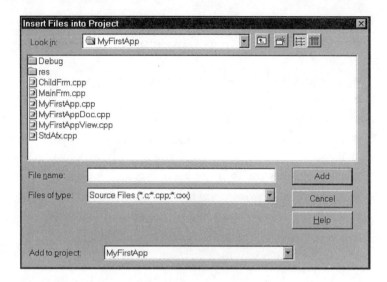

> **Note**
>
> You'll never add header files (.h or .hpp) to the project file, because you access them within a program's source code by using the #include preprocessor directive. In fact, the Developer Studio doesn't even allow you to add header files to a project.

The Project Command

Choose Insert, Project to insert an additional project into the current project workspace. The project has Debug and Release configurations for every platform selected. The command creates a subdirectory for the project files in the project workspace directory.

This command is invaluable if you're building an application with more than one executable, or any project with more than a single component. A single Visual C++ project can build your application, any DLLs it requires, and even device drivers or Windows NT services (if you have any).

The Component Command

The Component menu item enables you to insert prebuilt components into your project. Components are much like OLE custom controls or Visual Basic VBX controls; when you add a component from the Component Gallery dialog box (see fig. 2.17), its source files are added to your project. Some components even come with wizards that lead you through the process of choosing what component options are right for your project.

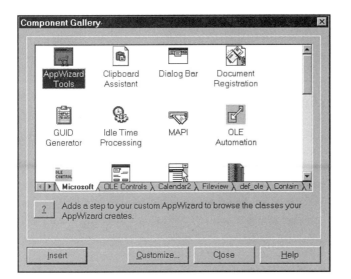

Fig. 2.17

*The Component Gallery
dialog box.*

The Build Menu

The Build menu's commands support building, rebuilding, debugging, and configuring your projects. The menu contains the following commands: Compile, Build *<your app.exe>*, Rebuild All, Batch Build, Stop Build, Update All Dependencies, Debug, Execute *<your app.exe>*, Settings, Configurations, Subprojects, and Set Default Configuration.

The Compile Command (Ctrl+F8)

The Compile command compiles the file in the currently active editor window. The Developer Studio displays the compilation's progress and outcome in the output window. If the compilation process results in any warnings or errors, you can use the Next Error/Tag (F4) and Previous Error/Tag (Shift+F4) commands or the Edit, Go To command to inspect the offending statements in the compiled source file.

The Build *<your app.exe>* Command (Shift+F8)

Use the Build command to build a source file (and the files included in that file). When you build the source files, the compiler uses the target that you selected. The two most common targets are Debug and Release. When you compile for the Debug target, the compiler and linker includes debugging information in the compiled program so that you can use the debugger. Use the Release target after you finish testing your program; it omits debugging information and turns on code optimization.

You can set the default configuration for the project by choosing Build, Set Default Configuration. You can also change the configuration target in the Project toolbar by choosing a target from the combo box.

The Developer Studio displays the progress and outcome of the build in the output window. If the compilation or linking results in any warnings or errors, you can use the Next Error/Tag (F4) and Previous Error/Tag (Shift+F4) commands or the Edit, Go To command to inspect the offending statements in the compiled source file.

The Rebuild All Command (Alt+F8)

The Rebuild All command enables you to force Visual C++ to build all the source files in the current project, regardless of their dependencies. You can rebuild the source files in any of the specified target modes, just as you can with the Build command.

The Batch Build Command

To build more than one type of target, choose Build, Batch Build. When you first choose the Batch Build command, the Batch Build dialog box displays (see fig. 2.18). From this dialog box, you can mark which of the target types you want to build.

Fig. 2.18

The Batch Build dialog box.

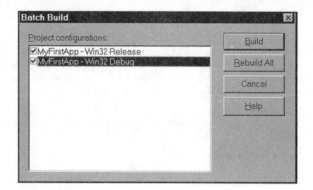

After you click the Build button, Visual C++ creates each of the target application types. To abort the operation, click the Cancel button. You can click the Help button to receive additional information about the batch build process.

The Stop Build Command (Ctrl+Break)

The Stop Build command enables you to interrupt a build or a rebuild operation. Typically, you choose to stop building a program when you remember that you need to make at least one more change in the source code before recompiling the program.

You might have noticed that Build and Stop Build have the same hot key: B. When you start a build, Stop Build is enabled and Build is disabled, so there is no conflict.

The Update All Dependencies Command

A typical Windows application involves multiple source-code files, header files, and resource files. The Developer Studio builds and maintains the list of files that are involved in a project. The Developer Studio first generates this list when you create a new project. The list includes source files (with .c and .cpp extensions), resource script files (with the .rc extension), and include files (which usually have .h or .hpp extensions). The Developer Studio maintains the interdependencies of the files in a project.

The Update All Dependencies command reconstructs the include file dependencies for all the files in the current project. Choose this command after adding new include files to the source code of several project source files. This command offers the convenience of updating the dependencies for the entire project at one time.

The Debug Submenu

The Debug submenu appears in the Build menu so that you can start the debugger with your application. It offers three commands:

- Go (F5) starts running your application in the debugger.
- Step Into (F8) starts running your application in the debugger and runs until it enters the first function in your application.
- Run To Cursor (F7) starts running your application in the debugger and runs until it encounters the function where the cursor's located.

The Execute *<your app.exe>* Command (Ctrl+F5)

The Execute command runs the program without the debugger. Contrast this with the Go command, which runs the program in the debugger. When you use Execute, your program runs as if you started it directly from Windows.

The Settings Command

Choose Build, Settings to display the Project Settings dialog box (see fig. 2.19), in which you can modify options related to the application that you are creating.

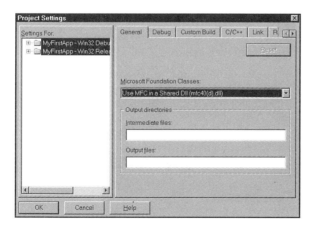

Fig. 2.19

The Project Settings dialog box.

The Project Settings dialog box is divided into sections by the tabs displayed along the top. The tabs enable you to access general, debug, C or C++, link, resource-related, OLE-type, and browse information settings. The dialog box's left side enables you to select the parts of the project to which you want the settings to apply, and the right side changes depending on which tab you select at the top of the dialog box.

The Project Settings diaog box's General page has options for choosing how to link the MFC class (static or dynamic) and the output location for your application's intermediate and output directories. The default location for intermediate and output directories is in the WINDEBUG directory in your project's current directory.

The Project Settings dialog box's Debug page has options for choosing the executable for the current debug session, selecting the working directory, setting program arguments, specifying additional DLLs to use with your application, and setting the remote executable path and file name.

The Project Settings dialog box's C/C++ page includes a list box from which you can choose the category of options to modify. Categories include General, Output, Input, Customize, and Debug. As you select each category, more compiler language options appear in the dialog box.

In the Project Settings dialog box's Link page, you can choose the output file name and the object module name. The page also presents check boxes for choosing to generate debug information, link incrementally, enable program profiling, ignore default libraries, generate mapfiles, and more.

The Project Settings dialog box's Resource page enables you to set information about the resources related to your application, including the target language (such as Dutch, German, or English) to use for resources, additional include file directories, and preprocessor definitions.

In the Project Settings dialog box's OLE Types page, you can specify the output file name, the output header file name, the include directories, and any additional preprocessor directives you want to define when building OLE applications.

The Project Settings dialog box's Browse Information page enables you to specify the browse information file name, and also presents options that enable you to suppress the startup banner and update browse information only on demand.

When you finish making changes in the Project Settings dialog box, click the OK button to make the change take effect. If you don't want your changes to take effect, click Cancel. To see online context-sensitive help, click the Help button.

The Configurations Command

Use the Configurations menu item to add a new configuration to an existing project or remove an existing configuration from a project. When you add a new configuration, you can select it and change its settings in the Project Settings dialog box, as described previously.

The Subprojects Command

Choose Build, Subprojects to add a subproject to an existing project in your project workspace. You can also create a new project and add it as a subproject by clicking the New button; if you do, it's the same as choosing the Insert, Projects command.

The Set Default Configuration Command

The Set Default Configuration command displays the available project configurations so that you can select which target you want to use as a default. All build commands apply to the selected project configuration. If you build a project that contains sub-projects, the same configuration is built in to all out-of-date subprojects.

The Debug Menu

When you start debugging an application or DLL, the Build menu is replaced by the Debug menu, which offers various commands to help you manage program debugging from within the Developer Studio. Don't confuse this Debug menu with the Build menu's Debug submenu.

The full Debug menu includes the following commands: Go, Restart, Stop Debugging, Break, Step Into, Step Over, Step Out, Run to Cursor, Step Into Specific Function, Exceptions, Threads, Settings, and QuickWatch.

As you can see from these commands, the Debug menu offers several methods to control stepping through a program in a debugging session. In addition to controlling program execution, the Debug menu's commands enable you to see values of local and global variables, as well as CPU registers. Chapter 4, "Debugging Visual C++ Applications," discusses the debugging commands in more detail and shows you how to use the debugger windows with different applications.

The Go Command (F5)

The Go command runs the program until it reaches a breakpoint or the end of the program. The command triggers execution from the current position in a program. If you just began running the program, this position is the start of the program. If you were at a breakpoint, the program starts executing there.

The Restart Command (Shift+F5)

The Restart command reloads the program into memory and discards the previous values in the program's variables. In other words, this command lets you start the program with a clean slate. If you built the program with the Debug target mode, the Restart command runs the program until it reaches the start of the program (either `main()` or `WinMain()`).

The Stop Debugging Command (Alt+F5)

By choosing Debug, Stop Debugging, you can end a debugging session while the program is at a breakpoint or while it is between steps when stepping through the code.

The Break Command

The Break menu item interrupts whatever the program is doing and causes the debugger to show the program's state. This is similar to the Stop Debugging menu item, except that instead of ending the debugging session, it returns control to the debugger. Break also terminates OLE applications that are waiting for communication from external applications.

The Step Into Command (F8)

By choosing the Step Into command, you can single-step through the next statement and trace into any available function calls in that statement. Use this command to investigate the action of called functions and member functions.

The Step Over Command (F10)

The Step Over command enables you to single-step through the next statement in your program without stepping into any called functions. Choose this command when you are certain that you do not need to trace the called functions.

The Step Out Command (Shift+F7)

The Step Out command offers a valuable counterpoint to the other step commands. It enables you to skip the remaining statements in a function and stop the debugger again at the last statement of a function. This command eases the frustrations of single-stepping through many nested function calls. With it, you can get out of a function just as easily as you got into it.

The Run to Cursor Command (F7)

When you choose the Run to Cursor command, the debugger executes your program until it reaches the line of source code where the cursor's currently located. This is handy for starting a program and stopping at a specific location (that is, the current cursor location) quickly.

Internally, the Run to Cursor command works by having the Developer Studio create a temporary breakpoint at the current cursor location. The program then executes (just as if you chose Debug, Go). On reaching the temporary breakpoint, the program halts execution and deletes the breakpoint.

The Step Into Specific Function Command

By choosing the Step Into Specific Function menu item, you can step through your code one function at a time. If you use this technique to step into a nested function call, you can choose which function the debugger steps into. Step Into Specific Function works for any number of nesting levels. In the following statement, for example, you can place the cursor in street, house, or room and step into the selected function:

```
street(house(room(foo)));
```

> **Note**
>
> The Step Into Specific function appears only when the active window is a source code or disassembly window. If you have an InfoViewer window up, you won't see this command.

The Exceptions Command

The Exceptions command displays the Exceptions dialog box (see fig. 2.20), which gives you ways to work with microprocessor, Windows, and C++ exceptions. Several common microprocessor exceptions include Divide by Zero, Stack Overflow, and Illegal Instruction.

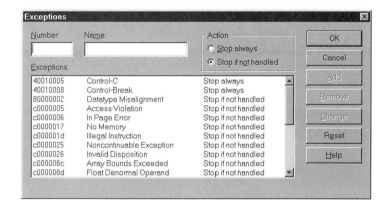

Fig. 2.20

The Exceptions dialog box.

Microprocessors use these exceptions to notify the operating system that something drastic has happened to the system. In the Exceptions dialog box, you can control the action that the debugger should take when these exceptions occur while debugging your application.

> **Note**
>
> For more information on using C++ exceptions, see Chapter 16, "Advanced Debugging Techniques."

The Threads Command

Windows NT and Windows 95 support *threads*—multiple paths of execution within a single process. Threads are like processes, but smaller. You can run several processes at once; each process in turn can have several threads.

To debug threads, choose <u>D</u>ebug, <u>T</u>hreads to display the Threads dialog box, which enables you to select the threads associated with your program. If your program is a single-threaded application (as most programs are), all that the dialog box lists is the `WinMain()` thread associated with many Windows applications. However, if you write your program to be multithreaded, the Threads dialog box displays each of the currently executing threads.

The Threads dialog box provides command buttons for suspending (<u>S</u>uspend) and resuming (<u>R</u>esume) execution of individual threads within your program. You can also switch the debugger's focus so that its information is displayed in your debugging session by clicking the Set <u>F</u>ocus button. Clicking the Close button removes the Threads dialog box from the screen.

The Settings Command

The <u>D</u>ebug menu's Settings command is the same as that of the <u>B</u>uild menu.

The QuickWatch Command (Shift+F9)

The QuickWatch command enables you to inspect and modify variables and members of class instances. The command displays the QuickWatch dialog box, shown in figure 2.21, which identifies the value for the selected variables by placing the cursor over the value.

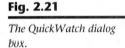

Fig. 2.21

The QuickWatch dialog box.

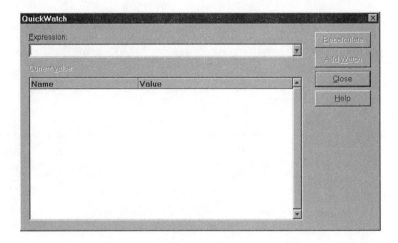

The <u>E</u>xpression pull-down list shows the name of the expression whose value is being displayed. You can choose other expressions by picking the one that you want from this pull-down list.

The Current <u>v</u>alue area displays structures and class instances in an outline form, like the Explorer or File Manager. Structures and classes that can be expanded are displayed with a plus sign (+) to the left of the data item; items that have already been expanded are flagged with a minus sign (–) to the left of the data item.

To expand or collapse the members of a structure or class instance, just click the plus or minus sign. The displayed structure then grows or shrinks as appropriate.

The Add Watch command button enables you to add the symbol selected in the Current Value list to the Watch window.

The Recalculate button forces QuickWatch to update the value of the selected expressions. This is handy when you want the debugger to redisplay a structure or item that has been changed.

You can also modify a variable's value in the QuickWatch window. Just double-click the entry in the Value column that you want to change, and you can edit it in place, just like an Excel cell.

The Tools Menu

The Tools menu's commands give you control over the look, feel, and behavior of Developer Studio and Visual C++. The menu contains the following commands: Browse, Close Browse Info, Profile, Remote Connection, Customize, Options, Record Keystrokes, and Playback Recording.

The Browse Command (Alt+F12)

When you build a program, the Developer Studio generates a database of the various symbols associated with your program. The database contains sophisticated information that tracks where a symbol is defined and referenced. This information is valuable for studying and debugging complex applications. You can access the information through the Browse command. To display the Browse dialog box, choose Tools, Browse or press Alt+F12.

Using the Browser. The Browse command opens the Browse dialog box (see fig. 2.22). It enables you to select a name on which to query and the type of query that you want to execute.

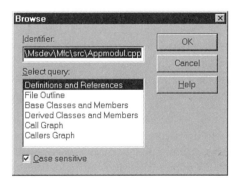

Fig. 2.22

The Browse dialog box.

The types of queries from which you can select include the following:

- Definitions and References shows class definitions and references to these definitions in your source code. This option indicates where your program defines and references symbols.

- File Outline enables you to browse the structure of the files associated with your application. This option displays all user-defined functions, classes, data, macros, and types that are in your program's source code.

- Base Classes and Members displays all classes from which the selected class inherits attributes.

- Derived Classes and Members displays all classes that inherit attributes from the selected class.

- Call Graph shows the relationships among all the functions that the selected function calls in your program.

- Callers Graph displays the relationships among the functions that call selected functions in your program.

If you put a value into the Identifier field, you can limit your browsing to symbols whose names match your specification. After you enter an identifier, choose one of the query types from the Select query list.

After pressing the OK button, you see the resulting browse window (see fig. 2.23). This window enables you to view graphically the relationships among symbols in your program. Each view contains specialized information.

Fig. 2.23

The Definitions and References dialog box is one of several browse windows that you can open from the Browse dialog box.

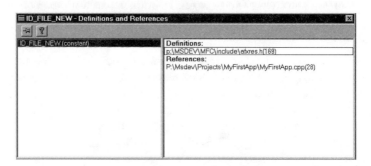

By default, the class browser window's left pane displays the functions and classes in the file. You can click to select a symbol from the list or double-click to open the source at the definition.

The right pane of the class browser window displays definitions and references for the item currently selected in the left pane. Again, you can double-click the location specified for the definition or reference to open the source at the definition or reference.

Navigating Definitions and References. You can jump to definitions and references in your source code by using the Edit, Go To command or the Go to Definition button on the Browse toolbar. Either of these commands locates the definition of a symbol. First, place the cursor to the left of, or anywhere on, the symbol's name. Then invoke the command by selecting Edit, Go To and choosing Definition, clicking the Go To Definition toolbar button, or pressing the shortcut key, F11. The Developer Studio responds by locating the definition of the targeted symbol.

By contrast, the Go to Reference command moves the insertion cursor to the first location that references the selected symbol. To jump to a reference, first place the cursor to the left of, or anywhere on, the symbol's name. Then invoke the command by selecting Edit, Go To and choosing Reference, clicking the Go To Reference toolbar button, or pressing the shortcut key, Shift+F11. The Developer Studio responds by locating the first reference to the targeted symbol.

Use the Next and Previous buttons on the Browse toolbar to navigate through all the references to the selected symbol in a project.

The Next Definition command moves the insertion cursor to the next location that references the selected symbol. The shortcut key for this command is Ctrl+(Numpad +). Similarly, the Previous Definition command moves the insertion cursor to the previous location that references the selected symbol. The shortcut key for this command is Ctrl+(Numpad –).

The Pop Context toolbar button moves back to the previous symbol that you browsed before you applied the final Go to Definition or Go to Reference command; its shortcut key is Ctrl+(Numpad *).

The class browser provides a handy way to examine the class symbols, functions, and variables used in your program.

The Close Browse Info Command

The Close Browse Info option closes the browse information file related to the current project. You might want to do this if your system is low on memory and you don't want the browse file to waste valuable memory space.

The Profile Command

Choose the Profile menu item to examine the behavior of an application when it runs. You can determine which parts of the code the application executes, which parts it never executes, the absolute amount of time that it spends executing any part of the code, or the relative amount of time that it spends executing any part of the code. You can use this information to determine where to optimize your code's performance and to determine what you gained after your optimizations.

The Remote Connection Command

Sometimes you need to run your application on another machine; for example, you might be writing a communications program, or testing some features of your program that require special hardware.

Visual C++'s remote debugging features let you run the debugger on one machine (the debugger host) and the program to be debugged on another machine (the debugger target). Choose the Remote Connection menu item to set the options that you want to another machine for debugging. For more details on two-machine debugging, see Chapter 16, "Advanced Debugging Techniques."

The Customize Command

Choose Tools, Customize to display the Customize dialog box (see fig. 2.24), which enables you to change a variety of settings.

Fig. 2.24

The Customize dialog box.

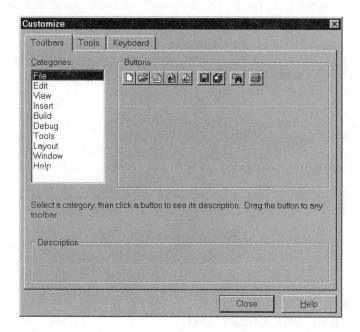

Along the top of the Customize dialog box are three tabs that you can select: Toolbars, Tools, and Keyboard.

The Customize dialog box's Toolbars page enables you to modify the buttons that appear on toolbars. You can drag a button from the dialog box and drop the button onto the toolbar. You can also remove buttons presently on a toolbar by dragging them from the toolbar and dropping them into the dialog box. When you finish customizing your toolbars, click the Close button to make your changes permanent.

The Tools page enables you to add functionality to the Developer Studio by adding utilities and programs to the Tools menu. You can add to the Tools menu any .exe program by clicking the Add button and specifying the file name of the utility (or tool) to execute. After specifying the file name, you can then specify the text to display at the bottom of the Tools menu, as well as any arguments to pass to the program.

You can also use the command to remove and reorganize the tools, like Spy++, listed as commands in the Tools menu. The dialog box contains edit controls that you can use to supply the following information for each newly added tool:

- The command line for invoking the tool
- The menu text
- The tool's argument
- The initial directory

The Tools dialog box contains a check box that you can select to make Developer Studio prompt you for arguments each time that it invokes the tool.

In the Customize dialog box's Keyboard page (which is shown in fig. 2.25), you can assign shortcut keys to existing menu commands. Controls in the dialog box enable you to specify how the keyboard commands should operate.

The Editor combo box lets you select the editor whose shortcut keys you want to customize. The Categories list box shows the menus available in the editor, which you selected from the Editor drop-down list. The Commands list box shows the commands available on the menu that you selected from the Categories list box.

To create a new shortcut key, enter the key or keys to which you want to assign values in the Press New Shortcut Key text box. If the key combination is currently assigned to another command, the Current Keys list box displays that command. To assign the new shortcut key combination, choose the Assign button.

The Current Keys list displays the shortcut key combinations currently assigned to the command selected in the Commands list box. The Assign button assigns the shortcut key combination displayed in the Current Keys list box to the command selected in the Commands list box.

The Remove button deletes the shortcut key combination selected in the Current Keys list box. The Reset All button restores the shortcut key combinations to their default settings.

The Options Command

Choose Tools, Options to display the Options dialog box (see fig. 2.25), which also enables you to change certain groups of settings. The dialog box has tabs along the top that enable you to choose the types of options that you want to modify. The tabs include Editor, Tabs, Debug, Compatibility, Directories, Workspace, Format, and InfoViewer. Each of these tabs displays options that relate to the selected tab.

Fig. 2.25

The Options dialog box.

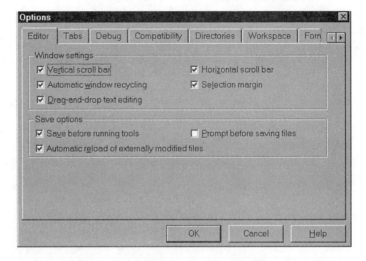

The Editor tab lets you control the behavior of Developer Studio's text editor, including which scroll bars to use and whether files should automatically be saved during compilation.

With the Tabs tab, you can set the editor's tabstop settings on a per-file-type basis. This is useful because individual programmers often have different indentation styles depending on the language of the file that they're editing.

The Debug tab gives you control over the format and appearance of data displayed in the debuggers' windows.

The Compatibility tab lets you tailor Developer Studio's behavior to match other editor environments to which you might be accustomed, including Visual C++ 2.x, BRIEF, and Epsilon.

The Directories tab lets you specify which directories the Developer Studio should use for include files, executable files, library files, and source files. You can make these settings by platform, so if you're developing for Win32 and Macintosh, for example, you can specify separate directories.

You can control the default workspace behaviors with the Workspace tab: which windows are displayed as dockable windows, whether the status bar contains a clock, whether projects are automatically loaded when you start Developer Studio, and so on.

The Format tab offers a way to customize the font, font size, and window colors, and text color for each kind of editor window.

Finally, the InfoViewer tab gives you control over how InfoViewer displays search dialogs and search results.

The Record Keystrokes Command (Ctrl+Shift+R)

By choosing Tools, Record Keystroke, you can record a series of keystrokes. When you select this command, two buttons display that enable you to stop or pause the recording of keystrokes. Type your keystrokes and click the Stop button to stop recording the keystrokes, or choose Tools, Stop Recording.

The Playback Recording Command

Choose the Playback Recording command to play back the keystrokes that you recorded by using the Record Keystroke menu item. For typing repetitive series of commands, you can't beat the functionality that Record Keystroke and Playback Recording provide.

The Window Menu

The Window menu commands enable you to arrange and manage the many windows in the Developer Studio. The menu contains the following commands: New Window, Split, Hide, Cascade, Tile Horizontally, Tile Vertically, and Close All. The menu also contains a list of all open source, header, and resource file windows, plus a Windows command.

The New Window Command

By choosing the New Window command, you can create an additional window in which to view a source file. With this functionality, combined with the Split command (see the next section), you can have an almost unlimited number of views on a file. All the views remain completely synchronized. Figure 2.26 shows one file open in four windows, with each window having four panes showing different parts of the file.

The Split Command

The Split menu item enables you to split a window into two panes. Each pane can contain different views of the same window's contents. Some programmers prefer to use this command instead of creating a new window, because running this command requires less physical space on the screen.

The Hide Command (Shift+Esc)

By choosing Window, Hide, you can make the current editor window invisible. This command is convenient when you want to keep a window available for your use, but you don't want it to clutter the space inside the Developer Studio.

Fig. 2.26

With the Split Window command, you can split your screen into multiple windows.

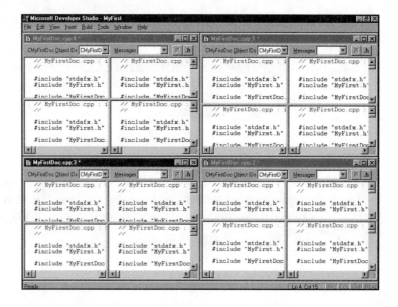

The Cascade Command

With the Cascade command, you can arrange the windows in the Developer Studio in a cascaded fashion. This command arranges the windows by their Z-order (that is, the order in which they overlay each other).

The Tile Horizontally Command

The Tile Horizontally command arranges the windows in the Developer Studio horizontally, side by side.

The Tile Vertically Command

By choosing Window, Tile Vertically, you can arrange the windows in the Developer Studio vertically, side by side. Because source code is usually taller than it is wide, you might find that this option provides a better viewing of editor windows than when they are tiled horizontally.

The Close All Command

The Close All command closes all the windows currently in the Developer Studio client area except the project and output windows. The command prompts you to save the contents of any window that you have modified but not yet saved.

The Windows Command

Developer Studio lists the first nine open windows as items in the Windows menu. You can also use the Windows command to display a dialog box listing all the open windows in your workspace. The Windows dialog box has buttons for activating, closing, or saving the windows that you select in the Select Window list.

The Help Menu

The Help menu's commands give you a variety of ways to find and view help. The menu contains the following commands: Contents, Search, Keyboard, Define Subset, Set Default Subsets, Open Information Title, Tip of the Day, Technical Support, and About Developer Studio. The Developer Studio uses the powerful Windows Help engine, which you are probably well acquainted with by now.

From Here...

This chapter introduced you to the commands and controls of the Developer Studio. Now that you've seen the environment, the following chapter will lead you into an in-depth examination of using the Developer Studio, Visual C++, and MFC to build applications.

To learn more about working with Developer Studio, you might want to review the following chapters of this book:

- To learn more about building applications with AppStudio and the ClassWizard, see Chapter 3, "Using AppStudio."
- To learn more about using the Developer Studio debugger, see Chapter 4, "Debugging Visual C++ Applications."
- For information on using the MFC libraries in your programs, see Chapter 6, "Using MFC."

CHAPTER 3

Using AppStudio

The Developer Studio provides powerful resource editors for creating and editing all Windows resource types. Windows resources are the parts of your program with which users interact. Windows has many predefined resources, including bitmaps, dialog boxes, and icons. This chapter shows you how to use the resource editors inside the Developer Studio.

Note

In Visual C++ version 1, AppStudio was a separate program that you could execute from the Developer Studio. In Visual C++ 2, AppStudio was an integrated part of the Visual Workbench. Visual C++ 4 seamlessly integrates the resource editors into the project workspace. You no longer have to work in separate windows and contexts to edit your Windows resources; Microsoft has integrated all resource editors into the Developer Studio's easy-to-use environment.

This chapter covers the following topics:

- The types of resources that you can create and edit in the Developer Studio
- How to access the resource editors
- How to use resource editor options
- How to use the resource editors built in to the Developer Studio to modify Windows resources
- How to use Developer Studio to add new controls to a dialog box

The Project Workspace Resource View Window

With the Developer Studio resource editors, you can create and edit accelerator, bitmap, cursor, dialog box, icon, menu, string table, toolbar, user-defined (custom), and version resources. You can invoke the Developer Studio resource editor to create new resources (by choosing Insert, Resource or pressing Ctrl+R), or you can work with the resources of the current project. In the latter case, you should select the Resource View tab from the Project Workspace window. Figure 3.1 shows a sample Project Workspace Resource View window.

When you use File, Open to open an .rc file, Developer Studio opens the Resource View tab of the Project Workspace window for you.

Fig. 3.1

Developer Studio Resource View screen.

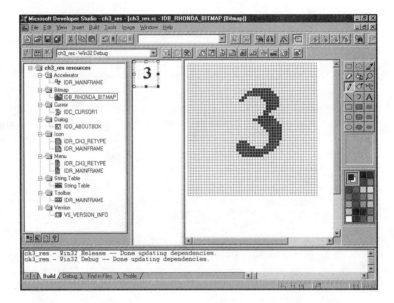

The Resource View window contains a list of the types of resources in the project. Clicking a resource type opens a tree-structured list of the currently named resources for the resource type.

The Insert, Resource command enables you to create a new resource. When you choose this command, the system displays the Insert Resource dialog box (see fig. 3.2), which enables you to select a resource type.

Fig. 3.2

The Insert Resource dialog box.

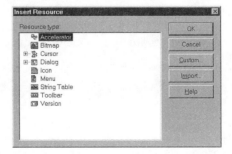

To edit a resource, double-click the resource name in the Resource View window. To delete a resource, highlight it and then press the Del key. You also can right-click the item in the Resource View window to display a context-sensitive menu that presents similar options. The Properties option displays the Properties dialog box, which enables you to fine-tune the properties of a resource or a resource component.

Windows provides eight predefined resource types and enables users to add custom resources. You can use the Developer Studio resource editor to create and edit the following types of resources:

■ Accelerator, which is a key combination (or *accelerator key*) that mimics menu commands.

■ Bitmap, which is a graphic image of any size.

■ Cursor, which is a special type of bitmap that shows the user the location of the mouse on-screen.

■ Dialog, which is a pop-up window that contains one or (usually) more interface objects—such as buttons, list boxes, and scroll bars—with which the user interacts.

■ Icon, which is a bitmap of a specified size that About dialog boxes use and that represents applications when minimized on-screen.

■ Menu, which is one of the standard hierarchical pull-down menus that are a feature of most Windows programs.

■ String Table, which is a special type of resource that enables you to store sections of text outside your program. This procedure conserves memory, because the program then loads the string resource only when needed.

■ Toolbar, which is a custom resource that enables you to create, edit, and use toolbars easily in your MFC applications.

■ Version, which is a type of resource that embeds information about the author, copyright holder, and version number inside an application. A version is useful for storing internal information about the program. Some install programs use this type of resource.

■ Custom, which is a user-defined resource that contains application-specific data. The data can have any format, and you can define the data as either a given file's content (if you specify the file name parameter) or a series of numbers and strings (if you specify the raw-data block). The Developer Studio provides a binary editor with which you can edit custom resources.

Each type of resource has an associated resource editor that is part of Developer Studio. This chapter cannot cover all these resource editors, but covers the most common ones: the icon, menu, toolbar, and dialog box editors.

The following sections provide examples of using Developer Studio resource editors for the following tasks:

- Modifying an existing menu and adding accompanying accelerators.
- Adding a new dialog box resource to replace the standard message dialog box. To add this resource, you draw the controls in the custom dialog box resource.
- Drawing the controls in a form view.

These examples describe a hands-on approach to working with the Developer Studio resource editors. However, this chapter doesn't attempt to cover every aspect of the Developer Studio resource editors.

What the Resource Editor Generates

When you create resources with AppStudio, you see a visual representation of the resource data. However, Developer Studio needs a resource definition that it can incorporate into your program. To solve this problem, AppStudio generates two files.

The first file, which usually has the name of your executable with the .rc extension added, is a text file called a *resource script*. If you open a resource script, you'll see that it's pretty readable. Here's an example that defines the TimeInABox dialog box that you build later in this chapter:

```
IDD_TIME_IN_A_BOX DIALOG DISCARDABLE  0, 0, 186, 71
STYLE DS_MODALFRAME ¦ DS_3DLOOK ¦ DS_CENTER ¦ WS_POPUP ¦ WS_CAPTION ¦
    WS_SYSMENU
CAPTION "The Current Time"
FONT 8, "MS Sans Serif"
BEGIN
    DEFPUSHBUTTON    "Close",IDOK,129,7,50,14
    LTEXT            "",IDC_TIMEBOX_TIME,5,5,115,32,SS_SUNKEN
    ICON             IDI_TIME_IN_A_BOX,IDC_STATIC,5,45,18,20
END
```

The second file, resource.h, is a C/C++ header file that defines numeric values for the constants defined in the .rc file. For example, `IDD_TIME_IN_A_BOX DIALOG` is defined as 130 in the resource.h file.

Modifying a Menu Resource

This section describes a simple application that supports the following features:

- Displaying the current system date and time
- Starting and stopping a simple timer
- Continuously displaying the current mouse location
- Echoing keyboard input in the view

The application supports the first two features through both mouse clicks and menu options. Right-clicking displays the current system date and time in a message dialog box. Left-clicking toggles the timer's start and stop. When you start the timer, the application displays a message dialog box that tells you that you started the timer. When you stop the timer, the application displays a message dialog box that shows the elapsed time. This action also resets the timer. The application supports these features by using menu options to display the date and time, to start the timer, and to stop the timer.

Now that you understand the application, you can use AppWizard to generate it. This process has four phases, which are described in the following sections.

Creating the Menu03 Application

The first phase uses AppWizard to create an application. To create a new application, select File, New, then choose Project Workspace from the file type dialog box. Name your project by using the Name field and select where the generated files should go by specifying a directory into the Location field. Keep the default selection of MFC AppWizard Application (.exe) in the project's Type field.

> **Note**
>
> For more details on using the AppWizard, see the section "Creating Applications with AppWizard" in Chapter 1, "Getting Started with Visual C++."

In the AppWizard dialog boxes that follow, make sure that you enable these features: Single Document Interface (SDI), Initial Toolbar, and Printing and Print Preview. In other words, create a minimal Windows application that uses the document and view classes. The application's view is a descendant of the class CView.

Editing the Menu Resource

After AppWizard generates the application skeleton, the second step of creating the application involves using the Developer Studio resource editor to edit the menu resource that AppWizard generated. This menu resource requires extensive editing. To edit the resource, follow these general steps:

1. Open the Developer Studio Resource View window (see fig. 3.1).
2. Select the menu resource type.
3. Right-click the IDR_MAINFRAME menu resource and choose Open from the context-sensitive menu. The Developer Studio menu editor displays the IDR_MAINFRAME menu resource. When you create an application by using AppWizard, it automatically provides the IDR_MAINFRAME menu definition.
4. Edit the current menu bar by deleting menus and menu commands and then adding new ones until you have the menu resource shown in figure 3.3.

Fig. 3.3

The menu editor.

To delete a menu command, click it and then press the Del key. To insert a command, select the empty menu-item placeholder and then press Enter or double-click the placeholder. The Developer Studio resource editor responds by displaying a Menu Item Properties dialog box for the new item. This dialog box enables you to enter the caption and identifier for the menu item and to fine-tune the item's properties. Use the identifiers ID_TIME_DATETIME, ID_TIME_STARTTIMER, and ID_TIME_STOPTIMER for the Date/Time, Start Timer, and Stop Timer commands, respectively. In addition, insert a separator menu item after the first command.

5. Close the menu editor window.

6. Select the accelerator resource type, and then choose the IDR_MAINFRAME accelerator resource. The Developer Studio resource editor displays the list of accelerators defined in the IDR_MAINFRAME accelerators resource.

7. Insert the new accelerator Shift+Ctrl+D for the Date/Time command by double-clicking in the open editing area. The Developer Studio accelerator resource editor window displays the Accel Properties dialog box, which enables you to specify the associated ID_XXXX identifier and accelerator key.

Figure 3.4 shows a sample session in which the user is adding a new accelerator key. The Accel Properties dialog box enables you to specify the accelerator key and to choose among the Ctrl, Alt, and Shift keys. In addition, you can specify whether the key value should be literally interpreted as an ASCII code or as a "virtual" key value. Systems that use Unicode or multibyte character systems may have different keyboard mappings, so ASCII keys may not work, but virtual keys will.

Fig. 3.4

The accelerator editor.

8. Repeat step 7 to add the accelerator keys Shift+Ctrl+S and Shift+Ctrl+T for the menu options Start Timer and Stop Timer, respectively.

9. Save the edited menu resource by choosing File, Save.

Adding Member Functions

The third phase of crafting the application involves the ClassWizard utility. Use ClassWizard to add the following member functions in the view class (fig. 3.5 shows the ClassWizard in action):

- The member function OnLButtonDown(), which responds to the Windows message WM_LBUTTONDOWN

- The member function OnRButtonDown(), which responds to the Windows message WM_RBUTTONDOWN

- The member function OnChar(), which responds to the Windows message WM_CHAR

- The member function OnMouseMove(), which responds to the Windows message WM_MOUSEMOVE

- The member function OnTimeDateTime(), which responds to the Windows command message CM_DATETIME

- The member function OnTimeStartTimer(), which responds to the Windows command message ID_TIME_STARTTIMER

- The member function OnTimeStopTimer(), which responds to the Windows command message ID_TIME_STOPTIMER

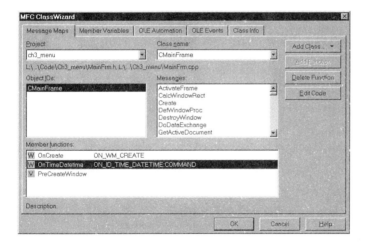

Fig. 3.5

Using ClassWizard to create member functions for the Time menu.

Modifying the Code

The fourth and final phase of creating the application is to modify the code by manually inserting the statements into the member-function definitions and then inserting other declarations. The manual code insertions are covered later in this section, with the related project listings. The appstud.rc resource file includes the following relevant resources:

- The customized `IDR_MMAINFRAME` menu resource, including the Time pop-up menu selection and its nested options
- The customized `IDR_MMAINFRAME` accelerators resource, with its three items: Shift+Ctrl+D, Shift+Ctrl+S, and Shift+Ctrl+T
- The customized string table resources created to display the one-line menu descriptions

Listing 3.1 contains the class definition for the view class, CChapter03MenuView.

Listing 3.1 ch3mView.h, the Class Definition for CChapter03MenuView

```
// ch3mView.h : interface of the CChapter03MenuView class
//
/////////////////////////////////////////////////////////////////////////////

class CChapter03MenuView : public CView
{
protected: // create from serialization only
    CChapter03MenuView();
    DECLARE_DYNCREATE(CChapter03MenuView)

// Attributes
public:
    CChapter03MenuDoc* GetDocument();

// Operations
public:

// Overrides
    // ClassWizard-generated virtual function overrides
    //{{AFX_VIRTUAL(CChapter03MenuView)
    public:
    virtual void OnDraw(CDC* pDC);  // overridden to draw this view
    virtual BOOL PreCreateWindow(CREATESTRUCT& cs);
    protected:
    virtual BOOL OnPreparePrinting(CPrintInfo* pInfo);
    virtual void OnBeginPrinting(CDC* pDC, CPrintInfo* pInfo);
    virtual void OnEndPrinting(CDC* pDC, CPrintInfo* pInfo);
    //}}AFX_VIRTUAL

// Implementation
public:
    virtual ~CChapter03MenuView();
#ifdef _DEBUG
    virtual void AssertValid() const;
    virtual void Dump(CDumpContext& dc) const;
#endif

protected:

// Generated message map functions
protected:
    //{{AFX_MSG(CChapter03MenuView)
```

```
        afx_msg void OnTimeDateTime();
        afx_msg void OnTimeStartTimer();
        afx_msg void OnTimeStopTimer();
        afx_msg void OnLButtonDown(UINT nFlags, CPoint point);
        afx_msg void OnRButtonDown(UINT nFlags, CPoint point);
        afx_msg void OnChar(UINT nChar, UINT nRepCnt, UINT nFlags);
        afx_msg void OnMouseMove(UINT nFlags, CPoint point);
        afx_msg void OnTimer(UINT nIDEvent);
        //}}AFX_MSG
        DECLARE_MESSAGE_MAP()
};

#ifndef _DEBUG  // debug version in ch3mView.cpp
inline CChapter03MenuDoc* CChapter03MenuView::GetDocument()
    { return (CChapter03MenuDoc*)m_pDocument; }
#endif

////////////////////////////////////////////////////////////////////////
```

ClassWizard customized the source code shown in listing 3.1 by inserting the declaration of the member functions in the view class. The following are the new member functions:

- `OnChar()` prints any character that is typed.
- `OnLButtonDown()` displays current date and time in a short format.
- `OnMouseMove()` displays the current mouse location.
- `OnRButtonDown()` displays current date and time in a long format.
- `OnTimeDateTime()` displays current date and time in a long format.
- `OnTimer()` displays the number of timer events and updates short and long current time strings.
- `OnTimeStartTimer()` starts a one-second timer.
- `OnTimeStopTimer()` stops the one-second timer.

ClassWizard inserts all these function definitions.

Listing 3.2 shows portions of the `CChapter03MenuView` class implementation; some of the unmodified AppWizard code has been trimmed from this listing.

Listing 3.2 ch3mView.cpp, Portions of the Source Code for the `CChapter03MenuView`

```
BEGIN_MESSAGE_MAP(CChapter03MenuView, CView)
    //{{AFX_MSG_MAP(CChapter03MenuView)
    ON_COMMAND(ID_TIME_DATETIME, OnTimeDateTime)
    ON_COMMAND(ID_TIME_STARTTIMER, OnTimeStartTimer)
    ON_COMMAND(ID_TIME_STOPTIMER, OnTimeStopTimer)
    ON_WM_LBUTTONDOWN()
    ON_WM_RBUTTONDOWN()
```

(continues)

Listing 3.2 Continued

```
        ON_WM_CHAR()
        ON_WM_MOUSEMOVE()
        ON_WM_TIMER()
        //}}AFX_MSG_MAP
        // Standard printing commands
        ON_COMMAND(ID_FILE_PRINT, CView::OnFilePrint)
        ON_COMMAND(ID_FILE_PRINT_DIRECT, CView::OnFilePrint)
        ON_COMMAND(ID_FILE_PRINT_PREVIEW, CView::OnFilePrintPreview)
END_MESSAGE_MAP()

/////////////////////////////////////////////////////////////////////////
// CChapter03MenuView message handlers

void CChapter03MenuView::OnTimeDateTime()
{
        // display current date/time in long format
        CClientDC dc(this);
        dc.TextOut(10, 40, CTime::GetCurrentTime().Format("%#c"));

}

void CChapter03MenuView::OnTimeStartTimer()
{
        // trigger a timer every second
        SetTimer(1, 1000, NULL);
}

void CChapter03MenuView::OnTimeStopTimer()
{
        // just shut it down
        KillTimer(1);
}

void CChapter03MenuView::OnLButtonDown(UINT nFlags, CPoint point)
{
        // display current date/time in standard format
        CClientDC dc(this);
        dc.TextOut(10, 20, CTime::GetCurrentTime().Format("%c"));

}

void CChapter03MenuView::OnRButtonDown(UINT nFlags, CPoint point)
{
        // display current date/time in long format
        OnTimeDateTime();

}

void CChapter03MenuView::OnChar(UINT nChar, UINT nRepCnt, UINT nFlags)
{
        CClientDC dc(this);
        char buffer[200];
        sprintf(buffer,
```

```
                    "Char: %c   Repeat Count: %2d   Flags: %08x    ",
                    (char)nChar,
                    nRepCnt,
                    nFlags);

        dc.TextOut(10, 60, buffer);

    }

    void CChapter03MenuView::OnMouseMove(UINT nFlags, CPoint point)
    {
        // TODO: Add your message handler code here and/or call default

        CClientDC dc(this);
        char buffer[200];
        sprintf(buffer,
            "Mouse: %4d,%4d   Flags: %08x        ",
            point.x,
            point.y,
            nFlags);

        dc.TextOut(10, 80, buffer);
    }

    void CChapter03MenuView::OnTimer(UINT nIDEvent)
    {
        static int count = 0;
        count++;
        CClientDC dc(this);
        char buffer[200];
        sprintf(buffer,
            "Total Timer Count: %4d",
            count);

        dc.TextOut(10, 100, buffer);
        OnLButtonDown(0,0);
        OnRButtonDown(0,0);
    } / Ch3View.cpp : implementation of the CAppstud1View class
```

In listing 3.2, ClassWizard inserted the following items:

- The message map macros to handle the various WM_XXXX and OnTimeXXXX messages

- The minimal definitions of the new OnXXXX member functions

You must still insert the implementation of these functions manually; AppWizard generates only a skeleton.

The following are the new OnXXXX member functions:

- The member function OnLButtonDown performs the following tasks:

    Declares the device context object dc as an instance of CClientDC.

Extracts the current time as a date and time representation appropriate for locale.

Draws this formatted string as the first line in the window.

■ The member function `OnChar` performs the following tasks:

Declares the device context object dc as an instance of `CClientDC`.

Formats the arguments of `OnChar()`, character value, repeat count, and flags as a string.

Draws this formatted information as the third line in the window.

■ The member function `OnRButtonDown` performs the following tasks:

Declares the device context object dc as an instance of `CClientDC`.

Extracts the current time as the long date and time representation, appropriate for current locale, as in `Tuesday, September 26, 1995, 12:41:29`.

Draws this formatted string as the second line in the window.

■ The member function `OnMouseMove` performs the following tasks:

Declares the device context object dc as an instance of `CClientDC`.

Creates a formatted string image for the mouse location. This task involves accessing the members x and y from the `CPoint` parameter point.

Draws this formatted string as the fourth line in the window.

■ The member function `OnTimeStartTimer` creates a local one-second timer for this window. `OnTimer()` processes the timer messages.

■ The member function `OnTimeStopTimer` destroys the local one-second timer created by `OnTimeStartTimer`.

■ The member function `OnTimer` performs the following tasks:

Declares the device context object dc as an instance of `CClientDC`.

Creates a formatted string that contains the total number of timer events generated by this application.

Draws this formatted string as the fifth line in the window.

Calls `OnLButtonDown` and `OnRButtonDown` to display the current date and time in both long and short formats.

Compile and run the program Ch3_menu.exe. Use the Time menu commands to view the current date and time and to manipulate the simple timer. Figure 3.6 shows a sample session with the program Ch3_menu.exe.

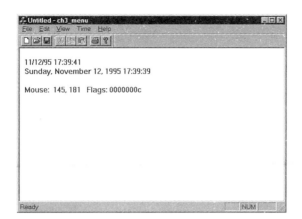

Visual C++ Tools

Fig. 3.6

Running Ch3_menu.exe.

Adding a New Dialog Box Resource

Now modify the preceding project to use a custom dialog box that displays the date and time. To create a new dialog box resource, you can use the Developer Studio dialog editor. This dialog box also includes a custom clock icon (or any other custom icon that you want to use), which you create with the Developer Studio icon editor. As long as you are using the Developer Studio dialog editor to create a new dialog box, you might as well customize the resource for the About dialog box. In addition, you use the ClassWizard utility to create a C++ class that supports the custom dialog box. You will attach the custom dialog box to the new menu item, Time in a Box, which will appear at the bottom of the Time menu.

Creating the Ch3_dial.exe Application

The initial phases for building and customizing this application Ch3_dial.exe include the same steps and tasks that you used in the Ch3_menu project. You can build the new application from scratch by using AppWizard, the Developer Studio resource editors, and ClassWizard.

The alternative to building the application from scratch is to create the Ch3_menu subdirectory, copy the files from Ch3_menu, rename some of these files (the ones that include the project name), edit the source files (to change the classes' names that depend on the project name), and then edit the project files to include the correct list of files.

This multiple-step operation might seem more elaborate than starting from scratch, but it's really not. Therefore, the first phase for creating the application is to copy the Ch3_menu project's files and edit them.

Creating the Icon and Dialog Box Resources

After you make the files of the Ch3_dial project equivalent to those of the Ch3_menu project, you can move on to the second phase. In this phase, you invoke the Developer Studio resource editors to create the new icon and dialog box resources. Perform the following steps:

1. Select the icon resource from the resource window.

2. Click the IDR_MAINFRAME icon, which is the icon that appears in the About dialog box. The Developer Studio resource editor responds by displaying the icon editor. This editor has two useful palettes: the Tools palette contains drawing tools, and the Colors palette enables you to choose the foreground and background colors that you use in your drawings. Figure 3.7 shows a sample session with the Tools palette as the IDR_MAINFRAME icon is being edited.

Fig. 3.7

The icon resource editor.

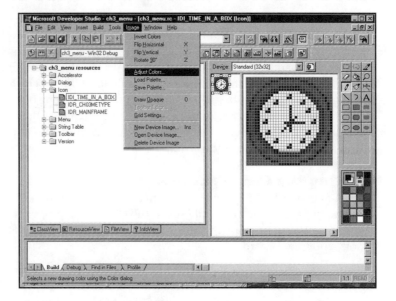

3. Alter the background colors for the IDR_MAINFRAME icon, using the colors of your choice. When you finish coloring, save the icon and close its window.

4. Create a new icon by choosing Insert, Resource. Then select Icon from the list of available resource types.

5. Select the colors and tools to draw a clock icon. (See fig. 3.7, which shows a sample session with the icon editor as the icon is being created.) When you finish drawing the icon, close its window.

6. Select the dialog box resource type in the Resource View window.

7. Choose the IDD_ABOUTBOX dialog box resource.

8. Edit the caption of the OK button, changing it to Close.

> **Note**
>
> To edit the title of any dialog box control, double-click the item to open its Properties dialog box. After making your changes in the dialog box, press Enter to close it.

9. Edit the static text controls to modify the version and copyright information. Figure 3.8 shows the types of changes that you might want to make. (You can insert your own name into the copyright line.) When you finish with the About dialog box resource, save and then close it.

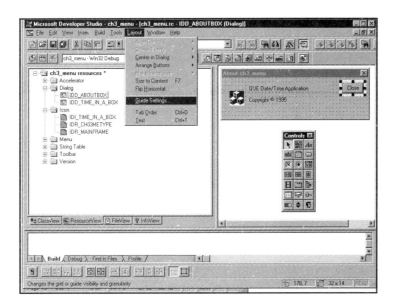

Fig. 3.8

Using the dialog box resource editor on the About dialog box.

10. Create a new dialog box resource by choosing Insert, Resource. In the Insert Resource dialog box, choose Dialog. The Developer Studio dialog box resource editor displays a dialog box that contains default OK and Cancel buttons.

11. Delete the Cancel button by selecting it and then pressing the Del key.

12. Double-click the OK button to display its Properties dialog box, type the caption **Close**, and move the control to the bottom of the dialog box.

13. Double-click the dialog box caption to open its Properties dialog box, and type the caption **Time in a Box**.

14. Select the static text tool from the Tools palette, and draw the static text control next to the Close button. In addition, center the text by choosing the Center option from the Properties dialog box's Text Align drop-down combo box. You should delete the static text control's default text, *Static*.

15. Select the picture control from the Tools palette to draw the icon in the dialog box. Then click the edge of the picture control to edit its properties. Double-click the picture control to select the icon picture type and to specify the ID IDI_TIME_IN_A_BOX. Figure 3.9 shows the Developer Studio dialog resource editor window as the IDI_TIME_IN_A_BOX dialog box resource is being created.

Fig. 3.9

Using the dialog box resource editor on the Time in a Box dialog box.

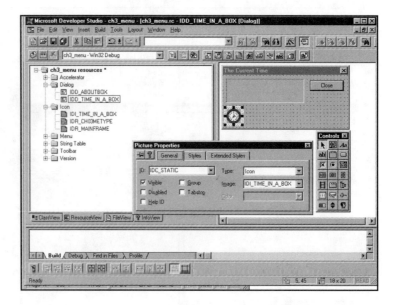

16. Save the new dialog box resource and close the resource window inside the Developer Studio.

Creating a New Class

In the third phase of creating the Ch3_dial.exe program, you use ClassWizard to create the class TimeInABox. Open the ClassWizard by choosing View, ClassWizard or pressing Ctrl+W. When the ClassWizard dialog box opens, click the Add Class button and select New from the pull-down menu. The Create New Class dialog box then appears as shown in figure 3.10. In the dialog box's Class Information group, specify TimeInABox in the Name text box and CDialog from the Base Class drop-down list. These selections make your new class a descendant of the CDialog class.

Fig. 3.10

Creating the `TimeInABox`
class.

After you create this class, use ClassWizard to add the message handler `OnInitDialog`
to the class `TimeInABox`. To do this, open the ClassWizard, click the Message Maps tab,
and select `TimeInABox` from the Class Name pull-down list. Select `TimeInABox` from
the Object IDs list; the Messages list then changes to reflect the messages that
`TimeInABox` can accept. Click `WM_INITDIALOG` in the Messages list, then click the Add
Function button to add the skeleton `OnInitDialog` handler. Figure 3.11 shows the
ClassWizard window after adding the `OnInitDialog` to the `TimeInABox` class.

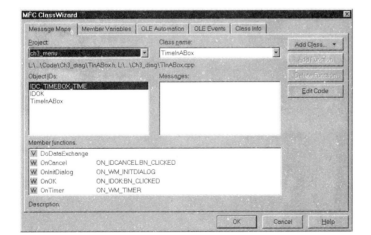

Fig. 3.11

*Using ClassWizard to
create* `TimeInABox` *class
members.*

Customizing the Code

In the fourth phase of creating this application, you manually customize the code for the relevant files, as discussed later in this section.

Listing 3.3 shows the resource.h header file. This listing shows the declarations of the identifiers for the menu, menu options, dialog boxes, and icons. The Developer Studio resource editor generates these declarations for you when it compiles your .rc file.

Listing 3.3   resource.h, Resource Definitions Generated from the Application's Resource File

```
//{{NO_DEPENDENCIES}}
// Microsoft Developer Studio generated include file.
// Used by ch3_menu.rc
//
#define IDD_ABOUTBOX                    100
#define IDR_MAINFRAME                   128
#define IDR_CH03METYPE                  129
#define IDD_TIME_IN_A_BOX               130
#define IDI_TIME_IN_A_BOX               131
#define IDC_TIMEBOX_TIME                1001
#define ID_TIME_DATETIME                32771
#define ID_TIME_STARTTIMER              32772
#define ID_TIME_STOPTIMER               32774
#define ID_TIME_TIMEDIALOG              32776

// Next default values for new objects
//
#ifdef APSTUDIO_INVOKED
#ifndef APSTUDIO_READONLY_SYMBOLS
#define _APS_3D_CONTROLS                1
#define _APS_NEXT_RESOURCE_VALUE        132
#define _APS_NEXT_COMMAND_VALUE         32777
#define _APS_NEXT_CONTROL_VALUE         1002
#define _APS_NEXT_SYMED_VALUE           101
#endif
#endif
```

You can find the AppWizard-generated resource file on this book's companion CD. The resource file defines the contents and appearance of the main menu, the accelerators, the About dialog box, and the new Time in a Box dialog box. AppWizard generated the initial version of the file, and you use the Developer Studio resource editors to customize it.

Listing 3.4 contains the source code of the TInABox.h header file. The file contains the declaration for the class TimeInABox, which is a descendant of class CDialog and which uses the resource ID ID_TIME_TIMEDIALOG to create the dialog box. ClassWizard generated most of the source code in the header file TInABox.h, including the declarations for the constructor, the untagged enumerated type, and the function DoDataExchange. ClassWizard also added the declaration for the member function OnInitDialog.

Listing 3.4   TInABox.h, the Class Definition of the TimeInABox Class

```
// TimeInABox dialog

class TimeInABox : public CDialog
{
// Construction
public:
    TimeInABox(CWnd* pParent = NULL);    // standard constructor

// Dialog Data
    //{{AFX_DATA(TimeInABox)
    enum { IDD = IDD_TIME_IN_A_BOX };
        // NOTE: the ClassWizard will add data members here
    //}}AFX_DATA


// Overrides
    // ClassWizard generated virtual function overrides
    //{{AFX_VIRTUAL(TimeInABox)
    protected:
    virtual void DoDataExchange(CDataExchange* pDX);   // DDX/DDV support
    //}}AFX_VIRTUAL

// Implementation
protected:

    // Generated message map functions
    //{{AFX_MSG(TimeInABox)
    virtual BOOL OnInitDialog();
    afx_msg void OnTimer(UINT nIDEvent);
    virtual void OnOK();
    virtual void OnCancel();
    //}}AFX_MSG
    DECLARE_MESSAGE_MAP()
}
```

Listing 3.5 contains the source code for the implementation of TimeInABox.

Listing 3.5   TInABox.cpp, the Source Code for the Implementation File

```
#include "stdafx.h"
#include "ch3_menu.h"
#include "TInABox.h"

#ifdef _DEBUG
#define new DEBUG_NEW
#undef THIS_FILE
static char THIS_FILE[] = __FILE__;
#endif
```

(continues)

Listing 3.5   Continued

```
//////////////////////////////////////////////////////////////////////
// TimeInABox dialog


TimeInABox::TimeInABox(CWnd* pParent /*=NULL*/)
    : CDialog(TimeInABox::IDD, pParent)
{
    //{{AFX_DATA_INIT(TimeInABox)
        // NOTE: the ClassWizard will add member initialization here
    //}}AFX_DATA_INIT
}


void TimeInABox::DoDataExchange(CDataExchange* pDX)
{
    CDialog::DoDataExchange(pDX);
    //{{AFX_DATA_MAP(TimeInABox)
        // NOTE: the ClassWizard will add DDX and DDV calls here
    //}}AFX_DATA_MAP
}


BEGIN_MESSAGE_MAP(TimeInABox, CDialog)
    //{{AFX_MSG_MAP(TimeInABox)
    ON_WM_TIMER()
    //}}AFX_MSG_MAP
END_MESSAGE_MAP()

//////////////////////////////////////////////////////////////////////
// TimeInABox message handlers

BOOL TimeInABox::OnInitDialog()
{
    CDialog::OnInitDialog();

    // Set the initial time
    SetDlgItemText(
        IDC_TIMEBOX_TIME,
        CTime::GetCurrentTime().Format("%#c"));
    // trigger a timer every second, to update the time
    SetTimer(1, 1000, NULL);

    return TRUE;   // return TRUE unless you set the focus to a control
                   // EXCEPTION: OCX Property Pages should return FALSE
}

void TimeInABox::OnTimer(UINT nIDEvent)
{
    // display current date/time in long format
    if (nIDEvent == 1) {
        SetDlgItemText(
            IDC_TIMEBOX_TIME,
            CTime::GetCurrentTime().Format("%#c"));
    }
    CDialog::OnTimer(nIDEvent);
```

```
    }

    void TimeInABox::OnOK()
    {
        // TODO: Add extra validation here

        CDialog::OnOK();
    }

    void TimeInABox::OnCancel()
    {
        // TODO: Add extra cleanup here

        CDialog::OnCancel();
    }
```

Listing 3.5 shows the implementation file for the TimeInABox class, which contains definitions for the following members:

- The constructor that invokes the constructor of the parent class. ClassWizard generated this function definition.

- The member function DoDataExchange, which simply invokes the function DoDataExchange of the parent class. AppWizard generated this definition.

- The member function OnInitDialog. ClassWizard generated the statements that invoke the function OnInitDialog of the parent class and return True. You must insert the call to the inherited member function SetDlgItemText. This call has the arguments IDC_TIMEBOX_TIME and the current time. The function SetDlgItemText assigns the string in the member szStr to the static text control in the dialog box. This member function also starts the one-second timer that keeps the displayed time up-to-date.

- The member function OnTimer, which updates the time string in the static control IDC_TIMEBOX_TIME. Again, the function SetDlgItemText updates the string.

- The member functions OnOK and OnCancel, which are the default functions generated by ClassWizard.

Listing 3.6 lists the changes to the source code from the ch3mView.cpp implementation file:

Listing 3.6 ch3mView.cpp, the Changed Source Code for the View's Implementation

```
// ch3mView.cpp : implementation of the CChapter03MenuView class

#include "stdafx.h"
#include "ch3_menu.h"

#include "ch3mDoc.h"
#include "ch3mView.h"
```

(continues)

Listing 3.6 Continued

```
#ifdef _DEBUG
#define new DEBUG_NEW
#undef THIS_FILE
static char THIS_FILE[] = __FILE__;
#endif

//////////////////////////////////////////////////////////////////////
// CChapter03MenuView

IMPLEMENT_DYNCREATE(CChapter03MenuView, CView)

BEGIN_MESSAGE_MAP(CChapter03MenuView, CView)
    //{{AFX_MSG_MAP(CChapter03MenuView)
    ON_COMMAND(ID_TIME_DATETIME, OnTimeDateTime)
    ON_COMMAND(ID_TIME_STARTTIMER, OnTimeStartTimer)
    ON_COMMAND(ID_TIME_STOPTIMER, OnTimeStopTimer)
    ON_WM_LBUTTONDOWN()
    ON_WM_RBUTTONDOWN()
    ON_WM_CHAR()
    ON_WM_MOUSEMOVE()
    ON_WM_TIMER()
    ON_COMMAND(ID_TIME_TIMEDIALOG, OnTimeTimeDialog)
    //}}AFX_MSG_MAP
    // Standard printing commands
    ON_COMMAND(ID_FILE_PRINT, CView::OnFilePrint)
    ON_COMMAND(ID_FILE_PRINT_DIRECT, CView::OnFilePrint)
    ON_COMMAND(ID_FILE_PRINT_PREVIEW, CView::OnFilePrintPreview)
END_MESSAGE_MAP()
.
.
.
#include "TInABox.h"

void CChapter03MenuView::OnTimeTimeDialog()
{
    // TODO: Add your command handler code here
    TimeInABox time_dialog;
    time_dialog.DoModal();
}
```

The customized source code shown in listing 3.6 includes definitions for the new member function OnTimeTimeDialog. This new function uses the class TimeInABox to display the dialog box, which typically involves creating the instance of the class TimeInABox and invoking it by sending it the C++ message DoModal.

Compile and run the program Ch3_dial.exe. Choose the commands from the Time menu (or click the left or right mouse button) to view the program's response, which involves displaying the custom dialog box. Figure 3.12 shows a sample session with the Ch3_dial.exe program.

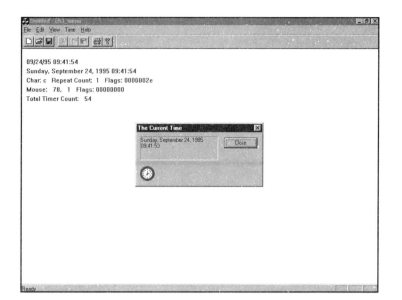

Fig. 3.12

Using ClassWizard to create TimeInABox *class members.*

Creating a Form View

Developer Studio enables you to create forms that are displayed and managed by the CFormView class. Forms, first implemented by Microsoft in Visual Basic, are very similar to dialog boxes. You can use the AppWizard utility to create an application that uses form views and then use the Developer Studio dialog box resource editor to draw the controls on the forms. Moreover, you can use ClassWizard to create any new classes and member functions that you need to make the form useful.

The following project, Ch3_form, is a form view created with the Developer Studio resource editor. Ch3_form, which is a variation on the projects presented earlier in this chapter, is a single document interface (SDI)-compliant application with a form view that contains the following controls:

- A borderless, read-only edit box that displays the current mouse coordinates
- A borderless, read-only edit box that displays the elapsed number of timers
- A borderless, read-only edit box that displays the current system date and time
- The Start command button control that starts and stops the simple timer
- The Date/Time command button control that displays the current system date and time in the borderless, read-only edit box just listed

AppWizard generates the Ch3_form.exe program's default menus.

Creating the Ch3_form.exe Application

For the first phase of creating the Ch3_form.exe application, you must use AppWizard. Create the new project Ch3_form as an SDI-compliant application. Check the classes that you are going to create and make sure that the view class is a descendant of the CFormView class rather than a descendant of the default parent class, CView. Then you can give AppWizard the green light to generate the application's core source code.

Adding Controls to the Form View Window

For the second phase of the project, you use the Developer Studio dialog box resource editor to add the controls. First, open the Resource View window. Developer Studio displays the resources IDD_ABOUTBOX and IDD_Ch3_form_FRM. Select IDD_CH3_FORM_FORM so that you can draw controls in the new, empty form. The Developer Studio dialog box resource editor displays the empty form, which contains the default message TODO: Place form controls on this dialog.

To customize the form, perform the following steps:

1. Select the initial static text control, the TODO string, and remove it by pressing the Del key.
2. Draw the three borderless, read-only edit boxes. Select from the Tools palette the control for each edit box, and draw the control in the form.
3. Draw the two command button controls. Select from the Tools palette each command button control, and draw the control in the form. Figure 3.9 shows the form with the command button and edit box controls drawn.
4. Double-click the mouse-position edit box to display its Properties dialog box, and type the control ID **IDC_FORM_MOUSE_COORD**. Figure 3.13 shows the Edit Properties dialog box with this information displayed.

Fig. 3.13

Using the dialog box editor to create the form's edit control for setting mouse coordinates.

5. Select the Styles tab at the top of the Edit Properties dialog box to display the options that enable you to customize the edit control's style. Select the Read-Only check box and make sure that the other check boxes are not selected (including Border). Figure 3.14 shows the Edit Properties dialog box with the appropriate option selected. When you finish, close the dialog box.

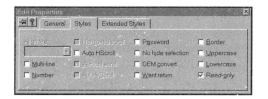

Fig. 3.14

In the Edit Properties dialog box's Styles page, you can specify that your new edit control is read-only.

6. Repeat steps 4 and 5 for the other two edit boxes. Use the ID IDC_FORM_DATE_TIME for the date and time edit box and IDC_FORM_TIMER_COUNT for the timer edit box.

7. Double-click the Update Date/Time button to display its Properties dialog box. Type the caption string **&Date/Time** and the ID **IDC_FORM_UPDATE**. Then close the Properties dialog box.

8. Double-click the Start button to display its Properties dialog box. Type the caption string **&Start** and the ID **IDC_FORM_START_TIMER**. Then close the Properties dialog box.

9. Save the updated resources. At this point, the dialog box should look like figure 3.15.

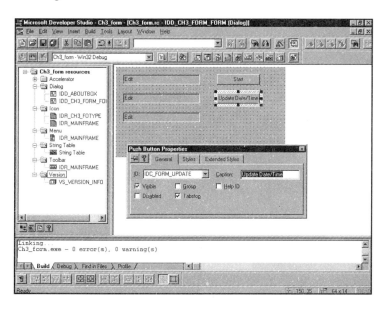

Fig. 3.15

The completed form view controls.

Adding Functions and Members

For the third phase of the project, use ClassWizard to add the message-handling member functions and the special data members for the form view class. Invoke ClassWizard and perform the following steps:

1. Select the Message Maps tab.

2. Add the member function `OnMouseMove`, which handles the Windows message `ON_WM_MOUSEMOVE` for the `CChapter3FormView` window.

3. Add to the Update Date/Time button (whose ID is `IDC_FORM_UPDATE`) the member function that handles the Windows notification message `BN_CLICKED`.

4. Add to the Start button (whose ID is `IDC_FORM_START_TIMER`) the member function that handles the Windows notification message `BN_CLICKED`.

5. Add the member function `OnTimer`, which handles the Windows message `WM_TIMER` for the `CChapter3FormView` window. Figure 3.16 shows ClassWizard after you create these new member functions.

Fig. 3.16

Using the ClassWizard to add the `CChapter3FormView` *member functions.*

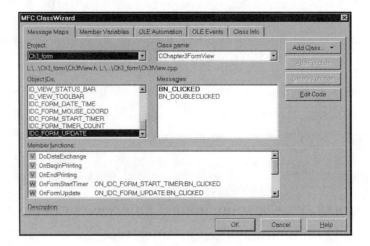

Customizing the Code

In the fourth and final phase of the project, you customize the source code manually. This section discusses this customization by presenting sections of the source-code files.

The partial script of the Ch3_form.rc resource file shown in listing 3.7 defines various resources. Of special interest are the About dialog box resource and the form resource. The form resource has the same syntax as that of an ordinary dialog box. The Ch3_form.rc file was created by AppWizard and then modified by the Developer Studio dialog box resource editor. Listing 3.7 shows the Ch3View.h header file, which the program uses with the resource script.

Listing 3.7 Ch3View.h, the Source Code for the Header File

```
// Ch3fView.h : interface of the CChapter3FormView class
//
/////////////////////////////////////////////////////////////////////////
```

```
class CChapter3FormView : public CFormView
{
protected: // create from serialization only
    CChapter3FormView();
    DECLARE_DYNCREATE(CChapter3FormView)

public:
    //{{AFX_DATA(CChapter3FormView)
    enum{ IDD = IDD_CH3_FORM_FORM };
        // NOTE: the ClassWizard will add data members here
    //}}AFX_DATA

// Attributes
public:
    CChapter3FormDoc* GetDocument();

// Operations
public:

// Overrides
    // ClassWizard-generated virtual function overrides
    //{{AFX_VIRTUAL(CChapter3FormView)
    public:
    virtual BOOL PreCreateWindow(CREATESTRUCT& cs);
    protected:
    virtual void DoDataExchange(CDataExchange* pDX);  // DDX/DDV support
    virtual BOOL OnPreparePrinting(CPrintInfo* pInfo);
    virtual void OnBeginPrinting(CDC* pDC, CPrintInfo* pInfo);
    virtual void OnEndPrinting(CDC* pDC, CPrintInfo* pInfo);
    virtual void OnPrint(CDC* pDC, CPrintInfo*);
    //}}AFX_VIRTUAL

// Implementation
public:
    virtual ~CChapter3FormView();
#ifdef _DEBUG
    virtual void AssertValid() const;
    virtual void Dump(CDumpContext& dc) const;
#endif

protected:

// Generated message map functions
protected:
    //{{AFX_MSG(CChapter3FormView)
    afx_msg void OnMouseMove(UINT nFlags, CPoint point);
    afx_msg void OnFormStartTimer();
    afx_msg void OnFormUpdate();
    afx_msg void OnTimer(UINT nIDEvent);
    //}}AFX_MSG
    DECLARE_MESSAGE_MAP()
};

#ifndef _DEBUG  // debug version in Ch3fView.cpp
inline CChapter3FormDoc* CChapter3FormView::GetDocument()
```

(continues)

Listing 3.7   Continued

```
    { return (CChapter3FormDoc*)m_pDocument; }
#endif

////////////////////////////////////////////////////////////////////////
```

The Ch3View.h header file shown in listing 3.8 contains the declaration of the view
class CChapter3FormView. The listing declares this class as a descendant of the class
CFormView. AppWizard created this file, and ClassWizard changed it according to the
steps followed earlier (when you were modifying the resources). ClassWizard added
the response-handling member functions OnFormUpdate, OnFormStartTimer, OnTimer,
and OnMouseMove. Listing 3.8 contains the Ch3View.cpp source file.

Listing 3.8   Ch3View.cpp, the Implementation of CChapter3FormView

```
// Ch3fView.cpp : implementation of the CChapter3FormView class

#include "stdafx.h"
#include "Ch3_form.h"

#include "Ch3fDoc.h"
#include "Ch3fView.h"

#ifdef _DEBUG
#define new DEBUG_NEW
#undef THIS_FILE
static char THIS_FILE[] = __FILE__;
#endif

////////////////////////////////////////////////////////////////////////
// CChapter3FormView

IMPLEMENT_DYNCREATE(CChapter3FormView, CFormView)

BEGIN_MESSAGE_MAP(CChapter3FormView, CFormView)
    //{{AFX_MSG_MAP(CChapter3FormView)
    ON_WM_MOUSEMOVE()
    ON_BN_CLICKED(IDC_FORM_START_TIMER, OnFormStartTimer)
    ON_BN_CLICKED(IDC_FORM_UPDATE, OnFormUpdate)
    ON_WM_TIMER()
    //}}AFX_MSG_MAP
    // Standard printing commands
    ON_COMMAND(ID_FILE_PRINT, CFormView::OnFilePrint)
    ON_COMMAND(ID_FILE_PRINT_DIRECT, CFormView::OnFilePrint)
    ON_COMMAND(ID_FILE_PRINT_PREVIEW, CFormView::OnFilePrintPreview)
END_MESSAGE_MAP()

////////////////////////////////////////////////////////////////////////
// CChapter3FormView construction/destruction

CChapter3FormView::CChapter3FormView()
    : CFormView(CChapter3FormView::IDD)
```

```
{
    //{{AFX_DATA_INIT(CChapter3FormView)
        // NOTE: the ClassWizard will add member initialization here
    //}}AFX_DATA_INIT
    // TODO: add construction code here

}

CChapter3FormView::~CChapter3FormView()
{
}

void CChapter3FormView::DoDataExchange(CDataExchange* pDX)
{
    CFormView::DoDataExchange(pDX);
    //{{AFX_DATA_MAP(CChapter3FormView)
        // NOTE: the ClassWizard will add DDX and DDV calls here
    //}}AFX_DATA_MAP
}

BOOL CChapter3FormView::PreCreateWindow(CREATESTRUCT& cs)
{
    // TODO: Modify the Window class or styles here by modifying
    //   the CREATESTRUCT cs

    return CFormView::PreCreateWindow(cs);
}

/////////////////////////////////////////////////////////////////////
// CChapter3FormView printing

BOOL CChapter3FormView::OnPreparePrinting(CPrintInfo* pInfo)
{
    // default preparation
    return DoPreparePrinting(pInfo);
}

void CChapter3FormView::OnBeginPrinting(CDC* /*pDC*/,
    CPrintInfo* /*pInfo*/)
{
    // TODO: add extra initialization before printing
}

void CChapter3FormView::OnEndPrinting(CDC* /*pDC*/,
    CPrintInfo* /*pInfo*/)
{
    // TODO: add cleanup after printing
}

void CChapter3FormView::OnPrint(CDC* pDC, CPrintInfo*)
{
    // TODO: add code to print the controls
}
```

(continues)

Listing 3.8 Continued

```
/////////////////////////////////////////////////////////////////////
// CChapter3FormView diagnostics

#ifdef _DEBUG
void CChapter3FormView::AssertValid() const
{
    CFormView::AssertValid();
}

void CChapter3FormView::Dump(CDumpContext& dc) const
{
    CFormView::Dump(dc);
}

CChapter3FormDoc* CChapter3FormView::GetDocument()
                                    // nondebug version is inline
{
    ASSERT(m_pDocument->IsKindOf(RUNTIME_CLASS(CChapter3FormDoc)));
    return (CChapter3FormDoc*)m_pDocument;
}
#endif //_DEBUG

/////////////////////////////////////////////////////////////////////
// CChapter3FormView message handlers

void CChapter3FormView::OnMouseMove(UINT nFlags, CPoint point)
{
    // TODO: Add your message handler code here and/or call default
    char buffer[200];
    sprintf(buffer,
        "Mouse: %d,%d  Flags: %08x",
        point.x,
        point.y,
        nFlags);
    SetDlgItemText( IDC_FORM_MOUSE_COORD, buffer);

    CFormView::OnMouseMove(nFlags, point);
}

void CChapter3FormView::OnFormStartTimer()
{
    // Start or stop the one-second timer
    static BOOL IsStarted = FALSE;
    if (IsStarted) {
        KillTimer(1);
        SetDlgItemText( IDC_FORM_START_TIMER, "Start");
        IsStarted = FALSE;
    } else {
        SetTimer(1, 1000, NULL);
        SetDlgItemText( IDC_FORM_START_TIMER, "Stop");
        IsStarted = TRUE;
    }
```

```
}
void CChapter3FormView::OnFormUpdate()
{
    // TODO: Add your control notification handler code here
    SetDlgItemText( IDC_FORM_DATE_TIME,
                    CTime::GetCurrentTime().Format("%#c") );
}

void CChapter3FormView::OnTimer(UINT nIDEvent)
{
    static int count = 0;
    if (nIDEvent == 1) {
        count++;
        char buffer[200];
        sprintf(buffer,
            "Timer Count: %d",
            count);
        SetDlgItemText( IDC_FORM_TIMER_COUNT, buffer);
        OnFormUpdate();
    }
    CFormView::OnTimer(nIDEvent);
}
```

The source code for the Ch3View.cpp implementation file shown in listing 3.8 was generated by AppWizard and then customized by ClassWizard. This customization incorporated the following elements:

- Inserting the message map macros for clicking the form's two command buttons and for moving the mouse and responding to timer messages
- Inserting the empty definitions of the OnXXXX member functions
- Inserting the calls to DDX_Control and DDX_Text for the form's controls

You must add the statements that define the member functions OnFormUpdate, OnFormStartTimer, OnTimer, and OnMouseMove. These statements are quite similar to those presented in the Ch3_Menu and Ch3_dial projects earlier in this chapter. Notice that these functions use the inherited member function SetDlgItemText to alter the text in the edit boxes or to alter the caption of the Start command button (the program toggles this caption between Start and Stop).

Compile and run the Ch3_form.EXE program. Move the mouse, and watch as the edit box in the upper-left corner displays the current mouse location. Click the Update Date/Time command button to view the current system date and time in the adjacent edit box. Click the Start command button, and watch its caption change and the Date/Time field update every second. Then click that button again to stop the automatic update. To exit, choose File, Exit.

Figure 3.17 shows a sample session with the Ch3_form.EXE program.

Fig. 3.17

Running the Ch3_form.exe application.

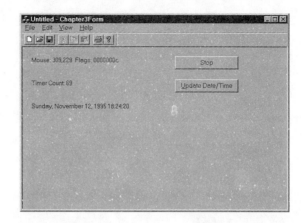

From Here...

In this chapter, you learned how to use AppStudio to generate resources for your MFC programs, and how to use the ClassWizard to breathe life into those resources by adding code that enables users to interact with the resources on-screen.

The combination of AppWizard and AppStudio makes for a powerful, fast tool set for building applications. Here are some related chapters that you might find useful:

- If you're ready to start using Visual C++ to debug your applications, see Chapter 4, "Debugging Visual C++ Applications."
- To learn more about the basic MFC classes, see Chapter 5, "Introducing MFC."
- If you're curious about how you can port an MFC application built with Developer Studio to other platforms, see Chapter 12, "Cross-Platform Development."

CHAPTER 4

Debugging Visual C++ Applications

The first compilers didn't furnish debuggers at all; you debugged your programs by looking at their output. As time passed, tools became more sophisticated, and debuggers emerged such as dbx and CodeView, which enabled programmers to inspect what a program did as it ran.

When you build a Windows program, you can inadvertently introduce a number of bugs in your code—the number of bugs is likely to increase as your programs become more complex. Visual C++ offers a built-in, integrated debugger to help capture and exterminate your bugs. With this debugger, you can monitor your program's behavior, see what code it's executing, look at and change variable values, and generally get an omniscient view of what your code is doing.

This chapter introduces the Developer Studio debugger and shows you how to apply its various features. This chapter covers the following topics:

- Reviewing the Debug menu commands
- Setting various kinds of breakpoints
- Using the Watch window to monitor variables and data members
- Managing the Watch window
- Using the Variables window to monitor local variables
- Using the Call Stack
- Viewing mixed source and assembly code

New Additions to the Debugger

It's obvious that the creators of Visual C++ are also users of Visual C++; in addition to making many other improvements in Developer Studio and Visual C++ 4, they've continued to make debugging easier and easier. Here's what they added to Visual C++ 4 debugging:

- DataTips provide pop-up information about a variable; when you simply point at a variable, the debugger displays the value as a ToolTip.

- AutoExpand automatically expands a variable to show the most important data at the top level.

- AutoDowncast automatically downcasts a pointer to show the data it points at by adding an extra member to the expanded object.

- The Variables window now includes Auto and Locals tabs, plus a *this* tab that shows you the contents of the current object's member variables.

- The Watch window now includes Watch1, Watch2, Watch3, and Watch4 tabs to help you organize how the variables that you're watching are grouped.

- The QuickWatch dialog box enables you to view or edit a variable's value quickly.

- The new toolbar button Breakpoint Toggle enables you to quickly toggle whether the current source line has a breakpoint.

- The Breakpoint dialog box now enables you to set breakpoints on locations, expressions, or a condition.

- The Step Into Specific function now provides you with nested function calls that enable you to control the location to which debugging steps.

- Remote Debugging now provides the capability to use serial or higher-performance TCP/IP connections to debug a program on two machines at once. One machine runs the program being debugged, and the other runs the debugger itself.

Reviewing the Debug Menu Commands

Table 4.1 summarizes the commands in the Debug menu, table 4.2 shows debugging commands available from the View menu, and table 4.3 lists the keyboard shortcuts that you can use to control the debugger's actions.

Table 4.1 Debug Menu Commands

Command	Shortcut Key	Description
Go	F5	Runs the program associated with the current project.
Restart	Ctrl+ Shift+F5	Reloads a program and restarts execution.
Stop Debugging	Shift+F5	Ends the debugging session.
Break		Halts program execution and returns control to the debugger without ending the program.
Step Into	F11	Single-steps through each program line.

Step Over	F10	Single-steps through each program line, but executes functions without entering them.
Step Out	Shift+F11	Runs the program to the first statement after the current function call.
Run to Cursor	Ctrl+F10	Runs the program until it reaches the insertion point.
Step Into Specific Function	F7	Step to a specific nested function.
Exceptions		Lets you set what debug actions are triggered for microprocessor and C++ exception handling.
Threads		Controls which thread is the current thread when debugging multithreaded applications.
Settings		Displays the breakpoints associated with a program and lets you clear and set breakpoints.
QuickWatch	Shift+F9	Opens the QuickWatch window to add, view the value of, or alter the value of a watched variable.

Table 4.2   The View Menu's Debug-Related Commands

Command	Shortcut Key	Description
Watch	Alt+3	Opens the Watch window.
Variables	Alt+4	Displays auto and local variables associated with a function.
Registers	Alt+5	Views microprocessor register values.
Memory	Alt+6	Views a raw memory dump.
Call Stack	Alt+7	Displays the Call Stack.
Disassembly	Alt+8	Opens a window showing assembler source code.

Table 4.3   Keyboard Commands for Debugging

Command	Shortcut Key	Description
DebugBreak		Stops program execution; breaks into the debugger.
DebugDisableAllBreakpoints		Disables all breakpoints.
DebugEnableBreakpoint	Ctrl+Shift+F9	Enables or disables a breakpoint.
DebugExceptions		Edits debug actions taken when an exception occurs.
DebugGo	F5	Starts or continues the program.
DebugGoToDisassembly		Activates the disassembly window for this instruction.

(continues)

Visual C++ Tools

Table 4.3 Continued		
Command	**Shortcut Key**	**Description**
DebugGoToSource		Activates the source window for this instruction.
DebugHexadecimalDisplay	Alt+F9	Toggles between decimal and hexadecimal format.
DebugMemoryNextFormat	Alt+F7	Switches the memory window to the next display format.
DebugMemoryPrevFormat	Alt+Shift+F7	Switches the memory window to the previous display format.
DebugQuickWatch	Shift+F9	Performs immediate evaluation of variables and expressions.
DebugRemoveAllBreakpoints		Removes all breakpoints.
DebugRestart	Shift+F5	Restarts the program.
DebugRunToCursor	F7	Runs the program to the line containing the cursor.
DebugSetNextStatement	Ctrl+Shift+F7	Sets the instruction pointer to the line that contains the cursor, skipping over code.
DebugSettings		Edits the project build and debug settings.
DebugStepInto	F8	Steps into the next statement.
DebugStepOut	Shift+F7	Steps out of the current function.
DebugStepOver	F10	Steps over the next statement.
DebugStepOverSource	Ctrl+F10	Steps over the next source-level statement.
DebugStopDebugging	Alt+F5	Stops debugging the program.
DebugThreads		Sets the debugger's thread attributes.
DebugToggleBreakpoint	F9	Inserts or removes a breakpoint.
DebugToggleMixedMode	Ctrl+F7	Switches between the source view and the disassembly view for this instruction.

About Debugging Your Programs

Almost all programs contain errors of some type during their development process. In fact, bugs are a common part of programming. A program rarely runs correctly on the first try. Programmers are constantly going back and correcting parts of their program to make it work correctly.

There are three types of errors:

- *Compile-time errors* are rather straightforward to fix because they result from an error in your program's syntax. Visual C++ catches these errors while compiling the program. Before you can even run the program, you must correct any compile-time errors. To correct compiler errors, you do not use a debugger. In fact, before you can use a debugger, you must eliminate the errors. (Before you can debug a program, it must be compiled.) When using Visual C++, you can press F4 to step through your compiler errors. Also, when Visual C++ highlights a compiler error, you can press F1 to find detailed information on the error.

- *Run-time errors* can cause your program to terminate and produce an error message. This type of error results from incorrect error checking within your program. Sometimes run-time errors occur because a program expected the user to enter a certain type of value and the user instead entered a different type of value (for example, the user might have entered a string into an edit control that expects to receive an integer value). Another typical run-time error is an uninitialized variable, in which a variable is supposed to be set to a specific value but is not set correctly.

- A *logical error* is one in which your program is doing something different from what you expected it to do. The computer always does what it is told. You might have thought that you told it something but inadvertently told it something else. When using a debugger, you can find out what your program told the computer to do, thus finding the difference between what you want the computer to do and what you actually told it to do. You can then change the program to work the way that you expected.

With the debugging commands in the Developer Studio, you can run your programs a line at a time and view the value of variables as the program executes. Visual C++ 4's debugger is considered an *integrated debugger* because it is part of the programming environment. Before Visual C++ 2, you had to run a separate program (which was called, appropriately enough, a *debugger*), which then enabled you to test your program. By using the special features of the Developer Studio's integrated debugger, you can examine memory locations and control program flow while the program executes.

Setting Breakpoints

The Developer Studio debugger supports various kinds of *breakpoints,* which range from simple to sophisticated. There are several ways to set and reset breakpoints in your source code. The simplest way is to use the context-sensitive pop-up menus that appear when you right-click the mouse button. When you are in a source file, this menu contains the Insert/Remove Breakpoints item. If the current line already contains a breakpoint, this pop-up menu contains Remove Breakpoint and Disable Breakpoint (or Enable Breakpoint if the breakpoint is disabled). In your source file's leftmost column, a small, solid red stop sign indicates an active breakpoint. A small, outlined red stop sign indicates a disabled breakpoint.

To set any kind of breakpoint, you can choose Edit, Breakpoints, or press Ctrl+B. The Breakpoints dialog box appears (see fig. 4.1).

Fig. 4.1

In the Breakpoints dialog box, you can define debugger breakpoints.

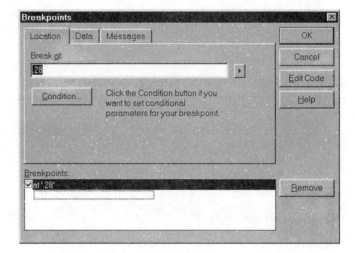

The Breakpoints dialog box contains the following controls:

- The OK command button closes the Breakpoints dialog box.
- The Cancel command button cancels any changes that you made since opening the Breakpoints dialog box.
- The Help command button accesses online Help.
- The Remove command button deletes the breakpoint currently selected in the Breakpoints list box.
- The Edit Code command button closes the dialog box and opens the source file to the currently selected breakpoint.
- The Breakpoints list box lists the current breakpoints. A check box appears to the left of an enabled or disabled breakpoint, respectively. Click the check box to toggle the breakpoint's status.
- The Location tab displays a page in which you can set, clear, disable, enable, or view location breakpoints. Use the Location tab and the Condition button to set conditional breakpoints.
- The Data tab displays a page in which you can set, clear, disable, enable, or view breakpoints on variables or expressions.
- The Messages tab displays a page in which you can set, clear, disable, enable, or view a breakpoint on a WndProc message.

Understanding the Various Breakpoints

Breakpoints tell the debugger where or when to break a program's execution. When the program halts at a breakpoint, you can examine your program's state, step through your code, and use the debugger windows to evaluate expressions.

The debugger supports the following types of breakpoints:

- *Location* breakpoints halt the debugger at a specified location.
- *Data* breakpoints halt the debugger when an expression becomes true or changes value.
- *Message* breakpoints halt the debugger at a WndProc function when a message is received.
- *Conditional* breakpoints halt the debugger at a specified location when an expression is true or changes value.

The Breakpoints dialog box, shown in figure 4.1, displays a list of all breakpoints set in the project. You can use this dialog box to set, remove, disable, and enable breakpoints. When you close a project, the debugger saves all breakpoints that you have set as part of the project information. The next time that you open the project, the breakpoints remain as you left them.

Location Breakpoints. The most common type of breakpoint is a location breakpoint. All location breakmarks do is stop when the program reaches a certain point in the source code; you use these breakpoints to stop the program before it executes a particular line of code. With the debugger, you can set location breakpoints as follows:

- On a specific line of source code
- At the beginning or the return point of a function
- At a label
- At a specified memory address

You can set or remove any of these location breakpoints without using the Breakpoints dialog box. You can disable and enable breakpoints on a source-code line or in the Disassembly or Call Stack window.

To set a breakpoint at a source-code line, follow these steps:

1. In a source window, move the insertion point to the line at which you want the program to break.

2. Choose the Insert/Remove Breakpoint toolbar button or press F9. A red dot appears in the left margin, indicating that you have set the breakpoint.

To set a breakpoint at the beginning of a function, follow these steps:

1. In the Find box on the Standard toolbar, type the function name. Then press Enter.

   2. Choose the Insert/Remove Breakpoint toolbar button or press F9.

To set a breakpoint at a function's return point, follow these steps:

   1. In the Call Stack window, move the insertion point to the function at which you want the program to break.

   2. Choose the Insert/Remove Breakpoint toolbar button or press F9.

To set a breakpoint at a label, follow these steps:

   1. In the Find box on the Standard toolbar, type the name of the label. Then press Enter.

   2. Choose the Insert/Remove Breakpoint toolbar button or press F9.

To set a breakpoint at a memory address, follow these steps:

   1. In the Disassembly window, move the insertion point to the line at which you want the program to break.

   2. Choose the Insert/Remove Breakpoint toolbar button or press F9.

The Developer Studio debugger supports various formats that specify breakpoint locations. You enter them in the Breakpoints dialog box. Table 4.4 presents these formats and offers an example of each.

Table 4.4   Breakpoint Location Formats

Format	Example	Comments
`.lineNumber`	`.125`	Line 125 of the active source file.
`Filename!lineNumber`	CTL.CPP!90	Line 90 in file ctl.cpp.
`Offset`	0x1A34	Offset 0x1A34 in the code segment.
`Offset`	IP	Instruction pointer offset to code segment CS.
`Segment:Offset`	0xA100:0x1A34	Offset 0x1A34 to segment 0xA100.
`Segment:Offset`	CS:0x1A34	Offset 0x1A34 to code segment CS.
`Segment:Offset`	CS:IP	Instruction pointer offset to code segment CS.

Data Breakpoints. Location breakpoints just stop when the program reaches a line of code; by contrast, data breakpoints make the debugger take control when an expression or variable value matches some condition that you set.

To set a breakpoint on a variable or expression, click the Breakpoints dialog box's Data tab. A data breakpoint breaks the program's execution when the value of the variable or expression changes from the value that it had when you set the breakpoint.

You can set a breakpoint on any valid C or C++ expression. Breakpoint expressions can also use memory addresses and register mnemonics. The debugger interprets all constants as decimal numbers unless they begin with 0 (octal) or 0x (hexadecimal).

> **Note**
>
> Except where noted, the following procedures work only for variables within the current scope. To set a breakpoint using a variable outside the current scope, you must specify the context in the Advanced Breakpoint dialog box; you can display this dialog box by clicking the small right-pointing triangle next to the Break At field.

To break execution when a variable changes value, follow these steps:

1. Click the Data tab.
2. In the text box Enter the Expression To Be Evaluated, type the variable name, such as **m_MyVar** or **class.member**.

To break when an expression is true, follow these steps:

1. Click the Data tab.
2. In the Expression text box, type an expression that contains a Boolean comparison operator, such as **Count==11** or **Houses>11**.

To break when an expression changes value, follow these steps:

1. Click the Data tab.
2. In the Expression text box, type an expression such as **x+y**.

To break on a variable outside the current scope, follow these steps:

1. Click the Data tab.
2. In the Expression text box, type the variable name.
3. Click the right-pointing triangle (it's really a drop-down menu) to the right of the text box.
4. From the menu that appears, choose Advanced. The Advanced Breakpoint dialog box appears.
5. In the Expression text box, type the function name and (if necessary) the file name of the variable.
6. Choose OK to close the Advanced Breakpoint dialog box. The information that you specified appears in the Breakpoints dialog box's Expression text box.
7. In the Breakpoints dialog box, choose OK to set the breakpoint.

Breaking on an Array. One common problem in C and C++ programming is managing arrays. You can easily miss an array count and end up writing data past the end of an array. Visual C++'s debugger enables you to set a breakpoint that gets triggered when an array element's value changes. To set a breakpoint when an array element changes, use the Data page's Number Of Elements text box. The number that you enter in this field determines how many elements of the array the debugger will monitor. This section provides some examples of how to use this field.

To break when the initial element of an array changes value, follow these steps:

1. In the Enter the Expression To Be Evaluated text box, type the first element of the array (**myArray[0]**, for example).

2. In the Number of Elements text box, type **1**.

3. Choose OK to set the breakpoint on myArray [0].

To break when an array's initial element has a specific value, follow these steps:

1. In the Expression text box, type an expression that contains the initial element of the array (**myArray[0]==1**, for example).

2. In the Number of Elements text box, type **1**.

3. Choose OK to set the breakpoint on myArray [0].

To break when an array's 12th element changes value, follow these steps:

1. In the Expression text box, type the 12th element of the array (**myArray[12]**, for example).

2. In the Number of Elements text box, type **1**.

3. Choose OK to set the breakpoint on myArray [12].

To break when any element of an array changes value, follow these steps:

1. In the Expression text box, type the first element of the array (**myArray[0]**).

2. In the Number of Elements text box, type **1**.

3. Choose OK to set the breakpoint on myArray.

To break when any of an array's first 10 elements change value, follow these steps:

1. In the Expression text box, type the array's first element (**myArray[0]**, for example).

2. In the Number of Elements text box, type **10**.

3. Choose OK to set the breakpoint on myArray[0] through myArray[10].

Breaking on a Pointer. If you set a breakpoint on a pointer variable, the debugger does not automatically dereference the pointer. If you want to set a breakpoint on the value to which you are pointing rather than the location to which you are pointing, you must explicitly dereference the pointer, as described in the following procedures.

To break when the location value of a pointer changes, type the pointer variable name in the text box Enter the Expression To Be Evaluated (**p**, for example).

To break when the value at a location pointed to changes, type the dereferenced pointer variable name in the Expression text box (***p** or **p->next**, for example).

To break when an array to which a pointer points changes, follow these steps:

1. In the Expression text box, type the dereferenced pointer variable name (***p**, for example).

2. In the <u>N</u>umber of Elements text box, type the length of the array in elements. For example, if the pointer is a pointer to double, and the array to which the pointer points contains 100 values of type double, type **100**.

Breaking on an Address or Register. To break when the value at a specified memory address changes, follow these steps:

1. In the text box <u>E</u>nter the Expression To Be Evaluated, type the memory address for the byte. For a word or doubleword memory address, enclose the address in parentheses, and precede it with a cast operator. For the word at memory location 00406036, for example, enter **WO(00406036)**. Use the cast operator BY for a byte (optional), WO for a word, or DW for a doubleword.

2. In the <u>N</u>umber of Elements text box, type the number of bytes, words, or doublewords to monitor. If you use the BY operator in the Expression text box, specify the number of bytes. If you used WO, specify the number of words. If you used DW, specify the number of doublewords.

To break when a register changes, follow these steps:

1. In the Expression text box, type a register mnemonic, such as **CS**.

2. In the <u>N</u>umber of Elements text box, type the number of bytes to monitor.

To break when a register expression is true, follow these steps:

1. In the Expression text box, type an expression that contains a Boolean comparison operator, such as **CS==0**.

2. In the <u>N</u>umber of Elements text box, type the number of bytes to monitor.

Conditional Breakpoints. Location breakpoints are useful, but sometimes you don't want to stop every time that a line of code is executed. For example, imagine trying to debug a function that parses input from a file but that crashed after the 405th input record. You wouldn't want to set a location breakpoint and then press F5 404 times to get to the crash condition!

Conditional breakpoints are location breakpoints that break execution only if a specified condition is met. To set conditional breakpoints, use the Breakpoint Condition dialog box. To open this dialog box, choose the <u>C</u>ondition button on the Location page of the Breakpoints dialog box.

The Breakpoint Condition dialog box looks and operates much like the Data page, but has one additional field. The text box Enter the Number of Times To <u>S</u>kip before Stopping enables the debugger to skip the breakpoint a specified number of times. If you type **4** in this text box, for example, the debugger stops the fifth time that your program reaches that location and meets the condition. If you set this field to **9**, the debugger stops the 10th time that your program reaches that location and meets the condition.

To set a plain conditional breakpoint, which will break every time that the condition you specify is true, follow these steps:

1. Click the Location tab. In the Break At text box, type a location as described in the section "Location Breakpoints."

2. Click the Condition button. The Breakpoint Condition dialog box appears.

3. Fill in the text boxes Enter the Expression To Be Evaluated and Number of Elements as you would for a data breakpoint. (See the section "Data Breakpoints" for detailed information.)

As mentioned in the previous example, you might want to skip a breakpoint some number of times before actually stopping. To set a conditional breakpoint with a skip count, follow these steps:

1. Fill in the Enter the Expression To Be Evaluated text box as you would for a data breakpoint. (See the section "Data Breakpoints" for detailed information.)

2. Fill in the Enter the Number of Times To Skip before Stopping text box. If you want your program to break every Nth time that the condition is met at the specified location, enter in this text box **N -1**. (The debugger then skips the breakpoint the first N times.)

You cannot set values for both Enter the Number of Times To Skip before Stopping and Enter the Number of Elements To Watch for the same breakpoint.

Message Breakpoints. You can use the Messages tab in the Breakpoints dialog box to set a breakpoint on a message received by an exported Windows function. You can select whether to break on a specific message or on any message from a class of messages.

To set a breakpoint on a message, follow these steps:

1. Click the Messages tab.

2. In the Break at WndProc combo box, type the name of the Windows function. If you are setting a breakpoint during a debug session, the list contains the exported functions in your project.

3. In the drop-down list box Set One Breakpoint for Each Message To Watch, select the message.

4. To set another breakpoint, press Enter and then repeat step 3 as needed, then press Enter again.

Debugging a Sample Program

This chapter's sample application is part of the Scribble tutorial application provided with Visual C++. If you didn't choose the "typical" installation when you installed Visual C++ back in Chapter 1, "Getting Started with Visual C++," you won't have the sample code. Because of Microsoft's copyright, the Scribble code isn't included on this book's CD.

Using Unconditional Breakpoints

In this section, you use simple, unconditional breakpoints to monitor local variables and data members while creating a new build of the Scribble application. Load the project workspace for Scribble (it should be in \MSDEV\SAMPLES\MFC\SCRIBBLE), and make sure that the project target is set to Win32 Debug. Rebuild the executable if necessary. Open the scribvw.cpp and scribdoc.cpp source files, and use the Edit, Breakpoints command to set the following breakpoints:

1. Move the cursor to line 150 of scribvw.cpp and choose Edit, Breakpoints. Click the Location tab, and then click the Break At pop-up combo box. Select line 150. Click OK to save the breakpoint.

2. Move the cursor to line 173 and repeat step 1.

3. Move the cursor to line 214 and repeat step 1.

4. Open the scribdoc.cpp file, and repeat step 1 to set a breakpoint at line 265 of scribdoc.cpp.

With these four breakpoints, the Breakpoints dialog box should appear as shown in figure 4.2.

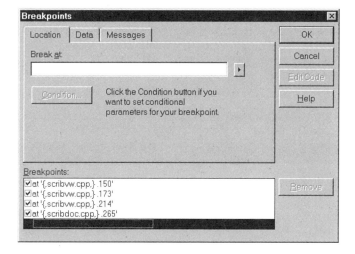

Fig. 4.2

The Breakpoints dialog box with four scribble breakpoints set.

Press F5 to load the debugging symbols and run the program.

Open the Watch window by choosing View, Watch. Then type the names of the data members that you want to watch. Type **theApp** from Scribble. In the Variables window, click the Locals tab and resize the three windows to an arrangement that resembles that shown in figure 4.3. (If you right-click in the window to display the pop-up context menu and then select Docking View, the Developer Studio manages the windows for you.)

Fig. 4.3

*The initial debugging
screen, stopped at
breakpoint* scribvw:214.

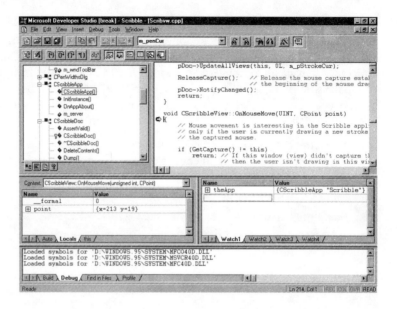

When the program starts to run, it triggers the OnMouseMove breakpoint. The Watch
window shows the data member theApp that contains the string Scribble, courtesy of
Visual C++ 4's new AutoExpand functionality. By clicking the + icon and expanding
theApp, you display the class hierarchy, courtesy of Visual C++ 4's new AutoDowncast
functionality (see fig. 4.4).

Fig. 4.4

*The Watch window using
AutoDowncast to display
the class hierarchy.*

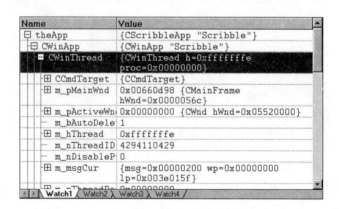

The Variables dialog box's Locals page shows the local variables _formal and
point. _formal is the unnamed first argument, and point is the named CPoint
argument.

Next, press Ctrl+Shift+F9 to disable this breakpoint. Then press F5 to reach the second
breakpoint. By left-clicking in the Scribble window, you trigger the next breakpoint,
located at line 150. There are four ways that you can examine the point variable's
value:

- The Variables dialog box's Locals page
- The Variables dialog box's Auto page (because the program passes the variable by value)
- The Watch window, if you drag the point variable into the window
- DataTip, if you pause the cursor over the point variable anywhere in the edit window

Using Breakpoints with Expressions

In this section, you use a conditional breakpoint to pause the program when an expression is true. For this exercise, assume that you want to stop anytime that the mouse x value is 300 or whenever you access the 10th element while drawing a stroke.

First, move the insertion point to line 184 of scribdoc.cpp. The statement on line 184 is a for loop that loops through all the points in the array of strokes. Next, choose Edit, Breakpoints to display the Breakpoints dialog box. Click the check boxes for the current four breakpoints in the Breakpoints area to disable the previous test's breakpoints. In the Location page, type **184**. Click the Condition button and type **y==0** into the Enter the Expression To Be Evaluated text box. Click the OK button to add this breakpoint, and then follow the same procedure to set a breakpoint on line 214 of scribvw.cpp, when `point.x==300`. At this point, the Breakpoints dialog box should look like figure 4.5.

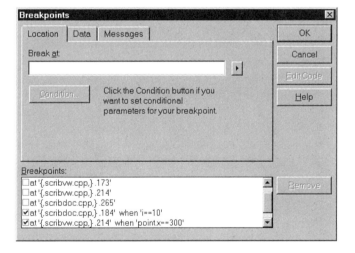

Fig. 4.5

The Breakpoints dialog box showing conditional breakpoints.

Now rerun Scribble and trigger these conditional breakpoints:

1. Press F5 to run the program in debug mode.
2. When the program's window appears, start drawing a scribble. As you move the mouse to the left, you should trigger the `point.x==300` breakpoint. The program pauses and displays a message dialog box informing you that the condition of the breakpoint at line 219 is true (see fig. 4.6).

Fig. 4.6

Developer Studio displays a breakpoint message when point.x==300.

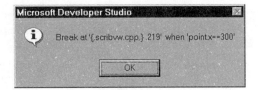

3. Press F5 to continue the program in debug mode. When the program's window appears, it tries to redraw the current scribble. This triggers the other conditional breakpoint when I==10. The program pauses and displays a message dialog box informing you that the condition of the breakpoint at line 186 is true (see fig. 4.7).

Fig. 4.7

The breakpoint message when i==10.

Now select the i variable and choose Debug, QuickWatch. The QuickWatch dialog box appears (see fig. 4.8) in which you can add, modify, and zoom in on a variable. The QuickWatch dialog box shows the name of the variable i.

Fig. 4.8

Using the QuickWatch dialog box to set i=100.

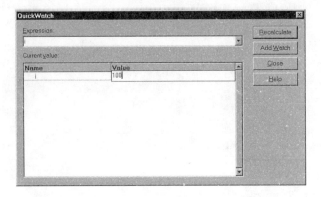

The QuickWatch dialog box shows its current value and enables you to edit the value. Select the current value, 10, and type **100** in the pop-up edit control. Close the QuickWatch dialog box by clicking the Close command button. The value of the variable i in the Locals window is now 100, not 10.

Next, single-step through the rest of the statements in the member function DrawStroke. Notice that when Scribble draws the stroke, the points from 10 to 99 are missing. Press Alt+F5 to stop the debugging session and terminate Scribble.

Viewing the Call Stack

The call stack is the set of all functions that lead to the currently executing function. If you're in the `DrawStroke()` function and view the call stack, you'll see the functions that the program has called to reach the member function DrawStroke().

The Developer Studio integrated debugger's Ⅴiew menu offers the Ⅽall Stack command, with which you can view the Call Stack. For example, to view the Call Stack for the member function `DrawStroke`, move the insertion point to line 178. Invoke the Breakpoints dialog box and clear all current breakpoints. Insert an unconditional breakpoint and close the dialog box.

Press F5 to run the program in debug mode. Next draw and scribble, and then trigger a redraw by maximizing the Scribble MDI child window. This triggers the breakpoint at line 178. To make the Call Stack visible, choose Ⅴiew, Ⅽall Stack. Figure 4.9 shows the Call Stack window; it's the topmost window on the left side of the figure.

Fig. 4.9

Using the QuickWatch window to set i=100.

The top of the Call Stack window's list shows the function `CStroke::DrawStroke()`. Below it is the member function `CScribbleView::OnDraw()`. The libraries incorporated in the project define the remaining functions in the Call Stack. The Call Stack window contains a pop-up menu that enables you to control what the window displays. To display the menu, just right-click anywhere over the Call Stack window. This displays a context-sensitive menu from which you can choose several useful commands, including the following:

- Parameter Values controls whether the Call Stack window includes the parameters used to call each function in the stack.

- Parameter Types toggles the display of the parameters' types (if parameters are being displayed).

- Hexadecimal Display toggles the display of the parameter values between hexadecimal or decimal.

Viewing Mixed Source/Assembly Code

With the Developer Studio debugger, you can view both the C++ statements and their equivalent assembly language instructions. When you choose View, Disassembly, the debugger displays a window that lists assembly language instructions. The shortcut key combination for the Disassembly menu option is Alt+8. By default, this new window appears at the location at which you have docked the source window. You can view both the source and disassembly windows side by side by undocking the disassembly window and rearranging the screen layout (see fig. 4.10).

Fig. 4.10

Viewing disassembly and source code windows.

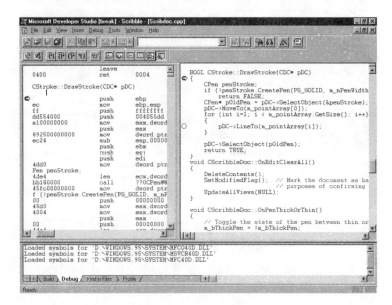

By choosing Tools, Options and then clicking the Options dialog box's Debug tab, you can customize the displayed information. The Debug page offers three options:

- Source Annotation annotates disassembled code with source code.

- Code Bytes displays the code byte values when disassembling code.

- Symbols displays symbols when disassembling code.

These viewing controls are also available in a pop-up menu available from the Disassembly window; to display the window, just right-click anywhere in the Disassembly window.

If you program in assembly language, this kind of information offers valuable insight on the low-level instructions that the program is executing. In addition, the assembly code can tell you whether Visual C++ is compiling your code correctly. Even if you are not an assembly language programmer, these instructions can help you gain insight into how C++ statements translate into assembly language instructions.

Managing the Watch Window

The Watch window lets you add, delete, and edit expressions. These expressions can include variables, operators, and constants, or they can consist only of the name of a variable or data member. The Developer Studio debugger evaluates the expression in the Watch window and displays its value. You access the Watch window by choosing View, Watch or by pressing the shortcut key Alt+3.

Adding and Deleting Expressions

Adding an expression is as easy as typing it. You can insert an expression before you begin a debugging session, while the session is paused between steps, or at a breakpoint. Just type the expression and press Enter—that's all there is to it. If you enter an expression during a debug session, the debugger evaluates the expression.

You also can use the QuickWatch dialog box to add a variable to the Watch window. Place the cursor to the left or within the name of the targeted variable and invoke the QuickWatch dialog box. Then choose the Add Watch command button to insert the targeted variable in the Watch window.

To view type information for a variable in a Watch window, follow these steps:

1. In the Watch window, select the line that contains the variable whose type you want to see.
2. Right-click in the Watch window and select Properties from the context-sensitive pop-up menu.

When the program pauses at a breakpoint or between steps, you can change the value of any non-const variable in your program. This gives you the flexibility to try changes and see their results in real time, or to recover from certain logic errors. To modify the value of a variable in the Watch window, follow these steps:

1. In the Watch window, double-click the value.
2. Type the new value and press Enter.

To delete an expression from the Watch window, you first must end the current debug session. After you end the session, simply select the entire line that contains the expression that you want to remove and press the Delete key.

Expanding and Collapsing Variables

The Watch and Variables windows often include objects, strings, arrays, structured variables, or data members; these items all have fields or other contents besides the variable's value itself. Simple variables, like int and char, don't have any other data. Fortunately, the Watch and Variables windows display a plus sign (+) or minus sign (–) to the left of the variable names for variables that have fields or member data. The + character indicates that the variable's information is collapsed. The – character indicates that the variable's information is expanded. To toggle between expanding and collapsing the information, click the variable or move the insertion point to that variable and press Enter. When you toggle the display, the contents of the window change to reflect your command. Figure 4.11 shows a Variables window with both collapsed and expanded variables displayed.

Fig. 4.11

Viewing variables in the Variables window.

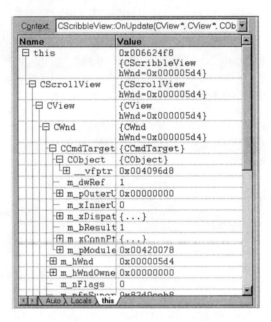

For more information on expanding and collapsing variable views, see the section "The QuickWatch Command" in Chapter 2, "Using the Visual C++ Developer Studio."

From Here...

In this chapter, you learned how to use the Visual C++ debugger to trace the execution of your programs. When you're trying to find out why your code isn't working right, a good debugger can be worth its weight in blood, sweat, tears, and toil.

For more information on debugging programs in Visual C++, you might want to review the following chapters of this book:

- To learn more about the Developer Studio environment, see Chapter 2, "Using the Visual C++ Developer Studio."
- For information on using C++ exception handling to make your code more bug-resistant, see Chapter 13, "Exception Handling."
- For more information about advanced debugging methods, see Chapter 16, "Advanced Debugging Techniques."

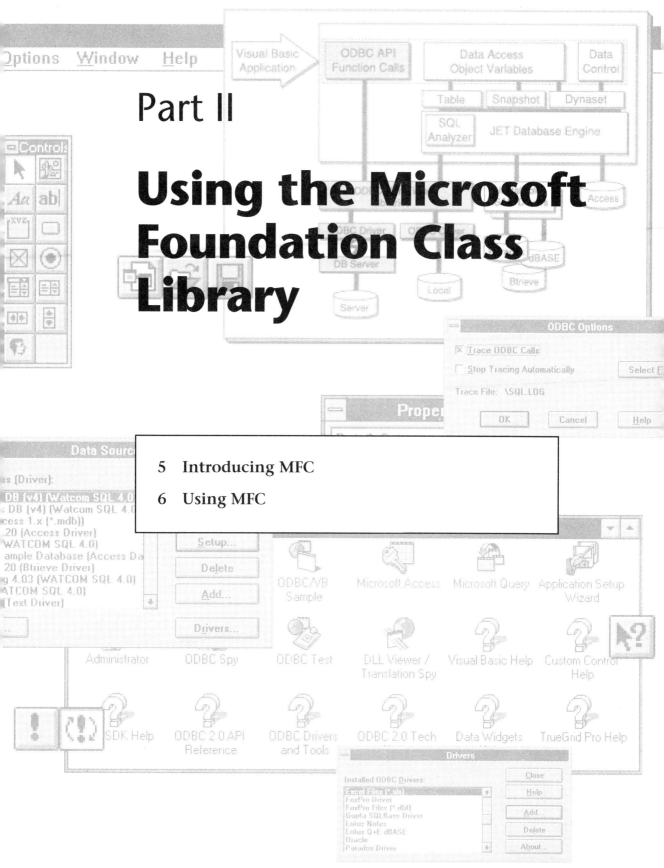

Part II

Using the Microsoft Foundation Class Library

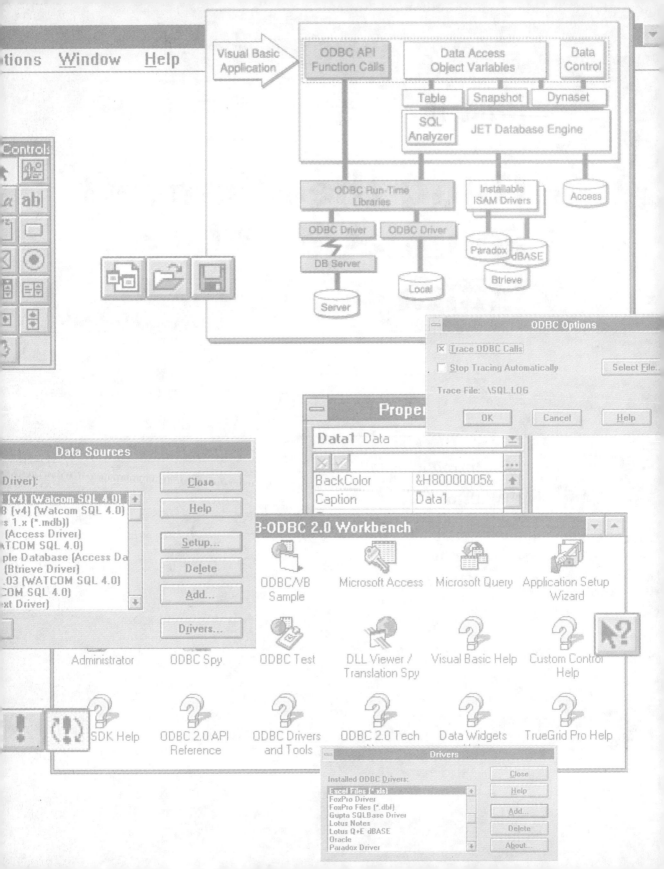

CHAPTER 5

Introducing MFC

If you're new to Visual C++ programming, you've probably read a lot about the Microsoft Foundation Classes, otherwise known as MFC. MFC provides an object-oriented approach to Windows development that not only can save you time, but also can make the development process much less painful than it is when you use the "raw" Windows API. This chapter introduces you to MFC and shows how it works with AppWizard to help you write applications.

By the end of this chapter, you will be familiar with the following:

- The files that AppWizard generates
- The classes used by an application developed with MFC
- MFC and what it provides for application developers

An Overview of MFC

MFC belongs to a category of software called *application frameworks*. Of course, if you've never used an app framework before, that statement probably doesn't tell you much. What exactly is an app framework?

Consider the process that you go through when you write a Windows application in C using the Windows SDK. You produce a source-code module that contains WinMain() (the starting point of all Windows programs). You write code to initialize your application, followed by a message loop (which never seems to change much, regardless of the type of program that you are writing). You register your window classes (with RegisterClass()) and write a window callback procedure (otherwise known as a WndProc) for each window class that you create. If your program uses dialog boxes, you create them either by using some sort of resource editor or by writing the .rc file by hand. Then you write a dialog procedure (or DlgProc) for each dialog box. Then you must hook the dialog procedure to your code so that it displays at the appropriate time. In your window procedures, you create a large switch statement, with a case statement for each message from Windows that you expect to handle. For each case statement, you must remember how to break apart the parameters that Windows passes to you (in the LPARAM and WPARAM variables), making sure that you pass back the right value to Windows (or calling DefWndProc, if necessary). If you had done some exploring in the header files provided with your C++ compiler, you might have discovered windowsx.h (which contains Microsoft's "message crackers") and used those to help you obtain values from the variables that Windows passes to you.

After going through this process a few times, most programmers go into "cookie-cutter" mode, in which you simply modify a previously written program to match your current need. The Windows SDK's *Guide to Programming* manual (supplied with earlier versions of Windows SDKs) and other popular Windows books taught this method of Windows program development, in which you have to examine each program to find the exact differences among them.

After using this programming method a while, you notice that you spend much of your time just setting down your programs' basics, which almost always look the same. At this point, you create a do-nothing program with which you can start any project. Also, after examining the code that you write, you notice all the silly rules that you have to remember—such as "use CreateBitmap() to create a bitmap, but use DeleteObject() to get rid of it" and "make sure that you use BeginPaint() and EndPaint() in your WM_PAINT code so that you won't confuse Windows."

If this sounds familiar to you, you probably wonder whether a better method exists. Why do you have to remember all these details? That is the job for which application frameworks were designed. Instead of making you churn out the same code every time that you start an application, a framework provides the "core components" that you need for every application that you write.

Frameworks actually perform two functions: defining the behavior of a basic application, and (under Windows) providing a class-based interface to the underlying API (the Windows API). Because a framework defines a basic application, you can write a simple program with very little code. The framework provides the application's default behavior, which your program simply inherits. When you want your program to do something different, you can override (or extend) the functionality that the framework provides. In the case of a C++ app framework, you can inherit large amounts of work from the framework to take advantage of its features.

In this chapter, you take a look at the extensive functionality that MFC provides.

How MFC Is Provided

MFC is provided in the form of C++ classes. These classes encapsulate all the details of dealing with the Windows API, including such complicated subjects as OLE (Object Linking and Embedding), ODBC (Open Database Connectivity), and Winsock (the Windows implementation of TCP/IP, which is the basis of any Internet-aware application). The classes provide the basis of writing an application for Windows and provide higher-level functionality for your applications.

MFC provides to an application some basic features. The framework provides support for applications that use single windows (otherwise known as SDI, or single-document interface, applications) or multiple windows inside an application window (otherwise known as MDI, or multiple-document interface, applications). MDI applications support "Last Files Used" lists, whereas MFC keeps track of the last few files that the application uses. MFC also enables a program to change menus when different windows become active.

The framework provides automatic support for toolbars (dockable and nondockable). But although MFC provides some toolbar bitmaps automatically, you must create your own bitmaps for custom toolbars. After creating the bitmaps, you give MFC a handle to the toolbar, and the framework then handles displaying the toolbar, handling mouse clicks on the toolbar, and providing automatic help for each toolbar button. If the toolbar is dockable, MFC automatically handles docking and undocking the toolbar for you.

MFC encapsulates all Windows graphics device interface (GDI) and user-interface elements. You can create pen objects, fonts, brushes, and so on, with the relevant classes automatically destructing the GDI object when it goes out of scope. Similarly, MFC provides classes for buttons (including buttons with custom bitmaps on them), list boxes, combo boxes, radio buttons, and text-entry fields. The framework also provides full support for the use of common dialog boxes, which are standard dialog boxes that Microsoft provides for opening files, choosing fonts, choosing colors, and selecting printer options.

The framework also provides automatic support for online Help, using standard Windows help files. As you will see later, AppWizard helps this process by providing "standard" help files that you can use as a starting point.

MFC also supports tasks that are not directly related to Windows, but are useful for writing robust applications. The framework provides classes to support the creation of abstract data structures, including linked lists, queues, and arrays. These abstract classes also know how to write themselves to and read themselves from files, making saving and restoring data rather easy. MFC also offers a string class that can deal with strings that change size.

If you work with complicated APIs such as OLE, the framework provides classes that make it easier to use the API. In essence, these classes give you 20,000 lines of OLE code to use as a base, freeing you from having to learn a lot of the gritty details of OLE. Similarly, the ODBC classes give you an abstract, table-oriented view of your databases.

Finally, like most application frameworks, MFC gives your application a high degree of portability. MFC supports not only Windows 95, but also Windows NT, Windows 3.1, and even Macintosh System 7. Your program doesn't have to deal with the differences among platforms; instead, MFC handles those details automatically. You just recompile your application.

However, all these features don't come for free. You have to do some of the work yourself. As you will soon see, MFC works with you to develop a complete application.

You can use AppWizard to generate code, but although that generated program runs, opens windows, and provides a toolbar and an About box, it doesn't do anything special. You have to make the program do what you want it to do. Instead of writing a bunch of code to get this far, however, you simply start adding classes and methods to respond when MFC gives your application control.

One aspect of many application frameworks (including MFC) that gives some programmers trouble is the use of a document/view architecture. This is a fancy way of describing how MFC works with your code to present your data and interact with the user. This architecture is nothing new to MFC; other frameworks also use document/view. If a framework doesn't use document/view, it simply treats the windows as areas to be painted, just as the Windows API does.

In a document/view architecture, the framework deals not with windows, but with a document. *Documents* are nothing more than classes to represent your data. They know how to read themselves to and from files, how to update themselves, and how to talk to views. *Views* are classes that show the contents of documents.

Consider, for example, a text editor. The document in a text editor is the underlying data (the text). The view shows the contents of the document. A view is much like a window. However, in an MDI application, you can have multiple views on the same data. And because documents know how to talk to views, if you change the appearance of one view (by modifying the data shown in the view), the other views on that document can change, too. A good example is a spreadsheet. For a spreadsheet, the underlying document is simply a table of numbers and formulas. You might have two views, one containing a graphical view of the data (rows and columns of numbers) and another view containing a graph of those numbers. In other words, you've got one document (the spreadsheet) with two views (a table and a graph). If you change a number in the table view, the document can update itself and tell the views to show the new data (causing the graph to update itself).

The document/view architecture clearly separates the program's actual data and the program's graphical display of data. It also requires you, as the program's developer, to think some before you start adding code. The architecture provides a great deal of abstraction (that is, it encourages you, the developer, to place a wall between the data and the part of your program that displays the data), because you can change the document code without affecting the view code. Because documents and views are separate classes, you provide access to each class through well-defined functions.

If documents and views seem confusing, don't worry. It takes a little time to get used to them. Later, in the section "Using AppWizard To Generate an Application," you will see how documents and views work together.

Essential MFC Classes

Before you examine in depth an application written with MFC, this section takes a look at several of the important classes that MFC supplies. Then you can generate an application with AppWizard and see these classes in use.

The first class that you should know about is `CObject`, otherwise known as "the mother of all classes." Many of the classes in MFC inherit behavior and capabilities from `CObject`. Most of the classes that you write with MFC will also inherit from `CObject`. Among other things, `CObject` gives classes the capability to serialize themselves through `CArchive`, which enables your classes to read and write themselves to and from files, with minimal coding on your part. `CObject` also supports the determination of class types at run time, through the `GetRuntimeClass()` and `IsKindOf()` methods. In addition, `CObject` enables MFC programs to verify their internal state, through the `IsValid()` method, whenever the developer wants. You can write for your class a version of `IsValid()` that a program can call at run time to verify that an instance of a class is "valid" (you determine exactly what "valid" means). Finally, `CObject` supports object dumping (through `Dump()`), so that classes can output their contents in a readable fashion at run time. Although `CObject` is the base class for most of MFC, not all classes inherit from `CObject`. However, when your classes inherit from `CObject`, you saddle them very little overhead.

When you create an application with MFC, you create one class that derives from `CWinApp`. The `CWinApp` class defines the *application object.* Normally, if you're writing an application in C with the Windows SDK, you provide a function, `WinMain()`, that Windows calls. In other words, `WinMain()` (as far as you're concerned) is the starting point of your application's lifetime. Under MFC, you instead create a class that derives from `CWinApp` and supply in that class methods that set up your application for you. You don't create `WinMain()` at all. Instead, buried inside MFC is a `WinMain()` function that is called for you. When your application starts, it automatically constructs your `CWinApp`-derived class and calls the methods inside it so that you have a chance to set up your application.

Any given application can have only one `CWinApp`-derived class, and that class must be global. `CWinApp`-derived classes provide information that is generally global to the application object (such as instance information). In Visual C++ 1.5, `CWinApp` was the main class for an application object. In Visual C++ 4, `CWinApp` inherits from a new class, `CWinThread`. `CWinThread` defines a program's thread of execution. All applications start with one main thread. You can create additional threads through `CWinThread`. In an MFC application, you must use `CWinThread` rather than the `CreateThread()` Win32 call; `CWinThread` knows about MFC, but `CreateThread()` doesn't.

`CDocument` is the base class used by any documents that your application creates. The `CDocument` class provides the basic functionality for all documents, including the creation, loading, and saving of documents. Documents are part of MFC's command routing, and thus receive from MFC messages that tell them what to do (for example, MFC usually routes File Open commands to a document class). The user does not modify documents directly; instead, the user uses views to pass changes to documents. Views know the document to which they are attached; documents know which views are currently active. Documents also use an abstract class called a *document template* to determine which resources a document uses.

The CDocTemplate class defines document templates. CDocTemplate is an abstract base class, so you do not use it directly. Instead, you define document templates as descendants of CDocTemplate. MFC uses document templates to define the relationship among a document class (descended from CDocument), a view class (descended from CView or one of the other view classes), and a frame window class (which contains the view). You must create one document template for each type of document in your application.

The CView class manages views. CView is the base view class; other view classes have more specialized features. The first of these is CScrollView, a view that knows how to scroll by using scroll bars. The second is CEditView, a view that knows how to perform text editing with Cut, Paste, and Copy commands. CEditView is much like an edit control. The final view class is CFormView, which contains controls. CFormViews also support scrolling. When a user interacts with your application, a view draws what the user sees in a window. If the user changes the window's contents, the program usually passes those changes back to the document so that it can update itself. Remember, a document represents the raw data with which an application works. The view just shows the contents of that document in some way. Remember, too, that although you can attach several views to a document, you can attach to a document only one view at a time.

MFC creates and manages Windows with the CWnd and CFrameWnd classes. Although a CWnd object is not exactly the same as a Windows window, it functions exactly like one. The CWnd class has member functions that handle all the basic API calls that you usually associate with a window. A CFrameWnd (which inherits from CWnd) usually contains views. CFrameWnds understand views and can handle the functionality that views depend on, such as updating the menu and toolbar. If a CFrameWnd is the main application window, the application terminates automatically (after notifying you that the user chose to close the application).

The framework handles file input/output (I/O) through two classes: CArchive and CFile. CArchives manage an archive stream and provide a class a way to write itself to and read itself from a file. CFiles perform unbuffered, binary I/O with disk files. Normally, you create a CFile and then attach it to a CArchive. Each open file can have only one CArchive. CArchive works with both primitive data types as well as classes that descend from CObject.

MFC provides many other classes, but the preceding are the ones that you must understand. The next section, "Using AppWizard To Generate an Application," uses FileView's source code as an example as it discusses the way that you normally use these classes.

Using AppWizard To Generate an Application

Now you can begin developing a program with MFC. In Chapter 6, "Using MFC," you develop a small program called FileView, which enables the user to view text files.

Instead of writing the beginning of the program, you can use AppWizard to generate a skeleton application.

AppWizard is one of the tools that Visual C++ provides to write Windows applications. AppWizard's job is quite straightforward. It asks you some questions about what you want your application to do, and then it generates several files for you, customized by the answers that you gave. You use AppWizard only once, at the beginning of development. You can't use this tool to generate an application and then later change your mind. If you run AppWizard a second time (and you've made changes to the original code generated by the first execution of AppWizard), your changes are silently deleted.

Keep one thing in mind about the code that AppWizard (and MFC in general) generates: None of this code is special or secret. Microsoft gives you the MFC source code, so you should take advantage of it and examine what that code provides to you. In other words, don't treat AppWizard and MFC as "black boxes." Too many MFC tutorials treat the skeleton code generated by AppWizard as something that programmers should not explore. Although AppWizard creates several structures and comments that you should not change manually (unless you know what you are doing), it is important to understand the code that the tool provides for you. The same principle applies to MFC. Although you probably shouldn't change the original MFC source code (because Microsoft doesn't support any changes that you make), examining the MFC source code can be quite enlightening. You can learn much about how the features in MFC are implemented.

Now create the skeleton application that you will need to create FileView. Later, you'll dissect and examine the code that AppWizard and MFC provide. This exercise will give you a good understanding of what you must do to turn this skeleton program into a functioning Windows application.

AppWizard's Questions

To generate the skeleton application, start the Microsoft Developer Studio and choose File, New. Developer Studio displays the New dialog box (see fig. 5.1), which asks which type of file you want to create. Select Project Workspace from the list box and click OK.

Note

From this point on in this discussion, when we say "Visual C++," we are actually talking about Developer Studio. However, because Visual C++ and Developer Studio are one and the same for the purpose of this discussion, we simply use the term *Visual C++*.

After you click OK, Visual C++ starts questioning you about the type of program that you want to create (see fig. 5.2). In the New Project Workspace dialog box, you tell Visual C++ that you want to create an AppWizard-generated application.

Fig. 5.1

Visual C++'s New dialog box.

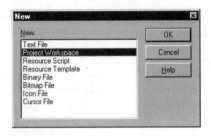

Fig. 5.2

Visual C++'s New Project Workspace dialog box.

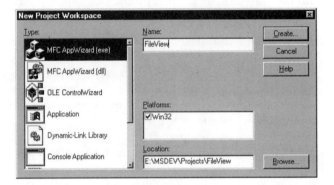

In the Name text box, you specify your project's name. By default, the name that you specify in this text box also specifies the directory in which all the files for this project will go. As you type a name, Visual C++ fills in the Location text box. In this case, type **FILEVIEW** in the Name text box, because that is the program that you'll be working on later. Note that Visual C++ changes the Location text box's entry to E:\MSDEV\PROJECTS\FILEVIEW.

The Type list box lets you specify the type of project that you want to create. Use the default, MFC AppWizard (exe), which generates just what it implies: an AppWizard program. The other choices are MFC AppWizard (dll), OLE ControlWizard, Application, Dynamic-Link Library, Console Application, Static Library, Makefile, and Custom AppWizard. When you select MFC AppWizard (exe), Visual C++ proceeds to ask questions about the features that you want in your application.

Finally, the New Project Workspace dialog box's Platform list enables you to specify the platform that you want to support. In figure 5.2, this copy of Visual C++ has only the Win32 libraries and tools installed, so you can't select any other platforms. After entering **FILEVIEW** into the Name text box, click Create, because the defaults for the rest of the fields are fine.

Step 1—the Type of Application and Language. After you click the Create button, AppWizard begins asking questions about the features that you want in your application. These questions consist of six "steps," with each step focusing on a specific part of the MFC framework. Each step has a set of Back and Next buttons, as you can see in figure 5.3. Therefore, if you get to Step 5 and realize that you made a mistake back in Step 2, you can go back to that step without losing any information that you've already entered. Figure 5.3 shows Step 1.

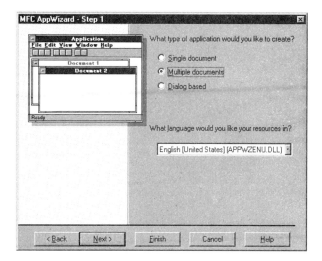

Fig. 5.3

Step 1 of AppWizard, in which you choose your application type.

Step 1 asks you which type of application you want to create. You can choose a Single document (one window inside of the main window), Multiple documents (like Microsoft Word or Sysedit, in which you can have multiple child windows open inside your main window), or Dialog based (in which your main window is simply a dialog box). For FileView, accept the default, Multiple documents, because you want to be able to view more than one file at once, and also because FileView will enable you to view the same file in more than one window.

AppWizard generates several text-based resources for your application (menu prompts, dialog boxes, and toolbar help). Step 1's Language list lets you choose the language that you want to use for these resources. You want to use the default, U.S. English, so simply click the Next button to go on to Step 2.

Step 2—Database Support. In Step 2, you decide whether your application will use the ODBC classes to access a database. Figure 5.4 shows Step 2's questions.

As you can see, the step presents four choices. The default is None, which includes no database support. Use this choice for FileView, because it doesn't need ODBC support. If you do want ODBC support, you can choose Header Files Only to have AppWizard include only the ODBC header files, or you can choose one of the last two options (Database View without File Support and Database View With File Support) to specify a database for your application. If you choose the last option, Database View With File Support, the database must already exist. AppWizard asks you to select the database before you can continue.

Fig. 5.4

Step 2 of AppWizard, in which you choose whether you want to use ODBC support.

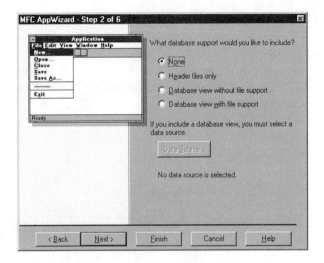

When you specify a database, AppWizard generates classes that derive from CRecordSet and CRecordView to support your database. The last two options generate a form-based application that enables you to view and update your database easily. When you add file support to your application, you also add document serialization, which enables your application to maintain, for example, a user profile file. Both options enable your application to maintain the database through ODBC. The absence of file support does not affect reading to or writing from the database.

FileView doesn't require database support, so click the Next button to go to the next step.

Step 3—OLE Support. Step 3 asks questions related to OLE 2 support. Figure 5.5 shows the dialog box.

Fig. 5.5

Step 3 of AppWizard, in which you select OLE support for your application.

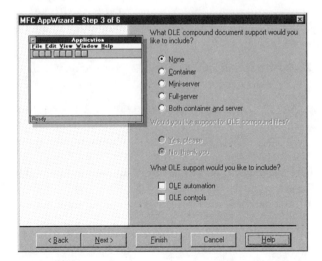

By default, your code doesn't support OLE. FileView doesn't need to be OLE-aware, so accept this default.

Your application can be an OLE container, a server, or both. If an application is an OLE container, it can contain linked and embedded objects. Containers don't provide support to other OLE programs; they just hold embedded objects. Servers, on the other hand, create compound-document objects that can be embedded in OLE containers. If you choose the Mini-Server option, your application will not run as a standalone program; instead, other programs will call it to create OLE objects for them. If you choose the Full-Server option, your server can run as a standalone program and create OLE objects for other applications. As you can see in the dialog box's list, an application can be both a container and a server at the same time.

If you want your application to include any OLE support, you can choose to support OLE compound files. When you do so, your application stores the OLE objects in one file (rather than multiple files) and must maintain access to individual OLE objects. You aren't telling AppWizard to generate support for OLE for FileView, so currently this option is inactive and thus unavailable.

If you want to expose your application to OLE Automation, select the OLE Automation check box. Otherwise, other programs that use OLE Automation will not have access to your application. Likewise, if you want to use OLE controls in your application, select the OLE Controls check box.

Note

If you want to learn more about OLE programming, several good books are available. For example, see Que's *Using OLE 2 in Application Development* for more information about OLE.

Click the Next button to go to Step 4.

Step 4—Application Features and Advanced Options. Step 4 (fig. 5.6) is the most complicated step because it presents many possible choices.

The questions in Step 4 concern the non-OLE and ODBC features from MFC that you want to include in your application. By default, Docking Toolbar, Initial Status Bar, Printing and Print Preview, and 3D Controls are selected.

MFC applications usually have a toolbar attached to the main window. AppWizard supplies a default set of bitmaps. You can add your own buttons. If you select Docking Toolbar, the application will support dockable toolbars, which can either stay attached to the top of the window or be "torn off" to float around like a child window. Dockable toolbars can also redock at the left, bottom, top, or right sides of your application's main window.

Initial Status Bar turns on a beveled status bar at the bottom of your application's main window. The generated application will use this status bar to provide helpful hints to users as they move around the interface. For example, a string table (in the language that you chose in Step 1) provides hints as the user selects menu options and toolbar buttons. You can also use this status bar in your code to provide messages to the users as they run your application. If you don't want a status bar initially (when your application starts), deselect this option.

Fig. 5.6

Step 4 of AppWizard, in which you choose other features for your application.

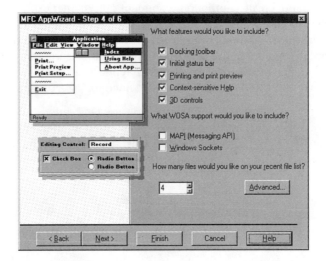

Selecting Printing and Print Preview adds code to the generated application to support unified printing and the capability to preview of printing on the screen. *Unified printing* means that AppWizard generates classes to help your code support printing without having to write separate printing routines. AppWizard also provides classes to support print preview (with one- or two-page-at-a-time preview, zooming previews, and so on). However, because the print preview code is rather generic, you probably will have to modify it to make the preview more palatable for most applications. The default code for print preview doesn't supply headers, footers, or special formatting. AppWizard supplies support for the Print common dialog boxes to enable the user to change printers and printer options and select ranges of pages to print.

If you choose Context Sensitive Help, AppWizard generates a set of .rtf (Rich Text Format) files, along with support files that the Windows Help Compiler uses. AppWizard then adds a Help menu to your application's menu bar. The .rtf files have placeholders for information about your application, but you must modify these files to make them useful for your application's users. Although you can use any editor to edit .rtf files, a program that understands .rtf (such as Microsoft Word) is necessary to modify help files easily. By default, Context-Sensitive Help is not selected. FileView will use online Help, so select this option now.

Finally, if you select 3D Controls, your application's interface will have a beveled look.

The next portion of the dialog box, What WOSA Support Would You Like To In-clude?, enables you to provide support for MAPI (Windows mail messaging) and Windows Sockets. FileView doesn't use either of these features, so don't select these options.

The next field affects the Most Recently Used list that MFC can maintain for your application. The default number is 4. MFC maintains for your application a Registry entry that lists the last files used by your application. This list appears at the bottom of your application's File menu.

Click the Advanced button to display a dialog box that presents options that affect the appearance of your application's windows. Figure 5.7 shows the first Advanced Options dialog box.

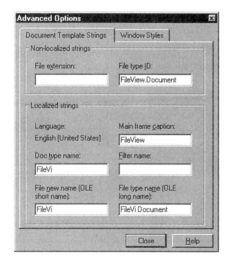

Fig. 5.7

Step 4's Advanced Options dialog box, which you use to select document template settings.

II

Using MFC

You use this dialog box to specify document template settings. In other words, the Advanced Options dialog box lets you specify settings for files used by the generated application. If your application is going to create files, you can use these options to identify your files. For example, if the files that your application will create will have a special extension, you can specify that extension in the Filter Name text box. When the application displays common dialog boxes for File Open and Save, these dialog boxes' File Type combo box automatically displays this extension for the listed files. FileView doesn't create files, so you don't change any of these options.

At the top of the dialog box are two *tabs*. By providing such tabs, a dialog box can display separate *pages,* with each page presenting a completely different set of fields, buttons, and other user-interface elements. You activate the different pages by click-ing their tab. MFC supports the creation of these tabs so that you can use them in your programs.

By clicking the Window Styles tab, you display the second part of the Advanced Options dialog box, shown in figure 5.8.

Fig. 5.8

The Advanced Options dialog box's Window Styles page.

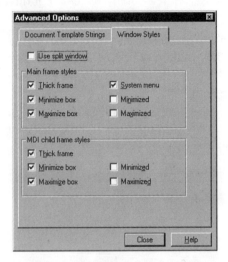

This dialog box consists of two groups of check boxes. You use the first group, Main Frame Styles, to specify options for your *main frame window,* which is the term by which MFC refers to your application's main window. It's the primary window that the user sees when your application starts, and it encloses any windows that you create. This group of options enables you to specify the text for your window's caption, as well as whether your application will have a sizing border, a minimize box, a maximize box, and a System menu. You can also specify whether you want your application's main window to start minimized or maximized.

In the second group of check boxes, MDI Child Frame Styles, you can specify similar options for your MDI child windows. All the options are exactly the same except that this group lacks a System menu check box (because MDI child windows cannot have System menus).

Finally, at the top of the dialog box is a Use Split Window check box. When you select this option, AppWizard generates code that enables your application to use splitter windows. A *splitter window* can be split into two parts with a line (or *bar*) near the top of the window. When you drag this bar, you essentially split the current child window into two independent views on the current document. If used properly, splitter windows add a helpful way to view large documents, enabling the user to determine what parts of and how much of the document he or she wants to see. However, the use of splitter windows changes the base classes that your application uses. Thus, you must specify whether you want to use splitter windows before generating your application code.

FileView doesn't change any of the default options, so click the Close button and then Next to go on to Step 5.

Step 5—Source File Comments and MFC Library Type. Step 5 deals with source-code comments, and how you want to tie MFC to your application. Figure 5.9 shows Step 5's dialog box.

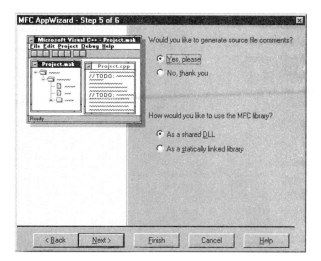

Fig. 5.9

AppWizard's Step 5, which deals with source-code comments and the MFC library type.

The options of this dialog box are fairly straightforward. The question Would You Like To Generate Source File Comments means exactly what it says. The option Yes, Please is selected by default, so AppWizard places in the code some comments that tell you where you need to add functionality, usually in the form of TODO comments. If you select No, Thank You, AppWizard doesn't generate any comments.

Finally, you must decide whether you want MFC bound into your application (by a static library) or whether you would prefer to use MFC as a dynamic link library. The choice is largely up to you. Linking with a DLL makes your executable file smaller. If you're developing many applications, this choice will save you hard drive space (because only one one copy of the DLL must be available, no matter how many applications use it). The default is to link with a DLL. However, linking with a static library means one less file to distribute with your application. The drawback is that your application might require more memory. If you write two applications that use MFC, and you use the DLL, you can place the DLL in your Windows directory and both applications will find it. DLLs are also shared between applications, so both applications will load a total of only one copy of the DLL. If you bind MFC to both applications statically, then both applications will load their own private copy of MFC, which will use more memory. It's becoming common to use the DLL option, because most of Microsoft's applications (including many that are distributed with Windows itself) use MFC and thus already have a copy of the MFC DLL in the Windows directory.

For this application, you can access all these default settings, so click the Next button and go to Step 6, the last step.

Using MFC

Step 6—Class Names and File Names. In Step 6, AppWizard tells you the names of the new classes that it is going to create, based on your answers to the questions in Steps 1 through 5. Figure 5.10 shows Step 6's dialog box.

Fig. 5.10

AppWizard's dialog box for Step 6, in which you specify the class names and file names that MFC generates for you.

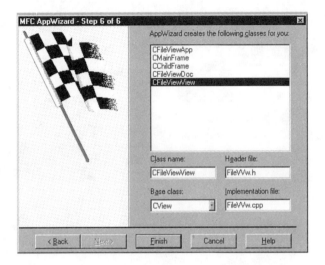

AppWizard is going to create four new classes for the FileView application. CFileViewApp is the application class, descending from CWinApp. As mentioned previously, all MFC applications must have one class that derives from CWinApp and that defines the application itself. The next class, CMainFrame, is a class to encompass your application's main window. CFileViewDoc and CFileviewView are this application's document and view classes.

If you don't like the names that AppWizard generates, you can change them. As you can see in figure 5.10, CFileviewView is highlighted in the Classes list box. Below the list box, AppWizard shows the class name in the Class Name text box. If you want to change CFileviewView to something else, you can just type the new name. For some classes, you might notice also that the other fields are grayed out. AppWizard doesn't let you change some of the names because doing so might undo work that it has already done or result in an unusable application.

In most cases, you don't need to change any of these settings. However, there is at least one case where you might. For example, AppWizard normally assumes that your generated view class should descend from CView (MFC's generic view class). However, you can inherit from several other view classes as well. You can change the inheritance in this dialog box. AppWizard knows the purpose of each class and doesn't let you change something that you shouldn't.

In most cases, you probably won't want to change any of these settings, and thus will simply choose the Finish button to finish generating the application. However, exceptions to this general rule exist. In fact, the programs on the companion CD provide an example. The software that was used to make the CD imposes an eight-character limit on the length of file names. The file name that AppWizard generates for the `FileViewView` class, FileViewView.cpp, exceeds the limit, so it had to be shortened to FileVVw.cpp. Likewise, although you would normally put the `CFileviewDoc` class into FileViewDoc.cpp, this file name is again too long, so it was changed to FileVDoc.cpp. As you perform the steps described in this chapter, however, feel free to leave the file names alone.

When you click the Finish button, you go to the last dialog box before AppWizard generates your application. Figure 5.11 shows the New Project Information dialog box.

Fig. 5.11

The New Project Information dialog box is your last step toward generating your application.

This dialog box summarizes what you've told AppWizard to do. At this point, AppWizard hasn't actually created anything. If you click Cancel now, you return to Step 6, where you can fix any mistakes that you made or cancel the entire AppWizard session. In the case of FileView, you have correctly answered all the questions, so click OK to move on. AppWizard then generates your application.

What Does AppWizard Generate?

Now that you've gone through all those dialog boxes, you have an application that you can compile and execute. After AppWizard finishes generating all the source files, Visual C++ loads the newly created project. Choosing Project, Build FileVFileView.exe results in an executable application, shown in figure 5.12.

Fig. 5.12

The newly created
application in action.

As you can see, you have a real application (and you haven't written any code yet!). The application has a complete menu bar, a functioning toolbar, online Help, and even an About box. However, this application doesn't do anything. You can open windows, resize the main window, or iconize the MDI child windows, but clicking in a window doesn't draw anything. In Chapter 6, "Using MFC," you extend this application to become FileView. But first, take a look at what you have generated with AppWizard.

If you look in the FILEVIEW directory, you see several .cpp and .h files, a .mak file, three directories (RES, DEBUG, and HLP), and a file named README.TXT. README.TXT contains a summary of what AppWizard did and what's in each file.

Note

Open README.TXT on your system to see the file in its entirety.

README.TXT gives you a brief overview of what's in each file. This chapter goes further and looks at each file in detail to see how an application built with MFC works. The next section begins with FileView's .mak (make) file.

> **Note**
>
> Although this chapter lists some files in their entirety (in particular the C++ source and header files), it does not list others (FileView.mak and the .rtf files in the HLP directory), simply because they are either too long to include (and you can look at them on your system) or because there is no crucial need to examine them in detail. FileView.mak, for example, is quite large and usually is not a file that you want to edit.

The Makefile (FileView.mak)

Visual C++ uses FileView.mak to manage your project's organization. The makefile tells Visual C++ which files to use for the project and what actions to take to build an executable file. FileView.mak also helps Visual C++ determine which files depend on what, so that it can track dependencies.

Either Visual C++ or Microsoft's Make utility, NMAKE, can use the makefile. You can use NMAKE if you want to rebuild your program without running Visual C++'s integrated environment. Because Visual C++ uses FileView.mak (and you never change the file), this chapter discusses the makefile's contents. However, this discussion is strictly for informational purposes. You should never change this file unless you are sure of what you are doing, because if you do something wrong, Visual C++ will not be able to build your project correctly.

A makefile consists of rules and actions. The *rules* are `if-then` constructs that Visual C++ uses to determine what to do each step of the way as it builds an executable file. The *actions* tell Visual C++ which programs to invoke to satisfy a sequence of events. Visual C++ knows about certain rules that it must follow to produce a program from a set of source files. Here's the rule for one of the files in your project:

```
##################################################### Begin Source File
```

Lines that begin with the # character are comments. Some, like the preceding one, tell Visual C++ where the information for one source file begins. Other comments, as you see later, modify the current options for different tools.

The following are definitions of "variables" for Visual C++:

```
SOURCE=.\stdafx.cpp
DEP_STDAF=\
.\stdafx.h
```

These definitions are like C and C++ #defines, in which one string is substituted for another. The preceding example defines SOURCE to be the current source file (stdafx.cpp), and DEP_STDAF lists the files on which stdafx.cpp depends. In other words, if stdafx.h changes, it affects stdafx.cpp and any files on which stdafx.cpp depends.

Makefiles support logical operators such as IF. In the following example, a variable named CFG is being examined:

```
!IF   "$(CFG)" == "Win32 Debug"
```

If the variable contains the string *Win32 Debug*, Visual C++ processes the lines following the IF statement (up to the corresponding ENDIF or ELSEIF statement). To reference the contents of a variable in a makefile, you use $(CFG). In this case, Visual C++ sets CFG to the type of program that you are building. If you use NMAKE from the command line, you can either set the value of CFG yourself or accept the default, Win32 Debug. At the top of the makefile, CFG is set to this value unless you specify something else.

The following action line demonstrates how to construct stdafx.obj:

```
# ADD BASE CPP /Yc"stdafx.h"
BuildCmds= \
        $(CPP) /nologo /MDd /W3 /Gm /GX /Zi /Od /D "WIN32" /D "_DEBUG"
              /D "_WINDOWS"\
/D "_AFXDLL" /D "_MBCS" /Fp"$(INTDIR)/FileView.pch" /Yc"stdafx.h"\
 /Fo"$(INTDIR)/" /Fd"$(INTDIR)/" /c $(SOURCE) \
"$(INTDIR)\StdAfx.obj" : $(SOURCE) $(DEP_CPP_STDAF) "$(INTDIR)"
      $(BuildCmds)
```

Visual C++ uses the comments before the action line to modify the compiler's standard options. Later you use stdafx.cpp to create a precompiled header file for this project. It takes Visual C++ a long time to parse all the header files that come with MFC, but precompiled headers greatly speed up the compile process, because Visual C++ can read the precompiled header quickly without having to parse it.

You can interpret the action line as follows. stdafx.obj depends on three variables: SOURCE, DEP_STDAF, and INTDIR. SOURCE and DEP_STDAF were set earlier to stdafx.cpp and stdafx.h. INTDIR is the intermediate directory to which the final compiled files should go. After processing, this line looks like the following (internally):

```
.\WinDebug/stdafx.obj: stdafx.cpp stdafx.h .\Debug
```

Therefore, you must build stdafx.obj if it doesn't already exist, or if stdafx.cpp, stdafx.h, or DEBUG change. If you must build stdafx.obj, the subsequent lines (until the next dependency line) tell Visual C++ how to do so. In this case, this means invoking the C++ compiler with a bunch of options (seen before as $(CPP) /nologo /MD /W3 /GX /Zo /Od /D "_DEBUG"...).

Visual C++ uses the remaining lines in this part of the makefile if you're building the Win32 Release software. As you can see, the lines are almost exactly like the previous ones; only compiler options have changed:

```
!IF   "$(CFG)" == "FileView - Win32 Release"
# ADD CPP /Yc"stdafx.h"
BuildCmds= \
        $(CPP) /nologo /MD /W3 /GX /O2 /D "WIN32" /D "NDEBUG"
              /D "_WINDOWS" /D\
"_AFXDLL" /D "_MBCS" /Fp"$(INTDIR)/FileView.pch" /Yc"stdafx.h"
```

```
                /Fo"$(INTDIR)/"\
 /c $(SOURCE) \
 "$(INTDIR)\StdAfx.obj" : $(SOURCE) $(DEP_CPP_STDAF) "$(INTDIR)"
    $(BuildCmds)
```

If you examine the makefile, you'll see that most of the source files don't have to be as complicated. Visual C++ sets up several default compiler options for most of the files. stdafx.obj is special because it builds a precompiled header file. The lines that deal with FileView.cpp, for example, aren't nearly as messy:

```
# Begin Source File
SOURCE=.\FileView.cpp
DEP_CPP_FILEV=\
      ".\ChildFrm.h"\
      ".\FileVDoc.h"\
      ".\FileVVw.h"\
      ".\FileView.h"\
      ".\MainFrm.h"\
      ".\StdAfx.h"\
```

Again, FileVFileView.cpp's section starts with a `Begin Source File` comment, followed by definitions for `SOURCE` and `DEP_CPP_FILEV` (FileVFileView.cpp's dependencies). When AppWizard creates a project, Visual C++ scans all the source files to build the dependency list. Here, FileVFileView.cpp depends on four header files.

The following example is a little easier to follow:

```
"$(INTDIR)\FileView.obj" : $(SOURCE) $(DEP_CPP_FILEV) "$(INTDIR)"\
 "$(INTDIR)\FileView.pch"
# End Source File
```

FileVFileView.obj depends on four "files": SOURCE, DEP_CPP_FILEV, INTDIR, and INTDIR/FileView.pch. Remember that Visual C++ will expand this line as follows, replacing the variables with their current values:

```
.\WinDebug/FileView.obj: .\FileView.cpp .\mainfrm.h .\FileVdoc.h
_.\FileVvw.h .\FileView.h .\ Debug .\ Debug/FileView.pch
```

If any of the files listed after the colon are more recent than FileView.obj, you must rebuild FileView.obj. But no line tells how to build FileView.obj. In this case, Visual C++ defined some rules earlier that told it how to build an .obj file from a .cpp file if necessary.

There's much more to the makefile, but this discussion gives you enough of an idea of its use. After all, you probably will never change this file. Now it's time to examine the source code.

The Main Header File (FileView.h)

FileView.h is FileView's main #include file. It declares the `CFileViewApp` class (which is FileView's application class) and includes other #include files that FileView uses:

```
// FileView.h : main header file for the FileView application
//
#ifndef __AFXWIN_H__
```

```
#error include 'stdafx.h' before including this file for PCH
#endif
```

The first thing that FileView.h does is check whether the precompiled copy of the
MFC headers is included. Visual C++ sets up the project file's compiler options to
make sure that this happens:

```
#include "resource.h"        // main symbols
```

Next the resource IDs are included. The resource.h file contains the definitions for any
resources that FileView uses:

```
/////////////////////////////////////////////////////////////////
// CFileviewApp:
// See FileView.cpp for the implementation of this class
//
class CFileviewApp : public CWinApp
{
public:
CFileviewApp();
// Overrides
// ClassWizard-generated virtual function overrides
//{{AFX_VIRTUAL(CFileviewApp)
public:
virtual BOOL InitInstance();
//}}AFX_VIRTUAL
// Implementation
//{{AFX_MSG(CFileviewApp)
afx_msg void OnAppAbout();
// NOTE - the ClassWizard will add and remove member functions here.
//    DO NOT EDIT what you see in these blocks of generated code!
//}}AFX_MSG
DECLARE_MESSAGE_MAP()
};
/////////////////////////////////////////////////////////////////
```

resource.h defines the application class CFileviewApp. This class is fairly simple, with
only three methods defined. You'll see the implementation of these methods in a
moment. Now examine the interesting declarations under the "Overrides" and
"Implementation" comments.

AppWizard declared a public virtual function called InitInstance(). Whenever you
inherit behavior from CWinApp, you must override InitInstance(), which is called
every time that an instance of your application starts. The generated version of
InitInstance() doesn't do much (see the next section). You can also override
InitApplication(), which is called the first time that your application starts.
ClassWizard uses the comments to mark virtual functions.

AppWizard then generates a section of code for ClassWizard to use when adding
member functions. As you can see, AppWizard blankets the section with AFX_MSG
comments (along with a note warning you not to edit the block of code). As you
add or remove member functions with ClassWizard, it updates this section of code
automatically.

`DECLARE_MESSAGE_MAP()` is an MFC macro that creates what MFC calls a *message map*. MFC programs often use message maps, so you need to understand exactly what they are.

When you design a class hierarchy for C++, you usually define a base class with methods. Classes that inherit from that base class probably have methods that have the same name and argument types as the base class, but do something entirely different. For example, suppose that you have a base class named Shape. Instances of the Shape class know how to do many things, including how to draw themselves, so suppose that this class includes a Draw() method. Thus, the definition for Shape might look like this:

```
class Shape
{
virtual void Draw();
// other methods and data, as needed...
};
```

If you define a class that is a type of Shape (for example, a circle), you declare Circle as inheriting from Shape:

```
class Circle : public Shape
{
virtual void Draw();
// other methods for Circle...
};
```

You can then write code that works with the Shape class (and classes that inherit from Shape) by passing a pointer to an instance of Shape or Circle, as in the following example:

```
Circle *s;
// do some operations with s
s->Draw();
doSomething(s);
```

This invokes Circle's Draw() method because you are dealing with a pointer to a Circle. However, if you pass the pointer s to a function that expects a Shape pointer (and that function invokes the Draw() method), how do you invoke the proper method? For example, suppose that you have a function called doSomething() that accepts a pointer to a Shape, and then invokes the Draw() method through the pointer:

```
void doSomething(Shape *shp)
{
shp->Draw();
}
```

How does the compiler know to invoke the Draw() method in Circle and not in Shape? From your reading of C++ books, you know that the compiler constructs a *virtual function table* to tell it what methods to invoke. Because Draw() is declared as virtual, the compiler keeps track of the class type with which you are dealing and uses the virtual function table (which is attached to each instance of the created class) to call the right method. Therefore, every time that you create an instance of the class Circle, there's a bit of overhead for the function table.

II

Using MFC

This table probably isn't too big for one to ten functions. But what about a class that has 50 methods that all must be virtual? Even worse, what if the classes that inherit from this 50-method class are likely to override only a few of the functions rather than all 50?

A message map is intended to handle this problem. The DECLARE_MESSAGE_MAP() macro creates a table of function pointers that point to messages that this class can handle. CFileViewApp currently has one entry in the table—OnAppAbout(), which is called whenever the application displays the About box. With this approach, a class has overhead only for the functions that it must support. When the user chooses the Help About menu item, Windows generates a message, and MFC begins looking for classes that might handle the message. To determine whether a class can handle a message, MFC uses the pointer table created by DECLARE_MESSAGE_MAP(). After finding such a class, MFC calls the appropriate method (in this case, OnAppAbout()). If MFC didn't use message maps, you would have to attach large virtual function tables to instances of some of your classes.

You can place DECLARE_MESSAGE_MAP() almost anywhere in the class definition. However, you must remember to declare any new methods' attributes (public, private, or protected) explicitly after DECLARE_MESSAGE_MAP().

The next section explores how this class is implemented.

The Application Class Source (FileView.cpp)

FileView.cpp (listing 5.1) contains the implementation of the CFileViewApp class.

Listing 5.1 FileView.cpp Defines the Class Behaviors for the Application

```
// FileView.cpp : Defines the class behaviors for the application.
//
#include "stdafx.h"
#include "FileView.h"
#include "MainFrm.h"
#include "ChildFrm.h"
#include "FileVDoc.h"
#include "FileVVw.h"
#ifdef _DEBUG
#define new DEBUG_NEW
#undef THIS_FILE
static char THIS_FILE[] = __FILE__;
#endif
/////////////////////////////////////////////////////////////////////////////
// CFileViewApp
```

FileView.cpp begins by including the header files for other classes and defining a variable called THIS_FILE, which contains the name of the current source file (FileView.cpp). The file then creates the message map, by defining which methods to call for each Windows message that this class can handle:

```
BEGIN_MESSAGE_MAP(CFileViewApp, CWinApp)
    //{{AFX_MSG_MAP(CFileViewApp)
    ON_COMMAND(ID_APP_ABOUT, OnAppAbout)
        // NOTE - the ClassWizard will add and remove mapping macros here.
        //    DO NOT EDIT what you see in these blocks of generated code!
    //}}AFX_MSG_MAP
    // Standard file-based document commands
    ON_COMMAND(ID_FILE_NEW, CWinApp::OnFileNew)
    ON_COMMAND(ID_FILE_OPEN, CWinApp::OnFileOpen)
    // Standard print setup command
    ON_COMMAND(ID_FILE_PRINT_SETUP, CWinApp::OnFilePrintSetup)
END_MESSAGE_MAP()
```

The `BEGIN_MESSAGE_MAP()` and `END_MESSAGE_MAP()` macros surround the message map. `BEGIN_MESSAGE_MAP()` sets up some methods for dealing with message maps and then begins the definition of the function pointer array. The arguments to `BEGIN_MESSAGE_MAP` are the current class (`CFileViewApp`) and the class from which the current class inherits (`CWinApp`). If the current class doesn't know how to handle a message, these macros cause unhandled messages to be passed up the class hierarchy.

There are several macros that can appear in a message map. Currently, the message map for `CFileViewApp` uses only the `ON_COMMAND()` macro, which tells MFC which methods handle *command messages,* which the `WM_COMMAND` Windows message generates. `CFileViewApp` can handle four messages. `ON_COMMAND(ID_APP_ABOUT, OnAppAbout)` means that if Windows generates a `WM_COMMAND` message, and the message's parameter is `ID_APP_ABOUT`, MFC should call the `OnAppAbout()` method of the `CFileViewApp` class. `ID_APP_ABOUT` is the Help About menu item's ID. The remaining three `ON_COMMAND()` macros handle standard Windows messages: File Open, File New, and File Print Setup. In each case, the message passes to methods within the `CWinApp` class.

AppWizard generates default constructors for classes and adds a TODO comment that explains the method's purpose:

```
/////////////////////////////////////////////////////////////////////////
// CFileViewApp construction

CFileViewApp::CFileViewApp()
{
    // TODO: add construction code here,
    // Place all significant initialization in InitInstance
}
```

In this case, `CFileViewApp`'s constructor doesn't do anything.

Your application object's declaration must be global, and there should be only one instance of the application class. AppWizard generates the declaration and assigns the variable `theApp` to be an instance of the class:

```
/////////////////////////////////////////////////////////////////////////
// The one and only CFileViewApp object

CFileViewApp theApp;
```

Now you have the actual methods of `CFileViewApp`. Here's `InitInstance()`:

```
/////////////////////////////////////////////////////////////////////////////
// CFileViewApp initialization

BOOL CFileViewApp::InitInstance()
{
    // Standard initialization
    // If you are not using these features and wish to reduce the size
    // of your final executable, you should remove from the following
    // the specific initialization routines you do not need.

#ifdef _AFXDLL
    Enable3dControls();     // Call this when using MFC in a shared DLL
#else
    Enable3dControlsStatic();
                            // Call this when linking to MFC statically
#endif

    LoadStdProfileSettings();
                        // Load standard INI file options (including MRU)
```

`InitInstance()` starts by setting up features that you selected during the AppWizard's code-generation process. Because you asked for 3-D controls, the application calls `Enable3DControls()` (or `Enable3DControlsStatic()`, if you linked the MFC run-time library directly into your code), followed by `LoadStdProfileSettings()`, which reads the .INI file maintained by MFC for your application. The .INI file contains information maintained between application invocations, most notably the list of recently used files:

```
    // Register the application's document templates. Document templates
    // serve as the connection between documents, frame windows, and views.

    CMultiDocTemplate* pDocTemplate;
    pDocTemplate = new CMultiDocTemplate(
        IDR_FILEVITYPE,
        RUNTIME_CLASS(CFileViewDoc),
        RUNTIME_CLASS(CChildFrame), // custom MDI child frame
        RUNTIME_CLASS(CFileViewView));
    AddDocTemplate(pDocTemplate);
```

Next, `InitInstance()` sets up, creates, and registers your document templates. Remember, a document template binds together the document, view, and frame window classes for a document in an MFC application. Because your application is an MDI application, `InitInstance()` creates an instance of the `CMultiDocTemplate` class, passing the file type for your documents along with pointers to the various classes that the template uses. `InitInstance()` then calls `AddDocTemplate()` to add the document template to the list of templates that the application knows about.

After registering the document template, `InitInstance()` creates the main frame window for the application:

```
    // create main MDI Frame window
    CMainFrame* pMainFrame = new CMainFrame;
```

```
if (!pMainFrame->LoadFrame(IDR_MAINFRAME))
return FALSE;◄─── Terminate App
m_pMainWnd = pMainFrame;
```

The main frame window is the normal Windows window that you see, with the menu and toolbar attached. AppWizard allocates an instance of CMainFrame, and then the LoadFrame() method loads the list of shared resources. This method brings into memory all the necessary resources, including the menu, toolbar, and accelerator table created by AppWizard. If LoadFrame() succeeds, the pointer to the CMainFrame object is saved in m_pMainWnd, which is part of the CWinThread class. By default, if the window pointed to by m_pMainWnd closes, MFC terminates the application.

If it cannot create the main window, InitInstance() returns to the caller (in this case, MFC) a value of False. If InitInstance() returns False, the application cannot start.

If it successfully loads and creates the main window, InitInstance() then creates a local instance of the CCommandLineInfo class. This variable, cmdInfo, passes to ParseCommandLine() to handle any parameters that were passed to the program:

```
// Parse command line for standard shell commands, DDE, file open
CCommandLineInfo cmdInfo;
ParseCommandLine(cmdInfo);

// Dispatch commands specified on the command line
if (!ProcessShellCommand(cmdInfo))
    return FALSE;
```

ParseCommandLine() examines the parameters and sets the correct values in cmdInfo, which the application can then pass to ProcessShellCommand(). ProcessShellCommand() then calls the appropriate methods in your application, depending on which command-line parameters were encountered. If your program received no parameters, it calls OnFileNew(), which makes your application act as if the user chose File, New. If you are familiar with prior versions of MFC, this call replaces the old explicit call to OnFileNew() that AppWizard used to generate.

AppWizard-generated applications understand several options. If you pass a file name to your program, ProcessShellCommand() calls the OnFileOpen() method, which enables your application to open the specified file. There are also command-line switches to make your program print a file automatically, to start and wait for a DDE session, to start your program as an embedded OLE object, and to start your program under OLE Automation. For more details, see the documentation for CCommandLineInfo.

In any case, if the call to ProcessShellCommand() fails (that is, if FileView couldn't execute a File, New command), the program doesn't start.

If you've gotten this far, you have created the main window and registered the document template. You're now ready to display the main window:

```
// The main window has been initialized, so show and update it:
pMainFrame->ShowWindow(m_nCmdShow);
pMainFrame->UpdateWindow();
```

To display the main window, you invoke `ShowWindow()` and `UpdateWindow()`. `m_nCmdShow`, a member of `CWinThread`, contains the value of `nCmdShow` that Windows passed to the application.

To signal that everything in `InitInstance()` succeeded, you return `TRUE`:

```
return TRUE;
}
```

Next are the declaration and implementation of your application's About box. AppWizard places both the class declaration and implementation in one place in your .cpp file:

```
/////////////////////////////////////////////////////////////////////////
// CAboutDlg dialog used for App About
class CAboutDlg : public CDialog
{
public:
CAboutDlg();
// Dialog Data
//{{AFX_DATA(CAboutDlg)
enum { IDD = IDD_ABOUTBOX };
//}}AFX_DATA
    // ClassWizard-generated virtual function overrides
    //{{AFX_VIRTUAL(CAboutDlg)
    protected:
    virtual void DoDataExchange(CDataExchange* pDX);  // DDX/DDV support
    //}}AFX_VIRTUAL
// Implementation
protected:
    //{{AFX_MSG(CAboutDlg)
        // No message handlers
    //}}AFX_MSG
    DECLARE_MESSAGE_MAP()
};
```

About boxes are simply modal dialog boxes, so AppWizard creates the class `CAboutDlg` that inherits its behavior from `CDialog`, which is MFC's dialog box class. In this case, AppWizard creates two methods: a constructor and `DoDataExchange()`. AppWizard also creates a member variable, `IDD`, to hold the About box resource's ID. And, as before, AppWizard creates a message map for the dialog box.

`DoDataExchange()` is used for a process called Dialog Data Exchange/Dialog Data Verification (DDX/DDV). This process enables dialog boxes to send data back and forth between the dialog box's controls and the dialog box class's data members. Because of this method, when you can transfer data between, for example, a text edit control in the dialog box and a string variable in the dialog box class, the process can be transparent to the developer. You simply set up the relationship and make the appropriate function calls. AppWizard generates an empty DDX/DDV method; then, when you create dialog boxes with AppStudio, you use ClassWizard to update this method.

`CAboutDlg`'s constructor doesn't do anything; it just passes the ID of the dialog back up to `CDialog` so that it can initialize the dialog box:

```
CAboutDlg::CAboutDlg() : CDialog(CAboutDlg::IDD)
{
//{{AFX_DATA_INIT(CAboutDlg)
//}}AFX_DATA_INIT
}
```

CAboutDlg's empty DDX/DDV method simply calls CDialog's DDX/DDV method:

```
void CAboutDlg::DoDataExchange(CDataExchange* pDX)
{
CDialog::DoDataExchange(pDX);
//{{AFX_DATA_MAP(CAboutDlg)
//}}AFX_DATA_MAP
}
```

Like all windows and dialogs, CAboutDlg has a message map:

```
BEGIN_MESSAGE_MAP(CAboutDlg, CDialog)
//{{AFX_MSG_MAP(CAboutDlg)
// No message handlers
//}}AFX_MSG_MAP
END_MESSAGE_MAP()
```

Simple modal dialogs can let CDialog handle all the messages, so your message map is currently empty.

As you'll recall, the message map for your CFileViewApp class contains an entry that causes MFC to call CFileViewApp's OnAppAbout() method. When this call occurs, OnAppAbout() creates an instance of the class CAboutDlg and sends it the DoModal() message, which creates and displays the dialog box:

```
// App command to run the dialog
void CFileViewApp::OnAppAbout()
{
CAboutDlg aboutDlg;
aboutDlg.DoModal();
}
```

AppWizard places the declaration for CAboutDlg in this .cpp file because only CFileViewApp handles the class. When OnAppAbout() terminates, the program calls CAboutDlg's destructor, cleaning up the dialog box.

Finally, AppWizard places a comment marker to show where new command handlers for CFileViewApp go:

```
/////////////////////////////////////////////////////////////////
// CFileViewApp commands
```

That pretty much covers the application object. Next you examine the code for the main window that InitInstance() invokes.

The Main Frame Header File (mainfrm.h)

The CMainFrame class maintains the application's main window. As mentioned previously, this is the window that most people associate with an application. The window includes the main caption, the System menu, the application menu bar, and the toolbar. By default, AppWizard generates mainfrm.h and mainfrm.cpp to define this class. Listing 5.2 shows mainfrm.h.

Listing 5.2 mainfrm.h, the Interface of the CMainFrame Class

```
// mainfrm.h : interface of the CMainFrame class
//
/////////////////////////////////////////////////////////////////
class CMainFrame : public CMDIFrameWnd
{
DECLARE_DYNAMIC(CMainFrame)
```

CMainFrame inherits its functionality from CMDIFrameWnd because this application is an MDI application (there is another class, CSDIFrameWnd, for non-MDI apps). AppWizard inserts into the class another macro, DECLARE_DYNAMIC(). This macro enables you to use CObject's IsKindOf() method to identify a class at run time. Why do you want to do this? As you'll see, methods in your code often are passed pointers to objects. These pointers are declared as pointers to classes high up in the MFC class tree. You can use methods like IsKindOf() to determine whether the pointer that you received points to a class in which you're interested. If it does, you can safely cast the pointer to the class that you want. DECLARE_DYNAMIC() inserts code that enables you to do this safely. mainfrm.cpp has a corresponding macro, IMPLEMENT_DYNAMIC(), to finish the job. Almost all MFC macros occur in such pairs, with one in the class declaration and another in the implementation code.

Next, CMainFrame's constructor is declared (as public), followed by empty public sections for your use. Then you come to the ClassWizard virtual overrides, where ClassWizard inserts method declarations each time that you use ClassWizard to add another handler.

```
public:
CMainFrame();
// Attributes
public:
// Operations
public:
// Overrides
// ClassWizard-generated virtual function overrides
//{{AFX_VIRTUAL(CMainFrame)
    virtual BOOL PreCreateWindow(CREATESTRUCT& cs);
//}}AFX_VIRTUAL
```

Notice the declaration of the PreCreateWindow() method. This method enables you to modify the window parameters before you actually create the window. The window's default implementation simply enables the CMDIFrameWnd class to perform its default action.

Next is the declaration for CMainFrame's ~~con~~structor, followed by comments that ClassWizard needs:

```
    // Implementation
    public:
    virtual ~CMainFrame();
    #ifdef _DEBUG
    virtual void AssertValid() const;
    virtual void Dump(CDumpContext& dc) const;
    #endif
```

AppWizard declares a virtual destructor for this class, followed by some methods surrounded by `#ifdef _DEBUG`. `_DEBUG` is defined only if you are compiling under the Debug settings, not the Release settings. In this case, AppWizard includes `AssertValid()` and `Dump()` only if you are building a debug version of your application. The next section discusses what these methods do.

The following two variables hold the status bar and toolbar for your main window. Your application constructs them when your main window receives a `WM_CREATE` message from the message map.

```
    protected:  // control bar embedded members
    CStatusBar  m_wndStatusBar;
    CToolBar    m_wndToolBar;
```

Here is `CMainFrame`'s message map:

```
    // Generated message map functions
    protected:
    //{{AFX_MSG(CMainFrame)
    afx_msg int OnCreate(LPCREATESTRUCT lpCreateStruct);
    // NOTE - the ClassWizard will add and remove member functions here.
    //    DO NOT EDIT what you see in these blocks of generated code!
    //}}AFX_MSG
    DECLARE_MESSAGE_MAP()
    };
    /////////////////////////////////////////////////////////////////////
```

Currently the message map has only one entry, `OnCreate()`, which MFC invokes after catching a `WM_CREATE` message.

The next section shows how to implement this class.

The Main Frame Source File (MainFrm.cpp)

MainFrm.cpp (listing 5.3) contains the implementation of the `CMainFrame` class, which defines the behavior of your application's main window.

Listing 5.3 MainFrm.cpp, the Implementation of the CMainFrame Class

```
// MainFrm.cpp : implementation of the CMainFrame class
//
#include "stdafx.h"
#include "FileView.h"
#include "MainFrm.h"
#ifdef _DEBUG
#define new DEBUG_NEW
```

(continues)

Using MFC

II

Listing 5.3 Continued

```
#undef THIS_FILE
static char BASED_CODE THIS_FILE[] = __FILE__;
#endif
```

Like all of your .cpp files, MainFrm.cpp begins by including the necessary header files, and declares a private character array to hold the name of the current source file.

The IMPLEMENT_DYNAMIC() macro finishes the code set up by the DECLARE_DYNAMIC() macro from MainFrm.h. It defines the necessary methods that MFC uses to determine the class type of an object at run time. Following this macro is CMainFrame's message map. Currently, CMainFrame handles only one message locally (ON_WM_CREATE()), which responds to the WM_CREATE message sent by Windows. The remaining entries automatically handle selections from the Help menu. In each case, the message is routed to the parent class, CMDIFrameWnd.

```
/////////////////////////////////////////////////////////////////
// CMainFrame
IMPLEMENT_DYNAMIC(CMainFrame, CMDIFrameWnd)
BEGIN_MESSAGE_MAP(CMainFrame, CMDIFrameWnd)
//{{AFX_MSG_MAP(CMainFrame)
// NOTE - the ClassWizard will add and remove mapping macros here.
//    DO NOT EDIT what you see in these blocks of generated code!
ON_WM_CREATE()
//}}AFX_MSG_MAP
// Global help commands
    ON_COMMAND(ID_HELP_FINDER, CMDIFrameWnd::OnHelpFinder)
    ON_COMMAND(ID_HELP, CMDIFrameWnd::OnHelp)
    ON_COMMAND(ID_CONTEXT_HELP, CMDIFrameWnd::OnContextHelp)
    ON_COMMAND(ID_DEFAULT_HELP, CMDIFrameWnd::OnHelpFinder)
END_MESSAGE_MAP()
```

The following array holds indicators for the status bar at the bottom of the main window. The default status bar has an area for messages, followed by a separator and space for showing the status of the Caps Lock, Num Lock, and Scroll Lock keys.

```
static UINT BASED_CODE indicators[] =
{
ID_SEPARATOR,           // status line indicator
ID_INDICATOR_CAPS,
ID_INDICATOR_NUM,
ID_INDICATOR_SCRL,
};
```

AppWizard generates a default constructor and virtual destructor for the main window. The default versions don't do anything special. If you add any members to the CMainFrame class, you can handle their construction and destruction here.

```
/////////////////////////////////////////////////////////////////
// CMainFrame construction/destruction
CMainFrame::CMainFrame()
{
// TODO: add member initialization code here
```

```
    }
    CMainFrame::~CMainFrame()
    {
    }
```

`CMainFrame`'s message map invokes the next method when Windows sends a `WM_CREATE` message to MFC for the main window. AppWizard passes a pointer to a `CreateStruct` structure that contains information about the window being created.

`OnCreate()` first calls the `OnCreate()` method of the base class, `CMDIFrameWnd`:

```
    int CMainFrame::OnCreate(LPCREATESTRUCT lpCreateStruct)
    {
    if (CMDIFrameWnd::OnCreate(lpCreateStruct) == -1)
    return -1;
```

If `CMDIFrameWnd::OnCreate()` fails, the call returns –1 to signal that the program cannot continue.

`OnCreate()` then attempts to create the toolbar, load the toolbar bitmaps (see fig. 5.13), and initialize the toolbar's buttons:

```
    if (!m_wndToolBar.Create(this) ¦¦
            !m_wndToolBar.LoadToolBar(IDR_MAINFRAME))
    {
    TRACE0("Failed to create toolbar\n");
    return -1;      // fail to create
    }
```

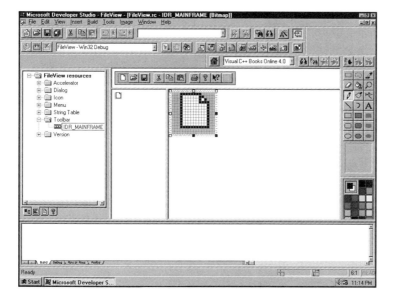

Fig. 5.13

The generated toolbar.

Again, if any of these operations fails, OnCreate() returns –1 to signal that CMainFrame couldn't create the window. Notice that if the class cannot create the toolbar, the TRACE0 macro is invoked. TRACE0 sends a message to the MFC diagnostic stream, afxDump. Your Windows configuration defines afxDump to be either the debugger, a debug terminal, or stderr. TRACE0 accepts one string as an argument. Other macros (TRACE1, TRACE2, TRACE3, and TRACE) accept other arguments. Remember that the TRACE macros work only when compiling a Debug release. If you are compiling a Release version of a program, the TRACE macros turn into a null statement. Therefore, you should not put expressions in a TRACE macro that have side-effects that you depend on.

Next AppWizard creates the status bar. Again, if AppWizard fails to create this feature, TRACE0 outputs a diagnostic message, and OnCreate() returns –1.

```
if (!m_wndStatusBar.Create(this) ||
!m_wndStatusBar.SetIndicators(indicators,
sizeof(indicators)/sizeof(UINT)))
{
TRACE0("Failed to create status bar\n");
return -1;       // fail to create
}
```

The last thing that OnCreate() does is enable toolbar docking and ToolTips (the tiny pop-up help messages that display when the user's mouse lingers over a toolbar button). You can comment out this code if you decide that you want to turn off these features.

```
// TODO: Remove this if you don't want ToolTips or a resizeable toolbar
    m_wndToolBar.SetBarStyle(m_wndToolBar.GetBarStyle() |
        CBRS_TOOLTIPS | CBRS_FLYBY | CBRS_SIZE_DYNAMIC);
    // TODO: Delete these three lines if you don't want the toolbar to
    //   be dockable
    m_wndToolBar.EnableDocking(CBRS_ALIGN_ANY);
    EnableDocking(CBRS_ALIGN_ANY);
    DockControlBar(&m_wndToolBar);
    return 0;
}
```

Next is the implementation of CMainFrame's PreCreateWindow() method:

```
BOOL CMainFrame::PreCreateWindow(CREATESTRUCT& cs)
{
    // TODO: Modify the Window class or styles here by modifying
    //   the CREATESTRUCT cs
    return CMDIFrameWnd::PreCreateWindow(cs);
}
```

As you can see, the default version simply calls CMDIFrameWnd's version. The parameter passed in by reference, cs, is a CREATESTRUCT. A CREATESTRUCT is a structure that defines all the parameters of a window (including its position, size, menu handle, and window class). If you want to modify a window before AppWizard actually creates it (because MFC handles most of the mechanics of window creation for you), you would do so in this method.

Finally, AppWizard generates diagnostic methods for use when debugging:

```
/////////////////////////////////////////////////////////////////
// CMainFrame diagnostics
#ifdef _DEBUG
void CMainFrame::AssertValid() const
{
CMDIFrameWnd::AssertValid();
}
void CMainFrame::Dump(CDumpContext& dc) const
{
CMDIFrameWnd::Dump(dc);
}
#endif //_DEBUG
/////////////////////////////////////////////////////////////////
// CMainFrame message handlers
```

You should set up `AssertValid()` to check the current object's internal state. If something is inconsistent, you should use the `ASSERT` macro to raise an error condition. You should not change the object (because `AssertValid()` is a const function). Before checking your object's internal state, you should pass the call up the class tree (as this example does). `Dump()` is used to output a readable copy of the current object. You can use `Dump()` to format (in a format of your choice) the member variables of a class and send an annotated string to the `CDumpContext` reference sent to dump. Then MFC (or you) can produce a readable dump of your class during a debugging session, or when you detect a problem while the application is executing.

At this point, you've seen the main window (`CMainFrame`) and the application object itself (`CFileViewApp`). In the next section, you examine the generated document class, `CFileviewDoc`.

The Document Class Source (FileVdoc.h)

If you review the implementation of `InitInstance()` in `CFileViewApp`, you'll remember that `InitInstance()` calls `OnFileNew()` as part of the application initialization. `CFileViewApp` doesn't provide an implementation of `OnFileNew()`, so the call passes back up the class tree to `CFileViewApp`'s parent class, `CWinApp`. Remember also that the message map for `CFileViewApp` routes the message `ID_FILE_NEW` back up to `CWinApp`. How does `CWinApp` know to create a FileView document (`CFileviewDoc`)?

If `CWinApp`'s implementation of `OnFileNew()` gets called, `OnFileNew()` looks at the registered document templates (remember, you registered your document template in `InitInstance()`). If you registered only one document template, `CWinApp` calls the constructor for that document. In the case of FileView, you registered only one template, so `CWinApp` calls `CFileviewDoc` (the document class for your document template). If you had registered more than one document template, `CWinApp` would display a dialog box that enables the user to select a document type. Listing 5.4 is the class definition for `CFileviewDoc`.

II

Using MFC

Listing 5.4 FileVdoc.h, the Class Definition for `CFileviewDoc`

```
// FileVdoc.h : interface of the CFileviewDoc class
//
/////////////////////////////////////////////////////////////////////
class CFileviewDoc : public CDocument
{
protected: // create from serialization only
CFileviewDoc();
DECLARE_DYNCREATE(CFileviewDoc)
```

Your document class, `CFileviewDoc`, inherits its behavior from MFC's main document class, `CDocument`. As usual, AppWizard has created a default constructor for this class, followed by the MFC macro `DECLARE_DYNCREATE()`. This macro (along with its counterpart in the .cpp file, `IMPLEMENT_DYNCREATE()`) allows this class to be dynamically constructed. All your document and view classes should have this macro, because MFC might have to create instances of these classes dynamically, for example, from a disk file.

AppWizard generates two overrides of virtual methods inside `CDocument`: `OnNewDocument()` and `Serialize()`. The application calls `OnNewDocument()` to set up a document every time that a new one is needed. `Serialize()` is used when a document is being read from or written to an archive object. Remember from the chapter introduction that archives are usually attached to `CFile` objects.

```
// Attributes
public:
// Operations
public:
// Overrides
// ClassWizard-generated virtual function overrides
//{{AFX_VIRTUAL(CFileviewDoc)
public:
virtual BOOL OnNewDocument();
    virtual void Serialize(CArchive& ar);
//}}AFX_VIRTUAL
```

Next is a virtual destructor for your document class, followed by another virtual function, `Serialize()`:

```
// Implementation
public:
virtual ~CFileviewDoc();
```

The rest of the class is quite similar to what you've seen before. AppWizard generates your Debug methods, `AssertValid()` and `Dump()`. It then generates an empty message map for the document class.

```
#ifdef _DEBUG
virtual void AssertValid() const;
virtual void Dump(CDumpContext& dc) const;
#endif
protected:
```

```
    // Generated message map functions
    protected:
    //{{AFX_MSG(CFileviewDoc)
    // NOTE - the ClassWizard will add and remove member functions here.
    //    DO NOT EDIT what you see in these blocks of generated code!
    //}}AFX_MSG
    DECLARE_MESSAGE_MAP()
    };
    //////////////////////////////////////////////////////////////////////
```

The implementation of your document class is fairly simple, as shown in listing 5.5.

> **Listing 5.5   FileVDoc.cpp, the Implementation of the CFileviewDoc Class**
>
> ```
> // FileVDoc.cpp : implementation of the CFileviewDoc class
> //
> #include "stdafx.h"
> #include "FileView.h"
> #include "FileVDoc.h"
> #ifdef _DEBUG
> #define new DEBUG_NEW
> #undef THIS_FILE
> static char BASED_CODE THIS_FILE[] = __FILE__;
> #endif
> //////////////////////////////////////////////////////////////////////
> // CFileviewDoc
> IMPLEMENT_DYNCREATE(CFileviewDoc, CDocument)
> ```

IMPLEMENT_DYNCREATE() is the counterpart to the DECLARE_DYNCREATE() macro in FileVDoc.h. Again, this macro just sets things up so that MFC can dynamically create instances of this class when necessary.

Like all your other classes, your document class gets a message map. AppWizard generates an empty message map for this class:

```
    BEGIN_MESSAGE_MAP(CFileviewDoc, CDocument)
    //{{AFX_MSG_MAP(CFileviewDoc)
    // NOTE - the ClassWizard will add and remove mapping macros here.
    //    DO NOT EDIT what you see in these blocks of generated code!
    //}}AFX_MSG_MAP
    END_MESSAGE_MAP()
```

When you add variables to your document class, you can handle their initialization, creation, and destruction in the constructor and destructor for the document class. AppWizard's code doesn't do anything. That's why your documents currently don't react at all.

```
    //////////////////////////////////////////////////////////////////////
    // CFileviewDoc construction/destruction
    CFileviewDoc::CFileviewDoc()
    {
    // TODO: add one-time construction code here
    }
    CFileviewDoc::~CFileviewDoc()
```

II

Using MFC

```
{
}
```

Here's the implementation of `OnNewDocument()`:

```
BOOL CFileviewDoc::OnNewDocument()
{
if (!CDocument::OnNewDocument())
return FALSE;

// TODO: add reinitialization code here
// (SDI documents will reuse this document)
return TRUE;
}
```

In this case, you just call `CDocument`'s `OnNewDocument()` method. If that call doesn't
succeed, something went wrong and you shouldn't continue. AppWizard adds a TODO
comment to show you where to put code that the application should execute every
time that the user requests a new document. This method is not the same as the constructor, because you might be reusing a document.

When a document needs to be read from or written to a file, `Serialize()` is called and
passed a reference to an instance of the class `CArchive`:

```
/////////////////////////////////////////////////////////////////////////
// CFileviewDoc serialization
void CFileviewDoc::Serialize(CArchive& ar)
{
if (ar.IsStoring())
{
// TODO: add storing code here
}
else
{
// TODO: add loading code here
}
}
```

`CArchive` provides overloaded operators for reading and writing to and from the
archive. Your generic document doesn't have any member variables, so this section
of code is empty, except for TODO comments to remind you of this code's purpose. In
Chapter 6, "Using MFC," when you enable FileView to read text files, you will change
`Serialize()`.

Last, but not least, are the Debug methods:

```
/////////////////////////////////////////////////////////////////////////
// CFileviewDoc diagnostics
#ifdef _DEBUG
void CFileviewDoc::AssertValid() const
{
CDocument::AssertValid();
}
void CFileviewDoc::Dump(CDumpContext& dc) const
{
CDocument::Dump(dc);
```

```
}
#endif //_DEBUG
//////////////////////////////////////////////////////////////////
// CFileviewDoc commands
```

The View Class Source (FileVVw.h and FileVVw.cpp)

Listing 5.6 shows the view class that goes with this document class.

```
// FileVVw.h : interface of the CFileviewView class
//
//////////////////////////////////////////////////////////////////
class CFileViewView : public CView
{
protected: // create from serialization only
    CFileviewView();
    DECLARE_DYNCREATE(CFileviewView)
```

Your view class starts just the same way as your document class did. CFileViewView is declared to inherit from CView (MFC's main view class). AppWizard generates a default constructor and inserts the DECLARE_DYNCREATE() macro to enable MFC to allocate instances of this class dynamically as needed.

Because you can attach views to only one document at a time, AppWizard generates a method, GetDocument(), that returns a pointer to the document to which a view is currently attached:

```
// Attributes
public:
CFileviewDoc* GetDocument();
```

Next, ClassWizard generates the virtual function overrides:

```
// Operations
public:
```

In some cases, an application does not use message maps to direct Windows-generated messages to a class. This is the case with the following methods:

```
// Overrides
// ClassWizard generated virtual function overrides
//{{AFX_VIRTUAL(CFileviewView)
public:
virtual void OnDraw(CDC* pDC);  // overridden to draw this view
    virtual BOOL PreCreateWindow(CREATESTRUCT& cs);
protected:
virtual BOOL OnPreparePrinting(CPrintInfo* pInfo);
virtual void OnBeginPrinting(CDC* pDC, CPrintInfo* pInfo);
virtual void OnEndPrinting(CDC* pDC, CPrintInfo* pInfo);
//}}AFX_VIRTUAL
```

II

Using MFC

OnDraw() is called whenever a view must repaint itself. OnDraw() is special in that the default implementation is a pure virtual function. In other words, you must provide an implementation of OnDraw() in your view class. The remaining three methods (OnPreparePrinting(), OnBeginPrinting(), and OnEndPrinting()) are used only if you selected printing and print preview support. Their default implementations do nothing. You'll look at their implementation and parameters in a moment.

Next you have the virtual destructor for CFileviewView, as well as the Debug methods and your message map. These should certainly be familiar to you by now.

```
// Implementation
public:
virtual ~CFileviewView();
#ifdef _DEBUG
virtual void AssertValid() const;
virtual void Dump(CDumpContext& dc) const;
#endif
protected:
// Generated message map functions
protected:
//{{AFX_MSG(CFileviewView)
// NOTE - the ClassWizard will add and remove member functions here.
//    DO NOT EDIT what you see in these blocks of generated code!
//}}AFX_MSG
DECLARE_MESSAGE_MAP()
};
```

You'll recall that the declaration of your view class defined a method called GetDocument() to retrieve the current document to which a view is attached. AppWizard generates two versions of GetDocument(). If you're not building a Debug release, GetDocument() is an inline function. If you are building a Debug release, GetDocument() resides in your .cpp file and is a true function. In either case, GetDocument() simply retrieves the value stored in m_pDocument, a member of the CView class (the main view class). Because m_pDocument is stored as a pointer to a CDocument, it is cast to a pointer to a CFileviewDoc.

```
#ifndef _DEBUG  // debug version in FileView.cpp
inline CFileviewDoc* CFileviewView::GetDocument()
{ return (CFileviewDoc*)m_pDocument; }
#endif
```

Now examine the implementation of the CFileviewView class, shown in listing 5.7.

Listing 5.7 FileVvw.cpp, the Implementation of the CFileviewView Class

```
/////////////////////////////////////////////////////////////////
// FileVvw.cpp : implementation of the CFileviewView class
//
#include "stdafx.h"
#include "FileView.h"
#include "FileVdoc.h"
#include "FileVvw.h"
#ifdef _DEBUG
```

```
#define new DEBUG_NEW
#undef THIS_FILE
static char BASED_CODE THIS_FILE[] = __FILE__;
#endif
/////////////////////////////////////////////////////////////////////
// CFileviewView
IMPLEMENT_DYNCREATE(CFileviewView, CView)
BEGIN_MESSAGE_MAP(CFileviewView, CView)
//{{AFX_MSG_MAP(CFileviewView)
// NOTE - the ClassWizard will add and remove mapping macros here.
//    DO NOT EDIT what you see in these blocks of generated code!
//}}AFX_MSG_MAP
// Standard printing commands
ON_COMMAND(ID_FILE_PRINT, CView::OnFilePrint)
    ON_COMMAND(ID_FILE_PRINT_DIRECT, CView::OnFilePrint)
ON_COMMAND(ID_FILE_PRINT_PREVIEW, CView::OnFilePrintPreview)
END_MESSAGE_MAP()
```

As usual, you start by including the necessary header files and declaring the THIS_FILE array. You also have the IMPLEMENT_DYNCREATE() macro to allow dynamic creation of this class, followed by the message map. Notice that there are map entries for ID_FILE_PRINT, ID_FILE_PRINT_DIRECT, and ID_FILE_PRINT_PREVIEW. Why are these entries here rather than in the document class? When the user chooses File, Print or File, Print Preview, he or she probably wants to print the contents of the current window. Going back to the spreadsheet analogy, if the user is viewing a graph and chooses File, Print, he or she probably wants to print the graph (which is shown in a view) and not the underlying numbers from the document that the graph is showing.

As in your other classes, AppWizard generates empty constructors and destructors:

```
/////////////////////////////////////////////////////////////////////
// CFileviewView construction/destruction
CFileviewView::CFileviewView()
{
// TODO: add construction code here
}
CFileviewView::~CFileviewView()
{
}
```

Again, for this class, AppWizard generates a default method to enable you to hook into the window-creation process before creating the window (view, actually). The default code just calls CView's version of PreCreateWindow():

```
BOOL CFileviewView::PreCreateWindow(CREATESTRUCT& cs)
{
    // TODO: Modify the Window class or styles here by modifying
    //  the CREATESTRUCT cs

    return CView::PreCreateWindow(cs);
}
```

The default implementation of OnDraw() doesn't do anything except get a pointer to the current document and verify that it is valid:

```
///////////////////////////////////////////////////////////////////
// CFileviewView drawing
void CFileviewView::OnDraw(CDC* pDC)
{
CFileviewDoc* pDoc = GetDocument();
ASSERT_VALID(pDoc);
// TODO: add draw code for native data here
}
```

Remember, the application calls OnDraw() whenever it has to repaint your view. The parameter that the application passes to OnDraw(), pDC, is a pointer to an instance of the CDC class (MFC's version of a device context). The CDC class has many methods for working with device contexts, including drawing, attribute selection, viewports, and GDI objects. You'll see CDC in action in Chapter 6, "Using MFC."

AppWizard generates the next three methods only if you selected Printing and Print Preview in Step 4 of AppWizard. The application calls OnPreparePrinting() before the actual printing takes place:

```
///////////////////////////////////////////////////////////////////
// CFileviewView printing

BOOL CFileviewView::OnPreparePrinting(CPrintInfo* pInfo)
{
// default preparation
return DoPreparePrinting(pInfo);
}
```

pInfo is a pointer to a CPrintInfo structure. This pointer enables your code to communicate with MFC about the print job. By setting fields of pInfo, you can control what the common Print dialog box displays. If you're going to set these fields, do so before the call to DoPreparePrinting(), because it displays the Print dialog box and creates a device context for the printer. The application also calls OnPreparePrinting() for Print Preview, but this call does not display a printer dialog box. If OnPreparePrinting() returns a value of FALSE (0), the print request is canceled.

The application calls OnBeginPrinting() after the printer device context (DC) is created, but before any printing actually occurs:

```
void CFileviewView::OnBeginPrinting(CDC* /*pDC*/, CPrintInfo* / *pInfo*/)
{
// TODO: add extra initialization before printing
}
```

As the TODO comment indicates, you typically use OnBeginPrinting() to set up GDI objects (and other types of initialization) where you need access to the printer DC. For example, you might need to know what paper size the user picked; because the user specifies this setting in the Printer common dialog box, you can't know this setting until after OnPreparePrinting() returns. By default, AppWizard comments out the pointers to the printer DC (pDC) and the printer info structure (pInfo) because this method is empty. This prevents the compiler from complaining about unused variables. When you write printer code, make sure that you remove the comments.

After the print job or print preview is finished, the application calls `OnEndPrinting()`:

```
void CFileviewView::OnEndPrinting(CDC* /*pDC*/, CPrintInfo* /*pInfo*/)
{
// TODO: add cleanup after printing
}
```

Typically, you use this method to free any resources that `OnBeginPrinting()` created. The default implementation does nothing. Again, you comment out the parameters to prevent compiler warning messages.

`CFileviewView`'s debug methods pass the call up the class tree to `CView`, because `CFileviewView` currently has no member variables to dump:

```
/////////////////////////////////////////////////////////////////////////
// CFileviewView diagnostics
#ifdef _DEBUG
void CFileviewView::AssertValid() const
{
CView::AssertValid();
}
void CFileviewView::Dump(CDumpContext& dc) const
{
CView::Dump(dc);
}
```

Typically, you should call `Dump()` in the parent class before dumping your class variables, which is what these methods do.

Finally, here is the version of `GetDocument()` for a Debug release:

```
CFileviewDoc* CFileviewView::GetDocument() // nondebug version is inline
{
ASSERT(m_pDocument->IsKindOf(RUNTIME_CLASS(CFileviewDoc)));
return (CFileviewDoc*)m_pDocument;
}
#endif //_DEBUG
/////////////////////////////////////////////////////////////////////////
// CFileviewView message handlers
```

This version of `GetDocument()` verifies that the document pointer points to an instance of `CFileviewDoc`, and if so, passes back the pointer. Remember, the Release version is inline and doesn't check the pointer. The comment at the end just highlights where ClassWizard is going to place the methods that it generates.

The Child Window Class (`CChildFrame`)

AppWizard generates two more source files: `ChildFrm.h` and `ChildFrm.cpp`. These two files define a class, `CChildFrame`, that implements the behavior of the MDI child windows for FileView. By default, all methods in this class just pass their work back up to `CMDIChildWnd`, the default class for MDI child windows.

The whole reason for this class is to enable you to modify the child windows easily. Earlier versions of AppWizard simply assumed that you wanted to use the standard MDI (or SDI, if you were developing a single-window app) behavior. Of course, if you wanted to modify the behavior, you first wrote a new class that inherits from CMDIChildWnd. AppWizard now saves you from having to perform that step.

FileView doesn't alter this behavior at all, so neither of these files changes. Listing 5.8 shows ChildFrm.h.

Listing 5.8 ChildFrm.h, the Interface of the CChildFrame Class

```
// ChildFrm.h : interface of the CChildFrame class
//
/////////////////////////////////////////////////////////////////////
class CChildFrame : public CMDIChildWnd
{
DECLARE_DYNCREATE(CChildFrame)
public:
    CChildFrame();
// Attributes
public:
// Operations
public:
// Overrides
    // ClassWizard-generated virtual function overrides
    //{{AFX_VIRTUAL(CChildFrame)
    virtual BOOL PreCreateWindow(CREATESTRUCT& cs);
    //}}AFX_VIRTUAL
// Implementation
public:
    virtual ~CChildFrame();
#ifdef _DEBUG
    virtual void AssertValid() const;
    virtual void Dump(CDumpContext& dc) const;
#endif
// Generated message map functions
protected:
    //{{AFX_MSG(CChildFrame)
    // NOTE - the ClassWizard will add and remove member functions here.
    //    DO NOT EDIT what you see in these blocks of generated code!
    //}}AFX_MSG
    DECLARE_MESSAGE_MAP()
};
/////////////////////////////////////////////////////////////////////
```

Listing 5.9 shows ChildFrm.cpp.

Listing 5.9 ChildFrm.cpp, the Implementation of the CChildFrame Class

```
// ChildFrm.cpp : implementation of the CChildFrame class
//
#include "stdafx.h"
#include "FileView.h"
#include "ChildFrm.h"
#ifdef _DEBUG
#define new DEBUG_NEW
#undef THIS_FILE
```

```
static char THIS_FILE[] = __FILE__;
#endif
/////////////////////////////////////////////////////////////////////////////
// CChildFrame
IMPLEMENT_DYNCREATE(CChildFrame, CMDIChildWnd)
BEGIN_MESSAGE_MAP(CChildFrame, CMDIChildWnd)
    //{{AFX_MSG_MAP(CChildFrame)
        // NOTE - the ClassWizard will add and remove mapping macros here.
        //     DO NOT EDIT what you see in these blocks of generated code!
    //}}AFX_MSG_MAP
END_MESSAGE_MAP()
/////////////////////////////////////////////////////////////////////////////
// CChildFrame construction/destruction
CChildFrame::CChildFrame()
{
    // TODO: add member initialization code here
}
CChildFrame::~CChildFrame()
{
}
BOOL CChildFrame::PreCreateWindow(CREATESTRUCT& cs)
{
    // TODO: Modify the Window class or styles here by modifying
    //  the CREATESTRUCT cs
    return CMDIChildWnd::PreCreateWindow(cs);
}
/////////////////////////////////////////////////////////////////////////////
// CChildFrame diagnostics
#ifdef _DEBUG
void CChildFrame::AssertValid() const
{
    CMDIChildWnd::AssertValid();
}
void CChildFrame::Dump(CDumpContext& dc) const
{
    CMDIChildWnd::Dump(dc);
}
#endif //_DEBUG
/////////////////////////////////////////////////////////////////////////////
// CChildFrame message handlers
```

That's all of the source code. Now take a look at the other files that AppWizard
generates.

Files for MFC (#include)

AppWizard generates stdafx.h and stdafx.cpp for each project that uses MFC. These
files' only purpose is to build your project's precompiled header. The main reason for
this header is to increase compile speed. MFC's header files are numerous and quite
large, consisting of many classes and methods. The first time that you build your
program (or choose Project, Rebuild All), you also build the precompiled header file.
Visual C++ parses the header files and produces a file with the .pch extension. It also
builds an .obj file for resolving references to the MFC classes. After you build this

precompiled header file, the compiler need only read it when you #include stdafx.h, which is much faster than parsing all those .h files every time, especially because they probably won't change while you develop your application.

stdafx.h #includes the main files for MFC, afxwin.h and afxext.h:

```
// stdafx.h : include file for standard system include files,
// or project-specific include files that are used frequently, but
// are changed infrequently
//
#define VC_EXTRALEAN    // Exclude rarely used stuff from Windows headers
#include <afxwin.h>     // MFC core and standard components
#include <afxext.h>     // MFC extensions
#ifndef _AFX_NO_AFXCMN_SUPPORT
#include <afxcmn.h>     // MFC support for Windows 95 Common Controls
#endif // _AFX_NO_AFXCMN_SUPPORT
```

stdafx.cpp just #includes stdafx.h. If you have any include files that won't change much, you can also include those files in stdafx.h.

```
// stdafx.cpp : source file that includes just the standard includes
//     FileView.pch will be the precompiled header
//     stdafx.obj will contain the precompiled type information

#include "stdafx.h"
```

The first time that you build your project, you'll see the difference between the two types of compiling. Building the .pch file can take anywhere from 45 seconds to several minutes (depending on your machine configuration), but each source file can be compiled in only about 10 seconds. Unless you build the .pch file, you have to wait for Visual C++ to parse the MFC header files for every file that gets compiled.

Resource IDs (resource.h)

AppStudio (and other parts of the Visual C++ environment) use resource.h (listing 5.10) for adding and deleting resources. At this point, this file doesn't contain much because you haven't added any new resources to the application. Generally, you won't touch this file much; instead, AppStudio modifies this file automatically.

Listing 5.10 resource.h, the File That Adds and Deletes Resources

```
//{{NO_DEPENDENCIES}}
// Microsoft Visual C++ generated include file.
// Used by FILEVIEW.RC
//
#define IDR_MAINFRAME                   128
#define IDR_FILEVITYPE                  129
#define IDD_ABOUTBOX                    100

// Next default values for new objects
//
#ifdef APSTUDIO_INVOKED
#ifndef APSTUDIO_READONLY_SYMBOLS
#define _APS_3D_CONTROLS                1
```

```
#define _APS_NEXT_RESOURCE_VALUE        130
#define _APS_NEXT_CONTROL_VALUE         1000
#define _APS_NEXT_SYMED_VALUE           101
#define _APS_NEXT_COMMAND_VALUE         32771
#endif
#endif
```

If you create a new resource in the integrated environment, resource.h is updated automatically. AppStudio uses the "Next default values" section to determine which value to assign to new resources.

The Default Resource File (FileView.rc)

FileView.rc contains the definitions for resources that your application uses. As you can see, AppWizard generates quite a few default resources when it creates an application. When this file is invoked, AppStudio parses it to display your resources as a hierarchical tree structure.

The first thing that FileView.rc does is #include resource.h. You'll recall that resource.h not only #defines resource values, but also tells AppStudio the values to use when creating new resources.

```
//Microsoft Visual C++ generated resource script.
//
#include "resource.h"
```

Next, FileView.rc brings in definitions required by AppStudio (and MFC). #define marks these symbols as READONLY so that you can't change them under AppStudio.

```
#define APSTUDIO_READONLY_SYMBOLS
/////////////////////////////////////////////////////////////////////
//
// Generated from the TEXTINCLUDE 2 resource.
//
#include "afxres.h"
/////////////////////////////////////////////////////////////////////
#undef APSTUDIO_READONLY_SYMBOLS
```

The following section of the .rc file is read-only if AppStudio is parsing the .rc file:

```
#ifdef APSTUDIO_INVOKED
/////////////////////////////////////////////////////////////////////
//
// TEXTINCLUDE
//
1 TEXTINCLUDE DISCARDABLE
BEGIN
"resource.h\0"
END
2 TEXTINCLUDE DISCARDABLE
BEGIN
"#include ""afxres.h""\r\n"
"\0"
END
3 TEXTINCLUDE DISCARDABLE
```

```
BEGIN
    "#define _AFX_NO_SPLITTER_RESOURCES\r\n"
    "#define _AFX_NO_OLE_RESOURCES\r\n"
    "#define _AFX_NO_TRACKER_RESOURCES\r\n"
    "#define _AFX_NO_PROPERTY_RESOURCES\r\n"
    "\r\n"
    "#if !defined(AFX_RESOURCE_DLL) ¦¦ defined(AFX_TARG_ENU)\r\n"
    "#ifdef _WIN32\r\n"
    "LANGUAGE 9, 1\r\n"
    "#pragma code_page(1252)\r\n"
    "#endif\r\n"
    "#include ""res\\FileView.rc2"""
            // non-Microsoft Visual C++ edited resources\r\n"
    "#include ""afxres.rc""      // Standard components\r\n"
    "#include ""afxprint.rc""   // printing/print preview resources\r\n"
    "#endif"
    "\0"
END
/////////////////////////////////////////////////////////////////////
#endif    // APSTUDIO_INVOKED
```

TEXTINCLUDE is a special directive that AppStudio uses to maintain multiple .rc files. Unfortunately, TEXTINCLUDE is not well-documented in the Visual C++ manuals. However, you can read Tech Note #35, "Using Multiple Resource Files and Header Files with Visual C++," which is distributed with Visual C++ (search for "Technical Notes" in Developer Studio). Fortunately, you should have little reason to mess with these statements. Tech Note #35 describes how AppStudio uses these constructs to maintain the integrity of resource files.

AppWizard provides two default icons for your application (along with the code page and language for the application):

```
/////////////////////////////////////////////////////////////////////
//
// Icon
//
// Icon with lowest ID value placed first to ensure application icon
// remains consistent on all systems.
IDR_MAINFRAME           ICON    DISCARDABLE      "res\\FileView.ico"
#if !defined(AFX_RESOURCE_DLL) ¦¦ defined(AFX_TARG_ENU)
#ifdef _WIN32
LANGUAGE 9, 1
#pragma code_page(1252)
#endif
IDR_FILEVITYPE          ICON    DISCARDABLE      "res\\FileVdoc.ico"
```

The first icon, IDR_MAINFRAME, is a default icon for the application itself. The application uses the second icon, IDR_FILEVITYPE, if you minimize one of the application's MDI child windows. Figure 5.14 shows these icons.

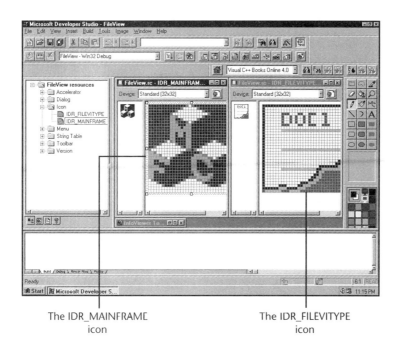

II

Using MFC

Fig. 5.14

The IDR_FILEVITYPE and IDR_MAINFRAME icons.

The IDR_MAINFRAME
icon

The IDR_FILEVITYPE
icon

These icons are generic, so you'll want to design new ones for your applications.

Your application has a toolbar, so AppWizard supplies a default bitmap, also named IDR_MAINFRAME, for the toolbar:

```
/////////////////////////////////////////////////////////////////////
//
// Bitmap
//
IDR_MAINFRAME          BITMAP  MOVEABLE PURE   "res\\Toolbar.bmp"
/////////////////////////////////////////////////////////////////////
//
// Toolbar
//
IDR_MAINFRAME TOOLBAR DISCARDABLE  16, 15
BEGIN
    BUTTON      ID_FILE_NEW
    BUTTON      ID_FILE_OPEN
    BUTTON      ID_FILE_SAVE
      SEPARATOR
    BUTTON      ID_EDIT_CUT
    BUTTON      ID_EDIT_COPY
    BUTTON      ID_EDIT_PASTE
      SEPARATOR
    BUTTON      ID_FILE_PRINT
    BUTTON      ID_APP_ABOUT
    BUTTON      ID_CONTEXT_HELP
END
```

You'll recall from the code that `InitInstance()` issues a `LoadFrame()` call, which loads all the resources associated with your main window. Therefore, your resources for the main frame window all have the same ID. Figure 5.14 shows the default toolbar bitmap.

AppWizard also generates two menus, `IDR_MAINFRAME` and `ID_FILEVITYPE`:

```
#if !defined(AFX_RESOURCE_DLL) || defined(AFX_TARG_ENU)
#ifdef _WIN32
LANGUAGE 9, 1
#pragma code_page(1252)
#endif
/////////////////////////////////////////////////////////////////////
//
// Menu
//
IDR_MAINFRAME MENU PRELOAD DISCARDABLE
BEGIN
POPUP "&File"
BEGIN
MENUITEM "&New\tCtrl+N",          ID_FILE_NEW
MENUITEM "&Open...\tCtrl+O",      ID_FILE_OPEN
MENUITEM SEPARATOR
MENUITEM "P&rint Setup...",       ID_FILE_PRINT_SETUP
MENUITEM SEPARATOR
MENUITEM "Recent File",           ID_FILE_MRU_FILE1,GRAYED
MENUITEM SEPARATOR
MENUITEM "E&xit",                 ID_APP_EXIT
END
POPUP "&View"
BEGIN
MENUITEM "&Toolbar",              ID_VIEW_TOOLBAR
MENUITEM "&Status Bar",           ID_VIEW_STATUS_BAR
END
POPUP "&Help"
BEGIN
MENUITEM "&Help Topics",          ID_HELP_FINDER
MENUITEM SEPARATOR
MENUITEM "&About FileView...",    ID_APP_ABOUT
END
END
IDR_FILEVITYPE MENU PRELOAD DISCARDABLE
BEGIN
POPUP "&File"
BEGIN
MENUITEM "&New\tCtrl+N",          ID_FILE_NEW
MENUITEM "&Open...\tCtrl+O",      ID_FILE_OPEN
MENUITEM "&Close",                ID_FILE_CLOSE
MENUITEM "&Save\tCtrl+S",         ID_FILE_SAVE
MENUITEM "Save &As...",           ID_FILE_SAVE_AS
MENUITEM SEPARATOR
MENUITEM "&Print...\tCtrl+P",     ID_FILE_PRINT
MENUITEM "Print Pre&view",        ID_FILE_PRINT_PREVIEW
MENUITEM "P&rint Setup...",       ID_FILE_PRINT_SETUP
MENUITEM SEPARATOR
MENUITEM "Recent File",           ID_FILE_MRU_FILE1,GRAYED
```

```
     MENUITEM SEPARATOR
     MENUITEM "E&xit",                  ID_APP_EXIT
     END
     POPUP "&Edit"
     BEGIN
     MENUITEM "&Undo\tCtrl+Z",          ID_EDIT_UNDO
     MENUITEM SEPARATOR
     MENUITEM "Cu&t\tCtrl+X",           ID_EDIT_CUT
     MENUITEM "&Copy\tCtrl+C",          ID_EDIT_COPY
     MENUITEM "&Paste\tCtrl+V",         ID_EDIT_PASTE
     END
     POPUP "&View"
     BEGIN
     MENUITEM "&Toolbar",               ID_VIEW_TOOLBAR
     MENUITEM "&Status Bar",            ID_VIEW_STATUS_BAR
     END
     POPUP "&Window"
     BEGIN
     MENUITEM "&New Window",            ID_WINDOW_NEW
     MENUITEM "&Cascade",               ID_WINDOW_CASCADE
     MENUITEM "&Tile",                  ID_WINDOW_TILE_HORZ
     MENUITEM "&Arrange Icons",         ID_WINDOW_ARRANGE
     END
     POPUP "&Help"
     BEGIN
     MENUITEM "&Help Topics",           ID_HELP_FINDER
     MENUITEM SEPARATOR
     MENUITEM "&About FileView...",     ID_APP_ABOUT
     END
     END
```

The first menu, IDR_MAINFRAME, is the application's default menu. It displays when no windows are open. The second menu, ID_FILEVITYPE, displays when a view on your document is open. This menu adds a few new items, such as ID_FILE_CLOSE, that apply only when a window is open.

AppWizard also creates a default accelerator key table, providing accelerators for common Windows operations (cut, copy, paste, new, and open):

```
     ///////////////////////////////////////////////////////////////
     //
     // Accelerator
     //
     IDR_MAINFRAME ACCELERATORS PRELOAD MOVEABLE
     BEGIN
     "N",          ID_FILE_NEW,          VIRTKEY,CONTROL
     "O",          ID_FILE_OPEN,         VIRTKEY,CONTROL
     "S",          ID_FILE_SAVE,         VIRTKEY,CONTROL
     "P",          ID_FILE_PRINT,        VIRTKEY,CONTROL
     "Z",          ID_EDIT_UNDO,         VIRTKEY,CONTROL
     "X",          ID_EDIT_CUT,          VIRTKEY,CONTROL
     "C",          ID_EDIT_COPY,         VIRTKEY,CONTROL
     "V",          ID_EDIT_PASTE,        VIRTKEY,CONTROL
     VK_BACK,      ID_EDIT_UNDO,         VIRTKEY,ALT
     VK_DELETE,    ID_EDIT_CUT,          VIRTKEY,SHIFT
     VK_INSERT,    ID_EDIT_COPY,         VIRTKEY,CONTROL
```

II

Using MFC

```
VK_INSERT,      ID_EDIT_PASTE,      VIRTKEY,SHIFT
VK_F6,          ID_NEXT_PANE,       VIRTKEY
VK_F6,          ID_PREV_PANE,       VIRTKEY,SHIFT
VK_F1,          ID_CONTEXT_HELP,    VIRTKEY,SHIFT
VK_F1,          ID_HELP,            VIRTKEY
END
```

Because you told AppWizard to include context-sensitive help for your application, the wizard provides accelerator keys for both general help and context-sensitive help.

You'll recall that AppWizard adds a class, CAboutDlg, to handle your application's About box. Here is the dialog box resource itself:

```
/////////////////////////////////////////////////////////////////////////
//
// Dialog
//
IDD_ABOUTBOX DIALOG DISCARDABLE  0, 0, 217, 55
CAPTION "About FileView"
STYLE DS_MODALFRAME ¦ WS_POPUP ¦ WS_CAPTION ¦ WS_SYSMENU
FONT 8, "MS Sans Serif"
BEGIN
ICON            IDR_MAINFRAME,IDC_STATIC,11,17,20,20
LTEXT           "FileView Version 1.0",IDC_STATIC,40,10,119,8,
                SS_NOPREFIX
LTEXT           "Copyright \251 1995",IDC_STATIC,40,25,119,8
DEFPUSHBUTTON   "OK",IDOK,178,7,32,14,WS_GROUP
```

By default, AppWizard generates a VERSIONINFO resource that is embedded in the executable:

```
/////////////////////////////////////////////////////////////////////////
//
// Version
//
VS_VERSION_INFO     VERSIONINFO
  FILEVERSION       1,0,0,1
  PRODUCTVERSION    1,0,0,1
 FILEFLAGSMASK 0x3fL
#ifdef _DEBUG
 FILEFLAGS 0x1L
#else
 FILEFLAGS 0x0L
#endif
 FILEOS 0x4L
 FILETYPE 0x1L
 FILESUBTYPE 0x0L
BEGIN
    BLOCK "StringFileInfo"
    BEGIN
        BLOCK "040904B0"
          BEGIN
                VALUE "CompanyName",     "\0"
                VALUE "FileDescription", "FILEVIEW MFC Application\0"
                VALUE "FileVersion",     "1, 0, 0, 1\0"
                VALUE "InternalName",    "FILEVIEW\0"
                VALUE "LegalCopyright",  "Copyright \251 1995\0"
```

```
                    VALUE "LegalTrademarks", "\0"
                    VALUE "OriginalFilename","FILEVIEW.EXE\0"
                    VALUE "ProductName",     "FILEVIEW Application\0"
                    VALUE "ProductVersion",  "1, 0, 0, 1\0"
            END
        END
        BLOCK "VarFileInfo"
        BEGIN
            VALUE "Translation", 0x409, 1200
        END
    END
    /////////////////////////////////////////////////////////////////////////
    //
    // DESIGNINFO
    //
    #ifdef APSTUDIO_INVOKED
    GUIDELINES DESIGNINFO DISCARDABLE
    BEGIN
        IDD_ABOUTBOX, DIALOG
        BEGIN
            LEFTMARGIN, 7
            RIGHTMARGIN, 210
            TOPMARGIN, 7
            BOTTOMMARGIN, 48
        END
    END
    #endif    // APSTUDIO_INVOKED
```

VERSIONINFO resources are underused in Windows development. They provide an easy way for an application to export version information. One use is for installation programs to determine which version of an application (or DLL) is currently installed. AppWizard also generates a DESIGNINFO resource for AppStudio's use.

AppWizard creates several string table resources for a generated application. The first one contains strings describing the document types, as specified to AppWizard:

```
/////////////////////////////////////////////////////////////////////////
//
// String Table
//
STRINGTABLE PRELOAD DISCARDABLE
BEGIN
IDR_MAINFRAME          "Fileview"
IDR_FILEVITYPE         "\nFilevi\nFilevi\n\n\nFileview.Document
_ \nFilevi Document"
END
```

The application uses the next string table during idle time:

```
STRINGTABLE PRELOAD DISCARDABLE
BEGIN
AFX_IDS_APP_TITLE      "FileView"
AFX_IDS_IDLEMESSAGE    "For Help, press F1"
AFX_IDS_HELPMODEMESSAGE "Select an object on which to get Help"
END
```

MFC provides for methods that can be called when the application is not busy. In this case, the application window will have a caption of *FileView* with *For Help, Press F1* in the status bar when nothing else is going on.

The application uses the following string table for the other part of the status bar, and contains indicators to show whether Num Lock is active, whether Scroll Lock is active, whether Caps Lock has been pressed down, and so on:

```
STRINGTABLE DISCARDABLE
BEGIN
ID_INDICATOR_EXT        "EXT"
ID_INDICATOR_CAPS       "CAP"
ID_INDICATOR_NUM        "NUM"
ID_INDICATOR_SCRL       "SCRL"
ID_INDICATOR_OVR        "OVR"
ID_INDICATOR_REC        "REC"
END
```

The next string table provides prompting when the menu item is highlighted:

```
STRINGTABLE DISCARDABLE
BEGIN
ID_FILE_NEW             "Create a new document\nNew"
ID_FILE_OPEN            "Open an existing document\nOpen"
ID_FILE_CLOSE           "Close the active document\nClose"
ID_FILE_SAVE            "Save the active document\nSave"
ID_FILE_SAVE_AS         "Save the active document with a new name
_ \nSave As"
ID_FILE_PAGE_SETUP      "Change the printing options\nPage Setup"
ID_FILE_PRINT_SETUP     "Change the printer and printing options
_ \nPrint Setup"
ID_FILE_PRINT           "Print the active document\nPrint"
ID_FILE_PRINT_PREVIEW   "Display full pages\nPrint Preview"
ID_APP_ABOUT            "Display program information,
_ version number and copyright\nAbout"
ID_APP_EXIT             "Quit the application; prompts to save
_ documents\nExit"
ID_CONTEXT_HELP         "Display help for clicked on buttons,
_ menus and windows\nHelp"
ID_HELP_INDEX           "List Help topics\nHelp Index"
ID_HELP_FINDER          "List Help topics\nHelp Topics"
ID_HELP_USING           "Display instructions about how to use
_ help\nHelp"
ID_HELP                 "Display help for current task or
_ command\nHelp"
ID_FILE_MRU_FILE1       "Open this document"
ID_FILE_MRU_FILE2       "Open this document"
ID_FILE_MRU_FILE3       "Open this document"
ID_FILE_MRU_FILE4       "Open this document"
ID_FILE_MRU_FILE5       "Open this document"
ID_FILE_MRU_FILE6       "Open this document"
ID_FILE_MRU_FILE7       "Open this document"
ID_FILE_MRU_FILE8       "Open this document"
ID_FILE_MRU_FILE9       "Open this document"
ID_FILE_MRU_FILE10      "Open this document"
ID_FILE_MRU_FILE11      "Open this document"
```

```
ID_FILE_MRU_FILE12      "Open this document"
ID_FILE_MRU_FILE13      "Open this document"
ID_FILE_MRU_FILE14      "Open this document"
ID_FILE_MRU_FILE15      "Open this document"
ID_FILE_MRU_FILE16      "Open this document"
ID_NEXT_PANE            "Switch to the next window pane\nNext Pane"
ID_PREV_PANE            "Switch back to the previous window
_ pane\nPrevious Pane"
ID_WINDOW_NEW           "Open another window for the active
_ document\nNew Window"
ID_WINDOW_ARRANGE       "Arrange icons at the bottom of the
_ window\nArrange Icons"
ID_WINDOW_CASCADE       "Arrange windows so they overlap\nCascade
_ Windows"
ID_WINDOW_TILE_HORZ     "Arrange windows as non-overlapping
_ tiles\nTile Windows"
ID_WINDOW_TILE_VERT     "Arrange windows as non-overlapping
_ tiles\nTile Windows"
ID_WINDOW_SPLIT         "Split the active window into panes\nSplit"
ID_EDIT_CLEAR           "Erase the selection\nErase"
ID_EDIT_CLEAR_ALL       "Erase everything\nErase All"
ID_EDIT_COPY            "Copy the selection and put it on the
_ Clipboard\nCopy"
ID_EDIT_CUT             "Cut the selection and put it on the
_ Clipboard\nCut"
ID_EDIT_FIND            "Find the specified text\nFind"
ID_EDIT_PASTE           "Insert Clipboard contents\nPaste"
ID_EDIT_REPEAT          "Repeat the last action\nRepeat"
ID_EDIT_REPLACE         "Replace specific text with different
_ text\nReplace"
ID_EDIT_SELECT_ALL      "Select the entire document\nSelect All"
ID_EDIT_UNDO            "Undo the last action\nUndo"
ID_EDIT_REDO            "Redo the previously undone action\nRedo"
ID_VIEW_TOOLBAR         "Show or hide the toolbar\nToggle ToolBar"
ID_VIEW_STATUS_BAR      "Show or hide the status bar\nToggle
_ StatusBar"
END
```

As the user moves the cursor over different menu items, the status bar updates with the appropriate entry from the string table.

The last string table has to do with nonapplication menu items, specifically the System menu. Like the previous string table, it provides prompts for the user when menu items are highlighted:

```
STRINGTABLE DISCARDABLE
BEGIN
AFX_IDS_SCSIZE          "Change the window size"
AFX_IDS_SCMOVE          "Change the window position"
AFX_IDS_SCMINIMIZE      "Reduce the window to an icon"
AFX_IDS_SCMAXIMIZE      "Enlarge the window to full size"
AFX_IDS_SCNEXTWINDOW    "Switch to the next document window"
AFX_IDS_SCPREVWINDOW    "Switch to the previous document window"
AFX_IDS_SCCLOSE         "Close the active window and prompts to
_ save the documents"
AFX_IDS_SCRESTORE       "Restore the window to normal size"
```

```
AFX_IDS_SCTASKLIST        "Activate Task List"
AFX_IDS_MDICHILD          "Activate this window"
AFX_IDS_PREVIEW_CLOSE     "Close print preview mode\nCancel Preview"
END
```

This last block of entries in the .rc file corresponds to the TEXTINCLUDE blocks at the beginning:

```
#ifndef APSTUDIO_INVOKED
/////////////////////////////////////////////////////////////////////////////
//
// Generated from the TEXTINCLUDE 3 resource.
//
#define _AFX_NO_SPLITTER_RESOURCES
#define _AFX_NO_OLE_RESOURCES
#define _AFX_NO_TRACKER_RESOURCES
#define _AFX_NO_PROPERTY_RESOURCES
#if !defined(AFX_RESOURCE_DLL) || defined(AFX_TARG_ENU)
#ifdef _WIN32
LANGUAGE 9, 1
#pragma code_page(1252)
#endif
#include "res\FileView.rc2" // non-Microsoft VC++ edited // resources
#include "afxres.rc"         // Standard components
#include "afxprint.rc"  // printing/print preview resources
/////////////////////////////////////////////////////////////////////////////
#endif    // not APSTUDIO_INVOKED
```

If AppStudio is reading the .rc file, the TEXTINCLUDE blocks will be used; if you are using the resource compiler, it ignores the AppStudio blocks and processes this last block.

The Resource Directory (RES)

Along with the .rc file, AppWizard also creates an RES directory, which holds resources that your application includes. As you create resources with AppStudio, it places them in this directory. Initially, this directory contains four files: the toolbar bitmap (toolbar.bmp; see fig. 5.14), the two icons (see fig. 5.15), and another resource file (FileView.rc2). In FileView.rc2, you can place references to resources that AppStudio does not create or edit (see listing 5.11). Initially, this file contains very little.

Listing 5.11 FileView.rc2, the Resource Directory

```
// FILEVIEW.RC2 - resources Microsoft Visual C++ does not edit
// directly
#ifdef APSTUDIO_INVOKED
#error this file is not editable by Microsoft Visual C++
#endif //APSTUDIO_INVOKED
/////////////////////////////////////////////////////////////////////////////
// Add manually edited resources here...
/////////////////////////////////////////////////////////////////////////////
```

As you can see, an #ifdef..#endif construct prevents you from loading this file into the integrated environment. However, FileView.rc #includes this file, so you can manually add resources here.

The Information File for ClassWizard (FileView.clw)

AppWizard generates FileView.clw for use by ClassWizard. Together with FileView.mak, this file constitutes a "project" (even though most people think of the makefile by itself as a project). Like the makefile, FileView.clw is one of the "don't touch" files. Although you can look at it (it's included on the companion CD), you should not change it. If ClassWizard doesn't like the contents, you probably cannot use ClassWizard at all on your project. As you will see, FileView.clw is much like a Windows .INI file.

Create the Online Help File (Makehelp.bat)

The rest of the files and directories have to do with online Help. Makehelp is a batch file that invokes the Windows help compiler to build your help file:

```
@echo off
REM — First make map file from Microsoft Visual C++ generated resource.h
ccho // MAKEHELP.BAT generated Help Map file.  Used by FILEVIEW.HPJ.
>"hlp\FileView.hm"
echo. >>"hlp\FileView.hm"
echo // Commands (ID_* and IDM_*) >>"hlp\FileView.hm"
makehm ID_,HID_,0x10000 IDM_,HIDM_,0x10000 resource.h >>"hlp\FileView.hm"
echo. >>"hlp\FileView.hm"
echo // Prompts (IDP_*) >>"hlp\FileView.hm"
makehm IDP_,HIDP_,0x30000 resource.h >>"hlp\FileView.hm"
echo. >>"hlp\FileView.hm"
echo // Resources (IDR_*) >>"hlp\FileView.hm"
makehm IDR_,HIDR_,0x20000 resource.h >>"hlp\FileView.hm"
echo. >>"hlp\FileView.hm"
echo // Dialogs (IDD_*) >>"hlp\FileView.hm"
makehm IDD_,HIDD_,0x20000 resource.h >>"hlp\FileView.hm"
echo. >>"hlp\FileView.hm"
echo // Frame Controls (IDW_*) >>"hlp\FileView.hm"
makehm IDW_,HIDW_,0x50000 resource.h >>"hlp\FileView.hm"
REM — Make help for Project FILEVIEW
echo Building Win32 Help files
start /wait hcrtf -x "hlp\FileView.hpj"
echo.
if exist Debug\nul copy "hlp\FileView.hlp" Debug
if exist Debug\nul copy "hlp\FileView.cnt" Debug
if exist Release\nul copy "hlp\FileView.hlp" Release
if exist Release\nul copy "hlp\FileView.cnt" Release
echo.
```

Makehelp constructs a "help map" and then calls the help compiler (hcrtf). Makehelp then copies the help file to both the Release and Debug directories (if they exist).

II

Using MFC

The Help Project File (FileView.hpj)

FileView.hpj is FileView's help project file. It tells the help compiler which .rtf files to include, as well as which bitmaps, cursors, and icons the help file needs. Generally, the help project file is not changed. Instead, you modify the .rtf source files and just run Makehelp again. To view this file, see the companion CD.

The Help Directory (HLP)

The .hpj file references several bitmaps and .rtf files. These files, which AppWizard generates, are placed in the HLP directory. The main help text is placed in two files: afxcore.rtf and afxprint.rtf. The subject of constructing help files is beyond the scope of this discussion. Although you update these files in Chapter 6, "Using MFC," for FileView, this section doesn't show them, simply because they are large (afxcore is about 50K of text, and afxprint is about 11K). When working with .rtf files, you should use a program that knows how to parse and display .rtf files. One program that fills this criteria quite well is Microsoft Word for Windows. If you must edit the .rtf file in "raw" form, look for lines of the form << .... >>. These markers indicate where you should place information specific to your application. However, you'll probably want to use tools designed for writing help files if you are going to add new sections to the generated help file.

That's it! By this point, you should be comfortable (or at least familiar) with the source code that AppWizard generates. As you can see, this code is only a starting point. In Chapter 6, you'll make this code do something useful.

Moving on To Finish FileView

After you use AppWizard to generate an application, you usually don't use the tool again. Generating an application is AppWizard's job, but you do that only once per application. In Chapter 6, "Using MFC," you use ClassWizard to add on to the code that you've just examined. As you use ClassWizard, it modifies the .cpp and .h files to add methods to the classes that you've already got. In Chapter 6, you'll examine what ClassWizard actually does and see how it uses those interesting-looking comments.

From Here...

So, what will you need to do to make FileView a "real" application? You must make it read text files, so you must modify the document class to read text and store it in an accessible form. You also must modify the view class to display what you've read, and enable the user to scroll the view.

You also must modify the printing and print preview code. If the user chooses to print a file, you'll want to make the output look nice, with footers and such. You'll also have to customize your application's online Help. In other words, you still have lots to do!

For information relating directly to MFC, you might want to see the following sources:

- Chapter 6, "Using MFC," tells you more about using MFC to write a functional Windows application.

- *Using OLE 2 in Application Development* (Que, 1994) will help you learn how to use OLE to enable your applications take advantage of Microsoft's OLE technologies.

Using MFC

In Chapter 5, "Introducing MFC," you used the AppWizard to create a skeleton application and learned about all the files that you generated in the process. Now you need to make this application do something practical. In this chapter, you turn that skeleton application into a program called FileView. Because you are interested in MFC's capability to make writing Windows applications easier, your primary purpose in this chapter is to use MFC to make your code changes as minimal as possible.

In this chapter, you learn about the following:

- Handling file input/output (I/O) through MFC's CArchive class
- Using TRACE() to output useful debugging information
- Catching and handling exceptions thrown by MFC
- Drawing text in a window
- Printing text on a printer, as well as supporting Print Preview
- Responding to scroll bar messages

Planning the FileView Application

Before writing any application (regardless of the language that you are using or the operating system for which you are writing), you should always write down exactly what you want the application to do. Although this preparatory stage isn't an absolute necessity, failing to do any planning can result in an application that seems "thrown together." You want your application's users to have a sense that you put some thought into your product. Few people want to use a poorly designed application.

> **Note**
>
> The FileView application is simple rather than elegant. Experienced MFC developers can easily nitpick various aspects of this program's code. However, the purpose of the application is to demonstrate how simple it can be to implement an application with MFC, not to show off complex C++ development methods.

What Do You Want FileView To Do?

FileView's purpose is simple. The program should enable the user to open and view text files in a scrollable window. Also, the program should let the user scroll both up and down and left and right, so that the user can view the entire file. While the user is viewing a text file, the program should use the file's contents to determine where line breaks occur. For this program design, a *line* is a stream of text followed by a carriage return or linefeed character.

How should the program store the text that is read from a file? Because the program will read the text files' contents as a sequence of lines, FileView should store the contents as a series of pointers to lines. To make things simple, you will restrict FileView to working only with files that fit in memory. This limitation isn't too bad, because Windows enables you to work with large amounts of memory. Also, FileView won't check a file's contents and will attempt to load the file independent of the length of a line. In other words, FileView won't balk at a text file containing lines of, say, 1,000 characters. As long as memory is available, FileView will read the file into memory.

FileView should also enable the user to print a file's contents. The contents that the program prints should be determined by the window that is active when the user chooses File, Print. When printed, a file should have a page footer, and display helpful information about the file.

The restrictions that you are placing on FileView limit its usefulness somewhat, but the program still serves as a good example of a "real" application. Occasionally in this chapter, you'll learn about various ways that you can make FileView better, but you'll have to implement those ideas as an exercise. A version of FileView with some of these enhancements is available on Que's CompuServe forum. Simply type **GO QUEBOOKS** at any CIS prompt. The file, FileView.zip, is in library 9, Programming.

This chapter discusses some aspects of the program only briefly, because a full discussion would take too much space. For example, you will customize the help file for FileView, but this chapter discusses only a portion of that process. However, the companion CD includes the complete .rtf source code.

So now that you know what FileView's capabilities and limitations are to be, you can begin implementing the program using MFC's document/view architecture.

What Exactly Are Documents and Views?

Chapter 5, "Introducing MFC," discussed MFC's document/view architecture. You now must decide how to implement FileView (at least as far as documents and views work). In other words, you need to decide what is contained in the document class and what is in the view class.

What should the document include? What should be in the view? For FileView, the answers to these questions are fairly simple. Documents should contain the data for a view to show. In other words, the document contains the raw data, and the view provides some type of window in which the user can view the data. For FileView, the document consists of the lines of text read from the file that the user specified. Thus, the document class should contain the pointers to each line of the file (after it is read into memory).

The view class must maintain information about itself, keeping track of the lines that it is currently showing, so that the user can easily update and scroll the view.

To create FileView, you make several changes to the skeleton application that you created in the last chapter. The following sections describe these changes one step at time. The first step is to change the skeleton application so that it can read a text file and set up a document.

Making FileView's Document Class Read Files

To enable FileView to open and read a text file, you must construct the document class for FileView.

Currently, if you compile and run the skeleton application and then choose File, Open, FileView displays the Windows File Open common dialog box. If you select a file from the file list, you get an empty window. You must change this behavior so that FileView prompts the user to select a text file. After the user selects the file, the program must open the file and read its contents into memory.

You can assume that the user will want to select files with the .txt extension, so the default type for the file that the user selects should be a text file. Currently, the Open dialog box doesn't specify a particular type of file, so you must change the code to implement this default behavior.

How does the code know which type of file you are interested in? The answer lies in the use of *document templates*. AppWizard automatically generates the code needed to create a document template. The file FileView.cpp contains the code in listing 6.1.

Listing 6.1   FileView.cpp, Code to Register a Document Template

```
CMultiDocTemplate* pDocTemplate;
pDocTemplate = new CMultiDocTemplate(
     IDR_FILEVITYPE,
     RUNTIME_CLASS(CFileViewDoc),
     RUNTIME_CLASS(CChildFrame),  // standard MDI child frame
     RUNTIME_CLASS(CFileViewView));
AddDocTemplate(pDocTemplate);
```

You are creating an MDI application, so the AppWizard creates an instance of the CMultiDocTemplate class and adds to MFC's internal list of document templates a pointer to that template. The constructor for CMultiDocTemplate takes four arguments: an ID number for the document resources (IDR_FILEVITYPE), and the names of the document, frame, and view classes. The ID number, IDR_FILEVITYPE, is a reference to resources for this document type. FileView's .rc file includes the code in listing 6.2.

Listing 6.2   FileView.rc, the Resource that Tells MFC What Type of Files Your Application Uses

```
STRINGTABLE PRELOAD DISCARDABLE
BEGIN
     IDR_MAINFRAME   "FileView"
     IDR_FILEVITYPE
  _    "\nFileVi\nFileVi\n\n\nFileView.Document\nFileVi Document"
END
```

The string resource referenced by IDR_FILEVITYPE tells MFC which type of file is associated with the document template. Therefore, if the user attempts to open a file whose type matches this string, AppWizard automatically constructs the associated document and view. You didn't specify anything special about the type of documents with which you are going to work, so AppWizard generates a default string resource for this application.

Understanding the Default String Resource

The IDR_FILEVITYPE string actually consists of seven strings that are separated by the newline character. Here are descriptions of each of these strings:

- The first string is used for a window title. MDI applications do not use this string, and thus leave it empty. For this reason, IDR_FILEVITYPE begins with \n.

- The second string, the docname, constructs the document's name if the user chose File, New. As new documents are created, MFC appends a number to the document's name so that each name is unique. FileView doesn't let the user create new files (and thus its File menu will not include a New command), so the program doesn't use this string. If no string is specified, MFC uses "Untitled" as the document name. The AppWizard uses a truncated form of your application name for this field (and for the other fields, except for the fourth and fifth strings).

- The third string, the filenewName, provides a type (such as "Spreadsheet") to the document. This type is displayed in the New dialog box. If no type is necessary, you can omit this string. FileView doesn't use it.

- The fourth string, the filterName, lets you specify a description for the types of files associated with this document. The Open dialog box's List Files of Type drop-down box list displays this description. For FileView, you change this string to Text Files (*.txt), because the program defaults to text files (files with the extension .txt).

- The fifth string, the filterExt, is used with the filterName to specify the extension for files associated with the document. For FileView, you change the string to .txt.

- The sixth and seventh strings are used for the Windows registration database. They enable you to register a document type with Windows applications (such as File Manager) that use this database. If you don't specify these strings, the document type cannot be registered. The sixth string, the `regFileTypeId`, is an internal type that identifies the document type. The seventh string, the `regFileTypeName`, provides a meaningful name to the registered type. FileView doesn't use either of these strings.

Thus, your modified `IDR_FILEVITYPE` string looks like this: *file types Assoc w/ doc*

```
IDR_FILEVITYPE     "\nFileVi\nFileVi\nText Files
    (*.txt)\n.TXT\nFileView.Document\nFileVi"
```
 5 → folder

Because of this one-line change, FileView now displays a list of text files when the user chooses File, Open.

Note

Alternatively, you can make this change by having the ClassWizard generate a handler for the `OnFileOpen()` method. If you use this alternative technique, you can customize the Open dialog box manually. However, you still must modify the resource string so that MFC can locate the proper document template after the user opens the file.

Figure 6.1 shows the application at this point.

Fig. 6.1

FileView's Open dialog box after you modify the `IDR_FILEVITYPE` *string.*

Notice that when the application starts, MFC creates, by default, an empty document window and gives the window the title FileVi1. This title is generated from the re-source string that you just changed. Later, in the section "Prompting the User for a File To Open," you change FileView so that it doesn't open an empty window like this when it executes. Next you enable FileView to read a file into memory.

Reading a Text File into RAM and Building a Document

When the user selects a file in the Open dialog box, MFC constructs the appropriate document class automatically. You want to modify your document class so that it initializes the class members that you use to hold the text file's contents.

Introducing Collection Classes. How should you store the lines of text that are read into memory? One way is to keep a list of pointers, each pointing to a line of the text file. As each line of text is read in, you store the characters in a string. Then, when you have a complete line of text, you store somewhere in memory a pointer to the string. If you were writing this program in C, you would probably allocate an area of memory to hold the pointers and construct routines to let you add, remove, and access individual pointers as needed. However, because you are using C++, MFC (like all good application frameworks) already has a solution for you: the *collection classes*.

The collection classes are C++ classes that construct abstract data structures in memory. MFC 3.0 includes many collection classes, which come in two types: collections based on templates, and collections not based on templates. Both types are similar, except that the template-based classes require you to do a little more work. The nontemplate classes are self-contained, but work only with certain predefined data types. For example, some collection classes work with WORDs. If you want to build one of these abstract structures for holding WORDs, a class has already been built for you. However, if you're working with custom data structures that you have built yourself, you'll probably have to use the template classes to construct your own abstract data structures. Previous versions of MFC did not offer the template classes, for one simple reason: Earlier versions of Microsoft C++ did not have built-in support for templates.

Regardless of whether you use the template classes, the collection classes fall into three general categories: arrays, lists, and maps (or dictionaries). Each category is based on a different type of basic data structure.

The *array classes* (CArray, CObArray, CStringArray, CPtrArray, and so on) construct an array in memory. Like an array in C, these array classes store each element of a fixed size contiguously in memory. Arrays can grow or shrink as you add and remove data. They can either grow one item at a time (as you add data) or you can preallocate elements in the array. Because arrays are stored as one contiguous piece of RAM, they must reallocate themselves periodically as the array grows. Arrays have the advantage of being capable of accessing any element at any time, with each element taking the same length of time to retrieve. However, inserting an item in the middle of an array can take time, because MFC has to move memory around to perform the insertion. The examples of the array classes listed earlier in this paragraph are just a few of the ones available. CArray is a "templatized" class, capable of storing any data type. CObArray, CStringArray, and CPtrArray are designed for specific data types (CObjects, CStrings, and void pointers).

You use the *list classes* (CList, CObList, CStringList, CPtrList, and so on) to build doubly linked lists of data. You can traverse the list in any direction, and inserting items at either the beginning or end of the list is a fairly fast process. Lists don't have to be contiguous in memory, so you don't have to reallocate them before adding new data. Lists also support searching for specific entries based on their value, but this search can be slow if the list is long. Accessing individual items of a list can also be slow, because you must traverse the list to reach the specified item.

The *map classes* (CMap, CMapPtrToPtr, CMapStringToPtr, and so on) construct *dictionaries,* which consist of a *key value* and a *data item.* The key value identifies the data item, and thus works much like a dictionary (in that you need to know only one data item to find another, larger data item). After you supply the key value, the map class can find the proper data item. The map classes enable you to build a data structure that can retrieve an item based on whatever key value you supply. However, a key value for a map, unlike those for arrays and lists, must be unique (you cannot have a map with two identical keys). Looking up an item in a map is very efficient, because a hash table performs the lookup. Maps are available in many permutations, enabling you to map CStrings to CObjects, pointers to pointers, CStrings to pointers, and much more.

Using the CPtrArray Class To Retrieve and Store Data. All three types of collections provide several methods for retrieving and storing data, none of which requires much work on your part. The collection classes are numerous (and can be complex) but enable you to store a text file's contents without having to write much code. For FileView, you use the CPtrArray class to hold the pointers to each line. A CPtrArray is used to hold an array of pointers; for FileView, you use the class to hold pointers to instances of CString, which is another MFC class. CString provides a convenient way to work with strings. You can think of a CString as an array of characters, but CStrings have more features than a simple array. As you examine the code for FileView, you'll learn more about the features of CStrings.

Because you are going to use a CPtrArray to hold the lines of text as they are read in, you must store a pointer to a CPtrArray in your document. You also must construct the CPtrArray when you create the document, and destroy the CPtrArray when you delete the document.

The document will own the CPtrArray, so you must add it to your class definition in FileVdoc.h. Here's the change:

```
class CFileViewDoc : public CDocument
{
    protected: // create from serialization only
    CFileViewDoc();
    DECLARE_DYNCREATE(CFileViewDoc)
    CPtrArray *lines;
```

You also must allocate the CPtrArray when you create the document. That code is in listing 6.3.

Listing 6.3   FileVdoc.cpp, Allocating Memory for the CPtrArray and Checking to Ensure That It Was Allocated

```
CFileViewDoc::CFileViewDoc()
{
    lines = NULL;
    try {
            lines = new CPtrArray();
}
catch (CMemoryException *e)
{
    AfxMessageBox("Can't allocate memory for reading file contents");
    TRACE0("Unable to allocate memory for file contents\n");
    e->Delete();
}
TRACE0("Allocated lines array\n");
}
```

You have simply changed CFileViewDoc's constructor to create a CPtrArray when it is invoked. This constructor builds an empty CPtrArray that grows as each pointer to a CString is added to it. When you attempt to create the CPtrArray, you must check whether the allocation succeeds. If it fails, a CMemoryException is thrown, and you have to catch it. To do so, you warn the user that memory couldn't be allocated. Finally, you issue a TRACE0 message so that you can see this code being invoked during the debugging process.

Likewise, you must delete the CPtrArray, as well as its contents, when you delete the document:

```
CFileViewDoc::~CFileViewDoc()
{
int i = 0;

if (lines != NULL)
        {
        while (i < lines->GetSize())
        delete (CString *) lines->GetAt(i++);
        lines->RemoveAll();
        delete lines;
        lines = NULL;
        }
TRACE0("Deleted lines array\n");
}
```

When the program calls the destructor for the document class, you must delete the array of pointers as well as that to which the pointers point. First, you check whether lines actually has a value. If a value exists, you delete the CPtrArray and its contents (lines will be NULL if it isn't storing anything, because lines is set to NULL when it is not being used or if it couldn't be created). To perform this deletion, you use GetSize() to ask the array how many elements are in it. As GetAt() returns each entry, you delete the entries. You then tell the array to remove all its elements (emptying the array) and finally, delete the array itself. Remember, deleting a collection does *not* delete the collection's contents. Also, remember that issuing a delete on a variable does not set its value to 0.

Modifying Serialize() To Construct a Document Class. Now that you have constructed a CPtrArray, you must read the text into it. Where should you do this? Chapter 5, "Introducing MFC," discussed serialization and the CArchive class. As you'll recall, the AppWizard adds the Serialize() method to your document class to support serialization. The application calls this method whenever a document is being read from or written to a file. To construct the document class, you can hook into the Serialize() method. Listing 6.4 shows how you do this.

Listing 6.4 FileVDoc.cpp, Modifying Serialize() to Read a Text File

```
void CFileViewDoc::Serialize(CArchive& ar)
{
        BYTE buf;
        CString s;
```

```
    if (ar.IsStoring())
    {
        // TODO: add storing code here
    }
    else
    {
        // TODO: add loading code here
        while (1)
        {
        try {
                ar >> buf;
        }
        catch (CArchiveException *e)
        {
            if (e->m_cause != CArchiveException::endOfFile)
            {
                TRACE0("Unknown exception loading file!\n");
                throw;
            } else
            {
                TRACE0("End of file reached...\n");
                e->Delete();
            } // end if
            break;
        } // End Catch
        s += buf;
        if (buf == '\n')
        {
                try {
                    lines->Add(new CString(s));
                }
                catch (CMemoryException *e)
                {
                    AfxMessageBox(
                        _"Not enough memory to load entire file");
                    TRACE1("Not enough memory to load file;
                        _only %d lines loaded\n", lines->GetSize());
                    e->Delete();
                    break;
                }
                s.Empty();
        }
    }
#ifdef _DEBUG
        afxDump.SetDepth(1);
        afxDump << lines;
#endif
    }
}
```

After calling the Serialize() method of your document class, MFC has already
opened the file that the user selected and has created an instance of the CArchive class
for it. You can use this CArchive to read from the text file. However, CArchive does not
know anything about the format of a text file, so you must interpret the format of the

file yourself. CArchive does know how to read primitive types, so you use this capability to read the file contents one byte at a time.

Serialize() starts by allocating a BYTE and a CString on the stack. You use the BYTE to hold each character as it is read in, and the CString to hold each line as you build it. When you reach the end of the line, the CString contains all the text from the current line.

If you are reading from the file (ar.IsStoring() is false), you enter a loop that reads one BYTE at a time from the archive. You don't have any code to execute if ar.IsStoring() is true, because FileView is incapable of creating files on disk (although you could easily add this capability). You want to know when you have reached the end of the file, so you must be prepared to catch the exception that CArchive throws when you reach the end-of-file (EOF) mark. To do so, you use the try/catch construct, just like you did in the document constructor, except that this time you want to catch a CArchiveException, not a CMemoryException.

The try block sets up code that could possibly throw an exception. If an exception does occur, the catch block determines who handles the exception. For FileView, you know that the CArchive is going to throw an exception when you reach the end of the text file, so you must be prepared for that exception. When the exception occurs, the catch block receives control. If not a CArchiveException, the exception is handed up the chain of control to check whether a handler exists for it. Exceptions are always passed up the class tree so that the base classes can catch the exception if they need to. By default, MFC doesn't catch many exceptions; if one occurs, you usually get an unhandled exception message.

For FileView, you catch any CArchiveExceptions that occur and examine the exception's cause. CArchiveExceptions have a member variable, m_cause, that contains the reason for the exception's occurrence. If the cause is CArchiveException::endOfFile (a constant in the CArchiveException class), you know that you reached the end of the file. If so, you print a debug message, delete the exception (so it won't hang around), and break out of the loop. As indicated in the documentation for CArchiveException, exceptions can also be thrown if you try to write to a read-only file, if you try to read from an archive that is opened for writing, if you are processing an archive that is the wrong version, or if other error conditions occur.

If the exception is a CArchiveException that you don't expect, you print another message and throw the exception again, so that the rest of MFC has a chance to see it. You must be prepared to catch exceptions that you expect. Otherwise, your application is likely to terminate with an unhandled exception failure.

If an exception doesn't occur, you add the character to your CString by using the + operator. CStrings know how to add to themselves character strings, other CStrings, and individual characters. The CString automatically grows to accommodate each character as it is added.

When you finally reach a newline character (\n), you know that you have reached the end of a line (because, by FileView's definition, all lines terminate with a newline). Your CStrings contain the text for the current line. You cannot simply add the CString to the array, however, because CPtrArrays expect a pointer, not a CString. You also cannot simply send your CString's address to the CPtrArray, because you will reuse this CString for every line. Instead, you use the Add() function to add a pointer to a new CString. By passing your CStrings to the constructor for this new CString, you obtain a pointer to a new CString that contains the contents of the CString that you have already built. The result is that you pass to Add() the address of a CString on the heap that contains the text that you have read in. After you use the Empty() function to empty the CString, you can continue reading characters. Again, you check whether a CMemoryException occurs when you allocate the new CString. If such an exception occurs, you issue a message and stop reading from the archive.

You should now understand why you must delete the contents of your CPtrArray when you call the document's destructor. The CPtrArray contains the *addresses* of your CStrings. If you don't delete these addresses, they hang around. Although Windows NT cleans up these allocations for you automatically, you should always clean up any memory that you allocate.

Finally, when building a debug release, you empty the contents of the CPtrArray after you build it. This is simply a safety measure for debugging.

Considering Alternative Solutions. Consider other ways that you could have read the file into memory, and why some would not work. For example, because you are building a CString to hold each line of text, you might wonder why you don't use the CStringArray class to hold the lines of text. Although you could do this, you would have to allocate a CString for each line that you read in, and CStringArrays can hold only CStrings, not pointers to CStrings. Therefore, because you are allocating each line as needed, it is easier to use a temporary CString and duplicate it when you know that it is complete.

Reading the text file a byte at a time is not the most efficient way to read a text file. You might consider simply having the archive transfer data directly to the CString, as follows:

```
ar >> s;
```

This scheme will not work as expected. Although you can easily serialize CStrings, this particular serialization does not result in the transfer of one line at a time into s. MFC has a class for processing text files (CStdioFile), but your CArchive is not attached to a CStdioFile. Instead, your CArchive is attached to a CFile, which reads and writes *binary* files, not text files. Therefore, transferring from the archive directly to a CString will get some of the file, but not a line as defined by FileView. Instead, this scheme would get a piece of a line, with the CString receiving an arbitrary amount of text. To process the archive a line at a time, you would have to override some of MFC's default behavior. Because you want to keep FileView simple, you just retrieve a byte at a time instead. Note that you cannot make buf a char because the CArchive class doesn't know how to serialize a char variable. The BYTE type is just about the same as a char, so you can use that type.

Now that you have the text in memory, the next step is to display it.

Making FileView's View Class Display Text

Your document class now contains pointers to lines of text, so you now must change your view class to display the text. The view class must be capable of accessing the lines that you have stored, so you add to your document class a method that, when called, returns the pointer to the lines of text. Here is the change to the document class header file (FileVdoc.h):

```
// Generated message map functions
    protected:
    //{{AFX_MSG(CFileViewDoc)
    // NOTE - ClassWizard adds and removes member functions here.
                // DO NOT EDIT what you see in these blocks of generated
                ➥code!
    //}}AFX_MSG
    DECLARE_MESSAGE_MAP()
    public:
    CPtrArray *GetLines()      { return lines; }
};
```

This new method, GetLines(), simply returns lines, which is your CPtrArray pointer. You also must add a member to the view class to keep track of which line is at the top of the view's window. Here is the change that you make to FileVvw.h:

```
class CFileViewView : public CView
{
protected: // create from serialization only
    CFileViewView();
    DECLARE_DYNCREATE(CFileViewView)
    int currentLine;
```

Next, you initialize the new variable while creating the view:

```
CFileViewView::CFileViewView()
{
    // TODO: add construction code here
    currentLine = 0;
}
```

Finally, you enable the view to display the actual text. The AppWizard generates for the view class a method called OnDraw() that is called when the view needs to paint itself. Listing 6.5 shows the version of OnDraw() that the AppWizard generates.

Listing 6.5 FileVVw.cpp, the OnDraw() Method Generated by the AppWizard and Then Modified

```
void CFileViewView::OnDraw(CDC* pDC)
{
    CFileViewDoc* pDoc = GetDocument();
```

```
            ASSERT_VALID(pDoc);
            CFont *ourFont;
            CFont *oldFont;
            ourFont = new CFont();
            ourFont->CreateFont(0, 0, 0, 0, FW_NORMAL, FALSE, FALSE,
            FALSE, ANSI_CHARSET, OUT_TT_PRECIS, CLIP_TT_ALWAYS,
            DEFAULT_QUALITY, DEFAULT_PITCH, "Courier New");
            oldFont = pDC->SelectObject(ourFont);
            CPtrArray *l = pDoc->GetLines();
            int y = 0;
            for (int i = currentLine; i < l->GetSize(); i++)
            {
            CString *line = (CString *) l->GetAt(i);
                pDC->TextOut(0, y, LPCTSTR(*line), line->GetLength() - 2);
            CSize lineHeight = pDC->GetTextExten (*line, line->GetLength());
                y += lineHeight.cy;
            }
            pDC->SelectObject(oldFont);
            delete ourFont;
    }
```

OnDraw() begins by declaring a few variables that you need. The method receives a pointer to an instance of the CDC class, which is MFC's encapsulation of a Windows device context. When working with the pointer to the CDC, you are working with whatever device context is currently being used, whether the context is for a view (window) or a printer. Like Windows DCs, CDCs, when created, have a set of default values for pens, fonts, brushes, and more. Because the default font for the CDC is not what you want, you must create a font for your text.

You declare two pointers to CFont, which is MFC's encapsulation of a GDI (graphics device interface) font. You need two pointers because you use one to create a font and another to hold the old font value that the CDC was using. When you finish using the CDC, you restore its old font and delete the font that you created.

When you create an instance of the class CFont, you don't actually create a font. The CFont constructor simply does some initialization of the class. After the constructor initializes an instance of CFont, you use the CreateFont() function to create a font. Alternatively, you can use two other functions to create fonts: CreateFontIndirect (which accepts a pointer to a LOGFONT structure that describes the font that you want) and FromHandle (which accepts a handle to a Windows font). You pass CreateFont() the information necessary for creating a plain font (not bold, italic, underlined, or overstruck, and of default quality) of the Courier New family. This plain Courier TrueType font is a reasonable default for the font width and height.

After you create your font, you select it for the CDC by using the SelectObject() method. This method knows that it is receiving a CFont pointer, so it returns a pointer to the old CFont that was selected for the CDC. (SelectObject() is overridden for different types of GDI objects, so it always returns a pointer to the old GDI object, no matter what type it is. If you pass a pointer to a CPen, you receive a pointer to the old CPen.) You store the returned CFont pointer so that when you finish you can reset the CDC the way it originally was.

The font is the only aspect of the CDC that you are going to change, so you are now ready to draw text. You start by getting a pointer to the lines of text, using the GetLines() method that you wrote earlier. The AppWizard generates a method, GetDocument(), that returns a pointer to the document associated with this view. By using this pointer, you can call GetLines() to gain access to the CPtrArray constructed for this document. Next, you initialize a variable, y, to keep track of your current y-position while you are drawing.

Your view has a member variable, currentLine, that keeps track of the line at the top of your view. Currently, the variable has a value of 0, because you set it to that when constructing the view. When you scroll the window, the program updates currentLine to keep track of the line currently at the top of the window. Therefore, you want to draw from line currentLine until you either fill the window or reach the last line in CPtrArray. To do so, you set up a loop to run from currentLine to the end of the array.

Using GetAt(), you retrieve a pointer to a line, casting it to a CString pointer in the process (remember, CPtrArray stores void pointers, so you must cast the pointer). After you get the pointer to the line, you can use TextOut() to draw the text. Because the y variable keeps track of the current y-position (and you are not handling horizontal scrolling yet), the coordinates for drawing are (0, y). You also pass to TextOut() the CString and its length.

You might wonder why you are using the LPCTSTR() operator on the CString. After all, you could simply pass the CString to TextOut() and let that method determine the string's length automatically. However, you don't yet use TextOut() here because the CString ends with a carriage return and linefeed pair, which show up as a rectangle on the screen. Because you convert the CString to an LPCTSTR() (a long pointer to a constant string), you can use a version of TextOut() that enables you to pass the string length. Then, by specifying the string's length minus two characters, you make TextOut() ignore the last two characters.

After drawing the string, you must determine the string's height so that you can update the y-position. GetTextExtent() returns a CSize variable that contains the string's width and height based on the current font selected for the CDC. The CSize contains two members, cx and cy, that contain the width and height of the line that you just drew, so you use the cy member to update the y-position. You then advance to the next line.

After you finish drawing, you select the old font for the CDC so that you can delete the font that you created. At this point, you can see this code work. Figure 6.2 shows FileView displaying the contents of a text file.

This view is nice, but has one problem: Because you have no way to scroll this window, you cannot view the rest of the file. So, your next major task is to make the view scrollable.

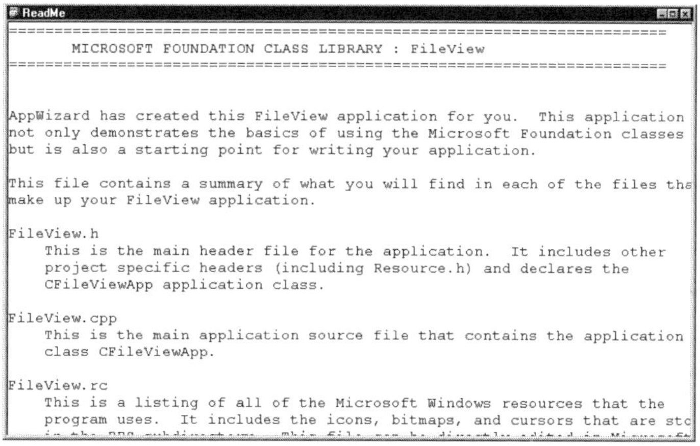
ReadMe

```
========================================================================
       MICROSOFT FOUNDATION CLASS LIBRARY : FileView
========================================================================


AppWizard has created this FileView application for you.  This application
not only demonstrates the basics of using the Microsoft Foundation classes
but is also a starting point for writing your application.

This file contains a summary of what you will find in each of the files tha
make up your FileView application.

FileView.h
    This is the main header file for the application.  It includes other
    project specific headers (including Resource.h) and declares the
    CFileViewApp application class.

FileView.cpp
    This is the main application source file that contains the application
    class CFileViewApp.

FileView.rc
    This is a listing of all of the Microsoft Windows resources that the
    program uses.  It includes the icons, bitmaps, and cursors that are stc
```

Fig. 6.2

FileView displaying a text file's contents.

Prompting the User for a File To Open

First, though, you should change FileView so that it doesn't create an empty document every time you start it up. To do this, you make a simple change to FileView.cpp in your `InitInstance()` method. As mentioned in Chapter 5, "Introducing MFC," when your application first starts, `InitInstance()` creates an instance of the class `CCommandLineInfo`. The application passes this variable to `ParseCommandLine()`, which fills in various members of this class based on the command line passed to the program. You then pass this instance of `CCommandLineInfo` to `ProcessShellCommand()`, which invokes the necessary methods in your program.

One member of `CCommandLineInfo` is an `enum` that contains a value based on what `ParseCommandLine()` found. To prevent FileView from creating an empty window every time that it starts, you must check this member to see whether any command-line parameters were passed to FileView. If none were passed, you must simulate a File, Open command rather than a File, New command (which is causing the empty window to occur). Here's the code change:

```
ParseCommandLine(cmdInfo);
if (cmdInfo.m_nShellCommand == CCommandLineInfo::FileNew)
    OnFileOpen();
else
{
// Dispatch commands specified on the command line
if (!ProcessShellCommand(cmdInfo))
    return FALSE;
}
```

After calling `ParseCommandLine()`, you check whether `m_nShellCommand` has a value of `FileNew`. If it does, no file name was passed to FileView, and you simply call `OnFileOpen()` to simulate a File, Open menu selection. Otherwise, let the old code do its work. Therefore, when FileView executes, it first prompts the user to select a file to view.

By adding a call to `OnFileOpen()`, you make FileView automatically prompt the user for a file to open when the user invokes the program.

Making the View Scrollable

To implement scrolling, the first change that you make is to the document class. The view windows need two scroll bars: one for horizontal scrolling, and one for vertical scrolling.

You should base the horizontal scrolling on the length of the longest line in the file. You can easily determine this length while the program is loading the file. To do so, you change the `Serialize()` method in the document class so that the method keeps track of the length of each line as it is read in. When the method finds a line that is longer than the previously longest line, you update the length that you store in the new variable, `maxLineLength`. You also must add to the document class the method `GetMaxLineLength()`, which returns the value stored in `maxLineLength`. You use this value when you update the view class to handle scrolling.

```
class CFileViewDoc : public CDocument
{
protected: // create from serialization only
CFileViewDoc();
DECLARE_DYNCREATE(CFileViewDoc)
CPtrArray *lines;
int maxLineLength;
.
.
.
CPtrArray *GetLines()     { return lines, }
int GetMaxLineLength()    { return maxLineLength; }
};
```

`Serialize()` calculates the variable `maxLineLength`. Again, this calculation requires a one-line change:

```
try {
lines->Add(new CString(s));
}
catch (CMemoryException *e)
{
AfxMessageBox("Not enough memory to load entire file");
TRACE1("Not enough memory to load file;
_ only %d lines loaded\n", lines->GetSize());
e->Delete();
break;
}
if (maxLineLength < s.GetLength())
maxLineLength = s.GetLength();
s.Empty();
```

Thus, when `Serialize()` finishes, `maxLineLength` contains the length (in characters) of the file's longest line. (Incidentally, you also could keep `maxLineLength` in the view class, and compute the value after creating the document.) Also, you must ensure that `maxLineLength` has a value, so initialize it to 0 in the constructor for the document class.

```
CFileViewDoc::CFileViewDoc()
{
lines = NULL;
maxLineLength = 0;
```

The changes required for the view class are a little more involved. The view class already knows how long the file is (in lines), because the class can call `GetLines()` in the document class and query the `CPtrArray` for the file's length. Also, because of the `currentLine` member variable (which until now has always had a value of 0), the view class knows which line is the current line. However, the code currently creates a font every time that it wants to draw text. You are using a fixed-pitch font (for which every character has the same width and height), although it would be more efficient for the view to create the font when the program initializes the view itself. Then the view class would create a font only once during the view's life. You also want to compute the width and height of a character only once, to make code of the `OnDraw()` method slightly faster. Here's the first change to the view class itself:

```
class CFileViewView : public CView
{
protected: // create from serialization only
CFileViewView();
DECLARE_DYNCREATE(CFileViewView)
int currentLine;
int margin;
CFont *ourFont;
int lHeight;
int cWidth;
```

In addition to `currentLine`, a variable called `margin` keeps track of your location for horizontal scrolling. When the user scrolls the window using the horizontal scroll bar, you must know where to begin showing each line. The `margin` variable holds this value. You also store a pointer to the font, as well as the height and width of a character in that font. Because we're assuming that every character in a font has the same height and width, FileView works well only with fixed-pitch fonts like Courier. `lHeight` contains the line's height, and `cWidth` contains the width (in pixels) of a single character.

The class itself requires some other changes, but because the ClassWizard handles these changes, they aren't listed in this section. When you use ClassWizard to add these methods, it automatically updates the class definition in FileVvw.h.

Now that you have added `margin`, you must ensure that it always has a valid value. To do so, you must initialize the variable in the view constructor:

```
CFileViewView::CFileViewView()
{
// TODO: add construction code here
currentLine = 0;
margin = 0;
}
```

You also want to initialize the other members of the view class when creating the view, but you first must wait until the program actually has constructed the view. To perform this initialization, you have the ClassWizard hook into a new method, OnInitialUpdate(). If you bring up the MFC ClassWizard dialog box and select the CFileViewView class in the Class Name drop-down list box, you see the screen shown in figure 6.3.

Fig. 6.3

The ClassWizard showing
CFileViewView.

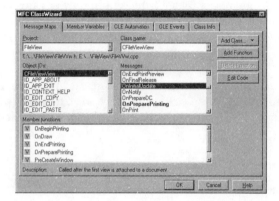

When you select CFileViewView in the Object IDs list box, the ClassWizard displays all the messages to which the CFileViewView class can respond. Scroll the contents of the Messages list box until OnInitialUpdate() is visible. Click the Add Function button. The ClassWizard then adds to the .cpp and .h files a message handler called OnInitialUpdate(). If you click the Edit Code button, you are placed in the editor and positioned at this new method. Listing 6.6 shows what the method should look like after you change it.

Listing 6.6 FileVVw.cpp, after the Change

```cpp
void CFileViewView::OnInitialUpdate()
{
        CFileViewDoc *pDoc = GetDocument();
        CPtrArray *l = pDoc->GetLines();
        SetScrollRange(SB_VERT, 0, l->GetSize());
        SetScrollPos(SB_VERT, 0);
        SetScrollRange(SB_HORZ, 0, pDoc->GetMaxLineLength());
        SetScrollPos(SB_HORZ, 0);
        CDC *pDC = GetDC();
        ourFont = new CFont();
        ourFont->CreateFont(0, 0, 0, 0, FW_NORMAL, FALSE, FALSE, FALSE,
        ANSI_CHARSET, OUT_TT_PRECIS, CLIP_TT_ALWAYS,
        DEFAULT_QUALITY, DEFAULT_PITCH, "Courier New");
        CFont *oldFont = pDC->SelectObject(ourFont);
        TEXTMETRIC tm;
        pDC->GetTextMetrics(&tm);
        lHeight = tm.tmHeight + tm.tmExternalLeading;
        cWidth = tm.tmAveCharWidth;
        CView::OnInitialUpdate();
}
```

The program calls `OnInitialUpdate()` after MFC attaches the document to the view, but before the program actually displays the view. `CView`'s version of `OnInitialUpdate()` eventually causes the program to call `OnDraw()` so that the view can paint itself. However, before this happens, you must set up some things for the view.

First, you set the values for the scroll bar ranges and positions. The vertical scroll bar should range from 0 to the number of lines read from the file. Likewise, the horizontal scroll bar should range from 0 to the length of the longest line. You also explicitly set the scroll bars to the beginning of the range. By setting the range and position of the scroll bars, you ensure that they automatically appear when the program displays the view.

Next, you create the font for drawing in the view. You need this font now because you must use it to determine the characters' height and width. Also, if you create the font now, you don't have to create it every time that the program calls `OnDraw()`. Using `GetDC()`, you get a device context for the view, create the font, and select the font for the DC. Then you can call `GetTextMetrics()` to obtain the height and width of a character in your font. Finally, you let `Cview`'s `OnInitialUpdate()` method do its work so that the program draws the view.

You have created an object (`ourFont`) on the heap here, so you must ensure that you delete it when you destroy the view. Therefore, you must change the view's destructor:

```
CFileViewView::~CFileViewView()
{
delete ourFont;
}
```

Now you must change `OnDraw()`, because it no longer needs to create a font, and also because the method needs to take into account whether the horizontal scroll bar was used. Listing 6.7 is the new version of `OnDraw()`.

Listing 6.7   FileVVw.cpp, after Modification

```
void CFileViewView::OnDraw(CDC* pDC)
{
CFileViewDoc* pDoc = GetDocument();
ASSERT_VALID(pDoc);
CFont *oldFont;
CRect clientRect;
oldFont = pDC->SelectObject(ourFont);
CPtrArray *l = pDoc->GetLines();
int y = 0;
GetClientRect(&clientRect);
for (int i = currentLine; i < l->GetSize(); i++)
{
CString *line = (CString *) l->GetAt(i);
if (line->GetLength() - 2 > margin)
pDC->TextOut(0, y, line->Mid(margin),
line->GetLength() - margin - 2);
y += lHeight;
```

(continues)

Using MFC

II

Listing 6.7 Continued

```
    if (y > clientRect.Height())
    break;
    }
    pDC->SelectObject(oldFont);
}
```

`OnDraw()` doesn't change much. It no longer creates the font (because `OnInitialUpdate()` now handles that task). It also takes into account the value of `margin` when drawing text. When drawing a line of text, the method considers the length of the string that it needs to draw. If `margin` is greater than the string's length, you have scrolled past the end of the line, so `OnDraw()` doesn't have to draw anything. If you want to draw text, the `CString::Mid()` method retrieves the portion of the `CString` that you want to draw. `Mid()` is much like the `MID$` function in Microsoft BASIC. In this case, the function returns a `CString` that contains the characters from the value of `margin` to the end of the string (`line[margin]`).

The line height that you calculate also increments to the next line. After you draw enough text to fill the view, you break out of the loop. To do so, you must know how tall the view is. `GetClientRect()` fills a `CRect` with the client window coordinates. The `Height()` method returns the view's height in pixels.

Finally, you need the view class to handle messages sent to you while the user is using the scroll bars. Again, you can have the ClassWizard notify you when the user clicks a scroll bar. Bring up the MFC ClassWizard dialog box and select the `CFileViewView` class in the Class Name drop-down list box. From the Object IDs list box, select `CFileViewView` (as you did previously). Now scroll down the Messages list box until you reach `WM_VSCROLL`, and then click the Add Function button, followed by the Edit Code button. The AppWizard then creates a new message handler called `OnVScroll()` and places you in the editor. Listing 6.8 shows the `OnVScroll()` message handler.

Listing 6.8 FileVVw.cpp, `OnVScroll()` with Code to Handle Scroll Messages

```
    void CFileViewView::OnVScroll(UINT nSBCode, UINT nPos,
    CScrollBar* pScrollBar)
    {
        CFileViewDoc *pDoc = GetDocument();
        CPtrArray *l = pDoc->GetLines();
        switch (nSBCode)
        {
            case SB_LINEUP:
                    if (currentLine > 0)
                        currentLine-;
                    break;
            case SB_LINEDOWN:
                    if (currentLine < l->GetSize())
                        currentLine++;
                    break;
            case SB_BOTTOM:
                    currentLine = l->GetSize();
                    break;
```

```
            case SB_TOP:
                    currentLine = 0;
                    break;
            case SB_PAGEUP:
                    {
                            CRect clientRect;
                            GetClientRect(&clientRect);
                            currentLine -= (clientRect.Height() / lHeight);
                            if (currentLine < 0)
                                    currentLine = 0;
                    }
                    break;
            case SB_PAGEDOWN:
                    {
                            CRect clientRect;
                            GetClientRect(&clientRect);
                            currentLine += (clientRect.Height() / lHeight);
                            if (currentLine > l->GetSize())
                                    currentLine = l->GetSize();
                    }
                    break;
            case SB_THUMBPOSITION:
            case SB_THUMBTRACK:
                    currentLine - nPos;
                    if (currentLine < 0)
                        currentLine = 0;
                    if (currentLine > l->GetSize())
                        currentLine = l->GetSize();
                    break;
    }
    SetScrollPos(SB_VERT, currentLine);
    Invalidate(TRUE);
    CView::OnVScroll(nSBCode, nPos, pScrollBar);
}
```

When the user clicks the vertical scroll bar, OnVScroll() is invoked and is passed three
parameters. The first parameter, nSBCode, tells which part of the scroll bar the user
clicked. The parameter can have one of the seven values listed in table 6.1.

Table 6.1   The Values of the nSBCode Parameter

Value	Meaning
SB_BOTTOM	The user moved the thumb of the scroll bar all the way to the bottom.
SB_LINEDOWN	The user clicked the down-arrow and wants to scroll down one line.
SB_LINEUP	The user clicked the up-arrow and wants to scroll up one line.
SB_PAGEDOWN	The user clicked the area between the thumb and the bottom of the scroll bar, indicating the desire to move down one page or one full screen.
SB_PAGEUP	The user clicked the area between the thumb and the top of the scroll bar, indicating the desire to move up one page or one full screen.

II

Using MFC

(continues)

Table 6.1 Continued	
Value	**Meaning**
SB_TOP	The user moved the thumb of the scroll bar all the way to the top of the scroll bar.
SB_THUMBPOSITION	The user grabbed the thumb with the mouse and dragged it to a new position.
SB_THUMBTRACK	The user is dragging the thumb, which calls OnVScroll().
SB_TOP	The user moved the thumb of the scroll bar all the way to the top of the scroll bar.

The second parameter, nPos, is valid only if nSBCode has a value of SB_THUMBPOSITION or SB_THUMBTRACK. The parameter contains the current position of the thumb within the scroll bar.

The last parameter, pScrollBar, is a pointer to a scroll bar control. The message handler uses this parameter only if the call to OnVScroll() was caused by a scroll bar that is a child control and not attached to a window. The FileView program doesn't have any scroll bars as child controls, so this parameter is always NULL.

If you get SB_LINEUP, SB_LINEDOWN, SB_TOP, or SB_BOTTOM, you simply adjust currentLine to a new value. If the value is SB_LINEUP or SB_LINEDOWN, you increment or decrement currentLine as needed. If the value is SB_TOP and SB_BOTTOM, you must set currentLine either to 0 (the first line) or l->GetSize() (the last line in the CPtrArray).

SB_THUMBPOSITION and SB_THUMBTRACK both invoke the same code, which simply sets currentLine to the value passed in nPos. When you initialized the scroll bar in OnInitialUpdate(), you set your scroll bar's range to be from 0 to l->GetSize(). Because you did so, the text in your window scrolls automatically as the user drags the thumb.

SB_PAGEUP and SB_PAGEDOWN require a bit more work. If the user wants to scroll a page at a time, you must figure out how big a page is. For FileView, a page is one full screen of text. Because you know how tall each line is (lHeight), you can divide the height of the client area by the height of one line to determine how many lines to scroll. You then adjust currentLine by that value.

In each case, you make sure that currentLine never goes below 0 or above the size of the CPtrArray. When the switch() statement finishes, you must reset the scroll bar's position so that it matches the value of currentLine. Finally, you invalidate the view (so that it will repaint) and call the base class to let it maintain itself. You then are done.

Now invoke the MFC ClassWizard dialog box and add the message handler for the WM_HSCROLL message. Listing 6.9 is the code for the OnHScroll() method.

Listing 6.9   FileVVw.cpp, the `OnHScroll()` Method

```
void CFileViewView::OnHScroll(UINT nSBCode, UINT nPos,
CScrollBar* pScrollBar)
{
    // TODO: Add your message handler code here and/or call default
    CFileViewDoc *pDoc = GetDocument();
    CPtrArray *l = pDoc->GetLines();
    switch (nSBCode)
    {
        case SB_LINELEFT:
            if (margin > 0)
                margin--;
            break;
        case SB_LINERIGHT:
            if (margin < pDoc->GetMaxLineLength())
                margin++;
            break;
        case SB_RIGHT:
            margin = pDoc->GetMaxLineLength();
            break;
        case SB_LEFT:
            margin = 0;
            break;
        case SB_PAGELEFT:
            {
                CRect clientRect;
                GetClientRect(&clientRect);
                margin -= (clientRect.Width() / cWidth);
                if (margin < 0)
                    margin = 0;
            }
            break;
        case SB_PAGERIGHT:
            {
                CRect clientRect;
                GetClientRect(&clientRect);
                margin += (clientRect.Width() / cWidth);
                if (margin > pDoc->GetMaxLineLength())
                    margin = pDoc->GetMaxLineLength();
            }
            break;
        case SB_THUMBPOSITION:
        case SB_THUMBTRACK:
            margin = nPos;
            if (margin < 0)
                margin = 0;
            if (margin > pDoc->GetMaxLineLength())
                margin = pDoc->GetMaxLineLength();
            break;
    }
    SetScrollPos(SB_HORZ, margin);
    Invalidate(TRUE);
    CView::OnHScroll(nSBCode, nPos, pScrollBar);
}
```

`OnHScroll()` is almost exactly like `OnVScroll()`, except that the code passed in `nSBCode` has different values, and you are adjusting `margin` rather than `currentLine`. When scrolling left or right by a full screen, you determine how much to scroll by dividing the width of your window's client area by the width of a character in your font (`cWidth`).

If you compile and execute FileView, you now have horizontal and vertical scroll bars with which you can view the whole file. Next you can move on to printing and print preview.

Improving Print Preview

The last major feature that you add to FileView is printing and print preview. The AppWizard generated code for printing and print preview (you might have noticed this code while building FileView), but the code isn't quite right. Currently, if you select Print Preview while viewing a text file, you notice that the text seems to run together. Also, FileView shows only one page of a file, no matter how long the file happens to be. Finally, the printed page has no identifiers (such as the name of the file that you are printing). In this section, you fix all these problems. Figure 6.4 shows what print preview currently looks like.

Fig. 6.4

FileView's print preview, which isn't quite right yet

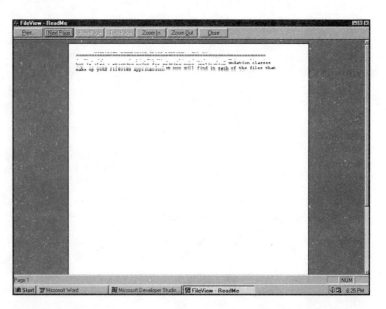

Like most MFC programming, printing (and print preview) with MFC is a cooperative process. The framework provides the basic, necessary functionality, but it can only go so far. You have to tell it exactly what you want it to do.

Consider the OnDraw() method for a moment. When OnDraw() executes, it receives a pointer to an instance of the CDC class. When you are working with a view inside of a window, this CDC represents a device context for the window in which you are supposed to draw. However, when you choose File, Print, this CDC no longer applies to the window, but to the printer. If you choose File, Print Preview, the CDC is the preview window's device context.

Although the Windows GDI is device-independent, when you draw in a window, you have to be aware of some details that are not normally issues. You can think of a window as having no boundaries (that is, you can draw outside the window without causing harm), but you cannot do so with a printed page. You must deal with your document in a format suitable for a piece of paper. For FileView, you break the lines of the file into pages so that you produce only one page at a time. You cannot simply dump out line after line and expect the printer to handle each correctly.

Consider what you need to do to make FileView print the way that you want. In Chapter 5, "Introducing MFC," you learned that the AppWizard generates several empty methods to handle printing. The first method, OnPreparePrinting(), is called when the user chooses File, Print or File, Print Preview:

```
BOOL CFileViewView::OnPreparePrinting(CPrintInfo* pInfo)
{
// default preparation
return DoPreparePrinting(pInfo);
}
```

OnPreparePrinting()'s job is to set up print job information. pInfo is a pointer to a CPrintInfo structure, which contains information about the print job. OnPreparePrinting() provides your first chance to customize the print job. However, you cannot do anything that requires a printer device context because no printer device context exists yet. The default code calls DoPreparePrinting(), which displays the Printer Selection common dialog box (if the user chose Print rather than Print Preview). The CPrintInfo structure includes methods that set such things as the minimum and maximum pages to print. The structure also contains a pointer to the Printer Selection common dialog box (a CPrintDialog object). Usually, you use OnPreparePrinting() to determine whether printing should occur. If OnPreparePrinting() returns FALSE, the print request is canceled. FileView doesn't need to change the default behavior, so you need not change this method.

The next method, OnBeginPrinting(), is called after OnPreparePrinting() but before any printing actually occurs. OnBeginPrinting() lets you examine the user's selections from the Printer Selection dialog box. Because the program calls OnBeginPrinting() after the user selects a printer, the method receives the printer's device context. This gives you a chance to use the printer CDC if you want to use it before printing actually begins. Listing 6.10 is FileView's version of this method.

Listing 6.10 FileVVw.cpp's `OnBeginPrinting()` Method, Which Initializes Variables before Printing Actually Starts

```
void CFileViewView::OnBeginPrinting(CDC* pDC, CPrintInfo* pInfo)
{
        // TODO: add extra initialization before printing
        CFont *oldFont = pDC->SelectObject(ourFont);
        saveLHeight = lHeight;
        saveCWidth = cWidth;
        TEXTMETRIC tm;
        pDC->GetTextMetrics(&tm);
        lHeight = tm.tmHeight + tm.tmExternalLeading;
        cWidth = tm.tmAveCharWidth;
        saveCurrentLine = currentLine;
        currentLine = 0;
        pDC->SelectObject(oldFont);
}
```

FileView's Print Preview screen looks so strange because `OnDraw()` is using the character heights of your font based on the height of the character when it was selected for a `CDC` for the screen, not for the printer. In this case, the character height on the screen is about 16 pixels. However, on the printer, the same font is about 50 pixels high. Therefore, `OnDraw()` is adding 16 to each line's y-coordinate when it actually should be adding 50. You fix this problem by saving the height and width of a character that you calculated when `OnInitialUpdate()` initialized the screen view and then getting the correct width and height from the printer (or print preview) `CDC`. Remember, when the user chooses File, Print, the program does *not* create a new view, only a new device context (this is also true for File, Print Preview).

Because `OnBeginPrinting()` received a `CDC` for the printer, you simply save the old width and height, select the font for the printer `CDC`, and use `GetTextMetrics()` to get the values again. You also save the value of `currentLine`, because you must manipulate this value when printing pages. The reason for manipulating `currentLine` is that you are printing the whole document, not just one screen. Currently, `OnDraw()` assumes that you are going to show only a portion of a file, not all of the file's contents.

Because you are saving these values, you need a place to store them. The most convenient place is the view class:

```
class CFileViewView : public CView
{
protected: // create from serialization only
     CFileViewView();
     DECLARE_DYNCREATE(CFileViewView)
     int currentLine;
     int margin;
     CFont *ourFont;
     int lHeight;
     int cWidth;
     int saveLHeight, saveCWidth;
     int saveCurrentLine;
     CRect printerRect;
```

You save your old character height and width in saveLHeight and saveCWidth, respectively. saveCurrentLine holds currentLine's old value. printerRect holds the rectangle that contains the coordinates of the printable area on a page of printer paper. Printers can't always print from edge to edge, so MFC supplies a CRect that contains the printable areas. OnDraw() uses this CRect to determine how much room it has for drawing.

The next method, OnEndPrinting(), is the inverse of OnBeginPrinting(). OnEndPrinting() is called after the print job finishes. Typically, you use this method to delete any data that you created in OnBeginPrinting(). FileView's version of OnEndPrinting() simply restores the values that were saved in OnBeginPrinting():

```
void CFileViewView::OnEndPrinting(CDC* /*pDC*/, CPrintInfo* /*pInfo*/)
{
    // TODO: add cleanup after printing
    lHeight = saveLHeight;
    cWidth = saveCWidth;
    currentLine = saveCurrentLine;
}
```

Therefore, when the user chooses File, Print, MFC calls OnPreparePrinting(), which calls DoPreparePrinting(). DoPreparePrinting() displays the Printer Selection dialog box. Unless the user then chooses the Cancel button, DoPreparePrinting() returns TRUE to OnPreparePrinting(). If the user doesn't click the Cancel button, OnPreparePrinting() returns TRUE also, which tells MFC that the print job can start.

MFC then sets up the print job and calls OnBeginPrinting(). You take the pointer to the CDC for the printer that you have received, select your font for the CDC, and determine how tall and wide each character is on the printer. You also make sure to save the old values (so that you can restore them in OnEndPrinting()) and then return.

Now MFC goes into a loop, generating print requests for each page of information. MFC doesn't know what a "page" is; it simply calls a method called OnPrint() for each page to be printed. However, you have overridden this method. Unless the user (or you) instructs MFC differently, it continues to send requests to print pages until the document has no more pages to print. You can tell MFC how many pages are in your document by using the SetMinPage() and SetMaxPage() members of the CPrintInfo structure. If you don't set these fields, MFC generates page requests until you tell it that the document has no more pages to print.

OnPrint() is not generated automatically, so you must add it by using the Class-Wizard. Like all the other methods that you have added with the ClassWizard, OnPrint() is a member of the CFileViewView class. In the MFC ClassWizard dialog box, you simply select OnPrint from the Messages list box and then click the Edit Code button. Listing 6.11 is your version of OnPrint().

II

Using MFC

Listing 6.11   FileVVw.cpp's `OnPrint()` Method, Which Actually Starts the Printing and Draws the Page Footer

```
void CFileViewView::OnPrint(CDC* pDC, CPrintInfo* pInfo)
{
    // TODO: Add your specialized code here and/or call the base class
    pInfo->m_rectDraw.InflateRect(0, -lHeight);
    printerRect = pInfo->m_rectDraw;
    int linesPerPage = (printerRect.Height() / lHeight)      - 1;
    currentLine = linesPerPage * (pInfo->m_nCurPage - 1);
    TRACE2("Printing page %d, starting with line %d\n", pInfo->m_nCur
    _ Page, currentLine);
    CView::OnPrint(pDC, pInfo);
    CString footer;
    CFont *oldFont;
    footer.Format("*** File %s ***", GetDocument()->GetPathName());
    oldFont = pDC->SelectObject(ourFont);
    pDC->TextOut(0, pInfo->m_rectDraw.Height() + lHeight, footer);
    pDC->SelectObject(oldFont);
}
```

The version of `OnPrint()` that the ClassWizard generates simply issues a call to `CView::OnPrint()`, which then calls `OnDraw()`. `OnPrint()` is the perfect place to add header or footer output, because the program calls the method just before printing a page. However, you must prepare your version of `OnPrint()` to do a little setting up before it lets the program do any printing.

First, because you are going to add a footer to the printed page, you adjust the rectangle that defines a printed page. To do so, you use `InflateRect()` to make the page one line smaller. This way, `OnDraw()` doesn't draw on the whole page and instead leaves alone an area that is one line high. You then calculate how many lines you can fit on a printed page.

You then must specify the line at which you want to start printing. For every page that FileView is to print, the program calls `OnPrint()` once. Therefore, the method is called first to print page 1, then to print page 2, and so on, until MFC is told to stop. `pInfo` contains a member variable that holds the number of the page that MFC wants to print. Using this variable, you set `currentLine` to the proper value, so that `OnDraw()` starts at the desired line. You must subtract 1 from the page number, because you want to set `currentLine` to point to the line that you want to appear at the top of the printed page. You also use a `TRACE()` macro to output some useful debugging information.

Now that you have adjusted the rectangle that holds the size of a printed page (and saved that value for `OnDraw()`), you can call `CView::OnPrint()` and let it call `OnDraw()`. `OnDraw()` prints a page of information. However, for this method to work, you must modify it a bit. You'll see how to modify it in a moment.

After you print a page, you construct a CString that contains your footer. Select your printer font for the printer CDC and use TextOut() to draw the footer at the bottom of the page. You made the printer area one line smaller, so you use the Height() method to determine where the bottom of the page is and then write your string there. You then set the printer CDC back to the way that it was originally.

As was mentioned earlier, you have to tell MFC when you are done printing. You haven't done this so far, so where do you do it? MFC calls another method in your code (if you have provided it) every time that it must set up the printer CDC for a printed page. You can use the OnPrepareDC() method to determine whether there is any more to print. Again, you use the ClassWizard to add a handler for the OnPrepareDC() message. Listing 6.12 is your version of this method.

Listing 6.12 FileVVw.cpp's `OnPrepareDC()` Method, Which Determines Whether Printing Should Continue

```
void CFileViewView::OnPrepareDC(CDC* pDC, CPrintInfo* pInfo)
{
    CView::OnPrepareDC(pDC, pInfo);
    if (pInfo != NULL)
    {
        if (currentLine < GetDocument()->GetLines()->GetSize())
        {
            TRACE1("currentLine = %d, continuing printing\n",
                currentLine);
            pInfo->m_bContinuePrinting = TRUE;
        }
        else
        {
            TRACE1("currentLine = %d, terminating printing\n",
                currentLine);
            pInfo->m_bContinuePrinting = FALSE;
        }
    }
}
```

OnPrepareDC() is actually called for both screen and printer CDCs. You are interested in doing something only if a print job is running. If OnPrepareDC() is called for a screen CDC, pInfo is NULL. By checking pInfo, you can determine whether the program is printing.

First, you call CView's version of OnPrepareDC(). Why do you call this method first, and not after you are done? MFC always assumes that documents are one page long. If you want the framework to assume something else, you have to specify it explicitly. (This is why FileView displayed only one page before you started modifying the program.) CView::OnPrepareDC() *always* sets the print job to terminate if the current page number is greater than 1, so you must override that behavior. The CPrintInfo structure contains another member variable, m_bContinuePrinting (a BOOL), that MFC examines to determine whether to continue the print job. By checking the value of currentLine, you can determine whether the last page caused currentLine to go beyond the end of the document. If so, you can set m_bContinuePrinting accordingly. GetDocument()->GetLines()->GetSize() is just another way to get the size of your CPtrArray without creating an explicit variable on the stack.

You now have only one more method to change, and that method, OnDraw(), requires only one change. Listing 6.13 is the new version of OnDraw().

Listing 6.13   FileVVw.cpp's OnDraw() Method, Modified To Handle Drawing to the Screen and Printer

```
void CFileViewView::OnDraw(CDC* pDC)
{
       CFileViewDoc* pDoc = GetDocument();
       ASSERT_VALID(pDoc);
       CFont *oldFont;CRect clientRect;
       oldFont = pDC->SelectObject(ourFont);
       CPtrArray *l = pDoc->GetLines();
       int y = 0;
       if (pDC->IsPrinting())
            clientRect = printerRect;
       else
            GetClientRect(&clientRect);
       for (int i = currentLine; i < l->GetSize(); i++)
       {
            CString *line = (CString *) l->GetAt(i);
            if (line->GetLength() - 2 > margin)
                 pDC->TextOut(0, y, line->Mid(margin),
            line->GetLength() - margin - 2);
            y += lHeight;
            if (y > clientRect.Height())
                 break;
       }
       pDC->SelectObject(oldFont);
}
```

The only change that you make to OnDraw() is to have it look at a different "client area" while printing is occurring. Remember, you saved a copy of the CRect corresponding to the printer page when you set up the print job. The IsPrinting() method of the CDC class tells you whether OnDraw() is being asked to print. If you are printing, you set clientRect to the printer page rectangle. Because you have already set up lHeight for the printer, and adjusted currentLine to point to the first line that you want to print on a page, OnDraw() dutifully draws the text on the printer CDC. Figure 6.5 shows the current version of FileView previewing a document.

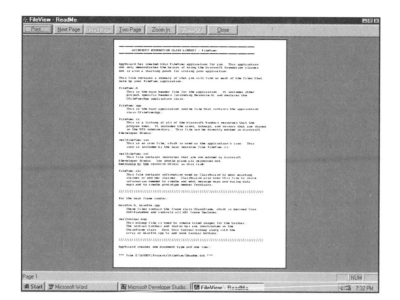

Fig. 6.5

FileView previewing a document (correctly).

From Here...

Basically, you are now finished developing FileView. You should make a few other modifications (such as making FileView's help file match the application) that are beyond the scope of this chapter. However, the .rtf source for the help files is on this book's companion CD.

You can improve FileView in many ways. However, to keep things simple, and to maintain the focus of simply getting you started using MFC, this chapter has not discussed these modifications. Here are some suggestions for enhancements that you can try to implement:

- FileView should not load the whole file into memory. Instead, it should load only a portion of a file and read only the pieces that it needs. The program could then load files more quickly and work with more files simultaneously.

- The program should print only portions of a file.

- You should enable the user to select the font in which FileView displays files.

- FileView should be capable of working with fonts that do not have a fixed pitch.

- Programmers would benefit if they could display a file's contents as a hexadecimal dump. This enhancement also would enable FileView to load nontext files as well as text files.

II

Using MFC

After making it through this chapter, you might want to see what else MFC has to offer. This chapter covered only a few of the many classes that MFC offers.

The following are chapters with related information:

- Chapter 13, "Exception Handling," explains catching and throwing exceptions in more detail.
- Chapter 15, "Memory-Management Techniques," helps you learn more about managing memory with Visual C++.

Part III

Object Linking and Embedding

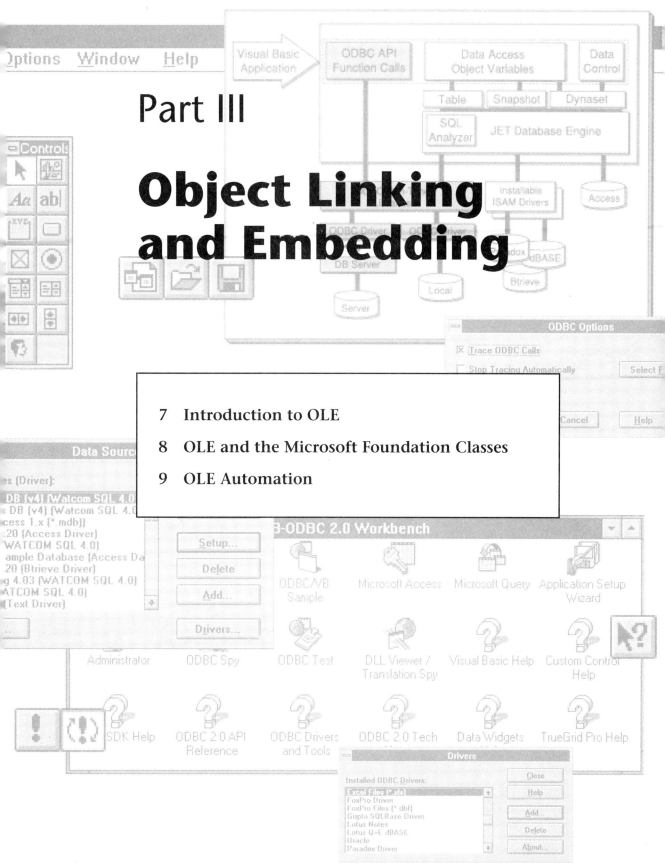

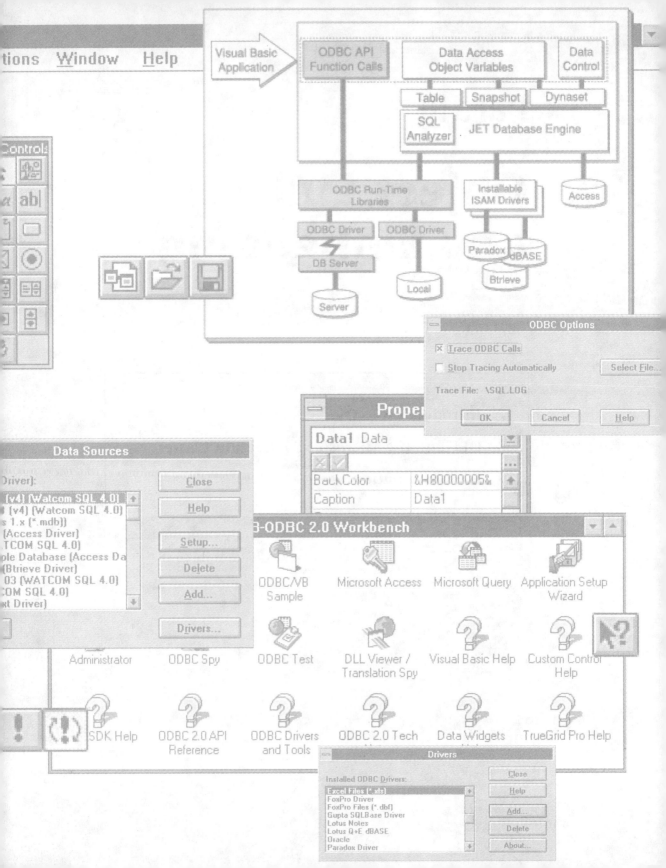

Window **Help**

Visual Basic Application

ODBC API Function Calls

Data Access Object Variables

Data Control

Table   Snapshot   Dynaset

SQL Analyzer   JET Database Engine

ODBC Run-Time Libraries

Installable ISAM Drivers

Access

ODBC Driver   ODBC Driver

Paradox   dBASE

DB Server

Btrieve

Server

Local

Control

ODBC Options

X Trace ODBC Calls

☐ Stop Tracing Automatically   Select File...

Trace File: \SQL.LOG

OK   Cancel   Help

Proper

Data1 Data

BackColor   &H80000005&
Caption   Data1

Data Sources

Driver):

[v4] [Watcom SQL 4.0]
[v4] [Watcom SQL 4.0]
s 1.x (*.mdb)]
(Access Driver)
TCOM SQL 4.0)
ple Database [Access Da
[Btrieve Driver)
03 (WATCOM SQL 4.0)
COM SQL 4.0)
xt Driver)

Close

Help

Setup...

Delete

Add...

Drivers...

B-ODBC 2.0 Workbench

ODBC/VB Sample   Microsoft Access   Microsoft Query   Application Setup Wizard

Administrator   ODBC Spy   ODBC Test   DLL Viewer / Translation Spy   Visual Basic Help   Custom Control Help

SDK Help   ODBC 2.0 API Reference   ODBC Drivers and Tools   ODBC 2.0 Tech   Data Widgets   TrueGrid Pro Help

Drivers

Installed ODBC Drivers:

Excel Files (*.xls)
FoxPro Driver
FoxPro Files (*.dbf)
Gupta SQLBase Driver
Lotus Notes
Lotus Q+E dBASE
Oracle
Paradox Driver

Close

Help

Add...

Delete

About...

CHAPTER 7

Introduction to OLE

This chapter introduces you to Object Linking and Embedding (OLE) version 2. You learn what OLE is, what benefits it provides to you as a developer, and what benefits it provides to your users. You then take a look at the OLE tools that come with Visual C++ and examine some fundamental terms and data types that you should know about when working with OLE.

The following topics are covered in this chapter:

- What OLE 2 is, and the features and technologies with which it empowers you
- The advantages and disadvantages of OLE 2 for users and developers
- What the Component Object Model is, how structured storage and compound files relate, what type of drag-and-drop operation OLE supports, what Uniform Data Transfer (UDT) is, what linking and embedding are, how in-place activation is related to embedding, and what OLE Automation is
- The OLE development and testing tools provided with Visual C++ 4
- Some of the ways that you can use OLE in your own applications

What Is OLE 2?

Try to remember when Microsoft introduced Windows 3.0. One result of this release was a change in the way that people work with computers. Specifically, users began to view the PC environment as being graphics-oriented rather than text-oriented. In a similar way, OLE 2 will change the way that people work with PC software. Windows 3.0 not only changed the way that people look at computers, it changed the standard hardware definition for computers and the big players in the software market. OLE 2 will affect the computer world as profoundly as Windows 3.0 has. The following sections discuss some of the ways that OLE 2 will cause this change in computing.

> **Note**
>
> Throughout this book, you will see references to Object Linking and Embedding, OLE, and OLE 2. Each of these terms refers to the same thing. You see the older version number (1.0) specified only when this book is referring to that particular version of OLE. Otherwise, the use of the number 2 emphasizes that you are working with the newest version of the technology.

Document-Centered Computing

OLE's focus is to enable the user to work in a computing environment that is document-centered rather than application-centered. A *document-centered* environment frees the user from having to start a specific application before working with data related to that application.

For example, the user no longer has to start a word processor before working with textual information or start a spreadsheet before working with numbers (see fig. 7.1). Instead, the user can work in almost any program and access information that belongs to any number of applications. An application's support of OLE makes this appearance of interapplication linking and embedding possible. One of the frequent uses for OLE is to embed an Excel chart into a Word for Windows document.

Fig. 7.1

OLE enables you to embed documents from one application into another application, such as this Excel chart embedded in a Word for Windows document.

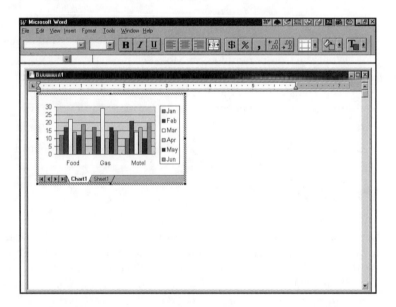

Today, Microsoft's top applications support OLE technology. Users no longer have to think of projects—such as reports, documents, spreadsheets, database listings, and e-mail—as separate tasks. Instead, the user can create an executive summary simply by using a drag-and-drop operation to put these elements together in a single document.

Component Software

Microsoft refers to this new concept of document-centered computing as *component software*. As its name suggests, the component software concept is based on the notion of a *component,* which is a reusable piece of software that you can easily "plug in to" other components from different vendors.

An example of such a component is a spell checker that you can plug in to multiple word-processing applications not sold by the spell checker's vendor. According to laboratory tests of a powerful West Coast software company (Microsoft), the ability to tie applications together into a closely knit unit results in a much more powerful computer system for the user.

Windows actually already has certain elements of interapplication communication. These elements include the Windows Clipboard, Dynamic Data Exchange (DDE), OLE 1.0, and dynamic link libraries (DLLs). However, as you will see, OLE 2 redefines the way that application programs communicate. In fact, interapplication communication takes on a new meaning as you learn about the features of OLE 2.

Why Is OLE Important?

OLE is important because Microsoft has made it an integral part of Windows, and Windows 95 and Windows NT use OLE functionality heavily. In fact, OLE is the technology behind Microsoft's own best-selling Office suite of applications (which consists of the Word for Windows word processor, the Excel spreadsheet program, the PowerPoint presentation graphics program, and the Access database program). According to distributors, Office is the hottest-selling application suite available today.

One of the reasons that Microsoft Office is such a hot seller is that Microsoft has designed the individual programs so that they can share data and operate together. By embracing OLE technology, you can get your applications to work together in just such a manner—not just among themselves, but also with other OLE applications.

The History of Object Linking and Embedding

OLE was originally designed by several PC vendors who were searching for ways to extend the Dynamic Data Exchange (DDE) protocol. A set of services built in to Windows, DDE enables applications to send and receive data among one another. The system is based on messages and relies on passing handles to globally allocated memory.

However, to integrate applications the way that they wanted, software engineers realized that they needed to provide a more robust set of interapplication specifications. In 1989, Microsoft and Aldus Corporation put together the first draft of the OLE specification. It was delivered to about 100 software developers at a software conference held by Microsoft.

During late 1989 and early 1990, several PC software vendors—including Lotus, WordPerfect, Aldus, Microsoft, Borland International, Metaphor, and Iris Incorporated—sent senior software developers to Redmond, Washington (headquarters of Microsoft), to provide additional input into the OLE specification and software.

III

OLE

At the November 1990 Comdex trade show, Microsoft announced a completed speci-fication, which was named Object Linking and Embedding version 1.0. The final OLE 1.0 specification was published in December 1990 and delivered to 230 software de-velopers. Lotus demonstrated a prerelease version of the Lotus Notes software that contained OLE capabilities.

The first applications to support the OLE 1.0 specification fully were Microsoft Excel 2.0 and Lotus Notes 2.0, which both shipped in February 1991. By the end of that year, many other vendors added OLE 1.0 capabilities to their applications.

Almost immediately, Microsoft began working on a more sophisticated set of OLE capabilities. These capabilities became the basis for the OLE 2 specification, which was developed during 1991 and 1992. Over 150 software development companies partici-pated in the OLE 2 beta test cycle, which had its own forum on CompuServe to facili-tate rapid response.

In May 1993, Microsoft held the first OLE 2 developers conference, at which over 1,200 developers were present. OLE 2 for Windows 3.1 was announced along with beta versions of OLE for the Apple Macintosh. The first products featuring OLE 2 were Microsoft Word for Windows and Excel, which were released in the summer of 1993.

The original OLE 2 specification has also been extended. In March of 1995, Microsoft, Intergraph, and a team of other computer-aided design (CAD) vendors introduced OLE for Design & Modeling (OLE4DM), a set of extensions to OLE 2 that made it more suitable for CAD and graphics applications. Regular OLE objects must be rectan-gular and cannot overlap, but OLE-DM includes support for transparent and translu-cent objects, as well as hooks for supporting three dimensional (3-D) objects. A full study of OLE-DM would require an entire book, but this book includes the specifica-tions for OLE4DM on the companion CD, in case you are interested.

User Advantages of OLE 2

The first advantage to your users is document-centered computing, which enables users to learn how to use applications more quickly and thus increases users' produc-tivity. Users no longer have to worry about working in different applications, because they now can accomplish their tasks from just about any single application.

Furthermore, using OLE 2 technology in your programs provides users with a greater range of software choices. As they discover the choices that component software makes available, users demand even more specialized components that they can plug in to multiple applications.

Most importantly, through specific OLE 2 features, such as Visual Editing, drag-and-drop support, and OLE Automation (this chapter discusses each of these features), applications become easier to use and more powerful. OLE 2 provides a more produc-tive way to work with applications and the operating environment.

Developer Advantages of OLE 2

Component software reduces the complexity of software development because developers can plug in prewritten software modules to accomplish specific tasks. As a result, component software should reduce software development costs and create opportunities for small software vendors to provide specialized software components.

OLE 2 is supported under Microsoft Windows 3.1, Windows 95, Windows NT 3.1 and later, and Apple Macintosh System 7, and it will continue to be integral to future versions of Microsoft operating systems. Because of this multiplatform support, software publishers can build applications that work the same way on different platforms. Users benefit because they can have the same functionality and a consistent linking and embedding model on three different operating systems.

If you develop custom libraries or DLLs that other programmers can use in their applications, these developers will appreciate how neatly packaged your OLE components are and how easily they can be integrated into their applications. As tools like Visual Basic enable more users to become developers, these benefits will become increasingly important.

For the developer, the greatest advantages of OLE 2 are the opportunities that it provides. Because OLE 2 changes the way that applications work, it provides a chance for smaller software developers to create new and compelling applications that users don't already have and are willing to purchase.

Disadvantages of OLE 2

You probably wouldn't take this chapter seriously if it continued to tell you that OLE 2 was the best thing since symbolic debuggers. Therefore, to give you the total picture, this section points out the disadvantages of OLE 2.

Although Microsoft might not admit it, anyone who wants either to use or program OLE 2 should own a fast machine. Specifying microprocessor types or memory requirements probably isn't useful, but keep the following golden rule in mind: the faster the better, and the more memory the merrier. Windows has created a demand for faster machines, which has resulted in lower prices for high-end hardware, and OLE 2 will continue these trends.

OLE 2 imposes a new disk storage mechanism that increases the storage requirements of your system. A simple one-sentence letter in Microsoft Word 6.0—with no special formatting— requires about 6K of disk space! This astonishing appetite for storage space will probably upset anyone working with limited disk space. Of course, this new storage requirement sounds ridiculous, but all new technologies require more resources. (Just wait until you find out about structured storage.)

Also, as powerful as OLE 2 is, you have to learn a lot of new concepts and facts before you can use it productively. The good news is that the Microsoft Foundation Classes (MFC) provide incredible support for OLE 2 and dramatically improve programmer productivity for creating applications that support OLE 2.

III

OLE

Finally, as is common with new technologies, not all applications support OLE 2. Microsoft used to be the only vendor that supported OLE 2 in its applications; however, the floodgates have opened, and many large and small software vendors (including Intergraph, Lotus, Borland, and Shapeware) have realized the benefits that OLE technology can offer their customers.

OLE Technologies Defined

Object Linking and Embedding version 2 is more than just a single piece of software. In fact, OLE 2 is a group of technologies. These technologies work together to provide a radical new type of Windows application. To the user, the most obvious use for OLE 2 is to link and embed documents among applications. However, in addition to providing this new view of computing for the user, OLE 2 provides many new services to the developer.

When you first took up Windows programming, you had to adopt a new mind set; likewise, OLE 2 requires that you learn several new programming ideas and concepts. If you think back hard enough, you might remember how difficult it was learning to work with hWnds, GDI objects, and message loops. Now, any seasoned Windows programmer uses them like a cook uses pots and pans.

Insiders at Microsoft call OLE 2 one-third of an operating system because OLE 2 alone has over 100 API functions—the entire original Windows version 1.0 had only about 350 functions. By the measure of the number of API functions, OLE 2 can be almost as confusing as Windows

The first key to learning OLE 2 is to realize that you don't have to learn to use every feature overnight. You first must understand a few fundamental concepts. Many of OLE 2's higher-level features build on lower-level features, so you must master the fundamentals before attempting to rewrite an application to support full Object Linking and Embedding capabilities.

The new technologies in OLE 2 include Windows objects, structured storage, compound files, UDT, drag-and-drop support, compound document technology, and OLE Automation. The following list describes each of the technologies:

■ Linking. When you *link* an object, you create a dynamic connection between the data in one application and the data in another application. For example, you can link a spreadsheet graph into a word processing document. Then, if graph data changes, the graph linked to the word processor changes to show the changes in the data.

■ Embedding. By *embedding* an object, you take linking to the next logical step— you actually store a copy of the graph in the word processor. Then, if you double-click an embedded graph, you launch a copy of the spreadsheet and can actually see the graph while working with the graph data in the spreadsheet. When you exit the spreadsheet application, the information is updated in the word processing document.

■ In-place activation, or Visual Editing. The hallmark of OLE 2 technology, *Visual Editing* enables users to activate and modify embedded objects in place directly, without switching to a different window. This activation includes operations such as editing, displaying, recording, and playing. Visual Editing is the technology that makes the entire notion of document-centered computing possible.

■ Component Object Model. This technology is partly a specification and partly an implementation. The *Component Object Model* defines a binary standard for object implementation that is independent of the programming language that you use. The OLE API functions enable you to instantiate a Windows object, which actually creates a standard object-creation technique for the system. The Component Object Model is the basis of OLE.

■ Structured storage. This specification describes how to create a file system within a file, by treating a single file as two types of objects, one resembling a disk subdirectory and the other a disk file. The specification is nearly identical to the hierarchical disk structure that DOS users have been accustomed to using since the release of DOS 2.0.

■ Compound files. This is a complete implementation of structured storage that you can use to replace traditional handle-based file functions. The implementation is independent of the rest of OLE 2. Visual C++ 4 includes DocFile Viewer, a tool that displays the structure of any compound file and enables you to view the file's hexadecimal data.

■ Drag-and-drop support. OLE 2's *drag-and-drop support* enables you to move data among applications simply by clicking and moving the mouse. This type of drag-and-drop support goes far beyond the simple drag-and-drop support that File Manager currently offers. With OLE 2's drag-and-drop support, you can write an application that accepts dropped data that previously you could transfer only only by using the Windows Clipboard.

■ UDT. This technology provides the functionality to represent all data transfers—Clipboard, drag-and-drop, DDE, and OLE—through a single piece of code called a *data object*. *UDT* is a powerful technology because it enables you to access data, no matter what the source, in a similar manner. In other words, you access data from the Clipboard the same way that you access data through DDE.

■ OLE Automation. This technology enables an object to expose a set of commands and functions that another piece of code can invoke. The intent is to enable the creation of system macro programming tools. *OLE Automation* provides a way to manipulate an application's objects from outside the application. Microsoft's Office applications, which feature a stripped-down version of Visual Basic as a macro language, use OLE Automation extensively to enable users to script them.

■ OLE custom controls. These are program modules that provide add-in support for language applications like Visual Basic, Visual C++, Borland C++, and dBASE for Windows. Chapters 11 and 12 cover OLE custom controls in detail.

III

OLE

As you can see, OLE is much more than simply the linking and embedding of objects. The following sections take a more in-depth look at each individual technology. At this point, you need at least a general understanding of each of these important concepts.

Windows Objects: The Component Object Model

The Windows Component Object Model defines a binary standard for object implementation that is independent of the programming language that you use. This standard enables two applications to communicate through object-oriented interfaces without either having to know anything about the other's implementation. An object that adheres to this standard is called a Windows object (see fig. 7.2).

Fig. 7.2

This diagram shows how the Component Object Model relates to the rest of OLE.

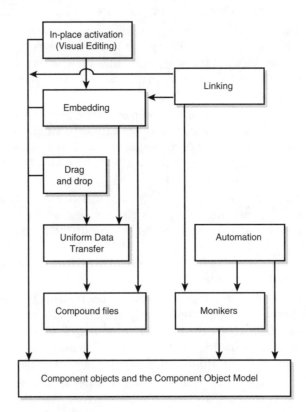

The Component Object Model is the key to OLE's extensible architecture, providing the foundation on which the rest of OLE is built. You can implement a Windows object in either a .DLL or an .EXE file.

Currently, you can choose to write Windows object modules either in C or C++. OLE is based on object-oriented programming concepts, which are inherent in C++. Although you can implement the same concepts with other languages, C++'s built-in support for objects makes the language easier to use for OLE development. Although you can implement OLE capability in almost any language, Microsoft prefers C++ because the language directly supports many of the concepts central to OLE.

Like C++, OLE supports the capability to inherit class functionality from a base class. Using a concept called *aggregation,* you can build a new object using one or more existing objects that support some or all of the new object's required interface. Thus, aggregation is the same concept as inheritance in C++.

Part of what makes OLE 2 so exciting is that it creates a binary model for object-oriented programming. C++ and SmallTalk are promoted as being object-oriented languages; however, you rarely hear about an object-oriented operating system (OOOS?). What C++ does for C is what OLE does for Windows.

MFC effectively insulates you from almost all the details of COM. Kraig Brockschmidt's excellent *Inside OLE* (Microsoft Press) is a comprehensive reference discussing every aspect of programming with COM.

Structured Storage

Structured storage provides a method for treating a single file-system entity as a structured collection of two types of objects: streams and storages. Both types of objects act like directories and files in a conventional tree-structured directory.

The OLE structured storage specification describes how data is saved and retrieved from disk storage. Using structured storage, multiple streams are stored in one underlying file, which results in a file that looks like a directory tree (see fig. 7.3, which shows what a structured storage file looks like in the DocFile Viewer utility). This concept contrasts sharply with the way that files currently are conceptualized—as one large continuous sequence of bytes on a disk that are manipulated through a single file handle and seek pointer.

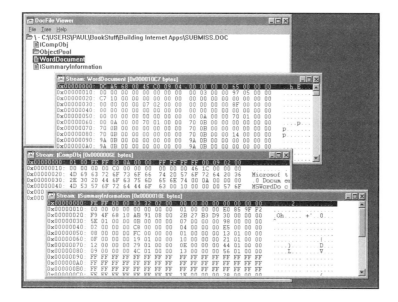

Fig. 7.3

The DocFile Viewer utility lets you view structured storage files and see both the data in them and how it's structured.

A *stream object* is the conceptual equivalent of a single disk file and is the basic building block of a file system. To name a stream object, you use a text string that can be as long as 31 characters. The stream's internal structure can have any structure you want; as far as OLE is concerned, the stream consists of arbitrary bytes. Your program no longer knows exactly where in the file to find the stream; however, by using API functions, you can gain access to the data in the stream.

A *storage object* is the conceptual equivalent of a subdirectory. Each storage object can contain any number of *storages* (subdirectories) and any number of *streams* (files). The number of storages that a file can contain is limited only by the amount of disk space available.

Structured storage is only a specification, so its use is optional. Furthermore, you can use structured storage independently of the other OLE 2 functions.

Compound Files

Compound files are a standardized implementation of structured storage that isolates your application from the exact placement of bytes within your files. If you adopt compound files for your storage system, the physical layout of your files on the disk is no longer under your direct control. However, you gain freedom from several nasty cross-platform issues. If you plan to write applications that run under Windows NT on non-Intel platforms, this freedom is a great blessing.

Compound storage is also important because it standardizes the layout of pieces of information within a file. Although the exact data format of each individual stream is still private, other programs can look into a compound file and enumerate the storages and streams that it contains.

By standardizing the names and contents of a few specific streams, the system shell and other applications can enable users to search within files for occurrences of data that match such attributes as the creation date, author, and keywords. Microsoft is currently defining standard names and structures for streams that contain information useful in queries. The long-range goal is to have all information on the file-system structure standardized in such a way that users can use the system shell to browse the contents of many streams.

With compound files, you can also provide features to make your applications more powerful. For example, you can easily provide features such as incremental saves that would be too difficult or time-consuming to add to a program without compound storage.

Drag-and-Drop Support

In testing laboratories, Microsoft found that the most widely used method of transferring data between applications is the Clipboard. However, to use the Clipboard, the user must choose Edit, Copy, move to the destination application, and choose Edit, Paste to place the data. These operations are repetitive, so Microsoft has found a more natural way to exchange data between applications: You simply click a data object, *drag* it to its destination, and *drop* it in place.

The OLE 2 drag-and-drop model supports three types of operations: interwindow dragging, interobject dragging, and dropping over icons. Figure 7.4 demonstrates drag-and-drop operations between two OLE applications.

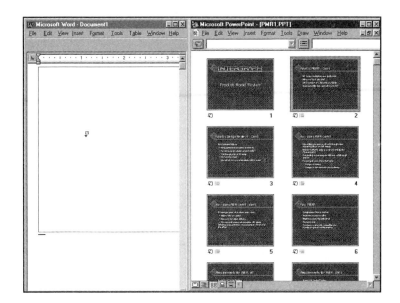

Fig. 7.4

Interapplication drag-and-drop operations enable users to move data between applications without using the Clipboard.

Interwindow dragging enables you to drag objects from one application window and drop them into another application window. For example, you can drag a graph from a spreadsheet window and drop it into a word processing document.

Interobject dragging enables objects nested within other objects to be dragged between not only windows but objects. In other words, you can drag an object to other windows and then drop it inside those windows.

Dropping over icons enables you to drag objects to a system resource on the Windows desktop, such as the printer, trash can, or mailbox icons. The appropriate action automatically occurs to the data object, depending on the icon on which you drop the object. This sort of drag-and-drop functionality far surpasses that which originally was available in Windows 3.1 and compares favorably to the drag-and-drop support provided by other platforms.

Uniform Data Transfer

Uniform Data Transfer (UDT), which is built on top of both the Component Object Model and compound files, provides a way for you to use a single piece of code to support all data transfers, including those performed through the Clipboard, drag-and-drop support, DDE, and OLE. This representation is done in an object-oriented fashion through a data object. This DataObject Viewer utility, shown in figure 7.5, displays the data that is available through the UDT mechanism.

III

OLE

Fig. 7.5

The IDataObject Viewer shows the data formats available for use with the Uniform Data Transfer mechanism.

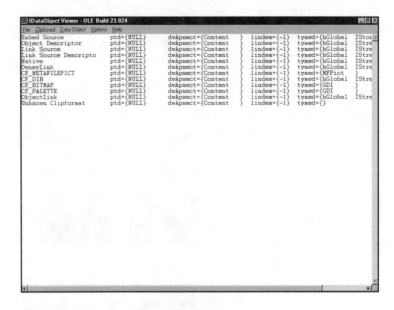

Using UDT in your applications gives you three great advantages:

- UDT data objects are not restricted to transferring data through global memory. Previously, all data transfers have used global memory to transfer information. In fact, UDT can also use compound files. This makes a lot of sense, because a large piece of data being transferred between applications often ends up being swapped out to disk anyway.

- With UDT, you can describe data using not only a Clipboard format, but also a specification about how much detail the data contains, the type of device (primarily printers) for which the data was rendered, and the sort of medium used to transfer the data. Instead of saying, "I have a bitmap," you can say "I have a bitmap rendered for 300 dots per inch on a LaserJet printer and stored as a data object." This capability enables you to choose the best possible representation of an object for use in your application when transferring data.

- OLE 2 separates the means of setting up a data exchange from the actual operation of exchanging data. Currently, each transfer protocol uses different functions and different data structures. Under OLE 2, however, applications use new API functions to transfer a pointer to a data object from the data source. These functions form the basis of the communication protocol. All exchange of data happens through the data object. Because the data object does not know anything about protocols, you can write one piece of code to perform an operation such as a Paste regardless of how you obtained the data object.

Linking

Linking is the first way to associate objects in a compound document with their object applications (fig. 7.6 shows an example). When you incorporate a Windows object into a document, that object maintains an association with the application that created it.

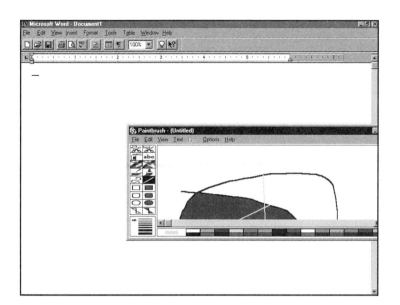

Fig. 7.6

A linked object, like this Paintbrush image linked into a Word document, is represented by a link in the target document.

When an object is linked, the source data continues to reside physically wherever it was initially created—either at another point within the document or in a different document altogether. Only a reference, or link, to the object and appropriate presentation data is kept with the compound document. Linked objects cannot move with documents to another machine; they must remain on the local file system or be explicitly copied.

One disadvantage of OLE 1.0 is that if you copy both a source object and a linked object to a new location, the source document no longer correctly points to the linked document. With OLE 2, linked objects that are moved or copied to the same destination maintain their links correctly. This new feature of OLE 2 is called *adaptable links*.

Object linking is efficient and keeps the size of documents small. A user can choose to link objects while another user is maintaining a source object, because a single instance of the object's data can serve many documents. Changes made to the source object are automatically reflected in any compound documents that have a link to the object. From the user's perspective, a linked object appears to be contained within a source document.

Embedding

Embedding is another way to associate a Windows object with your application. With an embedded object, a copy of the original object is physically stored in the compound document along with all the information needed to manage the object (see fig. 7.7). As a result, the object becomes a physical part of the document. A compound document containing embedded objects is larger than one that contains the same objects as links.

III

OLE

Fig. 7.7

Embedded objects are added to the contents of the target document instead of being referenced with a link.

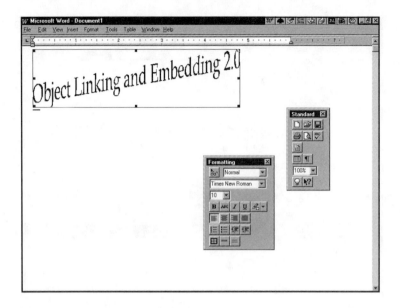

Embedding data offers several advantages that may outweigh the disadvantages of the extra storage overhead. For example, compound documents with embedded objects can be transferred to another computer and edited on that machine. A user of the document doesn't have to know where the original data resided because a copy of the object's source data travels with the compound document. Also, you can edit embedded objects in place—which brings this discussion to another capability of OLE 2: *in-place activation* or *Visual Editing*.

Visual Editing

With Visual Editing, the user can double-click an embedded object in a document and interact with the object at that exact location, without switching to a different window. Figure 7.8 shows an example.

The menus, toolbars, palettes, and other controls necessary to interact with the object temporarily replace the existing menus and controls of the active window. In other words, the application required to interact with the object takes control of the document window. When the focus returns to the main application, the original menus and controls are restored.

The advantage of Visual Editing is quickly apparent when you have documents that consist of many objects created by different applications. Instead of switching back and forth between different windows to update embedded objects, users can edit and interact within a single document window. The changes made to the objects are saved in the new document.

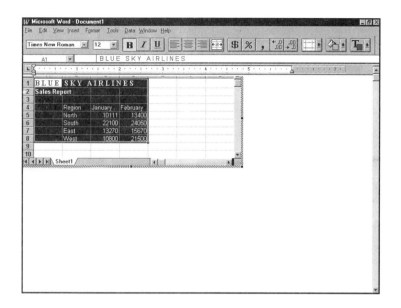

Fig. 7.8

You can activate embedded objects in place and edit them without leaving the container application.

OLE Automation

OLE Automation offers a powerful way to integrate applications through interapplication command operations. Applications can interact with one another without human intervention. OLE Automation uses OLE's Component Object Model, but you can implement Automation independently of other OLE features.

To use OLE Automation, the programmer must define a set of operations and expose them so that they're accessible to other applications. These operations can have argument lists and are similar to function calls in a regular programming language.

The possibilities of OLE Automation are enormous. Users can create macros and other command sets that work across applications. OLE Automation offers several advantages over macro languages:

- Users can bring the best pieces of different applications together to create completely new, specialized applications.
- Exposed objects are accessible from any macro language or programming tool that implements OLE Automation. Because the OLE Automation specification sets out a certain set of behavior, all macro languages that implement OLE Automation are fairly consistent. Users can choose tools based on their current knowledge and drive other tools with OLE Automation functions, instead of having to learn a new macro language for each application.
- Object names remain the same across application versions.
- OLE Automation provides built-in localization, because object names automatically conform to the user's national language (which is selected as a user preference in Windows).

Visual C++ 4 includes a tool, DispTest, that enables you to test OLE Automation objects (see fig. 7.9). You can also use Microsoft Visual Basic to work with the exposed objects in an OLE Automation application. For more information about DispTest, see Chapter 9, "OLE Automation."

Fig. 7.9

The DispTest utility provides OLE Automation testing features.

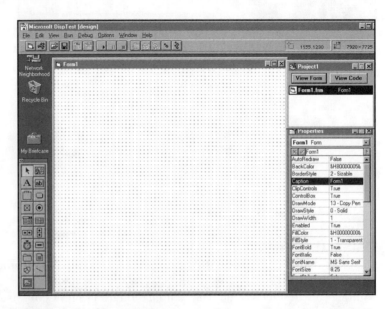

Note

DispTest is actually a scaled-down version of Microsoft Visual Basic 3.0. The only feature Visual Basic has that DispTest lacks (besides complete documentation) is the capability to create .EXE files.

OLE Custom Controls

An OLE custom control, or *OCX*, is a graphical software component that you can embed in an OLE 2 control container application.

Microsoft drew inspiration for the design of OLE custom controls from the VBX custom controls originally written as extensions to Visual Basic. The Visual Basic custom controls have become so popular that they created an entire market for developers writing software components for Visual Basic.

After VBX support was added to other languages like Visual C++, Borland Resource Workshop, and dBASE for Windows, Microsoft decided to create a new, more robust custom control specification based on an open standard. Visual C++ 4 provides several tools and components that make writing OLE custom controls easy. Chapters 10 and 11 cover OLE custom controls in more detail.

Uses for OLE 2 Technology

All this technology might sound great, but how can you use it in applications today, and why is it worth learning? This section explains some of the uses for OLE technology and how some of today's major categories of application software implement the technology.

Word Processors

Modern word processors are more than just text editors. Commercial-quality word processors are sophisticated document-generation tools that facilitate drawing, editing, layout, formatting, font manipulation, and a host of other capabilities.

Because they focus on documents, word processors are well suited to linking and embedding objects from other applications. Word processors benefit from OLE 2's drag-and-drop support because it simplifies moving graphics, text, and other objects around on a page. (Remember interobject dragging? The drag-and-drop operation does not have to be between applications.)

Word processors can also benefit from using OLE Automation in their macro languages to provide better integration between the word processor and other OLE Automated applications.

Spreadsheets

Spreadsheets are applications that work with numbers in rows and columns. Most modern spreadsheet applications also include graphing, database, and presentation graphics functions. Almost all the technologies found in OLE 2 can be used with spreadsheets.

For example, spreadsheet applications can use OLE 2's linking and embedding technology to offer ranges of cells as objects to be embedded in other applications. Such ranges map well to tables in a word processor. Users can also embed charts and text from a spreadsheet into another application.

Drag-and-drop operations are a natural for spreadsheets. You can move source text, charts, data, and virtually any portion of a spreadsheet within the spreadsheet as well as into other applications.

Databases

A database is an application for storing, retrieving, reporting on, and manipulating large amounts of data. Within database applications, the user can create tables of data, forms to view the data, and reports, and then program queries, macros, and code modules to manipulate the data.

A database can also benefit from most of the technologies that OLE 2 has to offer, although not as much as a word processor or spreadsheet can. For example, you can use OLE Automation to add capabilities for creating queries and accessing data with a macro language.

III

OLE

A database can also provide a way to link or embed data into another application. Mostly, you use OLE 2 inside a database to embed or link database information into other applications.

Comparing OLE 2 to OLE 1.0

OLE version 2 is to OLE version 1.0 what Windows 95 was to Windows 3.1. To put it mildly, OLE 2 is a major extension to the OLE 1.0 architecture.

OLE version 1.0 provided basic linking and embedding capabilities under 16-bit Windows. In fact, software publishers have used OLE 1.0 to add new data types—such as pictures, text, charts, video clips, and sound annotations—to their applications and insert them into other applications' documents.

Because OLE 2 is an extension to OLE 1.0, applications that follow the OLE 1.0 specification are 100 percent compatible with OLE 2. Applications that take advantage of OLE 2 have even greater capability to interact with other applications. OLE 2 offers substantial extensions to OLE 1.0 that provide users with a more powerful computing environment while remaining backwardly compatible with current OLE applications.

Also, Microsoft has rewritten portions of the OLE 1.0 infrastructure to optimize performance and reduce system resource usage. As a result, OLE 2 is not only more advanced than OLE 1.0 but also more efficient.

OLE 2 Definitions

Before you continue further in your exploration of OLE 2, this section takes a moment to define some OLE terminology.

Objects

The first term to define is the first word in OLE (Object Linking and Embedding). An *object* is a thing. In fact, the first place to look for objects is in the real world.

The best way to think of an object is as a component of something else. For example, an automobile consists of objects like tires, an engine, brakes, and a car stereo. For that matter, almost everything that you can think of is an object.

On your computer screen, objects include individual windows, bitmaps, menus, icons, and cursors. However, you normally don't link or embed any of these items in your documents. The types of objects that you embed in a document might include formatted text, 2-D or 3-D graphics objects, or exported data from database or spreadsheet applications.

Containers

A *container application* is a program that can incorporate embedded or linked OLE objects into its own documents. The documents managed by a container application must be capable of storing and displaying OLE objects as well as data created by the application itself. A container application must also enable users to insert new OLE objects or edit existing OLE objects. Figure 7.10 shows a program that is an OLE container and can contain OLE objects.

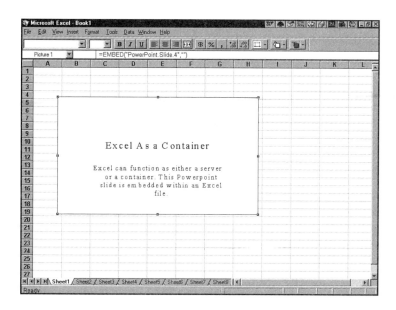

Fig. 7.10

Microsoft Excel can be an OLE container; this example shows an Excel spreadsheet with an embedded slide from a PowerPoint presentation.

Containers can simply hold embedded and linked objects, or they might be more sophisticated and enable other containers to link to their embedded objects.

Activations

After a user embeds an OLE object in a container application, the user can still modify the object. To do so, the user must activate the object, usually by double-clicking it.

When the user activates the object, the menus and toolbars in the container application change to reflect those that belong to the application that created the object. This behavior of activation promotes the concept of document-centered computing. The user can treat a compound document as a single entity, working on it without knowingly switching applications.

Servers

A *server application* creates OLE objects for use by container applications (see fig. 7.11). Some server applications support the creation of embedded items only, while others support the creation of both embedded and linked items. In rare instances, servers might support linking only. All server applications must support activation by container applications when the user wants to edit an item. The server not only provides data to be linked or embedded, it also provides the menu items, toolbars, and commands to enable the user to edit the embedded or linked data within another application's container. Figure 7.12 shows a server application that produces data that can be embedded in a container application.

III

OLE

Fig. 7.11

The WordArt component provided with Microsoft Excel is a server; you can embed its objects within OLE containers.

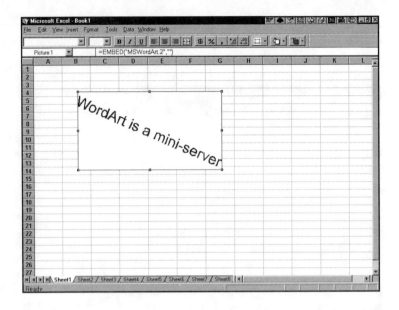

Full Servers

A *full server* can either be run as a standalone application or launched by a container application. A full server can store documents as files on disk. It can support embedding and linking, embedding only, or linking only. The user of a container application creates an embedded OLE object (and therefore uses the server) by choosing the Cut or Copy command in the server and the Paste command in the container.

Miniservers

A *miniserver* is a special type of server application that only a container can launch. A miniserver cannot run as a standalone application and is always run from another application. Miniservers, with their simplified user interface, can support only embedded objects, and they cannot open or save files on their own. A miniserver is useful when limited functionality is required or when a partnership with other container objects is predefined.

Along with the three main applications (Word for Windows, Excel, and PowerPoint) that can each be used as OLE servers (as well as containers), Microsoft Office comes with other miniservers, including the following:

- Microsoft WordArt, for creating logos and special effects
- Equation Editor, for creating mathematical equations
- Graph, for creating charts
- ClipArt Gallery, for accessing libraries of sample artwork

> **Note**
>
> An application can be both a container and a server at the same time. That is, it can both incorporate data into its documents and create data that can be incorporated as OLE objects into other applications' documents.

Marshaling

Marshaling is the process of passing function calls and parameters across process boundaries. Because the code of a Windows object can execute in another process's address space, the OLE system DLLs handle the translation of calling conventions and 16-bit to 32-bit parameter translation when the object and its user are running in a different process space. Fortunately, the Microsoft Foundation Classes handle this translation for you; however, you should be aware of what is occurring while your program runs.

For example, a container might be executing in a 32-bit process space, so it treats types such as UINT as 32-bit values. The server to that container might be running in a 16-bit address space and call a function in the container, passing a 16-bit world into a 32-bit world. Marshaling handles the translation between processes for you. Other data types, such as pointers, memory handles, and so on, are handled in a similar manner.

Interfaces

An *interface* is a group of related functions through which one application accesses the services of another. You can think of an interface, in C++ terms, as abstract base classes that specify behavior in a general manner with no implementation.

Interfaces are a binary standard for component object interaction. This is interesting because OLE provides an operating system standard for creating objects. This operating system standard is a great advantage over a language standard for creating objects because it enables you to implement objects that interact by using different programming languages.

Used by itself, the term *interface* refers to the definition (or prototype) of certain functions. MFC programmers do not use interfaces directly; they are used mostly by programmers who access the OLE API directly. Nevertheless, you will still see the term occasionally, so you need to understand it. In OLE, all interface names are prefixed with either IOle or I.

OLE 2 Tools in Visual C++ 4

When you install Visual C++ 4, the installer delivers a set of tools to help you provide OLE 2 support in your applications. This toolkit includes a set of dynamic link libraries (DLLs), sample code, online documentation, and viewing and browsing tools.

III

OLE

The tools are all installed in the \BIN subdirectory under the directory in which you installed Visual C++. Here are descriptions of each of these tools:

- IDataObject Viewer (dobjview.exe) displays a list of data formats currently available from a Clipboard or drag-and-drop operation. This tool is valuable when you work with UDT and implement a drag-and-drop operation.

- DocFile Viewer (dfview.exe) provides a method of examining the elements stored within a compound file used in structured storage. This tool is handy because its visual view of related data makes it easier to understand how structured storage works.

- Class ID Generator (uuidgen.exe) creates a unique class identifier, which is required when you register your application with OLE.

- Running Object Table Viewer (irotview.exe) displays information about the objects currently running. To experiment with this utility, try starting it while running an OLE 2 application. You might be surprised by the amount of information that this viewer presents.

- OLE2View (ole2vw32.exe), as its name suggests, enables you to view OLE 2 objects and their supported functions.

- Automation Test (disptest.exe), which is called DispTest and is very similar to Microsoft Visual Basic, enables you to test applications that implement OLE Automation.

- Type Library Generator (mktyplib.exe) is a small compiler that produces a type library (.TLB) file, which contains standard descriptions of data types and modules that you can use to expose functions for OLE Automation. You pass this tool a text file that contains code written in the ODL (Object Description Language) format. The compiler converts that file to a type library file; the system then uses the type library to keep track of which functions have been exposed for an application.

Note

The Visual C++ license agreement allows you to redistribute the core OLE 2 DLLs with your application. For your OLE 2 application to work correctly, the following files must ship with your application:

COMPOBJ.DLL	OLE2.DLL
OLE2.REG	OLE2CONV.DLL
OLE2DISP.DLL	OLE2NLS.DLL
OLE2PROX.DLL	STDOLE.TLB
STORAGE.DLL	TYPELIB.DLL

Make sure that you install these files into the Windows system directory on the user's hard drive. However, first use the Windows version control API functions to check whether these files already exist. If they do exist, you must ensure that you install these files only if they are newer than the files already on the user's machine.

Sample Programs

Microsoft's Developer Network (better known as MSDN) library contains several OLE sample programs. Some are written in C, and others use MFC. The examples implement an OLE server outline, a server test program, and an in-place server outline. There are also OLE container samples, including a base outline, a container outline, and a client test. Finally, the OLE Automation examples include Automation Calculator, Automation Polygon Server, and Simple Automation.

OLE 2 Hints

Make sure that you have SHARE installed on the system on which you plan to run OLE. If SHARE is not installed, your application won't work because the program initialization will fail. However, your program won't indicate any reason for this failure; it will simply start with an empty window, and the New command won't do anything. This problem can be a tough one to debug.

Also, watch out for different versions of the OLE system files installed on your computer. If you get strange results, you should definitely check for multiple OLE files on your system.

The OLE User Interface

When the user runs an OLE application (either a container or server), sometimes the application needs the user to supply certain information. OLE provides a set of dialog boxes (similar to the common dialogs found in Windows 95) that enable a program to interact with the user in a uniform way.

The OLE common dialog boxes handle such tasks as inserting objects, pasting objects, converting objects, and changing object icons. You should use the standard dialog boxes in your program for three reasons: They make programming easier, they make the size of your programs smaller, and (most importantly) they provide a consistent interface for your users.

III

Registering OLE Applications

When a user wants to insert an OLE object into an application, OLE presents a list of OLE object types currently available on the system, as shown in figure 7.12.

OLE gets this list from the system registration database, which is also called the *system Registry*. The system Registry uses structured storage to contain information provided by all OLE server applications.

OLE

Before you can use a server, it must first register itself in the registration database by storing entries that specify such information as each type of object for which it provides services and the file extensions and paths for each of its files. Container applications can use the information from the Registry to tell the user which object types are available.

Fig. 7.12

The Object dialog box gives the user a familiar, standard interface for inserting OLE objects into compound documents.

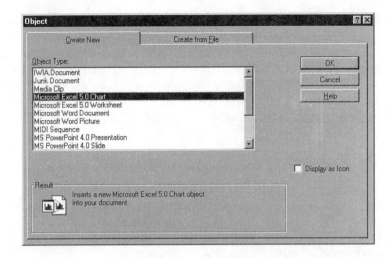

When a server application first installs itself, it should register all the types of OLE objects that it supports. You can also write the application so that it updates the Registry every time that it executes. This keeps the Registry updated if the server's executable file is moved.

The System Registry

The Registry is vital to OLE's operation because it stores important information about the software installed on the computer system. In addition to using the OLE object type data, Windows uses the Registry to store configuration information that is managed entirely by the operating system.

You can think of the Registry as a source of information about applications. Just like a compound document, you store and retrieve data kept in the Registry by using API routines, but you don't know exactly how the Registry is storing your data.

Developers can choose to store any type of application-related data in the Registry. Windows requires several types of data, including some data specific to OLE objects of your application. This information is used by system applications (such as Program Manager, File Manager, and the Windows 95 Explorer), as well as user applications.

Microsoft recommends that developers use the system Registry rather than Windows profile files. Profile files are text files with the .INI file extension. Initially, most programmers who have used the profile functions ask why they need to move to something different. The reasons for the system Registry include the following:

■ The Registry provides a convenient structure for storing data, and enables you to look up specific values by name. You no longer need to write parsers for .INI files.

■ You don't have to worry about whether the current path has multiple .INI files with the same name, or that your program is not accessing the correct file.

- Users are less likely to edit your program's configuration data manually, because they have to learn to use the Registry Editor. This is an advantage because sometimes users wreak havoc by setting values incorrectly.

- The system Registry uses a tree-structured approach to accessing information. Therefore, the programmer has more flexibility in storing data in the Registry.

The REG.DAT data file (located in the Windows system directory) stores Registry information. Windows creates and maintains this binary file, and Microsoft does not publish the file format. Windows also locks the file when it is first opened, so you cannot access it directly with file-manipulation routines.

The Registry Editor

As mentioned before, you can add, change, or remove data in the Registry from within your application by using the RegXXX() API routines. You can also manually modify the Registry by using the Registry Editor, shown in figure 7.13.

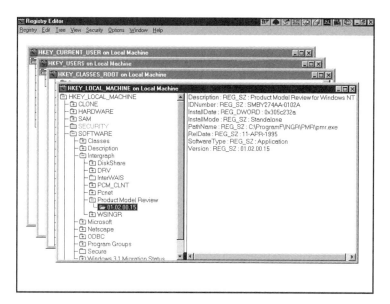

Fig. 7.13

The Registry Editor offers a manual way to edit data stored in the system's Registry.

The Registry Editor enables you to edit Registry *keys* and their *values*. A key is like a word in a dictionary and its value is like that word's definition. A key can have any number of subkeys, which in turn can have independent values.

The system Registry has four main *root keys*: one each for the local machine's configuration information, the current user, and all users on the local machine, plus one specifically for OLE class and mapping data. Each root key has its own window within the Registry Editor. These windows display the root keys' subkeys in a tree list similar to that of the Windows 3.1 File Manager.

From Here...

This chapter introduced OLE 2. You learned what OLE is, the benefits that it provides for both you and your applications' users, how it compares to older versions of OLE, and a bit about the utilities that are included with Visual C++ 4.

In the next chapter, you continue to study OLE by examining how to support OLE in your own programs by using the Microsoft Foundation Classes. Although you didn't get to examine any sample code in this chapter, you covered much information that is necessary to understand the samples in the next chapter.

To learn more about OLE 2, you can explore the following chapters:

- To learn how to write OLE applications using the MFC libraries, see Chapter 8, "OLE and the Microsoft Foundation Classes."
- For a discussion of OLE Automation and MFC, see Chapter 9, "OLE Automation."
- For information about writing your own OLE custom controls, see Chapter 11, "Building OLE Controls."
- For exhaustive coverage of the Component Object Model and the Windows OLE API, see Kraig Brockschmidt's *Inside OLE*, 2nd Edition (Microsoft Press).

OLE and the Microsoft Foundation Classes

In Chapter 7, "Introduction to OLE," you learned about the fundamental parts of OLE 2, and you saw the advantages and disadvantages of using OLE, along with some ideas for using OLE in your own applications. In this chapter, you'll learn how to build OLE 2 container and server applications using the Microsoft Foundation Class (MFC) libraries.

You'll learn how MFC simplifies OLE programming, as well as the type of OLE support that MFC provides. You also learn how to use AppWizard to take maximum advantage of the work that MFC can do for you.

In this chapter, you learn about the following:

- Why you should use MFC to build your OLE 2 applications
- What support the MFC classes provide for using OLE in your programs
- What the differences are among a container, miniserver, full server, and container-server
- How to display OLE objects in a container application
- How to add support for loading and saving OLE files to a container application
- How to create your own OLE server application

Why Use MFC To Program OLE?

The OLE 2 API can be overwhelming because it contains so many new routines, many for implementing concepts that are unfamiliar to some programmers. Normally, it is up to the programmer—you—to identify the OLE functionality that your application needs and then write the many functions required to add those features. Because OLE depends on the Component Object Model (COM), you also would have to learn and understand how COM works.

The Microsoft Foundation Classes make building OLE applications easy because all the code that you normally must write is already written for you. The MFC OLE classes implement the most commonly used OLE objects and interfaces and enable you to inherit their basic functionality. MFC provides usable classes for building servers, containers, and OLE custom controls (also called *OCXs*), as well as other utility classes.

To give you an idea of the amount of programming time that you save when you use MFC to add OLE features to your applications, consider this fact: The number of lines of source code for the MFC library increased *fourfold* when it added OLE 2 support. Before supporting OLE 2, the MFC source code consisted of about 5,000 lines. With OLE 2 support added, the code has about 20,000 lines. OLE support in MFC is about three-fourths of the entire class library. Think of this as the number of lines of source code that you don't have to write!

Of course, Microsoft wouldn't have done all this work unless the corporation believed putting OLE support into MFC. Microsoft's efforts pay off in making it easier for developers—that's you—to incorporate OLE support in new applications.

What MFC Provides

You've already seen that Visual C++'s AppWizard knows how to create applications with many Windows features, such as multiple document windows and floating toolbars. AppWizard can also build applications that support OLE 2 features. It can generate much of the code needed for basic container or server applications, leaving it to you to customize that code if necessary.

The OLE 2 classes in version 4.0 of the Microsoft Foundation Classes support the following features:

- *OLE 2 containers*—These containers enable you to embed OLE objects in your application.

- *OLE 2 servers*—With these servers, you can create an OLE object to embed in container programs.

- *OLE Automation*—This feature enables you to expose functions in your program to an outside application.

- *Drag and drop*—Classes provide functionality to enable your program to be the source as well as a target of a drag-and-drop operation.

- *Compound files*—The standard serialization routines automatically use OLE compound files without requiring any extra programming on your part.

- *Automatic registration*—You don't have to worry about working with messy .reg files or using the Registry Editor. Built-in functionality registers your programs for you.

- *OLE custom controls*—MFC 4.0 adds two types of support for custom controls. AppWizard can generate containers that can accept embedded custom controls, and MFC now includes several classes for building custom controls based on the COleControl class.

- *Standardized dialog box support*—The OLE user-interface guide recommends that you use consistent dialog boxes in your program (Insert Object, Paste Special, and so on). The OLE support in MFC enables you to call the OLE dialog boxes quickly and easily.

If you want to use a feature of OLE 2 that MFC doesn't provide, you can always work directly with the OLE 2 API functions. However, the MFC implementation is quite complete, so you usually have little need to interact directly with these OLE 2 API functions.

If you want to support any of the OLE Industry Solutions, like the OLE for Design & Modeling specification (which the companion CD includes), you must work directly with OLE routines. See the references in the "From Here…" section at the end of this chapter for more details on OLE programming.

OLE and AppWizard

The best way to get started writing an OLE application with MFC is to use AppWizard to create a skeleton application to which you can add functionality.

When working with AppWizard, the AppWizard OLE options dialog box is the most important step (see fig. 8.1).

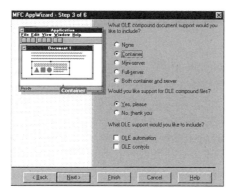

Fig. 8.1

The AppWizard OLE options dialog box (Step 3) enables you to specify what OLE support, if any, you want your generated application to include.

In this dialog box, you can choose the type of OLE functionality that you want to put into your application. If you select the first radio button, None, you specify a vanilla application with no OLE support. The following are the other buttons in that group:

- *Container*—An application that manipulates and stores OLE objects. Container applications can incorporate embedded or linked items into their own documents.

- *Mini-Server*—A special type of server that only a container can launch (the server is stored in a DLL). You cannot run a miniserver as a standalone application. Miniservers serve the OLE objects that are embedded in a container.

- *Full Server*—A server that you can run as a standalone application *or* embed in a container application.

- *Both Container and Server*—This option builds an application that provides the functionality of an OLE container and a server in one bundle. Both Excel and Word are container-server applications.

The next group of buttons enables you to specify whether you want your application to use MFC's support for compound files. If you select Yes, Please, the Serialize() methods for your document classes can store your application's data in standard compound documents.

The OLE Automation check box enables you to add OLE Automation support to your new application for further customization. This chapter doesn't cover OLE Automation, but you'll learn about it in Chapter 9, "OLE Automation."

Finally, the OLE Controls check box gives you control over whether you want your new container to support embedded OLE custom controls (OCXs). You can think of an OCX as an "embeddable" object that executes a function; it's not just a static data object like a chart. You learn more about using and building OCXs in Part IV, "Custom Controls."

What AppWizard Generates

You might remember from Chapter 5, "Introducing MFC," that AppWizard names the files based on the name that you supply for the project. As before, AppWizard generates files to implement your choice of an SDI or MDI application. When you run AppWizard and create a skeleton OLE application, the result is the following:

- One .txt text file listing the classes and files generated for the application; this file is a handy reference to see what AppWizard has done for you.

- Several .cpp source code files that implement classes for the application, its windows and views, a document class, and an embedded item class to be displayed by the view.

- One .rc resource script containing the application's resources, plus some .ico files for individual icons (one for the application, plus one for MDI child windows in MDI applications).

- Several .h header files—one for each generated .cpp file plus files to define the resources and precompiled headers for the project.

This might sound like a lot of files to keep track of; however, all these files also represent code that you don't have to create yourself. After taking a closer look at the created files, you examine what you have to add to the code that AppWizard generates.

All applications generated with AppWizard have an application class that derives from CWinApp, an About dialog box generated from CDialog, a view class that derives from CView, and a frame window class that derives from CFrameWnd for SDI applications or CMDIFrameWnd for MDI-based programs.

Container and Server Applications. For container applications, the application's document class derives from COleDocument. COleDocument, which derives from CDocument, provides support for embedding OLE objects and (optionally) OCXs in your documents. In addition, containers and container-servers also get an item object class that derives from COleClientItem; this item class represents the data that the container itself generates. MFC can then use this item class with compound files and the Uniform Data Transfer (UDT) mechanism. For example, an MFC-based drawing application would use the generated item class to store drawing graphics.

For miniservers, full servers, and container-servers, the document class derives from COleServerDoc rather than COleDocument. COleServerDoc provides additional methods for serving the contents of the document. Servers also have two additional classes that derive from COleFrameWnd (for in-place activation) and a server item class that derives from COleServerItem.

Application Resources. AppWizard generates a starting set of resources for your application, including the following:

- Accelerator key that support standard key definitions for either SDI or MDI applications, including the OLE operations that the application supports.
- An About dialog box, which you'll probably want to modify.
- Icons—one used both in the main window and the About dialog box, and another for MDI child windows (if your application supports MDI).
- Menus. The AppWizard provides a main menu bar for all SDI and MDI applications, including servers. In addition, programs that use MDI have another menu that they use when displaying MDI child windows. OLE container applications use another resource (IDR_CNTR_INPLACE) when displaying an OLE object.
- String resources, which provide information on the status line (optional).
- Class and object ID resources. Your application's object class (which derives from MFC's CWinApp) registers a server's objects with the system Registry.
- Bitmaps used in program toolbars (optional).

If AppWizard didn't generate these resources for you, you would have to create them manually by using AppStudio or another resource editor.

MFC Support for OLE 2

The MFC classes that provide support for OLE 2 fall into six groups:

- OLE base classes
- OLE Visual Editing classes
- OLE data transfer classes
- OLE dialog box classes
- OLE custom control classes
- Miscellaneous OLE classes

III

OLE

The OLE Base Classes

The OLE base classes exist so that you can inherit their behaviors in your own programs. Using the base classes gives you easy access to standard OLE behavior. The base classes include `COleDialog`, which provides common OLE dialog box implementations, `CDocItem`, which is an abstract base class that represents parts of documents, `COleDispatchDriver`, which calls OLE Automation servers from your program, and `COleDocument`, which implements OLE compound documents and provides basic container support. `COleDocument` is the base of the document class for container applications.

As you saw in the earlier section, "What AppWizard Generates," AppWizard can build classes that derive from these base classes for your application.

Visual Editing Classes

For Visual Editing, or in-place activation, to work, both the container *and* the server must support it. The container must know how to ask an embedded object to activate itself, and must be capable of relinquishing partial control of the event-handing process to the object. The server must know how to accept activation requests from the container, as well as how to take partial control when it gets such a request.

Visual Editing Classes for Containers. You probably won't be surprised to learn that container applications use the OLE Visual Editing container classes. These classes provide support for in-place activation. `COleLinkingDoc` provides the infrastructure for linking objects, and `COleClientItem` represents the client's side of the connection to an embedded or linked OLE item. All the container's items derive from this class.

Visual Editing Classes for Servers. Just like containers, servers have their own set of MFC classes for in-place activation. Server applications use these classes to handle the required tasks that OLE servers must (or should) support. The `COleObjectFactory` class creates items when other OLE containers request them. The `COleTemplateServer` class, which derives from `CDocTemplate`, uses the framework's document/view architecture to create OLE documents. `COleServerDoc`, the base class for server application document classes, provides the bulk of MFC's server support. The `COleServerItem` class implements the OLE interface to the `COleServerDoc` objects and allows links to portions of a document. The `COleIPFrameWnd` class provides the frame window used for generating a view when a server document is being activated for in-place editing. The `COleResizeBar` class provides the standard user interface for in-place resizing. Objects of this class are used with the `COleIPFrameWnd` class.

Note

An *object factory* is like a C++ constructor; you call it to create a new instance of some type of object. Microsoft's Component Object Model (COM), the model on which OLE is built, doesn't depend on C++, so COM specifies the use of class factories instead.

Data Transfer Classes

The OLE data transfer classes provide support for transferring data between applications by using OLE 2's interapplication drag-and-drop functionality. The COleDropSource class controls the drag-and-drop operation. The class provides feedback to your program to determine when a drag operation starts and when it ends. It also updates the cursor to let the user know which operations are taking place. The COleDropTarget class enables your program to be the target of a drag-and-drop operation (for example, to receive dragged text from Word). An application uses the COleDataSource class when providing data for a Clipboard transfer. Finally, you use the COleDataObject class to access the data that a COleDataSource object contains.

Standard Dialog Box Classes

The OLE dialog box classes supply predefined dialog boxes for handling common OLE user-interface tasks. You can think of them as common dialog boxes for OLE operations, just like the common file and print dialog boxes that Windows and MFC provide. This group includes seven dialog boxes, each deriving from COleDialog.

The COleInsertDialog class displays the Insert Object dialog box, which provides functionality for inserting new OLE linked or embedded objects. The COleConvertDialog class displays the Convert dialog box, in which the user can convert OLE items from one type to another. A program that uses the COleChangeIconDialog class can enable the user to change the icon associated with an OLE embedded or linked item. The COlePasteSpecialDialog implements the Paste Special dialog box for pasting OLE objects that are stored in the Clipboard. The COleLinksDialog displays the Edit Links dialog box, in which the user can modify information about linked items. The COleUpdateDialog class displays the Update dialog box, which indicates the progress of updating an object from one type of object to another. The COleBusyDialog class handles calls to busy server applications by displaying the Server Busy and Server Not Responding dialog boxes.

Custom Control Classes

Visual C++ 2 introduced the OLE Control Development Kit (CDK), a bundle of tools useful for developing OCX controls and OLE applications. Visual C++ 4 does away with the CDK as a separate item and includes its tools and classes for OCX support as part of the base product.

The most important CDK class is the CWnd-derived COleControl, which is the base class for MFC OCXs. COleControl has all the same functionality as CWnd, plus several specialized methods that can perform the same tasks as OCXs. COleControlModule provides an interface for initializing OCX control modules, while COlePropertyPage and CPropExchange give your OCXs a way to let users set a control's properties and store them as persistent objects in a structured storage container. Finally, CPictureHolder and CFontHolder provide an easy way to support font properties and bitmap displays within your controls.

III

OLE

Several changes to the container classes enable your container applications to support embedded OCXs. The fact that COleControl is based on CWnd greatly reduces the amount of work required to support OCXs.

Miscellaneous OLE Classes

The miscellaneous OLE classes provide several different services that enable you to track exceptions, display tracker information, and use compound storage. Both container and server applications use the COleException class to handle exceptions that result from failures in OLE processing. The CRectTracker class moves, resizes, and tracks objects that have been activated in place. The COleStreamFile class gives your program access to compound files. The COleDispatchException class handles exceptions resulting from OLE Automation. Finally, the COleMessageFilter class manages concurrency with local remote procedure calls (LRPCs).

Now that you have an overview of the OLE classes, take a look at an application that uses the OLE classes. First you'll examine a container application, then you'll implement an OLE server.

Creating an OLE Container with MFC

If you use AppWizard to generate a container-only application, the code that the wizard generates is straightforward. This section's listings omit boilerplate code (such as calls to enable 3-D controls and other similar calls that are common to all AppWizard-generated applications). Don't worry, though; full source is on the book's companion CD. This application adds some features, like tracker boxes, to the standard code that AppWizard generates for you.

> **Note**
>
> Throughout this section, you'll see that because the test application is called OContain, you use that name to generate the class and file names.

Initializing the Application

The first thing that an AppWizard-generated application does is to initialize the OLE system libraries by calling the afxOleInit function in your program's InitInstance member function.

The application must also tell MFC which menu to use when an in-place server is activated. You give MFC this information with a call to the SetContainerInfo function, specifying the resource ID of the menu resource to use.

Once OLE initialization is complete, the application continues with the by-now-familiar AppWizard code for initializing the document template, 3-D controls, and so on.

Displaying OLE Dialog Boxes

If you tell AppWizard to provide OLE support, it adds the Insert Object item to your application's Edit menu. When invoked, this menu item displays the Insert Object dialog box (see fig. 8.2).

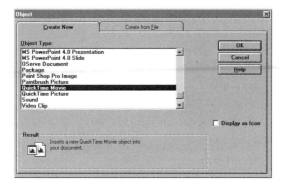

Fig. 8.2

You can easily include in your application the Insert Object dialog box, which is the standard way to enable the user to insert OLE objects within a container.

The standard behavior for this menu item is to display the standard OLE dialog box, which enables the user to select an object type (an Imagineer drawing, Excel worksheet, and so on) and a source (either a new object from the server, or an object already stored in a file). You'll see exactly how to use these dialog boxes in the section "The Container View Class." For now, rest assured that the OLE dialog boxes are just as easy to use as any other CDialog-based class. AppWizard automatically adds the dialog box resources to your application's resource file, and the default MFC behavior uses the OLE dialog boxes where appropriate.

Displaying OLE Objects

After inserting an object, you must display it in your document. As with all MFC applications, you add code to the View class in the OnDraw() member function, as follows:

```
void CContainView::OnDraw(CDC* pDC)
{
    CContainDoc* pDoc = GetDocument();
    ASSERT_VALID(pDoc);

    POSITION pos = pDoc->GetStartPosition();
    while (pos != NULL)
    {
        // draw the item
        m_pSelection = (CContainCntrItem*)pDoc->GetNextItem(pos);
        m_pSelection->Draw(pDC, m_pSelection->m_rect);
        // Draw tracker rectangle over the item
        CRectTracker tracker;
        SetupTracker(m_pSelection, &tracker);
        tracker.Draw(pDC);
    }
}
```

III

OLE

When it's time to redraw the view, this code gets all the `CContainCntrItem` objects that belong to the document and calls each embedded object's `Draw()` member function.

The last bit of code displays a Tracker window. The `CRectTracker` object is the hatched rectangular box that outlines an active OLE object; the program redraws this box to indicate to the user the application's active object.

Saving and Loading OLE Information

When you use the OLE classes in MFC, you save OLE information just as you normally do when writing MFC applications—by adding code to the `Serialize()` member function. The container item's `Serialize()` function looks like this:

```
void CContainCntrItem::Serialize(CArchive& ar)
{
    // Call base class
    COleClientItem::Serialize(ar);

    // Now store/retrieve data specific to ContainCntrItem
    if (ar.IsStoring())
    {
        // Save
        ar << m_rect;
    }
    else
    {
        // Load
        ar >> m_rect;
    }
}
```

> **Tip**
>
> If you examine the CContainCntrItem.h file on the companion CD, you'll notice that m_rect is added as a member to the container item. AppWizard didn't supply this member.

This code starts by calling the base class's `Serialize()` method to store the base class data. It then stores the coordinates of the embedded OLE objects, m_rect. In your own programs, you can store other important values similarly.

Internally, MFC uses OLE's structured storage to write the information to disk. However, you don't have to worry about adding any special code to access structured storage; the MFC implementation handles those details transparently for you.

A Simple Container Sample

Now look at the code for the OLE container program (see fig. 8.3). This is a bare-bones MFC application, with no status line or floating toolbars. This single-document interface application has an About dialog box, but that's about it. The application's most important feature is that it works as an OLE container, enabling you to insert multiple embedded or linked objects, move them around the window, and save and load files with the objects in them.

Fig. 8.3

The OContain example program, written with the MFC libraries, is a sample container application that accepts other applications' OLE objects.

A typical MFC application has many files, but this section shows only the most important ones. In addition, this section shows only those functions that you modify or that are interesting, not every single piece of code that AppWizard generates.

Tip

Remember, the companion CD that comes with this book includes all the source code for OContain.

The Container Application Class. You start with the container application's object. It has the fewest changes, because the document and view objects control most of the OLE functionality. In fact, you don't have to modify the code that AppWizard generates. Nevertheless, highlighting the differences in the `InitInstance()` member function (listing 8.1) is still useful.

III

OLE

Listing 8.1   OContain.cpp, Portions of the OContain Application Class

```
BOOL CContainApp::InitInstance()
{
    // Initialize OLE libraries
    if (!AfxOleInit())
    {
        AfxMessageBox(IDP_OLE_INIT_FAILED);
        return FALSE;
    }
    // Standard initialization
    // If you are not using these features and wish to reduce the size
    //  of your final executable, you should remove from the following
    //  the specific initialization routines you do not need.
#ifdef _AFXDLL
    Enable3dControls();
    // Call this when using MFC in a shared DLL
#else
    Enable3dControlsStatic();
    // Call this when linking to MFC statically
#endif
    LoadStdProfileSettings();
    // Load standard .INI file options (including MRU)
    // Register the application's document templates.
    // Document templates serve as the connection between
    // documents, frame windows, and views.
    CSingleDocTemplate* pDocTemplate;
    pDocTemplate = new CSingleDocTemplate(
        IDR_MAINFRAME,
        RUNTIME_CLASS(CContainDoc),
        RUNTIME_CLASS(CMainFrame),        // main SDI frame window
        RUNTIME_CLASS(CContainView));
    pDocTemplate->SetContainerInfo(IDR_OCONTATYPE_CNTR_IP);
    AddDocTemplate(pDocTemplate);
    // Parse command line for standard shell commands, DDE, file open
    CCommandLineInfo cmdInfo;
    ParseCommandLine(cmdInfo);
    // Dispatch commands specified on the command line
    if (!ProcessShellCommand(cmdInfo))
        return FALSE;
    return TRUE;
}
```

In this case, the differences appear to be minor. InitInstance() starts by calling the AfxOleInit() function, which MFC provides to handle all the necessary version checking and OLE initialization. If that call succeeds, you continue with normal AppWizard-style initialization. After registering your document template, you call the template's SetContainerInfo() function to tell the application which menu bar to use. The resource.h header file defines the IDR_OCONTATYPE_CNTR_IP identifier, which points to the main menu to use when an embedded item is activated in place. You'll find that the menu contains two separator bars between a standard File and Window main menu item. The two separator bars tell MFC where to insert menus provided by the server application when the embedded object is activated.

The Container Document Class. MFC encapsulates both views and OLE objects in documents, so this section examines the document class to see what changes it requires.

First, here's the CContainDoc object's constructor:

```
CContainDoc::CContainDoc()
{
     // Use OLE compound files
     EnableCompoundFile();
     // TODO: add one-time construction code here
}
```

The constructor includes the call to EnableCompoundFile() because you told AppWizard to provide compound document support in this application.

The application calls the OnNewDocument() function when the user requests a new document. In this application, the only difference between an OLE container and an ordinary SDI application is that the OLE container calls COleDocument::OnNewDocument() rather than the more familiar CDocument::OnNewDocument(). Here's the code:

```
BOOL CContainDoc::OnNewDocument()
{
     if (!COleDocument::OnNewDocument())
          return FALSE;
     // TODO: add reinitialization code here
     // (SDI documents will reuse this document)
     return TRUE;
}
```

You've already seen the code for CContainDoc::Serialize() in the section "Saving and Loading OLE Information."

The Container View Class. An MFC application's view class is responsible for displaying whatever information the document holds. In your container application, the document holds embedded or linked OLE objects, so your view must be capable of accepting new objects, dragging existing objects, and performing the standard cut, copy, and paste operations.

First examine the message map for the CContainView class. You add functions for WM_LBUTTONDOWN, WM_SETCURSOR, and the Copy and Paste comands. Here's the finished map:

```
BEGIN_MESSAGE_MAP(CContainView, CView)
     //{{AFX_MSG_MAP(CContainView)
     ON_WM_SETFOCUS()
     ON_WM_SIZE()
     ON_COMMAND(ID_OLE_INSERT_NEW, OnInsertObject)
     ON_COMMAND(ID_CANCEL_EDIT_CNTR, OnCancelEditCntr)
     ON_WM_LBUTTONDOWN()
     ON_WM_SETCURSOR()
     ON_COMMAND(ID_EDIT_COPY, OnEditCopy)
     ON_UPDATE_COMMAND_UI(ID_EDIT_COPY, OnUpdateEditCopy)
```

III

OLE

```
                ON_COMMAND(ID_EDIT_PASTE, OnEditPaste)
                ON_UPDATE_COMMAND_UI(ID_EDIT_PASTE, OnUpdateEditPaste)
                //}}AFX_MSG_MAP
        END_MESSAGE_MAP()
```

To be useful, the view must include methods to add new objects, draw and update the objects that it contains, and respond to mouse clicks and motions. The section "Displaying OLE Objects" has already shown your view's OnDraw() method. Now examine listing 8.2, the code that controls the inserting of objects.

Listing 8.2 ContainView.cpp, Showing the OnInsertObject() Method That Handles Inserted Objects

```
void CContainView::OnInsertObject()
{
    // Invoke the standard Insert Object dialog box to obtain
    //  information for the new CContainCntrItem object.
    COleInsertDialog dlg;
    if (dlg.DoModal() != IDOK)
        return;
    BeginWaitCursor();
    CContainCntrItem* pItem = NULL;
    TRY
    {
      // Create new item connected to this document.
      CContainDoc* pDoc = GetDocument();
      ASSERT_VALID(pDoc);
      pItem = new CContainCntrItem(pDoc);
      ASSERT_VALID(pItem);
      // Initialize the item from the dialog data.
      if (!dlg.CreateItem(pItem))
          AfxThrowMemoryException();  // any exception will do
      ASSERT_VALID(pItem);
      // If item created from class list (not from file), then launch
      //  the server to edit the item.
      if (dlg.GetSelectionType() == COleInsertDialog::createNewItem)
          pItem->DoVerb(OLEIVERB_SHOW, this);
      ASSERT_VALID(pItem);
      // As an arbitrary user-interface design, this sets the selection
      //  to the last item inserted.
      // TODO: reimplement selection as appropriate for your application
        m_pSelection = pItem;   // set selection to last inserted item
        pDoc->UpdateAllViews(NULL);
    }
    CATCH(CException, e)
    {
        if (pItem != NULL)
        {
            ASSERT_VALID(pItem);
            pItem->Delete();
```

```
        }
        AfxMessageBox(IDP_FAILED_TO_CREATE);
    }
    END_CATCH
    EndWaitCursor();
}
```

This code starts by creating a new COleInsertDialog object and using its DoModal() method to process the user's input. If the user cancels the dialog box, the code returns without further action.

In the more interesting case, in which the user chooses an object to insert, the code creates a new CContainerCntrItem object, copies the user's selection from the dialog box, and, if necessary, launches the server that can create new items of the type that the user selected.

> **Tip**
>
> CContainerCntrItem is the container item class discussed in the section "The Container Item Class."

Simply by passing the document object to the new item's constructor, you make the item a part of the document! That's all that you have to do to add the new item (much of the remainder of what you can do for the item, such as setting the hourglass cursor and turning it off again, is "window dressing"). The MFC OLE dialog box class handles the work of letting the user select from the available registered object types.

> **Tip**
>
> Did you notice the TRY and CATCH blocks in listing 8.2? Chapter 13, "Exception Handling," explains more about using exceptions to improve *and* simplify your code's error handling.

Handling Mouse Actions. You want to enable the user to use the mouse to manipulate items in your container, so you must add code for handling mouse actions. AppWizard-generated containers don't handle single- or double-clicks, and they don't let the user select from multiple items—but you'll fix that shortly.

First the application must be capable of determining which item the user has selected. The HitTestItems() function iterates through all the items embedded in the document until it finds one whose bounding rectangle encloses the mouse-down point (or until it finishes iterating through the items):

III

OLE

```
CContainCntrItem* CContainView::HitTestItems(CPoint point)
{
    CContainDoc* pDoc = GetDocument();
    CContainCntrItem* pItemHit = NULL;
    POSITION pos = pDoc->GetStartPosition();
    while (pos != NULL)
    {
        CContainCntrItem* pItem =
            (CContainCntrItem*)pDoc->GetNextItem(pos);
        if (pItem->m_rect.PtInRect(point))
            pItemHit = pItem;
    }
        // Return top item at point
    return pItemHit;
}
```

Later you use this function in your mouse-down event handlers.

Next the application needs a way to determine which embedded object the user has selected. When the user left-clicks an object (or chooses Edit, Paste), you want to high-light the object that the user intended to select. Listing 8.3 shows the SetSelection() function.

Listing 8.3   ContainView.cpp, Showing the SetSelection() Method

```
void CContainView::SetSelection(CContainCntrItem* pItem)
{
   // close in-place active item
   if (pItem == NULL || m_pSelection != pItem)
   {
      COleClientItem* pActiveItem
        = GetDocument()->GetInPlaceActiveItem(this);
      if (pActiveItem != NULL && pActiveItem != pItem)
        pActiveItem->Close();
   }
   // update view to new selection
   if (m_pSelection != pItem)
   {
      if (m_pSelection != NULL)
         OnUpdate(NULL, HINT_UPDATE_ITEM, m_pSelection);

     m_pSelection = pItem;
      if (m_pSelection != NULL)
         OnUpdate(NULL, HINT_UPDATE_ITEM, m_pSelection);
   }
}
```

This function closes any active in-place editing session, sets the active item to the selected item, and then sends the item an update message to redisplay the item if necessary.

To follow the OLE GUI guidelines, your container should display tracker rectangles, which graphically show the extent of a selected object. Your SetupTracker() method does just that:

```
void CContainView::SetupTracker(CContainCntrItem* pItem,
                                CRectTracker* pTracker)
{
    // Set up styles of tracker rectangle
    pTracker->m_rect = pItem->m_rect;
     if (pItem == m_pSelection)
        pTracker->m_nStyle |= CRectTracker::resizeInside;
     if (pItem->GetType() == OT_LINK)
        pTracker->m_nStyle |= CRectTracker::dottedLine;
     else
        pTracker->m_nStyle |= CRectTracker::solidLine;
     if (pItem->GetItemState() == COleClientItem::openState ||
        pItem->GetItemState() == COleClientItem::activeUIState)
     {
        pTracker->m_nStyle |= CRectTracker::hatchInside;
     }
}
```

You call `SetupTracker()` in the view's `Draw()` method to ensure that the application correctly highlights any selected items.

Now to the mouse actions method themselves. You've defined two: one for `WM_LBUTTONDOWN` and the other for `WM_LBUTTONDBLCLICK`. In keeping with good Windows behavior, a single left-click will select the object under the cursor, and a double-click will open the object. (In the case of this application, *open* means *in-place activation*.)

To handle single clicks, the `OnLButtonDown()` function can call `HitTestItems()` (defined earlier in this section) to check whether the mouse actually hit any items. If `HitTestItems()` returns a `CContainCntrItem`, you draw a tracker around it to indicate that it's selected and update the window (and the item) as long as the user continues holding down the button. Listing 8.4 shows the code that handles single-click events.

Tip

You also call the inherited `OnLButtonDown()` function to ensure that you keep the desired base class behavior.

Listing 8.4 ContainView.cpp, Showing the Method That Handles Mouse-Downs in the View

```
void CContainView::OnLButtonDown(UINT nFlags, CPoint point)
{
    CContainCntrItem* pItemHit = HitTestItems(point);
    SetSelection(pItemHit);
    if (pItemHit != NULL)
    {
        CRectTracker tracker;
        SetupTracker(pItemHit, &tracker);
        UpdateWindow();
        if(tracker.Track(this, point))
```

(continues)

Listing 8.4 Continued

```
        {
            pItemHit->InvalidateItem();
            pItemHit->m_rect = tracker.m_rect;
            pItemHit->InvalidateItem();

            GetDocument()->SetModifiedFlag();
        }
    }
    // Default processing
    CView::OnLButtonDown(nFlags, point);
}
```

The code for handling double-clicks is quite similar; in fact, you start by calling OnLButtonDown() to select the object. If that operation succeeds, you fire a command to the embedded object, asking it to activate itself in place for editing. Here's the code:

```
void CContainView::OnLButtonDblClk(UINT nFlags, CPoint point)
{
    OnLButtonDown(nFlags, point);
      if (m_pSelection != NULL)
    {
        m_pSelection->DoVerb(GetKeyState(VK_CONTROL) < 0 ?
            OLEIVERB_OPEN : OLEIVERB_PRIMARY, this);
    }
    // default processing
    CView::OnLButtonDblClk(nFlags, point);
}
```

Handling Menu Commands. Because your container enables the user to add objects, you should support some of the Edit menu commands so that users can copy, paste, and clear objects. Listing 8.5 shows the CContainView functions for executing these Edit menu commands and enabling or disabling menus depending on the program's state.

Listing 8.5 ContainView.cpp, Showing the Methods for Handling the Edit Menu's Actions

```
void CContainView::OnEditClear()
{
    if (m_pSelection != NULL)
    {
        m_pSelection->Delete();
        m_pSelection = NULL;
        GetDocument()->UpdateAllViews(NULL);
    }
}
void CContainView::OnEditCopy()
{
    // Implement the Copy command on the Edit menu.
    if (m_pSelection != NULL)
        m_pSelection->CopyToClipboard();
```

```
        }
void CContainView::OnEditPaste()
{
        CContainCntrItem* pItem = NULL;
        TRY
        {
            // Create new item connected to this document.
            CContainDoc* pDoc = GetDocument();
            ASSERT_VALID(pDoc);
            pItem = new CContainCntrItem(pDoc);
            ASSERT_VALID(pItem);
            // Initialize the item from Clipboard data
            if (!pItem->CreateFromClipboard())
                AfxThrowMemoryException();
            ASSERT_VALID(pItem);
            // Update the size before displaying
            pItem->UpdateFromServerExtent();
            // Set selection to newly pasted item
            SetSelection(pItem);
            pItem->InvalidateItem();
        }
        CATCH(CException, e)
        {
            if (pItem != NULL)
            {
                ASSERT_VALID(pItem);
                pItem->Delete();
            }
            AfxMessageBox(IDP_FAILED_TO_CREATE);
        }
        END_CATCH
}
void CContainView::OnUpdateEditClear(CCmdUI* pCmdUI)
{
        pCmdUI->Enable(m_pSelection != NULL);
}
void CContainView::OnUpdateEditCopy(CCmdUI* pCmdUI)
{
        pCmdUI->Enable(m_pSelection != NULL);
}
```

OnEditPaste() is noteworthy. When the user wants to paste an object into a document, you first create a new container item and initialize it from whatever is stored on
the Clipboard. If those two operations succeed, you update the display and set the
selection to the new item. Note that this isn't the same code that you would need to
support Paste Special for pasting in linked items.

Drawing the Item. One of the view's most important functions is drawing; after all, a
view that can't draw its data isn't very useful. Your view class is no different; it must
be capable of drawing the embedded items contained in the view. To accomplish this,
CContainView::OnDraw() iterates through all embedded objects, calls their Draw()
methods, and calls SetupTracker() to draw tracker boxes as needed:

III

OLE

```
void CContainView::OnDraw(CDC* pDC)
{
    CContainDoc* pDoc = GetDocument();
    ASSERT_VALID(pDoc);

    POSITION pos = pDoc->GetStartPosition();
    while (pos != NULL)
    {
        // draw the item
        m_pSelection = (CContainCntrItem*)pDoc->GetNextItem(pos);
        m_pSelection->Draw(pDC, m_pSelection->m_rect);
        // Draw tracker rectangle over the item
        CRectTracker tracker;
        SetupTracker(m_pSelection, &tracker);
        tracker.Draw(pDC);
    }
}
```

The Container Item Class. The container item is the heart of a container application. Most container applications enable the user to create some kinds of data in the application as well as accepting OLE objects. If you were writing a charting program, for example, you would implement the chart object in your container item class.

First examine what happens when the item gets changed. When the user is editing an item (either in place or fully open), it sends OnChange notifications for changes in the state of the item or the visual appearance of its content. Listing 8.6 shows the code for your OnChange() method, which catches OnChange notifications and redraws the object when necessary.

Listing 8.6 CntrItem.cpp, Showing the Method Triggered When the Object's Source Changes

```
void CContainCntrItem::OnChange(OLE_NOTIFICATION nCode, DWORD dwParam)
{
    ASSERT_VALID(this);
    COleClientItem::OnChange(nCode, dwParam);
    switch (nCode)
    {
      case OLE_CHANGED :
        InvalidateItem();
        UpdateFromServerExtent();
        break;
      case OLE_CHANGED_STATE :
      case OLE_CHANGED_ASPECT :
        InvalidateItem();
        break;
    }
}
```

This function redraws the object in one of two cases. If the object itself changes, you invalidate the object and have the UpdateFromServerExtent() function ask the server whether the object's size has changed. If the object's state or view aspect has changed, you invalidate the object.

Your `InvalidateItem()` function is pretty dumb—it asks the documents to update all views when the object changes:

```
void CContainCntrItem::InvalidateItem()
{
    GetDocument()->UpdateAllViews(NULL, HINT_UPDATE_ITEM, this);
}
```

Typically, your applications should be more careful to update only those views that contain data that has changed.

`UpdateFromServerExtent()` gets the server extent and redisplays the objects if the extents changed. First you call `GetExtent()` to get the object's extent; then, if the returned size differs from the object's m_size member, you change the size and redraw the affected objects. Listing 8.7 shows the complete code.

Listing 8.7   CntrItem.cpp, Showing the Routine That Updates the Object When the Server's Extent Changes

```
void CContainCntrItem::UpdateFromServerExtent()
{
    CSize size;
    if (GetExtent(&size))
    {
        // OLE returns the extent in HIMETRIC units
        //   however, we need pixels.
        CClientDC dc(NULL);
        dc.HIMETRICtoDP(&size);

        // Invalidate only if it has actually changed
        if (size != m_rect.Size())
        {
            // Invalidate old, update, invalidate new
            InvalidateItem();
            m_rect.bottom = m_rect.top + size.cy;
            m_rect.right = m_rect.left + size.cx;
            InvalidateItem();
            // Mark document as modified
            GetDocument()->SetModifiedFlag();
        }
    }
}
```

When the user moves one of your container items, the server sends an `OnChangeItemPosition` notification to change the location of the in-place editing window. You must handle these notifications, too, by both calling the base class method and redrawing any changed data. Listing 8.8 shows the `OnChangeItemPosition()` function.

III

OLE

> **Listing 8.8 CntrItem.cpp, Showing the Code for Reacting to a Change in the Object's Position**
>
> ```
> BOOL CContainCntrItem::OnChangeItemPosition(const CRect& rectPos)
> {
>     ASSERT_VALID(this);
>
>     if (!COleClientItem::OnChangeItemPosition(rectPos))
>         return FALSE;
>     InvalidateItem();
>     m_rect = rectPos;
>     InvalidateItem();
>     // Mark document as dirty
>     GetDocument()->SetModifiedFlag();
>     return TRUE;
> }
> ```

The container application that uses your item must know the item's size. To provide this data, your item gets a `GetItemPosition` notification to which you must respond. All your `OnGetItemPosition()` function needs to do is return the value of your `m_rect` member variable. This section doesn't show this function because it is so simple.

Creating an OLE Server with MFC

Containers provide a place for users to embed OLE objects. The other half of the OLE 2 equation is the server, which provides the data that is embedded into an OLE container. Although the processes for writing containers and servers are similar, you'll find that each type of program has its own unique properties.

When creating an OLE server with MFC, you first must choose between a full server or a miniserver. You know that a full server is a standalone application, and that a miniserver can only be embedded into an OLE container application and can't be started separately. For this example application, you create a full server.

When writing an OLE server, you must decide how much OLE support you are going to provide. For example, some server applications support only the creation of embedded items, whereas others support the creation of both embedded and linked items. If a server application supports linked items, it must be capable of copying its data to the system Clipboard.

Unlike a container, a server application must register itself with the system registration database. This enables container applications running on the system to know and access the server. AppWizard creates a .reg file that enables the Registry Editor to register the application; however, this file is not necessary for the OContain application because the MFC classes register your application dynamically at run time.

One of the important values that AppWizard creates is a class identifier (CLSID) that is unique for your program. For example, the CLSID declaration for the OServ application looks like this:

```
static const CLSID BASED_CODE clsid =
{ 0x519e21c0, 0x4303, 0x11b9,
{ 0xc0, 0x0, 0xe6, 0xf4, 0x2f, 0x7a, 0x6a, 0x9 } }
```

Each class of object must have a unique CLSID so that the particular object can be identified in the presence of any other objects. You can also create a CLSID with the help of the GUIDGEN.EXE utility, which ships as part of the Visual C++ 4 distribution.

Initializing the Server

A server application has to do all the standard OLE and MFC initializations, just like a container, but it must also take some additional steps. In addition to registering its object types with the Registry, a server application must register itself with the system (as was previously mentioned) and associate its document template with the object classes that it supports. The section "The Server Application Class" discusses in detail how this code works.

Drawing Server Items

When a container application launches a server, the server creates a *server item*. The server item (which is an object of the class COleServerItem) provides an interface between the server document and the container application.

To draw information with a server application, you must override the OnDraw() member of the derived COleServerItem class. The system calls this function to display the OLE item and to store it in a Windows metafile (.wmf). The container application then uses this Windows metafile to display the item in its own window.

As with most other applications, a server application has a view class. The view class has an associated OnDraw() function that displays the item when the user activates it in the container application. You should add code that can render the visual information provided by the server in the OnDraw() member functions so that users see an accurate representation when editing an item in place.

Your server can also override the OnGetExtent() member function. Containers can call this function to retrieve the item's size. You can use this function to return the size of window that you need to display your data.

A Simple Server Sample

The sample program, OServe, is a full OLE server application that does nothing but display a text string that proclaims that the application is a server. Building on this basic functionality is just a matter of adding message-processing functions to the program.

Server applications are actually easier to implement than containers, because they don't necessarily have to do as much. Miniservers are even simpler, because they don't have to include all the functionality of an MFC application.

III

OLE

The Server Application Class. As with the container, the server application class is quite similar to the standard AppWizard-generated code, so you examine this class first. Listing 8.9 shows the server's InitInstance() function.

Listing 8.9   oserver.cpp, the Sample Server's Application Class

```
BOOL COServerApp::InitInstance()
{
    // Initialize OLE libraries
    if (!AfxOleInit())
    {
        AfxMessageBox(IDP_OLE_INIT_FAILED);
        return FALSE;
    }
    // Standard initialization
    // If you are not using these features and wish to reduce the size
    //  of your final executable, you should remove from the following
    //  the specific initialization routines you do not need.
    LoadStdProfileSettings();
    // Load standard .INI file options (including MRU)
    // Register the application's document templates.
    //  Document templates serve as the connection between
    //  documents, frame windows, and views.
    CSingleDocTemplate* pDocTemplate;
    pDocTemplate = new CSingleDocTemplate(
        IDR_MAINFRAME,
        RUNTIME_CLASS(COServerDoc),
        RUNTIME_CLASS(CMainFrame),         // main SDI frame window
        RUNTIME_CLASS(COServerView));
    pDocTemplate->SetServerInfo(
        IDR_SRVR_EMBEDDED, IDR_SRVR_INPLACE,
        RUNTIME_CLASS(CInPlaceFrame));
    AddDocTemplate(pDocTemplate);
    // Connect the COleTemplateServer to the document template.
    //  The COleTemplateServer creates new documents on behalf
    //  of requesting OLE containers by using information
    //  specified in the document template.
    m_server.ConnectTemplate(clsid, pDocTemplate, TRUE);
    // Parse command line for standard shell commands, DDE, file open
    CCommandLineInfo cmdInfo;
    ParseCommandLine(cmdInfo);
    // Check to see if launched as OLE server
    if (cmdInfo.m_bRunEmbedded || cmdInfo.m_bRunAutomated)
    {
        // Register all OLE server (factories) as running.
        //  This enables the OLE libraries to create objects
        //  from other applications.
        COleTemplateServer::RegisterAll();
        // Application was run with /Embedding or /Automation.
        //  Don't show the main window in this case.
        return TRUE;
    }
    // When a server application is launched standalone,
    //  it is a good idea to update the system Registry
    //  in case it has been damaged.
```

```
        m_server.UpdateRegistry(OAT_INPLACE_SERVER);
        // Dispatch commands specified on the command line
        if (!ProcessShellCommand(cmdInfo))
            return FALSE;
        return TRUE;
    }
```

In addition to the ordinary application initialization code, this code does all the things that an OLE data server should:

- It uses the document template's `SetServerInfo()` member function to associate the `CInPlaceFrame` class with this server. This enables containers to know which of your server classes to use for your objects.

- It connects the server's document template to its `COleTemplateServer`. `COleTemplateServer` creates new documents for OLE containers by using information specified in the document template.

- It registers all the server's object types in the Registry.

The Server Document Class. The bulk of OServe's document class looks like all the other CDocument-based classes that you've already seen throughout the book. However, because your document class derives from `COleServerDoc`, it adds a new method: `OnGetEmbeddedItem()`. This function is responsible for returning a new embeddable item when called, so for OServe, all that the method does is use the new operator to build the item, as follows:

```
COleServerItem* COServerDoc::OnGetEmbeddedItem()
{
    // OnGetEmbeddedItem is called by the framework to get
    //  the COleServerItem that is associated with the document.
    //  It is called only when necessary.
    COServerSrvrItem* pItem = new COServerSrvrItem(this);
    ASSERT_VALID(pItem);
    return pItem;
}
```

That's it! Because your sample server doesn't do anything else, there's no other code in the document class.

The Server View Class. The only interesting thing that you do in your server's view class is to draw a representation for each embedded item. For OServe, you can draw the name of this book as a text string. Here's the code:

```
void COServerView::OnDraw(CDC* pDC)
{
    COServerDoc* pDoc = GetDocument();
    ASSERT_VALID(pDoc);
    CRect r;
    GetClientRect(&r);
    pDC->DrawText("Special Edition Using Visual C++, 95 Edition",
                    &r, DT_CENTER | DT_WORDBREAK);
}
```

III

OLE

Note that this code draws this banner string only when the user edits your server item in place (or when the server application itself is running). This code doesn't store a Windows metafile for later use, although you would probably want to do so in a real application.

The Server Item Class. At a minimum, your server item must be capable of drawing itself. To supply this capability, you must override the OnDraw() method and teach it how to draw. For OServe, all you want to do is draw a simple message, so you define a CString to hold that message, and use CDC::TextOut() to display it:

```
BOOL COServerSrvrItem::OnDraw(CDC* pDC, CSize& rSize)
{
    const CString kMessage =
      " Special Edition Using Visual C++, 95 Edition ";
    COServerDoc* pDoc = GetDocument();
    ASSERT_VALID(pDoc);
    pDC->SetMapMode(MM_ANISOTROPIC);
    pDC->SetWindowOrg(0,0);
    pDC->SetWindowExt(3000, 3000);
    pDC->TextOut(0, 0, kMessage, kMessage.GetLength());
    return TRUE;
}
```

The Server In-Place Frame Class. The in-place server frame contains server items when they're activated for in-place editing. This frame, which is based on the COleIPFrameWnd class, only provides a home for the server's view. The companion CD includes the source code for your server's in-place frame, but it's too simple to show here.

From Here...

This chapter explained how to start using the MFC OLE classes to build your own containers and servers. In the next chapter, you learn how to add OLE Automation support to your programs.

For more information on programming OLE support for your applications, you might want to refer to the following sources:

- Chapter 9, "OLE Automation," presents information about supporting OLE Automation.
- Part IV, "Custom Controls" (which consists of Chapters 10 and 11), explains how to write your own OLE custom controls.
- Chapter 19, "Using Common Controls with MFC," which is provided on this book's companion CD, explains how to use common controls with MFC.
- John Toohey's *Using OLE 2.x in Application Development* (Que, 1994), explains how to add OLE support to your applications.
- *Microsoft Visual C++ User's Guide, OLE 2 Classes,* presents detailed lists of all the OLE-related classes.

CHAPTER 9

OLE Automation

OLE Automation enables applications to expose a set of commands and functions that other applications can invoke. The feature provides a way to manipulate an application's objects and data from outside the application. Any OLE Automation *controller*, such as Visual Basic, can control applications that support OLE Automation.

In this chapter, you'll learn the following about OLE Automation:

- ■ What OLE Automation is, and how to use it
- ■ The difference between an Automation client and an Automation server
- ■ How to write an Automation server in Visual C++
- ■ How to use DispTest's client capabilities to access OLE Automation server applications

Introducing OLE Automation

Windows 3.0 provided Dynamic Data Exchange (DDE), a way for applications to control one another. Even without DDE, applications could always put their core functionality into a DLL and enable other programs to load the DLL and call functions within it.

OLE Automation is a more elegant solution than either of the above—and it's easier for developers to implement, too. The OLE Automation interface is stronger, faster, and more powerful than DDE ever was; it enables you to write applications that user-written programs can control.

You can add OLE Automation to your MFC application, whether the application is a container, a server, a miniserver, or a combined container and server. In general, OLE server applications are more likely to support Automation than OLE client applications; because servers provide data, it's usually logical to provide a way for the client to make requests through OLE Automation.

Just as OLE depends on containers (or *clients*) and servers, OLE Automation has two parts: the Automation client and the Automation server. The Automation server provides *properties* (or data) and *members* (or functions) for other applications to use. The Automation client uses the properties and members exposed by a server application.

Just as OLE depends on containers (or clients) and servers, OLE Automation support requires two parts: the Automation client and the Automation server. The Automation server provides objects for other applications to use. These objects can (and almost always do) have *properties*, or data, and *members* (or functions). The Automation client uses the properties and members exposed by a server application to manipulate the objects.

MFC enables you to write both Automation clients and Automation servers. The following sections briefly discuss the features and requirements of each.

OLE Automation Servers

OLE Automation servers are programs that enable other programs to control them through OLE Automation. A typical server provides methods for creating objects of whatever type it supports (graphic objects in a CAD program or spreadsheet objects in a spreadsheet) and for setting their properties.

Don't let this description worry you, though. Servers are just applications in which the developer has exposed some member functions (like the `Print` member of a document class) and properties (such as the number of words in a document object) so that other applications can use them.

In an MFC-based application, you expose members and properties by using the ClassWizard's OLE Automation property page. See the section "Creating an Automation Server in MFC" for more details.

OLE Automation Clients

OLE Automation clients (also called *Automation controllers*) can use OLE Automation to drive other applications. For example, the DispTest utility (included as part of Visual C++ 4) is an Automation client. It enables users to write programs in Visual Basic that can access the OLE Automation functions of almost any OLE Automation server. Of course, the full edition of Visual Basic can drive OLE Automation servers, and some applications include Visual Basic for Applications (VBA), a scaled-down version of Visual Basic.

> ### Tip
>
> If you're already used to using Visual Basic, you'll find DispTest very familiar, because it is based on Visual Basic 3.0.

OLE 2 specifies two types of Automation clients:

■ Dynamic clients acquire information about the properties of a server at run time. DispTest is a good example of a dynamic client, because it can work with any other OLE Automation server by interrogating the server to find out what it can do. MFC 4.0 does not provide support for this type of OLE Automation.

- Static clients are built with information about the properties and operations of the server at compile time. Static clients can't automatically figure out what features an Automation server provides.

MFC provides support for only the second type of Automation client. Because of this restriction, the programmer must know at compile time which Automation server application the Automation client will use and which properties it needs access to.

Benefits of OLE Automation

The possibilities of OLE Automation are enormous. You can create macros and other command sets that work across applications. OLE Automation offers several advantages over macro languages:

- You can bring together the best pieces of different applications to create completely new, specialized applications.

- You can easily integrate data that you already have stored in one program, like Excel or Access, and feed it to other applications.

- You can access exposed functions by using a programming tool such as DispTest or Visual Basic, as well as many applications' macro languages. With a program like DispTest or Visual Basic, you can easily write front-end applications that access the internal functions of other programs.

- Component object names remain the same across application versions, making it easier to update your application to work with the newest version of a product.

- OLE Automation provides built-in country localization features. Object names automatically conform to the user's preferred language, so you don't have to handle localization yourself.

Creating an Automation Server in MFC

Luckily, adding OLE Automation server support to your program is easy when you use MFC. If you also use Visual C++ to create your application, you gain the added benefits of being able to use the ClassWizard, which does much of the hard work for you.

MFC provides macros for OLE Automation support; these macros, known as *dispatch interfaces*, group and expose your server's functionality. Every Automation server program exposes both properties and methods.

Tip

Remember that MFC is available for a variety of other development environments, including Borland C++ and several UNIX platforms.

Exposing Properties

You can expose properties in two ways: by providing a pair of *accessor functions* to get and set an individual property's value, or by exposing the variable directly.

In most cases, accessor functions are a better solution. When you provide accessor functions that clients can call instead of depending on the presence of some variable with a particular name, the clients are insulated from any changes that you might make to the server's internal workings. This is important, because if clients break every time that you change your software's innards, most users will avoid your products. As long as you don't change the method interfaces, existing clients will still work with your server.

To expose a function, invoke ClassWizard, click the OLE Automation tab, and select the class that contains the function that you want to expose. Figure 9.1 shows the ClassWizard OLE Automation property page for the `CClikDoc` class. To add a new property, click the Add Property button to display the Add Property dialog box shown in figure 9.2.

Fig. 9.1

The ClassWizard OLE Automation page enables you to specify properties and methods that an OLE Automation server can call.

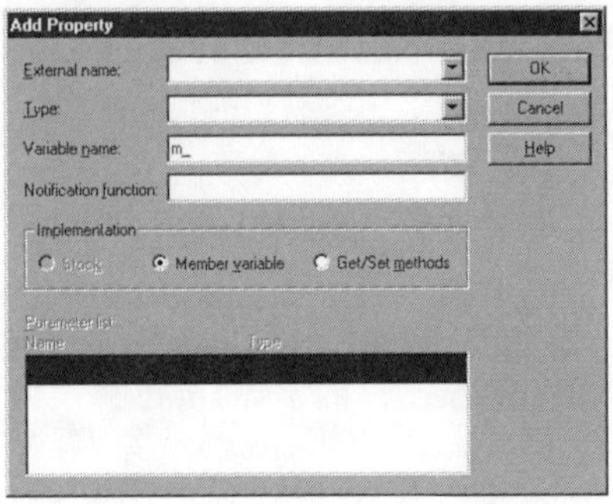

Fig. 9.2

In the Add Property dialog box, you can create new properties in your OLE Automation client application.

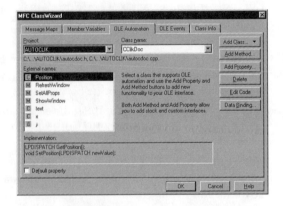

From the Add Property dialog box, you can choose the following:

- An external name for the property. Automation clients use this name to access the property. The name need not have anything to do with the names that you use to represent the property in your application.

- The property's data type (integer, string, and so on).

- The way to access the property. With MFC, you can use a member variable or accessor functions.

- A *notification function* to call when the property's value changes. This function is available only if you store the property as a member variable.

After you click OK, ClassWizard automatically creates new functions in your document class for the property that you added. It also adds an entry to the dispatch map, which OLE system files require. Finally, it updates the object description language (ODL) file to include a description of your new property.

Exposing Methods

Just as when you expose properties, when you expose methods, you make them available to clients. You expose methods from within your program by clicking the Add Method button in the OLE Automation page of the ClassWizard dialog box. The Add Method dialog box (see fig. 9.3) enables you to specify information about the method, including the external name (the name that clients use to trigger the method), the internal name (the name that your own code uses to refer to the method), and the data type that the method returns.

Fig. 9.3

In the Add Method dialog box, you can make functions in your Automation server available to other applications.

An OLE Automation Sample Program

The sample server in this section shows how to support OLE Automation in a server. This simple example provides properties for setting the position and content of a text string drawn in a window. The properties are named Position, Text, X, and Y, and you provide methods called RefreshWindow, SetAllProps, and ShowWindow. The program is a modified version of one of the sample programs that comes with Visual C++.

Because of the number of files in the entire MFC application, this section's code listings show only the most important files. In addition, the section shows only the modified functions or those that are particularly interesting, not every single thing that AppWizard generates.

> **Tip**
>
> Remember, this book's companion CD includes the complete source code for Autoclik.

The Server Application Class

Because AppWizard and MFC are so generous about providing automatic support for OLE functionality, the application class is exactly as it was generated by AppWizard. You don't have to make any changes to get OLE Automation support.

The Server Document Class

In the previous sections "Exposing Properties" and "Exposing Methods," you saw how to use ClassWizard to expose functions and data within your Automation server so that other programs could access them.

Depending on your application, exposing methods and properties from different parts of your program might make more sense. For example, a drawing application might expose some calls from the document, some from the view, and some for individual graphic objects. In this example, the server's document class, CClikDoc, contains all the properties and methods that you are exposing.

When you use ClassWizard to specify functions and properties to expose, it creates a *dispatch map*. Just like the message map, the dispatch map routes external events to your program. In this case, the events are requests for OLE Automation services. Again like message maps, the dispatch map has two parts. The first part appears in your C++ class's header file. Here's the dispatch map from autocdoc.h:

```
//{{AFX_DISPATCH(CClikDoc)
CString m_str;
afx_msg short GetX();
afx_msg void SetX(short nNewValue);
afx_msg short GetY();
afx_msg void SetY(short nNewValue);
afx_msg LPDISPATCH GetPosition();
afx_msg void SetPosition(LPDISPATCH newValue);
afx_msg void Refresh();
afx_msg void SetAllProps(short x, short y, LPCTSTR text);
afx_msg void ShowWindow();
//}}AFX_DISPATCH
DECLARE_DISPATCH_MAP()
```

The corresponding dispatch map from autocdoc.cpp looks like this:

```
BEGIN_DISPATCH_MAP(CClikDoc, CDocument)
        //{{AFX_DISPATCH_MAP(CClikDoc)
```

```
        DISP_PROPERTY(CClikDoc, "text", m_str, VT_BSTR)
        DISP_PROPERTY_EX(CClikDoc, "x", GetX, SetX, VT_I2)
        DISP_PROPERTY_EX(CClikDoc, "y", GetY, SetY, VT_I2)
        DISP_PROPERTY_EX(CClikDoc, "Position", GetPosition,
            SetPosition, VT_DISPATCH)
        DISP_FUNCTION(CClikDoc, "RefreshWindow", Refresh, VT_EMPTY,
            VTS_NONE)
        DISP_FUNCTION(CClikDoc, "SetAllProps", SetAllProps, VT_EMPTY,
            VTS_I2 VTS_I2 VTS_BSTR)
        DISP_FUNCTION(CClikDoc, "ShowWindow", ShowWindow, VT_EMPTY,
            VTS_NONE)
        //}}AFX_DISPATCH_MAP
    END_DISPATCH_MAP()
```

Each property and method that you've exposed has an entry in the dispatch table. MFC takes care of routing OLE events and messages to the appropriate functions.

The Visual C++ Autoclik sample provides a property and function for setting the text that's displayed when you click. You're going to extend the example by adding a property for the text's position, so you need to add member variables to the CClikDoc class definition. In this example, this member is called m_pt.

Exposed Properties. In this example, you define accessor functions for manipulating your properties. The simplest accessors are those for the individual X and Y coordinates of the window. Listing 9.1 shows those accessors.

> **Tip**
>
> If you want to make properties read-only, define a Get function only. Users can't set properties without a Set accessor.

Listing 9.1 Autoclik's Accessors for the Window's Individual X and Y Coordinates

```
short CClikDoc::GetX()
{
        return (short)m_pt.x;
}

void CClikDoc::SetX(short nNewValue)
{
        m_pt.x = nNewValue;
        Refresh();
}

short CClikDoc::GetY()
{
        return (short)m_pt.y;
}
```

(continues)

```
void CClikDoc::SetY(short nNewValue)
{
        m_pt.y = nNewValue;
        Refresh();
}
```

Exposed Methods. As you can see, the accessor functions for your properties are
quite simple. Because they operate only on individual data items, they're straightforward to code. In this application, though, you want to expose some more sophisticated capabilities. Because the window position is a coordinate pair, it would make
more sense to provide a pair of accessors for working with the position as a point
rather than individual coordinates. Here's what the GetPosition() accessor looks like:

```
LPDISPATCH CClikDoc::GetPosition()
{
        CClikPoint* pPos = new CClikPoint;
        pPos->m_x = (short)m_pt.x;
        pPos->m_y = (short)m_pt.y;

        LPDISPATCH lpResult = pPos->GetIDispatch(FALSE);
        return lpResult;
}
```

LPDISPATCH is a pointer to an OLE IDispatch interface, which is what OLE uses to
handle communications for OLE operations. Normally, MFC shields you from OLE
interfaces, but in this case the accessor must return an IDispatch pointer to be useful.

Note

In the Component Object Model (COM) specifications, an *interface* is a group of related functions that you access through an interface pointer. A complete description of COM is beyond
the scope of this book. Kraig Brockschmidt's *Inside OLE*, 2nd Edition (Microsoft Press) is a good
introduction if you want more detail.

SetPosition() is the opposite of GetPosition(); it converts the supplied LPDISPATCH
pointer into a CClikPoint, then uses the point's members to set the document's member data. In this case, LPDISPATCH is similar to an HWND: you use it in a function call to
get a more useful data type in return.

```
void CClikDoc::SetPosition(LPDISPATCH newValue)
{
        CClikPoint* pPos =
(CClikPoint*)CCmdTarget::FromIDispatch(newValue);
        if (pPos != NULL && pPos->IsKindOf(RUNTIME_CLASS(CClikPoint)))
        {
                m_pt.x = pPos->m_x;
                m_pt.y = pPos->m_y;
                Refresh();
        }
}
```

Of course, you can always define an exposed method that doesn't get or set any data itself. The ShowWindow() method doesn't manipulate any instance data; it just displays the application window. Consequently, it doesn't use any LPDISPATCH pointers or other OLE trappings—all it does is tell the CFrameWnd object to show the window. Here's what it looks like:

```
void CClikDoc::ShowWindow()
{
        POSITION pos = GetFirstViewPosition();
        CView* pView = GetNextView(pos);
        if (pView != NULL)
        {
                CFrameWnd* pFrameWnd = pView->GetParentFrame();
                pFrameWnd->ActivateFrame(SW_SHOW);
                pFrameWnd = pFrameWnd->GetParentFrame();
                if (pFrameWnd != NULL)
                        pFrameWnd->ActivateFrame(SW_SHOW);
        }
}
```

The Server Automation Object

In the Autoclik example, one of the properties that you enable users to control is the (X,Y) position of the Autoclik window. As you saw previously, this CClikPoint class derives from CCmdTarget, so it can receive dispatch events and respond to them. Because the CClikPoint objects can receive events directly, the class has its own dispatch map (helpfully provided by AppWizard). Here's what it looks like:

```
BEGIN_DISPATCH_MAP(CClikPoint, CCmdTarget)
      //{{AFX_DISPATCH_MAP(CClikPoint)
      DISP_PROPERTY(CClikPoint, "x", m_x, VT_I2)
      DISP_PROPERTY(CClikPoint, "y", m_y, VT_I2)
      //}}AFX_DISPATCH_MAP
END_DISPATCH_MAP() {
```

This map ties the X and Y coordinate properties of CClikPoint to the corresponding data members of the class. Think of the dispatch map for the Automation object as a directory entry: the map links a hidden internal name (the m_x and m_y members) with publicly visible names (x and y).

The ODL File

The Windows OLE subsystem needs to know what types of objects your OLE applications support. The *type library* provides a way for the system to keep track of which applications provide which object types.

To build a type library file (which usually has the .tlb extension), you create a file written in Microsoft's Object Definition Language (ODL). If you put an ODL file in your Visual C++ project, Visual C++ will compile it using the mktyplib tool and produce a .tlb file for you.

III

OLE

Tip

You should create a separate Visual C++ target for your type library file so that you can remake it when necessary.

The ODL file describes the properties and methods that your objects expose. Most importantly, the ODL definitions provide a Universal Unique ID (uuid) that identifies your object type. A complete discussion of ODL syntax, as well as what you need to do to build a type library file, is in Visual C++'s Books Online documentation. Listing 9.2 shows the Autoclik ODL file.

Listing 9.2   autoclik.odl, the Type Library Source for autoclik.exe

```
// autoclik.odl : type library source for autoclik.exe

// This file will be processed by the Make Type Library (mktyplib)
// tool to produce the type library (autoclik.tlb).

 [ uuid(0002180a-0000-0000-C000-000000000046), version(1.0) ]
library Autoclik
{
importlib("stdole32.tlb");

//  Primary dispatch interface for CClikDoc

[ uuid(0002180b-0000-0000-C000-000000000046) ]
dispinterface IACLIK
{
properties:
// NOTE - ClassWizard will maintain property information
//    here. Use extreme caution when editing this section.
//{{AFX_ODL_PROP(CClikDoc)
[id(1)] BSTR text;
[id(2)] short x;
[id(3)] short y;
[id(4)] IDispatch* Position;
//}}AFX_ODL_PROP

methods:
// NOTE - ClassWizard will maintain method information
//    here. Use extreme caution when editing this section.
//{{AFX_ODL_METHOD(CClikDoc)
[id(5)] void RefreshWindow();
[id(6)] void SetAllProps(short x, short y, BSTR text);
[id(7)] void ShowWindow();
//}}AFX_ODL_METHOD

};

//  Class information for CClikDoc

[ uuid(0002180c-0000-0000-C000-000000000046) ]
coclass CClikDoc
```

```
{
[default] dispinterface IACLIK;
};

//  Primary dispatch interface for CClikPoint

[ uuid(0002180d-0000-0000-C000-000000000046) ]
dispinterface IClikPoint
{
properties:
// NOTE - ClassWizard will maintain property information
//    here. Use extreme caution when editing this section.
//{{AFX_ODL_PROP(CClikPoint)
[id(1)] short x;
[id(2)] short y;
//}}AFX_ODL_PROP

methods:
// NOTE - ClassWizard will maintain method information
//    here. Use extreme caution when editing this section.
//{{AFX_ODL_METHOD(CClikPoint)
//}}AFX_ODL_METHOD

};

//  Class information for CClikPoint

[ uuid(0002180e-0000-0000-C000-000000000046) ]
coclass CClikPoint
{
[default] dispinterface IClikPoint;
};

//{{AFX_APPEND_ODL}}
};
```

Using DispTest as an OLE Automation Client

DispTest is an easy language to test your Automation servers. DispTest accesses OLE Automation's features through code written in Visual Basic.

This section describes the functions that DispTest provides for driving OLE Automation servers, and how to use those functions. DispTest provides two statements for creating OLE Automation objects:

- CreateObject() creates a new instance of an OLE Automation object.
- GetObject() retrieves an OLE Automation object from a file.

> **Note**
>
> Throughout this chapter, you can *almost* substitute the words *Visual Basic* whenever the word *DispTest* appears. DispTest is a version of Visual Basic 3.0 that does everything that the retail version does, except that it cannot create a final executable (.exe) file and (unfortunately) does not have help files.
>
> In DispTest, you can write only OLE client applications. You must use Visual C++ to write an OLE Automation server. The full versions of Visual Basic don't have the same limitation.

OLE Automation Objects

You access another application's exposed functions by creating an OLE Automation object. You use this object to reference the server application's exposed functions and properties. To create Automation objects, you use the `CreateObject()` function. `CreateObject()` requires a single parameter—a string variable that indicates the application name and type of object that you want to create.

Once you know the type of object that you want to create, use the `Set` keyword to assign the object returned by `CreateObject()` to the object variable, as in the following example:

```
Dim MyObject as Object
Set MyObject = CreateObject("Imagineer.Sheet")
```

When this code executes, it starts the application providing the object—in this case, Imagineer—and creates an OLE Automation object. Unlike the image displayed when you create a linked or embedded object, the object's image is not displayed anywhere in DispTest, and DispTest doesn't maintain the object's data.

The object is actually a part of the application that created it. DispTest code can reference this object by using the object variable returned from the `CreateObject()` function followed by a period (.) and the name of the exposed function in the server application that you want to call, as in the following example:

```
Dim MyObject as Object

Set MyObject = CreateObject("Imagineer.Sheet")

MyObject.SetLandscape
MyObject.Print
.
.
.
Set MyObject = Nothing
```

This code snippet creates the application object and then calls the functions named `SetLandscape` and `Print`. Finally, the code disposes of the object by setting the object variable to the `Nothing` keyword.

OLE Automation objects can use a significant amount of memory and system resources. Therefore, when you finish using OLE Automation, you should explicitly close any application that you no longer need and free its application object. To do this, set the object variable to the predefined value `Nothing`.

Activating OLE Automation Objects from a File

Most applications enable users to save application data in disk files. In the same spirit, most applications that support OLE objects store those objects in compound files on disk. The `GetObject()` function enables you to activate an OLE Automation object that has been saved to a disk file instead of creating a new one.

When you activate an OLE Automation object from a disk file, you need only specify the name of the file that you want to access. Windows determines which server application is associated with that data file by looking in the Registry for a type library that matches the object type. It then uses data from the type library to identify the server application and starts it, and then loads the data file that you specified.

To activate an OLE Automation object from a file, you first use DispTest to dimension an object variable. You then call the `GetObject()` function with a string variable that contains the name of the file that you want to activate. For example, suppose that you have an Excel spreadsheet data file named SALES.XLS and you want to create an OLE Automation object. You would use the following code:

```
Dim SpObj as Object
Set SpObj = GetObject("SALES.XLS")
```

When this code executes, the system invokes the spreadsheet, loads the data file SALES.XLS, and assigns the `SpObj` variable to this OLE Automation session. At this point, the contents of the entire data file become available to your Visual Basic application.

You can also activate only part of a data file. For example, you might want to access only specific cells in the spreadsheet. To activate only part of a file, add an exclamation point (!) or a backslash (\) to the end of the file name, followed by a string that identifies the part of the file that you want to activate.

Suppose that you want to activate the cells in the same spreadsheet from A1 to A10. You would use the following code to activate only the range of cells:

```
Dim SpObj as Object
Set SpObj = GetObject("SALES.XLS!A1:A10")
```

This code invokes the Excel application, and the object created contains and refers to only the specified range of cells.

III

OLE

Tip

Many other applications, like Intergraph's Imagineer Technical, follow Excel's Automation model.

When you use GetObject() to activate an OLE Automation object, the system uses data from the system Registry to determine which application to start. However, sometimes there may be some ambiguity, and some applications support multiple object types. For example, Excel has both chart and spreadsheet objects. You can provide more information by specifying the class of the OLE Automation object that you want to access as the optional second parameter to GetObject(), as in the following example:

```
Dim SpObj as Object
Set SpObj = GetObject("SALES.XLS", "Excel.Application")
```

The second parameter clarifies the exact type of object that you want to access. To access a chart, for example, you could specify Excel.Chart as the second parameter.

OLE Automation and the Future

OLE Automation is important because it offers an easy way for users to tie together different applications. Also, OLE Automation is becoming increasingly visible as a selling point. Users who want easy programmability are no longer satisfed with learning a separate macro language for each product that they use, and Visual Basic's success has set a high standard for Automation support. In the future, increasingly more applications will depend on OLE Automation instead of basing their standard scripting language on OLE Automation, giving OLE Automation more visibility in the marketplace.

You'll learn more about OLE Automation when you learn about OLE custom controls, because they are based on OLE Automation. In the meantime, here are some things that you might want to try:

- Add additional methods to the document class of this chapter's OLE Automation example. For example, you might consider adding Save() and Load() methods that call the document's Serialize() method. This will help you understand which functions you should dispatch to which parts of the application.
- Add richer error returning and exception reporting to this example. The OLE Automation specification provides a way for servers to return exact error codes ("that field must be a number") rather than mysterious numbers, but your server doesn't take advantage of that functionality.
- If you're multilingual, or know someone who is, try localizing this example so that it's in French, German, Spanish, Arabic, or whatever other languages you can think of.

From Here...

This chapter covered the basics of OLE Automation. You learned the difference between Automation servers and Automation clients, and you saw how to write an Automation server in Visual C++. Finally, you learned how to access servers from the DispTest utility included with Visual C++.

For more information on topics related to OLE Automation, see the following sources:

- For more information about writing OLE custom controls, see Chapter 10, "Using the ControlWizard."

- For more information on using OLE custom controls, see Chapter 19, "Using Common Controls with MFC," which is provided on this book's companion CD.

- For more details on including Automation support (including how to provide Automation in non-MFC programs), see John Toohey's *Using OLE 2.x in Application Development* (Que Publishing, 1994; ISBN 1-56529-991-4).

- For exhaustive coverage of the Component Object Model and the Windows OLE API, see Kraig Brockschmidt's *Inside OLE*, 2nd Edition (Microsoft Press).

III

OLE

Part IV

Custom Controls

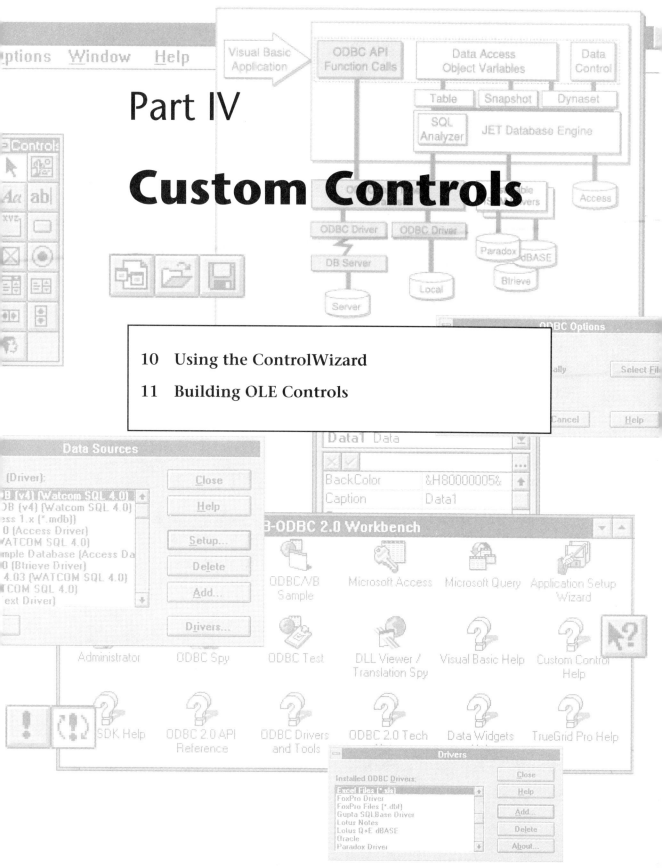

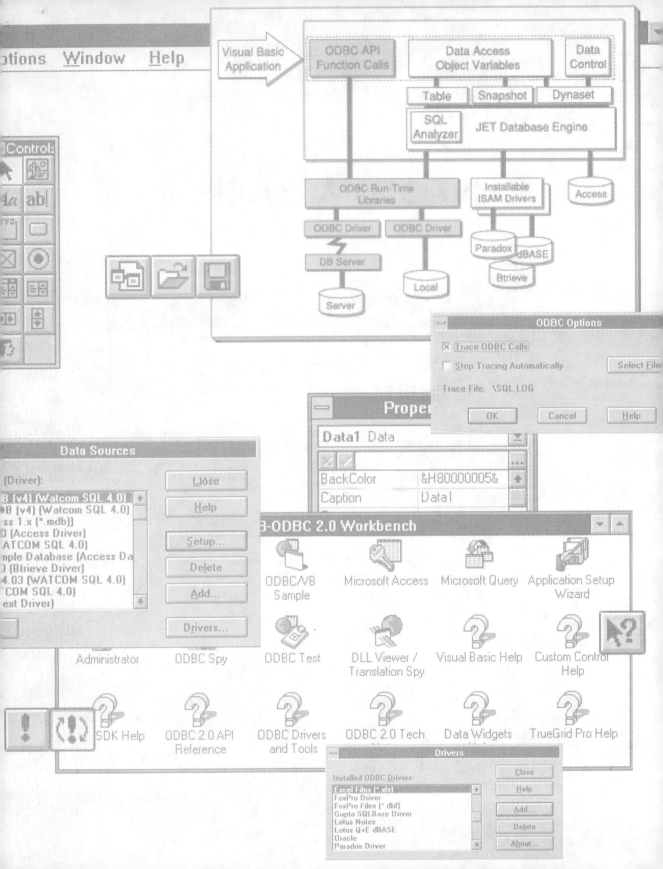

CHAPTER 10

Using the ControlWizard

The newest addition to the growing family of magicians (which includes AppWizard and ClassWizard) is the ControlWizard. The ControlWizard enables the developer to automate the process of creating OLE controls. OLE controls, otherwise known as *OCXs*, are the successors to the popular VBXs, the components created to extend the Visual Basic programming language. Only recently, as other development languages have begun using VBXs, their deficiencies have become apparent. The OCX specification was developed to bring software components into the world of OLE and 32-bit programming. VBXs began the component software revolution, and OLE and OCXs will carry it to all programming environments and into the operating systems of the future.

This chapter shows you how to create a trivial OCX, register the control, and test it using the Test Container utility. You learn about the following:

- What an OLE control is and what it can do for you
- Working with the ControlWizard to build an OLE control skeleton
- Adding licensing to your control
- Compiling and registering your OLE control
- Loading and testing your OLE control using the Test Container utility

The OLE Control

Microsoft is positioning Object Linking and Embedding (OLE) as an industry standard, and OLE controls are one more piece of the OLE puzzle. The original control specification, Visual Basic Extensions (VBX), was written for the 16-bit development environment. As Windows moves into the 32-bit environment with Windows NT and Windows 95, it makes sense to bring the custom control specification into the technology fold of the future.

What Is an OLE Control?

An OLE control, or OCX, is a piece of software that has been written to a very tight specification. Because of its specification's strictness, an OCX can be contained within other programs called *containers*. Creating a simple OCX is fairly easy, but the more you know about how they work, the more likely you are to succeed when you set out to build a sophisticated control.

An OLE control is basically an in-place server, and as such is loaded much more quickly than the average, everyday OLE server. OLE controls provide a direct interface to their methods and properties, unlike normal servers that route their interface through procedure calls. Because an OLE control loads quickly and provides a direct interface, it can change properties and execute function calls rapidly. Another thing that differentiates the OLE control in-place server from a normal OLE server is the event interface. The new event interface enables the in-place server to communicate directly with its container—something that a normal server does not do.

Note

Tests show that the current OLE control implementation is as fast, if not faster, than the equivalent VBX implementation. However, load time (the amount of time that it takes to load and display an OLE object) remains a concern. This delay is understandable when you consider the amount of work going on behind the scenes.

The OLE control specification sits comfortably on top of OLE. The internal features of an OLE control fall under three distinct categories:

- *Properties* are the control's data members. You use these data members to control the appearance and behavior of the control. You can provide direct access to the properties or you can limit access through get and set methods.

- *Methods* are the functions implemented by the control. You invoke methods to affect the control's appearance and internal variables. The control's methods affect appearance and data in exactly the same way as class methods in C++.

- *Events* are the interface through which the control communicates with its container. The control fires events to notify the container that something important is happening to the control, such as a mouse click or the arrival of data.

Methods are the most welcome addition to the OLE control specification. The original VBX specification lacked methods, so the independent software vendor had to implement a method through a single property or a combination of properties. The addition of methods opens OLE controls to any development environment capable of implementing an OLE container.

Why Use OLE Controls?

When Microsoft first introduced the idea of OLE controls, many in the industry asked why. After all, as the old adage says, "If it's not broken, don't fix it," and VBXs are (and continue to be) commercially successful. So, why mess with something that has created a component software industry? Here are a few reasons:

- The VBX specification was designed specifically for Visual Basic, and therefore has limits when used with other programming languages. The lack of methods is the most obvious of these limitations.

- VBXs assume that Visual Basic programs will be the containers. Therefore, they rely on Visual Basic for part of their programming interface. Other development tools must kludge their applications and development environment to work with VBXs.

- VBXs assume that the application will be built on 16-bit addresses. With the introduction of the 32-bit operating systems, this assumption is too restrictive.

The new OLE control specification is written to remedy these limitations. All Microsoft-supported operating systems are to implement OLE 2.

To understand the OCX philosophy fully, you need to know how to create OCXs. The rest of this chapter concentrates on developing a trivial OLE control.

A Trivial Control

A trivial OLE *control* contains the minimal code required to create a working OCX. This process is entirely automated by the ControlWizard. In contrast, you must create VBX controls manually.

> **Note**
>
> Thanks to the Microsoft Foundation Classes (MFC), the code necessary to implement a basic OLE control is minimal. Thanks to the ControlWizard, the effort is minimal as well.

To invoke the ControlWizard, choose File, New from the Developer Studio window's menu bar. When the New dialog box appears, choose Project Workspace from the list. The New Project Workspace dialog box opens as shown in figure 10.1.

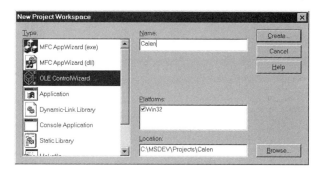

Fig. 10.1

The New Project Workspace dialog box enables you to build to a variety of project types.

From the Type list, select the OLE ControlWizard, and in the Name text box, enter **Calen**. In the Platform control, select Win32, and in the Location text box, accept the default location generated by Visual C++. Click the Create button to continue the specification process. This displays the first ControlWizard dialog box as shown in figure 10.2.

Fig. 10.2

The ControlWizard creates the skeleton control based on programmer inputs.

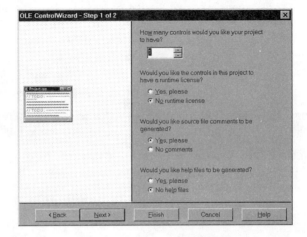

Accept the defaults in this dialog box and then click the Next button. This invokes the second dialog box, as shown in figure 10.3.

Fig. 10.3

The second ControlWizard dialog box enables you to specify further the details of the OCX that you are creating.

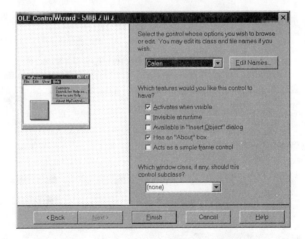

The ControlWizard dialog boxes contain several options that you can use to specify what the ControlWizard creates. With these options, you can choose to do the following:

- Create a single control or multiple controls in the same OCX.

- Add to your project support for licensing.

- Create the skeleton with or without source-line comments in the generated code.

- Create a help file for the OCX.

- Edit the names of various classes in your OCX.

- Specify whether the control is to activate when visible, be invisible at run time, be available in an Insert Object dialog box, have an About box, or act as a simple frame control.

- Specify another class from which your class is to be a subclass.

The rest of this chapter and Chapter 11, "Building OLE Controls," guide you step by step through the process of creating the Calen control, a custom OLE control for selecting a day of the month. These chapters cover all aspects of the ControlWizard, even if they don't apply to the creation of the Calen control. Therefore, you can easily change the attributes of your control to fit your specific needs.

To begin creating the Calen control, accept the project options that you have selected and click the Finish button. You then see the New Project Information dialog box shown in figure 10.4.

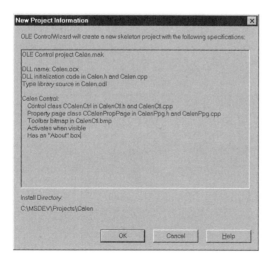

Fig. 10.4

The New Project Information dialog box tells you which files the ControlWizard has created for this project.

The new ControlWizard and MFC classes for writing OLE controls provide complete cross-platform compatibility. Therefore, you can compile your code in both the 16- and 32-bit development environments without changing the code.

Creating the skeleton of an OLE control is almost like magic. (After all, isn't that what a wizard is for?) Table 10.1 lists the most important files that the ControlWizard generates in the Calen directory.

Table 10.1   The Files Generated by the ControlWizard

File Name	Contents
Calen.mak	Project makefile
Calen.h	Header file for the control's application class
Calen.cpp	Implementation of the application class and registration functions
Calen.rc	Project resource file
Calen.def	Project-definition file for OLE controls
CalenCtl.h	Header file for your OLE control
CalenCtl.cpp	Implementation of your OLE control
CalenPpg.h	Header file for your control's property page
CalenPpg.cpp	Implementation of your control's property page
StdAfx.h	Header file for standard MFC include files
StdAfx.cpp	Implementation file for standard MFC include files
Resource.h	Header file for standard resources
Calen.ico	Icon resource for your control
Calen.odl	Project type library source

Microsoft has engineered the workspace to enable you to view your programs and classes in several different ways. Figure 10.5 shows the classes that the ControlWizard includes in your OCX project.

Fig. 10.5

The Class View enables you to locate methods in your project.

Double-clicking a method name moves your cursor to the method's location in the code window. Figure 10.6 shows the Resource View of your project.

Fig. 10.6

The Resource View enables you to manage the resources in your project.

By double-clicking the icon next to a resource, you bring up the appropriate editor to manipulate that resource. In this way, the Resource View enables you to work in a unified environment.

The final view available to the programmer is the File View. This view, shown in figure 10.7, enables you to manage all the files that make up this project.

Fig. 10.7

You can manage files in the File View.

As with the other views, double-clicking an icon in this view takes you to the appropriate file in the code window.

You have now completed creating the Calen control's skeleton. Before you compile and run the control, however, the following sections review the various source-code files created by the ControlWizard.

Note

The following sections do not discuss the project's makefiles or icon and bitmap files because they do little to inform you about the actual creation of OLE controls. As you develop your control, use the resource editor to customize both the icon and bitmap files.

The Calen.h File

Listing 10.1 shows the source code contained in the Calen's header file. The header file includes the definition for the Calen control's application class, as well as global variables used by the rest of the OCX.

Listing 10.1   Calen.h, the Calen Control's Header File

```
// Calen.h : main header file for CALEN.DLL

#if !defined( __AFXCTL_H__ )
     #error include 'afxctl.h' before including this file
#endif

#include "resource.h"        // main symbols

/////////////////////////////////////////////////////////////////////
// CCalenApp : See Calen.cpp for implementation.

class CCalenApp : public COleControlModule
{
public:
     BOOL InitInstance();
     int ExitInstance();
};

extern const GUID CDECL _tlid;
extern const WORD _wVerMajor;
extern const WORD _wVerMinor;
```

The Calen.cpp File

Listing 10.2 shows the source code for Calen.cpp. This file's contents include the implementation of the application class (CCalenApp) and the CCalenApp instance (theApp). You can add application entry and exit functionality to the CCalen::InitInstance() and CCalen::ExitInstance() methods. All MFC applications, including OCXs, have only one application instance. Of special interest are the OLE-specific code and data members. The class ID for the Calen control is stored in the

_tlid global variable. The standard functions DLLRegisterServer() and
DLLUnregisterServer() use this ID. As you might guess, these two functions register
and unregister the Calen control from the Registration database.

Listing 10.2   Calen.cpp, the Calen Control's Implementation File

```
// Calen.cpp : Implementation of CCalenApp and DLL registration.

#include "stdafx.h"
#include "Calen.h"

#ifdef _DEBUG
#define new DEBUG_NEW
#undef THIS_FILE
static char THIS_FILE[] = __FILE__;
#endif


CCalenApp NEAR theApp;

const GUID CDECL BASED_CODE _tlid =
          { 0xeb2a4940, 0x142b, 0x11cf, { 0x95, 0x2f, 0, 0x20,
            0xaf, 0x6e, 0x90, 0x3f } };
const WORD _wVerMajor = 1;
const WORD _wVerMinor = 0;


/////////////////////////////////////////////////////////////////////////
// CCalenApp::InitInstance - DLL initialization

BOOL CCalenApp::InitInstance()
{
     BOOL bInit = COleControlModule::InitInstance();

     if (bInit)
     {
          // TODO: Add your own module initialization code here.
     }

     return bInit;
}


/////////////////////////////////////////////////////////////////////////
// CCalenApp::ExitInstance - DLL termination

int CCalenApp::ExitInstance()
{
     // TODO: Add your own module termination code here.

     return COleControlModule::ExitInstance();
}


/////////////////////////////////////////////////////////////////////////
```

(continues)

Listing 10.2   Continued

```
// DllRegisterServer - Adds entries to the system Registry

STDAPI DllRegisterServer(void)
{
     AFX_MANAGE_STATE(_afxModuleAddrThis);

     if (!AfxOleRegisterTypeLib(AfxGetInstanceHandle(), _tlid))
          return ResultFromScode(SELFREG_E_TYPELIB);

     if (!COleObjectFactoryEx::UpdateRegistryAll(TRUE))
          return ResultFromScode(SELFREG_E_CLASS);

     return NOERROR;
}


/////////////////////////////////////////////////////////////////////////
// DllUnregisterServer - Removes entries from the system Registry

STDAPI DllUnregisterServer(void)
{
     AFX_MANAGE_STATE(_afxModuleAddrThis);

     if (!AfxOleUnregisterTypeLib(_tlid))
          return ResultFromScode(SELFREG_E_TYPELIB);

     if (!COleObjectFactoryEx::UpdateRegistryAll(FALSE))
          return ResultFromScode(SELFREG_E_CLASS);

     return NOERROR;
```

The Calen.rc File

The Calen.rc file, shown in listing 10.3, contains the resource script for resources that you can maintain with the resource editor. This file defines your About dialog box and the string table used by the Calen control. The resource script also includes the icon and bitmap used by your control.

Listing 10.3   Calen.rc, the Calen Control's Resource File

```
//Microsoft Visual C++ generated resource script.
//
#include "resource.h"

#define APSTUDIO_READONLY_SYMBOLS
/////////////////////////////////////////////////////////////////////////
//
// Generated from the TEXTINCLUDE 2 resource.
//
#include "afxres.h"


/////////////////////////////////////////////////////////////////////////
```

```
#undef APSTUDIO_READONLY_SYMBOLS

#ifdef APSTUDIO_INVOKED
/////////////////////////////////////////////////////////////////////////
//
// TEXTINCLUDE
//

1 TEXTINCLUDE DISCARDABLE
BEGIN
      "resource.h\0"
END

2 TEXTINCLUDE DISCARDABLE
BEGIN
      "#include ""afxres.h""\r\n"
      "\0"
END

3 TEXTINCLUDE DISCARDABLE
BEGIN
      "1 TYPELIB ""Calen.tlb""\r\n"
      "\0"
END

/////////////////////////////////////////////////////////////////////////
#endif    // APSTUDIO_INVOKED


/////////////////////////////////////////////////////////////////////////
//
// Version
//

VS_VERSION_INFO VERSIONINFO
 FILEVERSION 1,0,0,1
 PRODUCTVERSION 1,0,0,1
 FILEFLAGSMASK 0x3fL
#ifdef _DEBUG
 FILEFLAGS 0x1L
#else
 FILEFLAGS 0x0L
#endif
 FILEOS 0x4L
 FILETYPE 0x2L
 FILESUBTYPE 0x0L
BEGIN
    BLOCK "StringFileInfo"
    BEGIN
        BLOCK "040904B0"
        BEGIN
            VALUE "CompanyName", "\0"
            VALUE "FileDescription", "Calen OLE Control Module\0"
            VALUE "FileVersion", "1, 0, 0, 1\0"
            VALUE "InternalName", "CALEN\0"
            VALUE "LegalCopyright", "Copyright © 1995\0"
```

(continues)

Listing 10.3 Continued

```
                VALUE "LegalTrademarks", "\0"
                VALUE "OriginalFilename", "CALEN.OCX\0"
                VALUE "ProductName", "Calen OLE Control Module\0"
                VALUE "ProductVersion", "1, 0, 0, 1\0"
            END
        END
        BLOCK "VarFileInfo"
        BEGIN
            VALUE "Translation", 0x409, 1200
        END
    END


/////////////////////////////////////////////////////////////////////////////
//
// Icon
//

// Icon with lowest ID value placed first to ensure application icon
// remains consistent on all systems.
IDI_ABOUTDLL    ICON    DISCARDABLE     "Calen.ico"


/////////////////////////////////////////////////////////////////////////////
//
// Bitmap
//

IDB_CALEN   BITMAP DISCARDABLE  "CalenCtl.bmp"


/////////////////////////////////////////////////////////////////////////////
//
// Dialog
//

IDD_ABOUTBOX_CALEN DIALOG DISCARDABLE  34, 22, 260, 55
CAPTION "About Calen Control"
STYLE DS_MODALFRAME ¦ WS_POPUP ¦ WS_CAPTION ¦ WS_SYSMENU
FONT 8, "MS Sans Serif"
BEGIN
    ICON            IDI_ABOUTDLL,IDC_STATIC,10,10,20,20
    LTEXT           "Calen Control, Version 1.0",IDC_STATIC,40,10,170,8
    LTEXT           "Copyright \251 1995, ",IDC_STATIC,40,25,170,8
    DEFPUSHBUTTON   "OK",IDOK,221,7,32,14,WS_GROUP
END

IDD_PROPPAGE_CALEN DIALOG DISCARDABLE  0, 0, 250, 62
STYLE WS_CHILD
FONT 8, "MS Sans Serif"
BEGIN
    LTEXT           "TODO: Place controls to manipulate properties
                    ➥of Calen Control on this dialog.",
                    IDC_STATIC,7,25,229,16
END


/////////////////////////////////////////////////////////////////////////////
```

```
//
// DESIGNINFO
//

#ifdef APSTUDIO_INVOKED
GUIDELINES DESIGNINFO DISCARDABLE
BEGIN
    IDD_ABOUTBOX_CALEN, DIALOG
    BEGIN
        LEFTMARGIN, 7
        RIGHTMARGIN, 253
        TOPMARGIN, 7
        BOTTOMMARGIN, 48
    END
    IDD_PROPPAGE_CALEN, DIALOG
    BEGIN
        LEFTMARGIN, 7
        RIGHTMARGIN, 243
        TOPMARGIN, 7
        BOTTOMMARGIN, 55
    END
END
#endif    // APSTUDIO_INVOKED


/////////////////////////////////////////////////////////////////////////
//
// String Table
//

STRINGTABLE DISCARDABLE
BEGIN
        IDS_CALEN                "Calen Control"
        IDS_CALEN_PPG            "Calen Property Page"
        IDS_CALEN_PPG_CAPTION    "General"

END


#ifndef APSTUDIO_INVOKED
/////////////////////////////////////////////////////////////////////////
//
// Generated from the TEXTINCLUDE 3 resource.
//
1 TYPELIB "Calen.tlb"


/////////////////////////////////////////////////////////////////////////
#endif    // not APSTUDIO_INVOKED
```

The Calen.def File

The ControlWizard places the definitions in the Calen.def file, which is shown in listing 10.4. The library NAME and DESCRIPTION clauses contain the Calen project name, as well as the exports contained in the Calen OCX.

Listing 10.4   Calen.def, the Calen Control's Definition File

```
; Calen.def : Declares the module parameters.

LIBRARY      "CALEN.OCX"

EXPORTS
      DllCanUnloadNow     @1 PRIVATE
      DllGetClassObject   @2 PRIVATE
      DllRegisterServer   @3 PRIVATE
      DllUnregisterServer @4 PRIVATE
```

The CalenCtl.h File

Listing 10.5 shows the contents of the CalenCtl.h header file. This file contains the class definition for CCalenCtl. As you examine this class definition, keep in mind that CCalenCtl derives from the COleObject class, which provides so much of the functionality required by the Calen control. The derived class contains a public constructor, a protected destructor, the message-handling function OnDraw(), the property exchange function DoPropExchange(), and the control reset function OnResetState(). In particular, note the following macros, which further define your OLE control:

- DECLARE_OLECREATE_EX declares your control's class factory and provides the GetClassId() member function.

- DECLARE_OLETYPELIB declares the member function GetTypeLib(), which returns your control's type library. MFC uses the type library internally for your control's OLE interface.

- DECLARE_PROPPAGEIDS prepares your control for the binding of your property pages. Property pages provide a visual interface to your control's properties. You learn more about property pages in Chapter 11, "Building OLE Controls," when you actually implement property pages.

Listing 10.5   CalenCtl.h, the Header File for the CCalenCtrl Class

```
// CalenCtl.h : Declaration of the CCalenCtrl OLE control class.

/////////////////////////////////////////////////////////////////////
// CCalenCtrl : See CalenCtl.cpp for implementation.

class CCalenCtrl : public COleControl
{
      DECLARE_DYNCREATE(CCalenCtrl)

// Constructor
public:
      CCalenCtrl();

// Overrides

      // Drawing function
      virtual void OnDraw(
```

```
                    CDC* pdc, const CRect& rcBounds, const CRect& rcInvalid);

        // Persistence
        virtual void DoPropExchange(CPropExchange* pPX);

        // Reset control state
        virtual void OnResetState();

// Implementation
protected:
        ~CCalenCtrl();

        DECLARE_OLECREATE_EX(CCalenCtrl)      // Class factory and guid
        DECLARE_OLETYPELIB(CCalenCtrl)        // GetTypeInfo
        DECLARE_PROPPAGEIDS(CCalenCtrl)       // Property page IDs
        DECLARE_OLECTLTYPE(CCalenCtrl)        // Type name and misc status

// Message maps
        //{{AFX_MSG(CCalenCtrl)
          // NOTE - ClassWizard will add and remove member functions here.
          //    DO NOT EDIT what you see in these blocks of generated code!
        //}}AFX_MSG
        DECLARE_MESSAGE_MAP()

// Dispatch maps
        //{{AFX_DISPATCH(CCalenCtrl)
          // NOTE - ClassWizard will add and remove member functions here.
           //  DO NOT EDIT what you see in these blocks of generated code!
        //}}AFX_DISPATCH
        DECLARE_DISPATCH_MAP()

        afx_msg void AboutBox();

// Event maps
        //{{AFX_EVENT(CCalenCtrl)
          // NOTE - ClassWizard will add and remove member functions here.
           // DO NOT EDIT what you see in these blocks of generated code!
        //}}AFX_EVENT
        DECLARE_EVENT_MAP()

// Dispatch and event IDs
public:
        enum {
        //{{AFX_DISP_ID(CCalenCtrl)
        // NOTE: ClassWizard will add and remove enumeration elements here.
        // DO NOT EDIT what you see in these blocks of generated code!
        //}}AFX_DISP_ID
        };
```

The CalenCtl.cpp Implementation

Listing 10.6 shows the contents of the CalenCtl.cpp implementation file, which is where the majority of your control is written. Before you examine this listing, you need a more detailed overview of these contents. You can categorize these contents into 12 sections (keep in mind that Chapter 11 inspects each section more thoroughly):

- *The message map.* The ControlWizard inserts a basic message map that you will later modify with the ClassWizard. The current message map contains one entry, ON_OLEVERB, which responds to a request to edit the control's properties by calling the OnProperties() member function.

- *The dispatch map.* This map exposes functions and properties so that the outside world can discover which methods and properties your control possesses, and can access those functions and properties. The default entry in the dispatch map, AboutBox, activates the control's About dialog box.

- *The event map.* Listing 10.8 shows the shell of an empty event map. Later, you add more events to communicate with the control's container.

- *The property page IDs.* A new feature for OLE controls, these IDs identify the property pages that change the control's properties. All controls generated by the ClassWizard start with one property page, General, which is the only entry in the current set of property pages. You can also add user-defined property pages.

- *The OLE macros.* These two macros, IMPLEMENT_OLECREATE_EX and IMPLEMENT_OLETYPELIB, create the class factory and type library code needed to implement the control as an OLE object.

- *The interface IDs.* The two IIDs, IID_DCalen and IID_DCalenEvents, are the unique IDs for the Calen control and its events.

- *The CCalenCtrlFactory::UpdateRegistry() function.* You use this function to add or remove the entries in the Calen control's Registration database. The code and your control's default parameters are created for you automatically. The defaults are usually adequate. Chapter 11 explains more about what this function does. Note that the bRegister parameter determines whether the control is being registered or deregistered.

- *The constructor and destructor.* The Calen control's constructor initializes the control's IIDs. You should add additional class initialization code. The destructor is an empty shell. Add any additional cleanup code.

- *The OnDraw() function.* The ControlWizard places minimal code in this function so that your control draws at least something when this function is called. To enhance your control's appearance, you should replace the default code with your own.

- *The DoPropExchange() function.* This function provides *serialization* for your control; that is, the control's properties are loaded and saved to a stream in this function. The PX family of functions implements this functionality. You need only add the appropriate PX function for each of your properties that requires serialization.

- *The OnResetState() function.* This function resets the control's contents. Any properties included in DoPropExchange() should be reset to default values. You can also use this function to reinitialize internal class and data members.

- *The AboutBox() function.* Call this function to display your control's About dialog box. AboutBox() is also the only current member of the dispatch map. Visual C++ instantiates a CDialog object to display the About dialog box. The DoModal() member function is then executed to display the dialog box.

Listing 10.6   CalenCtl.cpp, the Calen Control's Implementation

```
// CalenCtl.cpp : Implementation of the CCalenCtrl OLE control class.

#include "stdafx.h"
#include "Calen.h"
#include "CalenCtl.h"
#include "CalenPpg.h"


#ifdef _DEBUG
#define new DEBUG_NEW
#undef THIS_FILE
static char THIS_FILE[] = __FILE__;
#endif


IMPLEMFNT_DYNCREATE(CCalcnCtrl, COleControl)


/////////////////////////////////////////////////////////////////////
// Message map

BEGIN_MESSAGE_MAP(CCalenCtrl, COleControl)
    //{{AFX_MSG_MAP(CCalenCtrl)
    // NOTE - ClassWizard will add and remove message map entries
    //    DO NOT EDIT what you see in these blocks of generated code!
    //}}AFX_MSG_MAP
    ON_OLEVERB(AFX_IDS_VERB_PROPERTIES, OnProperties)
END_MESSAGE_MAP()


/////////////////////////////////////////////////////////////////////
// Dispatch map

BEGIN_DISPATCH_MAP(CCalenCtrl, COleControl)
    //{{AFX_DISPATCH_MAP(CCalenCtrl)
    // NOTE - ClassWizard will add and remove dispatch map entries
    //    DO NOT EDIT what you see in these blocks of generated code!
    //}}AFX_DISPATCH_MAP
    DISP_FUNCTION_ID(CCalenCtrl, "AboutBox", DISPID_ABOUTBOX,
                    AboutBox, VT_EMPTY, VTS_NONE)
END_DISPATCH_MAP()


/////////////////////////////////////////////////////////////////////
// Event map

BEGIN_EVENT_MAP(CCalenCtrl, COleControl)
    //{{AFX_EVENT_MAP(CCalenCtrl)
```

(continues)

Listing 10.6   Continued

```
            // NOTE - ClassWizard will add and remove event map entries
            //     DO NOT EDIT what you see in these blocks of generated code!
            //}}AFX_EVENT_MAP
END_EVENT_MAP()


/////////////////////////////////////////////////////////////////////////////
// Property pages

// TODO: Add more property pages as needed.
//   Remember to increase the count!
BEGIN_PROPPAGEIDS(CCalenCtrl, 1)
      PROPPAGEID(CCalenPropPage::guid)
END_PROPPAGEIDS(CCalenCtrl)


/////////////////////////////////////////////////////////////////////////////
// Initialize class factory and guid

IMPLEMENT_OLECREATE_EX(CCalenCtrl, "CALEN.CalenCtrl.1",
      0xeb2a4943, 0x142b, 0x11cf, 0x95, 0x2f, 0, 0x20, 0xaf, 0x6e,
      0x90, 0x3f)


/////////////////////////////////////////////////////////////////////////////
// Type library ID and version

IMPLEMENT_OLETYPELIB(CCalenCtrl, _tlid, _wVerMajor, _wVerMinor)


/////////////////////////////////////////////////////////////////////////////
// Interface IDs

const IID BASED_CODE IID_DCalen =
            { 0xeb2a4941, 0x142b, 0x11cf, { 0x95, 0x2f, 0, 0x20,
              0xaf, 0x6e, 0x90, 0x3f } };
const IID BASED_CODE IID_DCalenEvents =
            { 0xeb2a4942, 0x142b, 0x11cf, { 0x95, 0x2f, 0, 0x20,
              0xaf, 0x6e, 0x90, 0x3f } };


/////////////////////////////////////////////////////////////////////////////
// Control type information

static const DWORD BASED_CODE _dwCalenOleMisc =
      OLEMISC_ACTIVATEWHENVISIBLE ¦
      OLEMISC_SETCLIENTSITEFIRST ¦
      OLEMISC_INSIDEOUT ¦
      OLEMISC_CANTLINKINSIDE ¦
      OLEMISC_RECOMPOSEONRESIZE;

IMPLEMENT_OLECTLTYPE(CCalenCtrl, IDS_CALEN, _dwCalenOleMisc)


/////////////////////////////////////////////////////////////////////////////
```

```
// CCalenCtrl::CCalenCtrlFactory::UpdateRegistry -
// Adds or removes system Registry entries for CCalenCtrl

BOOL CCalenCtrl::CCalenCtrlFactory::UpdateRegistry(BOOL bRegister)
{
    if (bRegister)
        return AfxOleRegisterControlClass(
            AfxGetInstanceHandle(),
            m_clsid,
            m_lpszProgID,
            IDS_CALEN,
            IDB_CALEN,
            FALSE,                          //  Not insertable
            _dwCalenOleMisc,
            _tlid,
            _wVerMajor,
            _wVerMinor);
        else
        return AfxOleUnregisterClass(m_clsid, m_lpszProgID);
}


/////////////////////////////////////////////////////////////////////////
// CCalenCtrl::CCalenCtrl - Constructor

CCalenCtrl::CCalenCtrl()
{
    InitializeIIDs(&IID_DCalen, &IID_DCalenEvents);

    // TODO: Initialize your control's instance data here.
}


/////////////////////////////////////////////////////////////////////////
// CCalenCtrl::~CCalenCtrl - Destructor

CCalenCtrl::~CCalenCtrl()
{
    // TODO: Clean up your control's instance data here.
}


/////////////////////////////////////////////////////////////////////////
// CCalenCtrl::OnDraw - Drawing function

void CCalenCtrl::OnDraw(
                CDC* pdc, const CRect& rcBounds, const CRect& rcInvalid)
{
    // TODO: Replace the following code with your own drawing code.
    pdc->FillRect(rcBounds,
CBrush::FromHandle((HBRUSH)GetStockObject(WHITE_BRUSH)));
    pdc->Ellipse(rcBounds);
}


/////////////////////////////////////////////////////////////////////////
```

(continues)

Listing 10.6   Continued

```
// CCalenCtrl::DoPropExchange - Persistence support

void CCalenCtrl::DoPropExchange(CPropExchange* pPX)
{
      ExchangeVersion(pPX, MAKELONG(_wVerMinor, _wVerMajor));
      COleControl::DoPropExchange(pPX);

      // TODO: Call PX_ functions for each persistent custom property.

}


/////////////////////////////////////////////////////////////////////////
// CCalenCtrl::OnResetState - Reset control to default state

void CCalenCtrl::OnResetState()
{
      COleControl::OnResetState();
                                  // Resets defaults found in DoPropExchange

      // TODO: Reset any other control state here.
}


/////////////////////////////////////////////////////////////////////////
// CCalenCtrl::AboutBox - Display an "About" box to the user

void CCalenCtrl::AboutBox()
{
      CDialog dlgAbout(IDD_ABOUTBOX_CALEN);
      dlgAbout.DoModal();
}


/////////////////////////////////////////////////////////////////////////
// CCalenCtrl message handlers
```

The CalenPpg.h Header File

Listing 10.7 shows the contents of the CalenPpg.h header file. This file contains the class definition for the CCalenPropPage class. This class provides the functionality for the General property page and derives from the CDialog MFC class.

Listing 10.7   CalenPpg.h, the Header File for the CCalenPropPage Class

```
// CalenPpg.h : Declaration of the CCalenPropPage property page class.

/////////////////////////////////////////////////////////////////////////
// CCalenPropPage : See CalenPpg.cpp.cpp for implementation.

class CCalenPropPage : public COlePropertyPage
```

```
{
    DECLARE_DYNCREATE(CCalenPropPage)
    DECLARE_OLECREATE_EX(CCalenPropPage)

// Constructor
public:
    CCalenPropPage();

// Dialog Data
    //{{AFX_DATA(CCalenPropPage)
    enum { IDD = IDD_PROPPAGE_CALEN };
        // NOTE - ClassWizard will add data members here.
        //   DO NOT EDIT what you see in these blocks of generated code!
    //}}AFX_DATA

// Implementation
protected:
    virtual void DoDataExchange(CDataExchange* pDX); // DDX/DDV support

// Message maps
protected:
    //{{AFX_MSG(CCalenPropPage)
        // NOTE - ClassWizard will add and remove member functions here.
        // DO NOT EDIT what you see in these blocks of generated code!
    //}}AFX_MSG
    DECLARE_MESSAGE_MAP()
```

The CalenPpg.cpp File

The CalenPpg.cpp file, which is shown in listing 10.8, contains the implementation of the CCalenPropPage class. The CalenPpg.cpp file also contains the following important items:

- *The message map.* The shell of the message map is included for later modifications.

- *The IMPLEMENT_OLECREATE_EX macro.* The CCalenPropPage is an OLE class and is registered in the Registration database. This macro declares the class factory for this control and the GetClassID() member function. The class factory registers the control.

- *The CCalenPropPageFactory::UpdateRegistry() function.* This function registers and deregisters the CCalenPropPage class.

- *The constructor.* This file includes the constructor's shell so that you can add your own initialization code.

- *The DoDataExchange() function.* This member function overrides the standard CHwnd::DoDataExchange() function to provide data transfer between the control and the control's property pages.

Listing 10.8 CalenPpg.cpp, the Implementation File for the `CalenPropPage` Class

```cpp
// CalenPpg.cpp : Implementation of the CCalenPropPage property
// page class.

#include "stdafx.h"
#include "Calen.h"
#include "CalenPpg.h"

#ifdef _DEBUG
#define new DEBUG_NEW
#undef THIS_FILE
static char THIS_FILE[] = __FILE__;
#endif


IMPLEMENT_DYNCREATE(CCalenPropPage, COlePropertyPage)


/////////////////////////////////////////////////////////////////////
// Message map

BEGIN_MESSAGE_MAP(CCalenPropPage, COlePropertyPage)
    //{{AFX_MSG_MAP(CCalenPropPage)
    // NOTE - ClassWizard will add and remove message map entries
    //    DO NOT EDIT what you see in these blocks of generated code!
    //}}AFX_MSG_MAP
END_MESSAGE_MAP()


/////////////////////////////////////////////////////////////////////
// Initialize class factory and guid

IMPLEMENT_OLECREATE_EX(CCalenPropPage, "CALEN.CalenPropPage.1",
    0xeb2a4944, 0x142b, 0x11cf, 0x95, 0x2f, 0, 0x20, 0xaf, 0x6e,
    0x90, 0x3f)


/////////////////////////////////////////////////////////////////////
// CCalenPropPage::CCalenPropPageFactory::UpdateRegistry -
// Adds or removes system Registry entries for CCalenPropPage

BOOL CCalenPropPage::CCalenPropPageFactory::UpdateRegistry
    (BOOL bRegister)
{
    if (bRegister)
        return AfxOleRegisterPropertyPageClass(AfxGetInstanceHandle(),
            m_clsid, IDS_CALEN_PPG);
    else
        return AfxOleUnregisterClass(m_clsid, NULL);
}


/////////////////////////////////////////////////////////////////////
// CCalenPropPage::CCalenPropPage - Constructor
```

```
CCalenPropPage::CCalenPropPage() :
        COlePropertyPage(IDD, IDS_CALEN_PPG_CAPTION)
{
        //{{AFX_DATA_INIT(CCalenPropPage)
        // NOTE: ClassWizard will add member initialization here
        //     DO NOT EDIT what you see in these blocks of generated code!
        //}}AFX_DATA_INIT
}


/////////////////////////////////////////////////////////////////////////
// CCalenPropPage::DoDataExchange - Moves data between page
// and properties

void CCalenPropPage::DoDataExchange(CDataExchange* pDX)
{
        //{{AFX_DATA_MAP(CCalenPropPage)
        // NOTE: ClassWizard will add DDP, DDX, and DDV calls here
        //     DO NOT EDIT what you see in these blocks of generated code!
        //}}AFX_DATA_MAP
        DDP_PostProcessing(pDX);
}


/////////////////////////////////////////////////////////////////////////
```

The StdAfx.h File

Listing 10.9 shows the StdAfx.h header file. It contains the single `#include` statement for the afxctl.h header file, which provides MFC support for OLE controls.

Listing 10.9   StdAfx.h, the Header File That Provides the `#include` Statement

```
// stdafx.h : include file for standard system include files,
//      or project specific include files that are used frequently,
//      but are changed infrequently

#define VC_EXTRALEAN      // Exclude rarely used stuff from Windows headers

#include <afxctl.h>       // MFC support for OLE Controls

// Delete the two includes below if you do not wish to use the MFC
//   database classes
#ifndef _UNICODE
#include <afxdb.h>                  // MFC database classes
#include <afxdao.h>                 // MFC DAO database classes
```

The StdAfx.cpp File

Listing 10.10 shows the contents for the StdAfx.cpp implementation file. The file provides a single `#include` statement that includes the StdAfx.h header file.

Listing 10.10   StdAfx.cpp, the Implementation File for the #include Statement

```
// stdafx.cpp : source file that includes just the standard includes
//  stdafx.pch will be the precompiled header
//  stdafx.obj will contain the precompiled type information
```

The Resource.h Header File

Listing 10.11 shows the contents of the Resource.h header file. This file contains several #define statements that the Calen.rc file uses. The #define statements correspond to the following:

IDS_??????	Strings in the string table
IDD_??????	Dialog box identifiers
IDB_??????	Bitmap identifiers
IDI_??????	Icon identifiers

When you load the Calen.rc file in the AppStudio, you will recognize these names as identifiers for the various resources that you can edit.

Listing 10.11   Resource.h, the Header File That Includes #define Statements for Calen.rc

```
//{{NO_DEPENDENCIES}}
// Microsoft Visual C++ generated include file.
// Used by Calen.rc
//

#define IDS_CALEN                1
#define IDS_CALEN_PPG            2

#define IDS_CALEN_PPG_CAPTION    100

#define IDD_PROPPAGE_CALEN       100

#define IDD_ABOUTBOX_CALEN       1

#define IDB_CALEN                1

#define IDI_ABOUTDLL             1

#define _APS_NEXT_RESOURCE_VALUE    201
#define _APS_NEXT_CONTROL_VALUE     201
#define _APS_NEXT_SYMED_VALUE       101
#define _APS_NEXT_COMMAND_VALUE     32768
```

The Calen.odl Type Library File

The Calen.odl file, shown in listing 10.12, the Calen control's type library information. The ClassWizard maintains the information stored in this file. Nevertheless, you should be aware of the contents of these types of files.

The Calen.odl type library file consists of three sections:

- *The dispatch interface.* The entries in the primary dispatch interface correspond directly to the dispatch map in CalenCtl.cpp. This information is added to the resources of your control so that the outside world can find out about the interfaces that your control supports. This section consists of properties and methods subsections.

- *The event dispatch.* This section stores information about the events that your OLE control generates. The container can then respond to events generated by your control. The event dispatch also consists of properties and methods subsections. Currently, the event interface has no properties, and the methods subsection corresponds to the events generated by the OLE object. In Chapter 11, you use the ClassWizard to add events to the event dispatch.

- *The class information.* This section exports the interface for both the primary dispatch interface and the event dispatch interface. Containers refer to this section to learn about the various interfaces that your OLE control supports.

Listing 10.12 Calen.odl, the Type Library File

```
// Calen.odl : type library source for OLE Control project.

// This file will be processed by the Make Type Library (mktyplib) tool
// to produce the type library (Calen.tlb) that will become a resource in
// Calen.ocx.

#include <olectl.h>

[ uuid(EB2A4940-142B-11CF-952F-0020AF6E903F), version(1.0),
  helpstring("Calen OLE Control module"), control ]
library CALENLib
{
    importlib(STDOLE_TLB);
    importlib(STDTYPE_TLB);

    //  Primary dispatch interface for CCalenCtrl

    [ uuid(EB2A4941-142B-11CF-952F-0020AF6E903F),
      helpstring("Dispatch interface for Calen Control"), hidden ]
    dispinterface _DCalen
    {
        properties:
        // NOTE - ClassWizard maintains property information here.
            //    Use extreme caution when editing this section.
            //{{AFX_ODL_PROP(CCalenCtrl)
            //}}AFX_ODL_PROP
```

(continues)

Listing 10.12 Continued

```
      methods:
            // NOTE - ClassWizard maintains method information here.
            //     Use extreme caution when editing this section.
            //{{AFX_ODL_METHOD(CCalenCtrl)
            //}}AFX_ODL_METHOD

            [id(DISPID_ABOUTBOX)] void AboutBox();
};

//   Event dispatch interface for CCalenCtrl

[ uuid(EB2A4942-142B-11CF-952F-0020AF6E903F),
  helpstring("Event interface for Calen Control") ]
dispinterface _DCalenEvents
{
      properties:
      //  Event interface has no properties

      methods:
            // NOTE - ClassWizard maintains event information here.
            //     Use extreme caution when editing this section.
            //{{AFX_ODL_EVENT(CCalenCtrl)
            //}}AFX_ODL_EVENT
};

//   Class information for CCalenCtrl

[ uuid(EB2A4943-142B-11CF-952F-0020AF6E903F),
  helpstring("Calen Control"), control ]
coclass Calen
{
      [default] dispinterface _DCalen;
      [default, source] dispinterface _DCalenEvents;
    };


      //{{AFX_APPEND_ODL}}
```

When building your project, the Visual Workbench compiles this file with the
mktyplib utility into the Calen.tlb file, which is then included in your control's
resources.

Adding Licensing Support to Your Control

Developers of third-party VBXs must implement their own scheme for licensing. The
methods used fall into three general categories:

■ *The license file.* The third-party control purchased by developers comes with an
.LIC file, which enables developers to use the control in their development environment. When the application is completed, it ships without the .LIC file,

preventing other people from developing with the control. The ControlWizard implements this method. Additional support is available for providing special licensing.

- *Separate controls.* The developer is provided with a control that works only in the development environment. A separate, run-time-only control ships with the application.

- *Time bombs and nag messages.* This method is used mostly by the shareware community. Many shareware VBXs are currently on the market, some of them of better quality than others. As the method suggests, either the control "blows up" after a certain length of time, or a nag message appears until the developer registers the control. After registering the control, the developer receives a "real" version that omits the time bomb or nag message.

The addition of licensing in the new OCX specification enforces a standard for control licensing. However, this standard leaves you enough flexibility in case you want to modify the licensing behavior. Most future OCXs on the market will support licensing. After all, the ControlWizard makes it easy.

To add licensing to the Calen control, use the ControlWizard as follows:

1. Use the ControlWizard to create a new control called Cal2.

2. When the ControlWizard dialog box appears, choose <u>Y</u>es, Please under the question about whether you want a run-time license for this control.

3. Click the <u>N</u>ext button and then the <u>F</u>inish button. The ControlWizard displays a summary of the project and the control options that you have selected. Figure 10.8 shows the New Project Information dialog box. Notice that the fifth line from the top reads `Runtime license validation using Cal2.lic`.

4. Click the OK button to generate the source code for the new Cal2 control.

Fig. 10.8

The New Project Information dialog box acknowledges the license validation.

Before compiling and running the Cal2 control, you must examine the important differences between the files in this project and the project that you created earlier in this chapter.

The Modified CalenderCtl.h Header File

The ControlWizard modifies the Cal2Ctl.h header file slightly so that it supports licensing.

The wizard replaces the DECLARE_OLECREATE_EX macro with BEGIN_OLEFACTORY and END_OLEFACTORY. These macros do manually what DECLARE_OLECREATE_EX does automatically. Sandwiched between these two macros are the member function declarations that support licensing:

- The VerifyUserLicense() function verifies that the control's container is licensed to contain the control.

- The GetLicenseKey() function gets a unique license key from the control and places it into the string pointed to by BSTR.

Listing 10.13 shows the new header file.

Listing 10.13   Cal2Ctl.h, the Modified Header File

```
// Cal2Ctl.h : Declaration of the CCal2Ctrl OLE control class.

//////////////////////////////////////////////////////////////////////
// CCal2Ctrl : See Cal2Ctl.cpp for implementation.

class CCal2Ctrl : public COleControl
{
    DECLARE_DYNCREATE(CCal2Ctrl)

// Constructor
public:
    CCal2Ctrl();

// Overrides

    // Drawing function
    virtual void OnDraw(
            CDC* pdc, const CRect& rcBounds, const CRect& rcInvalid);

    // Persistence
    virtual void DoPropExchange(CPropExchange* pPX);

    // Reset control state
    virtual void OnResetState();

// Implementation
protected:
    ~CCal2Ctrl();

    BEGIN_OLEFACTORY(CCal2Ctrl)          // Class factory and guid
        virtual BOOL VerifyUserLicense();
        virtual BOOL GetLicenseKey(DWORD, BSTR FAR*);
```

```
        END_OLEFACTORY(CCal2Ctrl)

        DECLARE_OLETYPELIB(CCal2Ctrl)        // GetTypeInfo
        DECLARE_PROPPAGEIDS(CCal2Ctrl)       // Property page IDs
        DECLARE_OLECTLTYPE(CCal2Ctrl)        // Type name and misc status

// Message maps
        //{{AFX_MSG(CCal2Ctrl)
            // NOTE - ClassWizard will add and remove member functions here.
            //   DO NOT EDIT what you see in these blocks of generated code!
        //}}AFX_MSG
        DECLARE_MESSAGE_MAP()

// Dispatch maps
        //{{AFX_DISPATCH(CCal2Ctrl)
            // NOTE - ClassWizard will add and remove member functions here.
            //   DO NOT EDIT what you see in these blocks of generated code!
        //}}AFX_DISPATCH
        DECLARE_DISPATCH_MAP()

        afx_msg void AboutBox();

// Event maps
        //{{AFX_EVENT(CCal2Ctrl)
            // NOTE - ClassWizard will add and remove member functions here.
            // DO NOT EDIT what you see in these blocks of generated code!
        //}}AFX_EVENT
        DECLARE_EVENT_MAP()

// Dispatch and event IDs
public:
        enum {
        //{{AFX_DISP_ID(CCal2Ctrl)
            // NOTE: ClassWizard adds and removes enumeration elements here.
            // DO NOT EDIT what you see in these blocks of generated code!
        //}}AFX_DISP_ID
        };
};
```

The Modified CalenCtl.cpp Implementation File

The ControlWizard also makes changes in the Cal2Ctl.cpp implementation file, as
shown in listing 10.14. The changes are not to the CCalenCtrl class, but to the
CCalenCtrlFactory class. The modifications implement the two functions defined in
Cal2Ctl.h, VerifyUserLicense() and GetLicenseKey(), and add the license strings
needed to implement the keys.

Listing 10.14. Cal2Ctl.cpp, the Modified Implementation File

```
// Cal2Ctl.cpp : Implementation of the CCal2Ctrl OLE control class.

#include "stdafx.h"
#include "Cal2.h"
#include "Cal2Ctl.h"
#include "Cal2Ppg.h"
```

(continues)

Listing 10.14   Continued

```
#ifdef _DEBUG
#define new DEBUG_NEW
#undef THIS_FILE
static char THIS_FILE[] = __FILE__;
#endif


IMPLEMENT_DYNCREATE(CCal2Ctrl, COleControl)


/////////////////////////////////////////////////////////////////////
// Message map

BEGIN_MESSAGE_MAP(CCal2Ctrl, COleControl)
     //{{AFX_MSG_MAP(CCal2Ctrl)
     // NOTE - ClassWizard will add and remove message map entries
     //     DO NOT EDIT what you see in these blocks of generated code!
     //}}AFX_MSG_MAP
     ON_OLEVERB(AFX_IDS_VERB_PROPERTIES, OnProperties)
END_MESSAGE_MAP()


/////////////////////////////////////////////////////////////////////
// Dispatch map

BEGIN_DISPATCH_MAP(CCal2Ctrl, COleControl)
     //{{AFX_DISPATCH_MAP(CCal2Ctrl)
     // NOTE - ClassWizard will add and remove dispatch map entries
     //     DO NOT EDIT what you see in these blocks of generated code!
     //}}AFX_DISPATCH_MAP
     DISP_FUNCTION_ID(CCal2Ctrl, "AboutBox", DISPID_ABOUTBOX,
                      AboutBox, VT_EMPTY, VTS_NONE)
END_DISPATCH_MAP()


/////////////////////////////////////////////////////////////////////
// Event map

BEGIN_EVENT_MAP(CCal2Ctrl, COleControl)
     //{{AFX_EVENT_MAP(CCal2Ctrl)
     // NOTE - ClassWizard will add and remove event map entries
     //     DO NOT EDIT what you see in these blocks of generated code!
     //}}AFX_EVENT_MAP
END_EVENT_MAP()


/////////////////////////////////////////////////////////////////////
// Property pages

// TODO: Add more property pages as needed.
//   Remember to increase the count!
BEGIN_PROPPAGEIDS(CCal2Ctrl, 1)
```

```
        PROPPAGEID(CCal2PropPage::guid)
END_PROPPAGEIDS(CCal2Ctrl)


/////////////////////////////////////////////////////////////////////////
// Initialize class factory and guid

IMPLEMENT_OLECREATE_EX(CCal2Ctrl, "CAL2.Cal2Ctrl.1",
     0xe5ed0ea9, 0x1493, 0x11cf, 0x95, 0x2f, 0, 0x20, 0xaf, 0x6e,
     0x90, 0x3f)


/////////////////////////////////////////////////////////////////////////
// Type library ID and version

IMPLEMENT_OLETYPELIB(CCal2Ctrl, _tlid, _wVerMajor, _wVerMinor)


/////////////////////////////////////////////////////////////////////////
// Interface IDs

const IID BASED_CODE IID_DCal2 =
            { 0xe5ed0ea7, 0x1493, 0x11cf, { 0x95, 0x2f, 0, 0x20,
              0xaf, 0x6e, 0x90, 0x3f } };
const IID BASED_CODE IID_DCal2Events =
            { 0xe5ed0ea8, 0x1493, 0x11cf, { 0x95, 0x2f, 0, 0x20,
              0xaf, 0x6e, 0x90, 0x3f } };


/////////////////////////////////////////////////////////////////////////
// Control type information

static const DWORD BASED_CODE _dwCal2OleMisc =
     OLEMISC_ACTIVATEWHENVISIBLE ¦
     OLEMISC_SETCLIENTSITEFIRST ¦
     OLEMISC_INSIDEOUT ¦
     OLEMISC_CANTLINKINSIDE ¦
     OLEMISC_RECOMPOSEONRESIZE;

IMPLEMENT_OLECTLTYPE(CCal2Ctrl, IDS_CAL2, _dwCal2OleMisc)


/////////////////////////////////////////////////////////////////////////
// CCal2Ctrl::CCal2CtrlFactory::UpdateRegistry -
// Adds or removes system Registry entries for CCal2Ctrl

BOOL CCal2Ctrl::CCal2CtrlFactory::UpdateRegistry(BOOL bRegister)
{
     if (bRegister)
          return AfxOleRegisterControlClass(
               AfxGetInstanceHandle(),
               m_clsid,
               m_lpszProgID,
               IDS_CAL2,
               IDB_CAL2,
               FALSE,                          // Not insertable
```

(continues)

Listing 10.14   Continued

```
                       _dwCal2OleMisc,
                       _tlid,
                       _wVerMajor,
                       _wVerMinor);
        else
               return AfxOleUnregisterClass(m_clsid, m_lpszProgID);
}


/////////////////////////////////////////////////////////////////////
// Licensing strings

static const TCHAR BASED_CODE _szLicFileName[] = _T("Cal2.lic");

static const WCHAR BASED_CODE _szLicString[] =
        L"Copyright  1995 ";


/////////////////////////////////////////////////////////////////////
// CCal2Ctrl::CCal2CtrlFactory::VerifyUserLicense -
// Checks for existence of a user license

BOOL CCal2Ctrl::CCal2CtrlFactory::VerifyUserLicense()
{
        return AfxVerifyLicFile(AfxGetInstanceHandle(), _szLicFileName,
               _szLicString);
}


/////////////////////////////////////////////////////////////////////
// CCal2Ctrl::CCal2CtrlFactory::GetLicenseKey -
// Returns a run-time licensing key

BOOL CCal2Ctrl::CCal2CtrlFactory::GetLicenseKey(DWORD dwReserved,
        BSTR FAR* pbstrKey)
{
        if (pbstrKey == NULL)
               return FALSE;

        *pbstrKey = SysAllocString(_szLicString);
        return (*pbstrKey != NULL);
}


/////////////////////////////////////////////////////////////////////
// CCal2Ctrl::CCal2Ctrl - Constructor

CCal2Ctrl::CCal2Ctrl()
{
        InitializeIIDs(&IID_DCal2, &IID_DCal2Events);

        // TODO: Initialize your control's instance data here.
}
/////////////////////////////////////////////////////////////////////
// CCal2Ctrl::~CCal2Ctrl - Destructor
```

```
CCal2Ctrl::~CCal2Ctrl()
{
    // TODO: Clean up your control's instance data here.
}


//////////////////////////////////////////////////////////////////////
// CCal2Ctrl::OnDraw - Drawing function

void CCal2Ctrl::OnDraw(
                 CDC* pdc, const CRect& rcBounds, const CRect& rcInvalid)
{
    // TODO: Replace the following code with your own drawing code.
    pdc->FillRect(rcBounds,
            CBrush::FromHandle((HBRUSH)GetStockObject(WHITE_BRUSH)));
    pdc->Ellipse(rcBounds);
}


//////////////////////////////////////////////////////////////////////
// CCal2Ctrl::DoPropExchange - Persistence support

void CCal2Ctrl::DoPropExchange(CPropExchange* pPX)
{
    ExchangeVersion(pPX, MAKELONG(_wVerMinor, _wVerMajor));
    COleControl::DoPropExchange(pPX);

    // TODO: Call PX_ functions for each persistent custom property.

}


//////////////////////////////////////////////////////////////////////
// CCal2Ctrl::OnResetState - Reset control to default state

void CCal2Ctrl::OnResetState()
{
    COleControl::OnResetState();
                          // Resets defaults found in DoPropExchange

    // TODO: Reset any other control state here.
}


//////////////////////////////////////////////////////////////////////
// CCal2Ctrl::AboutBox - Display an "About" box to the user

void CCal2Ctrl::AboutBox()
{
    CDialog dlgAbout(IDD_ABOUTBOX_CAL2);
    dlgAbout.DoModal();
}


//////////////////////////////////////////////////////////////////////
```

The final step is to give the control a meaningful name. If you build the control without doing this, the name that users will see when selecting your control in the application will be *Calen,* which is not very intuitive. A better name is *Que's Calendar Control.* To make this change, select the Resource View tab. Click the + signs next to Calen Resources and String Table. This displays the strings on the right side of the window. Double-click the string IDS_CALEN and type the name **Que's Calendar Control** in the dialog box that appears. Your screen should now look like figure 10.9.

Fig. 10.9

Control names should be intuitive to the user.

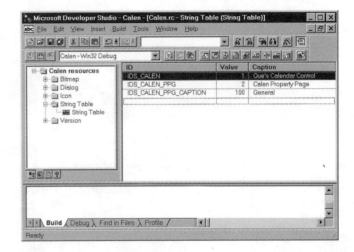

That's really all there is to generating a skeleton for an OCX control by using the ControlWizard. After creating half a dozen or so VBXs by hand, you quickly begin to appreciate the help provided by the ControlWizard. In the next section, you compile and register the new control.

Building the Calen Control

The next step is to choose File, Open Workspace to display the Open dialog box. Choose Calen.mak from the list to make Calen the current workspace. Then perform the following steps to prepare your control for testing:

1. In the Target drop-down list box, select Calen Win32 Debug.

2. Choose Build, Build Calen.ocx or press the F7 key. The Visual Workbench now compiles your control into Calen.ocx.

The Build process then registers the control for you. The Visual Workbench invokes the REGSVR32.EXE utility to register your control in the Registration database. REGSVR32.EXE loads your OCX as a DLL and calls the function DLLRegisterServer().

You are now ready to load your control into the Test Container utility.

The Test Container Utility

Developers of VBXs had to buy Visual Basic Professional Edition, not only to get the VBX CDK, but because they need Visual Basic to test the VBXs themselves. The new OCX CDK includes a Test Container program, which enables you to test all aspects and features of your control without requiring a third-party application.

A *container* is an application in which you can insert any number of OLE objects. With the Test Container, you can insert not only OLE controls, but any OLE objects stored in the Registration database.

The Test Container is an executable file that comes with the Visual C++. Its binary file name is TSTCON32.EXE. Figure 10.10 shows the Test Container utility after you invoke it.

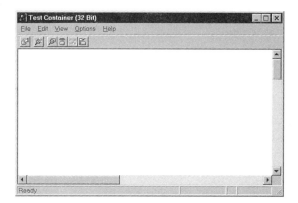

Fig. 10.10

The Test Container facilitates the testing of OCXs and other OLE controls.

To load the Calen control into the Test Container, choose Edit, Insert OLE Control.

You then see the dialog box shown in figure 10.11. The Object Type list box displays all the controls available for insertion into the container.

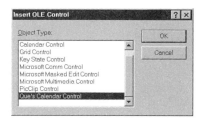

Fig. 10.11

The registered controls appear in a list box so that you can include them in the container application.

Select Calen Control from the list box and then click the OK button. The dialog box disappears and you return to the Test Container. Figure 10.12 shows the state of the Test Container after you insert the Calen control.

Custom Controls

Fig. 10.12

*The OCX control appears in
the container application.*

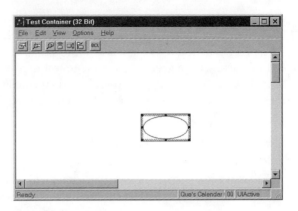

Several important things have now happened. The Test Container has located the
entry for the Calen control in the database, loaded and created the control inside the
container, and activated the control. The utility then called the control's OnDraw()
function to display the control. Notice that the Test Container's toolbar now includes
the control's default toolbar button. The bitmap for the toolbar is located in the resource file.

You can reposition your control by left-clicking the thick lines and then dragging and
dropping the control to its new location. Around the exterior of the control are
handles that you can use to resize the control.

The Test Container has many other options for testing your control. You use some of
these in Chapter 11, "Building OLE Controls." For now, here is a quick summary of
some of the more important features:

- The File menu's Save to Stream and Save to Substorage commands enable you to
  test your control's serialization. You can then invoke the Load command to
  create a new instance of your control in the Test Container.

- The File menu's Save Property Set and Load Property Set commands test serialization as well.

- The File menu's Register Controls command provides another convenient way
  to register and deregister your OLE controls.

- You can set the container's ambient properties by choosing Edit, Set Ambient
  Properties. If this command is not currently available, click the Test Container's
  client area. Clicking the client area causes the Test Container's menus to change
  to commands appropriate just for the Test Container. *Ambient* properties are
  those which belong to the container, such as font and background colors. Control developers can use ambient properties rather than custom properties when
  it is convenient for the control to have the same properties or characteristics as
  the container. Ambient properties provide consistency among all the controls in
  the container. You learn more about ambient properties in Chapter 11, "Building OLE Controls." You cannot take ambient properties for granted. A container
  can provide all, some, or no ambient properties.

IV

Custom Controls

- From the View menu, choose the Event Log and Notification Log command. Buttons four and six on the toolbar also invoke the Event Log and Notification Log respectively. The Event Log shows all the events that a control fires. The Notification Log shows changes to the properties of a control.

- The Edit menu also provides the Invoke Methods command, which enables you to test the control's methods. Button five on the toolbar is equivalent to the Invoke Methods command.

- The View menu provides the Properties command, which displays a generic Properties dialog box in which you can modify your control's properties. When you select a control in the Test Container, the bottom of the Edit menu contains a command for that specific type of control, such as Calen Control Object. Selecting the Calen Control Object command displays a submenu with another Properties command. The second Properties command displays the property pages for the currently selected control.

From Here…

In this chapter, you have learned how to create the skeleton of an OLE control both with and without control licensing. You also learned the basics about how to load and test your control with the Test Container utility. For further information, see the following chapters:

- For more information on Object Linking and Embedding, see Chapter 7, "Introduction to OLE."

- To build on the experience of this chapter by adding functionality to the Calen control, see Chapter 11, "Building OLE Controls."

Building OLE Controls

In Chapter 10, "Using the ControlWizard," you learned about creating the skeleton of OLE controls with the ControlWizard. In this chapter, you learn how to add the functionality that makes your control stand out from the crowd.

The calendar control, as it currently exists, is just a shell. You will add properties, events, and methods that provide the functionality. At minimum, the Calen control must correctly display a month in a typical calendar layout. The control must also respond to user-generated events and notify the container when the user selects a day of the month with a mouse click. Properties and methods for setting the month, day, and year will provide some additional flexibility.

In this chapter, you learn about the following:

- What the empty shell does now
- Understanding OCX properties
- Making the control look like a calendar
- Giving the user control through property pages
- Adding events and methods
- Converting a VBX to an OCX

The Empty Shell

AppWizard provided three important classes: CCalenApp, CCalenPropPage, and CCalenCtrl. As you build the Calen control, you will be making changes in these classes.

CCalenApp inherits from COLEControlModule, which inherits from CWinApp. Like the App objects in other applications, CCalenApp handles such application-wide operations as startup (through the InitInstance() function) and shutdown (through ExitInstance()).

CCalenPropPage inherits from COLEPropertyPage, which in turn inherits from CDialog. Therefore, you can change this control's property page as if it were a dialog box, by using the simple, intuitive tools in AppStudio. Property pages are impressive when you use them—but just wait until you see how easy they are to implement!

It's easy to get confused about what exactly a property page is. Is each one of the tabs on a dialog box a separate page? Or is the whole collection of tabs a page? Each tab is called a *page* and the collection of tabs is called a *sheet*. You set up each page as a dialog box and use ClassWizard to connect the values on that dialog box to member variables.

The CCalenCtrl class is the heart of your control. If you embed your control in a loaded or saved object, the class handles everything from loading and saving your control to drawing the control and handling events or property changes.

CCalenCtrl inherits from COLEControl, which has over 180 functions in addition to those that it inherits from CWnd. To see a list of all these functions, an explanation of their parameters, and a summary of what the functions do, check Books Online. Here is a list of the functions that you are likely to care about in CCalenCtrl:

- void OnDraw(CDC *pDC, CRect &rcBounds, CRect &rcInvalid)

  This function displays your control on the screen. In CCalenCtrl, you must override the function. AppWizard gives you an OnDraw() function that draws an ellipse in the control's client rectangle.

- void InvalidateControl(LPCRECT lpRect = NULL)

  Call this function to invalidate part of the control and force a redraw. If lpRect is NULL, the entire control is invalidated.

- COLORREF TranslateColor(OLE_COLOR clrColor, HPALETTE hpal = NULL)

  This function translates an OLE_COLOR (the type used to store properties that represent colors) into a COLORREF so that it can be passed to drawing functions.

COLEControl includes much more functionality that is of interest, especially concerning methods, events, and properties. Throughout this chapter, you learn about much of this other functionality in context.

OCX Properties

To make the control actually look like a calendar, you write an OnDraw() function that does something other than draw an ellipse inside the client rectangle. It makes sense to look at OnDraw() first, because the control cannot tell you anything until you write this OnDraw() routine, and it cannot draw anything until the control has some properties.

This control gives the user a visual presentation of its internal data variables. Most VBX controls used to do this as well, whether it was a "gas gauge" control indicating a "percent complete" variable, or a sophisticated tree control presenting a list of files.

Many OCX controls today go far beyond the simple presentation of internal data, performing calculations or operations for the user, but all still must present data visually. The list of internal data items for a calendar control is a short one, consisting of the year, month, and selected day. These data items are to become *properties* of the Calen control. An OCX control can have four kinds of properties: stock, ambient, extended, and custom.

Stock Properties

The framework provides stock properties that you can add to your control without having to do any coding:

- `Appearance`, which specifies the control's general look
- `BackColor`, which specifies the control's background color
- `BorderStyle`, which specifies the standard border or no border
- `Caption`, which specifies the control's caption or text
- `Enabled`, which specifies whether the control can be used
- `Font`, which specifies the control's default font
- `ForeColor`, which specifies the control's foreground color
- `Text`, which specifies the control's caption or text
- `hWnd`, which specifies the control's window handle

Stock properties are the easiest to deal with, but not surprisingly, the framework designers have not provided stock properties for the year, month, and day.

Ambient Properties

Ambient properties are properties of the environment that surrounds the control—that is, properties of the *container* into which you place the control. You cannot change ambient properties, but the control can use them to adjust its own properties; for example, the control can set its background color to match that of the container.

The container provides all support for ambient properties. If any of your code uses an ambient property that the container does not support, you should prepare that code to use a default value. Here's how to use an ambient property called `UserMode`:

```
BOOL bUserMode;
    if( !GetAmbientProperty( DISPID_AMBIENT_USERMODE,
        VT_BOOL, &bUserMode ) )
    {
        bUserMode = TRUE;
    }
```

This code calls `GetAmbientProperty()` with the display ID (*dispid*) and variable type (*vartype*) required. It also provides a pointer to a variable into which to put the value. This variable's type must match the vartype. If `GetAmbientProperty()` returns FALSE, `bUserMode` is set to a default value.

olectl.h lists the the following dispids:

- `DISPID_AMBIENT_BACKCOLOR`
- `DISPID_AMBIENT_DISPLAYNAME`
- `DISPID_AMBIENT_FONT`
- `DISPID_AMBIENT_FORECOLOR`
- `DISPID_AMBIENT_LOCALEID`
- `DISPID_AMBIENT_MESSAGEREFLECT`
- `DISPID_AMBIENT_SCALEUNITS`
- `DISPID_AMBIENT_TEXTALIGN`
- `DISPID_AMBIENT_USERMODE`
- `DISPID_AMBIENT_UIDEAD`
- `DISPID_AMBIENT_SHOWGRABHANDLES`
- `DISPID_AMBIENT_SHOWHATCHING`
- `DISPID_AMBIENT_DISPLAYASDEFAULT`
- `DISPID_AMBIENT_SUPPORTSMNEMONICS`
- `DISPID_AMBIENT_AUTOCLIP`
- `DISPID_AMBIENT_APPEARANCE`

Remember that not all containers support all these properties; some might not support any, and others might support properties not included in the preceding list.

Table 11.1 lists some vartypes.

Table 11.1   Description of Vartypes

Vartype	Description
VT_BOOL	BOOL
VT_BSTR	CString
VT_I2	short
VT_I4	long
VT_R4	float
VT_R8	double
VT_CY	CY
VT_COLOR	OLE_COLOR
VT_DISPATCH	LPDISPATCH
VT_FONT	LPFONTDISP

Remembering which vartype goes with which dispid and checking the return from `GetAmbientProperty()` is a bothersome process, so the framework provides member functions of `COLEControl` to get the most popular ambient properties:

- `OLE_COLOR AmbientBackColor()`
- `CString AmbientDisplayName()`
- `LPFONTDISP AmbientFont()` (don't forget to release the font by using `Release()`)
- `OLE_COLOR AmbientForeColor()`
- `LCID AmbientLocaleID()`
- `CString AmbientScaleUnits()`
- `short AmbientTextAlign()` (0 means General [numbers right, text left], 1 means left-justify, 2 means center, 3 means right-justify)
- `BOOL AmbientUserMode()` (TRUE means user mode, FALSE means design mode)
- `BOOL AmbientUIDead()`
- `BOOL AmbientShowHatching()`
- `BOOL AmbientShowGrabHandles()`

All these functions assign reasonable defaults if the container does not support the requested property. Again not surprisingly, the standard list of ambient properties does not include those that you need for the Calen control.

Extended Properties

The container handles extended properties, which typically specify the control's size and placement on the screen. Although the user thinks of these as properties of the control, the implementation of these properties is entirely up to the container developer. Therefore, a truly portable control will not use any extended properties.

Custom Properties

Custom properties are the internal data variables that a developer adds exclusively to a control. Other objects can access the variables in one of two ways: as a member variable or through `Get` and `Set` functions. Whenever a control must perform error checking on a property value, access to that property should be through `Get` and `Set` functions. When an outside object changes the value of a property being accessed as a member variable, a notification function is called to enable the control to react to the change, usually by redrawing.

For the Calen control, the year, month, and day are obvious candidates to be custom properties. `Month` and `Day` should have `Get`/`Set` access so that the control can ensure that the values represent valid dates. `Year` can have member variable access, because any number, even a negative one, is valid for a year. To add these custom properties, follow these steps:

1. Display the ClassWizard by choosing View, ClassWizard or by clicking the ClassWizard toolbar button (it looks like a magic wand waving a trail of stars over a class hierarchy).

2. Click the OLE Automation tab.

3. Click the Add Property button. The Add Property dialog box appears.

4. In the External Name combo box, type **Day**.

5. In the Type combo box, select short.

6. In the Implementation group, select the Get/Set Methods radio button.

The Add Property dialog box should look like figure 11.1. Notice how the ClassWizard automatically fills in the Get Function and Set Function fields. Click OK to add the property.

Fig. 11.1

Adding to your Calen control a custom property with Get / Set access.

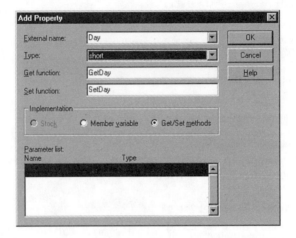

Click Add Property again and add Month as another short Get/Set variable in the same way as Day. Then add Year as follows:

1. Click the Add Property button.

2. In the External Name combo box, type **Year**.

3. In the Type combo box, select short.

4. In the Implementation group, select the Member Variable radio button.

The Add Property dialog box should look like figure 11.2. Notice that the ClassWizard automatically fills in the Variable Name and Notification Function field. Click OK to add the property. Then click OK in the MFC ClassWizard dialog box.

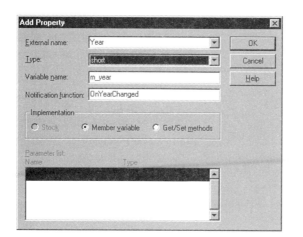

Fig. 11.2

Adding to your Calen control a custom property with member variable access.

IV

Custom Controls

Note

The Microsoft developers have decided to place limits on the year in their routines to calculate day of the week and similar date properties. This decision is sensible because calendar schemes have changed many times over the centuries. Entering any year earlier than 1900 causes an assertion failure in debug mode, an odd behavior in release mode. Therefore, Year should probably be a Get/Set access property as well, with error checking. In the Calen control, Year remains a member variable access property just for illustrative purposes. Alternatively, you could use a different package of date functions.

Drawing a Calendar

Typically a calendar presents the days of the month in a grid seven cells across, with the name of the month at the top, the words *Sunday, Monday, Tuesday,* and so on heading each column, and the numeric date in each cell. Because Calen is a 32-bit application, a three-dimensional effect provides a nice touch and isn't very hard to add.

OnDraw() first paints the background, then draws the border, the name of the month (such as *November*), the name of the day (such as *Wednesday*), and the individual days (such as *15*). Finally, the method again draws the current day in a different color.

Adding Properties

You want to give the user as much control as possible over the calendar's appearance, through stock properties like BackColor and additional custom properties like SelectedDayColor. In the MFC ClassWizard dialog box's OLE Automation page, click the Add Property button. Then, in the Add Property dialog box, add the following stock properties (you can choose their names by selecting from the External Name drop-down list):

- BackColor
- ForeColor
- Font

Even though your control will have a border, do not add BorderStyle, because the stock BorderStyle is just a yes-or-no flag. Adding the custom properties CtrlBorderStyle and DayBorderStyle enables the user to specify a raised or inset border, both around the whole calendar and around each day. In addition to these properties, the control needs colors for the rising and falling portions of the borders around each day and around the whole calendar. When your calendar is not three-dimensional, you need a color for the border around the whole calendar. The application needs a Font property to use for the day numbers, which probably will be bigger than the font that you use for the words on the control, and needs colors for the day numbers and the selected day's background.

Add the following custom properties (you must type their names in the Extenal Name combo box and select their types in the Type combo box):

Property Name	Type
CtrlBorderStyle	short
BorderRiseColor	OLE_COLOR
BorderFallColor	OLE_COLOR
BorderNormalColor	OLE_COLOR
ThreeD	BOOL
DayFont	LPFONTDISP
DayColor	OLE_COLOR
DayBorderStyle	short
DayRiseColor	OLE_COLOR
DayFallColor	OLE_COLOR
SelectedDayColor	OLE_COLOR

You can add all of these properties, with one exception, as member variable access properties. The type LPFONTDISP is not available for member variable properties; to choose this variable type, you must add DayFont as a Get/Set property.

After adding all the properties, you can examine your code and see which changes the ClassWizard has made. The first change is to your dispatch map, kept in calenctl.cpp (listing 11.1).

Listing 11.1   calenctl.cpp, the Dispatch Map

```
/////////////////////////////////////////////////////////////////////
// Dispatch map

BEGIN_DISPATCH_MAP(CCalenCtrl, COleControl)
    //{{AFX_DISPATCH_MAP(CCalenCtrl)
    DISP_PROPERTY_NOTIFY(CCalenCtrl, "Year", m_year, OnYearChanged,
        ➥VT_I2)
    DISP_PROPERTY_NOTIFY(CCalenCtrl, "CtrlBorderStyle",
        ➥m_ctrlBorderStyle, OnCtrlBorderStyleChanged, VT_I2)
    DISP_PROPERTY_NOTIFY(CCalenCtrl, "BorderRiseColor",
        ➥m_borderRiseColor, OnBorderRiseColorChanged, VT_COLOR)
    DISP_PROPERTY_NOTIFY(CCalenCtrl, "BorderFallColor",
        ➥m_borderFallColor, OnBorderFallColorChanged, VT_COLOR)
    DISP_PROPERTY_NOTIFY(CCalenCtrl, "BorderNormalColor",
        ➥m_borderNormalColor, OnBorderNormalColorChanged,
        ➥VT_COLOR)
    DISP_PROPERTY_NOTIFY(CCalenCtrl, "ThreeD", m_threeD,
        ➥OnThreeDChanged, VT_BOOL)
    DISP_PROPERTY_NOTIFY(CCalenCtrl, "DayColor", m_dayColor,
        ➥OnDayColorChanged, VT_COLOR)
    DISP_PROPERTY_NOTIFY(CCalenCtrl, "SelectedDayColor",
        ➥m_selectedDayColor, OnSelectedDayColorChanged, VT_COLOR)
    DISP_PROPERTY_NOTIFY(CCalenCtrl, "DayBorderStyle", m_dayBorderStyle,
        ➥OnDayBorderStyleChanged, VT_I2)
    DISP_PROPERTY_NOTIFY(CCalenCtrl, "DayRiseColor", m_dayRiseColor,
        ➥OnDayRiseColorChanged, VT_COLOR)
    DISP_PROPERTY_NOTIFY(CCalenCtrl, "DayFallColor", m_dayFallColor,
        ➥OnDayFallColorChanged, VT_COLOR)
    DISP_PROPERTY_EX(CCalenCtrl, "DayFont", GetDayFont, SetDayFont,
        ➥VT_FONT)
    DISP_PROPERTY_EX(CCalenCtrl, "Day", GetDay, SetDay, VT_I2)
    DISP_PROPERTY_EX(CCalenCtrl, "Month", GetMonth, SetMonth, VT_I2)
    DISP_STOCKPROP_BACKCOLOR()
    DISP_STOCKPROP_FORECOLOR()
    DISP_STOCKPROP_FONT()
    //}}AFX_DISPATCH_MAP
    DISP_FUNCTION_ID(CCalenCtrl, "AboutBox", DISPID_ABOUTBOX,
        ➥AboutBox, VT_EMPTY, VTS_NONE)
END_DISPATCH_MAP()
```

These macros define your control's properties. There are three types of macros:

- DISP_PROPERTY_NOTIFY is used for the member variable access properties. The parameters are the name of the control class, the external name of the property, the member variable, the notification function, and the variable type, which uses the same names (VT_I2 for short, and so on; see table 11.1) as the GetAmbientProperty() function discussed earlier in this chapter.

- DISP_PROPERTY_EX is used for the Get/Set access properties. The parameters are the name of the control class, the external name of the property, the Get function, the Set function, and the variable type.

■ DISP_STOCKPROP_BACKCOLOR is the macro for the stock property BackColor. This
macro doesn't need any parameters because it was set up just for BackColor.
The map also includes entries for ForeColor and Font.

calenctl.h (listing 11.2) includes another dispatch map.

Listing 11.2   calenctl.h, Another Dispatch Map

```
// Dispatch maps
    //{{AFX_DISPATCH(CCalenCtrl)
    short m_year;
    afx_msg void OnYearChanged();
    short m_ctrlBorderStyle;
    afx_msg void OnCtrlBorderStyleChanged();
    OLE_COLOR m_borderRiseColor;
    afx_msg void OnBorderRiseColorChanged();
    OLE_COLOR m_borderFallColor;
    afx_msg void OnBorderFallColorChanged();
    OLE_COLOR m_borderNormalColor;
    afx_msg void OnBorderNormalColorChanged();
    BOOL m_threeD;
    afx_msg void OnThreeDChanged();
    OLE_COLOR m_selectedDayColor;
    afx_msg void OnSelectedDayColorChanged();
    OLE_COLOR m_dayColor;
    afx_msg void OnDayColorChanged();
    short m_dayBorderStyle;
    afx_msg void OnDayBorderStyleChanged();
    OLE_COLOR m_dayRiseColor;
    afx_msg void OnDayRiseColorChanged();
    OLE_COLOR m_dayFallColor;
    afx_msg void OnDayFallColorChanged();
    afx_msg LPFONTDISP GetDayFont();
    afx_msg void SetDayFont(LPFONTDISP newValue);
    afx_msg short GetDay();
    afx_msg void SetDay(short nNewValue);
    afx_msg short GetMonth();
    afx_msg void SetMonth(short nNewValue);
    //}}AFX_DISPATCH
    DECLARE_DISPATCH_MAP()
```

In listing 11.2, you can see that the ClassWizard has added class member variables
and notification functions for the member variables access properties, and added Get
and Set functions for the Get/Set access properties. However, the ClassWizard hasn't
added any member variables for these properties; the Calen control will have to use its
own Get functions, or you will have to add member variables.

Writing Get and Set Functions

AppWizard provides skeletons of the Get and Set functions, but these skeletons don't
really do anything. Here's what the AppWizard provides for Day:

```
short CCalenCtrl::GetDay()
{
    // TODO: Add your property handler here
    return 0;
}
void CCalenCtrl::SetDay(short nNewValue)
{
    // TODO: Add your property handler here
    SetModifiedFlag();
}
```

The easiest way to handle Month, Day, and DayFont (the three Get/Set access properties) is to add member variables for them. In calenctl.h, add these three lines after the dispatch map:

```
CFontHolder m_dayFont;
short m_Day;
short m_Month;
```

CFontHolder is a class to hold font information. The class has methods to get and set the font that it holds. Because CFontHolder doesn't have a default constructor, you must change the declaration of the CCalenCtrl default constructor to look like this:

```
CCalenCtrl::CCalenCtrl()   : m_dayFont(NULL)
{
    InitializeIIDs(&IID_DCalen, &IID_DCalenEvents);
    m_dayFont.InitializeFont();
}
```

This declaration calls the CFontHolder constructor, which takes one parameter whenever the application calls the CCalenCtrl default constructor. This declaration also initializes m_dayFont to a default value.

You make Day a Get/Set access property to allow error checking, so that users cannot set the day to an incorrect value such as 64 or –7, or 31 if the month is February. To code this error checking, you need an array of days per month. At the top of calenctl.cpp and just before the include statements, add these lines:

```
int DaysInMonth[] = {
  31, 28, 31, 30, 31, 30,
  31, 31, 30, 31, 30, 31 };
```

Although you haven't yet written OnDraw(), you obviously can break up the method into several smaller parts—one that draws the name of the month, another that draws the days of the week, and so on, including a part that draws the selected day in a special color. Suppose that you plan to have a function called DrawSelectedDay() that takes TRUE if the user selects the day (which should then display in the special color) and FALSE if the user deselects the day (which then should display in the regular color), and that uses the member variable m_Day to determine which day is being drawn. In such a case, you then can call this function with FALSE before setting the new value for m_Day and then call the function again with TRUE after setting the new value. Listing 11.3 shows the Get and Set functions for Day.

Listing 11.3 calenctl.cpp, the `Get` and `Set` Functions for `Day`

```cpp
short CCalenCtrl::GetDay()
{
    return m_Day;
}
void CCalenCtrl::SetDay(short nNewValue)
{
    SetModifiedFlag();
    // Make some attempt to determine if the day is within a given
    // range.  Note that this does not check for leap years
    ASSERT(m_Month >= 1 && m_Month <= 12);
    if(nNewValue <1 ||nNewValue > DaysInMonth[m_selectedMonth-1] )
    {
    ThrowError(CTL_E_INVALIDPROPERTYVALUE,
        "Day is outside of allowable range");
    }
    else
    {
        CRect NullRect(0,0,0,0);
        DrawSelectedDay(FALSE,NullRect);
        m_Day = nNewValue;
        DrawSelectedDay(TRUE,NullRect);
    }
}
```

`ThrowError()` is a member function of `COLEControl`, which `CCalenCtrl` inherits. The function takes as its first parameter an error code, which is one of the values listed in table 11.?

Table 11.2 Error Codes for the `ThrowError()` Function

Error Code	Error
CTL_E_ILLEGALFUNCTIONCALL	Illegal function call
CTL_E_OVERFLOW	Overflow
CTL_E_OUTOFMEMORY	Out of memory
CTL_E_DIVISIONBYZERO	Division by zero
CTL_E_OUTOFSTRINGSPACE	Out of string space
CTL_E_OUTOFSTACKSPACE	Out of stack space
CTL_E_BADFILENAMEORNUMBER	Bad file name or number
CTL_E_FILENOTFOUND	File not found
CTL_E_BADFILEMODE	Bad file mode
CTL_E_FILEALREADYOPEN	File already open
CTL_E_DEVICEIOERROR	Device I/O error
CTL_E_FILEALREADYEXISTS	File already exists

Error Code	Error
CTL_E_BADRECORDLENGTH	Bad record length
CTL_E_DISKFULL	Disk full
CTL_E_BADRECORDNUMBER	Bad record number
CTL_E_BADFILENAME	Bad file name
CTL_E_TOOMANYFILES	Too many files
CTL_E_DEVICEUNAVAILABLE	Device unavailable
CTL_E_PERMISSIONDENIED	Permission denied
CTL_E_DISKNOTREADY	Disk not ready
CTL_E_PATHFILEACCESSERROR	Path/file access error
CTL_E_PATHNOTFOUND	Path not found
CTL_E_INVALIDPATTERNSTRING	Invalid pattern string
CTL_E_INVALIDUSEOFNULL	Invalid use of NULL
CTL_E_INVALIDFILEFORMAT	Invalid file format
CTL_E_INVALIDPROPERTYVALUE	Invalid property value
CTL_E_INVALIDPROPERTYARRAYINDEX	Invalid property array index
CTL_E_SETNOTSUPPORTEDATRUNTIME	Set not supported at run time
CTL_E_SETNOTSUPPORTED	Set not supported (read-only property)
CTL_E_NEEDPROPERTYARRAYINDEX	Need property array index
CTL_E_SETNOTPERMITTED	Set not permitted
CTL_E_GETNOTSUPPORTEDATRUNTIME	Get not supported at run time
CTL_E_GETNOTSUPPORTED	Get not supported (write-only property)
CTL_E_PROPERTYNOTFOUND	Property not found
CTL_E_INVALIDCLIPBOARDFORMAT	Invalid Clipboard format
CTL_E_INVALIDPICTURE	Invalid picture
CTL_E_PRINTERERROR	Printer error
CTL_E_CANTSAVEFILETOTEMP	Can't save file to TEMP
CTL_E_SEARCHTEXTNOTFOUND	Search text not found
CTL_E_REPLACEMENTSTOOLONG	Replacements too long

The second parameter to ThrowError() is a string with an error message. This function, which should be called only from within a property's Get or Set function, informs the control of the problem.

The Get and Set functions for Month are similar:

```
short CCalenCtrl::GetMonth()
{
    return m_Month;
}
void CCalenCtrl::SetMonth(short nNewValue)
{
    SetModifiedFlag();
    if(nNewValue>0&&nNewValue<13)
    {
        m_Month = nNewValue;
        InvalidateControl();
    }
    else
    {
        ThrowError(CTL_E_INVALIDPROPERTYVALUE,
            "Month is outside of allowable range");
    }
}
```

Notice that in this case you can't simply redraw part of the control, so a call to InvalidateControl() redraws the whole control.

The only remaining Get/Set access property is DayFont. Its functions look like this:

```
LPFONTDISP CCalenCtrl::GetDayFont()
{
    return m_dayFont.GetFontDispatch();
}

void CCalenCtrl::SetDayFont(LPFONTDISP newValue)
{
    SetModifiedFlag();
    m_dayFont.InitializeFont(NULL,newValue);
    InvalidateControl();
}
```

This property uses the CFontHolder functions GetFontDispatch() and InitializeFont() to get and set the font. Again, the Set function calls InvalidateControl() to force a redraw of the whole control.

Initialization and Persistence

Although it is nice to give the user control over all these properties, they should have sensible default values so that the control has a pleasing appearance even if the user doesn't set special property values. Also, after the user saves a document that contains a calendar control, you should restore the settings the next time that the user reloads the document. Both of these issues, initialization and persistence, are handled by the `DoPropExchange()` method.

AppWizard generates a skeleton `DoPropExchange()` method that looks like this:

```
/////////////////////////////////////////////////////////////////////////
// CCalenCtrl::DoPropExchange - Persistence support
void CCalenCtrl::DoPropExchange(CPropExchange* pPX)
{
    ExchangeVersion(pPX, MAKELONG(_wVerMinor, _wVerMajor));
    COleControl::DoPropExchange(pPX);
    // TODO: Call PX_ functions for each persistent custom property.
}
```

Remove the TODO comment that AppWizard left for you and add the following lines:

```
CTime time = CTime::GetCurrentTime();
PX_Bool(pPX,"ThreeD",m_threeD,FALSE);
PX_Short(pPX,"CtrlBorderStyle", m_ctrlBorderStyle,0);
PX_ULong(pPX,"BorderRiseColor", m_borderRiseColor, RGB(255,255,255));
PX_ULong(pPX,"BorderFallColor", m_borderFallColor, RGB(128,128,128));
PX_ULong(pPX,"BorderNormalColor", m_borderNormalColor, RGB(0,0,0));
PX_Font(pPX,"DayFont", m_dayFont,NULL,AmbientFont());
PX_ULong(pPX,"DayColor", m_dayColor, RGB(192,192,192));
PX_Short(pPX, "DayBorderStyle", m_dayBorderStyle, 0);
PX_ULong(pPX, "DayRiseColor", m_dayRiseColor, RGB(255,255,255));
PX_ULong(pPX, "DayFallColor", m_dayFallColor, RGB(128,128,128));
PX_Short(pPX, "Month", m_Month, time.GetMonth());
PX_Short(pPX, "Day", m_Day, time.GetDay());
PX_Short(pPX, "Year", m_year, time.GetYear());
PX_ULong(pPX, "SelectedDayColor", m_selectedDayColor, RGB(0,255,64));
```

You can call a variety of property exchange functions, one for each supported property type. All these functions have the same parameters:

- The pointer passed to `DoPropExchange()`
- The external name of the property as you typed it in the Add Property dialog box that you access from the MFC ClassWizard dialog box
- The member variable name of the property as you typed it in the Add Property dialog box that you access from the MFC ClassWizard dialog box
- The property's default value

The following are the PX_ functions:

- `PX_Blob()` (for binary large object [BLOB] types)
- `PX_Bool()`
- `PX_Color()`
- `PX_Currency()`
- `PX_Double()`
- `PX_Font()`
- `PX_Float()`

- PX_IUnknown() (for LPUNKNOWN types)
- PX_Long()
- PX_Picture()
- PX_Short()
- PX_String()
- PX_ULong()
- PX_UShort()

Filling in the property's default value is simple for some properties, but not so simple for others. You set all the colors with the RGB() macro, which takes values for red, green, and blue from 0 to 255 and returns a COLORREF. Table 11.3 explains the default colors.

Table 11.3 Default Color Properties for RGB()

Property	Red	Green	Blue	Overall Color
BorderRiseColor	255	255	255	White
BorderFallColor	128	128	128	Gray
BorderNormalColor	0	0	0	Black
DayColor	192	192	192	Light gray
DayRiseColor	255	255	255	White
DayFallColor	128	128	128	Gray
SelectedDayColor	0	255	64	Green

The sensible default for the month, day, and year is right now. The call to the static function CTime::GetCurrentTime() fills time with today's date and time; use its GetDay(), GetMonth(), and GetYear() functions to set the defaults for Day, Month, and Year.

The font's default should be whatever font the container is using. To get this font, call the COLEControl method AmbientFont().

The following are the defaults for the remaining values:

Property	Default
ThreeD	FALSE
CtrlBorderStyle	0 (raised)
DayBorderStyle	0 (raised)

Now when the user creates a new instance of your control, it will use these default values. When the user saves the control to file, the PX_ functions will save the property values; when the user reloads the control, the control will set the properties to the saved values.

Drawing the Control

After adding all the necessary properties, writing the Get and Set functions for the properties that need them, and writing DoPropExchange(), you are finally ready to use those properties to draw the control.

Listing 11.4 shows the code for OnDraw().

Listing 11.4   calenctl.cpp, the OnDraw() Function

```
void CCalenCtrl::OnDraw(CDC* pdc, const CRect& rcBounds,
                        const CRect& rcInvalid)
{
    // Fill in background
    CBrush brBack(TranslateColor(GetBackColor()));
    pdc->FillRect(&rcInvalid,&brBack);

    DrawBorder(rcBounds,pdc);
    DrawMonth(rcBounds,pdc);
    DrawDaysOfWeek(rcBounds,pdc);
    DrawDays(rcBounds,pdc);
    DrawSelectedDay(TRUE,rcBounds,pdc);
}
```

Note that this method breaks the drawing tasks into subtasks. There are two good reasons for doing so. First, by keeping the functions short, you can see more easily where problems are occurring or simply change just one part of the code. Second, your control can use these functions to redraw as little as possible, which makes re-drawing faster. Anywhere that your control calls InvalidateControl(), you might be able to call just one of these drawing functions instead. For example, after SetDayFont() changes the font used for displaying the days, you shouldn't have to redraw the border, the name of the month, or the names of the days of the week; instead, you should have to redraw only the days and the selected day. Keep these advantages in mind if you continue to tinker with the control.

This code demonstrates the use of a property: You access the background color (which is a stock property) with GetBackColor(). Custom properties are also important in DrawBorder(), as you can see in listing 11.5.

Listing 11.5   calenctl.cpp, the DrawBorder() Function

```cpp
void CCalenCtrl::DrawBorder(const CRect& rcBounds, CDC *pDC)
{
    BOOL nullDC = FALSE;
    CRect cRect(rcBounds);

    if(pDC==NULL)
    {
        pDC = GetDC();
        GetClientRect(cRect);
        nullDC = TRUE;
    }

    if(m_threeD)
    {
        // Determine the border colors based on the control style
        COLORREF clrOne, clrTwo;
        if (m_ctrlBorderStyle == 0)
        {
            //raised
            clrOne = TranslateColor(m_borderRiseColor);
            clrTwo = TranslateColor(m_borderFallColor);
        }
        else
        {
            //inset
            clrOne = TranslateColor(m_borderFallColor);
            clrTwo = TranslateColor(m_borderRiseColor);
        }

        CPen LeftTop;
        CPen RightBottom;

        // Make sure CreatePen succeeds and draw the 3-D border
        if(LeftTop.CreatePen(PS_SOLID,1,clrOne)
            && RightBottom.CreatePen(PS_SOLID,1,clrTwo))
        {
            CPen *OldPen = pDC->SelectObject(&LeftTop);

            pDC->MoveTo(cRect.left,cRect.bottom-1);
            pDC->LineTo(cRect.left,cRect.top);
            pDC->LineTo(cRect.right-1,cRect.top);

            pDC->SelectObject(&RightBottom);
            pDC->LineTo(cRect.right-1,cRect.bottom-1);
            pDC->LineTo(cRect.left-1,cRect.bottom-1);

            pDC->SelectObject(OldPen);
        }
    }
    else
    {
        CPen Pen;
        if(Pen.CreatePen(PS_SOLID,1,
            TranslateColor(m_borderNormalColor)))
```

```
        {
            CPen *OldPen = pDC->SelectObject(&Pen);

            pDC->MoveTo(cRect.left,cRect.top);
            pDC->LineTo(cRect.right-1,cRect.top);
            pDC->LineTo(cRect.right-1,cRect.bottom-1);
            pDC->LineTo(cRect.left,cRect.bottom-1);
            pDC->LineTo(cRect.left,cRect.top);

            pDC->SelectObject(OldPen);
        }
    }

    if(nullDC)
        ReleaseDC(pDC);
}
```

DrawBorder() uses m_threeD, m_ctrlBorderStyle, m_borderRiseColor, m_borderFallColor, and m_borderNormalColor to determine which kind of border to draw in what colors. These are all member variables that access custom properties. Notice how the call to SelectObject() saves the old pen so that the control can restore it later. In this way, drawing the control does not affect other drawing operations that might be going on. Whenever you change a device context, be sure to save the old value and restore it later.

After you draw the border, OnDraw() calls DrawMonth() (see listing 11.6).

Listing 11.6   calenctl.cpp, the DrawMonth() Function

```
void CCalenCtrl::DrawMonth(const CRect& rcBounds, CDC *pdc)
{
    int oldBkMode;
    CFont *oldFont;
    COLORREF oldColor;

    BOOL nullDC = FALSE;
    CRect cRect(rcBounds);

    if(pdc==NULL)
    {
        pdc = GetDC();
        GetClientRect(cRect);
        nullDC = TRUE;
    }

    // Draw the month in the top section of the frame
    CRect littleRect(cRect.left,cRect.top,
        cRect.left+7*30,cRect.top+30);
    oldFont = SelectStockFont(pdc);
    oldBkMode = pdc->SetBkMode(TRANSPARENT);
    oldColor = pdc->SetTextColor(TranslateColor(GetForeColor()));
```

(continues)

Listing 11.6   Continued

```
    pdc->DrawText(MonthsInYear[m_Month-1],
                lstrlen(MonthsInYear[m_Month-1]),
                littleRect,DT_VCENTER¦DT_CENTER¦DT_SINGLELINE);

    pdc->SetTextColor(oldColor);
    pdc->SelectObject(oldFont);
    pdc->SetBkMode(oldBkMode);

    if(nullDC)
        ReleaseDC(pdc);
}
```

DrawMonth() does not adjust the size of the month portion based on the control's current size. It draws a rectangle 210 pixels wide and 30 pixels high. The method saves the current font, background mode, and color, which the control restores after it finishes drawing. The array MonthsInYear stores the month's name. Add these lines to the beginning of calenctl.cpp:

```
    char *MonthsInYear[] =
    {
        "January",
        "February",
        "March",
        "April",
        "May",
        "June",
        "July",
        "August",
        "September",
        "October",
        "November",
        "December"
    };
```

After the control draws the border and month, OnDraw() calls DrawDaysOfWeek(), as shown in listing 11.7.

Listing 11.7   calenctl.cpp, the DrawDaysOfWeek() Function

```
void CCalenCtrl::DrawDaysOfWeek(const CRect& rcBounds, CDC *pdc)
{
    int oldBkMode;
    CFont *oldFont;
    COLORREF oldColor;

    CRect cRect(rcBounds);

    BOOL nullDC = FALSE;

    if(pdc==NULL)
    {
```

```
        pdc = GetDC();
        GetClientRect(cRect);
        nullDC = TRUE;
    }


    oldColor = pdc->SetTextColor(TranslateColor(GetForeColor()));
    oldFont = SelectFontObject(pdc,m_dayFont);
    oldBkMode = pdc->SetBkMode(TRANSPARENT);

    // Get a reasonable distance from the start of the days
    CSize cSize = pdc->GetTextExtent("X",1);
    CRect littleRect(cRect.left+16,cRect.top+60-(cSize.cy+10),
        cRect.left+45,cRect.top+60);

    // Draw the days of the week
    for(int i=0 ; i<7 ; i++)
    {
      pdc->DrawText(DaysOfWeek[i],lstrlen(DaysOfWeek[i]),
      littleRect,DT_VCENTER¦DT_CENTER¦DT_SINGLELINE);
      littleRect.SetRect(cRect.left+16+(i+1)*30,
          cRect.top+60-(cSize.cy+10),cRect.left+16+(i+1)*30+30,
          cRect.top+60);
    }

    pdc->SetTextColor(oldColor);
    pdc->SelectObject(oldFont);
    pdc->SetBkMode(oldBkMode);

    if(nullDC)
        ReleaseDC(pdc);
}
```

The DrawDaysOfWeek() method uses GetTextExtent() to get the size, in pixels, of the character "X" in the font kept in m_dayFont. The control uses this size to set the rectangle in which you write the names of the days. After writing each name, the method adjusts the rectangle to contain the next blank space, increasing the x-coordinates each time. The array DaysOfWeek keeps the names of the days. Add these lines to the beginning of calenctl.cpp:

```
char *DaysOfWeek[] =
{
    "Sun",
    "Mon",
    "Tue",
    "Wed",
    "Thu",
    "Fri",
    "Sat"
};
```

Only two functions remain: DrawDays() and DrawSelectedDay(). Listing 11.8 shows DrawDays().

Listing 11.8 calenctl.cpp, the DrawDays() and DrawSelectedDay() Functions

```
void CCalenCtrl::DrawDays(const CRect& rcBounds, CDC *pdc)
{
    int oldBkMode;
    CFont *oldFont;
    CPen *oldPen;
    COLORREF oldColor;

    CRect cRect(rcBounds);

    BOOL nullDC = FALSE;

    if(pdc==NULL)
    {
        pdc = GetDC();
        GetClientRect(cRect);
        nullDC = TRUE;
    }

    // Set up border colors
    COLORREF clrOne, clrTwo;
    if (m_dayBorderStyle == 0)
    {
        //raised
        clrOne = TranslateColor(m_dayRiseColor);
        clrTwo = TranslateColor(m_dayFallColor);
    }
    else
    {
        //inset
        clrOne = TranslateColor(m_dayFallColor);
        clrTwo = TranslateColor(m_dayRiseColor);
    }

    oldColor = pdc->SetTextColor(TranslateColor(m_dayColor));
    oldFont = SelectFontObject(pdc,m_dayFont);
    oldBkMode = pdc->SetBkMode(TRANSPARENT);

    CRect littleRect;
    CPen LeftTop, RightBottom;

     if(LeftTop.CreatePen(PS_SOLID,1,clrOne)
        && RightBottom.CreatePen(PS_SOLID,1,clrTwo))
    {
        oldPen = pdc->SelectObject(&LeftTop);

        int row=0;
        int col = 0;
        CTime time(m_year, m_Month, 1, 1, 1, 1);
        char day[4];
        int firstday = time.GetDayOfWeek() - 1;
            //day of week is 1-based; row and col are zero-based
        int lastday = firstday + DaysInMonth[m_Month-1];
        //notice this ignores leap years again
        int i;
```

```
        while (row < 6)
        {
            i = row*7+col;
            if ( (i >= firstday) && (i <= lastday) )
            {
                // draw the square
                  littleRect.SetRect(cRect.left+15+2+col*30,
                    cRect.top+60+row*30+2, cRect.left+45-2+30*col,
                    cRect.top+90-2+row*30);
                  pdc->MoveTo(littleRect.left,littleRect.bottom);
                  pdc->SelectObject(&LeftTop);
                  pdc->LineTo(littleRect.left,littleRect.top);
                  pdc->LineTo(littleRect.right,littleRect.top);

                  pdc->SelectObject(&RightBottom);
                  pdc->LineTo(littleRect.right,littleRect.bottom);
                  pdc->LineTo(littleRect.left,littleRect.bottom);

                // Draw the day number
                sprintf(day, "%d", (i - firstday + 1));
                pdc->TextOut(littleRect.left + 2, littleRect.top + 2,
                    day, lstrlen(day));
            }
            if (col == 6)
            {
                row++;
                col = 0;
            }
            else
            {
                col++;
            }
        }
    }

    pdc->SetTextColor(oldColor);
    pdc->SelectObject(oldPen);
    pdc->SelectObject(oldFont);
    pdc->SetBkMode(oldBkMode);

    if(nullDC)
        ReleaseDC(pdc);
}
```

The DrawDays() function loops through the rows of a typical calendar layout, drawing a number in each square except for the few blank ones at the beginning and end. Because it uses the DaysInMonth array, this function will never print *29* for the month of February. If you tinker with this control, one of the first things that you should do is replace the array with a function that returns 28 or 29 for February.

The only piece of drawing code that remains is DrawSelectedDay(), shown in listing 11.9.

Listing 11.9 calenctl.cpp, the `DrawSelectedDay()` Function

```cpp
void CCalenCtrl::DrawSelectedDay(BOOL bSelected,
    const CRect& rcBounds, CDC *pdc)
{
    int oldBkMode;
    CFont *oldFont;
    COLORREF clrColor, oldColor;

    CRect cRect(rcBounds);

    BOOL nullDC = FALSE;

    if(pdc==NULL)
    {
        pdc = GetDC();
        GetClientRect(cRect);
        nullDC = TRUE;
    }

    oldFont = SelectFontObject(pdc,m_dayFont);
    oldBkMode = pdc->SetBkMode(TRANSPARENT);

    CBrush cBrush;
    char day[4];

    // Determine the colors for brush and background
    if(bSelected)
    {
        oldColor = pdc->SetTextColor(TranslateColor(GetForeColor()));
        clrColor = TranslateColor(m_selectedDayColor);
    }
    else
    {
        oldColor = pdc->SetTextColor(TranslateColor(m_dayColor));
        clrColor = TranslateColor(GetBackColor());
    }
    if(cBrush.CreateSolidBrush(clrColor))
    {
        // Determine exactly what the day coordinates are,
        // fill the rectangle, and redraw the day text.
        CRect littleRect;
        CTime time(m_year, m_Month, 1, 1, 1 ,1);

        int maxPos = (time.GetDayOfWeek()-1+m_Day-1) * 30;
        int cx = maxPos % (7*30);
        int cy = maxPos / (7*30) * 30;

        littleRect.SetRect(cRect.left+15+cx+3,cRect.top+60+cy+3,
            cRect.left+45+cx-2, cRect.top+90+cy-2);
        pdc->FillRect(littleRect,&cBrush);

        // Draw the day number
        sprintf(day, "%d", m_Day);
        pdc->TextOut(littleRect.left+1, littleRect.top+1,
            day, lstrlen(day));
```

```
        }

        pdc->SetTextColor(oldColor);
        pdc->SelectObject(oldFont);
        pdc->SetBkMode(oldBkMode);

        if(nullDC)
            ReleaseDC(pdc);
    }
```

At this point, the control should be capable of drawing itself. To build it, choose Build, Build calen.ocx, or click the toolbar's Build All button. Then start the test container by choosing Tools, OLE Controls Test Container. Insert an instance of the control by choosing Edit, Insert OLE Control and then selecting Que's Calendar Control from the list.

If the control doesn't look quite right, grab the sizing square at the bottom-right corner and resize it. Your screen should look similar to figure 11.3.

Fig. 11.3

The Calendar control has sensible default values; your screen looks like this when ThreeD *is* FALSE.

Handling Property Changes

You've already implemented the three properties that are accessed with Get and Set functions. But when the rest of the custom properties and all the stock properties are changed, they inform the control by calling their notification function. For example, when the Year property changes, the control updates the value in m_year and calls the function OnYearChanged(). That function must ensure that the control is redrawn. Here's the code:

```
void CCalenCtrl::OnYearChanged()
{
    InvalidateControl();
    SetModifiedFlag();
}
```

Some of the functions can get away with only calling DrawBorder(), passing it a null rectangle that will be overridden later. For example, OnCtrlBorderStyleChanged() looks like this:

```
void CCalenCtrl::OnCtrlBorderStyleChanged()
{
    CRect NullRect(0,0,0,0);
    DrawBorder(NullRect);
    SetModifiedFlag();
}
```

You have already created the skeletons for all these functions. For the most part, completing each function is simply a matter of adding a call to DrawBorder() or InvalidateControl() and removing the ToDo comment. The following functions should call DrawBorder() in addition to SetModifiedFlag():

- OnCtrlBorderStyleChanged()
- OnBorderRiseColorChanged()
- OnBorderFallColorChanged()
- OnBorderNormalColorChanged()
- OnThreeDChanged()

These functions should call InvalidateControl() in addition to SetModifiedFlag():

- OnYearChanged()
- OnSelectedDayColorChanged()
- OnDayColorChanged()
- OnDayBorderStyleChanged()
- OnDayRiseColorChanged()
- OnDayFallColorChanged()

Now you can use the test container to set the value of any one of these properties. To change a single property, choose View, Properties (if you were to choose Edit, Properties, you would be attempting to display the property page, which you haven't written yet). Select the property name from the drop-down box. You'll notice a difference between stock and custom properties right away. When you select BackColor, a box with an ellipse (...) appears next to the value. By clicking this box, you display a page that includes a gray button that you can simply click to set the value to gray. When you select DayColor, no such button appears. Select ForeColor, which is black, and notice that its numerical value is zero. Select DayColor again and set the numerical value to zero. Click Apply and the control should resemble figure 11.4.

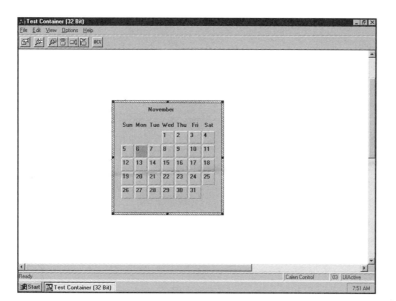

Fig. 11.4

You can customize the Calendar control in the test container. This figure shows the control with a gray background and black day color.

Minor Appearance Improvements

It's annoying to have to resize the calendar after creating it. By adding just one line to the control's constructor, you create the control at a more appropriate size:

```
CCalenCtrl::CCalenCtrl()  : m_dayFont(NULL)
{
    InitializeIIDs(&IID_DCalen, &IID_DCalenEvents);
    m_dayFont.InitializeFont();
    SetInitialSize(8*30,8*30);
}
```

Another annoyance is this control's icon. Because the icon consists of only the letters *OCX,* the user can easily confuse this control with other new OCX controls. Take a minute to set up a better bitmap. First select the Resource View, then double-click on the bitmap IDB_CALEN. Use the bitmap editor to transform the plain OCX bitmap into a more calendar-like bitmap such as the one shown in figure 11.5.

Fig. 11.5

Fig. 11.5

The Calendar control needs a new bitmap; this one resembles a calendar.

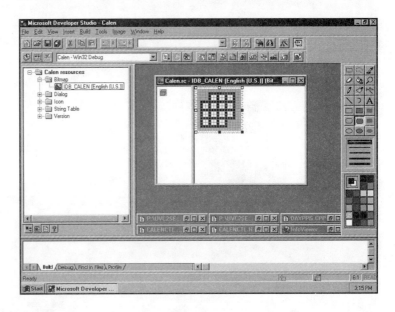

Property Pages

The test container enables you to change one property at a time, but most other containers do not. The control must have a property sheet—a collection of tabbed property pages. Actually, the control already has a property sheet, but it's a very boring one. As shown in figure 11.6, the property sheet has only one page that has nothing on it but a static control reminding you to do the property pages.

Fig. 11.6

When you first create the Calendar control, its property sheet has only one empty property page.

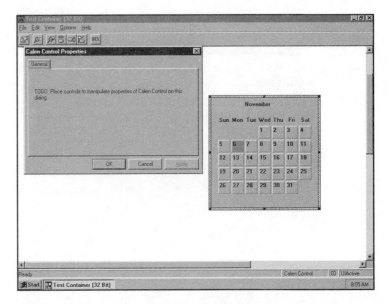

Stock Property Pages

The easy property pages to add are those for fonts and colors. Find the property page map in calenctl.cpp and add two lines to it, so that it looks like the following:

```
//////////////////////////////////////////////////////////////////////
// Property pages

// TODO: Add more property pages as needed.
//   Remember to increase the count!
BEGIN_PROPPAGEIDS(CCalenCtrl, 3)
    PROPPAGEID(CCalenPropPage::guid)
    PROPPAGEID(CLSID_CFontPropPage)
    PROPPAGEID(CLSID_CColorPropPage)
END_PROPPAGEIDS(CCalenCtrl)
```

Notice also that you are changing the number in the BEGIN_PROPPAGEIDS macro to 3, because the control now has three property pages. The two new ones are both stock property pages, but they work for both stock and custom properties—one page for colors and one page for fonts.

Build the control and load it into the test container, then choose Edit, Properties to display the new property sheet. Select the Color tab, then click the drop-down list box. It lists such custom properties as DayColor along with stock properties like BackColor, as shown in figure 11.7.

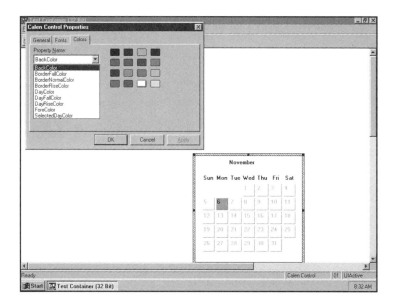

Fig. 11.7

The stock color property page handles both stock and custom properties.

General Property Page

Six properties remain that are neither fonts nor colors:

- CtrlBorderStyle
- ThreeD

■ DayBorderStyle

■ Year

■ Month

■ Day

CtrlBorderStyle and ThreeD both belong on the General property page. To add them, follow these steps:

1. Select the Resource View tab in the project window.

2. Double-click IDD_PROPPAGE_CALEN in the Dialog section.

3. Delete the TODO static control.

4. Add a check box with the caption Three D and a resource ID of IDC_THREED.

5. Add a combo box with a resource ID of IDC_CBORDERSTYLE. Edit the properties of the combo box, and in the E̲nter List Box Items box, add two lines: **0 - Raised** and **1 - Inset**. Change the combo box's style to Drop List. Then the value that the combo box returns is an index: 0 if the user selects the first one, 1 if the user selects the second, and so on. Widen the combo box so that these entries fit (to try out your new General property page, click the toolbar's light switch button).

6. Add a static control next to the combo box with the text **Control Border Style**. The General property page should resemble figure 11.8.

Fig. 11.8

You build the new General property page as you would any other dialog box.

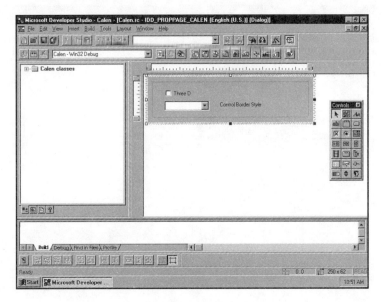

7. While editing the new property page, bring up ClassWizard. Select the Member Variables tab.

8. If the Class Name combo box doesn't show CCalenPropPage selected, open the drop-down list and select that class name.

9. Select IDC_THREED from the list of IDs and click the Add Variable button to connect this control to a member variable.

10. Enter **m_threeD** in the Member Variable Name edit box.

11. Leave Category as Value and Variable Type as BOOL.

12. Enter **ThreeD** in the Optional OLE Property Name combo box.

13. Click OK to connect the variable to the control.

14. Connect IDC_CBORDERSTYLE to an int member variable called m_ctrlBorderStyle with an OLE name of CtrlBorderStyle.

These member variable names might look familiar because the class CCalenCtrl has member variables with the same names. However, these are two different groups of variables. Both the member variables that you've just added to CCalenPropPage and the ones that were already in CCalenCtrl are connected to the OLE properties. When you use the property page, you change the value of (for example) IDC_THREED, which causes a change in CCalenPropPage::m_threeD, which causes a change in the OLE property ThreeD, which causes a change in CCalenCtrl::m_threeD and a call to CCalenCtrl::OnThreeDChanged. Try building the control and then testing it in the test container. This is certainly an easier way to change properties!

Custom Property Pages

Adding another property page all your own is a little more difficult than adding stock pages or modifying the general page that AppWizard provides. Still, the rewards are many; if your control has many properties, the better you organize them, the more usable you make your control.

In this section, you add a property page for Day-related properties. At first, the control will use this page only for the DayBorderStyle property. To add this property page, follow these steps:

1. Add a new dialog box to the project by right-clicking Dialog in the Resource View and choosing Insert, Dialog.

2. Delete the OK and Cancel buttons from the dialog box. Adjust the size to 250-by-100 pixels by moving the lower-right corner.

3. Choose Edit, Properties to display the Properties window. Change the resource ID to IDD_PROPPAGE_DAY. Then select the Styles tab and change Style to Child and Border to None.

4. Add a drop-down list box with the resource ID IDC_DBORDERSTYLE. This drop-down list box should be just like that which is in the General property page.

5. Invoke the ClassWizard. It prompts you to create a new class. Click OK.

6. In the Class Name box, type **CDayPropPage**. In the Base Class list box, select COlePropertyPage. Make sure that the Dialog is IDD_PROPPAGE_DAY. Click Create.

7. Select the ClassWizard's Member Variables tab, select IDC_DBORDERSTYLE, and click the Add Variable button.

8. Enter **m_dayBorderStyle** for the member variable name, leave the Category as Value, and select int as the Variable Type.

9. Enter **DayBorderStyle** in the Optional OLE Property Name combo box and click OK.

10. Click OK to close the ClassWizard.

11. Open the string table from the Resource View. Click the empty string at the bottom of the table. If the Properties window isn't already displayed, choose Edit, Properties.

12. Change the resource ID to IDS_DAY_PPG and the caption to **Day Property Page**. Add another string with the resource ID IDS_DAY_PPG_CAPTION and the text **Day**.

13. Close the string table.

So far, you have created the new dialog box and connected it to a class. However, you haven't done anything to connect it to the other property pages or to make it display with a tab. The tab is the easiest thing to take care of. In the CDayPropPage constructor, change the second parameter in the call to the base class constructor to IDS_DAY_PPG_CAPTION, the string that you just added to the string table. (AppWizard added a TODO comment reminding you to do this.) This change causes the dialog box to display with a tab that reads *Day*.

To connect the new dialog box to the control's property sheet, change CDayPropPage::CDayPropPageFactory::UpdateRegistry() This oddly named function registers the property page for you. Replace the 0 in the call to AfxOleRegisterPropertyPageClass() with IDS_DAY_PPG, the first string that you added to the string table. Again, AppWizard left a TODO comment reminding you to do this. Then return to the property page map in calenctl.cpp and add another line to the map so that it looks like the following:

```
//////////////////////////////////////////////////////////////////////
// Property pages

// TODO: Add more property pages as needed.
//   Remember to increase the count!
BEGIN_PROPPAGEIDS(CCalenCtrl, 4)
    PROPPAGEID(CCalenPropPage::guid)
    PROPPAGEID(CLSID_CFontPropPage)
    PROPPAGEID(CLSID_CColorPropPage)
    PROPPAGEID(CDayPropPage::guid)
END_PROPPAGEIDS(CCalenCtrl)
```

Don't forget to change the number of property pages to four, and to #include the header file for the CDayPropPage class. Build the control, load it into the test container, and display the property sheet. You then see the new page as shown in figure 11.9. As you can see, adding a whole new custom page is harder than adding a stock page or modifying the general page, but not much harder.

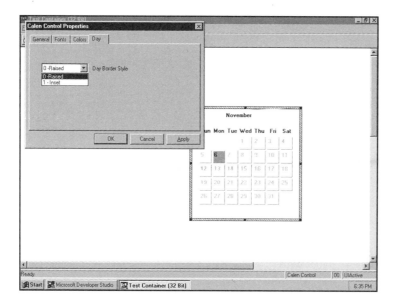

Fig. 11.9

The new Day property page connected to the control.

Methods and Events

Methods and events enable a container and a control to communicate about more than just property values. *Methods* are functions of the control that the container can call; *events* are ways that the control reports back to the container, typically so that the container can take action. Methods, which did not exist in VBX controls, significantly improve the way that containers and controls can interact.

Setting the Date

When on a form or dialog box that belongs to another program, your control should expose a method that enables the container to set the date. Two stock methods are available to any control: DoClick() and Refresh(). They are easy to add (as the word *stock* implies), but neither sets the date. To perform this task, you create a custom method called SetDate(), as follows:

1. Display the ClassWizard and select the OLE Automation tab. Make sure that CCalenCtrl is the selected class.

2. Click the Add Method button.

3. Enter **SetDate** for the name, and **BOOL** for the return type. Then fill in the parameter box. The three parameters are each short variables: month, day, and year.

4. Click OK to add the method, and then click OK to close the ClassWizard.

All that remains is to write SetDate(). AppWizard added a skeleton version. Fill it in as follows:

```
BOOL CCalenCtrl::SetDate(short month, short day, short year)
{
    BOOL RetVal = FALSE;

    if(month >= 1 && month <= 12)
    {
        if(day >= 1 && day <= DaysInMonth[month-1])
        {
            m_Month = month;
            m_Day = day;
            m_year = year;
            InvalidateControl();
            RetVal = TRUE;
        }
        else
            ThrowError(CTL_E_INVALIDPROPERTYVALUE,
                "Day is outside of allowable range");
    }
    else
        ThrowError(CTL_E_INVALIDPROPERTYVALUE,
            "Month is outside of allowable range");

    return RetVal;
}
```

This code should look pretty familiar from SetMonth() and SetDay(). To test it, build the control and load it into the Test Container. Choose Edit, Invoke Methods and then select SetDate from the Name drop-down list. Fill in the three parameters as 1, 1, and 1996, as shown in figure 11.10. Click the Invoke button and the date changes. Continue to explore in the Test Container for a while.

Fig. 11.10

The Test Container can invoke any control method.

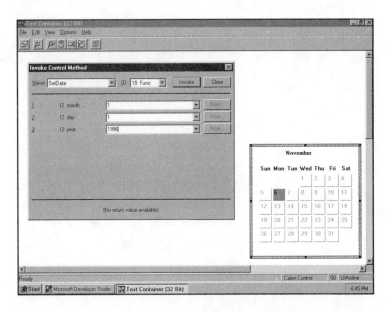

Adding the Stock Event `Click()`

Events are the ways that the control reports to the container. For example, the stock event `Click()` notifies the container that the user clicked the control. To add this event, display the ClassWizard as usual and select the OLE Events tab. Click the <u>A</u>dd Event button. Select `Click` from the External <u>N</u>ame drop-down list and click OK. Now every time that the user clicks the control, the container is notified.

You can confirm that this works in the Test Container. Load the control and choose <u>V</u>iew, <u>E</u>vent Log to watch the events as they happen. Click the container several times and it lists events in the log as shown in figure 11.11.

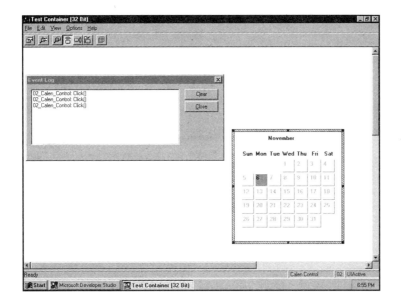

Fig. 11.11

The Test Container displays the `Click()` events that the control fires.

Adding the Custom Event `Select()`

Users can take actions that are more sophisticated than simply clicking the mouse, and the control should report these actions to the container. For example, if the user clicks a day (rather than the name of the month or of a weekday), the control should report the day that the user clicked. You add this custom event, `Select()`, much the same way as you add `Click()`, except that you type the name instead of selecting it from the list of stock events. The event has one parameter: a `short` variable called `Day`.

You then add a message map entry to handle mouse clicks, as follows:

1. Select the ClassWizard's Message Maps tab.
2. Select `CCalenCtrl` in both the Class <u>N</u>ame and Object <u>I</u>D lists.
3. Double-click `WM_LBUTTONDOWN`, the message generated when the user left-clicks. This adds the function `OnLButtonDown()`.
4. Click OK to close the ClassWizard.

Now when the user clicks the control, it calls the `OnLButtonDown()` function. If the user clicks a day, the control should fire a `Select()` event, so the first task is to determine whether the user is clicking a day. Traditionally, the `HitTest()` function (listing 11.10) performs this task.

Listing 11.10   calenctl.cpp, the `HitTest()` Function

```
short CCalenCtrl::HitTest(CPoint &point)
{
    short retval = -1;

    // Must be at least past the start of the days
    if(point.y>60)
    {
        // Must be at least between the first and last day on width
        if(point.x>15&&point.x<(15+30*7))
        {
            CTime cTime(m_year, m_Month, 1, 1, 1, 1);

            // Calculate the row and the column
            int row = (point.y-60)/30;
            int col = (point.x-15)/30;

            int day = row*7+col;
            day = day + 1 - cTime.GetDayOfWeek() + 1;

            // If the day is within the bounds, then return the value
            if(day > 0 && day <= DaysInMonth[m_Month-1])
                retval = day;
        }
    }

    return retval;
}
```

Here's how `OnLButtonDown()` uses `HitTest()`:

```
void CCalenCtrl::OnLButtonDown(UINT nFlags, CPoint point)
{
    COleControl::OnLButtonDown(nFlags, point);

    short day;

    if((day = HitTest(point))!=-1)
    {
        CRect NullRect(0,0,0,0);
        DrawSelectedDay(NullRect,FALSE);
        m_Day = day;
        DrawSelectedDay(NullRect,TRUE);
        FireSelect(day);
    }
}
```

The base class implementation handles the `Click()` event. If the user clicks a day, the `OnLButtonDown()` function changes the selected day and redraws the control, then fires the `Select()` event to notify the container.

Build the control, load it into the Test Container, display the event log, and click the control several times. Click both days and areas outside of days. Notice when the selected day changes and when it does not, then check the `Select()` and `Click()` events that the event log lists (an example log is shown in fig. 11.12). A `Click()` event fires every time that you click the mouse button, but a `Select()` event fires only when you click a day. Notice also that the log lists the `Select()` events' parameter—the day that you clicked.

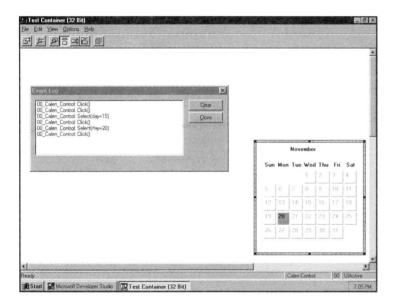

Fig. 11.12

The Test Container displays the `Click()` *and* `Select()` *events that the control fires. In this case, the user clicked twice outside area of the days and then clicked the 15th and the 20th.*

Converting VBX Controls

By now, you should be an ardent convert to the OCX way of doing things. Events are easier, methods are better than the kludgy old `Action` property, and usually the controls are quicker to make and easier to maintain. But do you have to rewrite all your old VBX controls from scratch?

Of course not. The ControlWizard can create an OCX from a VBX to save you much effort. Even if you did have to rewrite a VBX control, you could easily transfer to an OCX the work that you already put into the VBX's design.

First, make sure that your VBX has an exported function called `VBGetModelInfo()` that returns your `ModelInfo` structure. If the control lacks such a function, add one.

Next, run the VBX Template Tool. Earlier versions of the Control Developer's Kit included this tool, so VBX developers should still have it. Look for the files

CTLWZLIB.DLL and MFCCTLWZ.EXE in the directory MSVCCDK on the Visual C++ 1.52 CD. (You probably should copy these files to your hard drive.) Run MFCCTLWZ.EXE from a DOS prompt or choose File, Run.

This version of ControlWizard included the check box Use VBX Control as Template. When you select this check box on the Control Options dialog box, you enable the Select VBX Control button (that is, it is no longer grayed). Click this button and enter your VBX file name on the dialog box. Click OK and continue to work through the ControlWizard. After creating the skeleton control, the wizard copies the following implementations from your VBX:

- The stock properties `BorderStyle`, `Enabled`, `Font`, `Caption`, `Text`, `ForeColor`, `BackColor`, and `hWnd`.
- The stock events `Click`, `DblClick`, `KeyDown`, `KeyPress`, `KeyUp`, `MouseDown`, `MouseMove`, and `MouseUp`.
- All custom properties are copied as stubs. You must copy the source code manually.
- All custom events are copied as stubs. You must copy the source code manually.

Some properties that were standard in the VBX environment are extended properties in the OCX environment, which means that the control drops them and the container handles them. These properties include `Left`, `Height`, `Top`, and `Width`. Other implementations that the ControlWizard does not copy include the following:

- The stock properties `DragIcon`, `DragMode`, `MouseCursor`, and `MousePointer`.
- The stock events `DragDrop`, `DragOver`, `LinkOpen`, `LinkClose`, `LinkError`, and `LinkNotify`.

You should take the conversion slowly. Run the ControlWizard first and build the new control. Fill in the stubs for the custom properties and events a few at a time, building and testing the control after each addition. Once the control is working, add in the usual way whatever property pages you want.

Although converting a VBX to an OCX can sometimes be slow work, it's quicker than building the OCX from scratch. And the rewards of moving to an OCX are many, as you've seen. So hang in there! You might even end up specializing in converting controls from VBX to OCX—which is sure to be a growth industry.

From Here...

The Calendar OCX presented in this chapter is still only a shadow of what it could be. For example, it doesn't display the current year. Calendar controls in commercial products sometimes include little arrow buttons that enable the user to reset the month, the year, and so on. If you include a holiday file, the control could highlight holidays.

Also, the control can't handle leap years yet, and draws itself exactly the same no matter how it has been resized. Although it would be difficult to write code to draw the control scaled to the current size, such an effect is quite desirable. There is no limit to the capabilities that you can add to this little control.

For related information, see the following chapters:

- For a guide through the process of generating OLE custom control skeletons with the newest Visual C++ wizard, see Chapter 10, "Using the ControlWizard."

- For more information on controls and how you can use them with the Microsoft Foundation Classes, see Chapter 19, "Using Common Controls with MFC," which is provided on this book's companion CD.

IV

Custom Controls

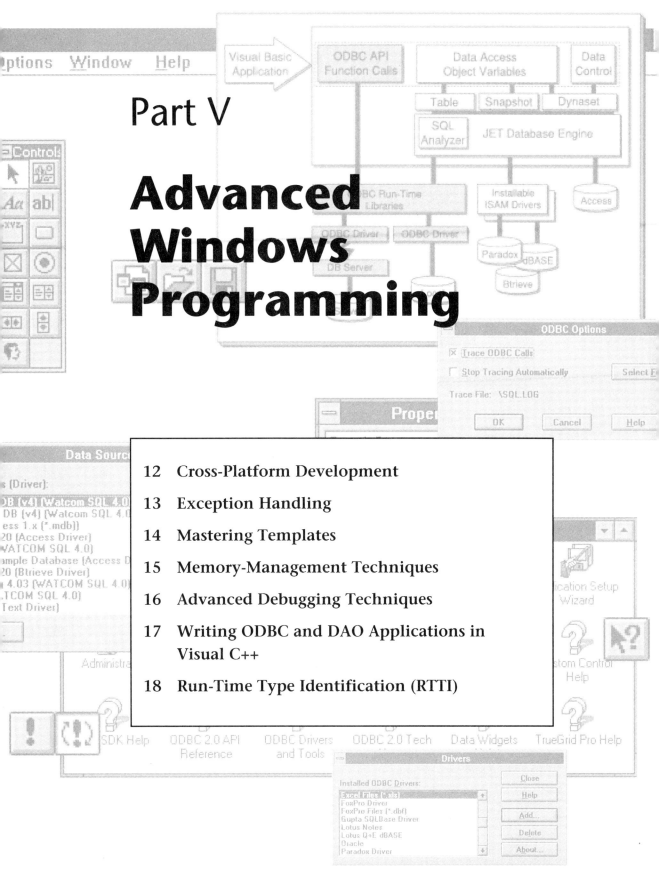

Part V

Advanced Windows Programming

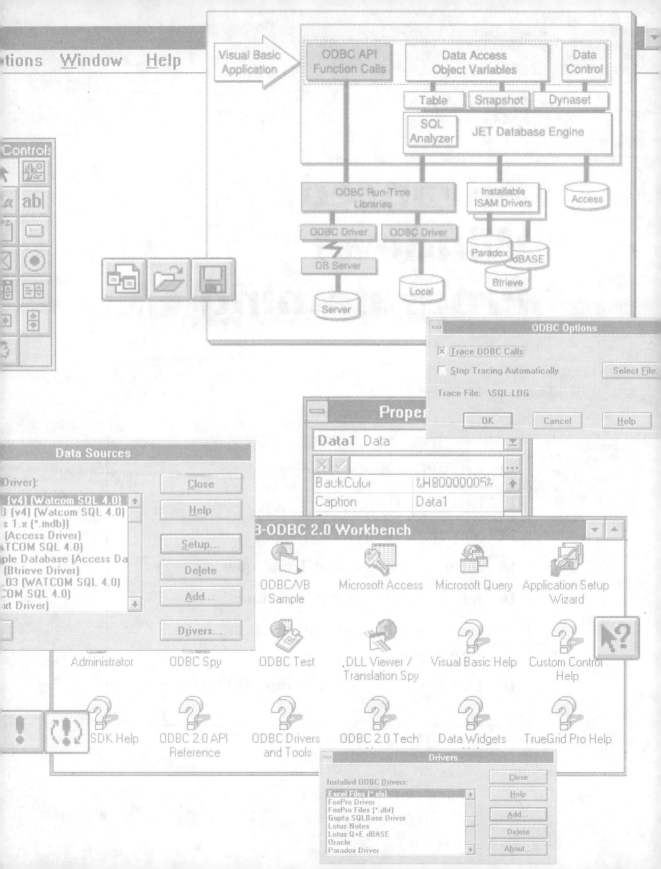

CHAPTER 12

Cross-Platform Development

Although Windows running on the Intel x86 processor owns the lion's share of the personal computer market, other processor types and operating systems obviously exist. You might find it desirable, or even necessary, to move your Win32-Intel programs to another platform, like DEC's Alpha running Windows NT or the Power Macintosh.

If you were just writing plain ANSI C or C++ programs, porting them would be fairly easy. However, if you've taken advantage of the MFC framework, your porting job can be much more difficult. Fortunately, Microsoft and other vendors have already ported MFC to other platforms. This chapter explains how to make your programs ready for movement to other operating systems and processor types.

In this chapter, you learn about the following:

- What to do to move your Win16 programs to Win32 and MFC
- What the structural differences are among the Intel x86, Motorola 68K, and various RISC processors on which you might want your code to run on
- The basics of porting your MFC application to the Macintosh OS
- The basics of porting your MFC application to UNIX, using the Wind/U portability libraries

Cross-Platform Tools for Advanced Programming

By using Win32 and the Microsoft Foundation Classes (MFC) for application development, you are already using cross-platform tools. Today, the Win32 API with MFC is available on several operating systems—including Windows, Macintosh OS (System 7) on 680x0 and PowerPC, several flavors of UNIX, and OpenVMS—and a wide variety of hardware architectures, from Intel 80386-based PCs to powerful 64-bit workstations. When developing cross-platform applications, you can use four types of development tools. The first two types are platform-specific versions of Visual C++ 4.

The third type consists of the add-on options that enable Visual C++ 4 to generate applications for the Apple System 7 operating system for Macintosh or PowerMac hardware. The last is a suite of tools loosely coupled to Visual C++, providing MFC 4 and Win32 on several UNIX operating systems platforms. Here are the four types of development tools:

- *Visual C++ 4 on Intel.* This version of Visual C++ runs under Intel Windows NT.

- *Multiplatform editions of Visual C++ 4 for Win32 on RISC under Windows NT.* These versions of Visual C++ 4 run under RISC (Reduced Instruction Set Computer) versions of Windows NT, such as MIPS and Alpha. The editions are similar to the standard version of Visual C++ 4, including all language and IDE features, full MFC, and wizards, but the compiler generates RISC object code, not Intel x86 object code. Your code should port without change.

- *Cross-development editions for Win32 on Macintosh and PowerMac under Intel Windows NT.* These cross-development products are add-ons that install on top of Visual C++ 4 running under Intel Windows NT. They enable Visual C++ 4 to generate Motorola 680x0 object code for the Macintosh, or PowerMac object code for the PowerMac. Both types of object code run on the Apple System 7 operating system. These editions enable you to develop core code with Visual C++ 4 in your Intel environment; you can then share most of this code across platforms. Your final application is a real Macintosh application with native speed, look, and feel.

- *UNIX/OpenVMS tools.* With these tools, you can port Visual C++ 4 developed applications to the UNIX and OpenVMS operating systems. Although not formal add-ons to Visual C++, these tools are provided by a Microsoft Windows Interface Source Environment (WISE) partner. Microsoft provides its WISE partner with ongoing access to Windows source code to maximize compatibility for MFC and Win32-based applications. This type of development uses the native UNIX compilers, linkers, and debuggers. The WISE partner provides the Win32 and MFC libraries, which enables you to develop core code with Visual C++ 4 and then share most code across all platforms. Your final application is a real UNIX/Motif application with native speed, look, and feel. Contact Bristol Technology for additional information on UNIX and OpenVMS support. You can contact this Microsoft WISE partner at info@bristol.com or http://www.bristol.com.

In the section "Portable Applications with the Win32 API and MFC," later in this chapter, you see what routines you can and cannot use on other platforms, and how to maximize your application's portability.

Table 12.1 lists the architectures for which you can write Visual C++ applications that use Win32 and MFC.

Table 12.1 Target Platforms					
CPU	**Vendor**	**OS**	**Win32**	**MFC**	**Visual C++ Tools**
Alpha	Digital	OpenVMS	Yes	Yes	No, native tools
Alpha	Digital	UNIX	Yes	Yes	No, native tools
Alpha planned	Digital	Windows NT	Yes	Yes	Multiplatform edition
HP-PA	Hewlett-Packard	HP-UX	Yes	Yes	No, native tools
Intel x86	Intel	Windows 3.1 with Win32s DLLs	Yes	Yes	Visual C++ 1.5
Intel x86	Intel	Windows 95	Yes	Yes	Visual C++ 4
Intel x86	Intel	Windows NT	Yes	Yes	Visual C++ 4
Intel x86	Intel	UNIX	Yes	Yes	No, native tools
Intel x86	Intel	DOS	Yes	Yes	No, native tools
Motorola 680x0	Apple Mac	System 7	Yes	Yes	Cross- development edition
MIPS	MIPS	Windows NT	Yes	Yes	Multiplatform edition planned
MIPS	SGI	IRIX 5	Yes	Yes	No, native tools
PowerPC	IBM	Windows NT	Yes	Yes	Cross-development edition
RS/6000	IBM	AIX	Yes	Yes	No, native tools
SPARC	Sun	Solaris	Yes	Yes	No, native tools
VAX	Digital	OpenVMS	Yes	Yes	No, native tools

The CPUs fall into two classes based on the complexity of their instruction set. The Intel x86 and Motorola 680x0 chips are Complex Instruction Set Computers (CISC) and the rest are Reduced Instruction Set Computers (RISC). CISC processors tend to have many instructions that make the CPU very flexible, while RISC processors have a smaller, less specialized set of instructions. The trade-off is that the smaller instruction set results in a smaller implementation of the CPU itself—which results in increased speeds. In general, most high-powered UNIX workstations are RISC-based and PCs are CISC-based.

As you have seen in this book, Visual C++ and MFC combine to make a very productive development environment. No longer are the results of this environment limited to Windows. By recompiling your source code, you can have native applications on almost any target environment.

Application Architecture

When you build a normal Windows application, you have MFC calling the Windows API, and the Windows API accessing the operating system and hardware. This structure is the basis for portability: By not accessing hardware or low-level operating system calls directly, you can replace the lower components without making any major changes to your application code. Figure 12.1 illustrates this application architecture.

Fig. 12.1

Windows NT application architecture across multiple CPUs.

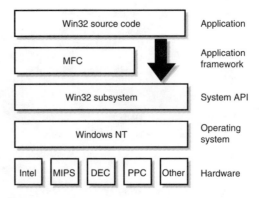

Fig. 12.2

For Win32-based Macintosh applications, you use the Microsoft Visual C++ 4 Cross-Development Edition for Macintosh. This edition consists of a set of add-on tools for Visual C++ 4 that enable you to compile and link Windows-based code for Macintosh applications, as well as native Macintosh code. You can do all your development work in the Visual C++ 4 environment running on a PC with Microsoft Windows NT. To run and debug code compiled for the Macintosh, you need an Ethernet-based AppleTalk network connection or a serial cable to connect your PC to your Macintosh. Visual C++ for Macintosh provides tools to transfer files and to debug applications from Visual C++ on your PC by running remotely on the Macintosh. When you create Win32-based applications for the Apple Macintosh, you change only the foundation of the application architecture, as figure 12.2 illustrates.

Fig. 12.2

Using MFC and Win32 for Macintosh applications.

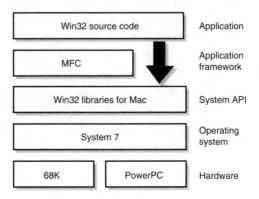

When developing Win32-based applications on UNIX, you mostly use Visual C++, but also use native UNIX tools to create the platform-specific executables. When you initially create the application, you use the Visual C++ 4 environment running on a PC with Microsoft Windows 95 or NT. To compile the application, you use UNIX compilers and other development tools. Just as when you create applications for the Macintosh, when you create Win32-based applications for UNIX, you change only the foundation of the application architecture (see fig. 12.3).

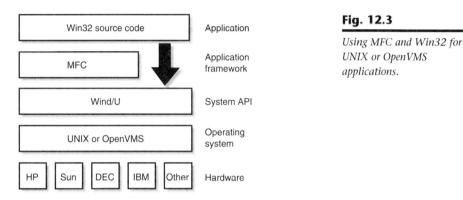

Fig. 12.3

Using MFC and Win32 for UNIX or OpenVMS applications.

Writing nonportable code with the Windows API and MFC is easy—simply call an OS-specific API or assume some API side-effect. Although using the Windows API and MFC does not guarantee a portable application, you *can* create a portable complex GUI application by using the Windows API and MFC. The information and guidelines presented in the rest of this chapter help you to transition current applications to other platforms, and to create more portable applications in the future.

Moving Win16 MFC Applications to Win32 MFC

This section quickly covers what has changed in the MFC library from Win16 MFC 2.5 to Win32 MFC 4.0. Moving a simple, large-model, AppWizard-generated application to MFC 4.0 is a straightforward process. The main differences in MFC 4.0 are the following:

- The packing of lParam and wParam parameters in the CWnd members OnCommand() and OnParentNotify() has changed from 16-bit MFC. This change is a result of Win32's widened WPARAM type. Normally, MFC hides the window procedure from you, unpacks wParam and lParam, and passes the properly unpacked values to you in a message handler. In the case of OnCommand(), wParam and lParam are actual parameters to the function. To determine whether you must update your code, you must examine how you are unpacking lParam and using wParam. For OnParentNotify(), MFC has changed the packing of lParam and no longer stores the child window identifier in `lParam`. Instead, `lParam` contains the 32-bit child window handle. If you need the child identifier, use the following two lines of code:

```
CWnd* pChild = FromHandle( (HWND)lParam );
int ChildID = pChild->GetDlgCtrlID();
```

In this code segment, the `FromHandle` function returns a temporary `CWnd` object for the specified child window handle. The `GetDlgCtrlID()` member function returns the child window ID. You also could retrieve the child ID by passing the child handle directly to the Windows `::GetDlgCtrlID()` function; however, the preceding code also retrieves a pointer to the child `CWnd` object, which your `OnParentNotify()` code probably uses elsewhere.

■ The `CTime` class has constructors that accept system and file times from Win32. The `CTime` class still has constructors that take MS-DOS time arguments. In addition, `CTime` supports `SYSTEMTIME` and `FILETIME` constructors.

■ Existing classes provide new member functions that wrap many of the new Win32 API functions, like new graphics device interface (GDI) functions and new functionality in the framework such as toolbar docking.

■ MFC has added new classes, such as `CWinThread` (which supports multithreaded programming).

■ Most of the MFC library is enabled for Unicode and for Double-Byte Character Set (DBCS) programming. The database classes are the exception. Because of this enabling, many class member functions now take character and string parameters of types based on the type `TCHAR`.

Win32s

When targeting multiple platforms, you should use only Win32s functions. Win32s is an operating system extension that enables Win32 applications to run on Windows 3.1 and Windows for Workgroups. Win32s offers software developers the following:

■ A 32-bit programming model for Windows 3.1 that shares binary compatibility with Windows NT and Windows 95.

■ Full OLE 2.x support, including 16-bit/32-bit interoperability.

■ Performance advantages of the 32-bit mode, including a flat 32-bit address range.

■ Win32 semantics for the API. However, some functions (for example, most GDI functions) have internal 16-bit limits despite their 32-bit interfaces.

■ A rich subset of the full Win32 API found on Windows NT, including the new Windows 95 common controls.

■ The capability to ship a single Win32 product for both Windows NT, Windows 95, and Windows 3.1+.

■ The key set of APIs to use for cross-platform development.

You already are familiar with much of the Win32s API because roughly 1,000 Win16 APIs were widened for Win32s. Most of the widening is due to the basic integer variable changing from two bytes to four bytes, and HANDLE changing to four bytes. Table 12.2 shows the number of bytes in the basic types.

Table 12.2 Basic Data Types		
Data Type	**Number of Bytes in Win16**	**Number of Bytes in Win32**
char, unsigned char	1	1
short, unsigned short	2	2
int, unsigned int	2	4
pointer, address	near = 2, far = 4	4 (8 on Digital UNIX)
long, unsigned long	4	4 (8 on Digital UNIX)
float	4	4
double	8	8

Table 12.3 shows the number of bytes in the basic Windows types.

Table 12.3 Windows Data Types		
Data Type	**Number of Bytes in Win16**	**Number of Bytes in Win32**
BOOL	2	4
DWORD	4	4
FARPROC	4	4
HANDLE	2	4
LPARAM	4	4
LPCSTR	4	4
UINT	2	4
WORD	2	2
WPARAM	2	4

By using the Windows types and minimizing assumptions about the size of data types, you can avoid most problems. Use the sizeof operator instead of relying on what you think should work. If you don't use sizeof, expect 64-bit pointers on Digital UNIX running on Digital Alpha to cause numerous problems.

Most of the 150 Win16 functions dropped from Win32s fall into two broad categories: functions that were OS-specific—that is, functions that accessed the hardware or DOS—and functions that have return values affected by word size differences. For example, `AllocDSToCSAlias` falls into the first category, and `GetViewportExt` falls into the second. Table 12.4 lists the dropped functions and alternatives for Win32.

Table 12.4 Win16 Functions Dropped from Win32s	
API Function	**Win32 Alternative**
`AccessResource()`	No Win32 equivalent; use LoadResource(), LockResource(), and FindResource()
`AddFontModule()`	None
`AdvancedSetupDialog()`	None
`AllocDiskSpace()`	None
`AllocDSToCSAlias()`	None
`AllocFileHandles()`	None
`AllocGDIMem()`	None
`AllocMem()`	None
`AllocResource()`	None (resource API in progress)
`AllocSelector()`	None
`AllocUserMem()`	None
`BM_GETIMAGE`	None
`BM_SETIMAGE`	None
`CallNextHookProc()`	CallNextHookProc()
`Catch()`	Use structure exception handling, MFC exceptions, or C++ exceptions
`ChangeSelector()`	None
`ClassFirst()`	None
`ClassNext()`	None
`CloseComm()`	CloseFile()
`CloseDriver()`	None
`CloseSound()`	Multimedia sound support
`CountVoiceNotes()`	Multimedia sound support
`CreateDIBIcon()`	None
`DeviceCapabilities()`	Portable DeviceCapabilitiesEx()
`DeviceMode()`	Portable DeviceModeEx()
`DlgDirSelect()`	Portable DlgDirSelectEx()
`DlgDirSelectComboBox()`	Portable DlgDirSelectComboBoxEx()
`DOS3Call()`	Named, portable Win32 API (see table 12.5)
`ExtCreateFontIndirect()`	None
`ExtDeviceMode()`	Portable ExtDeviceModeEx()

API Function	Win32 Alternative
FlushComm()	PurgeComm()
FreeAllGDIMem()	None
FreeAllMem()	None
FreeAllUserMem()	None
FreeSelector()	None
GCW_CURSOR	Get¦SetClassCursor()
GCW_HBRBACKGROUND	Get¦SetClassBrBackground()
GCW_HICON	Get¦SetClassIcon()
GetAspectRatioFilter()	Portable GetAspectRatioFilterEx()
GetBitmapDimension()	Portable GetBitmapDimensionEx()
GetBrushOrg()	Portable GetBrushOrgEx()
GetCharacterizationTable	None
GetCodeHandle()	None
GetCodeInfo()	None
GetCommError()	GetCommState()
GetCurrentPDB()	None
GetCurrentPosition()	Portable GetCurrentPositionEx()
GetDCOrg()	Portable GetDCOrgEx()
GetDOSEnvironment()	Portable GetEnvironmentStrings()
GetEnvironment()	None
GetInstanceData()	No equivalent; use alternative supported IPC mechanism
GetKBCodePage()	None
GetMetaFileBits()	Portable GetMetaFileBitsEx()
GetProcessExitCode()	None
GetSystemDebugState()	None
GetSystemDir()	Portable GetSystemDirectory()
GetTempDrive()	Not applicable to Win32; use GetTempPath()
GetTextExtent()	Portable GetTextExtentPoint()
GetTextExtentEx()	Portable GetTextExtentExPoint()
GetThresholdEvent()	Multimedia sound support
GetThresholdStatus()	Multimedia sound support
GetViewportExt()	Portable GetViewportExtEx()
GetViewportOrg()	Portable GetViewportOrgEx()

(continues)

Advanced Programming

V

Table 12.4 Continued

API Function	Win32 Alternative
GetWindowExt()	Portable GetWindowExtEx()
GetWindowOrg()	Portable GetWindowOrgEx()
GetWinFlags()	Portable GetSystemInfo()
GlobalDosAlloc()	None
GlobalDosFree()	None
GlobalEntryHandle()	None
GlobalEntryModule()	None
GlobalFirst()	None
GlobalFix()	None
GlobalInfo()	None
GlobalNext()	None
GlobalNotify()	Portable GlobalFlags()
GlobalPageLock()	None
GlobalPageUnlock()	None
GlobalUnfix()	None
GlobalUnWire()	Obsolete; use GlobalLock() and GlobalUnlock()
GlobalWire()	Obsolete; use GlobalLock() and GlobalUnlock()
GWW_HINSTANCE	GWL_HINSTANCE
GWW_HWNDPARENT	GWL_HWNDPARENT
GWW_ID	GWL_ID
GWW_USERDATA	GWL_USERDATA
InterruptRegister()	None
InterruptUnRegister()	None
IsGDIObject()	None
IsTask	GetExitCodeProcess()
LimitEMSPages()	None
LocalFirst()	None
LocalInfo()	None
LocalNext()	None
LocalNotify()	None
LockInput()	None
MAKEPOINT()	LONG2POINT()
MemManInfo()	None

API Function	Win32 Alternative
MemoryRead()	None
MemoryWrite()	None
ModuleFindHandle()	None
ModuleFindName()	None
ModuleFirst()	None
ModuleNext()	None
MoveTo()	Portable MoveToEx()
NetBIOSCall()	Named, portable Win32 API
NotifyRegister()	None
NotifyUnRegister()	None
OffsetViewportOrg()	Portable OffsetViewportOrgEx()
OffsetWindowOrg()	Portable OffsetWindowOrgEx()
OpenComm()	OpenFile()
OpenDriver()	None
OpenSound()	Multimedia sound support
PeekMessageEx()	None
PlaySoundEvent	None
ProfClear()	Visual C++ built-in profiling features
ProfFinish()	Visual C++ built-in profiling features
ProfFlush()	Visual C++ built-in profiling features
ProfInsChk()	Visual C++ built-in profiling features
ProfSampRate()	Visual C++ built-in profiling features
ProfSetup()	Visual C++ built-in profiling features
ProfStart()	Visual C++ built-in profiling features
ProfStop()	Visual C++ built-in profiling features
ReadComm()	ReadFile()
RegOpenRegistry()	None
RemoveFontModule()	None
ScaleViewportExt()	Portable ScaleViewportExtEx()
ScaleWindowExt()	Portable ScaleWindowExtEx()
SendDriverMessage()	None
SetBitmapDimension()	Portable SetBitmapDimensionEx()
SetCommEventMask()	SetCommMask()
SetEnvironment()	None

(continues)

Table 12.4 Continued

API Function	Win32 Alternative
SetMetaFileBits()	Portable SetMetaFileBitsEx()
SetOverprint	None
SetResourceHandler()	None (resource API in progress)
SetSoundNoise()	Multimedia sound support
SetViewportExt()	Portable SetViewportExtEx()
SetViewportOrg()	Portable SetViewportOrgEx()
SetVoiceAccent()	Multimedia sound support
SetVoiceEnvelope()	Multimedia sound support
SetVoiceNote()	Multimedia sound support
SetVoiceQueueSize()	Multimedia sound support
SetVoiceSound()	Multimedia sound support
SetVoiceThreshold()	Multimedia sound support
SetWindowExt()	Portable SetWindowExtEx()
SetWindowOrg()	Portable SetWindowOrgEx()
StackTraceCSIPFirst()	None
StackTraceFirst()	None
StackTraceNext()	None
StartSeparation	None
StartSound()	Multimedia sound support
StopSound()	Multimedia sound support
SwapRecording()	None
SwitchStackBack()	None
SwitchStackTo()	None
SyncAllVoices()	Multimedia sound support
SystemHeapInfo()	None
TaskFindHandle()	None
TaskFirst()	None
TaskGetCSIP()	None
TaskNext()	None
TaskSetCSIP()	None
TaskSwitch()	None
TerminateApp()	None
Throw()	Structure exception handling, MFC exceptions, or C++ exceptions

API Function	Win32 Alternative
UnAllocDiskSpace()	None
UnAllocFileHandles()	None
UngetCommChar()	None
ValidateCodeSegments()	None
ValidateFreeSpaces()	None
WaitSoundState()	Multimedia sound support
WM_CTLCOLOR	WM_CTLCOLOR type messages
WM_DDE_INIT	None
WM_OTHERWINDOWDESTROYED	None
WriteComm()	WriteFile()
Yield()	Obsolete in Win32

If you are using DOS3Call(), don't worry. The Win32 API has a function for the valid INT 21H operations. Table 12.5 outlines the equivalent Win32 API functions to use for various interrupts.

Table 12.5 DOS3CALL INT 21H **Functions and Their Win32 Equivalents**

INT 21H Subfunction	MS-DOS Operation under Win16	Win32 Equivalent
0EH	Select Disk	SetCurrentDirectory()
19H	Get Current Disk	GetCurrentDirectory()
2AH	Get Date	GetDateAndTime()
2BH	Set Date	SetDateAndTime()
2CH	Get Time	GetDateAndTime()
2DH	Set Time	SetDateAndTime()
36H	Get Disk Free Space	GetDiskFreeSpace()
39H	Create Directory	CreateDirectory()
3AH	Remove Directory	RemoveDirectory()
3BH	Set Current Directory	SetCurrentDirectory()
3CH	Create Handle	CreateFile()
3DH	Open Handle	CreateFile()
3EH	Close Handle	CloseHandle()
3FH	Read Handle	ReadFile()
40H	Write Handle	WriteFile()
41H	Delete File	DeleteFile()

V

Advanced Programming

(continues)

Table 12.5 Continued		
INT 21H Subfunction	**MS-DOS Operation under Win16**	**Win32 Equivalent**
42H	Move File Pointer	SetFilePointer()
43H	Get File Attributes	GetAttributesFile()
43H	Set File Attributes	SetAttributesFile()
47H	Get Current Directory	GetCurrentDirectory()
4EH	Find First File	FindFirstFile()
4FH	Find Next File	FindNextFile()
56H	Change Directory Entry	MoveFile()
57H	Get Date/Time of File	GetDateAndTimeFile()
57H	Set Date/Time of File	SetDataAndTimeFile()
59H	Get Extended Error	GetLastError()
5AH	Create Unique File	GetTempFileName()
5BH	Create New File	CreateFile()
5CH	Lock	LockFile()
5CH	Unlock	UnlockFile()
67H	Set Handle Count	SetHandleCount()

The 200 or so new APIs in Win32s, when compared to Win16, give the application programmer many additional building blocks. Here are the new Win32 functions included in Win32s:

AbnormalTermination	CompareFileTime	CreateProcess
accept	CompareString	DeleteCriticalSection
Animate_Close	connect	DeleteFile
Animate_Create	ContinueDebugEvent	DeviceCapabilitiesEx
Animate_Open	ConvertDefaultLocale	DisableThreadLibraryCalls
Animate_Play	CopyCursor	DM_GETDEFID
Animate_Seek	CopyFile	DM_SETDEFID
Animate_Stop	CopyIcon	DosDateTimeToFileTime
Beep	CreateDIBPatternBrushPt	DriverCallback
bind	CreateDirectory	DrvGetModuleHandle
CallNextHookEx	CreateDirectoryEx	DuplicateHandle
CloseHandle	CreateFile	EM_GETTHUMB
closesocket	CreateFileMapping	EnterCriticalSection
CommandLineToArgvW	CreateMappedBitmap	EnumCalendarInfo

EnumCalendarInfoProc	GetCommandLine	getservbyport
EnumCodePagesProc	GetCurrencyFormat	getsockname
EnumDateFormats	GetCurrentDirectory	getsockopt
EnumDateFormatsProc	GetCurrentProcess	GetStartupInfo
EnumFontFamProc	GetCurrentProcessId	GetStdHandle
EnumLocalesProc	GetCurrentThread	GetStringTypeA
EnumResLangProc	GetCurrentThreadId	GetStringTypeEx
EnumResNameProc	GetDateFormat	GetSystemDefaultLangID
EnumResourceLanguages	GetDiskFreeSpace	GetSystemDefaultLCID
EnumResourceNames	GetEffectiveClientRect	GetSystemTime
EnumResourceTypes	GetEnvironmentStrings	GetSystemTimeAdjustment
EnumResTypeProc	GetEnvironmentVariable	GetTempPath
EnumSystemCodePages	GetExitCodeProcess	GetThreadContext
EnumSystemLocales	GetExitCodeThread	GetThreadSelectorEntry
EnumThreadWindows	GetExpandedName	GetTimeFormat
EnumThreadWndProc	GetFileAttributes	GetUserDefaultLangID
EnumTimeFormats	GetFileSize	GetUserDefaultLCID
EnumTimeFormatsProc	GetFileTime	GetVersionEx
ExitProcess	GetFileType	GetVolumeInformation
ExitThread	GetFullPathName	GetWindowThreadProcessId
ExtEscape	gethostbyaddr	HANDLE_WM_NOTIFY
FileTimeToDosDateTime	gethostbyname	HeapAlloc
FileTimeToLocalFileTime	gethostname	HeapCreate
FileTimeToSystemTime	GetKBCodePage	HeapDestroy
FindClose	GetKerningPairs	HeapFree
FindFirstFile	GetLastError	HeapSize
FindNextFile	GetLocaleInfo	htonl
FlushFileBuffers	GetLogicalDrives	htons
FlushInstructionCache	GetNumberFormat	ImageList_Draw
FoldString	GetOpenFileName	ImageList_DrawEx
FormatMessage	getpeername	ImageList_EndDrag
FORWARD_WM_NOTIFY	GetProcessAffinityMask	ImageList_ExtractIcon
FreeDDElParam	getprotobyname	ImageList_GetBkColor
FreeEnvironmentStrings	getprotobynumber	ImageList_GetDragImage
FreeLibraryAndExitThread	GetSaveFileName	ImageList_GetIcon
GdiFlush	getservbyname	ImageList_GetIconSize

ImageList_GetImageCount	mciGetYieldProc	RemoveDirectory
ImageList_GetImageInfo	MenuHelp	ReplaceText
ImageList_LoadBitmap	mixerClose	ReuseDDElParam
ImageList_LoadImage	mixerGetControlDetails	SearchPath
ImageList_Merge	mixerGetDevCaps	select
ImageList_Read	mixerGetID	SelectObject
ImageList_Remove	mixerGetLineControls	send
ImageList_Replace	mixerGetLineInfo	sendto
ImageList_ReplaceIcon	mixerGetNumDevs	SetBrushOrgEx
ImageList_SetBkColor	mixerMessage	SetCurrentDirectory
ImageList_SetDragCursorImage	mixerOpen	SetEndOfFile
ImageList_SetIconSize	mixerSetControlDetails	SetEnvironmentVariable
ImageList_SetOverlayImage	mouse_event	SetErrorMode
ImageList_Write	MoveFile	SetFileApisToANSI
inet_addr	NDdeTrustedShareEnum	SetFileAttributes
inet_ntoa	NotifyChangeEventLog	SetFilePointer
InitCommonControls	ntohl	SetFileTime
InitializeCriticalSection	ntohs	SetLastError
ioctlsocket	OpenFileMapping	SetLastErrorEx
IoDBCSLoadByteFx	OpenProcess	SetLocaleInfo
IsTextUnicode	PackDDElParam	SetProcessWorkingSetSize
IsValidLocale	PlaySound	SetServiceBits
IsWindowUnicode	PostThreadMessage	setsockopt
LBItemFromPt	PrintDlg	SetStdHandle
LCMapString	RaiseException	SetSystemCursor
LeaveCriticalSection	ReadFile	SetSystemTime
listen	ReadProcessMemory	SetThreadAffinityMask
LoadCursorFromFile	recv	SetThreadContext
LoadLibraryEx	recvfrom	SetUnhandledExceptionFilter
LocalFileTimeToFileTime	RegCloseKey	ShellAbout
LockFile	RegCreateKeyEx	ShowHideMenuCtl
lstrcpyn	RegEnumValue	shutdown
MakeDragList	RegOpenKeyEx	Sleep
MapViewOfFile	RegQueryValueEx	socket
MapViewOfFileEx	RegSetValueEx	SystemTimeToFileTime
mciGetDeviceIDFromElementID	RegUnLoadKey	TlsAlloc

TlsFree	WM_CTLCOLORBTN	WSAAsyncGetServByName
TlsGetValue	WM_CTLCOLORDLG	WSAAsyncGetServByPort
TlsSetValue	WM_CTLCOLOREDIT	WSAAsyncSelect
ToAscii	WM_CTLCOLORLISTBOX	WSACancelAsyncRequest
UnhandledExceptionFilter	WM_CTLCOLORMSGBOX	WSACancelBlockingCall
UnlockFile	WM_CTLCOLORSCROLLBAR	WSACleanup
UnmapViewOfFile	WM_CTLCOLORSTATIC	WSAFDIsSet
UnpackDDElParam	WNetAddConnection	WSAGetLastError
VirtualAlloc	WNetGetConnection	WSAIsBlocking
VirtualFree	WriteFile	WSASetBlockingHook
VirtualProtect	WSAAsyncGetHostByAddr	WSASetLastError
VirtualQuery	WSAAsyncGetHostByName	WSAStartup
WaitForDebugEvent	WSAAsyncGetProtoByName	WSAUnhookBlockingHook
WideCharToMultiByte	WSAAsyncGetProtoByNumber	

Using MFC for Portability

The MFC library was designed with portability in mind. The following are the key portability benefits of MFC:

- Message maps and associated On functions
- Use of C++ objects rather than OS-dependent handles
- Stronger type checking
- The capability to use Win32s APIs internally

The message maps in an MFC application hide the unpacking of the WPARAM and LPARAM type parameters. Breaking apart message parameters not only is a portability hassle, but also is error-prone. The widening of handles to 32 bits has forced the re-packing of several messages, because Win16 packed 16-bit handles with other data into the 32-bit LPARAM. Most MFC 2.5 applications already use the medium or large programming model with 32-bit object pointers; in MFC 4.0, these object pointers remain 32 bits. Instead of dealing with the handles that have changed from 16 to 32 bits, the object pointers have not changed in size. Also, MFC 2.5 applications had to define STRICT, which increased the amount of type checking possible.

Portable Applications with the Win32 API and MFC

To create portable applications, you need not change most of your current code and coding practices. In some applications, you might not have to change a single line of code; after you recompile and relink them, they're ready to run. Other applications that have a long Win16 or C legacy might require a lot of conversion effort. Before looking at specific differences, here are some general guidelines to increase portability:

■ Include full file path names; use single-case names with forward slashes and no drive letters.

■ DOS linefeeds and carriage returns differ from the UNIX newline, so don't use \r in your code.

■ Don't rely on path names that start with drive letters.

■ Don't use private tools unless you plan to port them to every target environment.

■ Have clean compiles. Most warning messages generated with Warning level 3, /W3, indicate code with portability problems. To make sure that you fix these problems, select the Warnings as Errors option in the C/C++ tab of the Build Settings dialog box. This option ensures that files that generate such warnings are not compiled.

■ Never assume the following:

Byte ordering

The structure of the stack, heap, or memory

An internal structure layout

A single-tasking operating system

The case or format of a string or file name

The sign of a number

That undocumented functions are safe to use

■ Always use the following:

typedefs, which are safer than the native types

The sizeof operator (don't assume size)

ifdefs to isolate platform dependencies

Differences among Intel x86, Motorola 680x0, and RISC

Applications that use pointer arithmetic to address individual bytes within a variable, or to read and write binary data, must be aware of byte-ordering differences. There are two byte-ordering techniques, *little endian* and *big endian*. Some new CPUs allow the operating system to specify byte ordering, so never assume byte ordering based on the CPU. The MIPS CPU is an example. When running NT, the byte ordering matches Intel x86 style, but when running UNIX, the byte ordering is swapped. For each type of Win32-compatible processor, table 12.7 shows the byte ordering of specific operating systems.

Table 12.6 Byte Ordering

Processor	Operating System	Byte Order
Alpha	All	Little endian
HP-PA	NT	Little endian
HP-PA	UNIX	Big endian
Intel x86	All	Little endian
Motorola 680x0	All	Big endian
MIPS	NT	Little endian
MIPS	UNIX	Big endian
PowerPC	NT	Little endian
PowerPC	non-NT	Big endian
RS/6000	UNIX	Big endian
SPARC	UNIX	Big endian
VAX	OpenVMS	Little endian

Little endian byte ordering places the least significant byte first and the most significant byte last. The following layout represents four bytes of data:

```
bits: [  7  6  5  4  3  2  1  0 ]  Byte 0    < Address
bits: [ 15 14 13 12 11 10  9  8 ]  Byte 1
bits: [ 23 22 21 20 19 18 17 16 ]  Byte 2
bits: [ 31 30 29 28 27 26 25 24 ]  Byte 3
```

For example, a pointer to a four-byte integer contains the address of that integer's least significant byte (bits 0 through 7). Adding 1 to the pointer value causes it to point to the next higher byte of the value (bits 8 through 15), and so on.

Big endian byte ordering places the most significant byte first, followed by the next most significant byte, and so on, with the least significant byte last. The following layout represents four bytes of data:

```
bits: [ 31 30 29 28 27 26 25 24 ]  Byte 0    < Address
bits: [ 23 22 21 20 19 18 17 16 ]  Byte 1
bits: [ 15 14 13 12 11 10  9  8 ]  Byte 2
bits: [  7  6  5  4  3  2  1  0 ]  Byte 3
```

In this ordering, a pointer to an integer value contains the address of the integer's most significant byte. The individual ordering of bits within each byte does not differ between processors. Therefore, writing a single byte of data is the same on each machine, but writing a larger object, such as a two- or four-byte integer, will swap the bytes.

Structure Packing and Storage Alignment

Along with different byte ordering, the various processors have different storage-alignment requirements. The storage-alignment differences affect the location of fields within a structure. A common practice was to pack Win16 structures on one-byte boundaries to save memory. But now, most non-Intel x86 processors cannot access odd-memory addresses, so this packing is impossible.

Applications usually should align structure members at addresses that are "natural" for the data type and the processor involved. For example, a four-byte data member should have an address that is a multiple of four. This principle is especially important when you write code for porting to multiple processors. A misaligned four-byte data member which is on an address that is not a multiple of four causes a performance penalty with an Intel x86 processor and causes a hardware exception with a MIPS RISC processor. In the latter case, although the system handles the exception, the performance penalty is even greater than with the Intel processor.

Table 12.7 lists the proper and portable storage alignments for processors targeted by Win32.

Table 12.7   Type Alignment Requirements

Type	Alignment
char	Align on byte boundaries
short	Align on even byte boundaries
int, long, and float	Align on 32-bit boundaries
double	Align on 64-bit boundaries
structures	Largest alignment requirement of any member
unions	Alignment requirement of the first member

The compiler automatically aligns data in accordance with these requirements, inserting padding in structures up to the limit (the default pack size) specified by the /Zp option or #pragma pack. For example, /Zp2 allows up to one byte of padding, /Zp4 allows up to three bytes of padding, and so on. The default pack size for Windows 3.x is two bytes, and the default for Win32 is eight. You should search your code for all #pragma pack statements and consider removing them. You should also examine your code for any structure offsets that you might be assuming. Any hard-coded structure field offsets are a sure sign of nonportable code.

The default packing with MFC 4 is four bytes—in other words, /Zp4. Using four-byte structure packing saves a little more memory on Intel x86 processors, but is not the most portable. In fact, MIPS and Alpha NT, as well as the UNIX version of Win32, require eight-byte packing. MFC helps to enforce this requirement by specifying the eight-byte packing pragma for some target platforms. In the following MFC code segment, the source contains various ifdefs for alignment based on the target platform. For example, for MIPS, ALPHA, and PowerPC, which require eight-byte alignment, MFC overrides the default four-byte structure packing:

```
From: mfc/include/afxv_cpu.h
///////////////////////////////////////////////////////////////

#ifdef _MIPS_
// specific overrides for MIPS...
#define _AFX_PACKING    8        // default MIPS alignment (required)
#endif //_MIPS_


///////////////////////////////////////////////////////////////

#ifdef _ALPHA_
// specific overrides for ALPHA...
#define _AFX_PACKING    8        // default AXP alignment (required)
#ifdef _AFX_NO_DEBUG_CRT
extern "C" void _BPT();
#pragma intrinsic(_BPT)
#define AfxDebugBreak() _BPT()
#else
#define AfxDebugBreak() _CrtDbgBreak()
#endif
#endif  //_ALPHA_


///////////////////////////////////////////////////////////////

#ifdef _PPC_
// specific overrides for PPC...
#define _AFX_PACKING    8        // default PPC alignment (required)
#endif //_PPC_


///////////////////////////////////////////////////////////////
```

The preceding code indicates only the number of bytes to use, but does not contain a pack pragma. In mfc/include/afx.h, a pack pragma uses these _AFX_PACKING values:

```
From mfc/include/afx.h
#ifdef _AFX_PACKING
#pragma pack(push, _AFX_PACKING)
#endif
```

But MFC defaults to four-byte packing on Intel x86 and Motorola 680x0 processors. afxver_.h specifies this four-byte packing default as follows:

```
// From: mfc/include/afxver_.h
// set up default packing value
#ifndef _AFX_PACKING
#define _AFX_PACKING    4      // default packs structs at 4
// bytes
#endif
```

For portability, you must override this default and use eight-byte packing. One way to do this is in the Build Settings dialog box (which you access by choosing Build, Settings), by following these steps:

1. Select all projects in the Settings For list box.
2. Select the C/C++ tab.

3. Select General from the Category list.

4. Add **,_AFX_PACKING=8** to the end of the Preprocessor Definitions text box.

The following is an example of how storage-order assumptions affect your program. This example casts a simple three-byte structure to the type `long` because the application assumes the physical order in which the data is stored:

```
// nonportable code
struct time
{
char hour
char minute
char second
};
...
struct time now;
struct time alarm_time;
...
if ( *(long *)&now >= *(long *)&alarm_time ) {
// sound alarm
}
```

This code segment makes the nonportable assumption that the data for `hour` will be stored in a higher order position than `minute` and `second`. This works in little endian environments, but the alarm might never sound on a UNIX or Mac application.

To make this code segment portable, you can break the comparison between the two long integers into a component-by-component comparison, as follows:

```
// portable code
struct time
{
char hour
char minute
char second
};
...
long time_cmp(struct time t1, struct time t2)
{
long t1_seconds = t1.hour * 3600 + t1.minute * 60 + t1.second;
long t2_seconds = t2.hour * 3600 + t2.minute * 60 + t2.second;
return t2_seconds - t1_seconds;
}
...
struct time now;
struct time alarm_time;
...
if ( time_cmp(now, alarm_time) >= 0) {
// sound alarm
}
```

Again, as a general rule, search for any type casting and determine whether you should remove it.

Memory Allocation

All the standard Win32, C run-time library, and C++ memory-allocation schemes work across platforms. Only with the Macintosh do you need to be concerned with memory models and 16-bit limits. For portability on the Macintosh, always build with the large memory model /AL, also known as farCode and farData. This model removes most 16-bit limits for your applications. Also, check whether you have any #pragma data_seg or #pragma code_seg compiler directives. These directives force additional 16-bit limits on your application. Macintosh code segments are restricted to 32K, and the one near data segment is restricted to 32K. Also, your automatic variables on the stack are restricted to 32K. You can avoid these problems by dynamically allocating large automatic variables instead of assuming a nearly unlimited stack size.

File System Differences

Win32 applications must work with several file systems. Windows NT has three file systems: New Technology file system (NTFS), the DOS file allocation table (FAT) file system, and high-performance file system (HPFS). Windows 95 supports only FAT and VFAT (virtual file allocation table) file systems. The Macintosh file system, HFS, is another completely different beast, with creator types, file types, directory IDs, and more. The UNIX file system is a large tree structure with long file names and the possibility for other drives or network drives to be mounted anywhere in the tree. OpenVMS is hardly related at all to UNIX; it has a tree structure, but uses brackets ([ ]) as delimiters. Table 12.8 lists major differences among the file systems.

Table 12.8   File System Attributes

File System	Long File Names	Separator	Drives	Case-Sensitive
FAT	No	\ or /	A: ... Z:	No
HPFS	Yes	\ or /	A: ... Z:	No, preserves case
NTFS	Yes	\ or /	A: ... Z:	No, preserves case
VFAT	Yes	\ or /	A: ... Z:	No, preserves case
Mac	Yes	/	Named objects	Yes
OpenVMS	Yes	[ ]	Named objects	No
UNIX	Yes	/	Named objects	Yes

Standard Windows code that parses and manipulates path names does not work on the Macintosh or UNIX. Also, HFILE handles returned by Win32 functions do not work in the normal C run-time library functions.

File systems like NTFS and VFAT on Windows 95 preserve the case in which the file name was created, but all file system comparisons are case-insensitive. Thus, *Word, word,* and *WORD* all refer to the same file.

V

Advanced Programming

Even with all these differences, most applications that use the MFC library are easy to make portable. For example, in the MFC tutorial Scribble, the path name to the file is almost totally managed by the MFC framework. In the Scribble application, code that deals with the path name simply passes or prints the string. Here's the OnOpenDocument() method from Scribble document class:

```
From; mfc/scribble/step5/scribdoc.cpp
///////////////////////////////////////////////////////////////////
// CScribDoc commands

BOOL CScribDoc::OnOpenDocument(LPCTSTR lpszPathName)
{
if (!CDocument::OnOpenDocument(lpszPathName))
return FALSE;
InitDocument();
return TRUE;
}
```

The OnOpenDocument member function simply forwards the path name to the parent class CDocument. The application code does not parse or examine the path name; only MFC needs to deal with any file-system-dependent issues.

In the following code fragment, the CDocument::GetTitle member function creates a CString of the file name:

```
From; mfc/scribble/step5/scribvw.cpp
void CScribView::PrintTitlePage(CDC* pDC, CPrintInfo* pInfo)
{
// Prepare a font size for displaying the file name
...
// Get the file name, to be displayed on title page
CString strPageTitle = GetDocument()->GetTitle();

// Display the file name one inch below the top of the page,
// centered horizontally
pDC->SetTextAlign(TA_CENTER);
pDC->TextOut(pInfo->m_rectDraw.right/2, -100, strPageTitle);
...
}
```

The code doesn't parse or examine the file name, but simply uses TextOut to draw the file name. The MFC libraries, rather than your application, deal with any platform dependencies.

Your application might have to enable the user to choose a file name in some way that's inconvenient without high-level MFC classes. If so, use the MFC class CFileDialog, which uses the Windows common dialog boxes GetOpenFileName and GetSaveFileName. You can use this class to help create a layer between your application code and the various file systems. When using CFileDialog to build a file-system-independent layer, start by examining the implementation of CWinApp::OnFileOpen, CDocument::OnFileSave, and related functions in the MFC source code. The following code segment illustrates some differences that you must deal with between most Windows-based file systems and the Mac file system, and demonstrates how MFC deals with the differences:

```
From: mfc/src/doccore.cpp
#ifndef _MAC
// check for dubious file name
int iBad = newName.FindOneOf(_T(" #%;/\\"));
#else
int iBad = newName.FindOneOf(_T(":"));
#endif
```

In the preceding example, MFC uses an #ifndef to deal with the differences in the set of invalid characters allowed in a path name.

Some classes of programs must access the file system outside of the MFC class library. When your application needs direct access, start with the Win32 file system APIs and add #ifndefs as needed. Table 12.9 lists the Win32 file system API functions and indicates whether these APIs are available in the Macintosh and UNIX Win32 libraries.

Table 12.9 Win32 File System Functions

API Function	Win32s	Availability Macintosh	UNIX/OpenVMS
CloseHandle()	Yes	Yes	Yes
CopyFile()	Yes	Yes	Yes
CreateDirectory()	Yes	No	Yes
CreateDirectoryEx()	Yes	No	Yes
CreateFile()	Yes	Yes	Yes
DefineDosDevice()	No	No	No
DeleteFile()	Yes	Yes	Yes
FileIOCompletionRoutine()	No	No	No
FindClose()	Yes	Yes	Yes
FindCloseChangeNotification()	No	No	No
FindFirstChangeNotification()	No	No	No
FindFirstFile()	Yes	Yes	Yes
FindNextChangeNotification()	Yes	No	No
FindNextFile()	Yes	Yes	Yes
FlushFileBuffers()	Yes	Yes	Yes
GetCurrentDirectory()	Yes	No	Yes
GetDiskFreeSpace()	Yes	No	Yes
GetDriveType()	Yes	No	Yes (always fixed)
GetFileAttributes()	Yes	Yes	Yes
GetFileInformationByHandle()	No	Yes	Yes
GetFileSize()	Yes	Yes	Yes

(continues)

V

Advanced Programming

Table 12.9 Win32 File System Functions

API Function	Win32s	Availability Macintosh	UNIX/OpenVMS
GetFileType()	Yes	Yes	Yes
GetFullPathName()	Yes	Yes	Yes
GetLogicalDrives()	Yes	No	No
GetLogicalDriveStrings()	No	No	No
GetSystemDirectory()	Yes	No	Yes
GetTempFileName()	Yes	Yes	Yes
GetTempPath()	Yes	Yes	Yes
GetVolumeInformation()	Yes	No	Yes
GetWindowsDirectory()	Yes	No	Yes
_hread()	Yes	Yes	Yes
_hwrite()	Yes	Yes	Yes
_lclose()	Yes	Yes	Yes
_lcreate()	Yes	Yes	Yes
_llseek()	Yes	Yes	Yes
LockFile()	Yes	Yes	Yes
LockFileEx()	No	No	Yes
_lopen()	Yes	Yes	Yes
_lread()	Yes	Yes	Yes
_lwrite()	Yes	Yes	Yes
MoveFile()	Yes	Yes	Yes
OpenFile()	Yes	Yes	Yes
QueryDosDevice()	No	No	No
ReadFile()	Yes	Yes	Yes
ReadFileEx()	No	No	Yes
RemoveDirectory()	Yes	No	Yes
SearchPath()	Yes	No	Yes
SetCurrentDirectory()	Yes	No	Yes
SetEndOfFile()	Yes	Yes	Yes
SetFileAttributes()	Yes	Yes	Yes
SetFilePointer()	Yes	Yes	Yes
SetHandleCount()	Yes	No	No
SetVolumeLabel()	No	No	No

API Function	Win32s	Availability Macintosh	UNIX/OpenVMS
UnlockFile()	Yes	Yes	Yes
UnlockFileEx()	No	No	Yes
WriteFile()	Yes	Yes	Yes
WriteFileEx()	No	No	Yes

Note

If your applications have to deal with a series of related files, consider using the OLE structure storage library. Only the root of the storage object is an actual file-system name and must be portable. This OLE component manages the names of elements contained within storage objects. These names are portable to any environment.

Porting Applications to the Macintosh

This section outlines the steps for porting an existing application to the Macintosh. These steps assume that you have installed on your Intel x86 Windows-based computer the Visual C++ 4 Cross-Development Edition for Macintosh. You perform each of the following steps within this Visual C++ environment on your PC:

1. Add the Macintosh targets to your existing project.
2. Add to the project any Macintosh-specific code or resource files.
3. Configure the Macintosh target settings in the Link, Macintosh Resource, and Compiler tabs of the Build Settings dialog box.
4. Set the Debug tab options in the Build Settings dialog box for the Macintosh target.
5. Make any source file adjustments (.cpp, .c, .h, and so on).
6. Create Macintosh-specific resources and put them in the project's .r file.
7. Modify your Win32 resources as necessary (using `#ifdefs`) for use with the Macintosh version of the application.
8. Compile and link the application and resource files.
9. Prepare any WinHelp files for use on the Macintosh.
10. Copy the compiled files to the Macintosh.
11. Test and debug the application. The application runs and displays on the Macintosh. The debugger runs and displays on the PC.

V

Advanced Programming

Porting Visual C++ Applications to UNIX

The Win32/MFC APIs are available on several UNIX platforms. These tools, also known as Windows Interface Source Environment (WISE) cross-development products, provide the Windows APIs running on UNIX systems.

The UNIX operating system and the available development tools vary slightly with each hardware manufacturer. Lately, most UNIX systems derive from the AT&T System V Release 4 UNIX release, and C++ compilers are based on the AT&T Cfront 3.0 ANSI draft compiler. Also, the hardware manufacturers have agreed to use the X Window windowing system and Motif user interface look-and-feel standard. For the Win32 and MFC programmer on UNIX, the supplied WISE Win32 and MFC libraries hide most differences. For example, LoadLibrary() has different implementations on Sun and HP workstations, but to the Win32 application, the LoadLibrary() semantics are the same. There are also differences in compiler and linker switches, but again the WISE cross-development tools abstract these differences into platform-independent makefiles.

This section outlines the steps for porting an existing application to UNIX. These steps assume that you already have installed the Wind/U cross-development software. All these steps take place on the UNIX workstation:

1. Copy the source files to the UNIX workstation.
2. Convert the DOS source code to a format readable on UNIX. The cross-development software includes a utility that converts DOS end-of-line characters (carriage return and newline) to the UNIX end-of-line character (just newline). All cross-platform source code controls tools automatically handle this step.
3. Add any UNIX-specific code.
4. Create a UNIX makefile.
5. Compile the application using the makefile.
6. Compile the resource files.
7. Link the application and resource files.
8. Compile any WinHelp files for use on UNIX.
9. Test and debug your application using your UNIX debugger.

The following subsections describe an example of moving the DIBLOOK sample to a UNIX platform. DIBLOOK is one of the sample MFC applications that views device-independent bitmap (.dib) files or device-dependent bitmap (.bmp) files in MDI child windows.

Understanding the Wind/U Architecture

The Wind/U software architecture is similar to the Windows architecture, but is hosted on a different graphics, window, and operating system. Wind/U provides the three major sections of the Windows API: Kernel calls for core non-GUI functions, User calls for menus and dialog boxes, and the Graphics Device Interface (GDI) calls for device-independent drawing. These components are provided as shared libraries; most of the other WinAPI components are contained in DLLs that wrap around these three core libraries (see fig. 12.4).

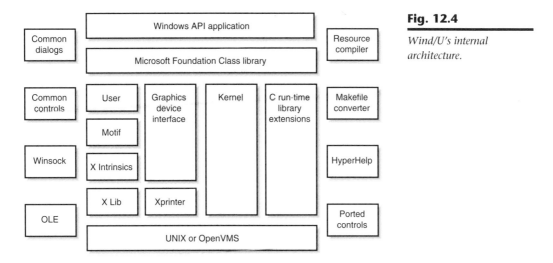

Fig. 12.4

Wind/U's internal architecture.

Converting the Files

Use the prepare_source utility to convert the files from DOS format to UNIX, as is done in listing 12.1.

Listing 12.1   File Conversion from DOS to UNIX

```
unix > prepare_source

prepare_source
==============

This utility resolves DOS and Visual C/C++ compiler differences in the
source code found in the current directory.  Only files ending in the
extensions .c, .rc, .dlg, .h, .C, and .rc2 will be processed.
The original code is backed up to the subdirectory ORIGINAL.

The script does the following:
1. Changes C++ // comments to ANSI standard /* */ in C source files.
2. Performs DOS to UNIX conversion (removes ^M and ^Z characters).
3. Scans the source code to identify potential problem spots.
Problem spots are reported in the file WARNINGS.

Do you wish to continue? (y¦n)
y

Linking .cpp files to UNIX .C files
```

(continues)

Listing 12.1 Continued

```
copying dibapi.cpp   to    dibapi.C
copying dibdoc.cpp   to    dibdoc.C
copying diblook.cpp  to    diblook.C
copying dibview.cpp  to    dibview.C
copying mainfrm.cpp  to    mainfrm.C
copying myfile.cpp   to    myfile.C
copying stdafx.cpp   to    stdafx.C

Creating directory ORIGINAL to contain your original files.

Converting files in the current directory.
Processing:
dibapi.C
dibapi.h
dibdoc.C
dibdoc.h
diblook.C
diblook.h
diblook.rc
dibview.C
dibview.h
mainfrm.C
mainfrm.h
myfile.C
resource.h
stdafx.C
stdafx.h
Processing Completed
Original files are saved in ORIGINAL directory.
```

Creating a UNIX Makefile

Visual C++ makefiles and UNIX makefiles differ enough to make it difficult to use a single makefile in both environments. Normally, you do not edit the internal Visual C++ makefile, .mak, directly. Instead, you make changes in the Build Settings dialog box and the project's workspace. The `make_windumakefile` utility creates a basic UNIX makefile directly from the Visual C++ makefile, providing functionality similar to the Project Files dialog box in Visual C++. The makefile generated by `make_windumakefile` works unchanged across UNIX platforms for applications that are contained within one directory, as DIBLOOK is. This makefile contains information about which source and resource files are included in the project, how to compile everything, and how to link the final executable. To generate the makefile, just type this command at your UNIX shell prompt:

```
unix > make_windumakefile diblook >Makefile
```

Cleaning Up DIBLOOK

The DIBLOOK MFC sample has a few nonportable constructs. The following code segments show the various pieces of code that you must change, along with comments on the changes. All the UNIX changes, like the Macintosh changes, are inside

`#ifdef`s so that the changes are backward-compatible to all platforms. This compatibility enables you to use one source code base for all platforms. Where differences are necessary, as in the following byte-ordering problems, these changes are visible only if a compile-time directive turns on the appropriate `#ifdef`.

Open the file myfile.cpp, which is in the directory /SAMPLES/MFC/DIBLOOK. The following code fragment begins on line 26 of that file; it shows the use of the Wind/U-provided macros for swapping byte ordering and accessing UNIX functions:

```
#include "dibapi.h"

#ifdef WU_APP          // included UNIX byte-swapping macros and functions
#include "wuExten.h"
#endif
```

The next code fragment begins at line 153 of the same file; it shows some code, bracketed with `#ifdef`s, that changes the way the file's written to ensure that byte ordering is correct on the UNIX platform:

```
TRY
{
#ifdef WU_APP
// Write the file header
// Use Wind/U extension functions
// to take care of byte-swapping issues
wuWriteBitmapFileHeaderToFile(file.m_hFile, &bmfHdr);
// Write the Bitmap Info Header
// Use Wind/U extension functions
// to take care of byte-swapping issues
wuWriteBitmapInfoHeaderToFile(file.m_hFile,
(LPBITMAPINFOHEADER) lpBI);
// Write the bits
file.WriteHuge((LPSTR) lpBI + lpBI->biSize,
_ dwDIBSize - lpBI->biSize);
#else
// Write the file header
file.Write((LPSTR)&bmfHdr, sizeof(BITMAPFILEHEADER));
...
```

The following code, which begins at line 246 of the same file, shows the reverse of the preceding snippet; here, the code calls Wind/U routines to swap bytes back into Win32 order when reading the bitmap file:

```
/*
* Go read the bits.
*/
#ifndef WU_APP
if (file.ReadHuge(pDIB, dwBitsSize - sizeof(BITMAPFILEHEADER)) !=
dwBitsSize - sizeof(BITMAPFILEHEADER) )
{
::GlobalUnlock((HGLOBAL) hDIB);
::GlobalFree((HGLOBAL) hDIB);
return NULL;
}
#else
```

V

Advanced Programming

```
  // Can't read directly - have to take into account byte-swapping
  // of the BITMAPINFOHEADER structure.
  // From start of file, seek to point after file header.
  */
  llseek(file.m_hFile,14,SEEK_SET);
  if (!wuReadBitmapInfoHeaderFromFile(file.m_hFile,
  _ (LPBITMAPINFOHEADER) pDIB))
  {
  ::GlobalUnlock((HGLOBAL) hDIB);
  ::GlobalFree((HGLOBAL) hDIB);
  return NULL;
  }
  lpBI = (LPBITMAPINFOHEADER) pDIB;
  if (file.ReadHuge(pDIB + ((LPBITMAPINFOHEADER)pDIB)->biSize,
  /* We've already read the INFOHEADER*/
  dwBitsSize - ((LPBITMAPINFOHEADER)pDIB)->biSize - 14)
  != dwBitsSize -((LPBITMAPINFOHEADER)pDIB)->biSize -14)
  {
  ::GlobalUnlock((HGLOBAL) hDIB);
  ::GlobalFree((HGLOBAL) hDIB);
  return NULL;
  }
  #endif

  ::GlobalUnlock((HGLOBAL) hDIB);
  return hDIB;
  }
```

Compiling DIBLOOK

Now that you have updated the code to handle the byte-swapping differences, you can build the UNIX executable. The UNIX make program uses the makefile created by make_windumakefile, compiles the source files and resource file, and links the applications:

```
unix > make
mkdir sol2
CC -O -c -Dsol2 -DWU_APP -D_PORTABLE ... -o sol2/stdafx.o stdafx.C
```

Running DIBLOOK

To run the application, type the following command at your UNIX shell prompt:

```
unix > sol2/diblook
```

The DIBLOOK application should be up and running. At first glance, DIBLOOK appears just as it does on Windows or Windows NT. But if you look closer, Motif has some slight differences, such as a more 3-D look to the menu bar and menu items. Click the File Open toolbar icon and open some of your favorite .dib or .bmp files.

From Here...

By now, you have learned that Win32 and MFC are cross-platform libraries and that Visual C++ 4 is the cornerstone to a productive cross-platform development environment. Today, from a single source base of MFC code, you can develop native applications for all Windows operating systems, as well as native Apple System 7 applications for the Macintosh and PowerMac, and native UNIX/Motif applications for RISC workstations.

For more information on related topics, see the following sources:

■ See Chapter 2, "Using the Visual C++ Developer Studio," for more information on changing project and build settings.

■ See Chapter 5, "Introducing MFC," and Chapter 6, "Using MFC," for an overview of the classes within MFC that you can use to replace some nonportable code in your application.

■ See *Using UNIX* (Que, 1994), for in-depth explanations of UNIX programming considerations.

V

Advanced Programming

CHAPTER 13

Exception Handling

Exception handling provides a structured and formalized service for dealing with exceptional events. Typically the term *exception handling* refers to handling error conditions; however, you can also use exception handling for a variety of other tasks. As you will see later in this chapter, traditional methods of error handling are flawed in several profound ways. Exception handling solves most of these problems.

C++ exceptions help programmers deal with several common programming headaches that typically require developers to write large amounts of tedious code that gets executed very infrequently. Specifically, exceptions do the following:

■ Help provide a standardized error-handling mechanism

■ Help programs deal with anticipated problems

■ Help programs deal with problems that were completely unanticipated when the program was built

■ Help the programmer recognize, track down, and fix bugs

This chapter begins by looking at some of the ways that programs currently handle error conditions. You learn about the following:

■ How exception handling accomplishes the same results as currently used procedures

■ Why exceptions are a superior method for getting these results

■ How to use and deploy exception handling throughout your Visual C++ programs

■ How to modify a larger program to take full advantage of C++ exceptions

Visual C++ 4 now supports many of the powerful extensions that will appear in the final ANSI C++ standard. Visual C++ 2 supported templates and exception handling. To these, Visual C++ 4 has added run-time type identification, namespaces, and template support robust enough to support the Standard Template Library. All these features are crucial for the development of sophisticated and reliable C++ programs.

This chapter focuses on exception handling. Understand that exception handling is *not* a cure-all. If you choose to use exceptions, you must put a significant amount of work into using them. And, as with any powerful tool, exceptions can be used improperly.

Software Development in an Imperfect World

Suppose that a fellow programmer claims to have developed a large C++ program that was totally bug-free after the first successful compile, and that can deal with any error condition, any abnormal event, and anything that could conceivably go wrong. How would you react?

Your first reaction would probably be to have your poor, deluded friend immediately institutionalized. Such a boast is not only difficult to believe, it's actually funny! After all, computer programmers are only human, and human beings are notoriously error-prone. Even if the person making this outrageous claim were a truly exceptional programmer, writing a program that can deal with every single conceivable problem is impossible. Such a program would be absolutely gigantic, and most of its code would be dedicated to coping with situations that might never arise.

This premise is somewhat unsettling. If programmers resign themselves to writing imperfect programs that can't deal with a wide range of potential problems, is computer software inherently unreliable? Maybe so.

Many industry insiders have talked at great length about the *software crisis*. Despite exciting new paradigms (for example, object-oriented programming) and productive new development environments (Visual C++, for example), the cost of developing software is increasing, but the reliability of software is not increasing at a corresponding rate.

This sorry state of affairs is due to several unique factors that all have conspired to make life miserable for programmers. The marketplace has forced software up a steep evolutionary path that has resulted in contemporary products that make the programs of 10 years ago look Cro-Magnon by comparison. The sophisticated users of today demand attractive, graphical applications that work together and provide immediate and tangible productivity benefits. Yikes! When you consider that users want all this without their applications becoming completely overwhelming, today's programmers clearly have their work cut out for them.

All these market-induced pressures lead to a single fundamental problem: complexity. Today's programs are so complex that it's no wonder that they're less reliable. They are, after all, doing much more. With increased complexity, things are much more likely to go wrong. And as Murphy's Law correctly asserts, "If something can go wrong, it will."

The problem is that you can't simply print Murphy's Law on the front of a software box or in a warranty disclaimer. You can't explain to an irate customer over a support line that he lost a week's worth of work because we live in an imperfect world (actually, you can try, but I wouldn't advise it). Instead, a concentrated effort must be made to ensure that new software is becoming more reliable.

Exception Handling: A Flagstone on the Road to Reliability

Several things can be done to alleviate the software crisis, and only a few of them have a direct relationship with Microsoft Visual C++. Some strategies, such as teaching specific techniques for writing solid code, are simply extensions of the normal education process. Other strategies, such as using object-oriented programming to facilitate code reuse, require a profound change in the way that developers traditionally have built programs.

The use of C++ exception handling falls into this latter category. Exception handling is a relatively new approach to an old problem: what a program should do when something unexpected happens. The underlying mechanisms might surprise you (to the uninitiated, exception handling smells an awful lot like the dreaded goto), but don't be fooled. Exceptions are an elegant and effective way to combat complexity and ensure that your programs run more reliably.

Coping with Error in C

Before jumping into the details of the exception-handling syntax, it's beneficial to take a look at some of more traditional ways that C programs (and pre-exception handling C++ programs) have dealt with error conditions. (Exception handling is useful for more than simply trapping error conditions. However, because trapping errors is the context in which programmers most often use exception handling, this chapter focuses on that purpose.)

A program that cannot handle exceptions still has several ways in which to trap and process error conditions. Although the following overview is not an exhaustive list of strategies, it covers the most commonly used ones.

Returning Error Values

By far the most common way to signal an error within a function or object method is simply to return a value that indicates whether something went wrong. All programmers have used these types of functions; after all, most C library functions use such functions to communicate error conditions. The class in listing 13.1, for example, has a single method that calculates a signed value that could theoretically be useful when used inside a program.

Listing 13.1 Using a Direct Return Value To Report an Error

```
// Our theoretically useful class
class AUsefulClass {
public:
```

(continues)

Listing 13.1 Continued

```
        long CalcAUsefulValue()
        {
           Do some processing and return the value
        }
   };

   // Now use the class
   AUsefulClass MyVar;
   long lAUsefulValue = MyVar.CalcAUsefulValue();
   if (lAUsefulValue != 0)
        cout << "The value is " << lAUsefulValue << "\n";
   else
   cout << "An error occurred!\n";
```

In this case, the program could return a calculated number as appropriate or return a value of zero if an error occurred. This code snippet checks the return value and flags an error if the returned value is zero.

This technique works fine, unless zero is a potentially valid return value. If the method can legitimately return zero, there's no way to differentiate between a calculated value of zero and an error.

You can often use a constant value or range of values as returnable error codes. In the preceding example, if zero were a valid return value, you could perhaps use –1 to signal an error instead. Still, this will not always be the case.

This method of reporting errors has three problems. First, for a program to check for an error condition, the programmer must remember what these "magic" error codes are. This strategy is quite error-prone. (Does –1 mean "Out of memory" or "Out of range"? Or are you thinking about a colleague's error codes for a SuperDooHicky class?) Forcing people to remember "magic" numbers is a remarkably effective way to introduce bugs into your programs.

Second, as alluded to previously, occasions *will* arise when it is very difficult (or even impossible) for the programmer to find a free value that an application can return as an error. Take the following function prototype, which simply adds two unsigned shorts:

```
   unsigned short Add(unsigned short addend1, unsigned short addend2);
```

It is possible to pass two numbers into this function that, when added, will overflow the returned unsigned short value. Clearly, this would be an error condition and should be reported as such. But what error value could you possibly return? Zero doesn't work because that's a perfectly valid answer if both addends are zero. In fact, *any* unsigned short value is a valid answer in this example. There simply aren't any free numbers that you can use as error codes. This problem is not completely insurmountable, however, as you will see in the next section.

You cannot say the same about the third problem, however. A program must go through the effort of checking the return value to determine that an error has occurred. If a programmer is lazy or simply forgets to check the return value, serious errors can slip by unnoticed. If you think that this seems unlikely, ask yourself when was the last time that you checked the return value of a call to `strcpy()` or `printf()`.

Clearly, although it is the most frequently used mechanism for reporting errors, simply returning an error code has some problems associated with it.

Returning Error Values in Function Arguments

This error-reporting strategy is a simple improvement on the previous strategy. Instead of reporting errors with return codes, programs can pass in a variable whose sole purpose is to be assigned an error code if something goes wrong. Using this strategy, the `Add()` function from the preceding section might use the following prototype. Notice that this prototype uses a reference to a `short` (it could also use a pointer to a `short`) because the `ErrorCode` variable must be modifiable.

```
unsigned short Add(unsigned short addend1,
                   unsigned short addend2,
                   short& ErrorCode);
```

Alternatively, you could have a variable return the addition's result and have the function return an error code. Clearly, this is just a variation on the same theme:

```
short Add(unsigned short addend1,
          unsigned short addend2,
          unsigned short& Result);
```

This strategy solves the problem of having to search for freely available error values. Still, the programmer must remember the potential error values and remember to check the returned error variable's contents.

A Global Error Variable

Instead of passing an error variable into a method, the programmer can simply rely on a global error variable. This technique saves the function's user from having to pass an extra argument into a method call; however, it's hard to view this savings as a huge productivity win. Listing 13.2 demonstrates how a programmer might use this error-reporting technique.

Listing 13.2 global.cpp, Using a Global Variable To Report an Error

```
// Get needed include files
#include <limits.h>
#include <iostream.h>

// Global error variable declaration
short ErrorCode;

unsigned short Add(unsigned short addend1, unsigned short addend2)
{
```

(continues)

Listing 13.2 Continued

```
        unsigned long sum = addend1 + addend2;
        if (sum > USHRT_MAX)
           ErrorCode = -1;
        return (unsigned short) sum;
}

void main()
{
        unsigned short Result = Add(12345, 54321);
        if (ErrorCode == -1)
           cout << "Overflow error!\n";
        else
           cout << "The answer is " << Result << "\n";
}
```

This technique is a valid mechanism for reporting errors, but has several serious problems as well. As in the previous two methods, the programmer calling the function still must remember the specific error codes for which to check. Also, the programmer still must remember to check the error variable after the call.

In addition, this strategy suffers from the simple fact that it relies on global data. Subsequent calls to other functions could change the error variable without the programmer realizing it. The problem is exacerbated under operating systems, such as Windows NT, that support multiple threads of execution. Under these operating systems, the error variable might change even before the program has a chance to check the value initially.

Using global variables for error codes has a long tradition, going back to the early days of programming in C under the UNIX operating system. The use of the errno variable continues to this day, although most compiler vendors support errno more for the sake of compatibility than as a serious error-reporting mechanism.

Using goto or setjmp/longjmp

Both goto and setjmp/longjmp interrupt the normal flow of execution, so an error-handling strategy based on one of these approaches cannot be ignored. This behavior is very valuable because potentially serious errors cannot slip by unnoticed. On the other hand, both of these techniques suffer from some serious problems when used with C++ objects.

Take a quick look at goto first. Listing 13.3 demonstrates how you might rely on goto to trap errors.

Listing 13.3 Using goto To Help Report an Error

```
unsigned long sum = addend1 + addend2;
if (sum > USHRT_MAX)
        goto OverflowError;
cout << "The sum is " << sum << "\n";
```

```
More relevant processing

OverflowError:
    cout << "An overflow occurred!\n";
```

In this example, if the code encounters an overflow condition, the programmer clearly is going to know about it. Unfortunately, goto has a serious limitation: You can use it only within a single function or method. Although you might be tempted to write such code in listing 13.4, you simply can't.

Listing 13.4   badgoto.cpp, an Illegal Use of goto To Help Report an Error

```cpp
// Get needed include files
#include <limits.h>
#include <iostream.h>

unsigned short Add(unsigned short addend1, unsigned short addend2)
{
        unsigned long sum = addend1 + addend2;
        if (sum > USHRT_MAX)
           goto OverflowError; // Illegal can't leave Add()
        return (unsigned short) sum;
}

void main()
{
        unsigned short Result = Add(12345, 54321);
        cout << "The answer is " << Result << "\n";
        return;

        // Error-handling section but you'll never get here using
        // this program
OverflowError:
        cout << "Overflow error!\n";
        return;
}
```

On the other hand, setjmp/longjmp—which is essentially a goto on steroids—can help you with this problem. Listing 13.5 shows a version of the same program that at least works.

Listing 13.5   jump.cpp, Using setjmp/longjmp To Help Report an Error

```cpp
// Get needed include files
#include <limits.h>
#include <iostream.h>
#include <setjmp.h>

jmp_buf jmp_info;

unsigned short Add(unsigned short addend1, unsigned short addend2)
```

(continues)

V

Advanced Programming

Listing 13.5 Continued

```
        {
            unsigned long sum = addend1 + addend2;
            if (sum > USHRT_MAX)
                longjmp(jmp_info, -1);
            return (unsigned short) sum;
        }

        void main()
        {
            int ErrorCode = setjmp(jmp_info);
            if (ErrorCode == 0) {
                unsigned short Result = Add(12345, 54321);
                cout << "The answer is " << Result << "\n";
                return;
            }

            // Error-handling section
            else {
                cout << "Overflow error!\n";
            }
        }
```

This strategy is better. It enables the programmer to design an error-handling infra-structure that cannot be ignored or forgotten. This increases reliability because the programmer must handle errors whether he or she wants to or not. There's still the problem of remembering error codes; however, because the error processing will be centralized (theoretically) into error-handling blocks, the program at least has the option of installing generic error handling that doesn't have to use specific error codes.

Unfortunately, the setjmp/longjmp strategy suffers from a fatal flaw: It doesn't know C++. This shortcoming might not seem like such a big deal, but think about what would happen in the pseudocode snippet in listing 13.6.

Listing 13.6 Creating a Memory Leak with longjmp

```
    void MyUsefulFunc()
    {
        MyMemoryHogClass   Hog;

        ... Some processing ...

        if (Some error condition)
            longjmp(jmp_info, -1);

        ... Continue with more processing ...
    }
```

Assume that MyMemoryHogClass dynamically allocates a substantial amount of memory from the heap and releases that memory when its destructor is called. If an error occurs and the `longjmp` executes, a memory leak occurs because the `Hog` object instance is never destructed.

You need an error-processing strategy that contains elements of the `setjmp`/`longjmp` approach but that is responsive to the needs of C++ programs when it comes to destructing object instances that move out of scope because of an error. Enter C++ exception handling, which does all of this and more.

A Better Way with Exceptions

At first glance, handling exceptions seems much like using `setjmp`/`longjmp`, but it quickly becomes apparent that exceptions are much more robust. For the most part, exception handling addresses many of the deficiencies of the error-processing strategies mentioned in previous sections while adding significant flexibility and additional functionality.

When using exception handling, programs have no choice but to respond to errors. As mentioned during the discussion of `setjmp`/`longjmp`, this increases reliability because errors cannot slip between the cracks and cause unanticipated problems later.

Exception handling enables programs to use any C++ object or built-in type to represent information about an error. Therefore, you need not rely on numeric error codes (unless you want to). Instead, you can create hierarchies of specialized classes dedicated to communicating information about abnormal events.

Finally, exception handling is inherently bound to the C++ language. If throwing an exception forces local object instances out of scope, you are assured that the appropriate destructors will be called.

Exception-Handling Fundamentals: Throwing, Catching, and Trying

Now that you have an understanding of the problems that exception handling addresses, it's time to see how to use Visual C++ exceptions. The easiest way to learn about exceptions is to see them in action, so take a close look at listing 13.7, which presents a trivial exception-handling example.

Listing 13.7   simple.cpp, a Trivial Example of Exception Handling

```
// Get needed include files
#include <limits.h>
#include <iostream.h>
#include <eh.h>

unsigned short Add(unsigned short addend1, unsigned short addend2)
{
        unsigned long sum = addend1 + addend2;
        if (sum > USHRT_MAX)
```

(continues)

Listing 13.7   Continued

```
                  throw 1;
            return (unsigned short) sum;
      }

      void main()
      {
            try {
               unsigned short Result = Add(12345, 54321);
               cout << "The answer is " << Result << "\n";
            }
            catch (int ErrorCode) {
                cout << "An overflow occurred! ErrorCode = "
                << ErrorCode << "\n";
            }
      }
```

The example in listing 13.7 has three interesting elements. Notice that the call to the Add() function is enclosed within a scope preceded by the try keyword. This *try block* indicates to the compiler that the program is interested in exceptions that might occur within this block. For this reason, code enclosed within a try block is sometimes said to be *guarded*.

Immediately following the try block is the *catch block* (more commonly referred to as the *exception handler*). Program execution jumps to this block if an exception occurs. Although this simple example has only a single handler, programs might have many different handlers that can process a multitude of different exception types.

The last element of the exception-handling process is the throw statement, found within Add(). The throw statement actually signals an exceptional event. The metaphor is simple and elegant: Program code *throws* exception objects that are *caught* by handlers. This process is sometimes called *raising an exception*. In this simple example, the exception that the code is throwing is in the form of a simple integer (the ErrorCode); however, as you will see later, programs can throw virtually any type of exception.

Listing 13.8 demonstrates a slight modification to the example. See if you can guess this program's output.

Listing 13.8   unwind.cpp, a Demonstration of Unwinding the Stack

```
Same #include Files as 13.7
class MyMemoryHogClass {
public:
        ~MyMemoryHogClass() { cout <<
        _ "In the MyMemoryHogClass destructor.\n"; }
};

unsigned short Add(unsigned short addend1, unsigned short addend2)
{
        MyMemoryHogClass Hog;
```

```
            unsigned long sum = addend1 + addend2;
            if (sum > USHRT_MAX)
                throw 1;
            return (unsigned short) sum;
     }
     main() same as listing 13.7
```

If you type this example and run it, you get something like the following:

```
    In the MyMemoryHogClass destructor.
    An overflow occurred! ErrorCode = 1
```

As you can see, the program calls the Hog object's instance's destructor when the exception forces execution from Add(). This is an absolutely crucial aspect of C++ exceptions that other error-handling techniques simply cannot emulate. The process of calling the destructors of local objects as exceptions to move them out of scope is often referred to as *unwinding the stack*.

Examining try Blocks

Take a closer look at what a try block is. The following is the official syntax of the try block:

```
    try-block :
            try compound-statement handler-list
```

This syntax makes two important points. You must follow the try keyword with a compound statement (a block of code separated from the current scope by braces). Single-line try blocks are *not* supported in a manner similar to that allowed by the if, while, and for statements. Listing 13.9 makes this distinction clear.

Listing 13.9   Examples of Legal and Illegal try Blocks

```
// Legal -- "if" doesn't require compound statement
if (a > b)
        cout << "a is greater than b.\n";

// Legal --_ "for" doesn't require compound statement
for (loop = 0; loop < numberOfElements; loop++)
        ProcessElement();

// Illegal -- try block needs a compound statement
try
        ProcessElement();

// Legal_-- try block uses a compound statement(enclosing a single line)
try {
        ProcessElement();
}

// Legal
try {
    ProcessFirstElements();
```

(continues)

Listing 13.9   Continued

```
        ProcessSecondElements();
}
```

The second important thing that the official syntax tells you is that you must follow a try block immediately with at least one handler. This makes sense. After all, what would it mean if you told the compiler that you wanted to catch exceptions for a particular block of code but you didn't tell the compiler where you wanted to route the exceptions? Listing 13.10 shows both legal and illegal examples demonstrating this rule.

Listing 13.10   Examples of Legal and Illegal Handler Placement

```
// Illegal -- No handler at all
try {
        ProcessElements();

// Illegal --- the catch handler doesn't immediately follow the try block
try {
        ProcessElements();
}
ProcessMoreElements();
catch (int ErrorCode) {
        ProcessException(ErrorCode);
}

// Legal
try {
        ProcessElements();
}
catch (int ErrorCode) {
        ProcessException(ErrorCode);
}

// Legal
try {
        ProcessElements();
}
catch (int ErrorCode) {
        ProcessException(ErrorCode);
}
catch (char * ErrorString) {
        cout << "Exception (" << ErrorString << ")\n";
}
```

You can place into a try block any code that you want, including calls to other local functions, functions in a DLL, or object methods. Any code in a try block, at any level of nesting, can throw exceptions.

You can nest try blocks inside of each other as appropriate. Examine listing 13.11, which shows one try block used within another.

Listing 13.11   nested.cpp, an Example of Nested try Blocks

```cpp
// Get needed include files
#include <stdlib.h>
#include <iostream.h>
#include <eh.h>

// Constants
const int MIN_FLAG_VALUE = 0;
const int MAX_FLAG_VALUE = 10;
const int FLAG_OUT_OF_BOUNDS = 0xFF;

// Processing
void DoSomethingElse()
{
        cout << "Inside DoSomethingElse.\n";
}


void DoSomethingUseful(int Flag)
{
        cout << "Inside DoSomethingUseful.\n";

        // Is our flag too big or too small?
        if (Flag < MIN_FLAG_VALUE || Flag > MAX_FLAG_VALUE)
           throw FLAG_OUT_OF_BOUNDS;

        // Do some processing
        try {
           if (Flag == 0) {
                   cout << "The flag was set to zero.\n";
                   DoSomethingElse();
           }
           else
                   throw "Flag is non-zero.";
        }
        catch (char *ErrorString) {
           cout << ErrorString << "\n";
        }
}

void main(int argc, char *argv[ ])
{
        // If no command-line arguments, set the flag to zero
        int UseFlag = (argc == 1 ? 0 : atoi(argv[1]));

        // Do some processing
        try {
           DoSomethingUseful(UseFlag);
        }
        catch (int ErrorCode) {
           cout << "Caught an exception (" << ErrorCode << ")\n";
        }
}
```

Although this example looks deceptively simple, it has a couple of levels of subtlety.

Table 13.1 shows the output of listing 13.11 depending on the command-line argument passed into it.

Table 13.1 Different Output Examples from Listing 13.11 (nested.cpp)	
Command-Line Argument	**Program Output**
No arguments	Inside DoSomethingUseful. The flag was set to zero. Inside DoSomethingElse.
Flag equal to 0	Inside DoSomethingUseful. The flag was set to zero. Inside DoSomethingElse.
Flag < 0 or flag > 10	Inside DoSomethingUseful. Caught an exception (255).
Flag between 1 and 10	Inside DoSomethingUseful. Flag is nonzero.

In the first and second case, the `try` block sets the flag to zero, calls `DoSomethingUseful()`, and checks to ensure that the flag value is within the allowed range. Because the value is within the range, the following `if` statement checks whether the flag is zero. Because the flag is zero, the block prints a message and calls `DoSomethingElse()`. These cases do not throw any exceptions and the program executes normally.

In the third case—when the flag is greater than 10 or less than 0—the block calls `DoSomethingUseful()` and the flag fails the "within valid range" check. This failure throws an exception (`FLAG_OUT_OF_BOUNDS`). This integer exception is caught by the handler that follows the `try` block in `main()`, which dutifully prints the exception value.

In the last case, the flag is passed in and passes through `DoSomethingUseful()`'s bounds check. However, it fails the `if`-statement check for a zero value and throws a string exception. This string exception is caught by the handler within `DoSomethingUseful()`, which simply prints the string.

In the next section, you see how Visual C++ determines which handler to call under various circumstances. As you might imagine, things can get complex quickly unless you plan adequately beforehand. (And complexity is exactly what you want to avoid!)

Catching Exceptions

Visual C++ exception handlers are tremendously important because they are responsible for determining the next course of action after catching an exception. Properly delegating responsibility to handlers is an important part of your program's design.

Handlers 101. The official syntax for a handler is the following:

```
handler-list :
        handler handler-list (opt)
handler :
        catch ( exception-declaration ) compound-statement
```

This syntax tells you several important things. A compound statement follows the handler, so you must enclose the handlers within braces just like try blocks. The syntax also shows that a handler list follows try blocks. This means that you can assign many different exception handlers to catch exceptions from a single try block. The only general limitation on this rule is that the exception type processed by each handler must be unique.

Take a quick look at listing 13.12. This listing shows some examples of both legal and illegal exception handlers.

Listing 13.12   Examples of Legal and Illegal Handlers

```
// Illegal -- the handler needs to be within a compound statement
try {
        ProcessStuff();
}
catch(int ErrorCode)
        ProcessError(ErrorCode);

// Legal
try {
        ProcessStuff();
}
catch(int ErrorCode) {
        ProcessError(ErrorCode);
}

// Illegal --_ both catch blocks handle the same exception type (int)
try {
        ProcessStuff();
}
catch(int CommError) {
        ProcessError(CommError);
}
catch(int ErrorCode) {
        ProcessError(ErrorCode);
}

// Illegal -- CommErrorType is still just an int
typedef int CommErrorType;
try {
        ProcessStuff();
}
catch(CommErrorType CommError) {
        ProcessError(CommError);
```

(continues)

Listing 13.12   Continued

```
}
catch(int ErrorCode) {
        ProcessError(ErrorCode);
}

// Legal --_CommErrorType is now a separate exception type
class CommErrorType {
public:
        int CommError;
};

try {
        ProcessStuff();
}
catch(CommErrorType CommError) {
        // Assuming ProcessError() is overloaded to handle CommErrorTypes
        ProcessError(CommError);
}
catch(int ErrorCode) {
        ProcessError(ErrorCode);
}
```

You can create a handler that specifies only the exception type and does not declare an exception object. Such a handler might be all that your program needs to process error conditions adequately. In fact, if you declare an exception object name but don't reference it, the Visual C++ compiler complains about an unused local variable. Listing 13.13 shows this behavior in action.

Listing 13.13   Specifying Only the Exception Type in a Handler Declaration

```
try {
        ProcessElements();
}
catch (int) {
        cout << "An error occurred in ProcessElements()!\n";
}
```

Programs use different exception types to distinguish among different kinds of error conditions. Each type must have a corresponding handler, because if the C++ run-time component cannot find an appropriate handler to which to route an exception, it terminates the program. (As you will see later, there are exceptions to this behavior—no pun intended!)

The Catch-All Handler. You can use a general-purpose handler that will match any type of exception. This handler, which is referred to simply as the *ellipsis handler*, is declared (appropriately enough) with an ellipsis for its exception argument. Listing 13.14 demonstrates this handler.

Listing 13.14   ellipsis.cpp, Using the Ellipsis Catch-All Exception Handler

```cpp
// Get needed include files
#include <limits.h>
#include <iostream.h>
#include <eh.h>

unsigned short Add(unsigned short addend1, unsigned short addend2)
{
        unsigned long sum = addend1 + addend2;
        if (sum > USHRT_MAX)
            throw 1;
        return (unsigned short) sum;
}

unsigned short Divide(unsigned short dividend, unsigned short divisor)
{
        if (divisor == 0)
            throw "Divide by zero";
    return (dividend / divisor);
}

void main()
{
        try {
            unsigned short Result = Add(12345, 12345);
            cout << "The first answer is " << Result << "\n";
            Result = Divide(55, 0);
            cout << "The second answer is " << Result << "\n";
        }
        catch (int) {
            cout << "An addition overflow occurred!\n";
        }
        catch (...) {
            cout << "Something else bad happened.\n";
        }
}
```

In this example, the call to Add() completes normally because the arguments to the function do not cause an overflow condition. The following call to Divide(), however, fails because a zero value passes in as the function's divisor argument. This raises a string exception that contains the words "Divide by zero". No exception handler is explicitly designed to deal with string exceptions. There is, however, an ellipsis handler, and the string exception is routed there.

The ellipsis handler *must* catch an exception, so you must make this handler the last handler in the handler list. At compile time, the code in listing 13.15 is flagged as an error.

Listing 13.15   Illegal Placement of the Ellipsis Handler

```
type {
        ProcessElements();
}
catch (...) {
        cout << "Some unidentifiable exception was raised.\n"
}
catch (int) {
        cout << "An integer exception was raised.\n";
}
```

The final thing to note about the ellipsis handler is fairly obvious: Because the ellipsis handler is a catch-all handler that can accept any type of exception, there is no way to actually get at the thrown exception object. Even if there was some way to get at the object reference, you would have no way to determine the object's type. Unless you know an exception's type, framing the processing of the exception into any sort of useful context is difficult. For this reason, ellipsis handlers are typically used to catch unanticipated exceptions and deal with them in a generic fashion.

The Great Handler Search. Depending on the circumstances, searching for the right handler might not be quite as straightforward as the contrived examples in this chapter might have led you to believe. In fact, it is very important that you carefully order handler lists and that you sufficiently consider the precise type that they handle.

The C++ run-time code follows several key rules when dispatching an exception. These rules can become confusing, so read them carefully.

- *Rule 1:* Exception handler lists are searched from the beginning of the list to the end. The exception is dispatched to the first capable handler. Therefore, if—because of one of the following rules—more than one handler can potentially handle an exception, the first handle in the list gets the exception.

- *Rule 2:* As discussed in the previous section, the ellipsis handler can handle any exception.

- *Rule 3:* Code can dispatch an exception to a handler for the appropriate exception type *or to a handler for a reference to that type.* Therefore, both the catch (MyClass&) and catch (MyClass) handlers can accept an exception of type MyClass. You can use the const and volatile modifiers, but they are not factored into the matching process. After an exception is caught, however, any const or volatile modifiers remain in full force.

The Visual C++ compiler does not let you provide a handler list that contains both a handler for a type and a handler for a reference to that type because the first handler in the list will always win. The section "The Subtleties of Throwing" explains in detail why you would provide one over the other.

- *Rule 4:* Code can dispatch an exception to a handler designed to accept objects having as their type a base class of the exception. Therefore, if class B derives from class A, a class A handler can accept a class B exception.

  The Visual C++ compiler does not enable you to provide a handler list that contains a handler for a base type before a handler for a derived type, because the base type handler would always process the exceptions meant for the derived type handler.

- *Rule 5:* In accordance with rule 3, you can route an exception to a handler that can accept a *reference* to an object whose type is a base class of the exception. Therefore, if class B derives from class A, a class A reference handler can accept a class B (or class B reference) exception.

  As in the previous examples, the Visual C++ compiler prevents you from shooting yourself in the foot: It doesn't let you provide a handler list that contains a handler for a reference to an exception's base class before a handler for the exception's type (or a reference to that type). This prevention is necessary because otherwise the first handler in the list would always process the exception.

- *Rule 6:* You can route an exception to a handler that accepts a pointer to which you can convert a thrown pointer by using standard pointer conversion rules.

- *Rule 7:* If the program cannot find in the current handler list a handler for an exception, search for another handler list in an enclosing level of scope. If the search for a handler progresses all the way to the first level of scope (main()) without success, the C++ run-time system terminates the program abnormally. You can modify this by using the set_terminate() function described in the section "Installing Your Own terminate() Handler," later in this chapter.

Because there's much going on in these rules, a few examples are probably in order. Listing 13.16 shows a program with nested try blocks. Try to predict the output of this code.

Listing 13.16 rule7.cpp, a Demonstration of Rule 7

```
// Get needed include files
#include <iostream.h>
#include <eh.h>

void Func1(int flag)
{
        try {
            cout << "In Func1.\n";
            if (flag)
                    throw "String exception";
        }
        catch (int) {
            cout << "Caught an integer exception.\n";
        }
}
```

(continues)

Listing 13.16 Continued

```
void main()
{
      try {
         Func1(1);
      }
      catch (char *str) {
         cout << "Caught a string exception: " << str << "\n";
      }
      catch (...) {
         cout << "Caught an unrecognized exception.\n";
      }
}
```

This example demonstrates rule 7. Passing in a nonzero value for `Func1()`'s flag variable causes the program to raise a string exception. However, there is no handler for string exceptions in `Func1()`'s try block, so the C++ run-time code drops to the next level of scope and searches the handler list in `main()`. That list does include a string exception handler, so this code dispatches the exception accordingly.

The next example, listing 13.17, demonstrates some of the implications of rules 1, 4, and 5.

Listing 13.17 rules145.cpp, a Demonstration of Rules 1, 4, and 5 Using Multiple Inheritance

```
// Get needed include files
#include <iostream.h>
#include <eh.h>

class First1 { };
class First2 { };
class Last : public First1, public First2 { };

Last MyLast;

void Func1(int flag)
{
      cout << "In Func1.\n";
      if (flag)
         throw MyLast;
}

void main()
{
      try {
         Func1(1);
      }
      catch (First1&) {
         cout << "Caught a First1 exception.\n";
      }
      catch (First2&) {
```

```
        cout << "Caught a First2 exception.\n";
      }
      catch (...) {
        cout << "Caught an unrecognized exception.\n";
      }
   }
```

This code contains a multiple inheritance hierarchy, with the Last class inheriting from both First1 and First2. When Func1() raises the MyLast exception, the program searches the handler list in main() for a match. The first handler checked is catch (First1&). The exception thrown is of type Last, so there is clearly no exact match with this handler. However, because Last derives from First1, this handler qualifies as an acceptable handler as stipulated by rule 4. Note also that even though the handler is designed to accept *references* to type First1, this handler is acceptable because of rule 5.

Suppose that you order this list with the First2& handler appearing before the First1& handler, as in the following example:

```
catch (First2&) {
      cout << "Caught a First2 exception.\n";
}
catch (First1&) {
      cout << "Caught a First1 exception.\n";
}
catch (...) {
      cout << "Caught an unrecognized exception.\n";
}
```

In this case, the First2& handler receives the exception because of rule 1.

As a final example, look at listing 13.18, which demonstrates how rule 6 affects the matching process. In this program, the exception being thrown is a pointer type. Because of rule 6, pointer-based exceptions are a little more adaptable than normal exceptions.

Listing 13.18 rules16.cpp, a Demonstration of Rules 1 and 6

```
// Get needed include files
#include <iostream.h>
#include <eh.h>

class Base { };
class Derived : public Base { };

void Func1(int flag)
{
      cout << "In Func1.\n";
      if (flag)
        throw new Derived;
}
```

(continues)

Listing 13.18   Continued

```
void main()
{
        try {
           Func1(1);
        }
        catch (Derived*) {
           cout << "Caught a Derived* exception.\n";
        }
        catch (Base*) {
           cout << "Caught a Base* exception.\n";
        }
        catch (void*) {
           cout << "Caught a void* exception.\n";
        }
        catch (...) {
           cout << "Caught an unrecognized exception.\n";
        }
}
```

The exception that this program is throwing—a Derived pointer—can be caught by *any* of the four handlers supplied. This is because you can legitimately cast a Derived pointer to either a Base pointer or a void pointer. Notice that you cast down anything to a void pointer, so a void pointer handler catches any type of pointer exception.

What Exactly Are You Throwing, Anyway?

Several times this chapter has noted that, even though most of the examples so far have concentrated on simple integer or string exceptions, an exception can actually be of any type. Your first reaction on hearing this might have been to ask why.

Maybe an appropriate (albeit somewhat coy) response to that question is, why not? Clearly a C++ object offers a much richer palette of functionality than a simple integral type. Class-based objects can present an interface to programs that imply a wide range of error-processing options, whereas a simple integer or string can only communicate a basic state or describe an error condition in a minimalist fashion.

Organizing exceptions into class hierarchies also gives programs the option of dealing with errors at several different levels of granularity. Take, for example, the simple exception hierarchy shown in figure 13.1.

In this hierarchy, the topmost exception class is named SimpleExp. MathExp derives from SimpleExp, which in turn has children exception classes IntegerOverflow and DivideByZero. A program that uses this class hierarchy throws a wide variety of very specific exception objects such as IntegerOverflow and DivideByZero. However, when it comes to actually catching these exceptions, the program has the option of treating the exceptions generically (as SimpleExps), somewhat generically but within a math context (as MathExps), or as the specific exceptions that they really are.

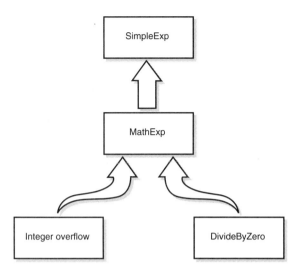

Fig. 13.1

A sample exception class hierarchy.

The Subtleties of Throwing. You already know that you dispatch exceptions to handlers by using the `throw` keyword, but this chapter still hasn't discussed two subtleties associated with `throw`.

Both of these subtleties are related to things that happen when a program throws an exception. The first is related to the concept of unwinding the stack. Remember that unwinding the stack refers to the process of calling the destructors of local class objects that the exception dispatch will move out of scope. This concept is pretty straightforward to understand and crucial to using exception handling effectively within C++ programs. Unwinding the stack, however, does *not* imply that objects created dynamically off the heap using the `new` operator will be destructed. For example, the `MyLocalGuy` object will get destructed in the following case:

```
void Func1()
{
        LocalGuy MyLocalGuy;
        throw 1;
}
```

However, the following case does not destruct the object:

```
void Func1()
{
        LocalGuy *MyLocalGuy = new LocalGuy;
        throw 1;
}
```

> **Caution**
>
> Your program must explicitly release dynamic allocations before raising the exception. Otherwise, your program could develop memory leaks. A program with too many memory leaks can use up some of the system's free memory and thus harm the system's performance.

The second subtlety relates to how you catch an exception after it is thrown. Remember that an exception can be caught by a handler designed to accept objects of the appropriate type *or references to objects of the appropriate type.*

When your program handles an object by value or by reference, Visual C++ makes a copy of the object instance being thrown. This copy is stored in a temporary variable whose existence is hidden from your program. If the compiler didn't do this and you threw an object that was declared locally, the thrown object would be out of scope and would no longer exist by the time the program called your handler. Your handler receives this mysterious "behind the scenes" copy—and not the instance that was originally thrown—as the exception argument.

The biggest implication here is that if you are throwing your exceptions by value or by reference, your classes must know how to copy themselves. If your class is complex and requires special copying behaviors, you must equip the class appropriately with a copy constructor that knows about these special requirements.

Contrast this to when you catch and throw an exception using a pointer. In this scenario, the run-time code directly passes the pointer into the handler, bypassing the copying that occurs when you throw by value or reference. Because the compiler does not make a copy, you are responsible for ensuring that the object is in a stable and completely constructed state.

Unfortunately, there are additional pitfalls associated with throwing exceptions using pointers. If you throw a pointer that refers to a local object, that object no longer exists by the time that your program calls your handler, and the pointer will be invalid. If, on the other hand, you create a new object off the heap using the new operator, you must remember to delete the pointer in your handler; otherwise, you introduce a memory leak.

Yet another technique has your program throw a temporary object:

```
void Func1()
{
        throw MyClass();
}
```

Visual C++ is smart enough to realize that you are throwing and catching with a temporary object and does not go through the unnecessary step of creating a clandestine copy (and triggering an invocation of your copy constructor). As you would expect, however, you must create the temporary object, so you do call its constructor.

Passing Exceptions. In the course of integrating exception handling into your programs, you might encounter a situation in which you want to field an exception in one `try` block, do some processing, and then pass the exception back up to another `try` block for additional processing. To do this, you use the `throw` keyword with no arguments. When the C++ run-time code encounters this syntax, it redispatches the current exception to the next matching exception handler. Listing 13.19 shows an example of how you might code this passing of exceptions.

Listing 13.19 rethrow.cpp, an Example of Passing Exceptions

```cpp
// Get needed include files
#include <eh.h>
#include <iostream.h>

void Func1()
{
        try {
           throw "Something went wrong!";
        }
        catch (char *) {
           cout << "Doing some initial processing...\n";
           throw;
        }
}

void main()
{
        try {
           Func1();
        }
        catch (char*) {
           cout << "Doing some secondary processing.\n";
        }
}
```

When run, this program displays the following:

```
Doing some initial processing...
Doing some secondary processing.
```

The program redispatches the exception to the next enveloping `try` block. The run-time code does not look for new handler matches that might exist farther down in the current handler list.

Throwing Exceptions from Inside Constructors. Before exception handling came along, one of C++'s great deficiencies was the lack of a simple way to signal errors from within object constructors. If, for example, a memory allocation within a constructor failed, programs typically had to rely on such hokey mechanisms as passed-in error variables (sound familiar?) and internal object state variables. For this reason, many C++ gurus have preached the virtues of not allocating resources within constructors at all.

All of that changes with the availability of exception handling. Exceptions can be thrown from within constructors just like anywhere else. When such an exception is thrown, the object construction process is aborted in a way that cannot be overlooked by the program initiating the creation of the new object. If any base classes are successfully constructed before the exception is raised, those classes' destructors are called in reverse order. If any objects are local to the constructor, those objects' destructors are guaranteed to be called.

To demonstrate these concepts, listing 13.20 shows a program with a Base class and Derived class that abort the construction of a Derived object in the constructor.

Listing 13.20   cnstruct.cpp, an Example of Raising Exceptions from within a Constructor

```
// Get needed include files
#include <iostream.h>
#include <eh.h>

class LocalGuy
{
public:
        LocalGuy() { cout << "In the LocalGuy constructor.\n"; }
        ~LocalGuy() { cout << "In the LocalGuy destructor.\n"; }
};

class Base
{
public:
        Base() { cout << "In the Base constructor.\n"; }
        ~Base() { cout << "In the Base destructor.\n"; }
};

class Derived: public Base
{
public:
        Derived(int flag)
        {
           LocalGuy MyLocalGuy;
           cout << "In the Derived constructor.\n";
           if (flag)
                   throw -1;
        }
        ~Derived() { cout << "In the Derived destructor.\n"; }
};

void main()
{
        try {
           Derived(1);
        }
        catch (int) {
           cout << "Caught the Derived class exception.\n";
        }
}
```

When run, the program displays the following output:

```
In the Base constructor.
In the LocalGuy constructor.
In the Derived constructor.
In the LocalGuy destructor.
In the Base destructor.
Caught the Derived class exception.
```

As you can see, the program successfully constructs the Base class (remember that constructors are called in the order of Base to Derived). Execution then proceeds into the Derived constructor, which raises an exception. The program destructs the Base class and dispatches the exception to the appropriate handler. The LocalGuy instance confirms that the program destructs local class objects appropriately.

Note that the program does not call the *destructor* for Derived before dispatching the exception. This makes sense; because the object's construction has not completed, it is inappropriate to call a destructor that you have written to destruct a fully constructed object.

Finally, remember that dynamically allocated resources are not automatically destructed when the program raises an exception. If a constructor allocates memory from the heap by using the new operator and you want to dispatch an exception from within the constructor, you must delete the allocated memory before dispatching the exception. If your class doesn't do this, you have no way to regain the pointer to the newly allocated memory, and your class introduces a memory leak.

Installing Your Own `terminate()` Handler

If your program throws an exception and the C++ run-time code returns all the way back to main() without finding a matching handler, your program will be terminated by default. The run-time code will stop program execution and display the on-screen message abnormal program termination.

If this behavior is too extreme for your taste, changing it is simple. The program calls the terminate() function when it cannot find an appropriate handler. You can install your own terminate() function by using set_terminate(). Listing 13.21 shows this procedure.

Listing 13.21   term.cpp, Providing Your Own `terminate()` Function

```
// Get needed include files
#include <eh.h>
#include <stdlib.h>
#include <iostream.h>

void MyTerminate()
{
        cout << "I regret to inform you that the exception could "
```

(continues)

Listing 13.21   Continued

```
            <<_"not be dispatched.\n";
        cout << "I'm going away now...\n";
        exit(-1);
}

void main()
{
        set_terminate(MyTerminate);
        try {
           throw "Won't somebody catch me?";
        }
        catch (int) { }
}
```

Set_terminate() takes as its single parameter a pointer to your new termination handler. The function's return value is a pointer to the new termination handler, which is simply the parameter that you are passing into the function (yes, the usefulness of this return value does seem somewhat dubious).

Exploring a Hypothetical Application

So far, this chapter has concentrated on presenting the semantics of exception handling using trivial examples. This is all fine and good, but without taking a look at a more substantial example, it's still difficult to get a feel for how profoundly the use of exception handling affects the entire program.

The rest of this chapter explores a hypothetical application called ExpSum. This application is quite small, but still sizable enough to demonstrate some techniques that you might want to use when integrating exceptions into your standard programming practices.

An Introduction to the ExpSum Application

The function of the ExpSum program is to take a text file that contains expense voucher information and display the file's contents to the screen in a report format. During the processing of the file, the program is responsible for doing some (very limited) analysis of the file's expense information to ensure that it is valid. Listing 13.22 is the output of the ExpSum application using a sample voucher file.

Listing 13.22   An Example of the ExpSum Application's Output

```
    +================================================================+
    |                    EXPENSE FILE PROCESSOR                      |
    +================================================================+


    Employee #9264
    Ben E. Eye
```

```
         123 Liberty Bell South Dr.
         Birmingham, AL 35244

         Expenses
         _____
         8/1/94     New security badge              4.00
         8/1/94     Phone calls                    47.89
         8/13/94    Rental car                     87.99
         ==========================================================
         Employee Total:                          139.88


         Employee #8394
         Jason R. Jordan
         40 Hurt Ln.
         Arlington, VA 22201

         Expenses
         _____
         7/12/94    Beverages                     227.58
         7/12/94    Taxi                           11.95
         ==========================================================
         Employee Total:                          239.53

         Employee #9520
         Chris K. Corry
         123 Car of Kings Blvd.
         Arlington, VA 22204

         Expenses
         _____
         8/4/94     Room rate                      77.00
         8/4/94     Lodging tax                     6.16
         8/6/94     In-room movies                104.97
         ==========================================================
         Employee Total:                          188.13


         +========================================================+
         ¦ EXPENSE FILE TOTAL:                     567.54 ¦
         +========================================================+
```

Actually, this discussion presents two programs. The first, ExpSum1, shows the
ExpSum application as it might be written by a programmer who was either unfamiliar with the use of exception handling or did not have the language extension at his
disposal. The application relies on a variety of error-handling techniques that are all
based on the traditional strategies discussed earlier in this chapter. For this reason, the
program suffers from many of the maladies of contemporary C++ code; despite its
small size, the program can be difficult to follow. There is no centralization of error-
handling logic, and the error-handling logic that does exist is cumbersome and
distracting.

The second example, ExpSum2, depicts ExpSum after the programmer overhauls it to take advantage of C++ exceptions. ExpSum2 is shorter (although that is not necessarily one of the goals of using exception handling), the program's error-handling facilities are consolidated into a single location, and the entire program benefits from the simplification of the error-reporting code.

The ExpSum Application Structure

At the heart of ExpSum are two simple classes: Employee and Expense. The program primarily uses these classes in a relatively unsophisticated context: as containers for data pertaining to employees and expense reports. Although the two classes are rather unremarkable, they can both dump themselves out to a standard C++ output stream or load themselves in from a standard C++ input stream. Therefore, the ExpSum application can easily save and retrieve relevant information to the file system.

Listing 13.23 is the header file that contains the class definition for the Employee class.

Listing 13.23   employee.h, the Definition of the Employee Class

```
#ifndef EMPLOYEE_H
#define EMPLOYEE_H

// Get needed include files
#include <iostream.h>
#include <afx.h>

class Employee {
public:
        Employee();

        void SetID(unsigned NewID)
          { EmployeeID = NewID; }
        void SetFirstName(const char* NewName)
          { FirstName = NewName; }
        void SetMiddleInitial(char NewInitial)
          { MiddleInitial = NewInitial; }
        void SetLastName(const char* NewName)
          { LastName = NewName; }
        void SetAddress(const char* NewAddress)
          { Address = NewAddress; }
        void SetCity(const char* NewCity)
          { City = NewCity; }
        void SetState(const char* NewState)
          { State = NewState; }
        void SetZip(unsigned long NewZip)
          { Zip = NewZip; }
        void SetNumExpenses(unsigned NewNumExpenses)
          { NumExpenses = NewNumExpenses; }

        unsigned    GetID() const { return EmployeeID; }
        CString     GetFirstName() const { return FirstName; }
        char        GetMiddleInitial() const { return MiddleInitial; }
        CString     GetLastName() const { return LastName; }
        CString     GetAddress() const { return Address; }
```

```
          CString      GetCity() const { return City; }
          CString      GetState() const { return State; }
          unsigned long GetZip() const { return Zip; }
          unsigned     GetNumExpenses() const { return NumExpenses; }

private:
          unsigned     EmployeeID;
          CString      FirstName;
          char         MiddleInitial;
          CString      LastName;
          CString      Address;
          CString      City;
          CString      State;
          unsigned long Zip;
          unsigned     NumExpenses;

          friend ostream& operator<<(ostream& ostr,
                         const Employee& _employee);
          friend istream& operator>>(istream& istr, Employee& employee);
   };

   #endif
```

Although these header files contain most of the class implementations, the C++ source files employee.cpp and expense.cpp (listings 13.24 and 13.26, respectively) contain the class operators.

Listing 13.24   employee.cpp, the Implementation of the Employee Class

```
// Get needed include files
#include <employee.h>

Employee::Employee() :
        EmployeeID(0),
        MiddleInitial('\0'),
        Zip(0UL),
        NumExpenses(0)
{ }

ostream& operator<<(ostream& ostr, const Employee& employee)
{
        ostr << employee.EmployeeID;
        ostr << employee.FirstName << " ";
        ostr << employee.LastName << " ";
        ostr << employee.MiddleInitial;
        ostr << employee.Address << "\n";
        ostr << employee.City << " ";
        ostr << employee.State << " ";
        ostr << employee.Zip << " ";
        ostr << employee.NumExpenses << " ";
        return ostr;
}
```

(continues)

Listing 13.24   Continued

```
istream& operator>>(istream& istr, Employee& employee)
{
        char TempBuffer[256];
        istr >> employee.EmployeeID;
        istr >> TempBuffer;
        employee.FirstName = TempBuffer;
        istr >> TempBuffer;
        employee.LastName = TempBuffer;
        istr >> employee.MiddleInitial;
        istr.getline(TempBuffer, 256);
        employee.Address = TempBuffer;
        istr >> TempBuffer;
        employee.City = TempBuffer;
        istr >> TempBuffer;
        employee.State = TempBuffer;
        istr >> employee.Zip;
        istr >> employee.NumExpenses;
        return istr;
}
```

Listing 13.25 is the header file that contains the class definition for the Expense class.

Listing 13.25   expense.h, the Definition of the Expense Class

```
#ifndef EXPENSE_H
#define EXPENSE_H

// Get needed include files
#include <iostream.h>
#include <afx.h>

class Expense {
public:
        Expense();

        void SetDate(const char* NewDate)
          { Date = NewDate; }
        void SetDescription(const char* NewDescription)
          { Description = NewDescription; }
        void SetExpenseAmount(float NewExpenseAmount)
          { ExpenseAmount = NewExpenseAmount; }

        CString GetDate() const { return Date; }
        CString GetDescription() const { return Description; }
        float   GetExpenseAmount() const { return ExpenseAmount; }

private:
        CString  Date;
        CString  Description;
        float    ExpenseAmount;

        friend ostream& operator<<(ostream& ostr, const Expense& employee);
        friend istream& operator>>(istream& istr, Expense& employee);
```

```
};

#endif
```

Listing 13.26 shows expense.cpp, the C++ source file that implements the Expense class.

Listing 13.26   expense.cpp, the Implementation of the Expense Class

```
// Get needed include files
#include "expense.h"

Expense::Expense() :
        ExpenseAmount(0.0F)
{ }

ostream& operator<<(ostream& ostr, const Expense& expense)
{
        ostr << expense.Date << " ";
        ostr << expense.Description << "\n";
        ostr << expense.ExpenseAmount << " ";
        return ostr;
}

istream& operator>>(istream& istr, Expense& expense)
{
        char TempBuffer[256];
        istr >> TempBuffer;
        expense.Date = TempBuffer;
        istr.getline(TempBuffer, 256);
        expense.Description = TempBuffer;
        istr >> expense.ExpenseAmount;
        return istr;
}
```

As you can see, the two classes do little more than manage access to their data members. You learned about the CString class found within the Microsoft Foundation Classes (MFC) in Part II, "Using the Microsoft Foundation Class Library." Although CString is the only MFC class that these programs use, they use the class extensively throughout.

Three separate programs use these two classes. As already discussed, ExpSum1 is the version of the application that uses traditional error handling, whereas ExpSum2 is the version of the application that relies on C++ exception handling. The third program, ExpMaker, is the program responsible for creating the voucher files in the first place. ExpMaker is not a terribly exciting program, but it is obviously a necessary one. Because ExpMaker is not really relevant to the topics that this chapter discusses, this chapter doesn't analyze the program's design aspects; however, for the sake of completeness, listing 13.27 presents the program. After all, without ExpMaker (and the code needed to build it), the two ExpSum programs would have no expense files to process.

Listing 13.27 expmaker.cpp, the Expense File Generator Program

```cpp
// Get our needed include files
#include <fstream.h>
#include <iomanip.h>
#include "employee.h"
#include "expense.h"

void GetNewExpenseItem(ofstream& outfile, const unsigned itemnum)
{
        Expense NewExpense;
        float   ExpenseAmount;
        char    TempBuffer[256], ChompNewline;

        // User-friendly stuff
        cout << "\nExpense #" << itemnum+1 << "\n";

        // Fill in the basics
        cout << "Expense date   : ";
        cin.get(TempBuffer, 256);
        cin.get(ChompNewline);
        NewExpense.SetDate(TempBuffer);
        cout << "Description    : ";
        cin.get(TempBuffer, 256);
        cin.get(ChompNewline);
        NewExpense.SetDescription(TempBuffer);
        cout << "Expense amount : ";
        cin >> ExpenseAmount;
        cin.get(ChompNewline);
        NewExpense.SetExpenseAmount(ExpenseAmount);

        // Write the expense record to the file
        outfile << NewExpense;
}

void GetNewEmployee(ofstream& outfile)
{
        Employee      NewEmployee;
        unsigned long NewZip;
        unsigned      loop, NewID, NewNumExpenses;
        char          TempBuffer[256], ChompNewline, NewInitial;

        // User-friendly stuff
        cout << "\nNew employee record\n";
        cout << "===================\n";

        // Fill in the basics
        cout << "Employee ID    : ";
        cin >> NewID;
        cin.get(ChompNewline);
        NewEmployee.SetID(NewID);
        cout << "First name     : ";
        cin.get(TempBuffer, 256);
        cin.get(ChompNewline);
        NewEmployee.SetFirstName(TempBuffer);
        cout << "Middle initial : ";
```

```
        cin >> NewInitial;
        cin.get(ChompNewline);
        NewEmployee.SetMiddleInitial(NewInitial);
        cout << "Last name      : ";
        cin.get(TempBuffer, 256);
        cin.get(ChompNewline);
        NewEmployee.SetLastName(TempBuffer);
        cout << "Address        : ";
        cin.get(TempBuffer, 256);
        cin.get(ChompNewline);
        NewEmployee.SetAddress(TempBuffer);
        cout << "City           : ";
        cin.get(TempBuffer, 256);
        cin.get(ChompNewline);
        NewEmployee.SetCity(TempBuffer);
        cout << "State          : ";
        cin.get(TempBuffer, 256);
        cin.get(ChompNewline);
        NewEmployee.SetState(TempBuffer);
        cout << "ZIP code       : ";
        cin >> NewZip;
        cin.get(ChompNewline);
        NewEmployee.SetZip(NewZip);
        cout << "\nNumber of expense items for this employee? ";
        cin >> NewNumExpenses;
        cin.get(ChompNewline);
        NewEmployee.SetNumExpenses(NewNumExpenses);

        // Write the employee record to the file
        outfile << NewEmployee;
        // Now get the expense records
        for (loop = 0; loop < NewEmployee.GetNumExpenses(); loop++)
          GetNewExpenseItem(outfile, loop);
}

void main(int argc, char *argv[])
{
        // Check for right number of command-line arguments
        if (argc != 2) {
          cout << "USAGE: expmaker <outfile name>\n\n";
          return;
        }

        // Open the outfile
        ofstream outfile(argv[1]);

        // Place our dummy employee count
        unsigned EmployeeCount = 0;
        outfile << setw(5) << EmployeeCount << setw(0) << " ";

        // Main employee loop
        char Again;
        do {
          char ChompNewline;
          EmployeeCount++;
          GetNewEmployee(outfile);
```

(continues)

Listing 13.27   Continued

```
                 cout << "\nEnter another employee (Y/N)? ";
                 cin >> Again;
                 cin.get(ChompNewline);
             } while (Again == 'y' || Again == 'Y');


             // Go to the beginning of the file and fill in the
             // real employee count
             outfile.seekp(0, ios::beg);
             outfile << setw(5) << EmployeeCount;

             // Close the outfile _ we're done!
             outfile.close();
         }
```

You can build the ExpMaker program and then use it to generate a variety of different expense report files, including files that contain contextual errors (expenses that are too large or small to be claimed, an invalid number of employees or expense reports, and so on). ExpMaker enables you to build incorrect expense report files so that the error-handling muscle of the two ExpSum applications can be tested. If ExpMaker ensured that it created valid expense files, determining whether this flashy exception-handling logic is working would be quite difficult.

ExpSum1: The Model T of Expense Reporting

Now take a look at the first of these applications, ExpSum1. This program, presented in listing 13.28, consists of three sections, ProcessExpenseItem(), ProcessEmployee(), and main(). As you read the source code, pay special attention to how it reports errors and passes them through each of these sections.

Listing 13.28   expsum1.cpp, the ExpSum Application Using Traditional Error Handling

```
// Get our needed include files
#include <employee.h>
#include <expense.h>
#include <fstream.h>
#include <iomanip.h>

// Definitions
const int MIN_ALLOWABLE_EMPLOYEES = 1;
const int MAX_ALLOWABLE_EMPLOYEES = 20;
const int MIN_NUM_EXPENSES = 1;
const int MAX_NUM_EXPENSES = 10;
const float MIN_ALLOWABLE_EXPENSE = 1.0F;
const float MAX_ALLOWABLE_EXPENSE = 1000.0F;
const float MAX_ALLOWABLE_REIMBURSEMENT = 5000.0F;

// Error codes
typedef enum {
```

```
            EXP_NO_ERROR,
            EXP_ERR_EXPENSE_TOO_SMALL,
            EXP_ERR_EXPENSE_TOO_LARGE,
            EXP_ERR_NO_EXPENSE_ITEMS,
            EXP_ERR_TOO_MANY_EXPENSE_ITEMS,
            EXP_ERR_TOTAL_EXPENSE_TOO_LARGE
} ErrorCode;

float ProcessExpenseItem(ifstream& infile, ErrorCode& rc)
{
        Expense NewExpense;

        // Init the return code
        rc = EXP_NO_ERROR;

        // Read in the expense record from the file
        infile >> NewExpense;

        // Check for problems
        if (NewExpense.GetExpenseAmount() < MIN_ALLOWABLE_EXPENSE) {
           cout << "Error! Expense item under the minimum amount
                    _ eligible for reimbursement.\n\n";
           rc = EXP_ERR_EXPENSE_TOO_SMALL;
           return 0.0F;
        }
        if (NewExpense.GetExpenseAmount() > MAX_ALLOWABLE_EXPENSE) {
           cout << "Error! Expense item greater than maximum amount
                    _ eligible for reimbursement.\n\n";
           rc = EXP_ERR_EXPENSE_TOO_LARGE;
           return 0.0F;
        }

        // Display the expense
        cout << "      " << setw(10) << NewExpense.GetDate();
        cout << setw(35) << NewExpense.GetDescription();
        cout.unsetf(ios::left);
        cout << setw(12)<<NewExpense.GetExpenseAmount()<< "\n"<< setw(0);
        cout.setf(ios::left);

        return NewExpense.GetExpenseAmount();
}

float ProcessEmployee(ifstream& infile, ErrorCode& rc)
{
        Employee NewEmployee;
        float    EmployeeTotal = 0.0F;
        unsigned loop;

        // Init the return code
        rc = EXP_NO_ERROR;

        // Read in the employee record from the file
        infile >> NewEmployee;

        // Check for problems
        if (NewEmployee.GetNumExpenses() < MIN_NUM_EXPENSES) {
```

(continues)

Advanced Programming

V

Listing 13.28   Continued

```
        cout << "Error! No expense items for this employee.\n\n";
        rc = EXP_ERR_NO_EXPENSE_ITEMS;
        return 0.0F;
    }
    if (NewEmployee.GetNumExpenses() > MAX_NUM_EXPENSES) {
        cout << "Error! Too many expense items for this employee.\n\n";
        rc = EXP_ERR_TOO_MANY_EXPENSE_ITEMS;
        return 0.0F;
    }

    // Display the employee record
    cout << "Employee #" << NewEmployee.GetID() << "\n";
    cout << NewEmployee.GetFirstName() << " ";
    cout << NewEmployee.GetMiddleInitial() << ". ";
    cout << NewEmployee.GetLastName() << "\n";
    cout << NewEmployee.GetAddress() << "\n";
    cout << NewEmployee.GetCity() << ", ";
    cout << NewEmployee.GetState() << " ";
    cout << NewEmployee.GetZip() << "\n\n";

    // Now get the expense records
    cout << "       Expenses\n";
    cout << "       _____\n";
    for (loop = 0; loop < NewEmployee.GetNumExpenses(); loop++) {
        EmployeeTotal += ProcessExpenseItem(infile, rc);
        if (rc != EXP_NO_ERROR)
        return 0.0F;
    }

    // Check for problems
    if (EmployeeTotal > MAX_ALLOWABLE_REIMBURSEMENT) {
        cout << "Error! Expense total greater than maximum
                _ amount eligible for reimbursement.\n\n";
        rc = EXP_ERR_TOTAL_EXPENSE_TOO_LARGE;
        return 0.0F;
    }

    // Display the employee total
    cout << " ================================================\n";
    cout << "       Employee Total:";
    cout.unsetf(ios::left);
    cout << setw(42) << EmployeeTotal << "\n\n\n";
    cout.setf(ios::left);

    return EmployeeTotal;
}

void main(int argc, char *argv[])
{
    // Check for right number of command-line arguments
        if (argc != 2) {
            cout << "USAGE: expsum1 <infile name>\n\n";
            return;
```

```
      }

      // Open the infile
      ifstream infile(argv[1], ios::nocreate);
      if (!infile) {
         cout << "Expense file \"" << argv[1] << "\" not found.\n\n";
         return;
      }

      // Read in our number of employees
      unsigned EmployeeCount;
      float    FileTotal = 0.0F;
      infile >> EmployeeCount;
      if (EmployeeCount < MIN_ALLOWABLE_EMPLOYEES ¦¦
         EmployeeCount > MAX_ALLOWABLE_EMPLOYEES) {
         cout << "Invalid number of employees specified in
                 _ expense file.\n\n";
         infile.close();
      }

      // Set the stream display flags
      cout.setf(ios::left ¦ ios::showpoint ¦ ios::fixed);
      cout.precision(2);

      // Display our main heading
      cout <<"+=====================================================+\n";
      cout << "¦              EXPENSE FILE PROCESSOR¦\n";
      cout <<"+=====================================================+\n\n\n";

      // Main employee loop
      ErrorCode rc;
      do {
         FileTotal += ProcessEmployee(infile, rc);
         if (rc != EXP_NO_ERROR) {
               infile.close();
               return;
         }
      } while (__EmployeeCount);

      // Display the file total
      cout <<"+=====================================================+\n";
      cout << "¦ EXPENSE FILE TOTAL: ";
      cout.unsetf(ios::left);
      cout << setw(43) << FileTotal << " ¦\n";
      cout.setf(ios::left);
      cout <<"+=====================================================+\n";

      // Close the infile -- we're done!
      infile.close();
   }
```

The ExpSum1 program takes a single command-line argument indicating the expense file's name. The program opens this file, displays it in a formatted manner, and then closes it. If the program identifies any errors in the file during processing, an appropriate error message displays and the program terminates.

A Quick Overview of How ExpSum Works. The ExpSum application's execution strategy is quite simple. The program obtains the expense file name from the command line, opens the file, and reads an initial value that indicates how many employee records that the file contains. The program proceeds into a loop that calls the ProcessEmployee() function for the appropriate number of times.

Inside ProcessEmployee(), the program reads in the next employee record from the file and displays the initial employee information (employee number, name, address, and so on). One of the pieces of information that the Employee class knows about is the number of expense items that a particular employee has outstanding. ProcessEmployee() proceeds to call ProcessExpenseItem() the appropriate number of times for each employee.

ProcessExpenseItem() works similarly to ProcessEmployee(). The function reads in the next expense item from the file and displays it to the screen. After moving through the file, the program displays some final totals and closes the input file.

ExpSum1's Error Handling. ExpSum relies on the error-reporting strategy explained previously in the section "Returning Error Values in Function Arguments." As calls are made to ProcessEmployee() and ProcessExpenseItem(), an error code variable is passed along with the function arguments. When problems occur, the program displays a message and modifies the contents of the error variable. The calling functions check the error variable when they regain control. If an error occurs, the functions return to their caller. This process continues until control reverts back to main(), where execution stops.

Although this program works the way that it's supposed to, ExpSum could do better. In ExpSum, error values are forced back through the calling chain like a large truck that has driven into a dead-end alley. This propagation code results in situations where the program initially catches and processes errors but then must reprocess them at every point in the calling sequence. This bloats the program and makes it significantly more difficult to follow. Code that's hard to read is hard to maintain, and that means that bugs will be harder to track down.

The error handling hardwired into ExpSum1 is also inflexible. Suppose, for example, that you later decide to have the employee ID return to main() when a particular error condition occurs. To implement this behavior, you would have to retrofit the program severely, and as you did so, you would leave your application susceptible to the introduction of new bugs. In turn, you would spend more time debugging when you could be adding functionality.

Fortunately, the ExpSum2 application resolves all these concerns.

ExpSum2: The Ferrari of Expense Reporting

Okay, perhaps it's a jump to call ExpSum2 an expense-reporting Ferrari, but the application certainly is a big improvement over ExpSum1. The use of exceptions enables

the program to consolidate error handling into a single place without sacrificing readability or flexibility.

ExpSum2's Exception Class Hierarchy. Listing 13.29 shows the contents of
except.h. This new header file contains definitions for the exception types used by
ExpSum2's new error-handling infrastructure.

Listing 13.29   except.h, the Definitions for ExpSum2's Exceptions

```
#ifndef EXCEPT_H
#define EXCEPT_H

// Get needed include files
#include <eh.h>
#include <afx.h>

// Error codes
typedef enum {
        EXP_NO_ERROR,
        EXP_GENERIC_ERROR,
        EXP_ERR_EXPENSE_TOO_SMALL,
        EXP_ERR_EXPENSE_TOO_LARGE,
        EXP_ERR_NO_EXPENSE_ITEMS,
        EXP_ERR_TOO_MANY_EXPENSE_ITEMS,
        EXP_ERR_TOTAL_EXPENSE_TOO_LARGE
} ErrorCode;

// Our base exception class
class ExpException {
public:
        ExpException(ErrorCode NewErrorCode,
                const char *NewReason = NULL) :
                    TheError(NewErrorCode),
                    TheReason(NewReason)
        { }

        void SetErrorCode(ErrorCode NewErrorCode)
          { TheError = NewErrorCode; }
        void SetReason(const char* NewReason)
          { TheReason = NewReason; }

        CString   Why() const { return TheReason; }
        ErrorCode GetErrorCode() const { return TheError; }

private:
        CString   TheReason;
        ErrorCode TheError;
};

// Specific exception classes
class ExpenseTooSmall : public ExpException
{
public:
        ExpenseTooSmall() :
          ExpException(EXP_ERR_EXPENSE_TOO_SMALL,
```

(continues)

Listing 13.29   Continued

```
                              "Expense item under the minimum amount eligible
                               for reimbursement.")
        { }
};

class ExpenseTooLarge : public ExpException
{
public:
        ExpenseTooLarge() :
          ExpException(EXP_ERR_EXPENSE_TOO_LARGE,
                       "Expense item greater than the maximum amount
                        eligible for reimbursement.")
        { }
};

class EmployeeException : public ExpException
{
public:
        EmployeeException(ErrorCode NewErrorCode,
                      unsigned NewEmployeeID,
                      const char *NewReason = NULL) :
          ExpException(NewErrorCode, NewReason),
                       EmployeeID(NewEmployeeID)
        { }
        unsigned GetEmployeeID() const { return EmployeeID; }
private:
        unsigned EmployeeID;
};

class NoExpenseItems : public EmployeeException
{
public:
        NoExpenseItems(unsigned NewEmployeeID) :
          EmployeeException(EXP_ERR_NO_EXPENSE_ITEMS,
                           NewEmployeeID,
                           "No expense items for this employee")
        { }
};

class TooManyExpenseItems : public EmployeeException
{
public:
        TooManyExpenseItems(unsigned NewEmployeeID) :
          EmployeeException(EXP_ERR_TOO_MANY_EXPENSE_ITEMS,
                           NewEmployeeID,
                           "Too many expense items for this employee")
    { }
};

class ExpenseTotalTooLarge : public ExpException
{
public:
        ExpenseTotalTooLarge() :
          ExpException(EXP_ERR_TOTAL_EXPENSE_TOO_LARGE,
                       "Expense total greater than maximum amount
```

```
                              _ eligible for reimbursement.")
            { }
    };

    #endif
```

The exception hierarchy used by ExpSum2 is pretty elaborate for a program of this size. For applications that are only a couple of pages long, the number of exception types used is generally quite small, but the exaggerated hierarchy found in listing 13.29 demonstrates some of the functionality that programs significantly larger than ExpSum2 would probably need. Figure 13.2 presents a graphical overview of the exception hierarchy.

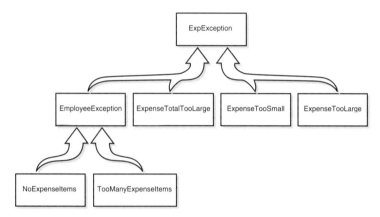

Fig. 13.2

ExpSum2's exception class hierarchy.

The topmost exception class is ExpException. This generic exception class provides the simplest of error-reporting services. When throwing an exception, the thrower can specify an error code and an optional description of the error, but there are no provisions for passing on any other contextual information. Still, with the ExpException class alone, the ExpSum2 application exhibits more error-processing functionality than ExpSum1 because of the addition of the error-description string.

New exception classes derive from ExpException as appropriate. This class hierarchy uses two different strategies. Classes deriving from ExpException serve to narrow the scope of a particular error. Although ExpException could represent virtually any error, classes such as ExpenseTooSmall leave little room for speculation about what went wrong. Given a class hierarchy with this level of granularity, an application has the option of interacting with errors in the abstract (treating all exceptions as ExpExceptions) or in the specific (treating exceptions as their actual type).

The second strategy used by classes within this hierarchy is to provide additional information. Recall the previous example about how difficult it is to return an employee ID through the calling chain. With exception handling, such a request becomes almost trivial and ExpSum2 does exactly this. The EmployeeException class provides the capability to throw an employee ID, and both the NoExpenseItems and TooManyExpenseItems classes take advantage of this service.

ExpSum2's Main Function. Instead of presenting ExpSum2 all at once and in its entirety, this subsection breaks the program into its component parts and discusses each with regard to its integration into the exception-handling framework. Listing 13.30 shows how `main()` changes between ExpSum1 and ExpSum2.

Listing 13.30   expsum2.cpp, ExpSum2's `main()` Function

```
// Get the needed include files
#include <fstream.h>
#include <iomanip.h>
#include "employee.h"
#include "expense.h"
#include "except.h"

// Definitions
const int MIN_ALLOWABLE_EMPLOYEES = 1;
const int MAX_ALLOWABLE_EMPLOYEES = 20;
const int MIN_NUM_EXPENSES = 1;
const int MAX_NUM_EXPENSES = 10;
const float MIN_ALLOWABLE_EXPENSE = 1.0F;
const float MAX_ALLOWABLE_EXPENSE = 1000.0F;
const float MAX_ALLOWABLE_REIMBURSEMENT = 5000.0F;

void main(int argc, char *argv[])
{
        // Check for right number of command-line arguments
        if (argc != 2) {
          cout << "USAGE: expsum2 <infile name>\n\n";
          return;
        }

        // Open the infile
        ifstream infile(argv[1], ios::nocreate);
        if (!infile) {
          cout << "Expense file \"" << argv[1] << "\" not found.\n\n";
          return;
        }

        // Main try block
        try {

          // Read in our number of employees
          unsigned EmployeeCount;
          float    FileTotal = 0.0F;
          infile >> EmployeeCount;
          if (EmployeeCount < MIN_ALLOWABLE_EMPLOYEES ||
          _ EmployeeCount > MAX_ALLOWABLE_EMPLOYEES)
                throw ExpException(EXP_GENERIC_ERROR,
                          "Invalid number of employees specified
                          _ in expense file.");

          // Set the stream display flags
          cout.setf(ios::left | ios::showpoint | ios::fixed);
```

```
        cout.precision(2);

        // Display our main heading
        cout <<"+==========================================+\n";
        cout << "¦               EXPENSE FILE PROCESSOR¦\n";
        cout <<"+==========================================+\n\n\n";

        // Main employee loop
        do {
                FileTotal += ProcessEmployee(infile);
        } while (_EmployeeCount);

        // Display the file total
        cout <<"+==========================================+\n";
        cout << "¦ EXPENSE FILE TOTAL: ";
        cout.unsetf(ios::left);
        cout << setw(43) << FileTotal << " ¦\n";
        cout.setf(ios::left);
        cout <<"+==========================================+\n";
    }

// Handlers
catch (EmployeeException& EmpExp) {
    cout << "\nError! ";
    cout << EmpExp.Why() << " (Employee " <<
        _ EmpExp.GetEmployeeID() << ")\n";
}
catch (ExpException& Exp) {
    cout << "\nError! " << Exp.Why() << "\n";
}
catch (...) {
    cout << "Caught an unrecognized exception.\n";
}

// Close the infile -- we're done!
infile.close();
    }
```

Start by looking at what hasn't changed. The program still processes the command-line argument the same way, and, at least from main()'s perspective, the general processing algorithm doesn't seem to have been modified. The formatting and display of banners and text-based frills has not been altered.

Now you can sink your teeth into what's different. The most obvious change is that the program now encloses most of the main() function within a single try block—the only try block in the program. This change enables you to consolidate all the application's error handling into a single handler list.

This try block has three handlers. None of them explicitly accepts any of the detailed exception types found in except.h. Instead, ExpSum2 relies primarily on two general-purpose handlers that catch EmployeeExceptions first and other instances of ExpException second. This handler list also has an ellipsis handler to ensure that no other exceptions slip by unnoticed. (Actually, they wouldn't go unnoticed at all;

unhandled exceptions would end execution and ExpSum2 wouldn't have a clue of what hit it!) These handlers display the description of what went wrong. In the case of the `EmployeeExceptions`, the program also displays the employee ID that was at fault.

Note that none of these handlers actually stops program execution. Although severe errors often require that a program stop, ExpSum2 has a good reason for not stopping execution. Note the last line of the program:

```
// Close the infile - we're done!
infile.close();
```

Although C++ streams know that they must close themselves if they are still open when destructed, you should still explicitly ensure that the program takes that responsibility. In this case, you can easily do so. More importantly, to close the file, you need not use the error-processing code that was previously scattered throughout the program. Notice, for example, the sections of `main()` that must close the file in ExpSum1:

```
do {
        FileTotal += ProcessEmployee(infile, rc);
        if (rc != EXP_NO_ERROR) {
           infile.close();
           return;
        }
} while (_EmployeeCount);
```

These sections need not worry about this task in ExpSum2:

```
do {
        FileTotal += ProcessEmployee(infile);
} while (_EmployeeCount);
```

Nor does the ExpSum2 code have to deal with returned error codes in any context. The code is free to concentrate on solving the problem instead of worrying about what to do if something goes wrong.

Processing Employees. Now focus your attention on `ProcessEmployee()`. Listing 13.31 contains the ExpSum2 code for this function.

Listing 13.31 expsum2.cpp, ExpSum2's `ProcessEmployee()` Function

```
float ProcessEmployee(ifstream& infile)
{
        Employee NewEmployee;
        float    EmployeeTotal = 0.0F;
        unsigned loop;

        // Read in the employee record from the file
        infile >> NewEmployee;

        // Check for problems
        if (NewEmployee.GetNumExpenses() < MIN_NUM_EXPENSES)
           throw NoExpenseItems(NewEmployee.GetID());
```

```
        if (NewEmployee.GetNumExpenses() > MAX_NUM_EXPENSES)
            throw TooManyExpenseItems(NewEmployee.GetID());

        // Display the employee record
        cout << "Employee #" << NewEmployee.GetID() << "\n";
        cout << NewEmployee.GetFirstName() << " ";
        cout << NewEmployee.GetMiddleInitial() << ". ";
        cout << NewEmployee.GetLastName() << "\n";
        cout << NewEmployee.GetAddress() << "\n";
        cout << NewEmployee.GetCity() << ", ";
        cout << NewEmployee.GetState() << " ";
        cout << NewEmployee.GetZip() << "\n\n";

        // Now get the expense records
        cout << "      Expenses\n";
        cout << "      _____\n";
        for (loop = 0; loop < NewEmployee.GetNumExpenses(); loop++)
            EmployeeTotal += ProcessExpenseItem(infile);

        // Check for problems
        if (EmployeeTotal > MAX_ALLOWABLE_REIMBURSEMENT)
            throw ExpenseTotalTooLarge();

        // Display the employee total
        cout << "==================================================\n";
        cout << "      Employee Total:";
        cout.unsetf(ios::left);
        cout << setw(42) << EmployeeTotal << "\n\n\n";
        cout.setf(ios::left);

        return EmployeeTotal;
    }
```

This function has really been cleaned up. Most of the ExpSum1 error checking has been replaced with exception-handling equivalents. ProcessEmployee() checks for various conditions. If something is not right, the function throws an exception. ProcessEmployee() doesn't have to worry about displaying error messages or setting return codes. These tasks are now either unnecessary or handled by main()'s handler list.

Notice also that ProcessEmployee() does not check for errors on the call to ProcessExpenseItem() because if anything goes wrong in that function, an exception is thrown back to main(). Still, apart from its error-processing aspects, this function is the same as the one in ExpSum1.

Processing Expense Items. The last part of the newly rejuvenated ExpSum application is the ProcessExpenseItem() function shown in listing 13.32.

Listing 13.32 expsum2.cpp, ExpSum2's `ProcessExpenseItem()` Function

```
float ProcessExpenseItem(ifstream& infile)
{
        Expense NewExpense;

        // Read in the expense record from the file
        infile >> NewExpense;

        // Check for problems
        if (NewExpense.GetExpenseAmount() < MIN_ALLOWABLE_EXPENSE)
           throw ExpenseTooSmall();
        if (NewExpense.GetExpenseAmount() > MAX_ALLOWABLE_EXPENSE)
           throw ExpenseTooLarge();

        // Display the expense
        cout << "     " << setw(10) << NewExpense.GetDate();
        cout << setw(35) << NewExpense.GetDescription();
        cout.unsetf(ios::left);
        cout <<setw(12)<< NewExpense.GetExpenseAmount()<< "\n"<< setw(0);
        cout.setf(ios::left);

        return NewExpense.GetExpenseAmount();
}
```

By now, you shouldn't be surprised that the same sort of things that were done to slim down error processing in `ProcessEmployee()` have been done in `ProcessExpenseItem()`. This function pares down the error checking on the expense amount range checking to the throwing of a simple exception. Everything else is the same as in ExpSum1.

Wrapping Up the ExpSum Application

The ExpSum example shows some of the techniques that you can use in your own programs. At the same time, you will quickly learn that using exception handling effectively is somewhat an acquired skill. For example, depending on your application's size and complexity, you might have to do multiphase error checking, in which nested `try` blocks partially process error conditions and then pass exceptions for processing by surrounding `try` blocks. Other applications might be better served by very simple exception hierarchies that utilize only one or two handlers. With experience, you will come to recognize the signs that favor one approach over another.

Regardless of ExpSum's ultimate applicability to larger programs, it is important to understand the fundamental lessons that the example implies. Exception handling increases a program's robustness and reliability by making it easier for the programmer to concentrate on the task at hand, whether that task is error handling or developing application logic.

Enabling and Disabling Visual C++ Exception Handling

Most of this chapter's discussion of exception handling is oriented toward C++ exceptions in general. To use exceptions in your programs, however, you must understand the compiler switches that Visual C++ makes available for modifying exception-handling behaviors.

More precisely, you should understand the compiler *switch;* the options that the Visual C++ compiler provides are pretty simple. To turn off exception handling (the default behavior), you use the /GX- command-line switch on the compiler. The /GX+ (or just /GX) switch turns on exception handling. This is the only compiler switch that you need to know.

If you are accustomed to using the Developer Studio, the setting for exception handling is in the Project Settings dialog box (shown in fig. 13.3). Select the C/C++ tab. From the Category combo box, choose C++ Language. As you might guess, the Enable Exception Handling check box is the toggle that turns exceptions on and off.

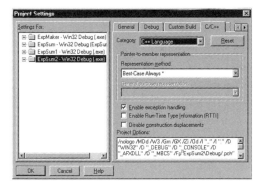

Fig. 13.3

The Project Settings dialog box, containing the Enable Exception Handling check box.

Why might you want to turn off exception handling? Probably the biggest drawback of using exceptions is that the compiler must perform much trickery to pull off the functionality that exception handling provides. This translates into additional "hidden" code embedded in your executables, which in turn means that your program sizes will be larger and that your programs will run a little slower. These are both faults that make programmers cringe. If you cannot accept the additional overhead that exception handling imposes on your programs, you might feel compelled to turn off the feature.

Portable Exceptions

Both the Windows NT and Windows 95 operating systems support an error-handling infrastructure called *structured exception handling.* Note that although structured exception handling is compatible with Visual C++'s language-based exceptions, they are *not*

V

Advanced Programming

the same thing. Languages other than C++ (most notably C) can use structured exception handling; C++ exception handling is obviously a language-dependent feature.

If you want to write more portable code, you should not use structured exception handling in a C++ program. Occasionally, however, you might want to mix C and C++ source code and thus need some facility for handling both kinds of exceptions. Because a structured exception handler has no concept of objects or typed exceptions, it cannot handle exceptions that C++ code throws; however, C++ catch handlers can handle C exceptions. Therefore, the C compiler does not accept C++ exception-handling syntax (try, throw, and catch), but the C++ compiler does support structured exception-handling syntax (try, except, and finally).

The structured exception-handling constructs that Visual C++ provides are interesting and beneficial for those non-C++ programs that must ensure that they deliver the most secure and robust performance possible. The vast majority of C++ programmers, however, should avoid structured exception handling.

MFC Exception Support: A Brief Overview

The early 32-bit versions of the Microsoft Foundation Classes were designed to work with the Visual C++ 1.0 compiler (32-bit edition). This early compiler's advanced C++ language support was quite limited. The compiler also did not support native, language-level exception handling.

Despite this fundamental limitation, the resourceful programmers at Microsoft came up with a macro-based framework that reasonably approximates C++ exceptions. These macros had some fundamental limitations (they could not unwind through the stack, for example) but enabled programmers to design their programs much like they would if the compiler supported exception handling natively.

With the release of MFC 3.0 (the version that shipped with Visual C++ 2), Microsoft began migrating the class library to native C++ exception handling. MFC 4.0 now uses a strictly native C++ error-handling infrastructure and adds migration code to provide backward compatibility for programs written to the macro-based exception-handling facilities provided by MFC versions released before version 3.0.

MFC provides several predefined kinds of exceptions, as listed in table 13.2.

Table 13.2   MFC Predefined Exceptions

Exception Class	Description
CException	Abstract class representing the top of the MFC exception hierarchy
CMemoryException	Out of memory
CFileException	File exception
CArchiveException	Archive/serialization exception

Exception Class	Description
CNotSupportedException	Response to request for unsupported service
CResourceException	Windows resource allocation exception
CDBException	ODBC database exceptions
CDaoException	DAO database exceptions
COleException	OLE exceptions
COleDispatchException	OLE Automation exceptions
CUserException	Exception that alerts the user with a message box, then throws a generic CException

As you start to write your MFC programs, take special note of those classes that can throw exceptions and plan accordingly.

From Here...

As this chapter has shown, if you choose to use exception handling, you might have to learn a few new tricks. But the new lessons that you must learn are fairly simple and straightforward. Remember that exception handling remedies many of the flaws of traditional error-handling strategies. Exceptions enable you to consolidate your error handling without worrying about whether your program will correctly destruct C++ objects when something goes wrong. And you can often retrofit your old programs to accommodate these new error-handling tactics with a relatively small amount of effort.

Several other chapters in this book address new and advanced issues in C++ programming. Be sure to check out the following chapters:

- Chapter 12, "Cross-Platform Development." Building applications that run under a variety of different operating systems can be a terribly difficult proposition. Visual C++ 4 and MFC help to make this process easier by supporting RISC-based Windows NT workstations, the Apple Macintosh, and even UNIX-based workstations. Chapter 12 explains how you can ensure that your programs make the portability leap with a minimal amount of effort.

- Chapter 14, "Mastering Templates." Templates are a powerful language extension that enables you to create "families" of classes that are all related through common functionality in ways that you cannot easily obtain through simple inheritance. Chapter 14 shows how to leverage templates effectively, by explaining both basic and advanced template implementations.

- Chapter 18, "Run-Time Type Identification (RTTI)." RTTI is a relative newcomer to the C++ feature set. It enables programmers to query objects and determine the type of objects at run time. Although this feature might sound rather esoteric, the chapter explains why this capability can be so valuable.

CHAPTER 14

Mastering Templates

Templates enable programs to create families of functions or classes. This explanation is, of course, rather dubious. Programmers who are unfamiliar with templates often complain that there seems to be little intuitive need for a class "family" that they cannot handle by such standard C++ mechanisms as inheritance and polymorphism. This reaction, however, is usually based on a rather shaky understanding of exactly what class families are and how programmers can use them. It usually takes only a few well-chosen examples to demonstrate the value of the generic class concept.

The problems that templates address have several names. What one author refers to as parameterized types another will refer to as generic classes, and yet another will call class families. This chapter uses the terms *generic classes* and *class families* interchangeably when discussing the abstract, theoretical problems that templates address, and uses the term *templates* (for obvious reasons) when referring to the C++ solution to these problems. Still the question remains: What are class families, and what is it about them that necessitates C++'s templates?

The following topics are covered in this chapter:

- Why function templates are superior to preprocessor macros
- How to declare and use function and class templates
- What a container class is and why you can build better containers using templates
- What is the Standard Template Library (STL)

Templates Are Here To Stay

Nothing is inherent in the idea of generic classes and functions that absolutely requires the use of template language extensions. For that matter, however, nothing is inherent in the tenets of object-oriented programming that requires class extensions to C. Templates, like exception handling and run-time type information, are ultimately conveniences that make certain programming tasks easier and less error-prone.

Although you can certainly simulate class families in a variety of different ways (most relying on the C++ preprocessor), adding templates to the language proper has several distinct advantages. Most important, by accepting templates into the still-evolving ANSI C++ standard, the user community creates a stable and dependable language extension that is source code compatible across compilers and operating platforms. If programmers had to rely on their own implementations of generic classes, everyone would have to "reinvent the wheel" whenever he or she wanted to create a class family. In the best of cases, you would have difficulty maintaining or even understanding code written by another programmer, unless you have significant knowledge of the original author's generic class implementation.

Luckily, a standard is emerging for templates, and most compiler vendors are scrambling to ensure that their compilers comply with the latest ANSI C++ standard's draft. Visual C++ 4 supports a complete and robust implementation of the draft ANSI standard. For these reasons, you cannot justify resisting the use of templates on the grounds that the extensions are too young or immature.

The larger problem is convincing programmers—novice and expert alike—that there is a compelling use for templates. To many programmers, template syntax and use is just foreign enough to appear intimidating. However, you shouldn't be intimidated. After you master a few basic abstractions and concepts, templates are as easy to use and understand as regular C++ classes.

Although you have now been exposed to such terminology as *generic classes* and *class families,* you still haven't gotten a good explanation of the template concept. So, the next section starts with step one.

Understanding Generic Functions and Classes

C++ provides a powerful set of features that enable you to approach complex programming problems by using convenient abstractions. You can use well-designed classes like a black box: You provide input data and concentrate on the output with little regard for how the class got there. Such abstractions free you from worrying about a host of compatibility and implementation issues, and, if you design your object interfaces well, enable you to focus on tying objects together.

A frustrating problem arises in those situations where you want to take a potentially disparate collection of these different "black boxes" and do the same thing to all of them. For example, how do you provide a function that, given three ordered objects of the same type, returns the object that is in the middle of the sort order? Listing 14.1 shows an implementation for integers.

Listing 14.1   intmid.cpp, Retrieving the "Middle" of Three Integers

```
#include <iostream.h>

int Middle(int a, int b, int c)
{
    return (a <= b ? (b <= c ? b : Middle(a, c, b)) :
        Middle(b, a, c));
}

void main()
{
cout << "Middle(3, 12, 5) is " << Middle(3, 12, 5);
}
```

When run, this program yields exactly what you would expect:

```
    Middle(3, 12, 5) is 5
```

This solution is nice enough for a simple problem. However, what if you want to do exactly the same thing for three floating-point numbers? You have to fire up the text editor and do a little bit of cutting and pasting. Listing 14.2 shows the new code that you need to support floating-point numbers. Note that C++'s function overloading enables you to keep the function name identical to the original code. The compiler uses the function arguments to decide which version of Middle() to call.

Listing 14.2   dblmid.cpp, Retrieving the "Middle" of Three Double Floating-Point Numbers

```
double Middle(double a, double b, double c)
{
    return (a <= b ? (b <= c ? b : Middle(a, c, b)) :
    Middle(b, a, c));
}
```

This really does seem like a waste. Here you have two code snippets that do exactly the same thing, but to different data types. To support an arbitrary number of integral and user-defined types, someone will have to write the same number of code snippets, most of which will be identical to listing 14.2 except for the type names.

Depending on the amount of experience that you have with C or C++, you might be wondering whether you can use a preprocessor macro to solve the problem. The answer is yes and no. Listing 14.3 shows a macro-based solution that appears to work. Note that the original implementation relied on recursion, which means that under certain circumstances the function must call itself until it meets a particular condition. Because C++ does not support recursive macros, the macro version is a little longer.

Listing 14.3   macromid.cpp, Using a Macro To Find the "Middle" of Three Ordered Objects of Arbitrary Type

```
#define _Middle(a, b, c)                               \
    ((a) <= (b) ? ((b) <= (c) ? (b) : ((a) <= (c) ?    \
    (c) : (a))) : ((a) <= (c) ? (a) : ((b) <= (c) ?    \
    (c) : (b))))
```

Listing 14.3 solves some of the problems inherent in applying Middle() to arbitrary types, but ends up causing more problems than it solves. Yes, this code enables you to call _Middle() with a variety of integral and user-defined types (as long as the objects support operator<=()). However, this approach also causes the compiled source code to become bloated and inefficient, and greatly compromises the strict type checking that is one of the hallmarks of C++.

Source Code Reuse and Efficiency

One of the great promises of object-oriented programming relates to code reuse. Inheritance is based on the premise that the more behaviors you can push into the base classes of a class hierarchy, the less code you have to add to newly derived classes. The spirit of reuse is at the core of what C++ is all about. As you will see, listing 14.3 is not a very good example of tight, reusable code.

The code presented in listing 14.3 appears to be relatively compact (readability is a completely different story). The operative word here is *appears,* because listing 14.3 can potentially cause your programs to grow significantly. Remember that _Middle() is a macro and that every occurrence of this macro in your code will be expanded. Examine the following rather innocuous assignment:

```
    float fMidValue = _Middle(34.23, 0.45, 396.27);
```

During compilation, this line is preprocessed and then passed to the compiler. Look at what the preprocessor comes up with for this single line of code:

```
    float fMidValue = ((34.23) <= (0.45) ? ((0.45) <= (396.27) ? (0.45) :
        ((34.23) <= (396.27) ? (396.27) : (34.23))) : ((34.23) <= (396.27) ?
        (34.23): ((0.45) <= (396.27) ? (396.27) : (0.45))));
```

Not a pretty sight. Now imagine this mess appearing in every place where your program calls the _Middle() macro. An application wouldn't have to call this macro too many times before noticeably increasing the program's size.

Obviously, the macro version of Middle() is also quite inefficient. To find the middle-ordered object, the expanded block of code requires a significant amount of processing. The biggest problem, however, is that the code is compiled everywhere that it is used. You might be tempted simply to wrap this expansion in a function declaration, but then you're back to where you started. Although placing this code in a function prevents the program from getting bloated, the function's prototype requires explicitly typed arguments.

Type Safety

There is another problem with using macros to implement generic classes. C++ benefits from being strongly typed. Because the language catches many inadvertent errors related to type at compile time, many bugs are resolved during development rather than run time.

> **Note**
>
> Unlike some object-oriented programming languages such as SmallTalk, C++ is a strongly typed language. In most cases, this means that the compiler can determine at compile time whether your program contains typing-related errors (such as passing arguments of the wrong type into methods, or calling methods that don't exist for a particular object class). It is only when programs take advantage of polymorphism and late-binding that C++ cannot perform type checking until run time.

The _Middle() macro opens the door for several subtle bugs related to its arguments' types. Foremost, the compiler lets arguments of different types call the _Middle() macro. Depending on what you're trying to accomplish, this behavior might not make sense. In this particular instance, however, the behavior is unlikely to make sense because comparisons of items usually have validity only when the items are all of the same type (you don't want to compare apples and oranges). The macro also has the compiler determine the result's type. If you're lucky, leaving this determination to the compiler will be appropriate; however, if you're unlucky, you might have to use a cast to ensure that the code compiles correctly.

Finally, certain expressions might not evaluate correctly in a macro. Calling _Middle() with arguments of 12, MyVar++, and 15 does not yield the desired result if the variable MyVar has a value of 14. This is because MyVar will have a value of 14 in some parts of the macro, but a value of 15 or 16 in others.

Templates as Function and Class Families

Without templates, you have no easy way to create implementations of function and class families that perform the same actions over a range of different data types. Although macros can work in some cases (and some uses of macros can get pretty elaborate), they suffer from the same problems of code size, efficiency, and type checking. Also, some hybrid mechanisms for creating generic classes rely on specialized C++ classes that are used with macros. These hybrid solutions might be a little better than the pure-macro approach, but ultimately both strategies suffer from many of the same failings. Templates enable you to create generic classes easily and without compromise.

V

Advanced Programming

> **Note**
>
> The primary aim of templates is to help programmers do more while writing less code. A single template definition can generate many different C++ functions or classes "under the covers." However, templates do not purport to reduce the sizes or amount of object code that is generated. Don't expect smaller executable and DLL files just because your programs use templates judiciously (in fact, you might actually see these files grow). You can expect your source files (.cpp and .h) to get smaller, which implies that you are spending less time writing and debugging code.

As alluded to earlier, templates are useful for creating families of functions in addition to families of classes. The `Middle()` example is a perfect candidate for a function template, and the next section explains how to write such a template definition. As you will see, function templates are similar to class templates, although there are a few differences in syntax and use.

A class template definition (as opposed to a function template definition) is neither a class nor an object instance. Instead, a class template is a description of how to create a new class given a particular type (or types). In C++, a class is useless unless you declare an object instance of that class. Similarly, a template is useless unless you declare a class instance of that template. If you find this concept a little confusing, don't worry. The following sections explain exactly how to write template definitions, and how to instantiate template classes and functions.

> **Note**
>
> After you define a class, you declare an instance of the class. After you define a template, you declare the type of class that you want to instantiate.

Function Templates

The `Middle()` example is the perfect place to start a practical discussion of how to use templates. Carefully examine the elements of the `Middle()` template, presented in listing 14.4.

Listing 14.4   templmid.cpp, a Template Function for Finding the "Middle" of Three Ordered Objects

```
#include <iostream.h>

// This is the function template definition
template <class Type>
Type Middle(Type a, Type b, Type c)
{
    return (a <= b ? (b <= c ? b : Middle(a, c, b))
```

```
        Middle(b, a, c));
}

void main()
{
    cout << "Middle(3, 12, 5) is " << Middle(3, 12, 5);
}
```

You might initially think that listing 14.4 looks very similar to listing 14.1. Well, it should. After all, both pieces of code are trying to do exactly the same thing. What makes listing 14.4 interesting is how it differs from listing 14.1. For the sake of convenience, listing 14.5 compares listing 14.1's prototype of Middle() to the declaration for the Middle() template definition.

Listing 14.5   A Comparison of Listing 14.1's Function Prototype to Listing 14.4's Template Declaration

```
// The "int" prototype of Middle
int Middle(int a, int b, int c);

// The template declaration
template <class Type>
Type Middle(Type a, Type b, Type c);
```

The most obvious difference is on the first line of the template declaration:

```
template <class Type>
```

This line tells the compiler to expect a template definition that describes a family of functions that utilize an arbitrary type, referred to as Type. Following the template keyword is a list of arbitrary type declarations enclosed in angled brackets (< >). This list of types is the template argument list.

Each type declaration in the argument list begins with the reserved word class followed by a user-provided name. A program can use whatever name is most appropriate to represent its types, but by convention, Type or simply T are two of the more commonly used symbolic names. After you define the generic type, you can use it throughout the function definition in the same way that you might use any integral C++ type. Although the first line of the template declaration includes only a single parameter, a template argument list can contain as many type declarations as necessary.

The second line of the template declaration in listing 14.5 provides the prototype for the function template:

```
Type Middle(Type a, Type b, Type c);
```

Instead of indicating explicit types for the arguments and the return value, however, this line indicates that the function takes three arguments of the same arbitrary type and returns a value of the same type. Listing 14.6 shows examples of both legal and illegal function template declarations.

> **Listing 14.6   Some Sample Function Template Declarations**
>
> ```
> // Legal
> template <class MyType>
> int DoSomething(MyType AValue, char *str);
>
> // Legal
> template <class T1, class T2>
> void PrintSomething(T1 page, T2 doc);
>
> // Illegal -- the "class" keyword must precede every
> // type argument (T2's is missing)
> template <class T1, T2, class MyType>
> void BlowSomethingUp(T1 target, T2 area, MyType val);
>
> // Illegal -- a template must have at least one type in
> // its argument list
> template <>
> char GetChar(unsigned char ch);
>
> // Illegal -- argument names must be unique
> template <class T, class T>
> void OpenFile(T FileAlias);
>
> // Illegal -- all arguments must appear in the function
> // prototype (T2 does not)
> template <class T1, class T2>
> void WriteFile(T1 FileAlias, char *str);
> ```

Note the difference between a template declaration and a template definition. A template declaration is the equivalent of a function prototype, except that it describes a family of functions that a template definition will define later. The last two lines of listing 14.5 comprise a template declaration:

```
template <class Type>
Type Middle(Type a, Type b, Type c);
```

A template definition, on the other hand, contains the actual implementation of a function template. Listing 14.4, for example, is a template definition.

You code the template definition virtually the same way that you write a normal C++ function. The only difference, apart from the obvious syntactical discrepancies already discussed, is that any of the types defined in the template argument list can be used in the definition as generic types.

Why Templates Do Not Work with Every Type

Template definitions are inherently generic, and this fact has some rather subtle implications. Consider, for example, the code fragment presented in listing 14.7.

Listing 14.7 addeq.cpp, the `AddEquals()` Function Template

```
        .
        .
        .
struct MyStruct {
      unsigned int a;
      unsigned int b;
};

template <class T>
unsigned int AddEquals(T val1, T val2, T compare)
{
      return (val1 + val2) == compare;
}

// Example 1 -- Legal
cout << "Does 4 + 5 = 9? ";
cout << (AddEquals(4, 5, 9) ? "Yes" : "No") << "\n";

// Example 2 -- Legal
cout << "Does 7.0 + 5.5 = 12.0? ";
cout << (AddEquals(7.0, 5.5, 12.0) ? "Yes" : "No") << "\n";

// Example 3 -- Illegal
MyStruct  a = { 23, 43 }, b = { 11, 19 }, c = { 34, 62 };
cout << "Does a + b = c? ";
cout << (AddEquals(a, b, c) ? "Yes" : "No") << "\n";
        .
        .
        .
```

This `AddEquals()` function takes two objects of a given type, adds them, and then compares them for equality to a third object of the same type. The template is very simple. The first two examples work as expected, but the third does not even compile. Why?

The reason is simple: The third example does not compile because the compiler doesn't know how to add `MyStruct`s or check them for equality. The `AddEquals()` template function applies the addition operator on its first two arguments and then checks whether the result of the addition is equal to the third argument. This scheme works fine for integral types that the compiler already knows how to add and compare. But the compiler does not understand how to add user-defined types like `MyStruct` or how to check them for equality. Indeed, the Visual C++ compiler does an excellent job of pointing out such an error by printing the following message:

```
LST07.CPP(11) : error C2676: binary '+' : 'struct MyStruct'
      does not define this operator or a conversion to a
      type acceptable to the predefined operator.
```

Listing 14.8 shows the changes that you would have to make to the `MyStruct` type to support the `AddEquals()` template.

Listing 14.8   addeq2.cpp, the Corrected `MyStruct` Type

```
typedef struct _MyStruct {
    unsigned int a;
    unsigned int b;

    // Operators
    MyStruct operator+(_MyStruct &o)
    {
        MyStruct temp = { a + o.a, b + o.b };
        return temp;
    }

    unsigned int operator==(_MyStruct &o)
    {
        return a == o.a && b == o.b;
    }

} MyStruct;
```

The third example in listing 14.7 works correctly with this version of the `MyStruct` type, displaying `Yes` when run.

Caution

The main lesson to learn from these examples is that templates are powerful constructs that you can use—potentially—with any integral or user-defined type. If, however, the type does not support the operations that the template needs, you cannot use the type with the template at all.

This limitation can be more problematic than it might initially seem. If, for example, you have purchased a set of template-based class libraries from a third-party vendor, you must know which operations have to be supported by types that will be used with the templates. You can often obtain this information by scanning header files or reading documentation, but you must somehow obtain the information.

Building the Class Template

At this point, you probably have a basic understanding of how you can use function templates to create generic functions that accept a variety of type-independent arguments. Class templates are in many ways similar to function templates. However, several complications arise when you take into account properties that are unique to classes, such as inheritance, member data, and class methods.

This section focuses on applying to the C++ class mechanism the concepts discussed in the function templates sections. This section also explores in more detail some of the finer points of the general template syntax. Some of these details also apply to function templates.

The Template Syntax

First review the "official" template syntax for functions and classes. You must have at least a general feeling for the precise syntax. Although the following definition is not very intuitive, you have actually already covered most of the parts of this syntax.

(a) template-declaration:

```
template < template-argument-list > declaration
```

(b) template-argument-list:

```
template-argument
template-argument-list, template argument
```

(c) template-argument:

```
type-argument
argument-declaration
```

(d) type-argument:

```
class identifier
```

This rather gruesome style is adopted from the Microsoft documentation (which, in turn, is adopted from *The C++ Annotated Reference Manual*). Although this syntax is complete, it certainly isn't easy to read.

But don't worry. The syntax is actually quite simple. In fact, section (a) summarizes the syntax. As discussed previously in the section "Function Templates," a template declaration (or definition) begins with the token `template` and is followed by an argument list enclosed in angled brackets:

```
template < template-argument-list > declaration
```

The declaration at the end of section (a) is simply a declaration or definition of a function or class.

Section (b) details exactly what makes up a template argument list:

```
template-argument
template-argument-list, template argument
```

Not surprisingly, this section indicates that a template argument list consists of one or more template arguments.

Next, section (c) indicates whether a template argument is a type argument or an argument declaration:

```
type-argument
argument-declaration
```

Section (d) explains the type argument, which is simply the class identifier syntax that you encountered when building the `Middle()` and `AddEquals()` template functions. The argument declaration, however, is something new. Template arguments can also consist of constant types that are not used as generic types at all. The section "Constant Expression Template Parameters" explains why you might want to use nongeneric types in a template declaration.

V

Advanced Programming

Defining the Template

This section provides some concrete examples. Suppose that you want to build a class that represents a railroad car. You could, for example, create a base class called `RailroadCar` that knows everything that you know about being part of a train. Then, as you learn about different types of railroad cars, you could inherit new classes from the original `RailroadCar` class.

The problem with this approach is that it requires many specialized classes (for example, `CowRailroadCar`, `PassengerRailroadCar`, and `CoalRailroadCar`), all of which are intrinsically linked to being a `RailroadCar`. This approach suggests that two different species of cow exist—the normal cow species and the cow-on-a-train species—when cows are simply cows, regardless of whether they are on a train.

Another problem occurs when you merge new code with previously written code. Suppose, for example, that you inherit a large inventory-management class library from your predecessor. Your boss asks you to add a set of rail shipment classes to the preexisting class library. This library already contains classes for all the products that the company produces, and each of these products can be shipped by rail.

If you use the inheritance method, you have to take all the existing objects and either insert the `RailroadCar` class high in the class hierarchy or use multiple inheritance to add the `RailroadCar` class functionality to each of the product classes.

To make matters worse, suppose that you don't even have the source code for the class library, that the library is a third-party product bundled in a Windows DLL, and that to use the classes you have to include header files and link with the DLL's import libraries. In this case, inserting the `RailroadCar` class into the middle of the inheritance tree isn't even an option.

Templates provide an easy solution to this problem. Because trains can haul virtually any type of commodity, a `RailroadCar` class must not make any immediate assumptions about what is inside the car. Templates don't have to make any assumptions about the characteristics of their generic types unless the programmer deems it appropriate. Listing 14.9 shows what a simple `RailroadCar` class template might look like.

Listing 14.9 train.cpp, a `RailroadCar` Class Template

```
#include <iostream.h>
#include <afx.h>

// Things to put in a RailroadCar
class Cow {
public:
    // Public member functions
    CString isA() { return "Cow"; }
    CString Moo() { return "Moo!"; }
};

class Passenger {
public:
```

```
    // Constructors and destructor
    Passenger(CString NewName) { Name = NewName; }

// Public member functions
CString isA() { return "Passenger"; }
CString GetName() { return Name; }
CString Complain() { return "Oh my poor back!"; }

private:
    CString Name;
};


// The RailroadCar class template
template <class T>
class RailroadCar {
public:
    // Constructors and destructor
    RailroadCar(int NewCarNumber, T& NewContents);
    ~RailroadCar();

// Public member functions
void ShowContents();
T* Unload();

private:
    T* pContents;
    int CarNumber;
};

// Constructor
template <class T>
RailroadCar<T>::RailroadCar(int NewCarNumber,
                    T&  NewContents)
{
    CarNumber = NewCarNumber;
    pContents = &NewContents;
}

// Destructor
template <class T>
RailroadCar<T>::~RailroadCar()
{
    Unload();
}

// Public member functions
template <class T>
void RailroadCar<T>::ShowContents()
{
    cout << "Railroad car #" << CarNumber;
    cout << " is filled with " << pContents->isA();
    cout << "s\n";
}

template <class T>
```

Listing 14.9   Continued

```
T* RailroadCar<T>::Unload()
{
    T* temp = pContents;
    pContents = NULL;
    return temp;
}


void main()
{
    // At Station 1
    Cow ACow;
    Passenger APassenger("Monty");

    RailroadCar<Cow> CarNumber1(1, ACow);
    RailroadCar<Passenger> CarNumber2(2, APassenger);

    CarNumber1.ShowContents();
    CarNumber2.ShowContents();

    // Go to Station 2...
    cout << "\n..Choo..Choo..\n\n";

    // At Station 2
    Cow* AtStation2Cow = CarNumber1.Unload();
    Passenger* AtStation2Passenger =
    CarNumber2.Unload();

    cout << "How was the trip, ",
    cout << AtStation2Passenger->GetName() << "?";
    cout << "  " << AtStation2Passenger->Complain();
    cout << "\n";
    cout << AtStation2Cow->Moo() << "\n";
}
```

Caution

This example, and others like it that use the CString class, rely on the Microsoft Foundation Classes (MFC). When these examples are compiled, the Project Settings notebook's General page must activate the appropriate settings. You must ensure that either the Use MFC in a Shared DLL or Use MFC in a Static Library option is selected in the Microsoft Foundation Classes combo box.

Listing 14.9 is actually a pretty complete (albeit silly) implementation of a template class. Although much of this program is self-explanatory, it presents several new concepts and a few things that merit additional discussion.

The following is the actual template definition. As you would expect, this definition looks almost exactly the same as a regular class definition.

```
// The RailroadCar class template
template <class T>
class RailroadCar {
public:
    // Constructors and destructor
    RailroadCar(int NewCarNumber, T& NewContents);
    ~RailroadCar();

    // Public member functions
    void ShowContents();
    T* Unload();

private:
    T* pContents;
    int CarNumber;
};
```

This template definition also has several parallels to the declaration of a function template. As you would expect after examining the formal template syntax, the first line uses the same syntax as the `Middle()` and `AddEquals()` examples earlier in this chapter:

```
template <class T>
```

This line tells the compiler that the template definition uses a single generic type, named T.

The rest of the definition holds no surprises; it simply describes the template class. The constructor takes an integer identification number as its first argument and a reference to a T for its second argument. This reference, which the class stores as a pointer to T, represents the railroad car's contents.

Other member functions include a method to display the car's contents, and a method to "unload" the car by returning a pointer to the car's contents. Not surprisingly, the template class's member data includes an integer for the car identification number, and, as was previously mentioned, a pointer of type T that points to the car's cargo.

With the definition of the template class's constructor and member functions, a new syntax is introduced. Examine the following definition for the `Unload()` method:

```
template <class T>
T* RailroadCar<T>::Unload()
```

The method prototype's definition is almost identical to a normal method declaration. However, instead of having a simple class name, the definition has a template name with the accompanying arguments:

```
// What you might expect
T* RailroadCar::Unload() ...

// The correct syntax
template <class T>
T* RailroadCar<T>::Unload() ...
```

You place the <T> between the template name and the double colons (::) for several reasons, but one of the most important reasons relates to a template feature called *specialization*. Specialization enables a program to override the default template behaviors for specific types. The section "Specialization" discusses this feature in more detail.

Almost everything that applies to coding normal C++ classes also applies to creating template code. You declare member functions by using a slightly different syntax, but otherwise you write the functions as you would any other class methods. You can use your generic type anywhere that you might use a normal integral or user-defined type. That is, after all, the real reason for using templates in the first place.

Instantiating Templates

A template definition by itself does nothing. To use a template, a program must create an instance of it, in much the same way that programs create object instances of classes. This process, like its class counterpart, is called *instantiation*.

Instantiating Function Templates. Instantiation for function templates and class templates is handled a little differently. Unlike class templates, a function template instantiation has no special syntax. All that a program has to do is to declare a normal function prototype with the appropriate types filled in. Therefore, to create an instance of the AddEquals() function template that accepts arguments of type Cow (see listing 14.9), all that is required is the following:

```
// Create an AddEquals template instance for Cows
unsigned int AddEquals(Cow val1, Cow val2, Cow compare);
```

Of course, this instantiation would work only if you define operator+() and operator==() for the Cow class.

Alternatively, a program can simply refer to a particular function template instance. The compiler then will realize that it must generate the instance. In listing 14.7, the compiler understands that it has to generate a version of AddEquals() for integers and for floating-point numbers when it encounters the use of these functions. Still, for readability and documentation purposes, you should declare your function template instances explicitly.

Instantiating Class Templates. Although the syntax for instantiating a class template is quite similar to the syntax for instantiating an object instance, there are a couple of important differences. Foremost, the process of instantiating a template is very different from the process of instantiating an object instance. On encountering a template instance, the compiler builds a whole new class definition custom tailored to the type (or types) that the template instance will be using. Compare this to instantiating a new object, where the compiler simply looks up the appropriate class and creates a new object of that type. Fortunately, new classes are generated from templates at compile time, so there are no run-time performance penalties. The following details the class template instantiation syntax:

(a) template-class-name:

```
template-name < template-arg-list >
```

(b) template-arg-list:

```
template-arg
template-arg-list , template-arg
```

(c) template-arg:

```
expression
type-name
```

As shown in section (a), the instantiation begins with a template name followed by an argument list that is enclosed in the obligatory angled brackets. As indicated by section (b), the argument list consists of one or more arguments.

More interesting is section (c), which describes what an argument is. The program is creating a new class, so all the generic type arguments specified in the template definition must be filled with specific types. Therefore, when instantiating a template, the program must pass in type names. Section (c) also indicates that the program can pass in constant expressions where appropriate. The section "Constant Expression Template Parameters" explores in more detail this variation on the normal instantiating syntax.

Listing 14.10 shows how you might use instantiation with the `RailroadCar` template.

Listing 14.10   Using the `RailroadCar` Class Template

```
void main()
{
    // At Station 1
    Cow ACow;
    Passenger APassenger("Monty");

    RailroadCar<Cow> CarNumber1(1, ACow);
    RailroadCar<Passenger> CarNumber2(2, APassenger);

    CarNumber1.ShowContents();
    CarNumber2.ShowContents();

    // Go to Station 2...
    cout << "\n..Choo..Choo..\n\n";

    // At Station 2
    Cow* AtStation2Cow = CarNumber1.Unload();
    Passenger* AtStation2Passenger =
    CarNumber2.Unload();
```

(continues)

V

Advanced Programming

Listing 14.10   Continued

```
        cout << "How was the trip, ";
        cout << AtStation2Passenger->GetName() << "?";
        cout << "  " << AtStation2Passenger->Complain();
        cout << "\n";
        cout << AtStation2Cow->Moo() << "\n";
}
```

The most important lines, from a template standpoint, are at the beginning of the listing:

```
    RailroadCar<Cow> CarNumber1(1, ACow);
    RailroadCar<Passenger> CarNumber2(2, APassenger);
```

These two lines are responsible for creating two railroad car classes: one that can be used with Cows and another that can be used with Passengers. The first part of each of these lines actually instantiates the new class. After the template class is instantiated, it can be used just like any other class; this program proceeds to declare two object instances of the newly created classes.

You could also write the preceding code as follows:

```
    // Create new types for template instantiations
    typedef RailroadCar<Cow> CowRailroadCar;
    typedef RailroadCar<Passenger> PassengerRailroadCar;

    // Now instantiate the object instances
    CowRailroadCar CarNumber1(1, ACow);
    PassengerRailroadCar CarNumber2(2, APassenger);
```

This style is a little more verbose, and therefore perhaps even a little more readable. The style also enables you to include further instantiations of CowRailroadCars and PassengerRailroadCars without having to type the cumbersome RailroadCar<...> syntax. The mechanism that you choose is a matter of personal preference. Keep in mind that you can use a template instantiation (such as RailroadCar<Car> and RailroadCar<Passenger>) in the same way, and in the same places, as any other type.

When you use the more verbose style, note that the Microsoft compiler does not actually generate the RailroadCar<Cow> and RailroadCar<Passenger> classes when it encounters the typedef statements. The classes aren't generated until the compiler encounters an instantiation of a CowRailroadCar or PassengerRailroadCar object. Because the typedefs result in little or no overhead, you can declare them liberally without concern about bloated object files or long compile times.

Using Static Template Member Data and Methods

Because the class generated by a template instantiation is really just a normal C++ class, static member functions and data are completely supported. The only tricky part is getting acclimated to the new syntax that the template definition requires, which isn't all that difficult.

For example, suppose that a program needs to implement a `GlobalValue` template. A `GlobalValue` is a global instance of some type that might differ for various programs (thus the template implementation). A `GlobalValue` class template has a static member function that returns the global value.

The `GlobalValue` example merits a quick digression about the value and dangers of using global data. Quite simply, programs shouldn't use global data unless you declare it `const`. The main problem is that classes and functions can inadvertently modify global data in ways that other objects in other parts of the program might not have anticipated. Such bugs are notoriously difficult to track down because you have to find the changes in an object's state retroactively and determine the parts of the program that were responsible for making those changes.

Such debugging becomes even trickier if the program runs under an advanced operating system (such as Windows 95, Windows NT, or OS/2) that supports multithreading. In such cases, the culprit responsible for modifying global data might be running concurrently in another thread, and might be behaving differently from run to run depending on ambiguous and hard-to-reproduce factors such as machine load.

Nevertheless, there are a few good excuses (and many bad ones) for using global data. In some cases, performance requirements dictate a quick way to modify program-wide control objects. Such requirements might apply particularly to multithreaded programs, in which threads might have to communicate with each other as quickly as possible, or programs such as those concerned with communications or low-level network plumbing, which must meet real-time processing requirements. In other cases, the burden (from both a performance and a coding perspective) of passing data through many levels of functions and objects can be too great to justify.

The `GlobalValue` template presented in listing 14.11 doesn't do much to alleviate the dangers of using global data, but does suggest a more formalized mechanism for declaring and accessing global information. At the very least, a `GlobalValue` class provides a convenient place to insert debugging routines that you can use to help track down tricky global data bugs. A full-blown `GlobalValue` template used in multithreaded environments could also implement semaphore mechanisms that would prevent contention on shared objects across multiple threads. Finally, if you use a `GlobalValue` class, global information does not have to reside in the global namespace. This makes inadvertent modification of global data much less likely, because a class or function must specifically obtain access to the global data through a static function call before being able to modify the global data.

Listing 14.11   global.cpp, a `GlobalValue` Template Using Static Member Data and Functions

```cpp
#include <iostream.h>

// Define the Boolean type
typedef unsigned char Boolean;
const Boolean TRUE = 1;
const Boolean FALSE = 0;

// GlobalValue template definition
template <class T>
class GlobalValue {
public:
    // Constructors and destructor
    GlobalValue();
    GlobalValue(T* pNewGlobalValue);
    ~GlobalValue();

    // Public member functions
    static T* GetGlobalValuePtr();

private:
    static T* pGlobalValue;
    static Boolean ShouldDelete;
};

// Initialize static data
template <class T>
T* GlobalValue<T>::pGlobalValue = NULL;
template <class T>
Boolean GlobalValue<T>::ShouldDelete = FALSE;

// Constructors
template <class T>
GlobalValue<T>::GlobalValue()
{
    pGlobalValue = new T;
    ShouldDelete = TRUE;
}

template <class T>
GlobalValue<T>::GlobalValue(T* pNewGlobalValue)
{
    pGlobalValue = pNewGlobalValue;
    ShouldDelete = FALSE;
}

// Destructor
template <class T>
GlobalValue<T>::~GlobalValue()
{
    if (ShouldDelete && pGlobalValue)
        delete pGlobalValue;
}
```

```
// Public member functions
template <class T>
T* GlobalValue<T>::GetGlobalValuePtr()
{
    return pGlobalValue;
}


// Now demonstrate use of a GlobalValue
void AFarAwayFunc()
{
    cout << "The int GlobalValue is ";
    cout << *GlobalValue<int>::GetGlobalValuePtr() << endl;
}

void main()
{
    int AVeryImportantInt = 123;
    GlobalValue<int> GlobalInt(&AVeryImportantInt);

    // Show the current value
    AFarAwayFunc();

    // Change the value
    AVeryImportantInt++;
AFarAwayFunc();
```

Advanced Programming

You find the template definition in the following lines:

```
// GlobalValue template definition
template <class T>
class GlobalValue {
public:
    // Constructors and destructor
    GlobalValue();
    GlobalValue(T* pNewGlobalValue);
    ~GlobalValue();

    // Public member functions
    static T* GetGlobalValuePtr();

private:
    static T* pGlobalValue;
    static Boolean ShouldDelete;
};
```

You declare the static member function GetGlobalValuePtr() and the static member data pGlobalValue and ShouldDelete the same as you would in a normal C++ class. In the constructors, destructor, and member functions, these data values are all manipulated just as you would expect. Similarly, you define the GetGlobalValuePtr() method just like any other class template member function.

As you can see in the following reprinted code, the syntax for initializing static member data is different than for normal classes because of the template relationship:

```
// Initialize static data
template <class T>
T* GlobalValue<T>::pGlobalValue = NULL;
template <class T>
Boolean GlobalValue<T>::ShouldDelete = FALSE;
```

Still, because the syntax is identical to the definition of class template member functions, this syntax doesn't present anything that this chapter hasn't already described previously.

Several things are noteworthy about the parts of listing 14.11 that actually use the GlobalValue template. The name of the AFarAwayFunc() function reinforces the point that any function or class method must access the global data through the GlobalValue class template, even if the class or function is defined in another source module. Because the AVeryImportantInt variable is declared only within the scope of main(), AFarAwayFunc() can access this value only through the appropriate class template. Notice also the syntax used to call the static method. This syntax is identical to that of a normal static member function call, except that you use a template qualifier rather than a class name.

Constant Expression Template Parameters

Previous sections that addressed template definition and instantiation referred to certain declaration forms that enable you to place nongeneric types within a template argument list. A program can use a regular integral or user-defined type and pass in a constant expression for that parameter during template instantiation. You can use this mechanism to introduce some flexibility in those classes that typically rely on fixed values.

The template declaration syntax lets you include type parameters or constant expressions in a template argument list. If a template uses an expression argument, it must be resolvable at compile time. Listing 14.12 shows examples of both legal and illegal uses of constant expressions in argument lists.

Listing 14.12   Using Constant Expressions in Template Argument Lists

```
const int MAX_NUM_BLAHS = 23;
const char* A_STR_NUM = "356";

template <int AnInt>
class BlahBlahBlah {
      ...Template definition omitted...
};

// All legal
BlahBlahBlah<22*4> Blahs1;
BlahBlahBlah<MAX_NUM_BLAHS>  Blahs2;
BlahBlahBlah<(MAX_NUM_BLAHS ? MAX_NUM_BLAHS : 1)> Blahs3;

// Illegal
BlahBlahBlah<atoi(A_STR_NUM)> Blah4;
```

```
// Illegal
void MyFunc(int NumBlahs)
{
    BlahBlahBlah<NumBlahs> InFuncBlah;
...
```

Constant expression template arguments are particularly useful in templates that use fixed-size data structures. For example, the following template typically declares an array of a constant size:

```
template <class T>
class MyClass {
    ...
private:
    T AnArray[A_CONST_VALUE];
    ...
};
```

You can make the same template class more flexible by declaring it with a constant expression argument and passing in the array's size during template instantiation:

```
template <class T, int ArraySize>
class MyClass {
    ...
private:
    T AnArray[ArraySize];
    ...
};

MyClass<double, A_CONST_VALUE> ADoubleMyClass;
```

While achieving the same general effect, the latter approach also allows for instantiations that may vary the array's size. You might not need such flexibility immediately, but other programs that use the same template can benefit from this sort of foresight. This approach does not affect run-time performance and affects code size only minimally, so the change is easy to justify.

Some Syntactical Pitfalls

Due to some subtleties in the argument list syntax, you must be particularly careful when a constant expression in a template argument list uses the greater-than operator (such as `operator>()`). Without parentheses, some expressions can prematurely close a template argument list:

```
MyClass<float, A_CONST > ANOTHER_CONST> AMyClass;
```

You can easily resolve (and avoid) such errors simply by enclosing all template argument list expressions inside parentheses:

```
MyClass<float, (A_CONST > ANOTHER_CONST)> AMyClass;
```

A similar case arises when a template class is instantiated with a nested template syntax. Note the following two classes, for example:

```
template <class T>
class FirstClass {
     ...Template definition omitted...
};

template <class T>
class SecondClass {
     ...Template definition omitted...
};

SecondClass<FirstClass<char *>> MySecondClass;
```

In this example, the two right-angled brackets (>>) in the MySecondClass declaration could be interpreted as being a right-shift operator. For the preceding code fragment, the Visual C++ compiler complains about two syntactical errors:

```
error C2146: syntax error : missing ',' before identifier 'MySecondClass'
error C2065: 'MySecondClass' : undeclared identifier
```

Tip

The key to avoiding these sorts of "red herring" errors is to use > > rather than >> for nested templates. The following declarations for MySecondClass compile without warnings or errors:

```
// This works fine
SecondClass<FirstClass<char *> > MySecondClass;

// As does this
SecondClass< FirstClass<char *> > MySecondClass;
```

How Generic Is a Template?

C++ templates are based on the idea of building (relatively) type-independent class families that all rely on a single definition. Unfortunately, in certain cases, you simply cannot describe a set of behaviors for every conceivable type. Two issues are involved:

■ What to do when a template must make assumptions about the generic types that it manipulates

■ What to do when a template makes assumptions about its generic types, and the type that you want to use doesn't conform to those assumptions

Type-Dependent Templates. Although templates can be useful for manipulating data generically, they become even more valuable if you can make a few well-chosen assumptions about the generic types with which they will be working. In some respects, you cannot avoid a certain amount of assuming. In the AddEquals() example (see listing 14.7), the template function assumes that it can add or compare for equality any types that are passed to the function. These two assumptions were of paramount importance for the function to accomplish its task. However, the template broke when passed the MyStruct type, which the template function could not add or compare.

Similarly, the RailroadCar example also makes an assumption. In the ShowContents() method, the template calls the isA() method of the item that the object is storing. Of course, many types of objects do not have an isA() method to call. In fact, the mere requirement of an isA() method precludes the use of any integral types as the template's generic type.

This logic has a catch-22. The more assumptions made about a template's generic type, the more capably the template can manipulate its data and the more useful the template becomes. On the other hand, the more assumptions made about a template's generic type, the fewer types can be used—which weakens the whole argument for using templates.

The reality is that a truly generic class is seldom a useful class. Because a truly generic template cannot make any assumptions about its data—about its T—you can expect only so much from the template. Without framing its data in a useful context, a template is restricted from performing its most useful functions.

The ideal goal, of course, is to find the middle ground between making the template too dependent on its types and making the template too generic to be very useful. In some cases, a template that is truly generic (or close to it) might be appropriate. Both the Middle() and AddEquals() template functions probably meet this criteria, although even these simplistic examples make some basic assumptions about their parameterized types. On the other hand, such a generic implementation would severely limit the RailroadCar class. After all, what good is a railroad car if you cannot look inside and determine its contents?

Specialization. Regardless of the kinds of compromises that you have to strike between functionality and generic approachability, you eventually encounter a situation in which the template that you want to use will not work with a desired type. Fortunately, a program can address these cases by using a template feature called *specialization*.

A template specialization enables you to overload a template function, template class, template class method, or template class static data member for a particular type. The AddEquals() example of listing 14.7 demonstrates how and why you might do so.

Recall that the AddEquals() function template takes two arguments of the same generic type, adds them together, and then compares the sum for equality with a third argument of the same type. But what happens when you try to use the AddEquals() template with character pointers, as in the following example?

```
char *pBig = "Big ";
char *pDog = "Dog";
char *pBigDog = "Big Dog";

unsigned int result = AddEquals(pBig, pDog, pBigDog);
```

This code does not compile. The Microsoft compiler complains that the template definition "cannot add two pointers." This makes sense, because adding two character pointers together is illegal. What you really want to do is concatenate the strings to which the character pointers refer.

This is a case, like the MyStruct example in listing 14.7, of the type not supporting the operations that the template must perform on it. Unlike the MyStruct example, in which you could add the operator+() semantic to the MyStruct class, you cannot add the operator+() semantic to character pointers because character pointers are an integral type. Even if you could add the addition semantic, the equality operation for character pointers compares only the pointer addresses and not the strings to which the pointers refer. So even if you could add character pointers, the template still wouldn't operate as expected.

The solution to this problem is to write a specialization that understands how to work with character pointers and provides the same sort of behavior with a type-specific implementation. Listing 14.13 details this specialization.

Listing 14.13 addeq3.cpp, the AddEquals() Function Template with a Character Pointer Specialization

```
#include <iostream.h>
#include <stdio.h>
#include <string.h>

template <class T>
unsigned int AddEquals(T val1, T val2, T compare)
{
    return (val1 + val2) == compare;
}

// Specialization for character pointers
unsigned int AddEquals(char *val1,
                char *val2,
                char *compare)
{
char Temp[512];
sprintf(Temp, "%s%s", val1, val2);
return !strcmp(Temp, compare);
}

void main()
{
    // Legal -- Uses template
    cout << "Does 4 + 5 = 9? ";
    cout << (AddEquals(4, 5, 9) ? "Yes" : "No") << "\n";

    // Legal -- Uses template
    cout << "Does 7.0 + 5.5 = 12.0? ";
    cout << (AddEquals(7.0, 5.5, 12.0) ? "Yes" : "No") << "\n";
```

```
        // Legal — Uses specialization
        cout << "Does \"Big \" + \"Dog\" = \"Big Dog\"? ";
        cout << (AddEquals("Big ", "Dog", "Big Dog") ? "Yes" : "No")
            << "\n";
    }
```

Apart from the obvious criticisms (the specialization uses a fixed-size character array that can be overflowed), this code will now work as expected with character strings. Note that a specialization makes no direct reference to function template syntax. Instead, you write the function as you normally would, regardless of whether there is a function template that tries to accomplish the same thing.

Similarly, you can specialize the ShowContents() member function from listing 14.9's RailroadCar template so that it supports types that might not have an isA() member function. Listing 14.14 shows how you can accomplish this.

Listing 14.14   train2.cpp, Specializing the RailroadCar Template's ShowContents() Member Function for Integers

```
#include <iostream.h>
#include <afx.h>

Definition of Cow class omitted...

Definition of Passenger class omitted...

Definition of RailroadCar template omitted...

// ShowContents specialization for integers
void RailroadCar<int>::ShowContents()
{
    cout << "Railroad car #" << CarNumber;
    cout << " is filled with an integer (" << *pContents;
    cout << ")\n";
}

void main()
{
    int IntegerCargo = 456;
    Cow Bessie;
    RailroadCar<int> CarNumber1(1, IntegerCargo);
    RailroadCar<Cow> CarNumber2(2, Bessie);

    // Calls the int specialization
    CarNumber1.ShowContents();

    // Calls the normal template member function that
    // relies on isA
        CarNumber2.ShowContents();
}
```

Unlike the `AddEquals()` function template specialization, the `RailroadCar` class specialization for integers does use template notation, although a `template <...>` line does not precede the member function definition. Aside from this slight discrepancy, the syntax and implementation are standard with respect to other member function definitions.

You can specialize static member functions in the same manner as normal member functions. You also can specialize static member data. A class that initializes a static class integer to one value for a particular generic type can initialize the same static integer to another value for a different generic type. For example, in the following class, the static integer `BufferSize` is normally initialized to 4K:

```
template <class T>
class NetworkCard {
    ...
    static int BufferSize;
    ...
};

// Initialize the static member data
template <class T>
int NetworkCard<T>::BufferSize = 4 * 1024; // 4K
```

If, however, the program needs a larger buffer size when the generic type T is a character pointer, the application need only initialize a specialization:

```
// Initialize the static member data for char*
// specialization
int NetworkCard<char*>::BufferSize = 16 * 1024; // 16K
```

If the program instantiates a `NetworkCard` template with a generic type of char*, `BufferSize` is 16K rather than the default 4K.

If all this specialization flexibility still isn't enough to meet a program's demands, you can specialize an entire class definition, as follows:

```
template <class T>
class MyClass {
    ...
    void DoSomething() { cout << "Apples\n"; }
    ...
};

// Class specialization for ints
class MyClass<int> {
    ...
    void DoSomething() { cout << "Oranges\n"; }
    ...
};

MyClass<char> ACharMyClass;
MyClass<int> AnIntMyClass;
```

In this case, the ACharMyClass object uses the normal class template. If the program calls ACharMyClass.DoSomething(), the object writes Apples to cout. The AnIntMyClass object, on the other hand, uses the specialization class for integers. If the program calls AnIntMyClass.DoSomething(), the object writes Oranges to cout.

Specializations provide enough flexibility to accommodate most situations in which a template definition appears to be either incomplete or inadequate to support the types that you want to use.

Inheritance and Templates

The classes that are generated when a template is instantiated are simply normal C++ classes, so it should come as no surprise that templates can be full and equal players in inheritance trees. You can also mix templates with regular classes in the inheritance tree, either as base classes or derived classes.

Therefore, three potential types of inheritance can involve templates: a template class can inherit from a normal C++ class, a normal C++ class can inherit from a template class, and a template class can inherit from another template class.

Inheriting a Template Class from a Nontemplate Class. Suppose that you have a normal base class (A) and a derived template (BTemplt). Listing 14.15 shows how you can code each of these definitions.

Listing 14.15   An Example of Inheriting a Template Class from a Nontemplate Class

```
// Base class definition
class A {
public:
    A(int aval) { Construct something for A }
    void FuncA() { Do something }
};

template <class T>
class BTemplt : public A {
public:
    BTemplt(int val1, int val2);
    ...
};

// Derived template definition
template <class T>
BTemplt<T>::BTemplt(int val1, int val2) :
A(val2)
{
    Construct something for Btemplt
}

// Create an instance and use it
BTemplt<int> MyStuff(1, 5);
MyStuff.FuncA();
```

This type of inheritance is straightforward. In this example, no matter what type is passed into the class template, all the public class A behaviors are available to MyStuff.

Inheriting a Nontemplate Class from a Template Class. Listing 14.16, which shows a template (ATmplt) and a derived normal class (B), is a little more interesting.

Listing 14.16   An Example of Inheriting a Nontemplate Class from a Template Class

```
// Base template definition
template <class T>
class ATemplt {
public:
    ATemplt(int aval);
    void FuncA() { Do something }
    ...
};

template <class T>
ATemplt<T>::ATemplt(int aval)
{
    Contruct something for ATemplt
}

// Derived class definition
class B : public ATemplt<int> {
public:
    B(int val1, int val2);
};

B::B(int, int val2) : ATemplt<int>(val2)
{
    Construct something for B
}

// Create an instance and use it
B MyStuff(1, 5);
MyStuff.FuncA();
```

Again, most of this example is pretty straightforward. However, one noteworthy item stands out. Because a normal class is being inherited from the template, you must specify the particular instance of ATemplt when declaring class B. In this case, class B doesn't derive from template ATemplt, but from class ATemplt<int>.

Because the generic type for ATemplt is hard-coded into the definition of class B, users of class B do not have to use any sort of template-specific syntax. In fact, programmers should be able to use objects of class B without ever being aware of the fact that some of the objects' behaviors are implemented with a base template.

Inheriting a Template Class from Another Template Class. Finally, listing 14.17 shows how a template class can be inherited from another template class. This scheme enables the generic types of one template to be linked intrinsically to the generic types of its base class.

Listing 14.17 An Example of Inheriting a Template Class from Another Template Class

```
// Base template definition
template <class T>
class ATemplt {
public:
    ATemplt(int aval);
    void FuncA() { Do something }
    ...
};

template <class T>
ATemplt<T>::ATemplt(int aval)
{
    Contruct something for ATemplt
}

// Derived template definition
template <class T>
class BTemplt : public ATemplt<T> {
public:
    BTemplt(int val1, int val2);
    ...
};

template <class T>
BTemplt<T>::BTemplt(int val1, int val2) :
ATemplt<T>(val2)
{
    Construct something for BTemplt
}

// Create an instance and use it
BTemplt<int> MyStuff(1, 5);
MyStuff.FuncA();
```

When one template class derives from another, as in this example, the base class can receive its generic types from the derived class, which in turn receives its generic types from a template instantiation.

The derived template doesn't necessarily have to use a generic type that is used only by a base template. However, the derived template must at least declare the generic type and pass it to the base template. To demonstrate this, listing 14.18 shows a derived class that requires two generic types, T1 and T2. The derived class, however, uses only T1 and accepts only T2, so the derived class can instantiate a base class that accepts a T2 generic type.

```
// Base template definition
template <class T2>
class BaseTemplt {
public:
    BaseTemplt(int aval);
    void FuncA() { Do something }
    T2 AnInstanceOfT2;
};

template <class T2>
BaseTemplt<T2>::BaseTemplt(int aval)
{
    Contruct something for BaseTemplt
}

// Derived template definition
template <class T1, class T2>
class DerivedTemplt : public BaseTemplt<T2> {
public:
    DerivedTemplt(int val1, int val2);
    T1 AnInstanceOfT1;
};

template <class T1, class T2>
DerivedTemplt<T1, T2>::DerivedTemplt(int val1, int val2) :
                    BaseTemplt<T2>(val2)
{
    Construct something for DerivedTemplt
}

// Create an instance and use it
DerivedTemplt<int, char*> MyStuff(1, 5);
MyStuff.FuncA();
```

Building Container Templates

A *container* is a programming construct designed to facilitate the storage, organization, and manipulation of objects. Programmers typically use containers throughout the run of a program so that they hold on to objects that they know they will need later.

The range of container types can be mind-boggling. Data structures like stacks, queues, trees, lists, vectors, bags, sets, dictionaries, associative arrays, and hash tables are all specialized examples of containers (and new types emerge from academia every year). Each of these different container types has compromises and trade-offs related to performance, ease of use, implementation size, and so on.

C++ provides myriad different ways to create and implement container objects. Before templates came along, most of these implementations depended on inheritance to provide the flexibility needed to build containers capable of storing arbitrary data types. However, the advent of templates has made it easier to create container classes and has eliminated many of the disadvantages of using an inheritance-based approach.

The Container Philosophy

People unfamiliar with containers usually wonder what they can accomplish with containers that they cannot accomplish with, for example, a standard C++ array.

The big problem with arrays is that you must declare them with a fixed size. Regardless of whether you declare an array on the stack or off the heap by using new, the array's subscript limits the array from growing or shrinking. If you specify a subscript that is too small, the program runs the risk of overflowing the array. If you specify a subscript that is too large, you waste memory and compromise both efficiency and speed.

Containers are typically implemented as dynamic data structures, so memory for their use is allocated off the heap as needed. If you add an item to a container, you use new to allocate memory for a reference or copy of that item (depending on the implementation). When you remove items from the container, this memory can be freed for use by other areas of the program.

Allocating and deallocating memory dynamically is certainly slower than using statically declared data structures, but the flexibility gained from a dynamic container usually compensates for the performance penalty. Sophisticated containers can play games with preallocating a certain number of items and allocating new items only when they are needed. Of course, such caching schemes suffer from some of the same problems as fixed-sized arrays if the initial number of created items is greater than the program will ever use, but such problems are more of an implementation concern than a reason not to use containers.

A full-fledged discussion of containers is beyond the scope of this chapter (indeed, it would very easy to write a long book just about implementing containers). Still, one of the most valuable uses of templates is to create container classes. For this reason, the next few sections take you step by step through the creation of a simple list container.

Note

The Microsoft Foundation Class library uses templates to implement six collection classes: CArray, CMap, CList, CTypedPtrArray, CTypedPtrList, and CTypedPtrMap.

The Inheritance-Based List Class

To give you a feel for some of the reasons that the template approach is superior to the inheritance approach, this section starts by building a linked-list class that relies on an inheritance approach. The list class that this section presents is by no means the definitive model for building a linked-list container. In fact, this fairly low-powered implementation has serious performance problems and supports only the most rudimentary operations. However, the goal of this section is not to provide instruction on how to best build containers in general, but to demonstrate how a template implementation is superior to an inheritance-based implementation. The linked-list class presented in this section serves this particular purpose quite nicely.

The List Class Implementation. A linked list is a container that consists of a list of nodes. Each of these nodes is connected to the others with link pointers in a linear fashion. The last node has a NULL link pointer. Figure 14.1 shows a conceptual representation of what a linked list looks like.

Fig. 14.1

A linked list.

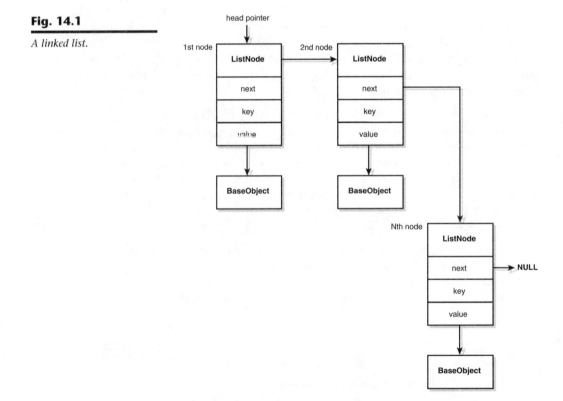

Your linked list implementation relies on three different classes: the linked-list class, a node class, and a base object class. Listing 14.19 shows the code for the node class.

Listing 14.19   inhlist.cpp, a Linked-List Node Class

```
class ListNode {
public:
    ListNode(int NewKey, BaseObject& NewObject);
    void SetNext(ListNode* pNewNext);
    BaseObject* GetContents() const;
    int GetKey() const;
    ListNode* GetNext() const;

private:
    ListNode* next;
    BaseObject* value;
    int key;
};

// Constructor
ListNode::ListNode(int NewKey, BaseObject& NewObject) :

    // Initialize member data
    next(NULL),
    value(&NewObject),
    key(NewKey)
{ }

// Public member functions
void ListNode::SetNext(ListNode* pNewNext)
{
    next = pNewNext;
}

BaseObject* ListNode::GetContents() const
{
    return value;
}

int ListNode::GetKey() const
{
    return key;
}

ListNode* ListNode::GetNext() const
{
        return next;
```

The ListNode object is not very sophisticated, which is just fine. Sophistication usually means larger objects and slower performance, which are not things that you want to introduce when building containers.

A ListNode consists of a key, a value, and a pointer to the next ListNode in the list. The key is an integer that is provided by the application that inserts items into the list. The application uses this key when it wants to find items in the list or to remove items from the list. The fact that the key is hard-coded as an integer is a potential problem, because an application might want to use a key other than a simple integer.

This template implementation will handle this problem, however.

The value pointer stores the node's contents. These contents consist of a pointer to an instance of the BaseObject class. The BaseObject class is essentially an empty class definition:

```
class BaseObject {
// Empty
};
```

The only objects that the linked-list class knows how to store are BaseObjects, so to put items into the list, users must derive them from the BaseObject class.

The final element of the linked list is the List class itself, which is presented in listing 14.20.

Listing 14.20   inhlist.cpp, the Main List Class

```
// Boolean type
typedef unsigned char Boolean;
const Boolean TRUE = 1;
const Boolean FALSE = 0;

class List {
public:
    List();
    ~List();
    Boolean Add(int NewKey, BaseObject& NewObject);
    Boolean Remove(int SearchKey);
    BaseObject* Find(int SearchKey) const;
    BaseObject* operator[](int OrderKey);
    int GetListSize() const;

private:
    ListNode* head;
    unsigned int NumItems;
};

// Constructor
List::List() :

    // Initialize member data
    head(NULL),
    NumItems(0)
{ }

// Destructor
List::~List()
{
    // Delete all the nodes in the list
    while (head) {
        ListNode* pTemp = head->GetNext();
        delete head;
        head = pTemp;
    }
```

```
}

// Public member functions
Boolean List::Add(int NewKey, BaseObject& NewObject)
{
    // Allocate memory for the new node
    ListNode* pNewNode = new ListNode(NewKey, NewObject);
    if (!pNewNode)
        return FALSE;

    // Insert the node into the list
    pNewNode->SetNext(head);
    head = pNewNode;
    NumItems++;
    return TRUE;
}

Boolean List::Remove(int SearchKey)
{
    ListNode* pCursor = head;

    // Is there a list?
    if (!pCursor)
        return FALSE;

    // Check the head first
    if (pCursor->GetKey() == SearchKey) {
        head = pCursor->GetNext();
        delete pCursor;
        NumItems_;
        return TRUE;
    }

    // Scan the list
    while (pCursor->GetNext()) {
        if (pCursor->GetNext()->GetKey() == SearchKey) {
            ListNode* pTemp = pCursor->GetNext();
            pCursor->SetNext(pTemp->GetNext());
            delete pTemp;
            NumItems_;
            return TRUE;
        }
    }
    return FALSE;
}

BaseObject* List::Find(int SearchKey) const
{
    ListNode* pCursor = head;
    while (pCursor) {
        if (pCursor->GetKey() == SearchKey)
            return pCursor->GetContents();
        else
            pCursor = pCursor->GetNext();
    }
    return NULL;
```

(continues)

```
                                                                    
  Listing 14.20  Continued                                          

  }

  int List::GetListSize() const
  {
      return NumItems;
  }

  // Operators
  BaseObject* List::operator[](int OrderKey)
  {
      ListNode* pCursor = head;
      int Count = 1;
      while (pCursor) {
          if (Count++ == OrderKey)
              return pCursor->GetContents();
          pCursor = pCursor->GetNext();
      }
          return NULL;
```

The List class is a little more exciting than the ListNode class because so many things are going on. As the class declaration indicates, this class supports inserting and deleting nodes, searching for a node based on its key, querying the list size, and retrieving a node based on its order in the list (rather than by its key).

The List constructor does nothing but initialize some local member data. The destructor moves through the list and deletes any nodes remaining in the list.

The Add() method allocates storage for a new ListNode object and sets the appropriate fields in the object through the ListNode constructor. The new node is then placed at the head of the list.

The Remove() method first checks whether the list includes at least one node, and if so, checks whether the list has only one node. If there is only one node (the head), this node is removed separately. Otherwise, a cursor moves through the list, looking one node ahead of its current position. If the List class finds the node that must be removed, the next pointer of the current node is set equal to the next pointer of the next node. The List class then uses the delete operator to remove the appropriate node.

The Find() method simply moves through the list until it finds a ListNode with a key equal to the search key. On finding such a key, Find() returns to the calling application the ListNode's value pointer.

The overloaded operator[] returns the value pointer of the Nth ListNode in the list. Note that this operation is independent of any node's key value. Therefore, MyList.Find(5) is not necessarily the same node as MyList[5]. The operator[] accomplishes this task by moving through the list and maintaining a count of its current position. On reaching the appropriate node, operator[] returns to the calling application the node's value pointer.

To demonstrate this List class in action, listing 14.21 shows a program that adds three items to a list and then removes them one at a time.

Listing 14.21   inhlist.cpp, Using the Inheritance-Based List

```
struct IntClass : public BaseObject {
    IntClass(int NewInt) { theInt = NewInt; }
    int theInt;
};

void ShowList(List& theList)
{
    int Loop;
    cout << "The list: ( ";
    for (Loop = 0; Loop < theList.GetListSize(); Loop++) {
        if (Loop) cout << ", ";
        IntClass* pIntClass = (IntClass*) theList[Loop+1];
        cout << pIntClass->theInt;
    }
    cout << " )\n";
}

void main()
{
    List theList;
    IntClass Int1(34), Int2(22), Int3(675);

    theList.Add(1, Int1);
    theList.Add(2, Int2);
    theList.Add(3, Int3);
    ShowList(theList);
    theList.Remove(2);
    ShowList(theList);
    theList.Remove(1);
    ShowList(theList);
    theList.Remove(3);
    ShowList(theList);
}
```

Problems with the List Class. The List class is a complete and usable implementation of a linked list, but it has some serious flaws. Although none of these flaws is fatal, they certainly make the List class less desirable to use.

The biggest problem with this implementation is that everything placed into the list must derive from the BaseObject class. Many programmers do not want to pick up the additional overhead of inheriting from BaseObject, even though in its current form the class does nothing. In a more practical form, however, a class like BaseObject would probably implement a whole range of behaviors that are common to an entire object inheritance tree. This range could include such things as a virtual isA() method that returns the name of the class, or support for trapping errors.

Merging different code bases together also presents problems. If you want to integrate your code with a third-party class library, placing any of the third-party objects into this List class becomes virtually impossible.

Finally, this sort of inheritance dependency makes it impossible to store integral types and simple, standard user-defined classes in the List class without the help of a wrapper class. Listing 14.21 demonstrates the sort of hoops that you must leap through just to store a series of integers. If you want a program to store a variety of integral types in a List class, you would have to wrap each type in a class that derives from BaseObject.

Of course, one alternative is to have the ListNode value pointer simply be a void pointer. But this is C++, not the dark and dangerous world of C! Using a void value pointer in the List class sacrifices any sort of type checking and requires that the application rely on intricate casting. With a void pointer implementation, there is no way to be completely sure that Find() or operator[] will return the item that you expect. If a void pointer is cast to a particular object type, and the pointer doesn't point to an instance of that object, a call to one of that object class's methods is almost certain to lead to a horrible program (or even system) crash.

Also, the List class requires that all the application keys be integers. This decision is pretty arbitrary, considering that some applications are sure to want to use strings and others will want to use user-defined types.

The solution to all these problems is to use a template-based container.

A Better Way with Templates

One great thing about porting the inheritance-based List class to templates is that you don't have to change any of the core logic. The code that actually performs operations remains almost completely intact, while only the definitions and declarations change. Even better, ugly constructs such as BaseObject and IntClass disappear completely.

Listing 14.22 shows the entire list template and a program that uses the template in a manner similar to listing 14.21. The name changes to ListT to reflect the fact that the list is implemented with templates.

Listing 14.22   tmpllist.cpp, the ListT Template

```
#include <iostream.h>
#include <afx.h>

// Boolean
typedef unsigned char Boolean;

// LIST NODE
template <class KeyType, class ValType>
class ListNodeT {
public:
    ListNodeT(KeyType NewKey, ValType& NewObject);
```

```
        void SetNext(ListNodeT* pNewNext);
        ValType* GetContents() const;
        KeyType GetKey() const;
        ListNodeT* GetNext() const;

private:
        ListNodeT* next;
        ValType* value;
        KeyType key;
};

// Constructor
template <class KeyType, class ValType>
ListNodeT<KeyType, ValType>::ListNodeT(KeyType  NewKey,
                              ValType& NewObject) :

        // Initialize member data
        next(NULL),
        value(&NewObject),
        key(NewKey)
{ }

// Public member functions
template <class KeyType, class ValType>
void ListNodeT<KeyType, ValType>::SetNext(ListNodeT* pNewNext)
{
        next = pNewNext;
}

template <class KeyType, class ValType>
ValType* ListNodeT<KeyType, ValType>::GetContents() const
{
        return value;
}

template <class KeyType, class ValType>
KeyType ListNodeT<KeyType, ValType>::GetKey() const
{
        return key;
}

template <class KeyType, class ValType>
ListNodeT<KeyType, ValType>* ListNodeT<KeyType, ValType>::GetNext() const
{
        return next;
}


// LIST
template <class KeyType, class ValType>
class ListT {
public:
        ListT();
        ~ListT();
        Boolean Add(KeyType NewKey, ValType& NewObject);
        Boolean Remove(KeyType SearchKey);
```

V

Advanced Programming

(continues)

Listing 14.22   Continued

```
        ValType* Find(KeyType SearchKey) const;
        ValType* operator[](int Position);
        int GetListSize() const;

private:
        ListNodeT<KeyType, ValType>* head;
        unsigned int NumItems;
};

// Constructor
template <class KeyType, class ValType>
ListT<KeyType, ValType>::ListT() :

        // Initialize member data
        head(NULL),
        NumItems(0)
{ }

// Destructor
template <class KeyType, class ValType>
ListT<KeyType, ValType>::~ListT()
{
        // Delete all the nodes in the list
        while (head) {
                ListNodeT<KeyType, ValType>* pTemp = head->GetNext();
                delete head;
                head = pTemp;
        }
}

// Public member functions
template <class KeyType, class ValType>
Boolean ListT<KeyType, ValType>::Add(KeyType  NewKey,
                                     ValType& NewObject)
{
        // Allocate memory for the new node
        ListNodeT<KeyType, ValType>* pNewNode =
                new ListNodeT<KeyType, ValType>(NewKey, NewObject);
        if (!pNewNode)
                return FALSE;

        // Insert the node into the list
        pNewNode->SetNext(head);
        head = pNewNode;
        NumItems++;
        return TRUE;
}

template <class KeyType, class ValType>
Boolean ListT<KeyType, ValType>::Remove(KeyType SearchKey)
{
        ListNodeT<KeyType, ValType>* pCursor = head;

        // Is there a list?
```

```
    if (!pCursor)
        return FALSE;

    // Check the head first
    if (pCursor->GetKey() == SearchKey) {
        head = pCursor->GetNext();
        delete pCursor;
        NumItems_;
        return TRUE;
}

    // Scan the list
    while (pCursor->GetNext()) {
        if (pCursor->GetNext()->GetKey() == SearchKey) {
            ListNodeT<KeyType, ValType>* pTemp =
                pCursor->GetNext();
            pCursor->SetNext(pTemp->GetNext());
            delete pTemp;
            NumItems_;
            return TRUE;
        }
    }
    return FALSE;
}

template <class KeyType, class ValType>
ValType* ListT<KeyType, ValType>::Find(KeyType SearchKey) const
{
    ListNodeT<KeyType, ValType>* pCursor = head;
    while (pCursor) {
        if (pCursor->GetKey() == SearchKey)
            return pCursor->GetContents();
        else
            pCursor = pCursor->GetNext();
    }
    return NULL;
}

template <class KeyType, class ValType>
int ListT<KeyType, ValType>::GetListSize() const
{
    return NumItems;
}

// Operators
template <class KeyType, class ValType>
ValType* ListT<KeyType, ValType>::operator[](int Position)
{
    ListNodeT<KeyType, ValType>* pCursor = head;
    int Count = 1;
    while (pCursor) {
        if (Count++ == Position)
            return pCursor->GetContents();
        pCursor = pCursor->GetNext();
    }
    return NULL;
```

(continues)

Listing 14.22 Continued

```
}

// Now use it all

template <class T>
void ShowList(T& theList)
{
    int Loop;
    cout << "The list: ( ";
    for (Loop = 0; Loop < theList.GetListSize(); Loop++) {
        if (Loop) cout << ", ";
        cout << *theList[Loop+1];
    }
    cout << " )\n";
}

void main()
{
    int Int1 = 34, Int2 = 22, Int3 = 675;
    ListT<int, int>  theIntList;
    theIntList.Add(1, Int1);
    theIntList.Add(2, Int2);
    theIntList.Add(3, Int3);
    ShowList(theIntList);
    theIntList.Remove(2);
    ShowList(theIntList);
    theIntList.Remove(1);
    ShowList(theIntList);
    theIntList.Remove(3);
    ShowList(theIntList);

    CString Str1("Here we are"), Str2("There you go"),
    Str3("What up?");
    ListT<CString, CString>  theStrList;
    theStrList.Add("Bob quote", Str1);
    theStrList.Add("Frank quote", Str2);
    theStrList.Add("Sally quote", Str3);
    ShowList(theStrList);
    theStrList.Remove("Frank quote");
    ShowList(theStrList);
    theStrList.Remove("Bob quote");
    ShowList(theStrList);
    theStrList.Remove("Sally quote");
    ShowList(theStrList);
}
```

This version of the linked list provides the same capabilities without the liabilities of the inheritance-based list. Because the application fills in both the types of the key and the value, this template allows for the creation of containers that can hold anything and that are indexed on almost any type of value.

One potential problem is that the key type must support `operator==()`. If you want to use the `ListT` template with a key type that doesn't have an `operator==()`, you must either add one or specialize `ListT::Remove`, `ListT::Find`, and `ListT::operator[]` to support the desired type. Still, the level of key flexibility in `ListT` compared to the plain `List` class is quite dramatic.

Because `ListT` no longer relies on `BaseObject`, you can store in the class any type, including all the integral types and user-defined types and classes that are a part of MFC. Even better, integrating third-party objects with `ListT` is easy because there are no inherent dependencies on the inheritance tree. You get all these advantages without compromising the built-in C++ type-checking mechanisms.

A Quick Word about the Standard Template Library (STL)

One of the largest and most dramatic additions to the ANSI standard occurred in the summer of 1994 with the acceptance of the *Standard Template Library* (usually referred to as *STL*). The STL is a container class library—implemented with templates—designed with generic programming techniques devised by Alexander Stepanov, Meng Lee, David Musser, and others. It tackles the problem of creating collection classes from an algorithmic vantage point. As a result, the STL classes perform efficiently but are very flexible and extendible.

Microsoft Visual C++ 4 does not ship with an officially supported version of STL. However, because the compiler's support for templates has improved radically since version 2.0, Visual C++ can now handle most STL products with aplomb. The distribution CD-ROM includes a public domain version of STL.

Before you can start using STL, you must have a firm grasp of three simple concepts: algorithms, iterators, and containers. A program uses containers to hold type instances, iterators to access and refer to items held by a container, and algorithms to process and manipulate container contents. For example, the following code fragment shows how you might code a search through an array of integers:

```
// Declare the array
vector<int>  MyVector(100, 0);

... Do some things ...

// Now see if the number 7 is in the array
int found = binary_search(MyVector.begin(), MyVector.end(), 7);
```

In this code, `MyVector` is the container. It holds integers, as indicated by its template argument. The `binary_search()` function encapsulates the algorithm. Algorithms know nothing about the containers on which they work. Instead, they interact only with iterators, which know how to move about in containers and provide a consistent interface for inserting and extracting items. In the preceding example, `MyVector.begin()` and `MyVector.end()` are two container methods that return iterators.

The STL is a large class library consisting of many different container and algorithm types. Although STL is efficient and sophisticated, it is surprisingly approachable and easy to learn.

Using Templates in the Default Manner

By default, when your program uses templates, the compiler scans each source module for template instantiations and generates class instances as needed. These classes are then placed in that module's object file. At link time, all the object files are combined and any duplicate class instantiations are discarded.

Using templates in the default manner has several advantages and disadvantages. The greatest advantage of this strategy is that it requires the least maintenance. The compiler does all the work of generating templates as needed and sorting through duplicates at link time. In fact, the programmer doesn't need to be concerned at all with tracking template instantiations.

The biggest problem with using templates in this manner is that, because every source file that uses templates might have to generate a template class, the entire template definition must be compiled in every module. This problem has two profound implications.

First, you cannot segregate templates into separate template modules. Instead, you have to define the entire template in an include file that is then read into any source file that might have to use that template.

Second, if you don't want your template's users to see how you get things done, you cannot use templates in the default manner. Because you must define all the templates in include files, your entire template is a public entity. If your template utilizes some amazing and proprietary computing algorithm, every nuance of its implementation will be open to public scrutiny. Even if your template doesn't contain any earth-shattering code, the fact remains that anyone who has access to the appropriate header file can view every aspect of the template. If you don't believe this, look in your compiler's \MSDEV\MFC\INCLUDE directory; the afxtempl.h header file contains all the implementations for the template-based classes within MFC!

Using Explicit Instantiation

An alternative to using templates in the default manner is to use what Microsoft calls *explicit instantiation*. This approach enables you to place template instances into template source modules and compile them together. You use template source modules with template user modules, which are the modules that actually use the templates. Template user modules use header files that describe only the template declaration and not the template definition (implementation). When a template user module is compiled, every instantiation is simply recorded as a reference to an external class definition. Because the compiler knows only about the template definitions and not how the template is actually implemented, the compiler does not—and indeed, cannot—generate a new class. Even if an instantiation is the first of its type that the compiler has encountered, a new class is not generated.

At link time, the linker takes all the references to templates from the template user modules and tries to match those references with template instantiations contained in template source modules.

This approach has the inverse advantages and disadvantages of using templates in the default fashion. Clearly, this method of template compilation requires much more effort in managing program template use. You must track specific template instantiations carefully and include them in the template source modules. If a template user module is changed later to use a new instantiation of an existing template, the new instantiation must be added to a template source module. This process is tedious and prone to error.

Also, because the template's provider must anticipate all the template instantiations that a program requires, this technique becomes unrealistic for programmers planning to provide shrink-wrapped class libraries. To meet every user's potential demands, the programmer would have to include a template source module that contains instantiations for all types. Meeting this need is clearly impossible, especially if the templates are to interact with user-defined object types.

Class library developers who depend on templates are caught between a rock and a hard place. Most commercial developers will want to keep their source code hidden and proprietary, which rules out placing template implementations in header files. However, they clearly cannot use explicit instantiation because they cannot anticipate or limit the potential template instantiation demand. Most programmers facing this dilemma will either have to bite the bullet and use the default method, or shy away from using templates altogether.

The upside is that the source code modules that use the templates need access only to the template declaration, not the entire template definition. Therefore, template header files can contain only declarations, and the template's actual implementation can be hidden in the template source modules. Proprietary algorithms and programming techniques used in the implementation of the templates can be safely hidden from prying eyes.

To demonstrate how to accomplish the rather cumbersome task, listing 14.23 shows how you can modify the `RailroadCar` example (listing 14.9) to use explicit instantiation.

Listing 14.23   templts.h, contents.h, templts.cpp, and train3.cpp—the `RailroadCar` Example Using Explicit Instantiation

```
// templts.h

// The RailroadCar class template
template <class T>
class RailroadCar {
public:
    // Constructors and destructor
    RailroadCar(int NewCarNumber, T& NewContents);
```

(continues)

Listing 14.23 Continued

```cpp
    ~RailroadCar();

    // Public member functions
    void ShowContents();
    T* Unload();

private:
    T* pContents;
    int CarNumber;
};

// contents.h

// Get needed include files
#include <afx.h>

// Things to put in a RailroadCar
class Cow {
public:
    // Public member functions
    CString isA() { return "Cow"; }
    CString Moo() { return "Moo!"; }
};

class Passenger {
public:
    // Constructors and destructor
    Passenger(CString NewName) { Name = NewName; }

    // Public member functions
    CString isA() { return "Passenger"; }
    CString GetName() { return Name; }
    CString Complain() { return "Oh my poor back!"; }

private:
    CString Name;
};

// templts.cpp

#include <iostream.h>
#include "templts.h"
#include "contents.h"

// Constructor
template <class T>
RailroadCar<T>::RailroadCar(int NewCarNumber,
    T&  NewContents)
{
    CarNumber = NewCarNumber;
    pContents = &NewContents;
}
```

```
// Destructor
template <class T>
RailroadCar<T>::~RailroadCar()
{
    Unload();
}

// Public member functions
template <class T>
void RailroadCar<T>::ShowContents()
{
    cout << "Railroad car #" << CarNumber;
    cout << " is filled with " << pContents->isA();
    cout << "s\n";
}

template <class T>
T* RailroadCar<T>::Unload()
{
    T* temp = pContents;
    pContents = NULL;
    return temp;
}

// Force instantiation of templates
template RailroadCar<Cow>;
template RailroadCar<Passenger>;


// train3.cpp

#include <iostream.h>
#include "templts.h"
#include "contents.h"

void main()
{
    // At Station 1
    Cow ACow;
    Passenger APassenger("Monty");

    RailroadCar<Cow> CarNumber1(1, ACow);
    RailroadCar<Passenger> CarNumber2(2, APassenger);

    CarNumber1.ShowContents();
    CarNumber2.ShowContents();

    // Go to Station 2...
    cout << "\n..Choo..Choo..\n\n";

    // At Station 2
    Cow* AtStation2Cow = CarNumber1.Unload();
    Passenger* AtStation2Passenger =
    CarNumber2.Unload();
```

V

Advanced Programming

(continues)

```
Listing 14.23   Continued
        cout << "How was the trip, ";
        cout << AtStation2Passenger->GetName() << "?";
        cout << "  " << AtStation2Passenger->Complain();
        cout << "\n";
        cout << AtStation2Cow->Moo() << "\n";
}
```

Perhaps the most noteworthy parts of this listing are the instantiations of the templates at the end of templts.cpp. These declarations ensure that the appropriate template classes are generated for use by the train3.cpp source file.

Note that in listing 14.9, the classes that represent items placed into railroad cars must be separated into a header file, because the instantiations used in templts.cpp rely on these classes.

If you are starting to believe that using explicit template instantiation is a painful process that is probably not worth the effort, you are not alone. Most users of Visual C++ templates will probably choose to use smart templates.

From Here...

This chapter covered a lot of ground and introduced many new concepts. Templates are a powerful language extension that enables you to create "families" of classes that are all related through common functionality in ways that you cannot easily obtain through simple inheritance. You've learned how to leverage templates effectively by utilizing both basic and advanced template implementations. The following chapters should aid you in further explorations and experimentation with C++ templates:

- To learn how to prepare your applications for porting into other environments, see Chapter 12, "Cross-Platform Development."

- For further code-refinement techniques, see Chapter 13, "Exception Handling."

- To learn about run-time type identification (RTTI), a relative newcomer to the C++ feature set, see Chapter 18, "Run-Time Type Identification (RTTI)." RTTI enables programmers to query objects and determine the type of objects at run time. Although this feature sounds rather esoteric, the chapter explains why this capability can be so valuable.

CHAPTER 15

Memory-Management Techniques

The memory-management techniques of Visual C++ 4 and the Win32 API are now both easier and more powerful than ever before. Memory management is easier due to the flat Win32 programming model; no longer do you have to deal with near and far pointers. The techniques are more powerful because of the new optional heap management functions that help you manage the free store.

In this chapter, you learn how to do the following:

- Program to the new Win32 flat memory model
- Choose between frame and dynamic memory allocation
- Choose between C and C++ memory allocation
- Overload a class to use a specific memory manager
- Debug memory corruption problems
- Detect and correct memory leaks
- Understand how OLE 2 client/server applications use memory

How Applications Access Memory

This chapter focuses on specific memory-management concerns for Visual C++ 4 and Win32. Before you delve into any new features, however, this chapter briefly contrasts memory access under the Win16 and Win32 APIs.

How Win16 Applications Access Memory

Among the key decisions that Visual C++ 1.5 and Win16 API application developers must make are which memory model and segment setup to use. Each of the available memory models has its advantages and disadvantages. Table 15.1 lists the six memory models available in Visual C++ 1.5 and Win16.

Table 15.1	Visual C++ 1.5 Memory Models	
Option	**Model**	**Comment**
/AT	Tiny	64K for both code and data
/AS	Small	64K for code, 64K for data
/AM	Medium	Multiple code segments, 64K for data
/AC	Compact	64K data, multiple data segments
/AL	Large	Multiple code segments, multiple data segments
/AH	Huge	Same as the large model, plus arrays can be over 64K

Most early Windows applications—that is, Windows 3.0 applications—used the *medium memory model*. The medium memory model is quite flexible, allowing the multiple code segments required to create sophisticated applications, and was friendly to the Windows 3.0 memory manager. Later, when Microsoft released Windows 3.1 and eliminated "real mode" Windows, most application developers switched to the *large memory model*. The large memory model eased programmers' memory-management tasks, but restricted applications to running on newer and more powerful hardware.

An additional concern to Win16 application developers is which segment setup to use. The *segment setup* affected how you accessed DLLs and Windows callback functions, again adding unnecessary complexity to the already arduous task of developing Windows applications. Table 15.2 lists the three segment setups available in Visual C++ 1.5 and Win16.

Table 15.2	Visual C++ 1.5 Segment Setups
Memory Model Option	**Comment**
d	Stack segment equals the data segment. This option is the default.
u	Stack segment is not equal to data segment. Load a data segment for each function entry.
w	Stack segment is not equal to data segment. Do not load data segment for each function entry.

If the preceding discussion confuses you, don't worry. It is history and no longer concerns most Visual C++ 4 programmers.

How Win32 Applications Access Memory

With Win32, you no longer have any options to select a memory model or segment setup. There is only one memory model; it has a flat address space with 32-bit pointers that can access anywhere in the 4G (2^{32} bytes) address space. Likewise, the model does not restrict the size of data items within this address range. On Windows NT, Windows 95, and Win32s, each process runs in a flat, linear address space with 32-bit addresses. This address space is divided into two main pieces. The high memory addresses from 8000 0000H to FFFF FFFFH are reserved for operating system process and data storage. The low memory addresses from 8000 0000H to 7FFF FFFFH are available for application code and data. If you're familiar with the VMX or UNIX operating environments, you'll recognize these ranges as the System and Process memory pools. The two 64K "no man's land" areas around the application address space help catch invalid memory accesses, such as attempting to write to a null pointer.

Figure 15.1 shows the Win32 virtual address space. It's "virtual" because the size of the virtual address space can be much larger than the amount of physical RAM that you have installed; Windows uses its virtual memory subsystem to map disk space to RAM and provide the larger space.

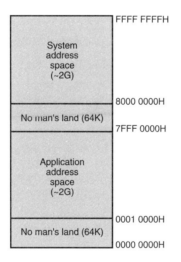

Fig. 15.1

Win32 virtual address space.

Memory-Management Functions

The Windows API provides a variety of ways to allocate memory. In Win16, you allocated memory from one or more local heaps (`LocalAlloc()`), the global heap (`GlobalAlloc()`), or the C library functions (`malloc()`, `free()`, and `realloc()`), or you used C++ operators (`new` and `delete`). Each method has its own advantages and disadvantages. Local heaps were tricky to create and switch between if you needed more than one, and each had a fixed size and a maximum size of 64K. The global heap allowed only about 8,000 allocations among all running applications. The C and C++ functions were convenient but created a lot of `__far` and `__near` hassles unless you were using the large memory model.

In Win32, you have all these options and new heap functions. However, Win32 removes most of the disadvantages of the old-style allocations. For example, local heaps are no longer restricted to 64K, the global heaps are no longer restricted to about 8,000 allocations, and `__near` and `__far` do not exist. In Win32, there is no difference between the local heap and the global heap.

The following tables list the various memory-management functions provided by Windows, the C run-time library, and MFC. Table 15.3 lists the Windows memory-management functions and shows which are available in Win16 and Win32. Table 15.4 lists the C library's memory-management functions, and table 15.5 lists the MFC functions, plus special MFC classes for memory management.

Table 15.3   Windows API Memory-Management Functions

Function	Availability Win16	Win32	Comments
CopyMemory()	No	Yes	Copies a block of memory from one location to another.
FillMemory()	No	Yes	Fills a block of memory with the specified byte value.
GetFreeSpace()	Yes	No	Gets the number of bytes in the global heap. For Win32, use `GlobalMemoryStatus()`.
GetFreeSystemResources()	Yes	No	Gets the percentage of free space for system, GDI, or USER resources.
GetProcessHeap()	No	Yes	Gets the heap handle of the calling process.
GetProcessHeaps()	No	Yes	Gets handles to all heaps that are valid for the calling process.
GetWinFlags()	Yes	No	Gets information on system and memory configuration. For Win32, use `GetSystemInfo()`.
GlobalAlloc()	Yes	Yes	Allocates a memory block. For Win32, use `malloc()`.
GlobalCompact()	Yes	No	Rearranges global memory.
GlobalDiscard()	Yes	Yes	Changes the memory block's size or `flags` to 0; same as calling `GlobalReAlloc()` with a size of 0.
GlobalDosAlloc()	Yes	No	Allocates the global memory that MS-DOS can access.
GlobalDosFree()	Yes	No	Frees global memory.
GlobalFix()	Yes	No	Prevents a memory block from moving in linear memory.
GlobalFlags()	Yes	Yes	Gets information about the memory block.
GlobalFree()	Yes	Yes	Frees a memory block.
GlobalHandle()	Yes	Yes	Gets the handle for the memory block.
GlobalHandleToSel()	Yes	No	Gets the selector for the global handle.
GlobalInfo()	Yes	No	Gets information on the global heap.
GlobalLock()	Yes	Yes	Locks a memory block.

Function	Availability Win16	Win32	Comments
GlobalLRUNewest()	Yes	No	Marks a memory block as the newest, least recently used.
GlobalLRUOldest()	Yes	No	Marks a memory block as oldest, least recently used.
GlobalMemoryStatus()	No	Yes	Gets information about current available memory.
GlobalNext()	Yes	No	Gets information on the next object in the global heap.
GlobalNotify()	Yes	No	Installs the callback function for the current task.
GlobalPageLock()	Yes	No	Marks a selector as fixed in physical memory.
GlobalPageUnlock()	Yes	No	Unmarks a selector as fixed in physical memory.
GlobalReAlloc()	Yes	Yes	Changes the size or flags of the memory block.
GlobalSize()	Yes	Yes	Gets the size of the memory block.
GlobalUnfix()	Yes	No	Enables a memory block to move in linear memory.
GlobalUnlock()	Yes	Yes	Unlocks the memory block.
GlobalUnWire()	Yes	No	Windows 2.x-specific function.
GlobalWire()	Yes	No	Moves an object to lock memory and increments the lock count. Windows 2.x only.
HeapAlloc()	No	Yes	Allocates a memory block from a heap.
HeapCompact()	No	Yes	Coalesces adjacent free blocks and decommits large free blocks of memory.
HeapCreate()	No	Yes	Creates a heap.
HeapDestroy()	No	Yes	Destroys a heap.
HeapFree()	No	Yes	Frees a memory block allocated from a heap.
HeapLock()	No	Yes	Attempts to acquire the critical section object, or lock, for the specified heap.
HeapReAlloc()	No	Yes	Changes the size of flags of the heap memory block.
HeapSize()	No	Yes	Gets the size of the heap memory block.
HeapUnlock()	No	Yes	Releases the ownership of the critical section object, or lock, for the specified heap.

V

Advanced Programming

(continues)

Table 15.3 Continued

Function	Availability Win16	Win32	Comments
HeapValidate()	No	Yes	Scans the memory blocks in the heap to verify that the control structures are in a consistent state.
IsBadCodePtr()	Yes	Yes	Checks for read access at the specified address.
IsBadHugeReadPtr()	Yes	Yes	Checks for read access in the specified address range.
IsBadHugeWritePtr()	Yes	Yes	Checks for write access in the specified address range.
IsBadReadPtr()	Yes	Yes	Checks for read access in the specified address range.
IsBadStringPtr()	Yes	Yes	Checks for read access to the complete string.
IsBadWritePtr()	Yes	Yes	Checks for write access in the specified address range.
LimitEmsPages()	No	No	Limits the amount of expanded memory assigned to an application. Windows 2.x only.
LocalAlloc()	Yes	Yes	Allocates a memory block. For Win32, same as GlobalAlloc().
LocalCompact()	Yes	No	Rearranges local memory.
LocalDiscard()	Yes	Yes	Changes the memory block's size or flags to 0; same as calling GlobalReAlloc() with a size of 0.
LocalFirst()	Yes	No	Gets information on the first object in the local heap.
LocalFlags()	Yes	Yes	Gets information about the memory block.
LocalFree()	Yes	Yes	Frees a memory block.
LocalHandle()	Yes	Yes	Gets the handle for the memory block.
LocalInfo()	Yes	No	Gets information on the local heap.
LocalInit()	Yes	No	Initializes an additional local heap at the specified address.
LocalLock()	Yes	Yes	Locks a memory block.
LocalNext()	Yes	No	Gets information on the next object in the local heap.
LocalReAlloc()	Yes	Yes	Changes the size or flags of the memory block.
LocalShrink()	Yes	No	Changes the size of the local heap.
LocalSize()	Yes	Yes	Gets the size of the memory block.

Function	Availability Win16	Win32	Comments
LocalUnlock()	Yes	Yes	Unlocks the memory block.
LockSegment()	Yes	No	Locks a segment at the specified address.
MoveMemory()	No	Yes	Moves a block of memory from one location to another.
SetSwapAreaSize()	Yes	No	Increases the amount of physical memory reserved for code segments.
UnlockSegment()	Yes	No	Unlocks a discardable memory segment.
VirtualAlloc()	No	Yes	Reserves or commits a set of virtual pages.
VirtualFree()	No	Yes	Releases a set of virtual pages.
VirtualLock()	No	Yes	Locks into physical memory a region of virtual memory.
VirtualProtect()	No	Yes	Changes the access protection on a set of virtual pages.
VirtualProtectEx()	No	Yes	Changes the access protection on a set of virtual pages in another process.
VirtualQuery()	No	Yes	Gets information about a set of virtual pages.
VirtualQueryEx()	No	Yes	Gets information about a set of virtual pages in another process.
VirtualUnlock()	No	Yes	Unlocks a set of virtual pages.
ZeroMemory()	No	Yes	Fills a block of memory with zeros.

Table 15.4   C Library Memory-Management Functions

Function	Availability Visual C++ 1.5	Visual C++ 4	Comments
_alloca()	Yes	Yes	Allocates memory from the stack.
_bfreeseg()	Yes	No	Destroys a based heap.
_bheapseg()	Yes	No	Creates a based heap.
calloc()	Yes	Yes	Allocates memory initialized to 0.
_expand()	Yes	Yes	Expands or shrinks a block of memory without moving it.
free()	Yes	Yes	Frees an allocated block.
_freect()	Yes	No	Gets available space in the near heap.

(continues)

V

Advanced Programming

Table 15.4 Continued

Function	Availability Visual C++ 1.5	Visual C++ 4	Comments
_halloc()	Yes	No	Allocates a memory block 64K or greater.
_heapadd()	Yes	Yes	Adds memory to the C library heap. This function was also available in Visual C++ 2.
_heapchk()	Yes	Yes	Checks the C library heap for consistency. This function is available only on Windows NT.
_heapmin()	Yes	Yes	Releases unused memory in the C library heap. This function is available only on Windows NT.
_heapset()	Yes	Yes	Fills free C library heap entries with a specified value. This function is available only on Windows NT.
_heapwalk()	Yes	Yes	Gets information about each entry in the C library heap. This function is available only on Windows NT.
_hfree()	Yes	No	Frees a block allocated by _halloc().
malloc()	Yes	Yes	Allocates a block of memory from the C library heap.
_memavl()	Yes	No	Gets the number of bytes available in the near heap.
_memmax()	Yes	No	Gets the size of the largest available block in the near heap.
_msize()	Yes	Yes	Gets the size of the allocated block.
_query_new_handler()	No	Yes	Gets the current new handler routine as set by _set_new_handler().
_query_new_mode()	No	Yes	Gets the new handler mode set by _set_new_mode for malloc().
realloc()	Yes	Yes	Reallocates a block to a new size.
_set_new_handler()	Yes	Yes	Enables the error-handling mechanism when the new operator fails to allocate memory.
_set_new_mode()	No	Yes	Sets the new handler mode for malloc().
_standard_new_handler()	No	Yes	Generates an xalloc() exception when new fails.
xalloc()	No	Yes	Throws an optional C++ exception when new fails.

Table 15.5 MFC Library Memory-Management Functions and Classes

Function	Availability MFC 2.5	MFC 4.0	Comments
AfxAllocMemoryDebug()	Yes	No	Internal MFC function to allocate a memory object with debugging information. Uses malloc() to allocate memory. Debug version only.
AfxCheckMemory()	Yes	Yes	Validates free store objects allocated by new.
AfxDoForAllObjects()	Yes	Yes	Iterates overall CObject objects in the free store. Debug version only.
AfxDumpMemoryLeaks()	Yes	No	Internal function to dump memory leaks when an application terminates.
AfxEnableMemoryTracking()	Yes	Yes	Enables or disables memory allocation tracking. Debug version only.
AfxFreeMemoryDebug()	Yes	No	Internal MFC function to free a memory object. Uses free to deallocate memory. Debug version only.
AfxIsMemoryBlock()	Yes	Yes	Checks whether the diagnostic version of new allocated the address.
AfxIsValidAddress()	Yes	Yes	Tests whether any address is with the program's memory space.
AfxIsValidString()	Yes	Yes	Tests whether the address points to a valid string.
afxMemDF	Yes	Yes	Global variable for tuning allocation diagnostics.
AfxSetAllocHook()	Yes	Yes	Defines a function to call before every memory allocation. Debug version only.
AfxThrowMemoryException()	Yes	Yes	Generates a CMemoryException() exception.
CMemoryException()	Yes	Yes	Predefined memory exception class for use when memory errors occur.
CMemoryState()	Yes	Yes	Class to help detect memory leaks.

Memory Allocation

There are two types of memory allocation: frame allocation and heap allocation. Frame allocation uses memory from the program stack. Heap allocation uses memory from the free store.

Frame Allocation

In C, frame-allocated variables are often called "automatic" variables because the compiler automatically allocates the space for them. The key difference between C and C++ is that in C++, if a given object has a destructor, the destructor is called when the frame variable goes out of scope.

As the following example shows, even simple frame allocation can create heap allocations:

```
void StackFrame(void)
{
        CString    scope0 = "0000"; // scope0 constructor called
        if (SomeTest()) {
            CString scope1 = "1111"; // scope1 constructor called
        } // scope1 destructor called
} //    scope0 destructor call
```

In this example, variables scope0 and scope1 are frame allocations. In the case of CString, however, a heap allocation is used to store the array of characters. Here's how a frame-allocated CString variable can cause objects to be allocated on the heap:

Note

Some of the code in this chapter consists of excerpts from the MFC class source code. To avoid violating Microsoft's copyright, we have not included such code on the companion CD.

```
Portions from mfc/src/strcore.cpp
...
///////////////////////////////////////////////////////////////////
// More sophisticated construction
CString::CString(LPCTSTR lpsz)
{
        int nLen;
        if ((nLen = SafeStrlen(lpsz)) == 0)
          Init();
        else
        {
          AllocBuffer(nLen);
          memcpy(m_pchData, lpsz, nLen*sizeof(TCHAR));
        }
}
...
void CString::AllocBuffer(int nLen)
// always allocate one extra character for '\0' termination
// assumes [optimistically] that data length will equal allocation length
```

```
        {
            ASSERT(nLen >= 0);
            ASSERT(nLen <= INT_MAX - 1);      // max size (enough room for 1
                                              //extra)
            if (nLen == 0)
            {
                Init();
            }
            else
            {
                m_pchData = new TCHAR[nLen+1];      // may throw an excpetion
                m_pchData[nLen] = '\0';
                m_nDataLength = nLen;
                m_nAllocLength = nLen;
            }
        }
```

The CString constructor takes the character string as a parameter. After ensuring that the string is not empty, the constructor calls the AllocBuffer() member function. This function call uses the new operator, triggering the heap allocation.

Stack Allocation

C++ directly supports heap allocation and deallocation of objects, and arrays of objects, by using the new and delete operators. These operators allocate memory for objects from a pool called the *free store*. In C, this free store is called the *heap*. Although the terms differ in most environments, the actual memory allocation from the operating systems differs little because most new operator functions use malloc() to allocate the memory. When you use new to allocate an object, the operator returns a pointer to the object. The default operator new returns NULL if there is insufficient memory for the allocation. The operator new is quite flexible. In the next section, you learn how MFC takes advantage of this flexibility to create a debug memory allocator.

Overloading new and delete

At first glance, the new and delete operators appear as simple memory allocators like malloc() and free. However, the operators are much more. They are a built-in part of the C++ language, and as C++ operators they can be overloaded and reimplemented like other operators can be. This flexibility has enabled Microsoft to build into MFC a complete diagnostic facility. The CObject class's operator definitions look like this:

```
Portions from mfc/include/afx.h:
class CObject
{
    public:
    // Object model (types, destruction, allocation)
    virtual CRuntimeClass* GetRuntimeClass() const;
    virtual ~CObject();  // virtual destructors are necessary

    // Diagnostic allocations
    void* AFX_CDECL operator new(size_t, void* p);
    void* AFX_CDECL operator new(size_t nSize);
    void AFX_CDECL operator delete(void* p);
```

```
#ifdef _DEBUG
        // for file name/line number tracking using DEBUG_NEW
        void* AFX_CDECL operator new(size_t nSize,
                LPCSTR lpszFileName, int nLine);
#endif
    ...
}
```

In afx.h, CObject appears to be always using a custom version of new; however, this is not the case. Examining afx.inl reveals that this new operator is simply defined to use the system new operator, ::operator new:

```
From: mfc/include/afx.inl
_AFX_INLINE void* CObject::operator new(size_t nSize)
{ return ::operator new(nSize); }
```

Later in this section, you see how to use a debug version of the new operator in MFC to track down memory corruption and memory leaks.

Handling Out-of-Memory Conditions

Like it or not, every application that you write should handle out-of-memory conditions. With Visual C++ 4, you have several options from which to choose:

- The new operator returning NULL (default)
- The new operator sending a CMemoryException exception (MFC)
- The new operator sending an xalloc C++ exception (ANSI C++ draft)

Using CMemoryException() leverages the MFC exception code and frees you from checking the return value of allocations.

Using the New Heap Memory Functions

Win32 has introduced a new suite of memory-management functions: the heap interface. The heap functions enable you to create a private memory-management area, referred to as a *heap* or *private heap* throughout the rest of this chapter. Private heaps can grow dynamically and have no size restrictions, except for the logical 1G application address space or physical hardware limitations. By using heaps, you can define working sets to reduce virtual memory page swapping, control fragmentation, simplify deallocation of memory, and minimize memory corruption problems. One method to reduce swapping is to use separate heaps for data units that are not needed at the same time. For example, in an MDI application, each document could use its own heap. This would tend to group all the data needed for a document near each other in memory, thus reducing swapping. This also enables you to destruct all data elements easily by destroying the heap, instead of individually deallocating hundreds—or possibly thousands—of small items when the user closes a document.

Heap Functions

This section briefly introduces the heap-management APIs. As you will see, the functions are modeled after the standard C run-time library memory-management functions.

The HeapCreate() function creates a private heap object:

```
HANDLE HeapCreate(
DWORD  flOptions;        // heap allocation flag
DWORD  dwInitialSize;    // initial heap size
DWORD  dwMaximumSize;    // maximum heap size
```

Other heap functions use the returned handle. The initial size determines the number of committed, read-write pages initially allocated for the heap. The maximum size determines the total number of reserved pages. These pages create a contiguous block in the virtual address space of a process into which the heap can grow. If the maximum size is nonzero, the heap cannot grow larger than the specified size. For maximum performance with single-threaded applications, use the HEAP_NO_SERIALIZE flag to prevent the overhead of mutual exclusion locks when allocating or freeing memory. Also, for increased performance, choose an initial size that is similar to the standard working set size of your application. This increases your ability to group objects together.

The GetProcessHeap() function gets the handle to the heap of the calling process:

```
HANDLE GetProcessHeap(VOID)
```

You can then use this handle in the calls to the HeapAlloc(), HeapReAlloc(), HeapFree(), and HeapSize() functions. Later, you use GetProcessHeap() as a default heap from which to allocate when overloading the new operator to take a heap object.

The HeapDestroy() function destroys the specified heap object:

```
BOOL HeapDestroy(
HANDLE  hHeap);          // handle of heap
```

HeapDestroy() decommits and releases all the pages of a private heap object, and invalidates the heap's handle. The destructors for any C++ objects in the heap are not called. If you count on the destructors being executed, do not call HeapDestroy().

The HeapAlloc() function allocates a block of memory from the heap:

```
LPVOID HeapAlloc(
HANDLE  hHeap;           // handle of the private heap block
DWORD   dwFlags;         // heap allocation control flags
DWORD   dwBytes)         // number of bytes to allocate
```

You cannot move the allocated memory. To clear the contents of the allocated block, use the HEAP_ZERO_MEMORY flag. The maximum element size is approximately 512,000 bytes. For larger elements, use GlobalAlloc().

The HeapReAlloc() function reallocates a block of memory from a heap:

```
LPVOID HeapReAlloc(
HANDLE  hHeap;          // handle of a heap block
DWORD   dwFlags;        // heap reallocation flags
LPVOID  lpMem;          // address of the memory to reallocate
DWORD   dwBytes;        // number of bytes to reallocate
```

This function enables you to resize a memory block and change other memory block properties. As with HeapAlloc(), you cannot move the allocated memory.

The HeapFree() function frees a memory block that the HeapAlloc() or HeapReAlloc() function allocates from a heap:

```
BOOL HeapFree(hHeap, dwFlags, lpMem)
HANDLE  hHeap;          // handle of the heap
DWORD   dwFlags;        // heap freeing flags
LPVOID  lpMem;          // address of the memory to free
```

The HeapSize() utility function returns the size, in bytes, of a memory block that the HeapAlloc() or HeapReAlloc() function allocates from a heap:

```
DWORD HeapSize(hHeap, dwFlags, lpMem)
HANDLE  hHeap;          // handle of the heap
DWORD dwFlags  ;        // heap size control flags
LPCVOID  lpMem;         // address of the memory
                        // to return size information for
```

The HeapSize() utility function returns the size, in bytes, of a memory block that the HeapAlloc() or HeapReAlloc() function allocates from a heap:

```
DWORD HeapSize(hHeap, dwFlags, lpMem)
HANDLE  hHeap;          // handle of the heap
DWORD dwFlags  ;        // heap size control flags
LPCVOID  lpMem;         // address of the memory
                        // to return size information for
```

The HeapCompact() utility function attempts to compact a specified heap:

```
DWORD HeapCompact(hHeap, dwFlags)
HANDLE  hHeap;          // handle of the heap
DWORD dwFlags  ;        // heap control flags
LPCVOID  lpMem;         // address of the memory
                        // to return size information for
```

HeapCompact() compacts the heap by coalescing adjacent free blocks of memory and decommitting large free blocks of memory. The function does not move any in-use memory blocks.

The HeapLock() utility function attempts to acquire the critical section object, or lock, that is associated with a specified heap:

```
DWORD HeapLock(hHeap)
HANDLE  hHeap;          // handle of the heap
```

If the function succeeds, the calling thread owns the heap lock. Only the calling thread will be capable of allocating or releasing memory from the heap. The function blocks any other thread of the calling process from executing if that thread attempts to allocate or release memory from the heap. Such threads remain blocked until the thread that owns the heap lock calls the `HeapUnlock()` function.

The `HeapUnlock()` utility function releases ownership of the critical section object, or lock, that is associated with a specified heap:

```
DWORD HeapUnlock(hHeap)
HANDLE  hHeap;           // handle of the heap
```

The `HeapUnlock()` function reverses the action of the `HeapLock()` function.

Controlling Fragmentation

In large applications, especially those that run for hours or days at a time, the system and private heaps can become fragmented. One way to control fragmentation is to use a set of fixed-size heaps, or *buckets*, for allocations. For example, a set of 10 bucket heaps with sizes 32 bytes, 64 bytes, 96 bytes...256 bytes, 288 bytes, large will eliminate most fragmentation.

In some cases, the use of buckets can cause a slight loss of performance, because the allocator has to work with the bucket handler instead of just taking space from the heap. However, this loss is rarely noticeable—but heap fragmentation often causes crashes, so the cure is not as bad as the disease.

Allocating C++ Objects in Heaps

At first, the heap APIs might seem best-suited for C-style allocation; however, you can take advantage of overriding the `new` and `delete` operators to provide C++ class-specific heaps. There are two main approaches: using separate heaps on a per-class basis or specifying a heap to use when creating a new object. In both approaches, you must create `new` and `delete` operators for the classes involved. The compiler calls the overloaded operators as needed.

Per-Class Heap Allocation. The following are the fundamental code segments for creating classes that use a private heap for memory block allocation. By default, the overloaded `new` operator for an object applies to all derived classes. For example, MFC overloads only the global and `CObject` `new` operators when providing the debug memory allocator. If you want to use a separate heap in a derived class, you need only duplicate the code in the derived classes. Having a heap for every class eliminates heap fragmentation because every object in each heap is the same size.

The following `CPerClass` class definition declares `m_Heap` and `m_HeapAllocatedCount` as static members:

```
Class CPerClass {
private:
static HANDLE m_Heap;
static UINT m_HeapAllocatedCount;
public:
void *operator new( size_t size );
void operator delete( void *block );
...
...  // other class members
};
```

You allocate static members of a class only once, not separately for each instance of the class. The m_Heap member contains the handle to the heap that you use to allocate all CPerClass objects. m_HeapAllocatedCount contains the number of CPerClass objects that currently exist. If m_HeapAllocatedCount is zero when you allocate an object, you create a heap. Likewise, if m_HeapAllocatedCount becomes zero after a delete, it destroys the heap, returning the memory pool to the operating system. A separate C++ source file must initialize these static members. This code declares an instance of CPerClass's static members and initializes them.

```
HANDLE CPerClass::m_Heap = NULL;
UNIT CPerClass::m_HeapAllocatedCount = 0;
```

The code for the new operator would be in the same file as these static member definitions. Most of the time that the CPU spends in this new operator is in the HeapAlloc() function, so creating an inline version of the new operator function has little advantage. The following code snippet shows the class's operator new:

```
void *CPerClass::operator new(size_t size)
{
// if no allocated blocks, create heap
if ( m_HeapAllocatedCount == 0 ) {
m_Heap = HeapCreate(HEAP_GENERATE_EXCEPTIONS, 4096, 0 );
}
// track allocations for destroy
m_HeapAllocatedCount++;
// allocate block from heap
return HeapAlloc( m_Heap, size )
}
```

If no heap has been allocated, the code allocates one before proceeding. In any case, the counter that tracks the number of objects allocated from the heap is incremented and the newly allocated block is returned as the operator's value.

You should change the flags and arguments used for HeapCreate() depending on your needs. If you are not using exceptions, you must remove the HEAP_GENERATE_EXCEPTIONS flag. Also, if you know that you will have to allocate many CPerClass objects, increase the initial heap size. After creating the heap, you use HeapAlloc() to allocate CPerClass objects. The HeapAlloc() call uses the static member heap and the size of the object that you pass to the operator new.

The code for delete is the logical mirror of new:

```
void CPerClass::operator delete( void *object)
{
// return the object to free pool
HeapFree( m_Heap, object);
m_HeapAllocatedCount_;
// check if heap can be destroyed
if ( m_HeapAllocatedCount == 0 ) {
HeapDestroy( m_Heap );
}
}
```

This overloaded `delete` operator takes one parameter: the address of the object to be freed. `delete` simply calls `HeapFree()` to release the memory block. Also, if this block is the last one that you allocated, the operator destroys the heap.

`new` **Operators Overloaded To Use a Heap Parameter.** The following code segments demonstrate how to create a suite of classes that share a single heap. Depending on your application structure, you might be able to access the correct heap dynamically. For example, your classes might always use the active document's heap. The following code segments save the heap ID in each allocated object to guarantee access to the correct heap when deleting the object. For reasonably sized objects, this four-byte overhead is small.

```
Class CSharedClassOne {
public:
void *operator new( size_t size, HANDLE heap );
void operator delete( void *block );
...
... // other class members
};
Class CSharedClassTwo {
public:
HANDLE m_Heap;
void *operator new( size_t size, HANDLE heap );
void operator delete( void *block );
...
};
```

The member `m_Heap` stores the heap ID or the `delete` operator. The code in these examples overrides the `new` operator and hides the global `new` operator. This prevents the code from creating any objects of `CSharedClassOne` or `CSharedClassTwo` without a heap parameter. Classes that need access to the global `new`—that is, classes that have a constructor without arguments—require an additional `new` operator with a single size parameter:

```
Class CSharedClassThree {
public:
HANDLE m_Heap;
void *operator new(size_t size);
void *operator new( size_t size, HANDLE heap );
void operator delete( void *block );
...
... // other class members
};
```

The implementations for operator `new` and `delete` functions are similar to the `CPerClass` versions. The `CSharedClass` classes supply the heap parameter instead of using a static class member such as `m_Heap` in `CPerClass`:

```
void * CSharedClassOne::operator new(size_t size, HANDLE heap)
{
// allocate block from heap
CSharedClassOne *object = (CSharedClassOne *)HeapAlloc( heap, size )
// save the heap for the delete operator
object->m_Heap = heap;
```

```
return (void *)object
}
void * CSharedClassTwo::operator new(size_t size, HANDLE heap)
{
// allocate block from heap
CSharedClassTwo *object = (CSharedClassTwo *)HeapAlloc( heap, size )
// save the heap for the delete operator
object->m_Heap = heap;
return (void *)object
}
void * CSharedClassThree::operator new(size_t size)
{
// no heap specified, use the system heap
HANDLE heap = GetProcessHeap();
// allocate block from heap
CSharedClassOne *object = (CSharedClassOne *)HeapAlloc( heap, size )
// save the heap for the delete operator
object->m_Heap = heap;
return (void *)object
}
void * CSharedClassThree::operator new(size_t size, HANDLE heap)
{
// allocate block from heap
CSharedClassOne *object = (CSharedClassOne *)HeapAlloc( heap, size )
// save the heap for the delete operator
object->m_Heap = heap;
return (void *)object
}
```

The implementation for all classes is similar. Each class saves the heap identifier in the member variable m_Heap and allocates the memory block by using HeapAlloc(). In C++, each class can have only one delete operator. To keep this function as simple as possible, the new operator function in CSharedClassThree that does not have a heap parameter uses GetProcessHeap() to get the main heap for the process.

To minimize your application's working set, you can use the following type of new and delete operator overloading:

```
void CSharedClass[One¦Two¦Three]::operator delete( void *object)
{
HeapFree((( CSharedClass[One¦Two¦Three] *)object)->m_Heap, object);
}
```

Sharing a heap among related data helps keep the memory blocks physically close and reduces page swapping.

The following code fragment shows how to share the heaps and identify constructs that will not compile:

```
SomeClass( HANDLE heap)
{
// The following line is an error, no operator new(size_t) is defined
CSharedClassOne *one = new CSharedClassOne;
// *** generates compiler error
// valid uses the specified heap
CSharedClassOne *one = new CSharedClassOne(heap);
```

```
    // also allocate a two object from the same heap
    CSharedClassTwo *two = new CSharedClassTwo(heap);
    // The following line is valid, operator new(size_t) is defined
    // Object process allocated from process default heap
    CSharedClassThree *process = new CSharedClassThree;
    // Object three allocated from shared heap
    CSharedClassThree *process = new CSharedClassThree(heap);
    ....
    delete one;
    delete two;
    delete process;
    delete three;
    }
```

As you have seen, the heap APIs are much more than a few primitive APIs for C programmers. They are a great foundation for implementing advanced C++ memory-management techniques.

New C Library and MFC Memory Diagnostic Facilities

One of the most frustrating bugs is a memory corruption error, such as attempting to use an object after it has been deleted, or writing past the end of a memory block. Often the impact of the memory corruption occurs nowhere near the actual bug, but in some unrelated code. Fortunately, MFC and the C run-time library include a robust set of functionalities to help find memory corruption problems. MFC and the C run-time library also include functionality to detect memory leaks, another problem that is very hard to find. Be sure to compile with _DEBUG and link with the debug MFC libraries. The memory diagnostic functions do not exist in the optimized MFC or C run-time libraries. The file mfc/src/afxmem.cpp implements all the MFC memory diagnostic functions, and the file crt/src/dbgheap.c implements all the C run-time memory diagnostic functions.

Memory Diagnostic Functions

In Visual C++ 2, MFC provided memory diagnostic functions, but if you weren't using MFC, you were out of luck. For Visual C++ 4, Microsoft has moved most of the functions into the C run-time library. Usually, the new C run-time functions have a similar function in MFC. Before you learn about the internals of the diagnostic functions, this section takes you on a brief tour of the most used functions. Most of the functions are global C functions that afx.h and crtdbg.h define.

AfxCheckMemory() and _CrtCheckMemory() validate the free memory pool and print error messages as required:

```
    BOOL AfxCheckMemory(void);
    int _CrtCheckMemory(void)
```

If the function detects no memory corruption, it prints nothing. The function checks memory objects allocated by the default new operator or any MFC new operators.

Visual C++ 4 checks memory allocated by direct calls to underlying memory allocators, such as malloc(), GlobalAlloc(), LocalAlloc(), or HeapAlloc(). Memory corruption messages are printed to afxDump, the CDumpContent object used for all MFC diagnostic messages. It looks for corrupt guard blocks and freed blocks that have been written on.

AfxDoForAllObjects() and _CrtDoForAllClientObjects() run the specified iteration function for all objects that derive from CObject and that have been allocated with new:

```
void AfxDoForAllObjects(
void (*pfn)(CObject* pObject, void* pContext),     // iteration function
void* pContext ); // user data to pass to iteration function

void _CrtDoForAllClientObjects(
void (*pfn)(void *, void *),
void *context );
```

The pContext pointer passes arbitrary information to the specified iteration function each time that the application calls it.

The Debug version of MFC normally enables diagnostic memory tracking. Use AfxEnableMemoryTracking() to disable tracking on sections of your code that you know are allocating blocks correctly:

```
BOOL AfxEnableMemoryTracking(
BOOL bTrack ); // use TRUE to turn on memory tracking
```

You disable memory tracking when you are allocating memory in a fully debugged subsystem and want to hide the allocations from subsystems that you are trying to debug. A good example of this is in the MFC library, CObject CHandleMap::FromHandle(HANDLE h). The implementation of FromHandle() turns off tracking because MFC users do not care about this temporary object.

The afxMemDF global variable, which you can access from a debugger or your program, tunes allocation diagnostics:

```
int afxMemDF;
```

The afxMemDF variable can have the following values:

Value	Name	Responsibility
0x01	allocMemDF	Turns on the debugging allocator (the default setting in the Debug library).
0x02	delayFreeMemDF	Delays freeing memory. While your program frees a memory block, the allocator does not return that memory to the underlying operating system. This places maximum memory stress on your program.
0x04	checkAlwaysMemDF	Calls AfxCheckMemory() every time that you allocate or free memory. These calls significantly slow memory allocations and deallocations, but provide integrity checks on every allocation and deallocation. This is a quick way to spot some memory corruption problems.

`AfxSetAllocHook()` sets a hook that you call before allocating each memory block:

```
AFX_ALLOC_HOOK AfxSetAllocHook(
AFX_ALLOC_HOOK pfnAllocHook ); // called just before every allocation
```

You call the hook function from `AfxAllocMemoryDebug()` to enable the user to monitor a memory allocation and to control whether the allocation is permitted. Allocation hook functions are prototyped as follows:

```
BOOL AllocHook( // return FALSE to fail the allocation
size_t nSize, // size of the proposed memory allocation
BOOL bObject, // TRUE for objects derived from CObject
LONG lRequestNumber ); // memory allocation sequence number
```

Debug Memory Allocator

Before you can understand how to use these functions to find memory corruption and leak problems, you must understand the basic data structures that the debug memory functions create.

```
typedef struct _CrtMemBlockHeader
{
// Pointer to the block allocated just before this one:
    struct _CrtMemBlockHeader *pBlockHeaderNext;
// Pointer to the block allocated just after this one:
    struct _CrtMemBlockHeader *pBlockHeaderPrev;
    char *szFileName;    // File name
    int nLine;           // Line number
    size_t nDataSize;    // Size of user block
    int nBlockUse;       // Type of block
    long lRequest;       // Allocation number
// Buffer just before (lower than) the user's memory:
    unsigned char gap[nNoMansLandSize];
} _CrtMemBlockHeader;
/* In an actual memory block in the debug heap,
 * this structure is followed by:
 *     unsigned char data[nDataSize];
 *     unsigned char anotherGap[nNoMansLandSize];
 */
```

The preceding variable size structure (taken from the C run time's header file) contains all the bookkeeping logic and the requested memory block. Figure 15.2 shows a diagram of what this structure looks like in memory.

These guard blocks (you'll also see them called *no-man's land)*, gap and anotherGap, are filled with a known pattern and checked by `AfxCheckMemory()`. The debug memory allocator uses three known patterns:

- bNoMansLandFill, 0xFD, which fills no-man's land
- bDeadLandFill, 0xDD, which fills objects after they're freed
- bCleanLandFill, 0xCD, which fills new objects right after they're allocated

Fig. 15.2

The debug memory allocator data structure.

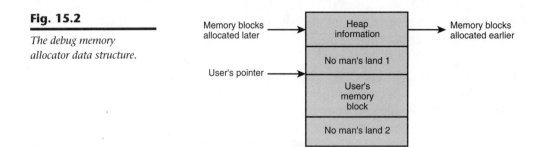

> **Caution**
>
> If you see any of these patterns appearing in your data structures, beware: Something is wrong with your code!

These values are designed to generate errors as fast as possible. They are nonzero, constant, odd, large, and atypical. Nonzero values help find bugs because some programs assume zero-filled data. Constant values are good because memory filling works the same way every time, which helps make bugs reproducible. (Of course, it is bad if constantly filling weird values masks a bug.) Mathematically odd numbers are good for finding bugs, assuming a cleared lower bit; they are useful also for trapping on processors like the 68000 and some RISC CPUs, which do not provide access to odd addresses. Atypical values (those which occur infrequently) are good because they typically result in early detection of errors in code. Large numbers are good for locating bad addresses because they're atypical too. For the case of no man's land and free blocks, if you create a pointer from a filled area and attempt to store data there, a memory integrity checker detects it.

In the next section, you examine where the debug memory allocator uses these patterns.

The No-Man's Land Fill Pattern. The four-byte guard block on both sides of the allocated memory block use the no-man's land fill pattern, bNoMansLandFill. The following code segments show how allocation functions fill in the guard blocks when the application allocates memory. Note the pointer arithmetic to access the upper land fill area. This arithmetic is required because the size of the memory block is not fixed. These no-man's land areas and the fill pattern are key to finding those loathsome writing-past-the-end-of-a-memory-block memory-trashing bugs.

> **Note**
>
> The code in this section comes from the Visual C++ run-time library's source; it's on your Visual C++ 4 CD.

```
                /* fill in gap before and after real block */
                  memset((void *)pHead->gap, bNoMansLandFill, nNoMansLandSize);
                  memset((void *)(pbData(pHead) + nSize), bNoMansLandFill,
                      nNoMansLandSize);
```

How does CheckMemory() verify that the land fills have not changed? The solution's quite simple: It checks for any of the "poison" patterns previously described. The following code checks for the bNoMansLandFill pattern in the guard blocks:

```
    /* check no-man's land gaps */
            if (!CheckBytes(pHead->gap, bNoMansLandFill,
                nNoMansLandSize))
                {
                _RPT3(_CRT_WARN,
                    "DAMAGE: before %hs block (#%d) at 0x%08X.\n",
                    blockUse, pHead->lRequest, (BYTE *) pbData(pHead));
                okay = FALSE;
            }

            if (!CheckBytes(pbData(pHead) + pHead->nDataSize,
                bNoMansLandFill, nNoMansLandSize))
    {
                _RPT3(_CRT_WARN,
                    "DAMAGE: after %hs block (#%d) at 0x%08X.\n",
                    blockUse, pHead->lRequest, (BYTE *) pbData(pHead));
                okay = FALSE;
            }
    ...
```

For these checks to be most useful, the realloc operator must fill the guard blocks when it resizes an already-allocated block:

```
    /* fill in gap after real block */
            memset(pUserBlock + nNewSize, bNoMansLandFill, nNoMansLandSize);
```

Finally, free() must check blocks for corruption as they're freed. This code checks the before- and after-data gap blocks for corruption:

```
    ...
    /* if we didn't already check entire heap, at least check this object */
            if (!(_crtDbgFlag & _CRTDBG_CHECK_ALWAYS_DF))
            {
                /* check no-man's land gaps */
                if (!CheckBytes(pHead->gap, bNoMansLandFill, nNoMansLandSize))
                    _RPT3(_CRT_ERROR,
                        "DAMAGE: before %hs block (#%d) at 0x%08X.\n",
                        szBlockUseName[_BLOCK_TYPE(pHead->nBlockUse)],
                        pHead->lRequest,
                        (BYTE *) pbData(pHead));
                if (!CheckBytes(pbData(pHead) + pHead->nDataSize,
                    bNoMansLandFill, nNoMansLandSize))
                    _RPT3(_CRT_ERROR,
                        "DAMAGE: after %hs block (#%d) at 0x%08X.\n",
                        szBlockUseName[_BLOCK_TYPE(pHead->nBlockUse)],
                        pHead->lRequest,
                        (BYTE *) pbData(pHead));
            }
```

Dead and Clean Land Fill Patterns. When you free a memory block, the dead land fill pattern, bDeadLandFill, fills the block. The bugs caused by using freed blocks usually show up after you fill the blocks with this dead land fill pattern. Likewise, when you allocate a memory block, the clean land fill pattern, bCleanLandFill, fills the block. Any bugs in your application resulting from the use of uninitialized data usually show up quickly and consistently after you fill the block with this known pattern.

MFC Debug Memory Operators

The debugging version of the MFC library overrides the global new and delete operators and implements additional debug new and delete operators for CObjects. For additional tracking, if you define DEBUG_NEW, the overloaded new operators include the file filename and the allocation's line number.

For optimized memory allocation, do not define _DEBUG when compiling files. For optimized nondebug compiles, afx.h defines the following:

```
// non-DEBUG version that assumes everything is OK
#define DEBUG_NEW new
#define AfxCheckMemory() TRUE
#define AfxIsMemoryBlock(p, nBytes) TRUE
#define AfxEnableMemoryTracking(bTrack) FALSE
```

If you have defined DEBUG_NEW in some source files, as MFC does, don't worry; they are optimized away when you compile a project with the Win32 Release target. In the following example, the two #define statements cancel each other out. The allocation of MyObject uses the normal new operator.

```
afx.h        ->
#define DEBUG_NEW new
somefile.cpp ->
#define new DEBUG_NEW
...
....MyOject p = new MyObject;
```

For debug memory allocation, define _DEBUG when compiling files. This defaults all CObject-derived allocations to void* AFX_CDECL CObject::operator new(size_t nSize) and other objects to void* AFX_CDECL operator new(size_t nSize) in afxmem.cpp. Both of these functions call AfxAllocMemoryDebug().

For debug memory allocation with allocation source-file tracking, define both _DEBUG and new=DEBUG_NEW. Normally, you specify _DEBUG on the command line as -D_DEBUG and define DEBUG_NEW as #define new DEBUG_NEW in source files. If you dcfine -Dnew=DEBUG_NEW on the compiler command line, the compiler will generate an error in afx.h and thus cannot use the file. afx.h defines DEBUG_NEW as follows:

```
#define DEBUG_NEW new(THIS_FILE, __LINE__)
```

Putting all these #define statements together leads to the following chain of macros for a simple new operation:

```
Step 1. MyOject p = new MyObject;
Step 2. MyOject p = DEBUG_NEW MyObject;
Step 3. MyOject p = new(THIS_FILE, __LINE__) MyObject;
```

These macros are not recursive, even though new translates to DEBUG_NEW, which translates to new. In C++, if the name of the macro that you are replacing is found during a macro scan or during subsequent rescanning, the application does not replace that macro.

The following code shows how these debug new operators use the new C run-time debug memory functions.

operator delete is a simple example:

```
    void PASCAL CObject::operator delete(void* p)
{
#ifdef _AFX_NO_DEBUG_CRT
    free(p);
#else
    _free_dbg(p, _CLIENT_BLOCK);
#endif
}
```

When debugging's enabled, this function calls free_dbg() (as previously discussed), which checks for corruption. operator new is quite similar:

```
#ifndef _AFX_NO_DEBUG_CRT
void* AFX_CDECL operator new(size_t nSize, LPCSTR lpszFileName,
    int nLine)
{
    return ::operator new(nSize, _NORMAL_BLOCK, lpszFileName, nLine);
}
void* PASCAL
CObject::operator new(size_t nSize, LPCSTR lpszFileName, int nLine)
{
    return ::operator new(nSize, _CLIENT_BLOCK, lpszFileName, nLine);
}
```

The debugging version of operator new accepts additional parameters for calling the debugging tools; in this case, these parameters include a name, block type, and line number that are passed to the run time's operator new.

Debugging Memory Corruption Problems

The most productive way to find memory corruption problems is to compile with -D_DEBUG, use #define new DEBUG_NEW in all source files that allocate memory, and set the checkAlwaysMemDF flag in the global variable afxMemDF. Then, every allocation and deallocation will scan the free store, looking for corrupt guard blocks.

Tracking memory allocation locations with DEBUG_NEW does not add storage overhead because the CBlockHeader structure always contains the file and line-number fields. These fields are set to NULL and 0 if you don't define DEBUG_NEW. By using the MFC convention of assigning the file name to a file-scoped variable, you can avoid any unnecessary run-time memory overhead:

```
#ifdef _DEBUG
#undef THIS_FILE
static char THIS_FILE[] = __FILE__;
#endif
```

All files generated by AppWizard contain this space-saving definition so that the name of the file does not appear repeatedly in the object file. Using the `checkAlwaysMemDF` flag slows a program; with large programs, the performance might not be acceptable. To minimize how much the program slows down, you can toggle the flag on and off or call `AfxCheckMemory()` as necessary. The following dummy function shows a simple memory-trashing error and the information that the debugger displays when you call the code:

```
void GenerateMemoryCorruptionError()
{
// turn on checking for every allocation/free
afxMemDF |= checkAlwaysMemDF;
// trash 1 byte of memory at end of string
char *string = new char[5];
strncpy(string, "Some long string", 5);
string[5] = 0; // bang, stepped past end of string
delete string;  // should generate an error
}
```

When you call `GenerateMemoryCorruptionError()`, the following TRACE messages are printed into the debug window:

```
Assertion Failed: flashy: File afxmem.cpp, Line 90
memory check error at $002E2B55 = $00, should be $FD.
DAMAGE: after Non-Object block at $002E2B50.
Non-Object allocated at file C:\MSVC20\SAMPLES\MFC\flashy_nt\
_ FLASHY.CPP(141).
Non-Object located at $002E2B50 is 5 bytes long.
```

This message correctly indicates that the guard block at the end of the allocated block was trashed. In this case, the guard value is zero and should be 0xFD.

You can also use external tools, like NuMega's BoundsChecker95. These tools tap into the system's memory allocator at the BIOS level and track allocations much as the MFC functions do. They also provide useful tools that validate the parameters that you pass to Win32 routines. Although expensive, such add-ons can save you much time and hair-pulling in some circumstances.

Debugging Memory Leak Problems

Another big headache with dynamic memory occurs when the application does not free all the allocated blocks. An allocation that is not freed and is no longer referenced by an application is called a *memory leak*. Again, the MFC debug memory allocator with the `CMemoryState()` structure can help track down memory leaks. Using the `Checkpoint` and `Difference` member functions enables you to detect memory leaks.

The `CMemoryState()` Structure. `CMemoryState()` is defined as a structure, which is the same as a class with all members public. Therefore, you can treat the `CMemoryState()` structure like a standard C++ object. The `CMemoryState()` diagnostics rely on the MFC debug memory allocator, so they can find only those leaks that were allocated with the MFC debug `new` operators. Here's the definition for the class:

```
      // Memory state for snapshots/leak detection
      struct CMemoryState
      {
            // Attributes
            enum blockUsage
            {
                  freeBlock,     // memory not used
                  objectBlock,   // contains a CObject-derived class object
                  bitBlock,      // contains ::operator new data
                  nBlockUseMax   // total number of usages
            };

            CBlockHeader* m_pBlockHeader;

            // pointer in the debug memory allocator
            LONG m_lCounts[nBlockUseMax]; // number of objects of each type
            LONG m_lSizes[nBlockUseMax]; // total size of object
            LONG m_lHighWaterCount;
                              // highest number bytes allocated at any time
            LONG m_lTotalCount; // total bytes allocated
            CMemoryState();     // constructor only sets m_pBlockHeader
                              // to NULL

            // Operations
            void Checkpoint(); // fill with current state
            BOOL Difference(const CMemoryState& oldState,
            const CMemoryState& newState);

            // Output to afxDump
            void DumpStatistics() const;
            void DumpAllObjectsSince() const;
      };
```

You populate a CMemoryState() object by calling the Checkpoint member function.
Checkpoint captures the current state of the MFC debug memory allocator. Thus, you
can use the following code segment to print current memory statistics:

```
      void DumpMemoryUsage()
      {
            CMemoryState Current;
            Current.Checkpoint();
            TRACE("Dumping current memory usage\n");
            Current.DumpStatistics();
      }
```

The following is a sample dump from the preceding example:

```
      Dumping current memory usage
      0 bytes in 0 Free Blocks.
      1112 bytes in 6 Object Blocks.
      886 bytes in 19 Non-Object Blocks.
      Largest number used: 7818 bytes.
      Total allocations: 22016 bytes
```

The first line describes the number of blocks whose deallocations were delayed if you
set afxMemDF to delayFreeMemDF. The second line describes how many objects remain
allocated on the heap. The third line describes how many nonobject blocks (arrays or

structures allocated with `new`) were allocated on the heap and not deallocated. The fourth line gives the maximum memory used by your program at any one time. The last line lists the total amount of memory used by your program.

MFC Automatic Memory Leak Detection. The MFC library automatically prints a list of memory leaks when a program terminates. It does this by creating a static object whose destructor checks for memory leaks. MFC creates the static object before your program calls `main` and calls the destructor after your program calls `exit`.

Your program should call the `afxExitDump` function only if MFC is not in a DLL. `AfxDumpMemoryLeaks()` does not initialize the `msEmpty` `CMemoryState` object with a call to `Checkpoint()`, so `msEmpty` points to the end of all allocated memory. Thus, `msEmpty.DumpAllObjectsSince` dumps all allocated objects that have not been deleted. For example, if you call the `GenerateMemoryLeak()` function as in the following example, three objects are leaked: `CPen`, `CString`, and `Crect`.

```
void GenerateMemoryLeak()
{
    CRect *rect = new CRect(0,1,2,3);
    CPen *pen = new CPen(PS_DASH, 5, RGB(255,100,200));
    CString *string = new CString("This is a leak.");
}
```

When you terminate the application after creating the preceding leaks, the program prints the following messages to the debug window:

```
Detected memory leaks!
Dumping objects ->
{89} strcore.cpp(78) : non-object block at $002E2C74, 16 bytes long
{88} C:\MSVC20\SAMPLES\MFC\flashy_nt\FLASHY.CPP(151) : non-object
_ block at $002E2C40, 12 bytes long
{87} C:\MSVC20\SAMPLES\MFC\flashy_nt\FLASHY.CPP(150) : a CPen at
_$2E2C10
m_hObject = 0x38
lgpn.lopnStyle = 0x1
lgpn.lopnWidth.x (width) = 5
lgpn.lopnColor = $C864FF
{86} C:\MSVC20\SAMPLES\MFC\flashy_nt\FLASHY.CPP(149) : non-object
_ block at $002E2BD8, 16 bytes long
Object dump complete.
```

Manual Memory Leak Detection. You also can check for memory leaks periodically while your program is running. The most important, and difficult, part is choosing where to make these checkpoints. In an MDI application, one logical place is before the application creates a new MDI window and after the application deletes the window. When choosing checkpoint locations in a single function, be sure to add an extra scope around the checkpoint area to ensure that any frame objects that allocate free store storage have their destructors called before the second checkpoint. Without this extra scoping, this secondary free store allocation shows up as a leak. Also, keep in mind that the `CMemoryState()` objects point into the internal data structures of the debug memory allocator. That is, `Checkpoint` does not make a copy of the memory pool; it simply points to the last allocated block. If you delete past this block and then use the pointer returned from the checkpoint, expect garbage results.

To detect a memory leak, follow these manual steps:

1. Create a `CMemoryState()` object and call the `Checkpoint` member function to get the initial snapshot of memory.

2. After you perform the memory allocation and deallocation operations, create another `CMemoryState()` object and call `Checkpoint` for that object to get a current snapshot of memory usage.

3. Create a third `CMemoryState()` object, call the `Difference` member function, and supply the previous two `CMemoryState()` objects as arguments. The return value for the `Difference` function is nonzero if there is any difference between the two specified memory states, which indicates that some memory blocks have not been deallocated.

Now examine a simple example of manual leak detection. First, you need a routine to generate a leak:

```
void GenerateMemoryLeak()
{
        CRect *rect = new CRect(0,1,2,3);
        CPen *pen = new CPen(PS_DASH, 5, RGB(255,100,200));
        CString *string = new CString("This is a leak.");
}
```

This code just allocates three objects from the heap without freeing them. Now you need a diagnostic routine to force the problem to show up:

```
void ShowMemoryLeakDiagnostics()
{
        // save the current memory state
        CMemoryState Initial;
        Initial.Checkpoint();

        // create a leak, so there is something to report
        GenerateMemoryLeak();

        // take a second snapshot, which will show the leak
        CMemoryState Final;
        Final.Checkpoint();

        // calculate the difference
        CMemoryState Difference;
        if (Difference.Difference(Initial, Final) ) {
                // print a summary of the dumped objects
                TRACE("Dumping memory leaks\n");
                Difference.DumpStatistics();
                // print the types of objects, but not the internals
                TRACE("_ leaked objects _\n");
                Initial.DumpAllObjectsSince();
        }
}
```

When you run the preceding leak generator, it creates output similar to the automatic leak detection. In this case, however, you do not use `afxDump.SetDepth(1)`, and thus do not call the `Dump()` function of `CObject`-derived objects. Here's what the output looks like:

V

Advanced Programming

```
Dumping memory leaks
0 bytes in 0 Free Blocks.
8 bytes in 1 Object Block.
44 bytes in 3 Non-Object Blocks.
Largest number used: 0 bytes.
Total allocations: 52 bytes.
_ leaked objects _
Dumping objects ->
{89} strcore.cpp(78) : non-object block at $002E2C74, 16 bytes long
{88} C:\MSVC20\SAMPLES\MFC\flashy_nt\FLASHY.CPP(151) : non-object
_ block at $002E2C40, 12 bytes long
{87} C:\MSVC20\SAMPLES\MFC\flashy_nt\FLASHY.CPP(150) : a CPen
_ object at $002E2C10, 8 bytes long
{86} C:\MSVC20\SAMPLES\MFC\flashy_nt\FLASHY.CPP(149) : non-object
_ block at $002E2BD8, 16 bytes long
Object dump complete.
```

OLE 2 Memory Management

OLE's purpose is to enable two applications to share information. In general, separate programming groups develop and test these applications. Sometimes part of this information sharing involves passing data structures between applications and having the two applications agree which is responsible for allocating and deallocating memory. To enable one application or DLL to allocate memory that another application or DLL can free, OLE introduced allocator objects. An application has two allocator objects: one for task allocation, and another for shared object allocation. Your application can overwrite the task allocator, but you cannot replace the shared object allocator. You use the shared allocator implementation in the Component Object library (COMPOBJ.DLL) to guarantee that the applications can share these objects.

The OLE memory-management conventions are for OLE public interfaces only; for internal memory allocation, you can use any Windows API, C library, or new/delete operators.

Choosing the correct allocator for OLE functions is critical. This choice depends on the usage of any pass-by-reference parameters. There are three categories of pass-by-reference parameters:

- *In* parameter (the callee accesses only parameter data)
- *Out* parameter (the callee initializes parameter data, for example, the function return value)
- *In-out* parameter (initially allocated by the caller)

For each group, the responsibility for allocating and freeing reference parameters is as follows:

Type	Allocator	Responsibility
In	Task or shared	Allocated and freed by the caller.
Out	Task	Allocated by the callee, freed by the caller.
In-out	Task	Initially allocated by the caller, then freed and reallocated by the callee as needed. The caller is responsible for freeing the final return value.

References passed as *in* parameters are inspected and, depending on the interface, modified by the callee. The callee must, however, copy the reference data to use it after the call returns. References passed as *out* or *in-out* parameters need special attention under failure conditions. If a function returns a failure code, the caller must know how to treat the returned reference. Follow these conventions for all *out* and *in-out* reference parameters on failure conditions:

Type	Failure Responsibility
Out	Must be set to a value that requires no action on the caller's part to clean up. That is, you must set all *out* parameters to NULL.
In-out	Must be left untouched by the callee, and thus remain at the value passed by the caller. The caller is responsible for freeing the initial value if necessary.

An allocator object implements the IMalloc interface. All allocator objects support this interface, which you must use to create reference parameters as described previously. The IMalloc interface is modeled after the standard C library memory and free APIs:

```
interface IMalloc : IUnknown {
virtual void * Alloc(ULONG size);
// allocates a block of memory
virtual int DidAlloc(void *block);
// determine if this Imalloc allocated the block
virtual void Free(void *block);
// frees a block of previously allocated memory
virtual void ULONG GetSize(void *block);
// returns size of memory block in bytes
virtual void HeapMinimize();
// release unused memory to the operating system
virtual void * Realloc(void *block, ULONG size);
// changes the size of previously allocated block
```

From Here...

In this chapter, you saw how to use the tools that Visual C++ provides to catch memory-management errors, including how the corruption detectors built in to the C run time and MFC work. You might also find some of the following sources useful:

- For information on building debug applications with Visual C++ , see Chapter 16, "Advanced Debugging Techniques."

- Steve Maguire's *Writing Solid Code* (Microsoft Press) is an invaluable guide filled with tips on catching *and* preventing memory allocation errors and all the other little nags that can keep your program from working right.

- Steve McConnell's *Code Complete* (Microsoft Press) is a thoughtful guide covering software construction. McConnell likens the process of building an application to building a house and gives a lot of insight into ways to build better software faster.

CHAPTER 16

Advanced Debugging Techniques

No matter how careful you are in constructing your programs, errors creep into them. As your programs become larger and more complex, you can be assured that errors will occur. These errors can make your life as a programmer less than ideal. Errors in your program can also make the lives of your users less than ideal.

In Chapter 4, "Debugging Visual C++ Applications," you learned how to use the integrated debugger to find and fix some typical program errors. In this chapter, you learn some techniques that help prevent errors from occurring in the first place.

In this chapter, you learn about the following:

- How to use the compiler and debugger to find the three major types of errors
- How to prevent bugs in your code from getting out into the world
- How to use basic debugging tools, including the ASSERT macro family
- How to use some of Visual C++ 4's advanced debugging features to debug DLLs, threads, and OLE 2

Note

Prior versions of Visual C++ contained a standalone debugger, CODEVIEW, that enabled the user to debug advanced features such as DLLs. Microsoft no longer provides CODEVIEW with Visual C++ 4, but has instead embedded several features of CODEVIEW into the integrated debugger.

Understanding the Three Types of Program Errors

Programmers encounter a myriad of errors during their careers, but most errors are one of three types: syntax errors, run-time errors, or logic errors. Syntax errors are easy to catch and correct. Most compilers and linkers, including those found in the Visual C++ Developer Studio, recognize such errors and report them to the programmer. Run-time errors occur while the program is executing and cause the program and its operating system to fail. These failures can be so catastrophic that they require the user to turn off the computer and start over again. But even when a program compiles, links, and executes to completion, it can still have logic errors. The results reported can be in error—that is, the program can make mistakes while calculating or displaying the results. Actually, the preceding statement is itself in error, because programs do exactly what they are programmed to do. Programs do not make mistakes—programmers make mistakes!

Syntax Errors

Syntax errors are the easiest errors to detect and usually to correct. Most compilers and linkers detect syntax errors and indicate each error's location within the source file, as well as the kind of syntax error detected. These errors range from misspelling C++ keywords (for example, `whlie` instead of `while`) to forgetting to place a semicolon at the end of a statement. Syntax errors can also include such mistakes as using a function name without providing a function definition.

If you need information about the detected error, you can place the cursor on the line that contains the error and press F1. A help window displays, containing information specific to the error. If you want to edit the source file to correct the error, you can double-click the line that contains the error. The Visual C++ Developer Studio automatically reads the indicated file into the editor and positions the cursor on the offending line. You can then edit the source code to correct the error.

The Visual C++ editor also helps you detect possible syntax errors by color-coding C and C++ keywords and data types. Table 16.1 summarizes techniques for resolving and minimizing syntax errors.

Table 16.1 Finding And Fixing Syntax Error

Technique	Description
Press F1 with the cursor on the error line in the output window	Displays detailed information on the error and tips on what caused the error.
Press F4	Displays the source statement that contains the next error.
Press Shift+F4	Displays the source statement that contains the previous error.
Choose Tools, Options	Controls the Visual C++ editor color-coding scheme.

Technique	Description
Choose <u>B</u>uild, <u>S</u>ettings	Controls the compiler warning level and whether warnings should be errors.
Double-click an error message	Displays the source statement that contains the error.

Run-Time Errors

Run-time errors occur while your program is executing. An example of a run-time error is an attempt to allocate memory with the C++ new operator when insufficient memory is available. Another example is trying to open a file that does not exist. You can test for and correct some run-time errors, but others can kill your process or lock up your machine. Fortunately, Visual C++ provides a new advanced feature, Just-In-Time (JIT) debugging, that can catch such errors and activate the integrated debugger before a catastrophic error occurs. JIT debugging is discussed near the end of this chapter.

Testing Function Return Values. Most C and C++ library functions return a value that indicates the function call's success or failure. You should get into the habit of checking these error codes after every function call. If you check for possible error conditions before continuing with the program, you have a chance to correct the condition, or at least to report the error to the user before exiting the application.

Because most Windows SDK and MFC functions return either a number or a defined constant, you have to search through the various header files to determine exactly what the return value really means. To make your life easier, you can collect all these values and their associated meanings into an error message table and then use the return code to search the table and display an appropriate message. Listing 16.1 is an example that demonstrates this technique for the 32-bit Windows _heapchk function.

> **Note**
>
> Because magic strings are not recommended in source code, and because your program might one day be ported to a foreign language, you should place into your application's resource file any messages to be displayed instead of hard-coding them into your application.

Listing 16.1 heaperrs.rc, the String Resources for _heapchk's Error Message Class

```
IDS_HEAPBADBEGIN
"Initial heap header information cannot be found or is bad"
IDS_HEAPBADNODE "Heap is damaged or a bad node was detected"
IDS_HEAPBADPTR "The pointer into the heap is not valid"
IDS_HEAPEMPTY "The heap is uninitialized"
IDS_HEAPOK "The heap is AOK!"
```

Listing 16.2 defines what the sample error table class looks like.

Listing 16.2   myerror.h, the Class Header for _heapchk's Error Message Class

```
#ifndef _MYERROR_
#define _MYERROR_

#define KEY_SIZE 5  // size of key
CMyErrorClass
{
public:
CMyErrorClass();
~CMyErrorClass();
void Init();
void display( int key );
private:
CMapStringToString err_msg;
};
#endif
```

Listing 16.2 declares a `CMapStringToString` collection class member variable for quick implementation of the class's lookup mechanism. The `Init` member function shown in listing 16.3 uses the `sprintf()` function to create a string representation of the error code's numeric value. The class then uses this string as the key to retrieve the error message.

Listing 16.3   myerror.cpp, a Sample Implementation of CMyErrorClass

```
CMyErrorClass :: Init()
{
char key[KEY_SIZE];
CString description;
sprintf(key,"%d",_HEAPBADBEGIN);
description.LoadString(IDS_HEADBADBEGIN);
err_msg[key] = description;
sprintf(key,"%d",_HEAPBADNODE);
description.LoadString(IDS_HEAPBADNODE);
err_msg[key] = description;
sprintf(key,"%d",_HEAPBADPTR);
description.LoadString(IDS_HEAPBADPTR);
err_msg[key] = description;
sprintf(key,"%d",_HEAPEMPTY);
description.LoadString(IDS_HEAPEMPTY);
err_msg[key] = description;
sprintf(key,"%d",_HEAPOK);
description.LoadString(IDS_HEAPOK);
err_msg[key] = description;
}
CMyErrorClass::display( int index )
{
char key[KEY_SIZE];
sprintf(key,index);
CString message;
if ( err_msg.Lookup( key, message ) )
```

```
    TRACE("Error message is : %s", (const char *) message);
    else
    TRACE1("No Error message for %d",index);
    }
```

The TRACE() macros are described later in this chapter, but you can replace them with a call to sprintf() and AfxMessageBox(), as follows:

```
    sprintf( buffer, "Error message is : %s", (const char *)message);
    AfxMessageBox(buffer);
```

Listing 16.4 is a sample application that uses this function.

Listing 16.4   How To Use the CMyError Class To Display an Error Message

```
CMyErrorClass msg;
.
.
.
msg.Init();
int err_code = _heapchk();
if( err_code )
    msg.display( err_code );
```

Exception Handling. One problem that you might encounter in C++ is an operation that does not generate an error, such as insufficient resources to initialize a class's member function in the constructor. You cannot test such operations for success or failure, because not all return a value; for example, the division operation does not return a value. Both the *Annotated Reference Manual (ARM)* (which is the *de facto* bible of the C++ community because its coauthor is Bjarn Stroustrup, the creator of C++) and the proposed ANSI C++ standard deal with such situations by using exception handling. As explained in Chapter 13, "Exception Handling," exceptions are abnormal program errors such as the failure to allocate sufficient memory. Exception handling is a mechanism for detecting and correcting such program errors. Exception handling enables programmers to handle such problems before they lead to a catastrophic failure. The syntax for this mechanism consists of a try/catch block: You try an operation and then catch any exceptions thrown by the program.

Early versions of Visual C++ simulated C++ exception handling with macros, but Microsoft has included with Visual C++ 4 true C++ exception handling. Visual C++ 4 also includes support for debugging exception handlers, as is demonstrated later in this chapter.

Logic Errors

Logic errors are the results of programmers instructing programs to perform incorrect actions. One type of logic error occurs when a program performs a calculation but yields an incorrect value. Another logic error occurs when a program takes an incorrect branch during execution. If you provide the wrong calculation or instruct your program to take the wrong path in an `if` statement, you have introduced an error in the program. Introducing such errors is referred to as *GIGO,* or "garbage in, garbage out." Remember that the program is simply following instructions that you have provided.

One way to spot a logic error is to follow the program's execution path. You can use a debugger to follow each step in a program's execution, as discussed in Chapter 4, "Debugging Visual C++ Applications."

A much simpler way is to print a statement to a debugging screen, indicating that the program has reached a particular point in the source code. You can also print the value of any variables before and after their use in a calculation. Even though you are adding program code that provides little functionality to your program's eventual user, the extra code helps you, the developer, create bug-free code. Because this code is excess baggage, you should consider wrapping the code in preprocessor macros so that it is available for debugging but omitted when you compile with a release target. The following lines of code demonstrate this technique:

```
#define DEBUG 1   // Include debugging code.
#ifdef DEBUG
cout << "Reached function X" << "value of var1 is " << var1 << endl;
#endif
```

In fact, Microsoft uses the same technique to include debugging code into its MFC class library, except that MFC uses the symbol _DEBUG rather than DEBUG. Microsoft also provides several macros that you can use to format and display such material.

Detecting Bugs before Users Do

When printing a variable's value no longer helps you investigate the problem, you must resort to the debugger. The easiest way to debug programs, though, is to write correct programs the first time. Unfortunately, perfect programs are found only in programmers' dreams and upper-management planning offices. Errors are a fact of life, but you can still try to minimize them as much as possible.

Using Desk Checks and Code Previews

Programs typically operate on a vast quantity of data and display the results in many different formats. During program development, you should test each section of code to make certain that it operates correctly. For testing purposes, you can write a generic `main()` function that enables you to pass parameters to the function that you are testing. You can then analyze the results to ensure that the function is providing the correct answers. This technique is sometimes referred to as *unit testing* or a *desk check.*

To create such a test, you first calculate the results of the program on a set of test data. Then you calculate (by hand or with a calculator) the expected results for the same set of input values. You should select input values to test the following types of conditions:

- Test the function with data that you normally expect the user to enter. Make sure that the function provides the correct answer for the input value.

- Test the function with the maximum and minimum values that it can handle or is designed to handle. Such values are called *boundary conditions*. An example is a function that operates on an array of N data types. Check what happens when the index is less than 0 or equal to 0, 1, $N–1$, N, or $N+1$, where N is the number of items in the array.
- Test the function for invalid inputs, such as those values that might result in division by 0.

The process of calculating the desk check can also help you, as programmer, better understand the problem at hand. Then you can construct a correct and more efficient application. You can think of this process as a design review or as Object-Oriented Analysis (OOA). You perform the Object-Oriented Analysis before you write a single line of code. The purpose of this process is to review the proposed variables, data structures, and algorithms that you plan to use to solve the given problem. You should consider including a fellow programmer in the code preview because "two heads are better than one." Perhaps the second programmer can show you a more efficient algorithm to use to calculate the answer. Like a computer program, an algorithm is simply a series of steps used to solve a problem; an algorithm is presented in written descriptions and mathematics, however, rather than in a programming language.

After you review your algorithms and select the test data, you can code and test the program. Then you can run and check the results against the values that you have calculated. If the calculated values match the desk check values, you can be confident that your program operates correctly. If the values do not match, you can be certain that your program contains errors that you must correct.

> **Note**
>
> A possibility always exists that the desk check data is incorrect. For this reason, someone other than the programmer should calculate the test results.

Using Code Reviews

In the last section, you learned that a code preview can help you spot errors before you code your program. However, sometimes bugs can survive such testing. You sometimes miss bugs in your code before you test it, and you can also overlook bugs while you test it. Before spending hours or possibly days tracking down a problem, you should have a fellow programmer take a look at the code that you have written. A programmer who has not been involved in writing a section of code is not accustomed to seeing the code day in and day out, so such a person might be able to spot an error that you have inadvertently overlooked.

As you examined the test.cpp program in listing 16.5, you probably noticed a few of the errors yourself and could have corrected them before you ever built and tested the program. But sometimes you can spend a long time working on a section of code and still never spot such errors; this is the programmer's version of the old expression, "You can't see the forest for the trees." In such instances, a second programmer reviewing your code can help you find and correct possible logic errors that you might have missed. A code review can also help you spot possible run-time error conditions that you have not anticipated.

You should also perform periodic process reviews. When you reach certain milestones in your project, you review the current path that your code takes to see whether you will reach your goal. For instance, if you're coding a robotic device to change a bottle in an assembly line, timing is everything. You would want to make sure that you properly position the arm over the bottle before lowering the arm downward; otherwise, the device will wreak havoc with the oncoming stream of bottles. This positioning would be a good place to perform such a process review, because the position is so critical.

Preventing Future Problems

Programs do not spring into existence and then suddenly disappear overnight. They have a distinct "life cycle," consisting of the following series of stages:

1. The need for a program is determined.
2. The problem to be solved is clearly defined.
3. A software construction plan is created, including testing criteria.
4. The program is designed.
5. The program is constructed.
6. The program is tested, debugged, and retested.
7. The program is released to the users.
8. The program is used and updated as new features are required and bugs are discovered.
9. Finally, the program is no longer needed, because the problem that it was originally designed to solve has changed, or because newer technology has made the program obsolete.

As you can see, a program has a birth, a life, and a death. A program is not a static object frozen in place or time. Because a program evolves over its lifetime, you must keep track of how the program changes. You track changes with internal comments so that future modifications can be made. The technique most often used for tracking overall software modifications is to include a list of comments. You place the list directly in the source-code files, usually at the beginning. These comments typically identify the original author of the source code, as well as the date (and perhaps the time) of its creation. The comments also indicate the purpose of the file's routines and how they interact with the rest of the program.

As the program matures and modifications are made, those who make changes, either to correct bugs or provide new features, add additional comments stating the changes made, who made the changes, and why the changes were needed. Sometimes the name of the person who authorized the change is added to the comments. These comments form a history of how and why the source code has evolved over time. Here's a sample comment header that lists all the pertinent information:

```
/********************************************************************/
// File: DBFUN1.CPP
//   Revision A - 3
// Author:  Joe E. Programmer
// Date :   August. 3, 1996
// Purpose: To demonstrate debugging techniques.
// Revision History:
//               A-3:      JEP 8/3/94
//                         : Fixed error #Q3456, added comments
//               A-2:      JEP 7/2/94
//                         : Added callback method for COMMUTIL.DLL
//               A -1:     JEP 6/25/94
//                         : Created.
/********************************************************************/
```

Placing comments at the beginning of the source file is inadequate, however. You must also comment your functions, describing what they do and any tricks that you used to achieve the correct result. By providing internal comments, you help future programmers maintain the code, even if that future programmer is you. It is not unusual for programmers to revisit code that they wrote months before and not understand what they have written!

The previous sections provide a process to help programmers detect and prevent program errors before the bugs make it into the application. But try as you might, errors do occur in programs, and when they do, you must debug. Chapter 4, "Debugging Visual C++ Applications," gave you an overview of the integrated debugger and its use in debugging typical MFC applications. The rest of this chapter highlights some of the advanced techniques that you can use when dealing with advanced MFC topics.

Back to Basics

Before you explore the advanced techniques, this section shows you what you can accomplish with simpler mechanisms. Sometimes you can get by without the debugger, by simply dumping the contents of a variable to an output device. Visual C++ supports several such mechanisms, including `AfxMessageBox()`, `TRACE()`, `_RPTn`, `_RPTFn`, and `OutputDebugString()`.

You can use `sprintf()` to format a string for use with these three functions, but MFC also supplies two functions, `AfxFormatString1()` and `AfxFormatString2()`, that accomplish the same task. The format of these functions is as follows:

```
AfxFormatString1( CString& rString, UINT nIDS, LPCSTR lpsz1);
```

`rString` is the string that you pass to `AfxMessageBox()`. `nIDS` is the ID for a string containing the special format charater %1, located in the application's string table. The following provides an example for using the `AfxFormatString1()` function:

```
// The string table entry in the application's resource file :
IDS_FMT1_STRING "Unable to Open File %1."
```

Here is the function call:

```
CString err_msg;
AfxFormatString1(err_msg, IDS_FMT1, "tempfile.000");
AfxMessageBox( err_msg );
```

The `AfxFormatString1()` function replaces the `%1` in the `IDS_FMT1_STRING` with the string passed in `lpsz1`, and then the `AfxMessageBox()` function displays the formatted string to the user.

Using the `AfxMessageBox()` Function

For "quick and dirty" debugging, the `AfxMessageBox()` function provides a great deal of functionality, not only for *ad hoc* debugging, but for communicating with the user in general. With this function, you can display various values on the screen without having to rebuild the application in debug mode or running the debugger. The various parameters have default values, so all you really have to do is pass the `AfxMessageBox()` function a string to display.

The following is the function's prototype:

```
int AfxMessageBox( LPCSTR lpszMsg, UINT nType = MB_OK, UINT nIDHelp = 0);
```

The `lpszMsg` parameter is a `CString` or null-terminated string to display. The `nType` parameter refers to the style of the message box and describes the buttons that appear, the modality of the message box, and the icons displayed. You can OR the values shown in tables 16.2 through 16.4 to achieve combined results. The `nIDHelp` parameter provides a context-sensitive help ID for the function.

Table 16.2 Message Box Button Types

Button Type	Description
MB_ABORTRETRYIGNORE	Displays three buttons: Abort, Retry, and Ignore. `AfxMessageBox()` returns IDABORT, IDRETRY, or IDIGNORE, depending on which button the user selects.
MB_OK	Displays the default button, OK. `AfxMessageBox()` returns IDOK.
MB_OKCANCEL	Displays the two buttons, OK and Cancel. The function returns IDOK or IDCANCEL, depending on which button the user clicks. Also, if the user presses Esc, the routine returns IDCANCEL.
MB_RETRYCANCEL	Displays a Retry and a Cancel button. The function returns IDRETRY or IDCANCEL, depending on the button selected. The function returns IDCANCEL if the user presses Esc.
MB_YESNO	Displays Yes and No buttons, and returns IDYES or IDNO, depending on which button the user selects.
MB_YESNOCANCEL	Displays the Yes, No, and Cancel buttons. The function returns IDYES, IDNO, or IDCANCEL, depending on which button the user selects. The function returns IDCANCEL if the user presses Esc.

You can indicate which button is the default (that is, the button to activate when the user presses the spacebar or the Enter key) by ORing with one of the following button types: MB_DEFBUTTON1, MB_DEFBUTTON2, or MB_DEFBUTTON3.

Table 16.3 lists the specifiers that control the message box's modality.

Table 16.3   Message Box Modality Specifiers

Specifier	Description
MB_APPMODAL	Specifies the default style and indicates that users must respond to this message before continuing with the application, but that they can switch to another application and work.
MB_SYSTEMMODAL	Indicates that users must respond to the message before they can do anything else in Windows.
MB_TASKMODAL	Used in routines that have no available Windows handle (like a DLL). This style has no use in an MFC program.

Table 16.4 lists the icons that you can display in the message box.

Table 16.4   Message Box Icons

Icon	Description
MB_ICONEXCLAMATION	Displays an exclamation point in the message box.
MB_ICONINFORMATION	Displays the "i" icon.
MB_ICONQUESTION	Displays the question mark icon.
MB_ICONSTOP	Displays the stop sign icon.

If the detected error is not severe, or one from which you can gracefully recover without trashing the application, you can use the AfxMessageBox() function as a quick way to alert the user and get simple feedback on how to proceed. The code fragment in listing 16.5 demonstrates this technique by displaying a message box with a question mark icon, a Retry and a Cancel button, and a prompt from the application's resource file. The message box also makes the Cancel button the default.

Listing 16.5   msgbox.cpp, Displaying and Responding to a Message Box

```
// string table entry in resource file :
IDS_SOCKET_ERR_OPEN    "Unable to Establish Connection, Retry or Cancel?"
// implementation code :
CString prompt;
prompt.LoadString(IDS_SOCKET_ERR_OPEN);
UINT response = AfxMessageBox(prompt, MB_RETRYCANCEL |
MB_ICONQUESTION);
switch( response )
{
case IDRETRY :
```

(continues)

V

Advanced Programming

Listing 16.5 Continued

```
// try this again
break;
case IDCANCEL :
// abandon this action
break;
default:
// should never reach here, but just in case....
break;
} // end switch
```

Debuggers are heavy-duty tools requiring time to set up and use, so many developers have continued to use the old standby, printf() (or its language equivalent), to pinpoint the location at which the error occurred. AfxMessageBox() provides you with the same functionality. The next section demonstrates another way to display diagnostic messages.

Asserting Yourself

MFC provides several macros for run-time validation. Run-time validation is important in Windows programs; events occur asynchronously, so it is difficult to predict exactly when and under what circumstances a function might be called. Run-time validation refers to checking the validity of a variable at run time rather than at compile time. For instance, you cannot determine the amount of memory available when you compile and link your application, so when a program requests memory or other system resources, you cannot ensure the request's success or failure until the program actually performs the operation at run time. This is especially true for Windows 95 and Windows NT, which support advanced operations such as giving applications different threads of execution. If the request for resources fails, catastrophic results, such as a program crash, can ensue. The following macros are available for run-time validation:

```
ASSERT(Boolean expression)

_ASSERT(Boolean expression)

_ASSERTE(Boolean expression)

ASSERT_VALID(CObject *pCObject)

VERIFY(Boolean expression)

TRACE(LPCSTR string)

_RPTn(reportType, format, [arg…])

_RPTFn(reportType, format, [arg…])
```

Only the VERIFY() macro compiles in release mode, so none of the other macros has side effects. The VERIFY() macro, when compiled in release mode, does not stop program execution, but does make any function calls that you specify between the parentheses.

The ASSERT() Macro. The ASSERT() macro is the same macro that you find in C. If the expression evaluates to 0, the program prints a message and aborts. The MFC source files contain many examples of this macro, including the following:

```
class CWin * ptr = AfxGetApp();
ASSERT( NULL == ptr );
```

If the AfxGetApp() function returns a pointer that is equal to NULL, the program displays a message box that indicates the file and line number of the instruction that caused the assertion.

You can also use the ANSI C/C++ assert() function or the C run-time library _ASSERT() or _ASSERTE() macros. These are all similar, except that _ASSERTE() includes the expression with the message text.

The ASSERT_VALID() Macro. The ASSERT_VALID(pCObject) macro checks to ensure that a pointer to an object is valid (in other words, that it is not NULL). The ASSERT_VALID() macro also calls the object's AssertValid() member function, if it is defined, to enable the object to validate itself. If either test fails, the macro aborts the program and displays a diagnostic message. You should supply the AssertValid() member function for any class that you derive from CObject, and then call the base CObject member function before performing your own checks, as the following example demonstrates:

```
// example for CObject::AssertValid derived functions
void CMassObject::AssertValid() const
{
TRACE("Entering AssertValid fn for CMassObject\n");
CObject::AssertValid();   // call the base class first
ASSERT( m_velocity < LIGHTSPEED_IN_VACUUM );
.... // test the other data members here
}
```

The VERIFY() Macro. The VERIFY() macro is similar to the ASSERT() macro in that if the expression evaluates to false, the macro prints the same error message and halts the program. The difference between the two macros is that, when compiled in release mode, VERIFY() still evaluates the expression but does not halt the program. Therefore, you can embed a function call in the macro and still have the program execute the function in release mode.

The TRACE() Macro. Previously you saw how to print debug messages with AfxMessageBox(). The TRACE() macro provides the same functionality plus much more. Like printf() and sprintf(), TRACE() uses a format string and a variable number of arguments. The macro prints its output to the AfxDump device when in debug mode, and does nothing in release mode.

Listing 16.6 demonstrates some sample uses for the TRACE() macro. The first call to the macro simply prints a message indicating entrance to the function. The next call then formats a string with information about the three variables m, v, and l.

V

Advanced Programming

Listing 16.6 Examples of Using the TRACE() Macro

```
TRACE("Entered function TEST\n");
int m(0), v(4), l(3);    // declare three ints and initialize them.
TRACE( "m=%d, v=%d, l=%d\n",m,v,l);
BOOL exceed(FALSE);
exceed = theApp.GetVelocity();
v = (exceed) ? m : l;
TRACE("END functions TEST\n");
```

Like TRACE(), the C run-time library macros _RPT and _RPTF can be used to track an application's progress. In nondebug builds, your executable does not include all versions of the TRACE(), _RPT(), and _RPTF() macros.

Specifying the Destination of Your Debug Output

The TRACE() macro provides the Visual C++ developer with printf()-type functionality in a non-Windows environment. But unlike printf(), which sends output to the default display, the TRACE() macro sends its output to the Visual C++ Developer Studio's debug window, as shown in figure 16.1. The Tracer tool controls which types of messages the output window displays as a series of check boxes (see fig. 16.2).

Fig. 16.1

TRACE() output from test.cpp.

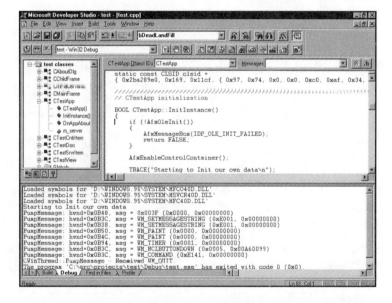

If the debug window is unavailable, the output goes to your system's AUX port. This can be a major problem, especially if you are developing an application that also uses your AUX port.

You can control how the framework responds to TRACE() messages by using the TRACER application located in the \MSVC20\BIN directory. Figure 16.2 shows the MFC Trace Options dialog box, which is the TRACER application's user interface.

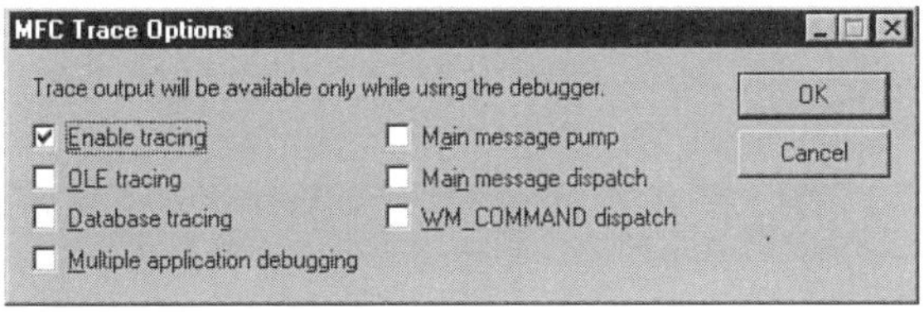

Fig. 16.2

The TRACER application's user interface, the MFC Trace Options dialog box.

The first option, Enable Tracing, activates the framework's tracing mechanism by inserting the following statement in the afx.ini file's DIAGNOSTICS section:

```
TraceEnabled = 1
```

You can provide the same functionality by inserting the following statement into your source code:

```
afxtrace = TRUE;
```

The rest of the options tell the framework which messages to display, such as those messages that deal with the Windows main message loop, OLE messages, and database messages.

The preceding techniques can help you debug your programs and avoid run-time catastrophes, but sometimes you need a full-featured debugger to detect and fix an errant program.

Setting Breakpoints

Chapter 4, "Debugging Visual C++ Applications," provides a good introduction to setting breakpoints while debugging MFC applications. Breakpoints are one of the most useful features of a debugger. By saving you from having to step through thousands of code lines to reach the program's trouble spot, breakpoints can also save you a lot of time and trouble. The "Setting Breakpoints" section of Chapter 4 explains in detail how to set breakpoints in MFC applications. Sometimes this process can be difficult. If you encounter such problems, the following function call, when compiled in debug mode, forces a break:

```
#ifdef _DEBUG
AfxDebugBreak();
#endif
```

The ifdef _DEBUG and endif macros ensure that only a debug build of the application calls the function.

Interrupting Your Application

Sometimes a program encounters a condition, such as an infinite loop, in which a breakpoint is not defined and the AfxDebugBreak() command is not inserted into the code. In such situations, you can attempt to regain control of the application by choosing Debug, Break. This command interrupts your program, returns program control to the integrated debugger, and also opens the disassembly window. When performing remote debugging under 32-bit Windows, you can use the shortcut key

Ctrl+Shift+F1 from a remote machine. (Remote debugging is discussed in more detail later in this chapter.)

Tip

Remember that Visual C++ switches between the <u>B</u>uild and <u>D</u>ebug menus, depending on whether your program is running or not.

Caution

If you're using Windows or Windows 95, interrupting an errant process can leave the application, the process, Visual C++, or the operating system in an unpredictable state.

Using I/O Redirection

The Visual C++ 4 Developer Studio enables you to redirect input/output (I/O) while you debug. The I/O redirection functionality is similar to Windows NT's CMD.EXE and is familiar to many DOS and UNIX programmers. I/O redirection enables a program to receive input from a file rather than stdin or to send its output to a file rather than stdout. A program can also redirect stderr.

To invoke I/O redirection, you must specify the proper I/O redirection commands to be used with your application. Display the Project Settings dialog box by choosing <u>P</u>roject, <u>S</u>ettings and clicking the Debug tab. In the Program Arguments text box, enter the desired redirection command in the Program Arguments text box; you cannot specify the commands on the Visual C++ 4 command line. Table 16.5 lists the I/O redirection commands. Figure 16.3 provides an example of redirecting I/O in a Visual C++ program.

Table 16.5 I/O Redirection Commands

Format	Action
<*file*	Read stdin from *file*
>*file*	Send stdout to *file*
>>*file*	Append stdout to *file*
2>*file*	Send stderr to *file*
2>>*file*	Append stderr to *file*
2>&1	Send the output from stderr to the (redirected) location of stdout (stderr > stdout)
1>&2	Send the output of stdout to the same location as stderr (stdout > stderr; the reverse of 2>&1)

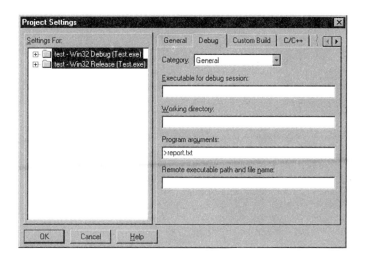

Fig. 16.3

Specifying I/O redirection.

Debugging Remote Applications

Sometimes you must debug an application executing on another system instead of executing both the debugger and the application on the same machine. You might be debugging a program that communicates with other machines, or testing your program on a different machine because of speed or system requirements. The system running the debugger is called the *host* machine, and the system running the application to be debugged is called the *remote* machine.

Running a Monitor

The remote machine must run a small program (much smaller than a full debugger), called a *monitor*. The monitor accepts and executes debugging commands from the host machine through a communications medium, usually the serial port. The remote machine can be an Intel, Macintosh, or Power Macintosh platform in Visual C++ 4.

You can use Visual C++ 4 to debug remote applications. You first set up the remote monitor program on the remote machine and then configure both systems. You then can use the integrated debugger to debug the remote machine as though the program were running on the same machine as Visual C++.

If the remote machine is a 32-bit Windows system, the appropriate debug monitor capability was automatically installed with the system. The program is called MSVCMON.EXE. If the remote machine is a Windows NT machine, the remote monitor consists of the following files, which you must copy manually to the remote machine: MSVCMON.EXE, TLN0COM.DLL, and DMN0.DLL.

Setting Up the Connection

After the remote monitor is in place, you must specify the connection between the two machines. The remote machine (sometimes called the target machine) determines the type and number of connections that are available. Use the following to install the remote debug monitor:

- On a Windows 95 or NT computer, the remote debug monitor consists of the following files: MSVCMON.EXE, MSVCRT40.DLL, TLN0COM.DLL, TLN0T.DLL, and DMN0.DLL. Copy these files to the remote computer.
- On a Win32s computer, the remote debug monitor consists of MSVCMON.EXE, TLW3COM.DLL, and DMW3.DLL. These files are installed automatically during setup.
- On a Macintosh, the remote monitor is a control panel, called VC++ Debug Monitor, which the Visual C++ for Macintosh Setup program installs automatically.
- On a Power Macintosh, the remote debugger is an application, called VC++ PowerMac Remote Monitor, that the Visual C++ for Macintosh Setup program installs automatically. Setup also installs the following files: VC++ Power Macintosh File Utility, VC++ Power Macintosh ADSP Transport, VC++ Power Macintosh TCP/IP Transport, and VC++ Power Macintosh Serial Transport.

The remote platform type determines the connections available. For Intel platforms, serial and TCP/IP connections are available. For Macintosh and Power Macintosh platforms, serial, TCP/IP, and AppleTalk connections are available. The AppleTalk connection is available only if the host is running Windows NT.

Figure 16.4 shows the Options dialog box's Debug page, which displays the different debug options. You activate this dialog box by choosing Tools, Options and then selecting the Debug tab.

Fig. 16.4

The Debug page of the Options dialog box.

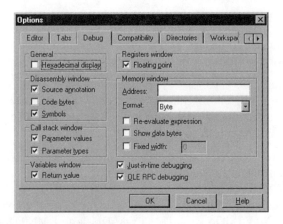

Choose Tools, Remote Connection to display the Remote Connection dialog box, in which you can select the connection type (see figure 16.5).

Fig. 16.5

The Remote Connection dialog box.

If you select the Network (TCP/IP) connection in the Connection list box, the Win32 Network (TCP/IP) Settings dialog box appears (see fig. 16.6).

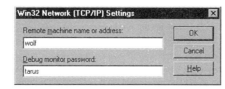

Fig. 16.6

The Win32 Network (TCP/IP) Settings dialog box.

In this dialog box, you select the appropriate communications settings for your system and then click the OK button. You then return to the Remote Connection dialog box.

After you select the proper settings in the Remote Connections dialog box, you must set the proper remote executable path and file name in the Project Settings dialog box's Debug page. Figure 16.7 shows the proper paths for a file named TEST.EXE located on the target machine in the C:\TEST directory.

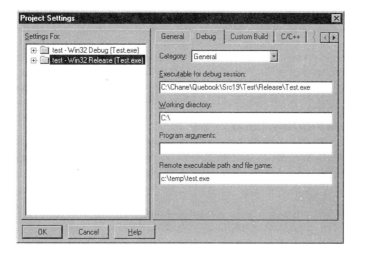

Fig. 16.7

The remote executable path and name entries.

Advanced Programming

V

The integrated debugger is now ready for remote debugging, but the target machine is not. To prepare the target (or remote) system, you must execute the MSVCMON.EXE program on the target machine. Then you can finally use the integrated debugger to debug the remote application.

Debugging Exceptions

The exception-handling facility in C++ enables programs to handle abnormal and unexpected situations in an orderly, structured manner. When a function detects an exception that you must handle, the function notifies the handler by using throw. The exception handler receives the notification by using catch. If no catch handler exists for an exception, the program typically calls terminate(). If you are debugging a program in Visual C++, however, the debugger notifies you that the exception handler did not catch the exception. Chapter 13, "Exception Handling," gave you an overview of the exception-handling mechanism available with Visual C++ 4 and the MFC 4 framework. This section provides an overview of how to debug such exception handlers.

To begin debugging exception handlers, you activate the Exceptions dialog box, shown in figure 16.8, by choosing Debug, Exceptions.

Fig. 16.8

The Exceptions dialog box.

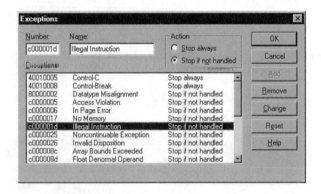

The Exceptions list box (see fig. 16.8) enables you to add, modify, or delete an entry.

Adding and Removing Exceptions

The Exceptions list box displays the system and user-defined exceptions defined for the current project. This list, which you can modify by adding and deleting list entries with the appropriate button, is saved in the project workspace file. Thus, you save the selection of exceptions from one debugging session to the next.

The Exceptions list box displays each exception that might occur in the application and indicates the action to take if the debugger detects the exception. After detecting an exception, the debugger can perform one of two actions: Stop Always or Stop If Not Handled.

To add an exception, you must place in the Number text box the DWORD associated with the exception. The number displayed in this text is either one that you have assigned to the exception or the value of the system-defined exception. The winbase.h header file defines most system exceptions, which have the prefix EXCEPTION.

Next, you can type in the Name text box the name of the exception; such a name is not required, however. You then use the Action group to indicate the type of action that the debugger should take when it encounters the exception. If you do not indicate an action, the Visual C++ Developer Studio defaults to the Stop If Not Handled action. Then click the Add button to add the exception to the list.

To modify any of these parameters, simply change the desired properties and click the Change button. To delete an entry in the list box, you must select the desired entry and then click the Remove button.

If you inadvertently (or purposely) delete some system exceptions from the list and want to restore the default system exceptions to the list, click the Reset button. You need not worry about the user-defined exceptions, because this action does not over-write any exceptions that have been added to the list.

Setting Exception Actions

Sometimes when an exception has been raised (or thrown), the debugger is notified about the exception twice. When the program reaches the point of execution that throws the exception, the debugger is always notified so that it has the first crack at handling the exception. If the debugger fails to handle the exception before the program continues executing, the debugger is notified again.

The Stop Always Action. If the action selected is Stop Always, the debugger stops the program and returns control to the user before the exception handler is called every time that it detects the specified exception. Thus, if you specify the action Stop Always, the debugger stops on both notifications. When the debugger stops, you can change the program and possibly fix the exception's cause.

The Stop If Not Handled Action. The Stop If Not Handled action instructs the debugger not to stop on the first-chance notification but to pass the exception to the program for processing. The debugger displays a notification line in the output window. If the program does not supply a handler for the exception, or if the handler fails, the debugger returns control to the developer. At this point, you have two choices:

- You can use the debugger's facilities to fix the cause of the exception.
- On the assumption that the debugger fixed the problem, you can simply ignore the exception and let the program continue executing.

The Stop If Not Handled action is the default for most of the system exceptions displayed in the Exceptions list box.

Debugging Threads

In the past, most applications had a single thread of execution—that is, they ran from beginning to end, executing only one set of instructions at a time. Modern operating systems—such as Windows 95, Windows NT, and UNIX—support the concept of application threads. Under this concept, an application can continue executing the application's main set of instructions, such as performing word processing tasks, while executing another set of instructions, such as saving a file to disk. The capability to spawn another thread of execution greatly increases an application's efficiency. Also, operating systems such as Windows NT can also run on machines with multiple processors. If a program has access to multiple CPUs, separate threads can have their own CPU instead of sharing a CPU with the main program. Although these concepts greatly increase efficiency, they also complicate the debugging of such programs.

Fortunately, Visual C++ 4 provides the capability to debug such applications with the integrated debugger, but only one thread at a time. To begin, choose Debug, Threads. You then see the Threads dialog box shown in figure 16.9.

Fig. 16.9

The Threads dialog box.

The Threads dialog box displays a list of all the current threads that exist for the application. The list displays status information for each thread. The thread ID is a unique DWORD that identifies the thread. The Thread ID field indicates the thread that currently has focus by placing an asterisk beside the listed thread ID.

The Suspend field indicates a value from 0 to 127. When a thread's Suspend value goes from 0 to 1, the thread is suspended and thus cannot execute until the value returns to 0.

The Priority field indicates the level of access that the operating system has granted the thread. This value can be one of seven priorities: Idle, Lowest, Below Normal, Normal, Above Normal, Highest, and Time Critical.

The Location field provides the thread's current address. This information is displayed as either an address or a function name. If the thread is executing in a module for which the debugger has no information, such as in a DLL or a system module, the Location field displays an address. Also, if you select the Address option, the field always displays the current address.

Debugging DLLs

Two methods exist for debugging dynamic link libraries. To use the first method, you must write both the DLL itself and the executable application (.EXE) that calls the DLL, and you must build both with debug information. You can use the second method if you are building only the DLL and not the executable application that calls the DLL.

DLLs and .EXEs

To debug both DLLs and .EXEs, you have to specify which DLLs a particular executable should load. To do this, open the application's project and then open the Project Settings dialog box by choosing <u>B</u>uild, <u>S</u>ettings. Choose Additional DLLs from the Category pull-down list and specify your DLLs in the <u>M</u>odule list.

The debugger then loads the DLL and makes it available for debugging. You can then set breakpoints in both the .EXE and the DLL. When you step from the .EXE file into a DLL function, the debugger can follow and allow symbolic debugging. *Symbolic debugging* refers to the capability to debug an application using source code. You can see the source code for the instructions that the application is currently executing instead of the assembly instructions for the compiled code. Symbolic debugging also enables the developer to examine the contents of variables by their names rather than by their memory addresses.

Standalone DLLs

If you are building only the DLL, debug information might not be available for the debugger. For example, if you are creating a DLL to use with Microsoft Word, Microsoft does not provide a version of Word that includes source code and symbolic information for debugging your DLL. However, the debugger can still execute the application and then provide support for only the DLL.

To debug such a project, you must specify the file name in the <u>E</u>xecutable for Debug Session text box on the Project Settings dialog box's Debug page.

You cannot do symbolic debugging in the application unless you use the disassembly window and can read the code. However, you can set breakpoints in your DLL and analyze your library.

Any information that you enter in the Project Settings dialog box's Debug page is saved with the project and loaded the next time that you load the project file.

Debugging OLE 2 Applications

Part III, "Object Linking and Embedding," provides a good introduction to OLE 2 programming with Visual C++ 4 and MFC 4. The integrated debugger provides the developer with the tools necessary to debug both OLE 2 client and server applications.

V

Advanced Programming

> **Note**
>
> For more information on the definitions of the terms *servers* and *clients,* see the "OLE 2 Defini-tions" section of Chapter 7, "Introduction to OLE."

The Limitations of the Debugger

The Visual C++ integrated debugger cannot debug two applications simultaneously. Therefore, you are limited, on the surface, to debugging only one application at a time. One way to work around this limitation is to have two versions of Visual C++ up and running, each debugging one of the OLE applications. If you are using Windows 95 and have another Windows 95 or Windows NT machine, you can use OLE remote procedure calls (RPCs) to debug the system. In the Options dialog box's Debug page, select the OLE RPC Debugging check box to ensure that the second debugging session is spawned when the debugger steps into the OLE application. To enable the OLE RPC Debugging option, you must have Windows NT administrator privileges.

To debug only one OLE application, you can build the application in debug mode and proceed as normal—with the caveats discussed in the following section.

Debugging OLE 2 Server Applications

Debugging OLE 2 server applications can pose some interesting problems. If you do not need symbolic information from the client application, you can build the server program with debug information and start a typical debug session. Then, to start the container application, choose the Run command from the Windows 95 Task Man-ager, the Windows NT File Manager, or Program Manager's File menu.

To debug an SDI (single document interface) server, you first choose Build, Settings. Then, in the Project Settings dialog box's Debug page, set the Program Arguments text box either to /Automation or /Embedding, as appropriate. You must set the server's command line in the Arguments text box so that the debugger can execute the appli-cation as if a container program had activated the server. Any container program that you now launch will use the instance of the server program started by the debugger.

Tools for Debugging OLE 2 Applications

Visual C++ provides several sample programs and tools to aid you in debugging OLE applications. The sample test applications give you various types of OLE projects against which to test your programs. You can also use well-known OLE applications such as Microsoft Word and Microsoft Excel to test your projects. The tools included with Visual C++ 4 and the OLE 2 SDK enable you to examine the OLE objects and the messages sent among them.

Sample Applications. Visual C++ provides several OLE examples for MFC program-ming. The MFC samples Calcdriv, Drawcli, Hiersvr, Inproc, Lpdrive, MFCcacl, Oclient,

Oleview, Superpad, Wordpad, and the Scribble tutorial (Step 7) provide complete source code for OLE applications. The Win32 SKD samples Browse, Browseh, Cmallspy, Common, Defo2v, Dfview, Dispcalc, Dspclac2, Hello, Lines, Outline, Simpcntr, Simpdnd, Simpsvr, Spoly, Spoly2, and Tibrowse are also on the Visual C++ 4 installation CD-ROM. For testing various OLE API calls for both container and server applications, check out the CL32TEST and SR32TEST sample programs. Visual C++ also provides a complete outline series that demonstrates how to convert non-OLE applications to OLE client/server applications.

OLE 2 Tools. Tools come in two flavors: viewers and spies. Both enable you to peer inside the OLE object and also to see what type of conversations occur between objects. These tools include the OLE2Viewer, the Docfile Viewer (DFView), the IDataObject Viewer, and the Running Object Table Viewer.

The OLE 2 Object Viewer. The OLE 2 Object Viewer displays all the OLE objects installed on the system and the interfaces that these objects support. The tool also enables you to edit the Registry entries and inspect the type libraries. Figure 16.10 shows the OLE 2 Object Viewer tool.

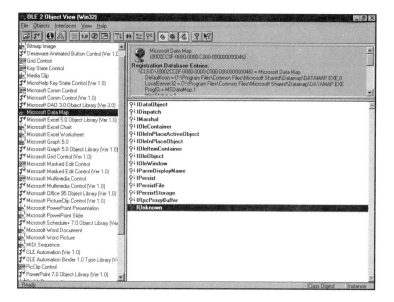

Fig. 16.10

The OLE 2 Object Viewer tool.

The Docfile Viewer (DFView). The Docfile Viewer displays all the contents of a compound document containing embedded objects. The source code for DFView is located in the \MSDEV\SAMPLES\SDK\OLE2\TOOLS\DFVIEW directory. The code provides an interesting look into OLE objects.

The IDataObject Viewer (DOBJVIEW). The IDataObject Viewer lists the data formats offered by OLE data objects created by either Clipboard or drag-and-drop operations. Figure 16.11 shows DOBJVIEW.

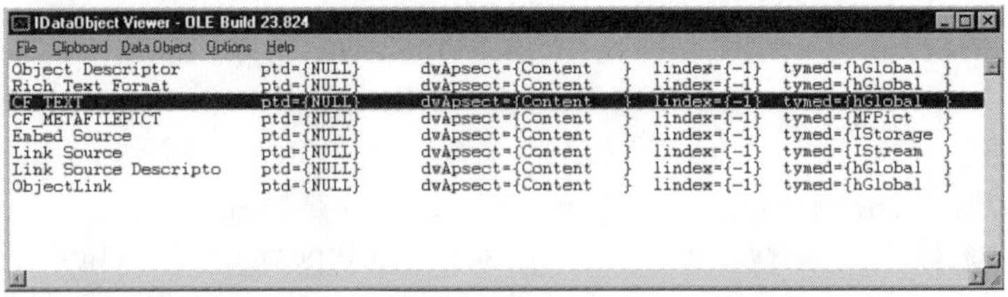

Fig. 16.11

The IDataObject Viewer tool.

The Running Object Table Viewer (IROTVIEW). The Running Object Table Viewer supplies information about OLE objects currently existing in memory. Figure 16.12 shows the IROTVIEW tool.

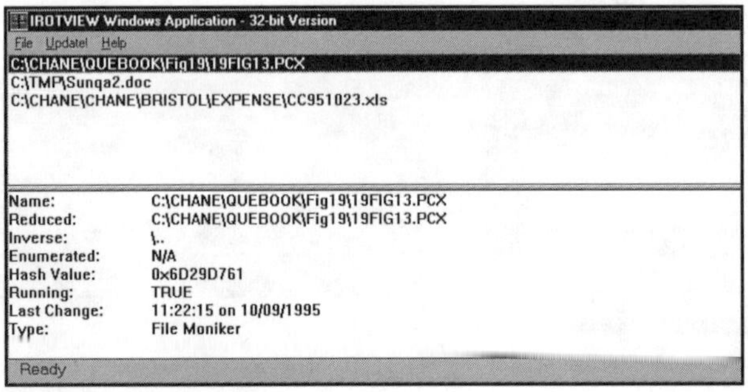

Fig. 16.12

The Running Object Table Viewer tool.

Just-In-Time Debugging

Visual C++ 2 introduced Just-In-Time (JIT) debugging, which enables Visual C++ Developer Studio to activate the integrated debugger when the application generates an unhandled exception or assertions. The application can thus execute at full speed without taking time to load the necessary symbols and prepare the debugger for operation. The Visual C++ Developer Studio detects the error and then activates the debugger "just in time" to prevent the application from crashing. You can then use the debugger to analyze the situation and possibly detect the bug causing the problem. The full analytical power of the debugger is available, as if the program originally had been executed under the debugger.

To activate Visual C++ 4 Just-In-Time debugging support, just select the Just-In-Time Debugging check box in the Options dialog box's Debug page.

From Here...

In a perfect world, you could always ensure that your programs never need a debugger. However, we live in an imperfect world, so this chapter described some advanced techniques that can help you bag those subtle bugs that sometimes occur with unusual development tasks. You might find the following chapters to be useful, too:

- Chapter 4, "Debugging Visual C++ Applications," provides an overview of the use of the integrated debugger. This chapter shows how to set breakpoints, control program execution, and examine and modify variables while a program is running.

- Chapter 11, "Building OLE Controls," discusses OLE custom controls.

- Chapter 13, "Exception Handling," covers in-depth the tricky subject of catching and dealing with exceptions.

- Part III, "Object Linking and Embedding," presents three chapters (7, 8, and 9) that provide an overview of OLE 2, and explain in detail how to use OLE with MFC and how to use OLE Automation.

CHAPTER 17

Writing ODBC and DAO Applications in Visual C++

Open Database Connectivity (ODBC) is Microsoft's standard API for database access, and Data Access Objects (DAO) provide the interface to the Microsoft Jet database engine. Both are supplied with Visual C++ 4. ODBC and DAO both supply abstractions that simplify working with databases, complete with the speed, power, and flexibility of C++. They both integrate your data access work with the MFC application framework. Both DAO and ODBC enable you to write applications that are independent of any particular database management system (DBMS). As usual in MFC, if you need finer control, you can call DAO or ODBC directly in addition to accessing them through the classes. MFC attempts to simplify programming for Windows, but also stays out of your way if you want access to the underlying APIs.

In this chapter, you explore the following:

- Basic ODBC concepts
- Basic DAO concepts
- Basic SQL concepts
- SQL grammar
- Setting up ODBC
- Using MFC database classes and wizards
- Using the ODBC API directly

An Introduction to ODBC Concepts

Program developers spend much of their time and effort writing code to access data in a DBMS. To write such code, many developers learn a unique API for each DBMS. With ODBC, learning all these APIs is no longer necessary.

What Is ODBC?

ODBC is a relational database API that uses Structured Query Language (SQL) to accomplish many of its tasks. An application that uses ODBC connects to a database through a driver written specifically to access that database.

ODBC is part of the Windows Open Services Architecture (WOSA). WOSA is Microsoft's vision for providing a unified set of services for enterprise-wide systems. Other services include the messaging API (MAPI) and the telephony API (TAPI).

The Origin of ODBC. Where did ODBC come from? Microsoft did *not* originate all components of the standard, but instead chose to base ODBC on portions of existing standards. The X/Open and SQL Access Group compiled two standards on which ODBC is based. The SQL syntax supported is based on their standard. The functions supported at the ODBC core level comply with Microsoft's Call Level Interface (CLI) specification.

The X/Open and SQL Access Group standards were not developed in a vacuum. Most of the SQL grammar evolved from a *de facto* standard influenced by such relational database management system (RDBMS) vendors as IBM and Oracle. The Call Level Interface resembles the native APIs of several database products. ODBC is an evolutionary step, not a revolutionary one.

Why Use ODBC? The initial reaction of many developers to ODBC is, "Why learn yet another database API?" Learning a database API is an expensive and time-consuming process. Most people are reluctant to embark on such a task without an immediate and pressing motivation.

ODBC provides several advantages that no other database API offers. You can use ODBC to access *any* database that has an available ODBC driver. ODBC is also SQL-based, providing a sophisticated and uniform interface to data sets as dissimilar as a comma-delimited text file and a multidimensional, hierarchical DBMS.

Most popular databases have ODBC driver support. Many new client/server projects require a Windows front end, and DBMS vendors want a share of this market. If a database vendor shows no interest in developing a driver, a third party often steps in to market its own. You seldom have to eliminate ODBC for lack of driver support.

The MFC database classes are also based on ODBC. These are a major benefit to Visual C++ programmers. The classes are relatively easy to use, and resemble the database access functions of Visual Basic 3.0, Professional Edition.

The Components of ODBC

ODBC consists of the following components:

- Your application
- The ODBC Administrator
- The driver manager
- The ODBC Setup application
- ODBC drivers
- ODBC data sources

To write effective applications with ODBC, you must be familiar with all these components. The following sections examine the role of each.

Your Application. Before your application can use ODBC, you must add the correct header files and libraries. If you are using Visual C++ and the MFC ODBC classes, you should let the AppWizard add these for you (see the section "The AppWizard" later in this chapter).

If you choose to use "raw" ODBC, you should add the extra components manually. You should include sql.h and sqlext.h in each source file that makes ODBC calls. The basic function prototypes and structure definitions for ODBC appear in sql.h. The sqlext.h file adds elements needed to use advanced features and itself includes sql.h. Both files depend on windows.h for data types.

You must link your application with ODBC.LIB, which is an import library for ODBC.DLL, the primary component of ODBC. If you are going to have ODBC support cursor operations (see the section "The CRecordset Class" later in this chapter), you should also link in ODBCCURS.LIB.

The ODBC Administrator. The ODBC Administrator is a Control Panel applet essential to the use of ODBC. It handles installed drivers and assists in managing data sources. It also provides access to call tracing of ODBC function calls.

When you installed Visual C++, the setup program should have added the ODBC icon to the Control Panel window (see fig. 17.1). If you don't see the icon in your Control Panel window, you must reinstall Visual C++. The Administrator and its support files enable you to manipulate sections of the Registry required for ODBC operation. This process also installs ODBC.DLL, which all ODBC applications call.

Fig. 17.1

The ODBC Administrator on the Control Panel window.

The ODBC Administrator is a redistributable file, as are all of ODBC's DLL components. If your application uses MFC, you are free to distribute drivers from the Desktop Driver set with your application (included with Visual C++). You must distribute with your application all the components that you need for ODBC.

Figure 17.2 shows the Administrator's main window, the Data Sources dialog box. It consists primarily of a list of data sources. Each item in the list has a user-defined name for the data source. It is followed by the name of the driver used by that source. This window is an interface to the ODBC section of the Registry, which stores the source configuration data.

Fig. 17.2

The ODBC Administrator configures data sources.

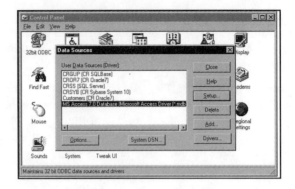

The ODBC Driver Manager. ODBC.DLL contains the ODBC driver manager, which is the most essential component of ODBC. The driver manager primarily controls the drivers' configuration and settings; it handles ODBC initialization and manipulating the sections of the Registry or ODBC.INI that deal with drivers.

The driver manager also provides drivers with entry points to ODBC functions and validates parameters for calls made from your application. Connecting to a data source actually occurs through the driver manager.

The ODBC Driver. ODBC drivers are DLLs that provide an interface from your application to the data inside a specified database. These DLLs are similar to the database libraries that you may have used before. ODBC and these libraries differ in one significant way, however: ODBC provides a nearly *uniform* interface to all databases that a driver supports.

Drivers differ widely, both in capability and modes of operation. The ODBC standard classifies drivers based on the following three criteria:

- API conformance level
- SQL grammar conformance
- Driver type

API Conformance Level. A driver's API conformance level places limits on the functions that your application can call. Driver developers may not implement every ODBC function. They are encouraged to conform to one of three levels of functionality:

- Core API conformance
- Extension Level 1 API conformance
- Extension Level 2 API conformance

Core API conformance entails a bare minimum of functionality. The 23 functions that comprise the core involve allocating and freeing environments, database connections, and SQL statements. The functions provide basic support for passing parameters into statements and accessing the results returned. The core also provides limited cataloging functions and error-message retrieval.

The core level suffices for very basic applications. However, this level is adequate only if you know the schema for each table when you're writing your application. If you must determine a table's schema at run time, you'll need to hold out for a more capable driver. Fortunately, the number of strictly core-level drivers is *very* small and decreasing.

> **Note**
>
> The best way to find a function's API conformance level is to check the ODBC API online Help. Most versions of this file enable you to view functions in groups according to their conformance level. This help file should be named ODBCAPI.HLP or ODBC20.HLP.

Extension Level 1 adds 19 more functions for you to use in your applications. This level completely supports obtaining a table's schema. You can learn which conceptual data types are available and what each is called. This ability is indispensable if your program is to work with several different drivers. You also can query the driver about support for different SQL conformance features.

Most drivers conform to this level. If your application is to reach the widest possible audience, this level is your target. You can write dynamic applications that, until run time, know nothing about the tables that they will manipulate.

> **Note**
>
> Developers using ODBC without the MFC database classes will find the API conformance level of great importance. If you are using the MFC database classes, you should have few problems if you obtain drivers of Extension Level 1 or higher. The database classes usually will protect you from minor differences in driver characteristics.

Extension Level 2 extends Level 1 with 19 more functions. You can now get information about both primary and foreign keys. Among other additional functionality, you can get information about table and column permissions, and you can use and create stored procedures. Among the most welcome features, however, are enhancements to cursor and concurrency control.

These levels are general guidelines. Some drivers omit several functions from their claimed level of support. Almost all drivers implement functions that belong to a higher conformance level. Microsoft has announced no plans for a true certification program to enforce adherence to these levels. Until such a program emerges, driver developers will continue to view the API conformance levels as informal guidelines.

SQL Grammar Conformance. The SQL conformance level of a driver determines which structured query language grammars you can use in ODBC statements. It also specifies which data types are available. The conformance levels defined for ODBC are the following:

V

Advanced Programming

- Minimum SQL grammar
- Core SQL grammar
- Extended SQL grammar

Minimum SQL grammar contains most of the features that you will need. You can CREATE and DROP tables and SELECT, INSERT, UPDATE, and DELETE records. The character field type can vary. It might correspond most closely with the standard types CHAR, VARCHAR, or LONG VARCHAR.

Core SQL grammar adds several useful features. The grammars enable you to ALTER tables and CREATE and DROP indexes and views. You also can GRANT and REVOKE a particular user's permission to create, read, and write records. Core grammar adds several data types to those that minimum grammar provides, and introduces integer types for both short and long integers. Core grammar also adds floating-point types of both single and double precision.

Extended SQL grammar completes the feature set with several advanced concepts. Extended grammar adds the DATE data type, along with several obscure variations on the standard types. The most important addition in the extended SQL grammar is the concept of *cursor control*. This feature enables you to alter the current row of a query after you have fetched it.

Note

Although DATE is technically part of the extended SQL grammar, nearly all drivers support dates.

The Driver Type. The driver type characterizes the division of labor between the driver and the associated database management system. There are two basic types:

- Single-tier drivers
- Multiple-tier drivers

Single-tier drivers process both the ODBC function calls and the SQL statements. The driver *is* the DBMS. For example, the dBASE driver from Microsoft's Desktop Driver Set can manipulate dBASE tables and indexes like a standalone DBMS. The driver also contains a SQL parser to translate the strings passed to the driver into function calls. Single-tier drivers are common on single-machine systems, because none of the traditional database products available on the PC started as SQL-based products.

Multiple-tier drivers talk to a separate DBMS. The driver must process function calls from ODBC applications, but it does not have to process all the SQL statements. That is a job for the DBMS.

A multiple-tier driver is often a communication manager for a true client/server DBMS. The driver might be the interface to a network communication protocol. The driver does not directly manipulate data files, and does not have to parse any SQL statements. It can simply pass them directly to the DBMS. Because multiple-tier drivers are usually front ends for powerful client/server systems, they usually have Extension Level 1 API or higher conformance.

Data Sources. Data sources combine the following:

- An ODBC database driver
- A target database
- Characteristics of the database or a connection to it, such as a user ID and password

A SQL Primer

Structured Query Language is a text-based language specifically designed to manipulate relational databases. IBM originated the language, but it has since been adopted by almost every major client/server database vendor. SQL is an essential component of ODBC.

Relational Objects

SQL operates on various objects in the relational model. The most basic of these objects are the following:

- The statement
- The database
- The table
- The column
- The row

SQL Statements. A SQL statement is a string that contains valid SQL grammar. Often, a semicolon terminates the statement. A statement can manipulate other relational objects or extract data from them. Here is a simple SQL statement that retrieves all data from a table called books:

```
SELECT * FROM books;
```

Some SQL users follow the convention of typing all SQL keywords in uppercase. They also type the names of all relational objects, such as tables and columns, in lowercase. This convention, which takes advantage of the fact that SQL is case-insensitive, makes the statements more readable. The only exception to this convention is that strings inside quotation marks maintain their case.

SQL Databases. The term *database* often causes confusion among developers new to the client/server world. In the relational model, the term refers to a related group of tables. In common parlance, you might refer to a relational database management system as a database. The terms *field* and *record* also are holdovers from the days when mainframe file systems were the state of the art. These terms have been replaced by the relational terms *column* and *record*.

When an ODBC driver's Setup dialog box refers to a database, it actually is referring to a related group of tables. Some DBMS systems enable you to change the current database by issuing the following statement:

```
DATABASE dbname
```

where *dbname* is the name of a relational database.

SQL Tables, Rows, and Columns. The *table* is the central concept of the relational database. A table consists of columns and rows, like a spreadsheet. Each *row* is what you may have seen referred to as a *record*. It is a data point, or entry, into a table. Each row consists of one or more *columns*. (You might have seen a column referred to as a *field*.)

SQL Taxonomy

SQL grammar is organized into several different functional groups:

- *Data definition language* consists of grammars to create, alter, and destroy tables and indexes. CREATE TABLE, CREATE INDEX, and ALTER TABLE statements perform data definition.

- *Data manipulation language* consists of grammars to insert, update, and delete rows inside tables. To perform these tasks, you use INSERT, UPDATE, and DELETE statements.

- *Data control language* consists of grammars to grant and revoke access rights to particular users or groups. The syntax for data control language statements varies more than it does for the other functional groups, but you almost always perform these tasks by using GRANT and REVOKE statements.

- *Data query language* consists of grammars to extract data from one or more tables. The SELECT statement is the group's only statement type.

SQL Grammar

Structured Query Language is a nonprocedural language that strongly resembles English. That is, a valid SQL statement often resembles a grammatically correct English sentence. Most statements start with a verb that summarizes the statement's purpose. SQL, like most computer languages, follows a syntax that is stricter than that of a spoken language.

Creating Tables and Indexes with CREATE. When you set up a database, the first step is to define tables and their indexes. The process of defining a table consists of giving the table a name and specifying the fields. You give the fields names and associate the fields with a data type.

Many databases include interactive utilities that enable you to create tables and indexes without resorting to SQL. Using SQL to create your tables, however, still provides advantages. You can save verified scripts to a file and use them later to rebuild or duplicate your database quickly.

> **Note**
>
> A series of SQL statements is called a *script*.

The CREATE TABLE Syntax. Here is the basic syntax of a CREATE TABLE statement:

```
CREATE TABLE tablename
 (
columnname1 datatype1 ,
columnname2 datatype2 ,
...
columnnamex datatypex ,
 )
```

tablename specifies the name of the table that you are creating. Each *columnname* parameter specifies the name of a column, and its accompanying *datatype* specifies the data type.

Data Types. A major objective of ODBC is to deal with all databases consistently. The ODBC standard has had limited success regarding data types. This is because there is such a wide variation in the data types that might be available.

Compounding the problem, the *datatype* parameter is usually a data type's *native* name. Therefore, a CHAR(12) column in one DBMS might be an ALPHANUMERIC(12) in another. In general, you should consult the help file that usually accompanies the ODBC driver to find the label for each data type. Otherwise, you must find the labels in the DBMS's written documentation.

Most DBMS systems support at least a character type, a numeric type, a logical type, and a date. More advanced client/server databases also support long integers, various floating-point types, BLOBs, and other data types.

> **Note**
>
> A *BLOB*, or *binary large object*, is an object of any arbitrary size. A BLOB is often used to store graphics.

NULL Values. Most client/server RDBMSs support the concept of *NULL*. A column with no value for a row is said to be NULL. A NULL value is not the same as an empty string in a character column or zero in a numeric column. The value is *undefined*. NULL refers to the fact that no SQL statement has defined any value for a column in a row.

The existence of a NULL does not necessarily flag an error. The NULL concept allows you to determine what columns do not contain information. Without this concept, you have no way to differentiate between an empty string or zero and undefined data.

As you might imagine, allowing a column to assume a NULL value can cause problems. There is only one unique NULL value, for instance. If the column that contains the NULL is a unique key, only one row can have a NULL. An attempt to add another row with a NULL in that column will fail.

There is a variation of the CREATE TABLE syntax that enables you to specify that every row in a table *must* define a value for specified columns. An attempt to INSERT a record that does not define a value for the specified columns will fail. You can add a NOT NULL clause after the definition of any column in which you want to prevent NULLs. The following is an example of the use of this syntax:

```
CREATE TABLE car ( driver CHAR(12) NOT NULL, passenger CHAR(12) )
```

where the passenger column can contain NULLs, but the driver column cannot.

If you are a PC database developer, you might find the concept of the NULL value to be somewhat foreign. This is because most traditional PC databases do not support it. Furthermore, ODBC cannot add the NULL value to a DBMS that does not already possess it.

Creating Indexes. Most real-world databases use indexes to improve performance or enforce a uniqueness constraint. ODBC supports the creation of indexes; like table creation, however, this support is limited by the native capabilities of the underlying DBMS.

Some DBMSs support only a single index for a file or limit the index to be built on one column. Again, you must reference the driver help file or other documentation to get the capabilities available and the syntax to access them. The basic syntax for a CREATE INDEX statement follows:

```
CREATE INDEX indexname
ON tablename
  (
columnname [ASC/DESC]
  )
```

indexname is the name of the index to be associated with the *tablename* table. The *columnname* parameter is the name of the column for which the statement is to generate an index. A CREATE INDEX statement usually creates an index with ascending values, but by placing ASC or DESC after the index name, you explicitly specify whether the index is ascending or descending.

Removing Tables and Indexes with DROP. After creating a table, you can remove it at any time with the DROP TABLE statement. This command's syntax is as follows:

```
DROP TABLE tablename
```

where *tablename* is the name of the table to drop. When you drop a table, you also remove attached indexes and other objects associated with the table.

Removing an index requires a syntax similar to removing a table:

```
DROP INDEX indexname
```

where *indexname* is the name of the index to remove. Special syntax, unique to the driver, is required to remove an index that does not allow the naming of indexes.

Adding Rows with INSERT. After creating a table, you can add data to it. To add a row of data to a table, you use the INSERT statement. There are several forms of the INSERT statement, most of which are supported by ODBC. The following is the syntax for the most basic INSERT statement:

```
INSERT INTO tablename
  ( columnname1, columnname2, columnname3, ... )
VALUES
  ( value1, value2, value3, ... )
```

where `tablename` is the name of the table to which you are inserting a row. The list of `columnnames` is case-insensitive. You should be careful that this list corresponds exactly to the list of `values`, however.

The values passed as parameters in an INSERT statement must be in a format appropriate to the column's data type. ODBC drivers handle some of the conversion for you. For example, they convert integers to floating-point types. The following are examples of formatting for various data types:

- Characters should be surrounded by single quotes, as in `'DOORS'`
- Integers should consist entirely of digits, as in `23421`
- Floats should be stated with the correct precision, as in `12.23`

Dates present a problem. Different DBMS systems expect dates to appear in various formats. Don't attempt to handle these formats on a case-by-case basis. Instead, use the shorthand syntax that remains fixed from driver to driver. The shorthand for dates is as follows:

```
{d 'YYYY-MM-DD' }
```

where YYYY is the four-digit year, MM is the two-digit month, and DD is the two-digit day of the month.

The INSERT statement has a short version. To use this version, you must know the order of the columns inside the table. Here is the statement's syntax:

```
INSERT INTO tablename
VALUES
  ( value1, value2, value3, ... )
```

where the `values` appear in the same order as they do in the CREATE TABLE statement. Note that this version of the INSERT statement simply omits the list of `columnnames` from the other version. If you have columns that will contain no information, give them a value of NULL.

Removing Rows with DELETE. To remove rows from tables, you use a DELETE statement. You can use a single DELETE statement to delete as many rows as you want. The syntax for DELETE is as follows:

```
DELETE FROM tablename
WHERE whereclause
```

where `tablename` is the table from which to remove records, and `whereclause` identifies the row or rows to remove.

You use the WHERE clause in several types of statements. The clause is a logical statement that can be resolved to TRUE or FALSE for any column. The WHERE clause has much the same syntax wherever it appears. The following are its simplest forms:

```
WHERE
fieldname operator fieldvalue

WHERE
fieldname1 operator fieldname2
```

where *fieldname* is the name of a field, *operator* is a mathematical comparison operator (see table 17.1), and *fieldvalue* is the value to use in that comparison. The clause's second line is called a *subclause*. By removing the WHERE clause completely, you cause the DELETE statement to remove *all* columns in a table.

Table 17.1 Basic Comparison Operators

Operator	Meaning
=	Equal to
!=	Not equal to
>	Greater than
>=	Greater than or equal to
<	Less than
<=	Less than or equal to

The basic comparison operators are the same ones that you might have used for math However, they are not just for numbers; you can also use them to compare strings alphabetically.

You can string subclauses together with a logical AND or OR. This gives you a great deal of power to specify a set of columns. You also can apply the logical NOT to a subclause if you want to invert its result.

Updating Rows with UPDATE. The UPDATE statement changes a column's value. You can use the statement to change one column or several, on one row or many. The syntax for UPDATE is as follows:

```
UPDATE tablename
SET
columnname1 = value1,
columnname2 = value2, ...
WHERE
whereclause
```

where *tablename* is the table that contains rows to update, and *columnname* is the name of a column to set to *value*. You can set the value of one column to the value of another by setting *value* to a column name.

Like the `DELETE` statement, the `UPDATE` statement enables you to use a `WHERE` clause to define the set of records on which to act. If you omit the `WHERE` clause, the statement updates all columns of the table.

Choosing Rows and Columns with SELECT. A *query* is a request for information. In SQL, a `SELECT` statement performs a query. The syntax for `SELECT` is more complex than the others, so this section reviews only the more commonly used clauses. With `SELECT`, you can specify a set of tables, rows, and columns with which to work and the order in which they will appear. The following is the syntax for `SELECT`:

```
SELECT
columnlist
FROM
table
WHERE
whereclause
ORDER BY
sortcolumnlist [ASC/DESC]
```

`columnlist` is a list of columns from a `table` to be shown. The `whereclause` defines the result set of the query, whereas the columns in `sortcolumnlist` define the sorted order of the results.

In an interactive system, entering a query displays a listing of the results. In a database API such as ODBC, a query returns a *result set.* You can then fetch the result set, one row at a time, into a buffer.

The `columnlist` can include items in addition to columns. The asterisk (*) is a shorthand notation representing all columns in a table. Another type of item that you can use is the *column function,* which has the following forms:

```
functionname( columnname )

functionname( * )
```

where `functionname` is the name of the column function and `columnname` is the name of the column on which the function will act.

Note

The following are common column functions:

`AVG()`	The average of the values in the column
`SUM()`	The sum of the values in the column
`MIN()`	The lowest value found in the column
`MAX()`	The greatest value found in the column
`COUNT()`	The number of values found (usually refers to * columns)

Relating Tables with Joins. The most useful type of query is the *join*. A common type of join is a query on two or more tables with a `whereclause` that compares the value of a column in one table to the value of a column in the other (usually by equality).

Relational tables store much of their information as *attributes* of a single kind of *entity*. Joins are useful in finding relationships *between* entities. A join between two tables can yield more information than either of the individual tables contains.

SQL grammar is not always simple. There is no SQL compiler to flag problems. Finding syntax errors in SQL statements has been traditionally a matter of trial and error. Fortunately, inexpensive, simple-to-use tools are available now.

One such tool is Microsoft Query. Query, an ODBC-based interactive query utility, is included as part of Visual C++ 4. Microsoft's flagship applications, such as Word and Excel, also include the utility as an applet.

Query uses wizards and a feature called Cue Cards to lead you through the process of attaching to a data source or executing a SQL statement. Step-by-step instructions are available to perform most common operations.

All in all, Query is a marvelous way to learn SQL. You can also use it to test your statements or create tables. The utility should work with any data source.

Testing SQL Statements

To execute a SQL statement, choose File, Execute SQL. Then click the Data Sources button to select a data source. You can now enter the statement in the SQL Statement edit control.

When you click the Execute button, Query attempts to execute your statement. If your statement contains a syntax error, you get an error message that describes it. If your statement succeeds but has no result set (such as an INSERT), a dialog box informs you of success or failure.

If your statement has a result set, Query can show you much more. A query window opens with two panes. The top pane is a graphical diagram representation of the tables in your query and the relationships between them. The bottom pane is a grid that contains the result set of the query.

Although you can easily test your own SQL statements with Query, the program's most powerful feature is the capability to write new queries. You can use it to further your SQL skills or just to avoid figuring out a complex query.

You can start a new query by choosing File, New Query. After choosing a data source, you are shown a list of tables from which to select. You can select any or all the tables listed for your query by double-clicking the table name. Click the Close button when you are done.

Now you can choose the column to include in your query by double-clicking on the column name or on * to select all columns. You can also define a join by dragging the name of the join fields on one table to the field that you want to join on the other table.

As you manipulate the tables in the upper pane, the grid in the lower pane changes to reflect the changes. When the results reflect exactly what you want, click the SQL button in the toolbar. The SQL dialog box appears with the query corresponding to the result set. If you want to keep the query's text, select the contents of the SQL Statement edit control and press Ctrl+Insert to paste it to the Clipboard.

ODBC Setup

After installing ODBC, you can add capabilities by adding drivers that enable you to access new DBMSs. To provide access to a particular database, you set up a new data source. A data source associates a driver, a database, and all information required to attach to the source.

Setting Up Data Sources

You usually add data sources through the ODBC Administrator, by following these steps:

1. Invoke the ODBC Administrator; its icon, titled ODBC, should appear in the Program Manager's Control Panel window.

2. Click the Add button.

3. Choose a driver from the list.

4. After you choose a driver, the driver configuration dialog box appears. Figure 17.3 shows the ODBC Oracle Driver Setup dialog box. Other driver configuration dialog boxes might look quite different.

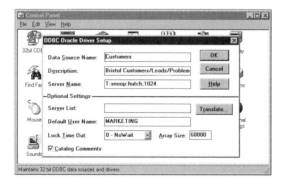

Fig. 17.3

In the ODBC Oracle Driver Setup dialog box, you can configure a data source.

5. Enter whatever information is needed to link your data source to the actual database. Read the driver documentation to find out what information is needed.

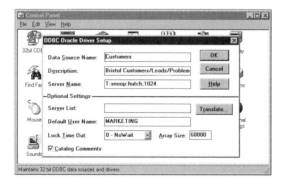

Setting Up Drivers

Before setting up a data source, you must have the applicable driver installed. Driver vendors usually write standard Windows install programs to help distribute their products. Invoking the install program should copy the driver files and add the correct items to the Registry.

Note

Under Windows NT, you must have Administrator privileges to add drivers or data sources.

Some drivers might not have an install program. Instead, you will use the ODBC Administrator to install the driver. To do this, click the Drivers button on the Administrator's main window. When the Drivers dialog box appears, click the Add button. You then can browse to the location of the driver files. The Administrator will use the ODBC.INF file at that location to determine how to install the driver.

After installing the driver, you can configure it. Some setup is specific to a data source. You can also use the driver configuration dialog box to set up global properties that apply to all data sources using this driver.

Using the MFC Database Classes

The MFC database classes enable you to access information stored in an ODBC data source in a very simple and straightforward manner. They also provide methods to integrate your application's views and data.

What Are DAO and ODBC?

DAO is familiar to database programmers who use Microsoft Access Basic or Microsoft Visual Basic. DAO uses the Microsoft Jet database engine to provide a set of data access objects—database objects, `tabledef` and `querydef` objects, `recordset` objects, and others. DAO is optimally useful for working with .MDB files like those created by Microsoft Access, but you can also access ODBC data sources through DAO and the Microsoft Jet database engine.

ODBC provides an API that different database vendors implement through ODBC drivers specific to a particular DBMS. Your program uses this API to call the ODBC driver manager, which passes the calls to the appropriate driver. The driver, in turn, interacts with the DBMS by using SQL.

Although internally MFC's implementations of DAO and ODBC are quite different, the similar interfaces make it relatively easy to port your applications from one to the other, particularly from ODBC to DAO. In the MFC programming model, when you use DAO or ODBC, you work with a database object for each open database. The database object represents your connection to the database. You make queries and updates through `CRecordset` objects. As described later, DAO provides additional objects for such tasks as working with table structure and saving queries for reuse. MFC supplies classes for each of these objects: one set of classes for DAO and another set for ODBC.

Choosing between DAO and ODBC

Which choice is best—DAO and ODBC? This is a very loaded question. Here are some guidelines:

- Use the ODBC classes if you are working strictly with ODBC data sources, particularly in client/server situations, where the MFC ODBC classes provide better performance.

- Use the DAO classes if you are working primarily with Microsoft Jet (.MDB) databases or with other database formats that the Microsoft Jet database engine can read directly.

One reason for choosing the DAO classes is that they provide a richer data access model, with support for data definition language (DDL) as well as data manipulation language (DML).

Because DAO also supports access via ODBC (through the Microsoft Jet database engine), the following are your primary reasons for choosing the DAO classes over the ODBC classes:

- Better performance in some cases, particularly when using Microsoft Jet (.MDB) databases

- Compatibility with the ODBC classes, Microsoft Access Basic, and Microsoft Visual Basic

- Access to validation rules

- The ability to specify relations between tables

Table 17.2 summarizes the key differences to help you choose between DAO and ODBC.

Table 17.2 Choosing between MFC's DAO and ODBC Classes

Task	DAO Classes	ODBC Classes
Access .MDB files	Yes	Yes
Access ODBC data sources	Yes	Yes
Available for 16-bit	No	Yes
Available for 32-bit	Yes	Yes
Database compaction	Yes	No
Database engine support	Microsoft Jet database engine	Target DBMS
DDL support	Yes	Only through direct ODBC calls
DML support	Yes	Yes

(continues)

V

Advanced Programming

Table 17.2 Continued

Task	DAO Classes	ODBC Classess
Nature of the MFC implementation	"Wrapper" of DAO core functions	Simplified abstraction rather than a "wrapper" of the ODBC API
Use for access to .MDB files (Microsoft Access)		Any DBMS for which you have a driver, especially in client/server situations
Transaction support	Per workspace or, for ODBC data, per database	Per database

If you are working solely with ODBC databases rather than Microsoft Jet (.MDB) databases, you might want to use the ODBC classes and avoid DAO's overhead.

The Wizards

A wizard presents a series of dialog boxes to lead you through a task. Microsoft has added wizards to each of its recent applications. These wizards can be a great help as you create MFC applications that use the database classes.

The AppWizard. The AppWizard leads you through the process of generating an application. To create an MFC database application with the AppWizard, perform the following steps:

1. Choose File, New.
2. Set the project name and its subdirectory.
3. Set the project type to MFC AppWizard (exe).
4. Click the Create button to invoke AppWizard.
5. In the MFC AppWizard - Step 1 dialog box, select the main window type and your application's language.
6. Click the Next button to move to the MFC AppWizard - Step 2 dialog box.
7. Select one of the radio buttons in the group What Database Support Would You Like To Include?:

   None (the default) causes AppWizard to leave out database support in the generated application.

   Header Files includes only the needed ODBC and DAO header files in your project, but doesn't include any of the MFC classes and doesn't generate new classes for you.

   Database View without File Support gives you access to ODBC data sources and provides a `CView`-derived class for your query results, but doesn't enable you to serialize query results.

   Database View with File Support gives you access to ODBC data sources and provides a `CView`-derived class for your query results, and you can serialize query results by using `CDocument`-based classes in your application.

8. If you selected either of the Database View radio buttons, you must include a data source. Click the <u>D</u>ata Source button to invoke the Select Data Source dialog box.

9. Select a DAO or ODBC data source and press Enter. If you selected an ODBC database, you now see the Logon dialog box. Once you log in, a list of available tables appears.

10. Select a table to associate with your database view.

11. Complete the AppWizard process by selecting your preferences in AppWizard Steps 3 through 6 and clicking the <u>F</u>inish button.

The AppWizard now generates all the files that your application needs.

The ClassWizard. You can use the ClassWizard to maintain the database classes that the AppWizard creates or to create new classes. You invoke the ClassWizard by choosing <u>V</u>iew, Class<u>W</u>izard, or pressing Ctrl+W. To add a database view class, follow these steps:

1. Use AppStudio to create a dialog box to hold your database view controls. You should add a control for each field that you want to display.

2. Invoke the ClassWizard.

3. Click the Add C<u>l</u>ass button and select New from the pop-up menu. The Create New Class dialog box appears.

4. Enter a class name in the Class Name edit control, then set the <u>B</u>ase Class to `CRecordView` or `CDaoRecordView`. Click the Create button to create the new class.

5. The Database Options dialog box appears. Select an <u>O</u>DBC or <u>D</u>AO data source from those listed. If you select an ODBC source, you must log in to the database before proceeding. The Select Database Tables dialog box appears. Select the tables that you want used in your `CRecordset` object, then click OK.

6. Click the Member Variables tab in the MFC ClassWizard dialog box.

7. Click the <u>B</u>ind All button to define the default bindings.

You have created a new `CRecordView` or `CDaoRecordView` and associated it with a `CRecordSet` or `CDaoRecordSet`. You can now use the class in your application.

The DAO Classes

There are six major classes that you instantiate directly to facilitate ODBC data access:

■ `CDaoDatabase` represents the connection to the DAO data source.

■ `CDaoWorkspace` maintains a named, password-protected database session, from login to logoff, by a single user.

■ `CDaoQueryDef` is the SQL statement that describes a query and its properties.

■ `CDaoTableDef` contains the stored definition of a base table or an attached table.

■ `CDaoRecordset` holds a query's result set as a set of individual records.

■ `CRecordView` is the user interface to the DAO data; it provides a `CView`-based class for displaying database results.

The ODBC Classes

The ODBC classes are similar to the DAO classes, but there aren't as many of them. You can directly instantiate three ODBC classes to talk to ODBC data sources:

- CDatabase represents the connection to the ODBC data source.
- CRecordset holds the result set of a query as a set of individual records.
- CRecordView provides the user interface to the ODBC data; it provides a CView-based class for displaying database results.

The CDatabase Class. The CDatabase class represents a connection with an ODBC data source. The class contains methods to open, close, and configure the connection. CDatabase also enables you to execute SQL statements that return no result set. You can also use the class to control when and if SQL statements executed against the connection will actually execute.

The following are the most basic methods of the CDatabase:

- Open() connects the CDatabase object to an ODBC data source.
- Close() disconnects the CDatabase object from a data source.
- IsOpen() indicates whether the CDatabase object is actually connected to a data source.
- ExecuteSQL() performs any SQL statement that does not return a result set, such as INSERT, UPDATE, or DELETE.

For many applications, you make a connection only once. The connection opens when the user starts the application, and closes when the user terminates the application. You might want to follow this practice because some drivers take several seconds to respond. Staying connected has few disadvantages.

In true client/server data sources, network traffic and other inherent delays can slow the response time to a logon or query. The transaction might actually fail to make the complete trip between client and server. To keep your application from hanging when such a failure occurs, you must set appropriate waiting periods. You set these timeouts with the following methods:

- SetLoginTimeout() sets the amount of time to wait for a login to complete before returning a failure indication.
- SeqQueryTimeout() sets the amount of time to wait for a query to complete before returning a failure indication.

Your application might have to execute a sequence of statements, all of which must succeed to be valid. If you find yourself in this "all or nothing" situation, you should try using transactions. Transaction support must be present in the DBMS because ODBC cannot supply it. The methods to avail yourself of this capability are the following:

- CanTransact() determines whether the DBMS supports the capability.
- BeginTrans() is called at the beginning of the critical section.

- `CommitTrans()` is called if all the statements in the transaction succeed. The database reflects the changes that the statements make.

- `RollBack()` is called if any statement in a transaction fails. The application does not complete changes that reflect statements executed since the last call to `BeginTrans()`. Instead, the application behaves as if the changes never happened.

The `CDatabase` class has several other methods. If it lacks some ODBC-supported capability that you want, you can use any API call that uses the database connection handle. The class has the public data member `m_hdbc`, which you can use to call ODBC API functions.

The `CRecordSet` Class. The `CRecordset` class is the workhorse of the MFC database classes. The `CRecordset` object stores both a query against a database and the results from that query. The class contains methods to set the conditions of the query. It also provides methods to navigate the current position in the result set and manipulate the rows. The minimum set of methods consists of the following:

- `Open()` defines and performs the current query and opens the result set. The syntax that you use in the query can determine which rows are in the result set and in which order they will appear.

- `Close()` closes the result set and destroys the query.

The `Open()` method sets all the query's important properties. You can determine these properties by setting the values of some public data members before calling `Open()`. If you want to change these properties later, you must call `Requery()`. This method performs a new `SELECT` statement that returns a new record set.

To choose which rows from a table will be in the record set, set a value for the `CString` data member `m_strFilter`. The value that you set in `m_strFilter` will appear in the query's `WHERE` clause. The following is an example of a value that you might use:

```
state = 'CA' AND county = 'MARIN'
```

where `state` and `county` are column names and `'CA'` and `'MARIN'` are values that these fields can take.

> **Note**
>
> You might want to review the syntax of the `SELECT` statement in the section "Choosing Rows and Columns with `SELECT`," earlier in this chapter.

To choose the order in which rows will appear in the record set, set a value for the `CString` data member `m_strSort`. The value that you set in `m_strSort` appears in the query's `ORDER BY` clause. The following is an example of a value that you might use:

```
state DESC, county DESC
```

Advanced Programming

V

where state and county are column names, and DESC specifies that the sort will occur from highest to lowest.

The current position in the result set is called the *cursor*. Moving the cursor is referred to as *scrolling*. The properties of the cursor can be important to the operation of the record set. The Open() method sets these characteristics, which last until the cursor closes. The different cursors create different record set types when you specify the following values of the enum OpenType:

- dynaset
- snapshot
- forwardOnly

Calling Open() with the dynaset value creates a new cursor that can scroll in both directions. When you scroll to a new record, its contents reflect changes that other users have made since your call to Open(). You can edit the current row's contents.

Calling Open() with the snapshot value creates a new cursor that can scroll in both directions. When you scroll to a new record, its contents reflect those values in the database at the time of your call to the Open() method. You can edit the current row's contents.

Calling Open() with the forwardOnly value creates a new cursor that can scroll in only the forward direction. When you scroll to a new record, its contents reflect those values in the database at the time of your call to the Open() method. You cannot edit the current row's contents.

You might wonder why anyone would ever create a snapshot or forwardOnly cursor rather than a dynaset. Your data source might not support dynaset functionality. Also, the snapshot also provides much better performance than the dynaset. If you know that you will need only forward, read-only scrolling, you will get much better performance by using a forwardOnly cursor rather than a dynaset or snapshot. Try to use the minimum functionality that fits your requirements.

> **Note**
>
> If your data source does not support the scrolling cursor concept, CRecordset might be capable of supporting the concept by loading the ODBC cursor library. This library, contained in ODBCCURS.DLL, simulates scrolling cursors by caching records before and after the current position.

CRecordset has several methods to determine the cursor's current position. The class also provides navigation methods to change the cursor's position:

- IsBof() determines whether the user has scrolled the cursor to a position before the record set's first row. If IsBof() returns TRUE, there is no current record.

- `IsEof()` determines whether the user has scrolled the cursor to a position after the record set's last row. If `IsBof()` returns TRUE, there is no current record.

- `IsDeleted()` determines whether the current record has been deleted. If `IsDeleted()` returns TRUE, the current record is invalid and cannot be updated.

- `MoveFirst()` moves the cursor to the record set's first record.

- `MoveLast()` moves the cursor to the record set's last record.

- `MoveNext()` moves the cursor to the record set's next record.

- `MovePrevious()` moves the cursor to the record set's previous record.

- `Move()` changes the cursor position forward or backward the given number of records relative to the current position.

You can usually edit the record at the current cursor position (the `Open()` method sets this property). Although you can perform INSERT, UPDATE, or DELETE statements through the `CDatabase::ExecuteSQL()` method, performing these operations on the current record is often more convenient. To perform these operations, you call the following methods:

- `AddNew()` creates a new, empty row and a buffer in which to store the new row values. You should set the columns to the desired values and call `Update()` to complete the process.

- `Delete()` deletes the current row.

- `Edit()`, which you call before setting an existing row's new column values, creates a buffer in which to edit the row's columns. You should call `Update()` to update the database's current row.

- `Update()` saves the value of the row from an edit buffer to the database's current record.

`CRecordset` provides several methods that you can use to get the information about the record set. These methods include the following:

- `GetRecordCount()` returns the number of rows (or the best available estimate) that the record set contains.

- `GetSQL()` returns the SQL string that defines the record set.

The `CRecordView` Class. The `CRecordView` class provides the user-interface elements to display and edit the current record of the record set. You should associate the class with a dialog box template to define a form for data entry. The `OnMove()` method handles the transfer of data between the data members in `CRecordView` and `CRecordset`, as well as navigation within the record set.

Using the ODBC API

You do not have to use the MFC database classes to use ODBC. You might prefer to use the ODBC API directly. You can even use a combination of the two.

V

Advanced Programming

This section's discussion of the ODBC API is, by necessity, brief. It gives little more than a glimpse of the API's power and versatility, exploring only a bare minimum of the available functionality.

Comparison with the MFC Classes

The ODBC API is more versatile than the MFC database classes. MFC is generally geared toward creating a record set and providing navigation methods through it. The framework usually displays one row at a time. The API lets you perform almost any action to a database and display the results in any manner that you choose.

The API can be, at times, somewhat faster than MFC. This is not because the classes are inherently slower but because it is much easier to customize the API calls to your specific purpose. This difference is probably insignificant unless you are dealing with a fairly large number of records.

The MFC database classes are much easier to learn and use than the API. If you have used Visual Basic, you will note that many of the methods in MFC share the same names. Usually, you call far fewer methods with MFC than with the API to perform the same actions.

The Environment and the Connection

Before manipulating a data source, you must create an ODBC environment. This environment initializes ODBC and enables you to establish a connection. Before you exit the application, you should destroy the environment handle.

After allocating the environment, you should create a connection. The connection enables you to access a database. You should connect to a database before attempting to manipulate it, and also disconnect from the database before destroying the environment. Listing 17.1 outlines the entire sequence of events.

Listing 17.1 How To Handle an Environment and Connection in an Application

```
HENV henv;          // Environment handle
HDBC hdbc;          // Connection handle
RETCODE retcode;    // Error Code
retcode = SQLAllocEnv( &henv );   // Try to allocate henv
if( retcode==SQL_SUCCESS )        // How did it go?
{
if( retcode==SQL_SUCCESS )
{
retcode = SQLAllocConnect( henv, &hdbc )
// Allocate the connection
// Connect to the database
SQLConnect(
hdbc,     // Database connection handle
"MyDB",   // Pointer to name of data source
SQL_NTS,  // "MyDB" is a null-terminated string (NTS)
```

```
"Rsmith", // Pointer to user name
SQL_NTS,  // "Rsmith" is a null-terminated string (NTS)
"Pword",  // Pointer to password, if necessary
SQL_NTS   // "Pword" is a null-terminated string (NTS)
);
// Do more ODBC...
if( hdbc != SQL_NULL_HDBC )
{
SQLFreeConnect( hdbc );  // Free the connection
}
}
}
// Do some other cleanup...
if( henv!= SQL_NULL_HENV )        // Was the handle valid?
{
SQLFreeEnv( henv );          // Free the handle.
}
```

Error Handling

All ODBC API functions have the same return type, the RETCODE. It is important to check the return value of all ODBC functions. The RETCODE can assume a simple, uniform set of values:

Returned Value	Meaning
SQL_SUCCESS	The function succeeded.
SQL_ERROR	The function failed due to an error.
SQL_INVALID_HANDLE	The function failed due to an invalid handle (HENV, HDBC, or HSTMT).
SQL_NEED_DATA	This function succeeded, but you must call other functions to supply more data.
SQL_NO_DATA_FOUND	The function succeeded. The query involved did not return any data, however.
SQL_SUCCESS_WITH_INFO	The function succeeded, but an abnormal condition occurred.

The ODBC Statement

The ODBC statement is the workhorse of the API. This statement is where you actually manipulate the database. You usually use the statement as follows:

1. Call SQLAllocStmt() to allocate the statement.
2. Call SQLExecDirect() to execute the statement.
3. Call SQLBindCol() to assign storage for each column in the result set.
4. Call SQLFetch() to retrieve each row of the result set.
5. Call SQLFreeStmt() to discard the statement when the query is complete.

The ODBC API is quite powerful, and contains more than 50 functions. Again, this section has covered only the barest essentials. From this point, you should be ready to expand your knowledge by studying the ODBC help files and example programs included with Visual C++ 4.

From Here...

In this chapter, you learned how to use ODBC to add database access to your MFC applications. ODBC provides a powerful way for your programs to work with database data regardless of the database itself—as long as the database software supports ODBC, you can use it.

To learn more, see the following chapters:

- Chapter 12, "Cross-Platform Development," shows you how to prepare your MFC applications for porting into other environments.

- Chapter 13, "Exception Handling," teaches you how to use C++ exceptions to improve your code's error handling. External data sources might not be available when you query them; exception handling provides a good way to handle such occurrences.

- Chapter 14, "Mastering Templates," offers help in using Visual C++'s template feature to write optimized and concise code. For example, you can write a template class to create the proper type of CRecordset object for you automatically.

CHAPTER 18

Run-Time Type Identification (RTTI)

The Visual C++ 4 compiler provides full support for a recently adopted ANSI/ISO extension called run-time type identification (RTTI). Although not widely used today, RTTI provides a variety of important services that can help make your code more robust and portable.

Programs can use the features of RTTI for several different purposes. Specifically, using RTTI enables your programs to do the following:

- Determine the precise type of an object instance, even if the pointer used to perform the query is of a type higher up in the class hierarchy.
- Safely cast a pointer up and down an inheritance hierarchy. This includes casting pointers to virtual base classes down to derived classes (a practice that has been illegal until now).
- Utilize object instance types in expressions.

At first glance, these features appear to be fairly uninspired; but, as you will see throughout the rest of this chapter, these simple and somewhat pedestrian language features, when correctly applied, can actually provide some important capabilities. In this chapter, you do the following:

- Investigate the different components of RTTI
- Walk though the steps required to integrate RTTI features into your programs
- Learn that the most important aspects of RTTI involve the `dynamic_cast` and `typeid` operators and the `type_info` class

Portability and Compatibility Concerns

In March of 1993, the standards committee accepted run-time type identification into the working draft of the X3J16 ANSI standard. To date, however, few compiler vendors have supported the RTTI extensions (particularly on Intel-based operating systems). You, however, will have to wait no longer. Being the proud owner of a shiny new copy of Visual C++ 4 places you into the select group of programmers using a compiler with a full-fledged implementation of RTTI.

Unfortunately, the rest of the world appears to be approaching RTTI more conservatively. Although Microsoft and Borland have full RTTI implementations, and second-tier players like Symantec and Watcom are close behind, many other compiler venders are still struggling to provide full RTTI support in their development products. The implications, at least for the time being, are pretty obvious. If you use RTTI features in your code, your programs might not compile on other operating systems or with other compilers. If portability is not of immediate concern to you, use these RTTI features with reckless abandon (well, maybe not *reckless* abandon). After all, they are destined to be part of the final ANSI C++ specification anyway, and ultimately all C++ compiler vendors will have to support these features.

On the other hand, if portability is important to you, don't feel guilty about skipping the rest of this chapter. Although RTTI provides useful services, its features are not absolutely essential. You are better off waiting until all your compilers support these capabilities.

Dealing with C++ Objects

C++ enables programmers to abstract complex problems and break them into descriptions about the relationships among different object classes. This arrangement is fine, but the C++ object model breaks down somewhat when compared to the tangible interaction that takes place between humans and objects on a day-to-day basis.

When you pick up an apple, you are relatively certain that you are holding an apple, not a kiwi fruit. All human beings have a range of experiences that tell them what an apple looks and feels like, and there is little chance that they will confuse it with another fruit.

Things can get a little trickier when dealing with C++ objects. Generally, C++ programs have a pretty good idea of what object types they are dealing with at any given time. If your code does its job right, an initialized pointer to an Apple object actually points to an Apple object, and that object behaves as expected.

Assuming, however, that your Apple class derives from a generic Fruit class, and a program is given a pointer to a Fruit, there is no easy way to determine whether the pointer refers to an Apple, a KiwiFruit, or any other class derived from Fruit. To make matters worse, if Fruit derives from a top-level GenericObject class (as is typical in many Smalltalk-like class libraries) and you give your code a pointer to a GenericObject, your code might be working with an Apple, a KiwiFruit, or a Boeing747. If you have ever tried to peel a 747, you know how undesirable such confusion can be.

Casting a GenericObject pointer to an Apple and then calling its Peel() method can have disastrous results if the pointer is actually pointing to a Boeing747 object. Clearly C++ classes could benefit greatly from some mechanism that enables programs to identify the precise type of an object pointer. Unfortunately, knowing your fruit in C++ is not as straightforward as it is in real life.

There isA( ) Way

To a large degree, C++ programmers solved the problem of type identification back when the language was in its infancy. The most common solution is to declare a virtual function—sometimes named isA()—at the highest level of the class hierarchy that is responsible for returning the unique name of the class. As the class hierarchy evolves, each derived class is responsible for overloading isA(), so that it returns the name of the new class. This structure makes possible code similar to that in listing 18.1.

Listing 18.1   Using isA( ) To Perform Class-Specific Actions

```cpp
void MakeSalad(GenericObject* pObject)
{
      switch(pObject->isA()) {

            case OBJ_APPLE:
            case OBJ_ORANGE:
            case OBJ_BANANA:
                  pObject->Peel();
                  break;

            case OBJ_LETTUCE:
                  pObject->Chop();
                  break;

            case OBJ_BOEING747:
                  cout << "Very funny, wiseguy!\n";
                  break;
      }
}
```

In this example, the code declares the isA() function so that it returns a numerical value that a switch statement can check. Each object class presumably has been assigned a unique class ID that corresponds to the appropriate OBJ_* constant or enumeration member.

Unfortunately, implementing isA() in this way can result in several problems. Returning a number implies that all classes can coordinate in such a way that doesn't duplicate any class IDs. Using numerical constants for class ID constants is easily accomplished for smaller class libraries, in which the developer possesses all the library source code. In some cases, however, the programmer might not have access to all the library sources. This lack of access, at the very least, precludes using an enumeration to store the class ID constants.

Using constant numerical values can be quite useful, but it can quickly become a maintenance and managerial nightmare. For that reason, programmers often prototype their isA() methods to return a character string representation of the class name. The code to check whether a GenericObject is an Apple, for example, is similar to the following:

```
// Is this pointer referencing an Apple?
if (!strcmp(pObject->isA(), "Apple")) {
    // Yes it is, do Apple stuff
    ...
}
else {
    // Nope, do otherwise
    ...
}
```

This code is a bit messier than it would be if isA() simply returned an integer, but it provides a little more flexibility. With isA() coded this way, the chance that two different class designers will inadvertently implement overlapping isA() return values is considerably less likely.

Problems with the isA() approach remain, however. What happens if a programmer forgets (or ignores) the requirement to provide an isA() method? An object instance of the new class will return the isA() value of its parent class, which is simply wrong. Even if the programmer implements the method, the possibility (albeit a slim one) remains that the programmer might return a value from isA() that is identical to a value already in use (talk about a hard bug to track down). Finally, what if you want to integrate one of your class libraries with another one, but that class library's type identification method is called IsA()? Or GetTypeID()? Or even worse, what if the other developer didn't even use and implement a type identification method?

Ultimately the problem boils down to an issue of standard practices. *If* you always follow the rules, and *if* you're fortunate enough to avoid overlapping type IDs, and *if* you don't need to interface with third-party class libraries, then the isA() approach will probably work well for you. On the other hand, all these "ifs" should probably make you feel a little nervous. Writing code on a foundation of "ifs" is just asking for trouble.

Enter the `dynamic_cast`

The Visual C++ compiler's run-time type identification system offers a better way for you to provide isA()-type services (among other things) without worrying about politically charged development mandates, or relying on error-prone programmatic devices built in to your class libraries.

dynamic_cast **Basics**

One way that RTTI provides improved isA()-type services is through a new casting operator: the dynamic_cast. Essentially, a dynamic_cast is designed to cast a pointer safely up and down an inheritance hierarchy. The operative word here is *safely* because a normal C++ cast usually enables you to cast pointers up and down inheritance trees as well.

A dynamic_cast pointer uses the following syntax:

```
dynamic_cast<T*>(ptr)
```

T, as used here, refers to a valid C++ type, and ptr is the source pointer. The cast returns a pointer of type T if ptr points to an object of type T. If ptr doesn't point to a T, the dynamic_cast fails and returns NULL.

Keep these important caveats in mind when using dynamic_cast; however, dynamic_cast (and other RTTI constructs) are designed to be used only with polymorphic classes. A *polymorphic class* is a class that contains at least one virtual (or pure-virtual) function. Further, classes that inherit virtual functions from a superclass also qualify to use RTTI.

> **Note**
>
> Because integral types are not polymorphic, the compiler does not support RTTI operations and manipulations on these types. Only user-defined classes and structures are eligible for RTTI use. Notice that this rule does *not* exclude the ANSI string class or the xalloc exception class.

Using the dynamic_cast Salad, Anyone?

Listing 18.2 shows the dynamic_cast in action (your use of this language feature is certain to be more profound than this frivolous example). The program simulates the preparation of salad ingredients and, obviously, is not designed to be particularly useful. Take special note of the dynamic_cast used in the ProcessIngredient() function.

Listing 18.2 salad.cpp, Using the dynamic_cast To Discern an Object Instance Type

```cpp
#include <iostream.h>

// Some miscellaneous definitions we will need
typedef enum {
      WHOLE,
      SHREDDED,
      GRATED,
      SLICED,
      CHOPPED
} FoodState;

// The top of the inheritance tree
class Food {
public:
      // Constructor
      Food(const FoodState = WHOLE);

      // Virtual methods - all food
      // must be able to set and return
      // its state. These functions also
      // ensure that Food is polymorphic
      // and can use RTTI.
```

(continues)

V

Advanced Programming

Listing 18.2 Continued

```
            virtual FoodState GetState() const;
            virtual void SetState(const FoodState);

    private:
            // Private member data
            FoodState theFoodState;
    };

    // Food constructor
    Food::Food(const FoodState newState)
    {
            SetState(newState);
    }

    // Getter and setter virtual methods
    FoodState Food::GetState() const
    {
            return theFoodState;
    }

    void Food::SetState(const FoodState newState)
    {
            theFoodState = newState;
    }

    // Overload << so we can display our state
    ostream& operator<<(ostream& outstrm,
                    Food&     theFood)
    {
            switch(theFood.GetState()) {
                case WHOLE:    outstrm << "Whole";
                        break;
                case SHREDDED: outstrm << "Shredded";
                        break;
                case GRATED:   outstrm << "Grated";
                        break;
                case SLICED:   outstrm << "Sliced";
                        break;
                case CHOPPED:  outstrm << "Chopped";
                        break;
                default:
                        outstrm << "Bad state!";
            }
            return outstrm;
    }


    // Individual food types
    class Apple : public Food {
    public:
        void Chop() { SetState(CHOPPED); }
        void Slice() { SetState(SLICED); }
    };
```

```
class Cheese : public Food {
public:
     void Grate() { SetState(GRATED); }
};

class Lettuce : public Food {
public:
     void Shred() { SetState(SHREDDED); }
};


// Process a single ingredient
void ProcessIngredient(Food* pIngredient)
{
     // Is this an Apple?
     Apple* pApple =
          dynamic_cast<Apple*>(pIngredient);
     if (pApple) {
          pApple->Chop();
          return;
     }

     // Is this a head of Lettuce?
     Lettuce* pLettuce =
          dynamic_cast<Lettuce*>(pIngredient);
     if (pLettuce) {
          pLettuce->Shred();
          return;
     }

     // Is this a piece of Cheese?
     Cheese* pCheese =
          dynamic_cast<Cheese*>(pIngredient);
     if (pCheese)
          pCheese->Grate();

     return;
}

// Let's prepare a salad
void main()
{
Lettuce       MyLettuce;
Apple         MyApple;
Cheese        MyCheese;

     // Process the vegetables
     ProcessIngredient(&MyLettuce);
     ProcessIngredient(&MyApple);
     ProcessIngredient(&MyCheese);

     // Show what we've done
     cout << "The lettuce is ";
     cout << MyLettuce << "\n";
     cout << "The apple is ";
     cout << MyApple << "\n";
```

(continues)

Listing 18.2 Continued

```
        cout << "The cheese is ";
        cout << MyCheese << "\n";
    }
```

This program defines a high-level Food class that knows only that food always exists in a certain state. The Food class enables you to set, query, and display the food's state, but is generally uninteresting. In fact, within a class hierarchy of any appreciable complexity and size, the Food class would probably have several pure virtual methods returning more detailed information about the specific type of food—an arrangement that is not part of this particular program.

Several specific food classes derive from Food. Each of these classes makes methods available that correspond to different ways that these foods might be processed. No rocket science going on here!

The most interesting part of the program is the ProcessIngredient() function. This function accepts a pointer to an object of type Food; after all, you don't want to limit your programs to just using fruits and vegetables. Maybe you like cheese on your salads, and maybe someone else likes croutons or peanut butter (there's no accounting for taste!). The point is that ProcessIngredient() should not limit the types of objects that can be processed, except to insist that they be foods and not wide-bodied aircraft (or something equally unappetizing).

ProcessIngredient() takes this Food pointer and proceeds to attempt casts to various object pointer types. Because a dynamic_cast is safe and returns NULL if the requested cast is inappropriate, each of these casting attempts fails until the correct cast succeeds. Once a dynamic_cast succeeds, the function knows the type of Food to which the pointer refers and can process the object accordingly.

dynamic_cast **versus Virtual Functions**

Just because you can use dynamic_cast to determine the identity of an ambiguous pointer doesn't mean that you should. The dynamic_cast can be tremendously useful for ensuring that your pointers are referencing what you think they are and for providing a generalized mechanism for determining object types. On the other hand, dynamic_cast isn't intended to be used as a crutch when a design can accomplish the same thing through virtual functions.

Take the previous salad-making example. Assume that the classes in that example are more concerned with making salad than they are with providing a generic Food class hierarchy. In this case, you can write the program better using virtual functions. Listing 18.3 shows how this program might look.

Listing 18.3   salad2.cpp, Using Virtual Functions to Create a Better Salad

```cpp
#include <iostream.h>

// Some miscellaneous definitions we will need
typedef enum {
      WHOLE,
      SHREDDED,
      GRATED,
      SLICED,
      CHOPPED
} FoodState;

// The top of the inheritance tree
class Food {
public:
      // Constructor
      Food(const FoodState = WHOLE);

      // Virtual methods -- all food
      // must be able to set and return
      // its state. These functions also
      // ensure that Food is polymorphic
      // and can use RTTI.
      virtual FoodState GetState() const;
      virtual void SetState(const FoodState);

private:
      // Private member data
      FoodState theFoodState;
};

// Food constructor
Food::Food(const FoodState newState)
{
      SetState(newState);
}

// Getter and setter virtual methods
FoodState Food::GetState() const
{
      return theFoodState;
}

void Food::SetState(const FoodState newState)
{
      theFoodState = newState;
}

// Overload << so we can display our state
ostream& operator<<(ostream& outstrm,
                Food&     theFood)
{
      switch(theFood.GetState()) {
          case WHOLE:    outstrm << "Whole";
                       break;
```

(continues)

Listing 18.3 Continued

```
                case SHREDDED:  outstrm << "Shredded";
                        break;
                case GRATED:    outstrm << "Grated";
                        break;
                case SLICED:    outstrm << "Sliced";
                        break;
                case CHOPPED:   outstrm << "Chopped";
                        break;
                default:
                    outstrm << "Bad state!";
        }
        return outstrm;
}


// Intermediate class grouping
class SaladIngredient : public Food {
public:
        // Pure virtual function which any
        // salad ingredient class must
        // provide
        virtual void ProcessIngredient() = 0;
};


// Individual food types
class Apple : public SaladIngredient {
public:
        void ProcessIngredient() { SetState(CHOPPED); }
};

class Cheese : public Food {
public:
        void ProcessIngredient() { SetState(GRATED); }
};

class Lettuce : public Food {
public:
        void ProcessIngredient() { SetState(SHREDDED); }
};


// Let's prepare a salad
void main()
{
        Lettuce     MyLettuce;
        Apple       MyApple;
        Cheese      MyCheese;

        // Process the vegetables
        MyLettuce.ProcessIngredient();
        MyApple.ProcessIngredient();
        MyCheese.ProcessIngredient();
```

Enter the dynamic_cast **603**

```
        // Show what we've done
        cout << "The lettuce is ";
        cout << MyLettuce << "\n";
        cout << "The apple is ";
        cout << MyApple << "\n";
        cout << "The cheese is ";
        cout << MyCheese << "\n";
}
```

As you can see, this salad-making variant completely removes RTTI use. This is because the `ProcessIngredient()` virtual function that is forced on any class derived from `SaladIngredient` assumes the responsibility for changing the object's state as appropriate. Using virtual functions in this case is much cleaner than having to rely on the cascading `if` statements and `dynamic_casts` in the listing 18.2 `ProcessIngredient()` function.

> **Tip**
>
> Anytime that you are tempted to use a `dynamic_cast` to determine a pointer's type (as opposed to simply providing a safe cast), ask yourself whether there is a way to accomplish the same thing using virtual functions. Leveraging polymorphism is superior to using the brute force capabilities of RTTI's `dynamic_cast`.

Of course, the program might want to use some of the specific food classes in a context different than simply making salads. The class hierarchy, for example, can have a `PizzaIngredient` class. The `Cheese` class then can use multiple inheritance and derive from both `SaladIngredient` and `PizzaIngredient`. Be careful, though; if a program adopts this approach, it must ensure that the `Food` class is a virtual base class. Additionally, the program must change the `ProcessIngredient()` method names in `SaladIngredient` and `PizzaIngredient` to avoid any naming conflict. In some cases, you might decide to use the RTTI approach of listing 18.2 because it alleviates the need for multiple inheritance and its messy problems.

dynamic_cast **and References**

You also can use the `dynamic_cast` operator to create a reference to a particular type. The syntax for this operation is as follows:

```
dynamic_cast<T&>(ref)
```

T, as used in this syntax, refers to a valid C++ type, and `ref` is the source reference. The cast returns a reference of type T only if `ref` refers to an object of type T. Because a NULL reference is not possible, you have no way to compare the result of a dynamic reference cast to determine whether it has failed. In the case of an invalid dynamic reference cast, a `bad_cast` exception is thrown. (For a thorough discussion of exception handling, see Chapter 13, "Exception Handling.") The following code snippets demonstrate the differences in checking for invalid dynamic pointer casts and invalid dynamic reference casts:

```
        // Checking for errors with dynamic pointer cast
        Derived* pDerived = dynamic_cast<Derived*>(pBase);
        if (!pDerived) {
              // Whoops! This was an invalid cast
              ...
        }

        // Checking for errors with dynamic reference casts
        try {
              Derived& MyDerived = dynamic_cast<Derived&>(MyBase);
        }
        catch (bad_cast) {
              // Whoops! This was an invalid cast
              ...
        }
```

In every other way, using the dynamic reference is just like using the dynamic pointer cast, except that the former obviously returns a reference rather than a pointer.

Boring Classes Need Not Apply (Usually)

The "polymorphic class only" RTTI limitation is not exactly a hard and fast rule. There is an important exception: casting from a derived class object pointer up to a base class pointer. Examine the code sample in listing 18.4.

Listing 18.4   dyncast1.cpp, Using the `dynamic_cast()` with Nonpolymorphic Classes

```
#include <iostream.h>

class Base {
      // Do nothing (not a polymorphic class)
};

class Derived : public Base {
      // Do nothing (not a polymorphic class)
};

void main()
{
      Derived  MyDerived;
      Derived* pMyDerived = &MyDerived;

      // Successful upcast
      Base* pBaseTest = dynamic_cast<Base*>(pMyDerived);
      cout << "pMyDerived ";
      cout << (pBaseTest ? "is" : "is not");
      cout << " a Base*.\n";
}
```

This code compiles and runs as expected. As it turns out, the Microsoft compiler enables you to dynamic_cast *up* a class hierarchy (for example, from a derived class to a base class) even if the classes involved are not polymorphic. Listing 18.5, however, shows a change to this code that breaks the program.

Listing 18.5   dyncast2.cpp, Incorrect Use of the `dynamic_cast` for Downcasting

```cpp
#include <iostream.h>

class Base {
    // Do nothing (not a polymorphic class)
};

class Derived : public Base {
    // Do nothing (not a polymorphic class)
};

void main()
{
    Derived  MyDerived;
    Derived* pMyDerived = &MyDerived;

    // Successful upcast
    Base* pBaseTest = dynamic_cast<Base*>(pMyDerived);
    cout << "pMyDerived ";
    cout << (pBaseTest ? "is" : "is not");
    cout << " a Base*.\n";

    // Successful(??) downcast
    if (pBaseTest) {
        Derived* pDerivedTest =
         dynamic_cast<Derived*>(pBaseTest);
        cout << "pBaseTest ";
        cout << (pDerivedTest ? "is" : "is not");
        cout << " a Derived*.\n";
    }
}
```

This program cannot even compile, because the second use of `dynamic_cast` attempts to cast a base pointer down to a derived pointer, and neither class is polymorphic. The Microsoft compiler complains that `'Base' is not a polymorphic type`, just as you would expect.

You can fix listing 18.5 simply by adding a single line to the definition of `Base`, as shown in listing 18.6.

Listing 18.6   dyncast3.cpp, Fixing the Compiler Error

```cpp
class Base {
// Do nothing
void virtual Nothing() { } // Now polymorphic
};
```

This change rids you of the troublesome compiler error and enables the program to compile, link, and run as expected.

V

Advanced Programming

RTTI and Multiple Inheritance

Before RTTI, programmers often were frustrated in their attempts to construct a piece of code to cast a pointer down a class hierarchy that incorporated a virtual base class. C++ simply does not support this sort of coding with the normal casting syntax.

Listing 18.7 shows a very simple class hierarchy consisting of a Base class, two Middle classes deriving from the base class, and then a main Derived class deriving through multiple inheritance from both of the middle classes. The program itself simply tries to take a pointer to a Derived class instance, cast the pointer down to the Base level, and then cast the pointer back up to the Derived level.

Listing 18.7   vrtbase1.cpp, a Simple Multiple Inheritance Hierarchy

```
#include <iostream.h>

class Base {
public:
      // Do nothing (not a polymorphic class)
      void BaseFunc() { cout << "In Base.\n"; }
};

class Middle1 : public Base {
public:
      // Do nothing (not a polymorphic class)
      void Middle1Func() { cout << "In Middle1.\n"; }
};

class Middle2 : public Base {
public:
      // Do nothing (not a polymorphic class)
      void Middle2Func() { cout << "In Middle2.\n"; }
};

class Derived : public Middle1, public Middle2 {
public:
      // Do nothing (not a polymorphic class)
      void DerivedFunc() { cout << "In Derived.\n"; }
};

void main()
{
      Derived  MyDerived;
      Base*    pBase = (Base*) &MyDerived;
      pBase->BaseFunc();
      Derived* pDerived = (Derived*) pBase;
      pDerived->DerivedFunc();
}
```

This program does not compile. The compiler gives you the following error message: `ambiguous conversion from 'Derived*' to 'Base*', could be to the 'Base' in base 'Middle1' of class 'Derived' or to the 'Base' in base 'Middle2' of class 'Derived'`.

You can easily fix this first error message. Because Derived indirectly inherits from Base twice, you have the classic multiple-instance problem that often plagues users of multiple inheritance. Clearly, you must make Base a virtual base class. Listing 18.8 shows the changes to the Middle1 and Middle2 classes that accomplish this task.

Listing 18.8   vrtbase2.cpp, Changes To Make Base a Virtual Base Class

```
#include <iostream.h>

class Base {
public:
      // Do nothing (not a polymorphic class)
      void BaseFunc() { cout << "In Base.\n"; }
};

class Middle1 : virtual public Base {
public:
      // Do nothing (not a polymorphic class)
      void Middle1Func() { cout << "In Middle1.\n"; }
};

class Middle2 : virtual public Base {
public:
      // Do nothing (not a polymorphic class)
      void Middle2Func() { cout << "In Middle2.\n"; }
};

class Derived : public Middle1, public Middle2 {
public:
      // Do nothing (not a polymorphic class)
      void DerivedFunc() { cout << "In Derived.\n"; }
};

void main()
{
      Derived  MyDerived;
      Base*    pBase = (Base*) &MyDerived;
      pBase->BaseFunc();
      Derived* pDerived = (Derived*) pBase;
      pDerived->DerivedFunc();
```

The solution shown in listing 18.8 works—almost. The program still doesn't compile. Instead, you now get the following error: cannot convert from 'class Base *' to 'class Derived *'. The fact that you can't perform a simple cast from a virtual base class down to a derived class is simply a limitation of C++, and without RTTI there isn't an easy or safe way to get around this problem.

Of course, because the Microsoft compiler supports the dynamic_cast, you have a simple and safe solution to this problem. Listing 18.9 shows the changes that you must make to the program to get it to work properly.

Listing 18.9 vrtbase3.cpp, Changes Needed To Incorporate RTTI and Make the Program Finally Work

```cpp
#include <iostream.h>

class Base {
public:
     // Do nothing
     void BaseFunc() { cout << "In Base.\n"; }

     // Now polymorphic so we can use RTTI
     virtual void Nothing() { }
};

class Middle1 : virtual public Base {
public:
     // Do nothing (not a polymorphic class)
     void Middle1Func() { cout << "In Middle1.\n"; }
};

class Middle2 : virtual public Base {
public:
     // Do nothing (not a polymorphic class)
     void Middle2Func() { cout << "In Middle2.\n"; }
};

class Derived : public Middle1, public Middle2 {
public:
     // Do nothing (not a polymorphic class)
     void DerivedFunc() { cout << "In Derived.\n"; }
};
void main()
{
     Derived  MyDerived;
     Base*    pBase = dynamic_cast<Base*>(&MyDerived);
     pBase->BaseFunc();
     Derived* pDerived = dynamic_cast<Derived*>(pBase);
     pDerived->DerivedFunc();
}
```

This version of the program not only compiles but runs as expected. Although you might find that you rarely need to perform an operation as relatively esoteric as this one, you certainly will appreciate dynamic_cast on those occasions when you do need this sort of casting manipulation.

As a final note on using the dynamic_cast operator with inheritance trees that utilize multiple inheritance, understand that RTTI enables programs to cast pointers and references *across* inheritance trees. Conceptually, this action is like casting a base pointer down to the lowest class in the inheritance tree and then casting the same pointer back up the tree, but through a different inheritance path. Listing 18.10 shows how you can change the vrtbase3.cpp example to demonstrate this lateral casting capability.

Listing 18.10   vrtbase4.cpp, Hopping across a Multiple Inheritance Hierarchy

```
// All class declarations and definitions the same as vrtbase3.cpp

1 void main()
2 {
3    Derived  MyDerived;
4    Middle1* pMiddle1 = dynamic_cast<Middle1*>(&MyDerived);
5    pMiddle1->Middle1Func();
6    Middle2* pMiddle2 = dynamic_cast<Middle2*>(pMiddle1);
7    pMiddle2->Middle2Func();
8 }
```

In this example, you set the pMiddle1 pointer to point to a class in the middle of the inheritance tree (line 4). On line 6, the program uses the dynamic_cast operator to move across the inheritance tree to another class located between Base and Derived. Notice that the syntax makes absolutely no reference to Derived and that the compiler is responsible for "finding a path" from one class in the tree to another.

A Brief Aside: Declarations inside Conditions

The ANSI C++ standards committee has adopted a language change that enables you to declare variables inside conditional statements (such as if, while, and switch). You can use these declarations with dynamic_cast. Unfortunately, Visual C++ does not support this feature in version 4's compiler.

Briefly, conditional declarations refer to the fact that standard C++ enables a variable declaration to return a value and that is usable inside an expression evaluation. Consider, for example, the following C++ declaration:

```
MyClass* pMyClass = new MyClass;
```

With conditional declarations, this syntax now yields a value that indicates whether pMyClass has been correctly initialized. A programmer could rewrite the declaration so that it is evaluated within an expression designed to trap memory-allocation errors:

```
if (MyClass* pMyClass = new MyClass) {
    // Do something
}
else {
    // The call to new failed
}
```

A full-fledged discussion of the implications of using valued declarations is beyond the scope of this chapter—and somewhat pointless, considering the Microsoft compiler doesn't support the feature yet. Nevertheless, you should at least recognize the feature's use. The Microsoft compiler will support conditional declarations sooner rather than later, and the feature's use will appear in code snippets that you might find in books, magazines, and other users' code.

V

Advanced Programming

The most important use of valued declarations, at least with respect to RTTI and dynamic_cast, is in conditionally creating variable instances with limited scope. Examine closely the following code snippet:

```
1 void DoNothing(Base* pBase)
2 {
3     Derived* pDerived = dynamic_cast<Derived*>(pBase);
4     if (pDerived) {
5         // Do something with the object
6         cout << "It's a Derived!\n";
7     }
8     // pDerived is still in scope and is accessible
9 }
```

As the comment on line 8 indicates, the variable pDerived is still in scope and fully accessible to the rest of the function, even though clearly this program declares pDerived simply to determine whether pBase is also a Derived instance.

You can solve this semantic problem by explicitly creating a new level of scope, as follows:

```
1   void DoNothing(Base* pBase)
2   {
3       { // Start of new scope
4         Derived* pDerived = dynamic_cast<Derived*>(pBase);
5         if (pDerived) {
6             // Do something with the object
7             cout << "It's a Derived!\n";
8         }
9       } // End of new scope
10      // pDerived is not in scope and is unaccessible
11  }
```

Line 10 and subsequent lines do not have access to pDerived, so technically this code does solve the problem—but the solution isn't pretty. You can use conditional declarations to solve the problem more elegantly:

```
void DoNothing(Base* pBase)
{
if (Derived* pDerived =
            dynamic_cast<Derived*>(pBase)) {
// Do something with the object
cout << "It's a Derived!\n";
}
// pDerived is not in scope and is unaccessible
}
```

As you can see, conditional declarations enable you to combine the declaration of pDerived, its initialization, and the evaluation of the result into a single unit. This combination helps to avoid errors that often result from using variables before they have been validated. This approach also resolves ugly scoping problems and makes the resulting function smaller and easier to understand.

Conditional declarations soon will be appearing in compilers. Although the feature is hardly earth-shattering, it is so convenient that programmers are sure to latch on to it and use it often. Be prepared.

`type_infos` **and the** `typeid` **Operator**

Obviously the capability to determine whether a pointer or reference is of a particular type can be quite useful. Occasionally, however, you want even more information about a particular class than you can obtain through the `dynamic_cast` operator.

The standard C++ implementation of RTTI includes a specification for a `type_info` class that you can use to describe various attributes of a particular type. Listing 18.11 shows the specific structure of Microsoft's `type_info` class.

Listing 18.11   The `type_info` **Class**

```
class type_info {
public:
virtual ~type_info();
    int operator==(const type_info& rhs) const;
    int operator!=(const type_info& rhs) const;
    int before(const type_info& rhs) const;
    const char* name() const;
    const char* raw_name() const;
private:
    ...
};
```

> **Note**
>
> For a Visual C++ 4 program to utilize `type_infos` and the `typeid` operator, it must include the typeinfo.h header file.

Now take a brief look at some of things that you can do with `type_info`. As evidenced by the overloaded equality and inequality operators, `type_infos` can be compared to each other. Using the `name` method, a program can retrieve the name of a type in the form of a character string. The `raw_name` method returns a string that doesn't mean much to humans but is unique to a class and can be used for comparisons. Finally, a program can determine the lexical order of two types (based on their name) by using the `before` method.

> **Note**
>
> Because both the copy constructor and the assignment operator are declared as private, you cannot copy `type_infos`.

> **Caution**
>
> Early drafts of the ANSI C++ draft standard specified that certain RTTI type names should have mixed-case names (specifically `Bad_cast`, `Bad_typeid`, and `Type_info`). These names have now been changed to their lowercase equivalents, which might cause you problems when porting code from compilers supporting the older naming conventions. RTTI-aware code developed with the Borland C++ 4.x compiler is probably the most pervasive culprit in this regard. To reinstate the old names, you can define `__RTTI_OLDNAMES` before including typeinfo.h.

How does a program create or otherwise access these `type_info` instances? RTTI provides an operator called `typid` that is designed expressly to return `type_infos`. `typeid` takes a single argument that can be either a simple type name or an expression. The operator returns to the program a `type_info` reference that corresponds to the requested type, or a `type_info` reference that corresponds to the type of the supplied expression.

The `typeid` operator does not require that you feed it exclusively polymorphic types. Consider, for example, the following code snippet:

```
// Show some integral type names
cout << typeid(int).name() << "\n";
cout << typeid(unsigned long).name() << "\n";
cout << typeid(char*).name() << "\n";
```

As you might expect, these three lines of code output `int`, `unsigned long`, and `char *`, respectively.

Because the typeid operator can accept expressions, you can pass variable names to the operator and manipulate the resulting `type_info` reference. As expected, the following code displays `class Apple`.

```
// Define our class
class Apple {
      // Do nothing
};

// Create an instance
Apple MyApple;

// Display the instance's name
cout << typeid(MyApple).name() << "\n";
```

In cases where the expression being evaluated is an instance of a polymorphic type, the `typeid` operator checks the actual object and returns an appropriate `type_info` object. The following code displays `class Derived`:

```
// Define our classes
class Base {
      // Do nothing
      // We have to make this class polymorphic
      // for this example to work correctly
virtual void Nothing() { }
```

```
    };

    class Derived : public Base {
        // Do nothing
    };

    // Create an object instance
    Derived  MyDerived;
    Base*    pBase = dynamic_cast<Base*>(&MyDerived);

    // Now show the "true" type of pBase
    cout << typeid(*pBase).name() << "\n";
```

Notice that in this example the classes must be polymorphic to get the correct behaviors. If you omit the stub definition of the Nothing method in the class Base, this code snippet reports that the type name is class Base.

> **Caution:**
>
> If RTTI features are disabled (as they are by default), the typeid operator still functions, but might not return the results that your program expects. If RTTI is off and a program passes a polymorphic pointer or reference into typeid, typeid returns a reference to a type_info instance that represents the declared type of the argument and not the type_info for the actual object to which the pointer or reference is pointing.

Salad Making Revisited

You can use type_infos in many of the same ways that you use the dynamic_cast operator. Recall that in the salad.cpp program (listing 18.2) you used the dynamic_cast operator to query the type of a provided base pointer. If the base pointer was not of the correct type, dynamic_cast returned a NULL, and you could determine that you needed to process the pointer differently. Listing 18.12 shows how you can use the typeid operator to make the same sort of determination.

Listing 18.12 salad3.cpp, Using typeid To Determine an Object's Type

```
#include <iostream.h>
#include <typeinfo.h>

// The definitions of FoodState, Food, Apple, Cheese,
// and Lettuce are the same as in salad.cpp

// Process a single ingredient
void ProcessIngredient(Food* pIngredient)
{
// Is this an Apple?
if (typeid(*pIngredient) == typeid(Apple)) {
    ((Apple*) pIngredient)->Chop();
    return;
}
```

(continues)

Listing 18.12 Continued

```
// Is this a head of Lettuce?
if (typeid(*pIngredient) == typeid(Lettuce)) {
    ((Lettuce*) pIngredient)->Shred();
    return;
}

// Is this a piece of Cheese?
if (typeid(*pIngredient) == typeid(Cheese))
    ((Cheese*) pIngredient)->Grate();

return;
}

// Let's prepare a salad
void main()
{
    Lettuce MyLettuce;
    Apple   MyApple;
    Cheese  MyCheese;

    // Process the vegetables
    ProcessIngredient(&MyLettuce);
    ProcessIngredient(&MyApple);
    ProcessIngredient(&MyCheese);

    // Show what we've done
    cout << "The ";
    cout << typeid(MyLettuce).name() << " is ";
    cout << MyLettuce << "\n";
    oout << "The ";
    cout << typeid(MyApple).name() << " is ";
    cout << MyApple << "\n";
    cout << "The ";
    cout << typeid(MyCheese).name() << " is ";
    cout << MyCheese << "\n";
}
```

As you can see, salad3.cpp explicitly checks the `type_info` of the passed-in ingredient pointer with the `type_info` of each of the possible food types. Because all the classes are polymorphic, the `type_info` returned by `typeid(*pIngredient)` refers to the actual object, which makes this comparison possible.

So which way should you write this program? It's a toss-up. Using the `type_info` method is a little easier to read and looks more obvious. However, the `type_info` method also relies on dangerous and unprotected C-style typecasts rather than the safer `dynamic_cast`. Because `dynamic_cast` essentially performs two jobs simultaneously—checking for the correct pointer type and then safely performing the cast—you probably are safer using the `dynamic_cast` solution rather than the `typeid` solution in this case.

The type_info before() **Enigma**

Recall that the type_info class contains a method called before() that is a mechanism to help collate a class hierarchy. Unfortunately, before() is actually of limited use (to say the least). Take a close look at listing 18.13.

Listing 18.13   before.cpp, Using the type_info before() Method

```cpp
#include <iostream.h>
#include <typeinfo.h>

// Define our classes
class Base {
      // Do nothing
      // Force polymorphism
      virtual void Nothing() { }
};

class Middle : public Base {
      // Do nothing
};

class Derived : public Middle {
      // Do nothing
};

// Show before relationship
void ShowBefore(const type_info& info1,
          const type_info& info2)
{
      cout << info1.name();
      cout << (info1.before(info2) ? " is " : " is not ");
      cout << "before " << info2.name() << "\n";
}

void main()
{
      // Show the relationships
      ShowBefore(typeid(Base),    typeid(Middle));
      ShowBefore(typeid(Base),    typeid(Derived));
      ShowBefore(typeid(Middle),  typeid(Base));
      ShowBefore(typeid(Middle),  typeid(Derived));
      ShowBefore(typeid(Derived), typeid(Base));
      ShowBefore(typeid(Derived), typeid(Middle));
}
```

The most useful implementation of before() would enable you to tell whether one class derives from another (for example, Base is before Derived). Using that implementation, listing 18.13 would output the following:

Class Base is before class Middle.

Class Base is before class Derived.

Class Middle is not before class Base.

Class `Middle` is before class `Derived`.

Class `Derived` is not before class `Base`.

Class `Derived` is not before class `Middle`.

This output, however, is not what Visual C++ returns. Instead, the Microsoft product outputs what appears at first glance to be almost random ordering information:

Class `Base` is before class `Middle`.

Class `Base` is before class `Derived`.

Class `Middle` is not before class `Base`.

Class `Middle` is not before class `Derived`.

Class `Derived` is not before class `Base`.

Class `Derived` is before class `Middle`.

According to the compiler, the ordering of this class hierarchy is `Base`, `Derived`, then `Middle`. This ordering certainly does not describe the inheritance relationship. What's going on here?

When the *names* of the classes change from `Base`, `Middle`, and `Derived` to A, B, and C, the compiler returns the following results:

Class A is before class B.

Class A is before class C.

Class B is not before class A.

Class B is before class C.

Class C is not before class A.

Class C is not before class B.

By now, you undoubtedly have realized that the compiler is just sorting the names of the classes alphabetically. If you don't understand the advantage of this order, don't worry—neither does anyone else. Ultimately, Microsoft's implementation of the `before()` method appears to have limited utility. If you can find a good use for it, more power to you.

Tip

Even though the `before()` method probably doesn't strike you as being particularly interesting or useful, you still can use the `dynamic_cast` operator to get at the sort of information that you might have hoped that `before()` would provide.

Setting the Visual C++ RTTI Compiler Switch

The Visual C++ compiler has only one command-line compiler switch that relates to run-time type identification. The /GR switch, which is off by default, controls whether RTTI information is created and stored for polymorphic classes. You effectively activate RTTI by placing /GR on your compiler command line or by checking the Developer Studio's Enable Run-Time Type Information check box, which you can find in the Project Settings dialog box's C/C++ page (see fig. 18.1).

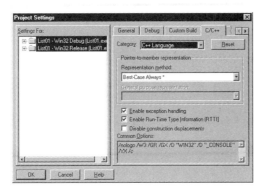

Fig. 18.1

Turning on RTTI.

From Here...

Run-time type identification is a relative newcomer to the C++ feature set. RTTI enables programmers to query objects and determine the type of objects at run time. Although this feature might sound somewhat esoteric, this chapter has explained why this capability can be valuable. You also might want to investigate some of the other chapters in this book that discuss advanced C++ language extensions:

- Exception handling enables programmers to localize error-processing logic and logically structure the way that their programs deal with abnormal execution events. For more information, see Chapter 13, "Exception Handling."

- Templates are probably the most frequently used C++ extension. They enable programs to build class families that function similarly, but perform operations on a wide variety of different data types. For more information, see Chapter 14, "Mastering Templates."

If you are interested in learning more about run-time type identification, see the following publications.

- Stoustrup, B. and D. Lenkov. *Run-Time Type Identification for C++* (revised yet again), X3J16/92-0121 = WG21/N0198, 1992.

- Stoustrup, B. and D. Lenkov. "Run-Time Type Identification for C++," *C++ Report,* 4(3):32-42, 1992.

- Stoustrup, B. and D. Lenkov. "Run-Time Type Identification for C++ (revised)," *Proceedings of the USENIX C++ Conference,* Portland, Oregon, August 1992.

- Lajoie, Josèe. Standard C++ Update: "The New Language Extensions," *C++ Report,* 5(6):47-52, 1993. (This list of supplementary publications was taken from this article.)

Index

Symbols

223

X-Y-Z

PLUG YOURSELF INTO...

MACMILLAN INFORMATION SUPERLIBRARY™

que   SAMS PUBLISHING   Hayden Books   que COLLEGE   NRP   alpha books   Brady   ADOBE PRESS

THE MACMILLAN INFORMATION SUPERLIBRARY™

Free information and vast computer resources from the world's leading computer book publisher—online!

FIND THE BOOKS THAT ARE RIGHT FOR YOU!

A complete online catalog, plus sample chapters and tables of contents give you an in-depth look at *all* of our books, including hard-to-find titles. It's the best way to find the books you need!

- **STAY INFORMED** with the latest computer industry news through our online newsletter, press releases, and customized Information SuperLibrary Reports.

- **GET FAST ANSWERS** to your questions about MCP books and software.

- **VISIT** our online bookstore for the latest information and editions!

- **COMMUNICATE** with our expert authors through e-mail and conferences.

- **DOWNLOAD SOFTWARE** from the immense MCP library:
  - Source code and files from MCP books
  - The best shareware, freeware, and demos

- **DISCOVER HOT SPOTS** on other parts of the Internet.

- **WIN BOOKS** in ongoing contests and giveaways!

TO PLUG INTO MCP: →

GOPHER: gopher.mcp.com

FTP: ftp.mcp.com

WORLD WIDE WEB: http://www.mcp.com

Home Page | What's New | Bookstore | Reference Desk | Software Library | Macmillan Overview | Talk to Us

Complete and Return this Card
for a *FREE* Computer Book Catalog

Thank you for purchasing this book! You have purchased a superior computer book written expressly for your needs. To continue to provide the kind of up-to-date, pertinent coverage you've come to expect from us, we need to hear from you. Please take a minute to complete and return this self-addressed, postage-paid form. In return, we'll send you a free catalog of all our computer books on topics ranging from word processing to programming and the internet.

Mr. ☐   Mrs. ☐   Ms. ☐   Dr. ☐

Name (first) ☐☐☐☐☐☐☐☐☐☐☐ (M.I.) ☐ (last) ☐☐☐☐☐☐☐☐☐☐☐☐☐☐☐☐

Address ☐☐☐☐☐☐☐☐☐☐☐☐☐☐☐☐☐☐☐☐☐☐☐☐☐☐☐☐☐☐☐☐

☐☐☐☐☐☐☐☐☐☐☐☐☐☐☐☐☐☐☐☐☐☐☐☐☐☐☐☐☐☐☐☐

City ☐☐☐☐☐☐☐☐☐☐☐☐☐☐☐ State ☐☐ Zip ☐☐☐☐☐☐☐☐☐

Phone ☐☐☐ ☐☐☐ ☐☐☐☐ Fax ☐☐☐ ☐☐☐ ☐☐☐☐

Company Name ☐☐☐☐☐☐☐☐☐☐☐☐☐☐☐☐☐☐☐☐☐☐☐☐☐☐

E-mail address ☐☐☐☐☐☐☐☐☐☐☐☐☐☐☐☐☐☐☐☐☐☐☐☐☐☐

1. Please check at least (3) influencing factors for purchasing this book.

Front or back cover information on book .... ☐
Special approach to the content .... ☐
Completeness of content .... ☐
Author's reputation .... ☐
Publisher's reputation .... ☐
Book cover design or layout .... ☐
Index or table of contents of book .... ☐
Price of book .... ☐
Special effects, graphics, illustrations .... ☐
Other (Please specify): _____ ☐

2. How did you first learn about this book?

Saw in Macmillan Computer Publishing catalog .... ☐
Recommended by store personnel .... ☐
Saw the book on bookshelf at store .... ☐
Recommended by a friend .... ☐
Received advertisement in the mail .... ☐
Saw an advertisement in: _____ ☐
Read book review in: _____ ☐
Other (Please specify): _____ ☐

3. How many computer books have you purchased in the last six months?

This book only .... ☐   3 to 5 books .... ☐
2 books .... ☐   More than 5 .... ☐

4. Where did you purchase this book?

Bookstore .... ☐
Computer Store .... ☐
Consumer Electronics Store .... ☐
Department Store .... ☐
Office Club .... ☐
Warehouse Club .... ☐
Mail Order .... ☐
Direct from Publisher .... ☐
Internet site .... ☐
Other (Please specify): _____ ☐

5. How long have you been using a computer?

☐ Less than 6 months   ☐ 6 months to a year
☐ 1 to 3 years   ☐ More than 3 years

6. What is your level of experience with personal computers and with the subject of this book?

	With PCs	With subject of book
New	☐	☐
Casual	☐	☐
Accomplished	☐	☐
Expert	☐	☐

Source Code ISBN: 1-7897-0401-3

7. Which of the following best describes your job title?

Administrative Assistant .... ☐
Coordinator .... ☐
Manager/Supervisor .... ☐
Director .... ☐
Vice President .... ☐
President/CEO/COO .... ☐
Lawyer/Doctor/Medical Professional .... ☐
Teacher/Educator/Trainer .... ☐
Engineer/Technician .... ☐
Consultant .... ☐
Not employed/Student/Retired .... ☐
Other (Please specify): _____ ☐

8. Which of the following best describes the area of the company your job title falls under?

Accounting .... ☐
Engineering .... ☐
Manufacturing .... ☐
Operations .... ☐
Marketing .... ☐
Sales .... ☐
Other (Please specify): _____ ☐

Comments: _____
_____
_____

9. What is your age?

Under 20 .... ☐
21-29 .... ☐
30-39 .... ☐
40-49 .... ☐
50-59 .... ☐
60-over .... ☐

10. Are you:

Male .... ☐
Female .... ☐

11. Which computer publications do you read regularly? (Please list)

_____
_____
_____
_____
_____
_____
_____
_____
_____
_____

Fold here and scotch-tape to mail.

Licensing Agreement

By opening this package, you are agreeing to be bound by the following: